Hebrew
With Ease

by Shifra JACQUET-SVIRONI and
Roger JACQUET

Adapted for English-speaking learners
by Shaul VARDI

Illustrated by J.-L. GOUSSÉ

B.P. 25
94431 Chennevières-sur-Marne Cedex
FRANCE

ISBN 978-2-7005-0538-2

Contents

Introduction

We would like to welcome you to the world of Hebrew. As you sit in your armchair, let us take you on a journey to Israel. You will discover a modern country with more than its share of political drama, but with its own special spirit. Your studies will also introduce you to the complex layers of history and thought that have flourished in this land.

Our focus is firmly on the present, however. Some seven million Israelis speak Hebrew – passionately and often loudly. It has been suggested that twelve Israelis out of ten spend most of their day glued to their mobile phones. Many other people around the world, Jews and non-Jews, also study Hebrew in all kinds of contexts.

Hebrew With Ease aims to provide you with a modern, practical vocabulary. At the same time, we have not forgotten Hebrew's Biblical roots, which are always fascinating and often provide a better understanding of this interesting and multilayered language.

A long history

Hebrew was never a dead language. Although for many centuries it was not used as a daily spoken language, Jews continued to pray and study in Hebrew, to read and write it, and, on occasions, even to speak it. The Bible contains valuable records of the ancient Hebrew language, but does not enable us to state with certainty when the language emerged. Archaeologists suggest that Egyptian clay tablets dating to the 15th and 14th centuries BCE (Before Common Era) include texts in a language spoken at the time in Canaan (on the eastern shores of the Mediterranean Sea and its hinterland) that is similar to an archaic Hebrew.

The Hebrew Bible as we now know it includes fragments from these ancient times, but was mainly edited after the Jews returned from Exile in Babylon, around the 6th century BCE. Accordingly, it documents the evolution of the language over some eight centuries.

The Babylonian and Jerusalem Talmuds were redacted in the 4th to 7th centuries CE (Common Era). Written in a mixture of Hebrew and Aramaic (a Semitic language closely related to Hebrew), these texts provide extensive information about the later development of Hebrew.

These sources provided the basis for the development of Medieval Hebrew, and later for the modern Hebrew that has become the language of the State of Israel. Over the centuries, Hebrew texts were written in Spain, Italy, France and elsewhere, including outstanding works of philosophy, religious thought and poetry. It should also be noted that many Christian Hebraists studied and mastered the language throughout this period (as is still the case).

From the late 19th century, the growing waves of Jewish immigration to Palestine (as the area – first under Ottoman control and from 1922 a British mandate – was then called) raised an interesting question. What language would serve this new society, formed by immigrants from countless traditions? Some of the immigrants favoured Yiddish, while others felt that German could best serve as a language of modern culture and education. However, these languages were alien to large numbers of immigrants. In the end, Hebrew won the day, though not without opposition. Many Orthodox circles opposed the use of Hebrew for everyday purposes, claiming this was offensive to the sacred tongue. The struggle was won mainly by the young generation.

Native-born 'Israelis' (though the State of Israel had not yet been founded) learned Hebrew at kindergarten and elementary school and took the language home, often teaching it to their parents. Long before Israel gained its independence in 1948, it was obvious that its official language would be Hebrew. In 1953, the Knesset (Israel's parliament) established the Academy of the Hebrew Language to encourage the development of the ancient tongue for modern use. Although some of the academy's suggestions provoke amusement, and Israelis have no hesitation about adopting foreign words (mainly from English), there has been some success in inventing new words from the ancient roots, as you will see in the course of your studies.

The origins of the Hebrew alphabet

The earliest known written languages used pictographs – for example, a stylized outline of a camel meant 'camel'. There are those who see remnants of this ancient system in the Hebrew alphabet even today. Take the sixth letter of the Hebrew alphabet, **vav** ו. The name of this letter means *hook*, and in fact it looks like a hook (the original version had two 'horns').

The next great step forward in writing was Egyptian hieroglyphics, which used pictures to represent ideas, sounds and grammar. These were inscribed on papyrus, wood or clay and later, carved into stone. This system, which originated around 3200 BCE, was borrowed by workers in the Sinai Peninsula around the middle of the second millennium BCE and simplified drastically into an alphabet.

This alphabet was used by the peoples of Canaan and the Near East, and was spread further by the Phoenicians to Europe and beyond. Most alphabets, including the Arabic, Hebrew, Greek, Cyrillic and Latin alphabets, ultimately derive from this original alphabet.

The form of the Hebrew alphabet most people are familiar with is the one consisting of the square letters seen in Torah scrolls, in the prayer book and on most signs in modern-day Israel. Yet there is also another form of the alphabet. As its name implies, the cursive alphabet has a more flowing and rounded appearance, although, as with the square script, the letters are not usually joined together but written separately. Most of the cursive letters are very similar to their 'square' equivalents. We will introduce the cursive alphabet gradually.

The logic of Hebrew

Your Hebrew studies will surely present you with some challenges, but they also offer an opportunity to become acquainted with a language that is very different from English and that has its own kind of logic.

The majority of Hebrew words are formed from three-letter roots that contain the essence of the word's meaning. Different forms of the word are constructed from the root in various ways, such as inserting vowels, doubling consonants or adding prefixes or suffixes. The root letters are predominantly consonants, and vowels are added above or below the root letters as diacritical marks or 'points'. However, as we will discover, in modern Hebrew, these vowels are rarely written – this may seem very strange to an English speaker, but don't worry, we'll help you get used to this over the course of the lessons!

If you have studied another foreign language (such as French, Spanish or German), you may find some aspects of Hebrew grammar familiar. Like French and Spanish, all nouns are either masculine or feminine, even if they refer to objects that have no intrinsic 'gender' – such as *book*, *sun* or *cucumber*. If a noun is accompanied by an adjective (*big book*, *hot sun* or *fresh cucumbers*), the adjective also changes according to the gender (masculine or feminine) and number (singular or plural) of the noun.

In some ways, you may find Hebrew complicated at first. For example, the simple past tense in English (*I/you/he/she/we/they walked*, all with the same form of the verb) compared to the equivalent in Hebrew (**halachti, halachta, halacht, halach, halchah** הָלַכְתִּי, הָלַכְתָּ, הָלַכְתְּ, הָלַךְ, הָלְכָה, to give just the singular forms) makes the latter seem a bit daunting. On the other hand, you'll be relieved to learn that in Hebrew, there is just one main tense for any action completed in the past. In contrast, take a moment to consider how many different past tenses there are in English depending on when the action took place in relation to the current time: *I walked, I have walked, I was walking, I had walked, I have been walking, I used to walk* … and so it goes on. Hebrew is also much more regular than English. Pity the Israeli school student who has to learn that the past of *I go* is *I went* – two completely unrelated words!

Another point that may comfort you as you begin your studies is related to the fact that Israel is a country of immigrants. A large proportion of Israelis learned Hebrew as a second language and, as a result, they don't always apply the strictest grammatical rules. This may be annoying for purists, but it's good news for you. In most cases, as long as you say something reasonably close to the proper form, people will understand you. We will, of course, teach the correct grammatical forms (while also mentioning some slang words and phrases), but as we emphasize throughout the book – don't obsess too much about this. As you get used to listening to Hebrew speech, you'll find yourself choosing the right form more and more effortlessly.

How to use this course

Our method is based on regular and gradual progress. A point of grammar will be introduced briefly at one point, and in later lessons further details and explanations will be provided. This approach mimics the way we learn our first language. Our goal is to help you gain an intuitive feel for Hebrew grammar and syntax. We have planned the learning stages carefully in order to help you absorb the material as easily as possible.

Now – over to you! For the best results, we suggest that you devote half an hour a day to your Hebrew studies. If you have a particularly busy day, you can cut back a little, but try not to miss our daily meetings. Like learning a musical instrument or going to the gym, language learning is a discipline. Once you make the commitment and start to see results, we are sure you will feel that the effort is worthwhile.

Comprehension: the first wave

The first 50 lessons concentrate on comprehension and assimilation of the language. The main goal is to try to understand what you read, and, if you have the recordings, hear.

We recommend the following:
1) Listen to the recording of the lesson, to get a feel for how Israelis pronounce the words and phrases you are about to learn.
2) Read the lesson carefully. Don't be embarrassed to read out loud, line by line, using the phonetic transcriptions to approximate the pronunciation. Look over the English translation to help you understand what you're reading.
3) Listen to the audio recording again, and repeat every phrase.
4) Read the notes, which provide important explanations about grammatical points, as well as additional information about the etymology and meaning of new words.
5) Work through the exercises in each lesson, which give you a chance to practice what you have learned.

After every group of six lessons, a review lesson summarizes all the main grammatical points introduced in that set of lessons.

Consolidation: the second wave

This is what we call the 'active' phase. Beginning from lesson 50, you will continue to move forward with your studies, but at the same time you will go back to review a previous lesson, starting from lesson 1. This time, however, instead of translating the first exercise in each lesson from Hebrew to English, try to translate in the other direction: that is, into Hebrew. This will develop your active knowledge of Hebrew alongside your developing comprehension of it.

The audio recordings

It is difficult to learn the sounds and rhythms of a language from written explanations. Listening to real Hebrew spoken by Israelis is the best way to get a feel for this. The audio recordings that accompany this course will help you improve your pronunciation. They will also help you learn where the stress goes (which part of each word is pronounced more forcefully). The stress in Hebrew is generally on the last syllable, but not always. The recordings are read by native Hebrew speakers and consist of the lesson text and the first exercise in each lesson. For the first 14 lessons, we have provided two recordings: a slow reading to give you time to follow along and repeat the text aloud, and a reading at normal speed.

Don't forget to learn the Hebrew numbers. The ordinal numbers are given at the beginning of every lesson, and the cardinal numbers with the page numbers at the bottom of every page.

Learning a new language offers a chance to see the world from a different angle. You may well find that the logical and structured nature of Hebrew makes it an easier language to learn than you imagined. Enjoy your studies, and …

בְּהַצְלָחָה! **Behatzlachah!** *Good luck!*

The Hebrew alphabet

The following table presents the Hebrew alphabet in alphabetic order – by which we mean the Hebrew order of the alphabet! The table shows the 'square' and 'cursive' scripts (the former is used in printed materials and the latter in handwriting), as well as the phonetic transliteration used in this book.

The Hebrew alphabet has 22 letters. Certain letters have two different pronunciations, and five letters have a different written form when they appear at the end of a word. All these forms appear in the table. Variations of the same letter share the same number in the first column.

	Square letter	Cursive letter	Name	Transliteration and pronunciation
1	א	א	**`alef**	` (glottal stop)
2	בּ	ב	**bet**	**b**
2	ב	ב	**vet**	**v**
3	ג	ג	**gimel**	**g** (as in ***game***)
4	ד	ד	**dalet**	**d**
5	ה	ה	**hey**	**h**
6	ו	ו	**vav**	**v**
7	ז	ז	**zayin**	**z** (as in *zoo*)
8	ח	ח	**chet**	**ch** (as in Scottish *loch*)
9	ט	ט	**tet**	**t**
10	י	י	**yod**	**y** (as in ***yes***, `at the beginning of a syllable) **i** (like the *ee* in ***meet***)

11	כּ	כּ	**kaf**	**k**
11	כ	כ	**khaf**	**kh** (as in Scottish *loch*)
11	ך	ך	final **khaf**	**kh**
12	ל	ל	**lamed**	**l**
13	מ	מ	**mem**	**m**
13	ם	ם	final **mem**	**m**
14	נ	נ	**nun**	**n**
14	ן	ן	final **nun**	**n**
15	ס	ס	**samekh**	**s** (as in ***s**even*)
16	ע	ע	**'ayin**	**'** (glottal stop)
17	פּ	פּ	**pe**	**p**
17	פ	פ	**fe**	**f**
17	ף	ף	final **fe**	**f**
18	צ	צ	**tsadi**	**tz** (as in *matzah*)
18	ץ	ץ	final **tsadi**	**tz**
19	ק	ק	**qof**	**q** (like the *k* in ***k**eep*)
20	ר	ר	**resh**	**r**
21	שׁ	שׁ	**shin**	**sh** (as in ***sh**ell*)
21	שׂ	שׂ	**sin**	**s** (as in ***s**even*)
22	ת	ת	**tav**	**t**

Vowel marks

Hebrew vowels are represented as diacritical marks (symbols added to letters) called **niqud**. (X in the table below is used to represent any letter.)

i	Xִ or Xִי	**i** pronounced like *ee* in ***meet***, but shorter
a	Xָ Xַ Xֲ	**a** as in ***apple***
o	וֹ	**o** as in ***dog***
e	Xֶ Xֵ Xְ	**e** as in ***met***
u	Xֻ וּ	**u** pronounced like *oo* in ***noon*** (but shorter)
ey	Xֵי	**ey** as in ***they***

Note: As you'll find out in the lessons, these vowel marks are not written in Hebrew for everyday use, and neither are the dots that distinguish between the forms **bet** and **vet**, **kaf** and **khaf**, **pe** and **fe**, and **shin** and **sin**. These letters usually appear simply as ב כ פ and ש.

Before starting the lessons, it is important to read the introduction to the course, even if you're not a total beginner.

1 First lesson (Shi'ur rishon) *(lesson first)*

The first line of each phrase, in **bold** *type, gives the pronunciation. The second line, in italic type, is a literal translation following the Hebrew word order. English words linked by a hyphen represent a single word in Hebrew. The third line gives the meaning of the phrase in everyday English.*

Boqer
Morning

1 – **Boqer tov!**
morning good
Good morning!

2 – **Boqer `or!**
morning-of light
Good morning!

Pronunciation note
1 Try to keep Hebrew vowels short and simple – the *o* in **boqer** is short as in *box*, not long as in *most*. Above all – don't worry! Israelis are used to hearing people speak Hebrew with American, British and other accents. They may smile, but they'll be delighted you're making the effort to speak their language.

1 שִׁעוּר רִאשׁוֹן

בּוֹקֶר

1 – בּוֹקֶר טוֹב!

2 – בּוֹקֶר אוֹר!

Transliteration

As you may already know, Hebrew is written and read from right to left. This is a big difference from English, and will take some getting used to. The good news is that there are no capital letters in Hebrew, and the punctuation marks are the same as in English. Hebrew has two types of script. 'Square script' is usually used in printed material, whereas 'cursive script' is used in handwriting. In lessons 1 to 14, we use the square script only. Then we will gradually introduce the cursive script, which will be used alongside the square script from lesson 29.

To help you decipher the Hebrew, in the first lessons, after the dialogue, a transliteration in English letters is given under each Hebrew word. These transliterations will be provided until you can manage reading the Hebrew script alone – don't worry, this will happen sooner than you think!

In these transliterations, separate letters are shown in capitals. The Hebrew vowel marks (the dots and dashes around the letters) appear as lower-case letters.

To help you match the Hebrew letters with the corresponding English characters, the Hebrew letters have been colour-coded alternately in black and blue: the same colours are then used in the transliteration. For example, let's look again at the word **boqer** בּוֹקֶר : in the transliteration that follows, the B is in blue as it transliterates the Hebrew בּ. The next letter, the ו, is in black and transliterated with the capital letter O. Next, the letter ק is printed in blue, along with the vowel written under it ֶ. As the vowel is

1

not written as a separate letter, it appears in lower-case. Finally, the Hebrew ר is printed in black, and transliterated as a black R.

By chance, the other two words introduced in this lesson – **tov** טוֹב *good* and **`or** אוֹר *light* – also include the vowel **o** in the same form. In the transliteration, the letter **`alef** א is represented by the sign ` . At the beginning of a word, this letter is barely heard, but in the middle of a word it is pronounced as a glottal stop (an example of this sound is the dropping of the 'tt' sound in the word *bottle* in a London Cockney accent; you can also hear it in the word *cooperative* just after the first *o*.

← (reading direction)

בּוֹקֶר

R Qe O B ←

boqer

טוֹב	בּוֹקֶר	**1**
V O T	R Qe O B	←
tov	**boqer**	
אוֹר	בּוֹקֶר	**2**
R O `	R Qe O B	←
`or	**boqer**	

Alphabet

In this section, the letters used in the lesson are introduced according to Hebrew alphabetical order. In ancient times, there was a strong connection between letters and images. Many of the Hebrew letters have traditional meanings and associations, some of which we mention here.

• **`alef** א is the first letter of the Hebrew alphabet. It represents the glottal stop, the sound represented by the hyphen in 'uh-oh'. At the beginning of a word, it essentially shows that the word begins with a vowel. For example, the word **`or** אוֹר *light* begins with an *o* sound. The letter א at the beginning of the word has no sound, but marks the opening of the mouth to begin the word.

• **bet** בּ: has a hearth-like shape, and the dot in the centre is its fire.

The word **bayit** means *house* and evokes a sense of warmth and intimacy. This letter is pronounced *b* as in *butter.*
• **vet** ב: this is the same letter as **bet**, but without the dot in the middle. It is pronounced *v* as in *van*. We will transcribe it simply by the letter **v**.
• **vav** ו: looks like a hook, and that's exactly what the word **vav** means! We also use **v** to represent this sound, which is identical to the sound of the letter **vet**. However, **vav** can also serve as a vowel. In the word **boqer** בּוֹקֶר, it is used to express the vowel **o**.
• **tet** ט: this letter is pronounced *t* as in *tennis*. In our transliteration it appears as **t**.
• **qof** ק: looks a little like an axe, but the word **qof** actually means *monkey*. We will use **q** to transliterate **qof**.
• **resh** ר: looks like the curve of the neck and head, and the Hebrew word for *head* is **rosh** רֹאשׁ. **Resh** ר can mean *beginning* or *origin*. This letter is pronounced *r* – try to make it a strong, rolled *r* like an actor in the theatre.

Vowels

For many centuries, Hebrew was written with only inaccurate vowel indications, and readers would fill in the correct vowel sounds according to their knowledge of the language. Somewhere between 600 and 800 CE, Jewish sages living in Tiberias on the shores of the Sea of Galilee adopted a system of dots and dashes placed above or below the letters to represent vowel sounds. Knowledge of Hebrew was fading at that time, and the sages were afraid that people would eventually forget how to read the sacred texts correctly.

Today, Hebrew has once again become a fully living language used in daily life. Israelis do not usually use the vowel marks in everyday writing, although sometimes a vowel or two may be added to a word to prevent confusion or clarify the pronunciation of a rare or foreign word.

In this course, we will start getting used to texts without the extra vowel marks from the beginning – there are no vowel marks in the Hebrew in exercise 1. Don't be alarmed – the words are all ones you have already seen, and the phonetic transliterations will help remind you of the correct pronunciation.

Modern Hebrew has six basic vowel sounds: **a** as in *man*, **o** as in *box*, **u** as in *food*, **e** as in *pen*, **i** as in *mint* and **ey** as in *they*. Here are the two we have seen so far:

o וֹ
e ֶ (the mark appears under the consonant that precedes the vowel)

1 *To do the exercises, we recommend that you use a notebook starting from the back cover (which of course in Hebrew would be the front!) because Hebrew is written from right to left, just as it is read. Whether using the square or cursive script, write each letter*

Targil rishon – Targem — תַרְגִיל רִאשׁוֹן – תַרְגֵם
Exercise 1 – Translate

Boqer	❶ בוקר
Tov	❷ טוב
\`Or	❸ אור
Boqer tov.	❹ בוקר טוב.
Boqer \`or.	❺ בוקר אור.

Targil sheni – Hashlem — תַרְגִיל שֵׁנִי – הַשְׁלֵם
Exercise 2 – Fill in the missing letters

Each dash represents one Hebrew letter (together with its vowel).

❶ Morning
boqer — בּ _ קֶ _

❷ Good
tov — _ וֹב

❸ Light
\`or — _ וֹר

separately – don't join them together. The words in the exercises do not include vowel marks, to get you used to seeing them the way they appear everywhere in Israel. Don't panic! You've already encountered all these words in the lesson.

Answers to Exercise 1

❶ Morning ❷ Good ❸ Light ❹ Good morning *(Morning good).* ❺ Good morning *(Morning-of light).*

Answers to Exercise 2 – Missing letters

❶ בּוֹקֶר
❷ טוֹב
❸ אוֹר

1 **Boqer `or** בוֹקֶר אוֹר *'morning of light' is a common morning greeting. If someone wishes you* **boqer tov**, *reply with* **boqer `or**. *Perhaps this custom comes from living in a country full of sunshine, where light is a symbol of happiness.*

Hebrew was never a dead language. It has evolved and changed over the centuries from Biblical times to the digital age, but it has always been in use. Even today, most modern Hebrew words can be easily traced to their Biblical roots. The history of Israel and its different immigrants have influenced the Hebrew spoken in the country today. Ashkenazim (Jews from Europe, particularly Eastern Europe and Germany) and Sephardim ('Sephardi' means 'Spanish', so refers to Jews exiled from the Iberian Peninsula, but has come to refer broadly to Jews who originate from Arab lands) have historically pronounced Hebrew differently; modern Israeli pronunciation is a hybrid of these two accents.

In modern times, the first wave of Jewish immigration began in 1881. Most of the newcomers came from Russia, Poland, Lithuania, Romania and Yemen. This is known as the First **'Aliyah** עֲלִיָּה ascent, *since wherever Jews come from, they 'ascend' or 'go up' to Israel. The first immigrants from Eastern Europe were fleeing the series of pogroms that followed the assassination of Czar Alexander II in March 1881. They spoke Hebrew with an Ashkenazi accent, but they soon adopted the local accent. Yemenites began to come to Israel in the same year out of religious fervour. Each of the* **'aliyot** *(*ascents *– the plural of* **'aliyah***) brought its own accents to the country.*

The Second **'Aliyah** *occurred from 1903 to 1913, as Jews continued to flee pogroms such as that in Kishinev (now Chişinău, the capital of Moldova). The Dreyfus Affair in France also had an influence on immigration to Israel, as well as on the ideas of Theodor Herzl, the founder of modern Zionism.*

The Third **'Aliyah** *(1918–23) brought newcomers from Europe and some Arab countries.*

The Fourth **'Aliyah** *(1924–28) brought mainly Jews from Poland. For the first time, the number of Jews heading East exceeded the number migrating to the United States.*

The Fifth **'Aliyah** *(1933–39) included many who entered the country illegally. A high level of immigration, illegal in the eyes of the British Mandate authorities who ruled the country at the time, continued from 1945 through 1948 in the aftermath of the Second World War. The story of the ship* Exodus *is the best-known example of this dramatic period.*

Following the establishment of the State of Israel in 1948, the gates opened, and immigrants flooded into Israel from many different countries.

Today, all Israelis speak Hebrew. Many of them have the accent typical of their country of origin. There is also a standard Israeli accent common among those born in the country.

Now you've learned your first few Hebrew letters. You're still a beginner, but next time you see Hebrew writing, we hope at least you won't feel that it all looks Greek to you ...

2 Second lesson (Shi'ur sheni)

Shalom
Hello

1 – Shalom Li`or!
peace Lior
Hello Lior!

2 – Shalom Shirli!
peace Shirli
Hello Shirli!

Pronunciation note
1, 2 Here the letter **yod** י is used to lengthen the *i* sound of the preceding vowel. Look at the names **Li`or** לִיאוֹר and **Shirli** שִׁירְלִי: the dot representing *i* appears under the consonant before the **yod** י..

2 שִׁעוּר שֵׁנִי

שָׁלוֹם

1 – שָׁלוֹם לִיאוֹר!

2 – שָׁלוֹם שִׁירְלִי! □

Transliteration

Here each Hebrew letter is shown with its English transliteration underneath it. The vowels shown by vowel marks are in lower-case and the other letters in upper-case. Don't forget to read from right to left! We have written the vowel sound **o** with a capital O when it represents the **vav** ו used to carry the vowel sound.

←

שָׁ ל וֹ ם

M O L SHa

shalom

1

שָׁ ל וֹ ם — לִ י א וֹ ר

← M O L SHa — R O ` I Li

shalom — **Li`or**

2

שָׁ ל וֹ ם — שִׁ י ר לְ י

← M O L SHa — I Li R I SHi

shalom — **Shirli**

Alphabet

• In the words in this dialogue, **yod** י has the sound *ee* as in *meet*. In other contexts, it can represent the consonant *y* as in *yes*. When the preceding letter carries the vowel ֵ , the combination is pronounced *ey* as in *they*. The name of this letter is similar to the word **yad** *hand*, but its shape is more like a thumb.

• **lamed** ל is pronounced *l* as in *lemon*. Its shape is like a lion-tamer's whip. The name of this letter also means *to learn*. This is the only Hebrew letter that rises above the line of letters with its tall neck. Hebrew seems to be telling us that through learning we can train ourselves to rise higher.

• **mem** ם is pronounced *m* as in *melon*. The form shown here is a final **mem**, used only when this letter appears at the end of a word.

Targil rishon – Targem / תַּרְגִּיל רִאשׁוֹן – תַּרְגֵּם
Exercise 1 – Translate

Shalom.	❶ שלום.
Shalom Li\`or.	❷ שלום ליאור.
Shalom Shirli.	❸ שלום שירלי.
Boqer \`or, Li\`or.	❹ בוקר אור, ליאור.
Boqer tov, Shirli.	❺ בוקר טוב, שירלי.

A different form is used at the beginning or in the middle of a word. Five Hebrew letters have distinct final forms – we'll meet them along our way.

• **shin** שׁ is pronounced *sh* as in *shell*, so naturally we will transcribe it as **sh**. The dot on the right-hand prong of this letter is not a vowel. It shows that the letter is to be pronounced *sh*. As we will see later, a dot on the left-hand prong turns the letter into **sin**, which is pronounced *s*.

Vowels

We encountered two new vowels in this lesson:

a ָ
i ִ

Answers to Exercise 1

❶ Hello *(Peace).* ❷ Hello Lior. ❸ Hello Shirli. ❹ Good morning *(Morning-of light)*, Lior. ❺ Good morning *(Morning good)*, Shirli.

Targil sheni – Hashlem תַרגִיל שֵנִי – הַשלֵם
Exercise 2 – Fill in the missing letters

❶ Hello.

Shalom. _ לוֹם

❷ Li`or – יא – ר

❸ Shirli – יר – י

❹ Good morning *(Morning good)*, Lior.
Boqer tov, Li`or. – וֹקֶר טוֹ – , לִי – וֹר

❺ Good morning *(Morning-of light)*, Shirli.
Boqer `or, Shirli. בּוֹקֶ – – וֹר, שִיר – –

Shalom שָלוֹם *is one of the most important words in the Hebrew language and is known all over the world. Though its basic meaning is* peace, **shalom** *is also used to mean* hello, goodbye, good morning, good evening *and so on.*

Like all Hebrew names, **Li`or** לִיאוֹר *has a positive meaning. In this case, the name means 'for-me-light' – in other words,* I have

Answers to Exercise 2

❶ שָׁלוֹם ❷ לִיאוֹר ❸ שִׁירְלִי ❹ בּוֹקֶר טוֹב, לִיאוֹר.
❺ בּוֹקֶר אוֹר, שִׁירְלִי.

light. *Another Hebrew name has the same combination in reverse:* **`Orli** אוֹרְלִי *'light-for-me'*. **Shirli** שִׁירְלִי *means 'poem-for-me' or* I have a poem.

Since you know Hebrew now, we can simply say **shalom** שָׁלוֹם *– until the next lesson.*

3 Third lesson (Shi'ur shlishi)

Kakhah, kakhah
Not bad

1 – Mah ① shlomkha ② Li`or?
what peace-your(masc.) Lior
How are you, Lior?

2 – Tov.
good
Good.

3 Mah shlomekh Shirli?
what peace-your(fem.) Shirli
How are you, Shirli?

4 – Kakhah, kakhah ③.
like-that like-that
Not bad (so-so).

Pronunciation notes
Title When the letter **hey** ה appears at the end of a word without an accompanying vowel, as it does here, it is not pronounced. Otherwise, it is pronounced *h* as in *hello*. You may find that many Israelis drop the *h* sound, particularly at the beginning of words, but you should pronounce it clearly (unless it's at the end of a word!).
• The letter **kaf** כּ is pronounced *k* as in *keep*.
• The letter **khaf** כ is a guttural or throaty sound, like the *ch* in the Scottish word *loch* or the German *achtung*. When **khaf** comes at the end of the word it is written differently (ך), but the pronunciation is the same.

3 שִׁעוּר שְׁלִישִׁי

כָּכָה, כָּכָה

1 – מַה שְׁלוֹמְךָ לִיאוֹר?

2 – טוֹב.

3 מַה שְׁלוֹמֵךְ שִׁירְלִי?

4 – כָּכָה, כָּכָה.

☐

Notes

① **mah** מַה means *what/which.* It is a vital word for forming questions.

② The words **shlomkha** שְׁלוֹמְךָ (masc.) (line 1) and **shlomekh** שְׁלוֹמֵךְ (fem.) (line 3) are written with the same letters, and both are formed from the word **shalom** שָׁלוֹם *peace*. The only difference is the vowels. The masculine form ends in *a*, while the feminine form has the vowel *e* under the **mem**.

Mah shlomkha (to a man) and **mah shlomekh** (to a woman) are the usual way to ask someone *How are you?* Literally, the Hebrew means 'What is your peace?' or 'What is your well-being?'.

③ Here, the letter **hey** ה comes at the end of the word, but it can also appear at the beginning or in the middle. In the word **mah** מַה *what*, the **hey** ה makes the word possible, since a Hebrew word must have at least two letters. A single letter with a vowel forms a syllable, but not a word. So the ה at the end is a vital part of the word, even if it's not pronounced. To give another example: if we remove the ה from **kakhah** כָּכָה, we would be left with **kakh** כָּךְ *so*, and the last consonant in the word, the **khaf**, would change to its final form ךְ.

כָּ כָ ה	כָּ כָ ה
H KHa Ka	H KHa Ka
kakhah	**kakhah**

1	מַ ה	שׁ ל וֹ מ ךָ	לִ י א וֹ ר
←	H Ma	KHa M O L SH	R O ` I Li
	mah	**shlomkha**	**Li`or**
2	ט וֹ ב		
←	V O T		
	tov		
3	מַ ה	שׁ ל וֹ מֵ ךְ	שִׁ י ר לִ י
←	H Ma	KH Me O L SH	I Li R I SHi
	mah	**shlomekh**	**Shirli**
4	כָּ כָ ה	כָּ כָ ה	
←	H KHa Ka	H KHa Ka	
	kakhah	**kakhah**	

תַרְגִיל רִאשׁוֹן – תַרְגֵם

Targil rishon – Targem

1. מה שלומך, שירלי? — Mah shlomekh, Shirli?
2. טוב. — Tov.
3. מה שלומך, ליאור? — Mah shlomkha, Li`or?
4. ככה, ככה. — Kakhah, kakhah.
5. שלום, מה שלומך? — Shalom, mah shlomkha?

Alphabet

• **hey** ה represents a breath of air. This letter is transliterated *h*.

• **kaf** כּ means the open palm of a hand. In modern Hebrew, **kaf** also means *spoon*.

• **khaf** כ is also a palm, but this time it is empty.

• final **khaf** ך. Now we can see the handle of the spoon.

• **mem** מ already made an appearance in its final form ם in lesson 2. The letter **mem** makes us think of the word **mayim**, which means *water*. You can imagine what an important letter this is in a country flooded with sunshine!

Answers to Exercise 1

❶ How are you, Shirli? ❷ Good. ❸ How are you, Lior? ❹ Not bad *(So-so)*. ❺ Hello, how are you*(masc.)*?

3

Targil sheni – Hashlem תַּרְגִּיל שֵׁנִי – הַשְׁלֵם

❶ What? *(Which?)*
Mah? מַ – ?

❷ Your peace *(masc.)*.
Shlomkha. שְׁלוֹמ – .

❸ Your peace *(fem.)*.
Shlomekh. שְׁלוֹ _ ךְ.

❹ Not bad *(So-so)*.
Kakhah, kakhah. _ כָה, כָּ _ ה.

❺ How are you, Shirli?
Mah shlomekh, Shirli? _ה _ לוֹמֵךְ, שִׁ _ רְל _?

Answers to Exercise 2

❶ מַה? ❷ שלומךָ. ❸ שלומֵך. ❹ כָּכָה, כָּכָה. ❺ מַה שלומֵך, שִׁירלִי?

You've reached the end of lesson 3! This is a good point to ask how you're doing. We hope your answer is **tov** טוֹב *and not just* **kakhah, kakhah** כָּכָה, כָּכָה.

4 Fourth lesson (Shi'ur revi'i)

Todah
Thanks

1 – Mah `atah shoteh ① ?
what you(masc.) drinking(masc.)
What are you drinking?

2 – Teh, todah.
tea thanks
Tea, thanks.

3 – Mah `at shotah?
what you(fem.) drinking(fem.)
What are you drinking?

4 – Birah todah.
beer thanks
Beer, thanks.

Pronunciation note
In modern Hebrew, the letters **tet** ט and **tav** ת have the same sound. However, it is important to learn the correct spelling, as the use of one or the other of these letters can make all the difference to the meaning of the written word.

Notes
① **shoteh** שׁוֹתֶה: this verb is in the present tense – the action is happening now. In English, we conjugate the verb differently depending on who is doing the action, e.g. *I drink, you drink, he/she drinks*. In Hebrew, the same form is used in the present tense for all singular pronouns – that is, when one person is doing the action – BUT the verb changes if the person doing the action is male or female. ▶

4 שִׁעוּר רְבִיעִי

תּוֹדָה

1 – מַה אַתָּה שׁוֹתֶה?

2 – תֵּה, תּוֹדָה.

3 – מַה אַתְּ שׁוֹתָה?

4 – בִּירָה, תּוֹדָה.

• In line 1, the *you* refers to a man, so the subject pronoun **`atah** אתה and the verb **shoteh** שׁוֹתֶה are in the masculine.
• In line 3, the *you* refers to a woman, so the subject pronoun **`at** את and the verb **shotah** שׁוֹתָה are in the feminine.

Notice that the only difference between **shoteh** שׁוֹתֶה and **shotah** שׁוֹתָה is in the final vowel sound accompanying the letter **hey**. When written without the vowel symbols, the two words look identical – the difference is all in the pronunciation. As you can imagine, it is important to get this right when you're talking to someone!

In Hebrew, almost any time you talk to or about someone, or even about objects, you will have to decide whether to use the feminine or masculine form. It takes some getting used to, but in time you'll do it without even thinking about it. In this book, we use the abbreviation (fem.) to indicate a word in the feminine form and (masc.) to indicate the masculine form.

←
תוֹדָה
H Da O T
todah

שׁוֹתֶה H Te O SH **shoteh**	אַתָה H Ta `a **`atah**	מַה H Ma **mah**	**1** ←
	תוֹדָה H Da O T **todah**	תֵה H Te **teh**	**2** ←
שׁוֹתָה H Ta O SH **shotah**	אַת T `a **`at**	מַה H Ma **mah**	**3** ←
	תוֹדָה H Da O T **todah**	בִּירָה H Ra I Bi **birah**	**4** ←

Targil rishon – Targem תַרְגִיל רִאשׁוֹן – תַרְגֵם

❶ אתה שותה בירה.
`Atah shoteh birah.

❷ את שותה תה.
`At shotah teh.

❸ תודה.
Todah.

❹ שלום, את שותה בירה?
Shalom, `at shotah birah?

❺ בוקר טוב, אתה שותה תה?
Boqer tov. `Atah shoteh teh?

Alphabet

• **dalet** ד is pronounced *d*. The name of this letter means *door*.
• **tav** ת. The word **tav** means *mark* or can refer to a musical note. This letter is pronounced *t*, just like the letter **tet**. We transliterate both as **t**, but make sure to write the correct letter in each case.

Vowels

The sound *e* can be written in two ways: either with the symbol ֶ (which we've already seen) or ֵ , both of which are placed under the consonant that comes before the vowel sound. There is no real difference in pronunciation – the distinction is grammatical. Don't let it worry you – pronounce both vowels like the *e* as in *pen*.

Answers to Exercise 1

❶ You*(masc.)* drink/are drinking beer. ❷ You*(fem.)* drink/are drinking tea. ❸ Thanks. ❹ Hello, are you*(fem.)* drinking beer? ❺ Good morning. Are you*(masc.)* drinking tea?

Targil sheni – Hashlem תַרְגִיל שֵׁנִי – הַשְׁלֵם

❶ You*(masc.)* drink/are drinking.
`Atah shoteh. _תָה שׁוֹ_ה.

❷ You*(fem.)* drink/are drinking.
`At shotah. אַ_ שׁוֹ_ה.

❸ Beer, tea.
Birah, teh. _ירָה, תֵ_.

❹ Thanks.
Todah. תוֹ_ה.

❺ What are you*(masc.)* drinking?
Mah `atah shoteh? מַ_ אַתָ_ _וֹתֶה?

---

5 Fifth lesson (Shi'ur chamishi)

'ivrit ①
Hebrew

1 – Boqer tov, Dan!
morning good Dan
Good morning, Dan!

2 Mah `atah lomed ②?
what you(masc.) learning(masc.)
What are you learning?

Pronunciation note
Most Israelis pronounce the letter **'ayin** just like **`alef**, that is to say, as a glottal stop within a word or barely pronounced at the beginning of a word, though some pronounce it as a more forceful, guttural sound.

Answers to Exercise 2

❶ אַתָּה שׁוֹתֶה. ❷ אַת שׁוֹתָה. ❸ בִּירָה, תֵּה. ❹ תוֹדָה. ❺ מַה אַתָּה שׁוֹתֶה?

Good work! You deserve a cup of tea, perhaps while learning to write the word coffee **kafeh** קָפֶה. **Todah** תוֹדָה *for your efforts.*

5 שִׁעוּר חֲמִישִׁי

עִבְרִית

1 – בּוֹקֶר טוֹב, דָּן!

2 מַה אַתָּה לוֹמֵד?

Notes

① **'ivrit** עִבְרִית *Hebrew* comes from the root עבר *to cross.* Hebrew words are derived from root words, which typically consist of three letters. A range of related words are formed by adding prefixes or suffixes to the root, or by changing the vowels.

② **lomed** לוֹמֵד *(I, you, he) learn/learns* or *am/are/is learning*: this is the masculine singular form of the present tense verb. In other words, this is the form we use when one male person is doing the learning. To say *you learn* to a man or boy, you say: **`atah** *you* (masc.) **lomed** *learn* (masc.). To say *I learn* if you are a man or boy, you say **`ani** (*I*) **lomed**.

3 – \`Ani lomed 'ivrit.
I learning(masc.) Hebrew
I am learning Hebrew.

4 – Le\`ah, mah \`at lomedet ③**?**
Leah what you(fem.) learning(fem.)
Leah, what are you learning?

5 – \`Ani lomedet latinit.
I learning(fem.) Latin
I am learning Latin.

Notes

③ **lomedet** לוֹמֶדֶת (*I, you, she*) *learn/learns* or *am/are/is learning*: this is the feminine singular of the present tense – the form to use when <u>one female person</u> is doing the learning. To say *you learn* to a woman or girl, you say **\`at** *you* (fem.) **lomedet** *learn* (fem.). To say *I learn* if you are a woman or girl, you say **\`ani** (*I*) **lomedet**. In this case, the sound **-et** is added to the masculine verb to form the feminine. You may have noticed that the word **\`ani** אֲנִי *I* is the same whether you are male or female.

3 – אֲנִי לוֹמֵד עִבְרִית.

4 – לֵאָה, מַה אַת לוֹמֶדֶת?

5 – אֲנִי לוֹמֶדֶת לָטִינִית.

□

Transliteration

עִבְרִית
← T I Ri V 'i
'ivrit

1	בּוֹקֶר	טוֹב	דָן	
←	R Qe O B	V O T	N Da	
	boqer	**tov**	**Dan**	
2	מַה	אַתָּה	לוֹמֵד	
←	H Ma	H Ta `a	D Me O L	
	mah	**`atah**	**lomed**	
3	אֲנִי	לוֹמֵד	עִבְרִית	
←	I Ni `a	D Me O L	T I Ri V 'i	
	`ani	**lomed**	**'ivrit**	
4	לֵאָה	מַה	אַת	לוֹמֶדֶת
←	H `a Le	H Ma	T `a	T De Me O L
	Le`ah	**mah**	**`at**	**lomedet**
5	אֲנִי	לוֹמֶדֶת	לָטִינִית	
←	I Ni `a	T De Me O L	T I Ni I Ti La	
	`ani	**lomedet**	**latinit**	

Alphabet

• **nun** נ : this letter is pronounced *n* (the name of the letter is pronounced *noon*). This letter has a distinct final form ן, which looks different, but is pronounced in exactly the same way. The final form, with its small head and long body, is similar to that of a snake. In a hot country, much of which is desert, is it really so surprising to find a snake lurking before us?
• **'ayin** ע : The ancient Hebrew alphabet used a representation of an eye for this letter, so it's no coincidence that to this day the word **'ayin** means *eye*. The same word also means *spring* or *source of water*. We will transliterate this letter by a straight apostrophe before the vowel it accompanies. As we explained in

Targil rishon – Targem — תַּרְגִּיל רִאשׁוֹן – תַּרְגֵּם

1. לאה לומדת עברית. — Le`ah lomedet 'ivrit.
2. דן לומד לטינית. — Dan lomed latinit.
3. אתה לומד. — `Atah lomed.
4. את לומדת. — `At lomedet.
5. מה שירלי לומדת? — Mah Shirli lomedet?

Targil sheni – Hashlem — תַּרְגִּיל שֵׁנִי – הַשְׁלֵם

1. Leah
Le`ah — לֵאָ _
2. Hebrew
'Ivrit — עִבְרִ _ _
3. Latin
Latinit — לָטִינִ _ _
4. Dan [is] learning.
Dan lomed. — דָ _ לוֹ _ ד.
5. Leah [is] learning.
Le`ah lomedet. — לֵ_ה לוֹמֶדֶ _.

the pronunciation section of this lesson, it is usually pronounced the same as **`alef**.

Vowels

We've already seen two ways of writing the sound *a*: ַ and ָ . There is also a third form: ֲ . We couldn't possibly explain here all the reasons for these differences. To be honest, it doesn't really matter: in modern Hebrew all these forms are pronounced identically. In any case, the aim is to get you reading Hebrew without the vowel signs as soon as possible.

Answers to Exercise 1

❶ Leah learns/is learning Hebrew. ❷ Dan learns/is learning Latin. ❸ You*(masc.)* learn/are learning. ❹ You*(fem.)* learn/are learning. ❺ What is Shirli learning?

Answers to Exercise 2

❶ לֵאָה. ❷ עִבְרִית. ❸ לָטִינִית. ❹ דָּן לוֹמֵד. ❺ לֵאָה לוֹמֶדֶת.

In the Bible, we read how Abraham travelled from Haran (in the east of modern-day Turkey), crossed the River Euphrates and reached the land of Canaan, now Israel. Abraham was the first person referred to as **'ivri**, *a Hebrew. When Moses left Egypt, he crossed the Red Sea to lead his people to the Promised Land. Joshua crossed the River Jordan to enter Canaan. These events all recall the name* **'ivri**, *which comes from the Hebrew root* עבר*. Not coincidentally, the same root is used in the verb* **'avar** עָבַר to pass *or* to cross.

In a way, you are like the **'ivrim** עִבְרִים, the Hebrews. *You have also begun a journey, and we hope you will soon feel completely at home in their language.*

6 Sixth lesson (Shi'ur shishi)

Beseder
Okay

1 – **Mah nishma'** ①**, Ya'el?**
what is-heard Yael
What's up, Yael?

2 – **Tov, todah, beseder** ②**.**
good thanks okay
[I'm] fine, thanks, OK.

3 **Mah chadash Dani`el?**
what new Daniel
What['s] new, Daniel?

4 – **`Eyn** ③ **chadash.**
there-is-no new
Nothing's new.

Pronunciation notes
2 The letter **samekh** ס, which we transliterate as *s*, is pronounced as in *seven*.
3 The letter **chet** ח, which we transliterate as **ch**, is pronounced by most Israelis exactly the same as the letter **khaf** כ. Originally it had a different pronunciation, like a very strong *h* and without the rasping, throaty sound of **khaf**. Some Israelis maintain this pronunciation, but if you pronounce the two letters in the same way everyone will understand you. In any case, remember not to pronounce this like the *ch* as in *check*!
4 `Eyn אֵין *there is no* rhymes with *rain*. The combination אֵי lengthens and softens the *e* sound; it should be pronounced like the diphthong *ey* as in *they*.

6 שִׁעוּר שִׁישִּׁי

בְּסֵדֶר

1 – מַה נִּשְׁמַע, יָעֵל?

2 – טוֹב, תּוֹדָה, בְּסֵדֶר.

3 מַה חָדָשׁ דָּנִיאֵל?

4 – אֵין חָדָשׁ.

Notes

① The verb **nishma'** נִשְׁמָע literally means 'is heard'.

② **beseder** בְּסֵדֶר *in order, okay.* This word consists of the prefix **b(e)** בּ *in* (it can also mean *by* or *by means of*), followed by the word **seder** סדר meaning *order.* בּ never appears on its own, but is always attached to a word that follows it.

③ **`eyn** אֵין means *there is no* or *there are no*. Have you noticed that Hebrew can say a lot with very few letters or words? A book translated from Hebrew into English expands considerably, and the reverse is also true, of course. There are several reasons for this. Firstly, some Hebrew sentences do not require a verb, as we have seen. Secondly, the vowels are not always written, keeping the words short. Thirdly, most Hebrew words are formed from three- or four-letter roots, often with a small number of additional letters. There are few very long words in Hebrew – bad news for Scrabble players, but good news for you!

5 – Chaval, lehitra`ot!

pity, to-see-each-other

Pity, see you!

Transliteration

בְּסֵדֶר

← R De Se Be

beseder

1	מַה ← H Ma **mah**	נִשְׁמַע ' Ma SH Ni **nishma'**	יָעֵל L 'e Ya **Ya'el**
2	טוֹב ← V O T **tov**	תּוֹדָה H Da O T **todah**	בְּסֵדֶר R De Se Be **beseder**
3	מַה ← H Ma **mah**	חָדָשׁ SH Da Cha **chadash**	דָנִיאֵל L `e I Ni Da **Dani`el**
4	אֵין ← N Y `e **`eyn**	חָדָשׁ SH Da Cha **chadash**	
5	חֲבָל ← L Va Cha **chaval**	לְהִתְרָאוֹת T O ` Ra T Hi Le **lehitra`ot**	

5 – חֲבָל, לְהִתְרָאוֹת!

Alphabet

• **chet** ח. The word **chet** חֵת means *fear*, while the letter has the shape of a door or barrier. We might learn from this that fear creates an invisible barrier in the soul.

• **samekh** ס. The name of this letter means *support*. Its round shape may strike us as a symbol of encircling protection.

Vowels

In lesson 4, we learned two ways of writing the sound *e*. Here is a third way: ֱ.

Targil rishon – Targem — תַּרְגִּיל רִאשׁוֹן – תַּרְגֵּם

Mah nishma'?	❶ מה נשמע?
Beseder.	❷ בסדר.
`Eyn chadash.	❸ אין חדש.
Lehitra`ot, Dani`el.	❹ להתראות, דניאל.
Mah chadash, Ya'el?	❺ מה חדש, יעל?

Targil sheni – Hashlem — תַּרְגִּיל שֵׁנִי – הַשְׁלֵם

❶ Pity. Chaval.	_ בָל.
❷ See you. Lehitra`ot.	לְ _ תְרָ _ וֹת.
❸ New Chadash	חָ _ שׁ
❹ Okay *(In order)*. Beseder.	_ סֵדֶר.
❺ There is no beer. `Eyn birah.	אֵ _ ן בִּירָ _ .

Answers to Exercise 1

❶ What's up? *(What is-heard?)* ❷ Okay *(In-order).* ❸ Nothing's new *(There-is-no new).* ❹ See you, Daniel. ❺ What's new, Yael?

Answers to Exercise 2

❶ חֲבָל. ❷ לְהִתְרָאוֹת. ❸ חָדָשׁ. ❹ בְּסֵדֶר. ❺ אֵין בְּעָיָה.

As you can see, there is always something **chadash** חָדָשׁ new *to learn. Is everything* **beseder** בְּסֵדֶר okay? *Then* **lehitra`ot** לְהִתְרָאוֹת see you soon!

7 Seventh lesson (Shi'ur shvi'i)

חֲזָרָה Chazarah – Review

Congratulations! You've nearly finished your first set of Hebrew lessons. Let's take a moment to go over what you've learned so far.

1 Alphabet

The table below summarizes all the letters we've seen so far, arranged in Hebrew alphabetical order. The slots still to be filled by letters we haven't learned yet are marked with /. The numbers indicate the lesson in which the letter appeared for the first time.

א	**`alef**	`	1	מ	**mem**	**m**	3
בּ	**bet**	**b**	1	ם	final **mem**	**m**	2
ב	**vet**	**v**	1	נ	**nun**	**n**	5
	/	/	/	ן	final **nun**	**n**	5
ד	**dalet**	**d**	4	ס	**samekh**	**s**	6
ה	**hey**	**h**	3	ע	**'ayin**	**'**	5
ו	**vav**	**v**	1	/	/	/	
/	/	/		/		/	
ח	**chet**	**ch**	6	/	/	/	
ט	**tet**	**t**	1	/	/	/	
י	**yod**	**y**	2	/	/	/	
כּ	**kaf**	**k**	3	ק	**qof**	**q**	1
כ	**khaf**	**kh**	3	ר	**resh**	**r**	1
ך	final **khaf**	**kh**	3	שׁ	**shin**	**sh**	2
ל	**lamed**	**l**	2	/	/	/	
				ת	**tav**	**t**	4

7 שִׁעוּר שְׁבִיעִי

2 Vowel marks

X here is used to represent any letter.

i	Xִ or Xִי	**a**	Xָ Xַ Xֲ
o	וֹ	**e**	Xֶ Xֵ Xְ

The only vowel missing is **u** – we'll get to that soon!

3 Three personal pronouns

`ani	אֲנִי	*I* (masc./fem.)
`atah	אַתָּה	*you* (masc.)
`at	אַתְ	*you* (fem.)

In the lessons to come, you'll learn the third-person singular pronouns (*he, she, it*), and later on the plural forms (*we, you, they*). You may well be a bit exhausted by the need to constantly think about masculine and feminine forms, something we hardly ever need to do in English. But spare a thought for the Hebrew speaker who learns English and has to cope with *I learn, I am learning, I do learn* and *I have been learning* – all of which in Hebrew would simply be **`ani lomed** אֲנִי לוֹמֵד for a man and **`ani lomedet** אֲנִי לוֹמֶדֶת for a woman.

4 Verbs

In fact, Hebrew verbs come in just four tenses: past, habitual past (e.g. *I used to*), present and future. You'll appreciate that if you've ever had to struggle with the tenses in languages such as French, Spanish or German. So far, we've been introduced to the present tense, in the first-person singular (*I*) and the second-person singular (*you*, in its masculine and feminine forms). In the present tense, Hebrew verbs only have four different forms: masculine singular, masculine plural and feminine singular, feminine plural. Here are some examples of the two forms we've learned so far.

4.1 Feminine singular

`ani shotah	אֲנִי שׁוֹתָה	*I drink*
`at shotah	אַת שׁוֹתָה	*you drink*
`ani lomedet	אֲנִי לוֹמֶדֶת	*I learn*
`at lomedet	אַת לוֹמֶדֶת	*you learn*

4.2 Masculine singular

`ani shoteh	אֲנִי שׁוֹתֶה	*I drink*
`atah shoteh	אַתָּה שׁוֹתֶה	*you drink*
`ani lomed	אֲנִי לוֹמֵד	*I learn*
`atah lomed	אַתָּה לוֹמֵד	*you learn*

As you can see, the feminine singular in the present tense ends either in **-ah** ָה or in **-et** ֶת ֶ.

Review exercise

Listen to the following text, if you have the recording. Repeat each phrase aloud and then translate it.

❶ בּוֹקֶר טוֹב, שִׁירְלִי. ❷ מַה שְׁלוֹמְךָ, דָּן? ❸ כָּכָה, כָּכָה. ❹ מַה חָדָשׁ? ❺ אֲנִי לוֹמֵד עִבְרִית בְּאַסִּימִיל. ❻ אַת שׁוֹתָה תֵּה? ❼ תּוֹדָה.

Congratulations! You've just reached a milestone. This revision exercise is presented without a phonetic transcription or transliteration. We're confident that you'll be able to read and understand it. Try to listen to the recording first and understand the phrases before reading them. Keep in mind that in the lessons, we will gradually phase out the phonetic transcriptions and transliterations.

Answers

❶ Good morning, Shirli. *(morning good Shirli)* ❷ How are you, Dan? *(what your-peace [masc.] Dan)* ❸ Not bad. *(so-so)* ❹ What's new? *(what new)* ❺ I'm learning Hebrew with Assimil. *(I am-learning Hebrew by-Assimil)* ❻ Are you drinking tea? *(you are-drinking [fem.] tea)* ❼ Thanks.

Eighth lesson (Shi'ur shmini)

Diburim
Speaking

1 – **`Atah medaber 'ivrit ①?**
you(masc.) speak(masc.) Hebrew
Do you speak Hebrew?

2 – **Lo ② raq 'ivrit. `Ani miPolanyah, `ani medaber polanit.**
not only Hebrew. I from-Poland I speak(masc.) Polish.
Not only Hebrew. I ['m] from Poland, I speak Polish.

3 – **VeAnatol?**
and-Anatol
And Anatol?

Pronunciation notes
The letter **vav** ו is used in three ways:
• As the equivalent of the vowel *o*, it is written וֹ. We've already come across this form.
• As the equivalent of the vowel *u* (*oo* as in *moon*), it is written וּ.
• As the equivalent of the consonant *v*, it is written ו.

Notes
① **'ivrit** עִבְרִית *Hebrew.* Almost all language names in Hebrew end in the suffix **-it** ית and are grammatically feminine. There are several examples in this lesson, such as **rusit** רוּסִית *Russian* from **Rusyah** רוּסְיָה *Russia.*

② **lo** לֹא *no.* This word is the equivalent of the English *no*, for example, when replying to questions demanding a yes/no response. It can mean *not* when it appears before a verb, or *no* when used before a noun, as we shall learn soon. Notice that the *o* sound is represented here by a dot above the **lamed**, followed by an **`alef**. As in a few other words in Hebrew, the **`alef** is completely silent here and does not represent a glottal stop. Accordingly, we do not use the ` symbol to represent the **`alef** in these cases.

8 שִׁעוּר שְׁמִינִי

דִבּוּרִים

1 – אַתָּה מְדַבֵּר עִבְרִית?

2 – לֹא רַק עִבְרִית. אֲנִי מִפּוֹלָנְיָה, אֲנִי מְדַבֵּר פּוֹלָנִית.

3 – וְאַנָטוֹל?

Transliteration

דִ בּ וּ רִ י ם
← M I Ri U B Di
diburim

1
אַ תָּ ה — ← H Ta `a — **`atah**
מְ דַ בֵּ ר — R Be Da Me — **medaber**
עִ בְ רִ י ת — T I Ri V 'i — **'ivrit**

2
לֹ א — ← ` Lo — **lo**
רַ ק — Q Ra — **raq**
עִ בְ רִ י ת — T I Ri V 'i — **'ivrit**

אֲ נִ י — ← I Ni `a — **`ani**
מִ פּ וֹ לָ נְ יָ ה — H Ya N La O P Mi — **miPolanyah**
אֲ נִ י — I Ni `a — **`ani**

מְ דַ בֵּ ר — ← R Be Da Me — **medaber**
פּ וֹ לָ נִ י ת — T I Ni La O P — **polanit**

4 – Hu meRusyah; hu medaber rusit, yidish ve'ivrit shel `ulpan ③.
he from-Russia he speaks(masc.) Russian Yiddish and-Hebrew of ulpan
He is from Russia; he speaks Russian, Yiddish and Ulpan Hebrew.

5 – VeRinah?
and-Rinah
And Rinah?

6 – Rinah? Hi medaberet 'ivrit shel shabat!
Rinah she speaks(fem.) Hebrew of shabbat
Rinah? She speaks Shabbat Hebrew!

You're probably wondering how you're expected to know which of these sounds is intended when you read text without the vowel marks. Our response to you is: be patient! You'll soon get the hang of it. For the moment, rely on the phonetic transcriptions. Over time, you'll find the correct pronunciation comes naturally.
In **boqer** *morning* בּוֹקֶר the וֹ is pronounced *o*.
In **Rusyah** *Russia* רוּסְיָה the וּ is pronounced *u*.
In **vered** *rose* וֶרֶד the ו is pronounced like *v* in *vet*.

Notes

③ If you're wondering what Ulpan and Shabbat Hebrew (line 6) are, read on! You'll find out at the end of this lesson.

Alphabet

• **pe** פּ : the name of this letter (pronounced more or less like *pay*) is also a word meaning *mouth*. Note the dot inside the curl of the letter; we will meet the dotless cousin of **pe** in lesson 10.

Vowels

Now introducing the last vowel mark you haven't seen yet: written וּ (note the position of the dot near the middle of the letter), this is pronounced *oo* as in *moon* (though the Hebrew sound is shorter than in English). The vowel mark ֻ is pronounced in the same way. We will discuss this vowel sound more later.

4 – הוּא מֵרוּסיָה; הוּא מְדַבֵּר רוּסִית, אִידִישׁ וְעִבְרִית שֶׁל אוּלְפָּן.

5 – וְרִנָה?

6 – רִנָה? הִיא מְדַבֶּרֶת עִבְרִית שֶׁל שַׁבָּת! □

3 וְאַנָטוֹל
← L O T Na `a Ve
ve`Anatol

4 הוּא — מֵרוּסיָה — הוּא
← ` U H — H Ya S U R Me — ` U H
hu — **meRusyah** — **hu**

מְדַבֵּר — רוּסִית — אִידִישׁ
← R Be Da Me — T I Si U R — SH I Di I `i
medaber — **rusit** — **yidish**

וְעִבְרִית — שֶׁל — אוּלְפָּן
← T I Ri V 'i Ve — L SHe — N Pa L U `
ve'ivrit — **shel** — **`ulpan**

5 וְרִנָה
← H Na Ri Ve
VeRinah

6 רִנָה — הִיא — מְדַבֶּרֶת
← H Na Ri — ` I Hi — T Re Be Da Me
Rinah — **hi** — **medaberet**

עִבְרִית — שֶׁל — שַׁבָּת
← T I Ri V 'i — L SHe — T Ba SHa
'ivrit — **shel** — **shabat**

Targil rishon – Targem תַּרְגִּיל רִאשׁוֹן – תַּרְגֵּם

❶ אנטול מדבר עברית של אולפן.
Anatol medaber 'ivrit shel `ulpan.

❷ רנה מדברת עברית של שבת.
Rinah medaberet 'ivrit shel shabat.

❸ הוא מרוסיה; הוא מדבר רוסית.
Hu meRusyah; hu medaber rusit.

❹ היא מפולניה; היא מדברת פולנית.
Hi miPolanyah; hi medaberet polanit.

❺ אני מדברת אידיש ועברית.
Ani medaberet yidish ve'ivrit.

Targil sheni – Hashlem תַּרְגִּיל שֵׁנִי – הַשְׁלֵם

❶ Shabbat Hebrew
'Ivrit shel shabat
_ בְרִית _ל שַׁבָּ_.

❷ Ulpan Hebrew
'Ivrit shel `ulpan.
עִבְרִ_ _ שׁ_ _ _לְפָּן.

❸ He speaks Polish.
Hu medaber polanit.
הוּ_ _דַבֵּר פּוֹלָנִ_ _.

❹ She speaks Yiddish.
Hi medaberet Yidish.
הִ_א מְדַבֶּרֶ_ _ יִדִישׁ.

❺ He is not from Russia.
Hu lo miRusyah.
_וּא לֹ_ _רוּסְיָ_.

Answers to Exercise 1

❶ Anatol speaks Ulpan Hebrew. ❷ Rina speaks Shabbat Hebrew. ❸ He is from Russia; he speaks Russian. ❹ She is from Poland, she speaks Polish. ❺ I speak*(fem.)* Yiddish and Hebrew.

Answers to Exercise 2

❶ עִברִית שֶׁל שַׁבָּת. ❷ עִברִית שֶׁל אוּלפָּן. ❸ הוּא מְדַבֵּר פּוֹלָנִית. ❹ הִיא מְדַבֶּרֶת אִידִישׁ. ❺ הוּא לֹא מֵרוּסיָה.

8

The Yiddish language ('Yiddish' אִידיש simply means Jewish*) developed among the Jews of Central Europe from the 10th century. From the 14th century, Yiddish spread to Eastern Europe and became the main language of most Ashkenazi Jews for several centuries. Yiddish is written in Hebrew letters, though some of the letters are used differently. The vocabulary and grammar of Yiddish is mainly German, along with Slavic and other influences. Many Hebrew words and expressions are used in Yiddish.*

The word **`ulpan** אולְפָּן *is of Aramaic origin, and is used to refer to a place of intensive study. In particular, the word is used to refer to the crash courses in Hebrew provided for* **'olim chadashim** עוֹלִים חֲדָשִׁים *– literally 'new comers-up' – the term used to refer to new Jewish immigrants to Israel. These six-month courses provide not only a basic grounding in Hebrew, but also an introduction to Israeli culture. The term 'Ulpan Hebrew' suggests a slightly academic and theoretical knowledge of the language. By the way, an* **`ulpan** *can also be a radio, television or recording studio.*

As for 'Shabbat Hebrew' - **'ivrit shel shabat** עִבְרִית שֶׁל שַׁבָּת*, this term is used to refer to an extremely precise and grammatical use of Hebrew, practiced by those with a rich vocabulary drawing*

on all the historical stages of this both ancient and modern language. Why is this referred to as Shabbat (Sabbath) Hebrew? Because Shabbat is both a reference to religious ceremonies, with their rich and complex language, and an important day in the Jewish religion.

Shabat *(spelled 'Shabbat' in English) is the Jewish day of rest. The word comes from the root* שבת *meaning 'to rest' or 'to stop work'. This is the word used in the Bible's Book of Genesis to indicate that God rested on the seventh day, after the six days of Creation.* **Shabat** *begins before sunset on Friday. In many families, the mother lights two candles placed on a white cloth; others follow the custom of lighting one candle for each member of the family. The father says the blessing over the wine and two braided loaves of Challah – the special bread for Shabbat. Most Israelis, whether or not they are religiously observant, eat with their families on Friday night, often along with assorted relatives and friends. On Saturday evening,* **shabat** *ends when three stars can be seen in the night sky. Most shops and businesses close around Friday lunchtime and reopen on Saturday evening. The word* **shabat** *has entered the English language as the Sabbath, and the word sabbatical also comes from the same source.*

Like the people conversing in this dialogue, you should soon be able to say that you speak Hebrew – Assimil Hebrew עִבְרִית שֶׁל אַסִימִיל *that is! We hope you're finding it easier going than you expected!*

Ninth lesson (Shi'ur tshi'i)

Machshevim
Computers

1 – **Shalom!**
peace
Hello!

2 **Boqer tov!** ①
morning good
Good morning!

3 **Mah `atem rotzim?**
what you(masc. plural) want(masc. plural)
What would you like?

Pronunciation notes
3 The letter **tsadi** צ is pronounced **tz**. Although English does not have a separate letter for this sound, it is exactly the same sound as at the end of the word *cats*. This sound can also be heard in the words *tsunami* and *tsetse*.

Notes
① **boqer tov** בּוֹקֶר טוֹב *good morning*, literally 'morning good'. In Hebrew, the adjective always follows the noun it describes. You may be familiar with this word order from French or Spanish – in Hebrew, there are no exceptions to this rule!

Alphabet
• **sin** שׂ : we came across the basic shape of this letter in lesson 2. The only difference between **shin** and **sin** is the position of the dot; here, it is on the left-hand fork of the letter.
• **tzade** or **tsadi** צ : the form of the letter we see here is used at the beginning or in the middle of a word (it takes a different form at the end of a word, which we'll find out about later).

מַחְשֵׁבִים

1 – שלום!

2 בּוֹקֶר טוֹב!

3 מַה אַתֶּם רוֹצִים?

Transliteration

מַ ח שֵׁ בִ י ם

← M I Vi SHe CH Ma

machshevim

1 שָׁ ל וֹ ם

← M O L SHa

shalom

2 בּ וֹ קֶ ר ט וֹ ב

← R Qe O B V O T

boqer **tov**

3 מַ ה אַ תֶ ם ר וֹ צִ י ם

← H Ma M Te `a M I TZi O R

mah **`atem** **rotzim**

4 – \`Anachnu rotzim machshev ② laben ③.
we want(masc.) computer for-the-son
We want a computer for our son.

5 Hu rotzeh machshev veinternet ④.
he wants(masc.) computer and-internet
He wants a computer with internet.

6 – Vehabat?
and-the-daughter
And your daughter?

7 – Hi rotzah machshev ⑤ nisa.
she wants(fem.) computer portable
She wants a laptop.

Notes

② The Hebrew word for computer is **machshev** מַחְשֵׁב. The root חשב means *to think*, *to calculate*. The initial letter **mem** מ is not found in the root, but is a letter used to help create names of objects. So you can see how Hebrew has created a word for a very modern device, drawing on a root found in the Bible. In this way, modern Hebrew preserves its connection with its Biblical past (as well as with other periods of its long history). One of the roles of the Academy of the Hebrew Language is to suggest new words from Hebrew roots, rather than adopting loanwords from other languages.

③ **laben** לַבֵּן *for our* ('the') *son*. The לַ **la-** at the beginning of the word is a contraction of the preposition **le** לְ, which means *to*, *for*, and the definite article **ha** הַ *the*. Compare this with **vehabat** וְהַבַּת *and your* ('the') *daughter* in line 6, where the **ha** הַ remains intact after the conjunction **ve** וְ *and*.

④ **ve** וְ is the Hebrew word for *and*. In Hebrew, a single letter is never written on its own, but attached to the following word. Just as the prepositions **le** לְ (see note 3) or **mi** מִ (see lesson 8) are added to the word that follows, so is וְ **ve**.

⑤ You'll notice that in lines 4, 5 and 7, the word **machshev** מַחְשֵׁב *computer* appears without any article, whereas in English we would need to say 'a computer'. Remember that Hebrew doesn't have an indefinite article (*a/an*), although it does have a definite article (*the*). Another word commonly used for a laptop computer is **machshev nayad** מַחְשֵׁב נַיָּד.

4 – אֲנַחנוּ רוֹצִים מַחשֵׁב לַבֵּן.

5 הוּא רוֹצֶה מַחשֵׁב וְאִנטֶרנֶט.

6 – וְהַבַּת?

7 – הִיא רוֹצָה מַחשֵׁב נִשָּׂא.

4 ← אֲנַחנוּ רוֹצִים מַחשֵׁב
U N CH Na `a — M I TZi O R — V SHe CH Ma
`anachnu **rotzim** **machshev**

← לַבֵּן
N Be La
laben

5 ← הוּא רוֹצֶה מַחשֵׁב
` U H — H TZe O R — V SHe CH Ma
hu **rotzeh** **machshev**

← וְאִנטֶרנֶט
T Ne R Te N `i Ve
ve`internet

6 ← וְהַבַּת
T Ba Ha Ve
vehabat

7 ← הִיא רוֹצָה מַחשֵׁב נִשָּׂא
` I Hi — H TZa O R — V SHe CH Ma — ` Sa Ni
hi **rotzah** **machshev** **nisa`**

9

Targil rishon – Targem תַּרְגִּיל רִאשׁוֹן – תַּרְגֵּם

❶ הבן והבת רוצים מחשב.
Haben vehabat rotzim machshev.

❷ הוא רוצה מחשב נשא.
Hu rotzeh machshev nisa.

❸ היא רוצה אנטרנט.
Hi rotzah `internet.

❹ מה אתם רוצים?
Mah `atem rotzim?

❺ אנחנו רוצים מחשבים.
`Anachnu rotzim machshevim.

Targil sheni – Hashlem תַּרְגִּיל שֵׁנִי – הַשְׁלֵם

❶ Laptop (portable computer)
Machshev nisa`
מַח _ ב נְ _ א

❷ The son wants internet.
Haben rotzeh `internet.
_ בֵּן רוֹ _ ה _ נְטֶרְנֶ _.

❸ The daughter wants a computer.
Habat rotzah machshev.
_ בַּת רוֹ _ ה מַחְשֵׁ _.

❹ We want some tea.
`Anachnu rotzim teh.
אֲנַ _ נוּ רוֹצִ _ _ תֵּ _.

❺ The son and daughter want computers.
Haben vehabat rotzim machshevim.
הַבֵּ _ _ הַבַּ _ רוֹצִ _ _ מַחְשְׁבִ _ _.

Answers to Exercise 1

❶ The son and the daughter want a computer. ❷ He wants a laptop. ❸ She wants internet. ❹ What do you want? ❺ We want computers.

Answers to Exercise 2

❶ מַחשֵׁב נִשָּׂא. ❷ הַבֵּן רוֹצֶה אִנטֶרנֶט. ❸ הַבַּת רוֹצָה מַחשֵׁב.
❹ אֲנַחנוּ רוֹצִים תֵּה. ❺ הַבֵּן וְהַבַּת רוֹצִים מַחשֵׁבִים.

10 Tenth lesson (Shi'ur 'asiri)

Beveyt qafeh
At a café

1 – 'Erev tov. Mah `aten rotzot?
evening good. what you(fem. plural) want(fem. plural)?
Good evening. What would you like?

2 – Qafeh ve'ugah ① **bevaqashah** ②**.**
coffee and-cake by-request
Coffee and a cake, please.

Pronunciation notes
1 'ayin ע – as we explained in lesson 5, most Israelis pronounce this letter just like **`alef**, although some pronounce it as a more forceful, guttural sound.

Notes

① Hebrew does not have an indefinite article (*a/an*), and no special word is needed to indicate *some* in phrases such as *I want some cake* or *some coffee*. Another important point: like many languages, nouns in Hebrew have grammatical gender, which means they are classed as either masculine or feminine. The gender of the noun makes a difference to any adjectives that are used with it, because these have to 'agree' with the gender by appearing in their masculine or feminine form. Here, **'ugah עוּגָה** *cake* is feminine (as are almost all words that end in ָה), and accordingly the adjective *good* describing the cake also appears in the feminine singular form: **tovah טוֹבָה** *good*, as seen in line 4. The masculine singular form is **tov טוֹב**. You can see the plural forms in review lesson 14.

② **bevaqashah בְּבַקָּשָׁה** *please* includes the preposition **be בְּ**, which means *by* in this case, and the noun **baqashah בַּקָּשָׁה** meaning *request*. So the expression literally means 'by request', but it is used like the English word *please*. You may ▸

10 שִׁעוּר עֲשִׂירִי

בְּבֵית קָפֶה

1 – עֶרֶב טוֹב. מַה אַתֶּן רוֹצוֹת?

2 – קָפֶה וְעוּגָה בְּבַקָּשָׁה.

• **tav** ת, which we already came across in lesson 4, is pronounced **t** as in *table*. In modern Israeli Hebrew, it sounds exactly the same as the letter **tet** ט.
3 gimel ג is pronounced *g* as in *game* (and never like the *g* in *page*).

be wondering why the word **baqashah** בַּקָּשָׁה begins with a **bet** בַּ, whereas in the word **bevaqashah** בְּבַקָּשָׁה the dot within the letter disappears and the word becomes **vaqashah** בַקָּשָׁה. As we've seen, several Hebrew letters have two forms, with or without a dot (known in Hebrew as **dagesh** דָּגֵשׁ), which changes the pronunciation. Certain contexts require the use of the form with the dot, while in others the dot is omitted. For example, when the letter appears at the beginning of a word, without a preceding preposition or conjunction, the form with the dot is always used. So at the beginning of a word, the letter **be** בּ is used, which is pronounced as a *b*.

This change from *b* to *v* can also be seen in the title of this lesson: **beveyt qafeh** בְּבֵית קָפֶה *in a café*. However, many Israelis don't observe these rules strictly in all cases and might pronounce this **bebeyt qafeh**, so the best thing to do is just try to remember that **be** בּ can be pronounced in one of two ways.

3 **Yesh** ③ **'ugat** ④ **gvinah?**
there-is cake-of cheese?
Is there cheesecake?

4 – `Eyn 'ugat gvinah, `aval yesh 'ugat pereg tovah ⑤**.**
there-is-no cake-of cheese but there-is cake-of poppy good
There isn't any cheesecake, but there's a good poppyseed cake.

5 **`O 'ugat shoqolad.**
or cake-of chocolate
Or chocolate cake.

Notes

③ **yesh** (line 3) and **`eyn** (line 4): it's worth memorizing this useful pair of words – **yesh** יֵשׁ meaning *there is* or *there are*, and **`eyn** אֵין meaning *there is not* or *there are not*. You'll be glad to hear that these words do not vary for masculine and feminine or singular and plural, so just learn them as they are and start using them to form simple sentences!

④ **'ugat gvinah** עוּגַת גְבִינָה : why does the word **'ugah** עוּגָה *cake* (line 2) turn into **'ugat** עוּגַת in lines 3, 4 and 5? This is an example of a special trick Hebrew uses for associating two nouns without using the word *of*. In this construction, the written form and pronunciation of the first noun often changes. Here, the feminine ending **ah** ָה changes into **at** ַת. We will learn more about this construction in later lessons.

⑤ **'ugah tovah** עוּגָה טוֹבָה : literally, 'cake good'. Just a reminder that this is the feminine version of the adjective **tov** טוֹב *good* (which appears in the expression **'erev tov** עֶרֶב טוֹב *good evening* in line 1). The feminine singular form of many adjectives is made by adding **-ah** ָה to the masculine form.

3 יֵשׁ עוּגַת גְבִינָה?

4 – אֵין עוּגַת גְבִינָה, אֲבָל יֵשׁ עוּגַת פֶּרֶג טוֹבָה.

5 אוֹ עוּגַת שׁוֹקוֹלָד. □

Transliteration

	בְּבֵית		קָפֶה
←	T Y Ve Be		H Fe Qa
	beveyt		**qafeh**
1	עֶרֶב	טוֹב	
←	V Re 'e	V O T	
	'erev	**tov**	
	מַה	אַתֶן	רוֹצוֹת
←	H Ma	N Te `a	T O TZ O R
	mah	**`aten**	**rotzot**
2	קָפֶה	וְעוּגָה	בְּבַקָשָׁה
←	H Fe Qa	H Ga U ' Ve	H SHa Qa Va Be
	qafeh	**ve'ugah**	**bevaqashah**
3	יֵשׁ	עוּגַת	גְבִינָה
←	SH Ye	T Ga U '	H Na I Vi G
	yesh	**'ugat**	**gvinah**
4	אֵין	עוּגַת	גְבִינָה
←	N Y `e	T Ga U '	H Na I Vi G
	`eyn	**'ugat**	**gvinah**
	אֲבָל	יֵשׁ	עוּגַת
←	L Va `a	SH Ye	T Ga U '
	aval	**yesh**	**'ugat**

טוֹבָה	פֶּרֶג	
H Va O T	G Re Pe	←
tovah	**pereg**	

שׁוֹקוֹלָד	עוּגַת	אוֹ	5
D La O Q O SH	T Ga U '	O `	
shoqolad	**'ugat**	`o	←

Targil rishon – Targem   תַּרְגִּיל רִאשׁוֹן – תַּרְגֵּם

❶ Yesh 'ugat gvinah tovah.   יֵשׁ עוּגַת גְּבִינָה טוֹבָה.

❷ `Eyn 'ugat pereg.   אֵין עוּגַת פֶּרֶג.

❸   קָפֶה וְעוּגַת שׁוֹקוֹלָד בְּבַקָּשָׁה.
Qafeh ve'ugat shoqolad bevaqashah.

❹ Mah `aten rotzot?   מָה אַתֶּן רוֹצוֹת?

❺ `Anachnu beveyt qafeh.   אֲנַחְנוּ בְּבֵית קָפֶה.

Targil sheni – Hashlem   תַּרְגִּיל שֵׁנִי – הַשְׁלֵם

❶ Cheesecake
   'Ugat gvinah   עוּגַ _ גְּבִינָ _

❷ Poppyseed cake
   'Ugat pereg   _ וּגַת פֶּרֶ _

❸ Do you*(fem. plural)* want some coffee?
   `Aten rotzot qafeh?   אַתֶּ _ רוֹצ _ _ קָפֶ _?

❹ Please
   Bevaqashah   _ _ קָשָׁה

❺ *(House-of)* café
   Beyt qafeh   בֵּי _ קָ _ ה

Alphabet

• **fe** פ is the same letter as **pe** פּ, which was introduced in lesson 8, but without the dot inside it. As explained in note 2 in this lesson, this is another of the letters that have two pronunciations depending on whether there is a dot inside them.

• **gimel** ג sounds like the Hebrew word for *camel*, **gamal** גָּמָל, and the letter itself seems to have a small hump.

Answers to Exercise 1

❶ There is a good cheesecake. ❷ There isn't any poppyseed cake. ❸ Coffee and chocolate cake, please. ❹ What would you like/ What do you want? ❺ We are at a café.

Answers to Exercise 2

❶ עוּגַת גבִינָה ❷ עוּגַת פֶּרֶג ❸ אַתֶן רוֹצוֹת קָפֶה? ❹ בְּבַקָשָׁה ❺ בֵּית קָפֶה

Israelis are particularly fond of cakes made from cream cheese or poppy seeds, sometimes garnished with fruit. You'll find them everywhere – in Israeli homes as well as in cafés and cake shops. If you prefer a drink alongside your slice of cake, hang on until the next lesson, when we'll be pleased to offer you a selection of beverages.

11 Eleventh lesson (Shi'ur achat 'esreh)

Baqafeteryah ①
At the cafeteria

1 – **Shalom. Mah `atem shotim?**
hello what you(masc. plural) drink(masc. plural)
Hello. What are you drinking?

2 – **Mah yesh?**
what there-is
What is there?

3 – **Yesh qafeh filter, qafeh botz, qafeh turqi, qafeh hafukh venes qafeh.**
there-is coffee-of filter, coffee-of mud, coffee Turkish, coffee reversed and-miracle-of coffee
There's filter coffee, unfiltered coffee, Turkish coffee, milky coffee and instant coffee.

4 **Sukar `o sukrazit?**
sugar or sweetener
[With] sugar or sweetener?

5 **Ve`aten?**
and-you(fem. plural)
And you?

6 – **`Anachnu shotot mitz tapuzim ②.**
we drink(fem.) juice-of oranges
We're drinking orange juice.

Notes

① In the last lesson, we learned the preposition **be** בְּ. Here, though, we see it in the form **ba** בַּ, which is the combination of **be** בְּ and **ha** הַ *the*. **Beqafeteryah** בַּקָפֶטֶרְיָה means *in a cafeteria*. **Baqafeteryah** בַּקָפֶטֶרְיָה means *in the cafeteria*. ▶

11 שִׁעוּר אַחַת עֶשְׂרֵה

בַּקָפֶטֶרְיָה

1 – שָׁלוֹם. מַה אַתֶּם שׁוֹתִים ?

2 – מַה יֵשׁ?

3 – יֵשׁ קָפֶה פִילְטֶר, קָפֶה בּוֹץ, קָפֶה טוּרְקִי, קָפֶה הָפוּךְ, וְנֵס קָפֶה.

4 סוּכָּר אוֹ סוּכָּרָזִית?

5 וְאַתֶּן?

6 – אֲנַחְנוּ שׁוֹתוֹת מִיץ תַּפּוּזִים. ☐

▸ ② **tapuzim** תַּפּוּזִים *oranges* is the plural form of **tapuz** תַּפּוּז. This word is a combination of **tapuach** תַּפּוּחַ *apple*, and **zahav** זָהָב *gold*. It is based on a form that appears just once in the Bible (Proverbs 25:11). The 'gold' component probably refers not only to the colour of this fruit, but also to its rarity and high price at the time.

בַּקָּפֶטֶרְיָה
H Ya R Te Fe Qa Ba ←
baqafeteryah

שׁוֹתִים	אַתֶּם	מַה	שָׁלוֹם	**1**
M I Ti O SH	M Te \`a	H Ma	M O L SHa	←
shotim	**\`atem**	**mah**	**shalom**	

יֵשׁ	מַה	**2**
SH Ye	H Ma	←
yesh	**mah**	

קָפֶה	פִילְטֶר	קָפֶה	יֵשׁ	**3**
H Fe Qa	R Te L I Fi	H Fe Qa	SH Ye	←
qafeh	**filter**	**qafeh**	**yesh**	
קָפֶה	טוּרְקִי	קָפֶה	בּוֹץ	
H Fe Qa	I Qi R U T	H Fe Qa	TZ O B	←
qafeh	**turqi**	**qafeh**	**botz**	

Targil rishon – Targem | תַּרְגִּיל רִאשׁוֹן – תַּרְגֵּם

1. אתם שותים קפה בוץ. — \`Atem shotim qafeh botz.
2. מה יש בקפטריה? — Mah yesh baqafeteryah?
3. אנחנו שותים מיץ תפוזים. — \`Anachnu shotim mitz tapuzim.
4. אתן שותות נס קפה. — \`Aten shotot nes qafeh.
5. יש קפה הפוך? — Yesh qafeh hafukh?

קָפֶה	וֶנֶס	הָפוּךְ	
H Fe Qa	S Ne Ve	KH U F Ha	←
qafeh	**venes**	**hafukh**	

סוּכְּרָזִית	אוֹ	סוּכָּר	4
T I Zi Ra K U S	O `	R Ka U S	←
sukrazit	**`o**	**sukar**	

וְאַתֶּן	5
N Te `a Ve	←
ve`aten	

תַּפּוּזִים	מִיץ	שׁוֹתוֹת	אֲנַחְנוּ	6
M I Zi U P Ta	TZ I Mi	T O T O SH	U N CH Na `a	←
tapuzim	**mitz**	**shotot**	**`anachnu**	

Alphabet

• final **tsadi** ץ. We introduced the letter **tsadi** in lesson 9. Here you see the form of the letter used at the end of a word.
• **zayin** ז. The name of this letter means *weapon*, but we should probably warn you that in slang it means *penis* and is used to form some vulgar but popular swear words. Respectable organizations and businesses are careful to avoid using the letter prominently in their branding.

Answers to Exercise 1

❶ You drink/are drinking 'mud' coffee. ❷ What is there in the cafeteria? ❸ We drink/are drinking orange juice. ❹ You drink/are drinking instant coffee. ❺ Is there milky coffee?

11

Targil sheni – Hashlem תַּרְגִּיל שֵׁנִי – הַשְׁלֵם

1. Milky coffee *(coffee reversed)*
   Qafeh hafukh
   קָ_ה הָפוּ_
2. Unfiltered coffee *(coffee mud)*
   Qafeh botz
   _פֶה בּוֹ_
3. Sugar or sweetener?
   Sukar `o sukrazit?
   סוּ_ר אוֹ סוּכְּרָ_ית?
4. Orange juice
   Mitz tapuzim
   מִי_ תַּפּוּ_ים
5. We drink*(masc.)* instant coffee.
   `Anachnu shotim nes qafeh.
   אֲנַ_נוּ שׁוֹתִ_ _ נֵ_ קַפֶ_.

A quick guide to Israeli coffee:

Qafeh turqi קָפֶה טוּרְקִי *: boil water in a small pan, add coarse-ground coffee and bring to the boil again while stirring.*

Qafeh botz קָפֶה בּוֹץ *: put the same coarse-ground coffee in a glass and add boiling water. After the 'sediment', or coffee grounds, settles at the bottom of the glass, enjoy your drink.*

Qafeh hafukh קָפֶה הָפוּךְ *: add milk to your preferred variety of black coffee. Why do Israelis call this 'reverse' coffee? Maybe because adding the milk 'reverses' the colour from black to white, but probably because it is very milky – a lot of milk with a little coffee, rather than the opposite.*

Nes qafeh נֵס קָפֶה *: add boiling water to instant coffee. This term is slightly out of date now, as Israelis have moved on to latte, macchiato and endless other varieties of coffee drinks. The word* **nes** נֵס *means* miracle, *and Israelis sometimes joke that if there is any coffee in this drink, it must be a miracle!*

Answers to Exercise 2

❶ קָפֶה הָפוּךְ ❷ קָפֶה בּוֹץ ❸ סוּכָּר אוֹ סוּכָּרָזִית? ❹ מִיץ תַפּוּזִים ❺ אֲנַחְנוּ שׁוֹתִים נֵס קַפֶה.

> *After all your hard work, you deserve one of the coffees described here, maybe with one of the cakes from lesson 10. If you have the audio recordings, listen to them while you enjoy some refreshments and try to absorb all the new Hebrew words and information you've learned.*

12 Twelfth lesson (Shi'ur shteym 'esreh)

Qniyot ①
Shopping

1 – **Uf! `ani 'ayef.**
oof I tired(masc.)
Oh! I [am] tired.

2 – **Lamah?**
why
Why?

3 – **Haqanyon ② me'ayef ③.**
the-mall tires(masc.)
The mall is tiring.

4 – **Mah `atah qoneh?**
what you(masc.) buy(masc.)
What are you buying?

Notes

① **qniyot** קְנִיּוֹת *purchases, shopping* is the plural noun of **qniyah** קְנִיָּה *a purchase, shopping* from the root קנה *to buy.* The plural is used as the general word for what you've bought – your 'shopping' – possibly because no Israeli could imagine going to the shops to buy just one item. As we've mentioned before, roots of three or four letters form the basis of most Hebrew words. When we indicate roots, they are not meant to be pronounced with any particular vowel marks. Our goal is to show you the basic letters that you will see in all kinds of words formed from a given root. For the sake of convenience, we translate the root with an English infinitive (to buy, to learn, etc.), but this is just to give a general idea of the root's meaning. Sometimes one of the root letters may 'drop out' in a particular formation, as we will see in note 2. ▶

12 שִׁעוּר שְׁתֵּים עֶשְׂרֵה

קְנִיּוֹת

1 – אוּף! אֲנִי עָיֵף.

2 – לָמָה?

3 – הַקַּנְיוֹן מְעַיֵּף.

4 – מַה אַתָּה קוֹנֶה?

▸ ② **qanyon** קַנְיוֹן *mall* is a relatively new word in Hebrew, created to translate the concept of a mall or shopping centre (we use the American term 'mall' here as a convenient one-word equivalent). This word comes from the root קנה that we discussed in note 1. This word ends with the suffix **-on**, וֹן which is often used to form names of places. Note that the third root letter – **hey** ה – has disappeared in this form. Nevertheless, Hebrew speakers still instinctively recognize the word's origins in the root קנה.

③ **me'ayef** מְעַיֵּף *tires/is tiring* is a verb formed from the root עיף. This lesson also introduces two other forms from the same root: the masculine adjective **'ayef** עָיֵף *tired* (line 1), and its feminine equivalent **'ayefah** עֲיֵפָה *tired* (line 5). Don't forget that in Hebrew, the ending of the adjective changes to 'agree' with a masculine or feminine noun.

5 – `Ani lo qoneh, `aval `ishti ④ qonah vehi lo 'ayefah!

I not buy(masc.) but my-wife buys(fem.) and-she no tired

I'm not buying, but my wife is buying, and she [is]n't tired!

Notes

④ **`ishti** אִשְׁתִּי *my wife* is formed from the word **`ishah** אִשָּׁה *woman, wife* with the addition of the first-person possessive (i.e. the equivalent of the English *my*) as a suffix at the end of the word. Just take our word for it for now – we'll soon see more about how to make possessive forms.

Alphabet

• final **fe** ף. This final **fe** is a big moment – you have now been introduced to all the letters of the Hebrew alphabet. Admit it: it was a bit easier than you expected, wasn't it?!

Transliteration

קְנִיּוֹת

T O Y Ni Q ←

qniyot

1

אוּף ← F U ` — **`uf**

אֲנִי ← I Ni `a — **`ani**

עָיֵף ← F Ye 'a — **'ayef**

2

לָמָּה ← H Ma La — **lamah**

5 – אֲנִי לֹא קוֹנֶה, אֲבָל אִשְׁתִּי קוֹנָה וְהִיא לֹא עֲיֵפָה!

מְ עַ יֵּ ף	הַ קַ נ י וֹ ן	3
F Ye 'a Me	N O Y N Qa Ha	←
me'ayef	**haqanyon**	

ק וֹ נֶ ה	אַ תָ ה	מַ ה	4
H Ne O Q	H Ta `a	H Ma	←
qoneh	**`atah**	**mah**	

אֲ בָ ל	ק וֹ נֶ ה	לֹ א	אֲ נִ י	5
L Va `a	H Ne O Q	` Lo	I Ni `a	←
`aval	**qoneh**	**lo**	**`ani**	

וְ הִ י א	ק וֹ נָ ה	אִ שְׁ תִּ י	
` I Hi Ve	H Na O Q	I Ti SH `i	←
vehi	**qonah**	**`ishti**	

עֲ יֵ פָ ה	לֹ א	
H Fa Ye 'a	` Lo	←
'ayefah	**lo**	

Targil rishon – Targem   תַּרְגִּיל רִאשׁוֹן – תַּרְגֵּם

❶ אני עיף.
`Ani 'ayef.

❷ היא לֹא עיפה.
Hi lo 'ayefah.

❸ הוא קונה, אבל היא לֹא קונה.
Hu qoneh, `aval hi lo qonah.

❹ למה הקניון מעיף?
Lamah haqanyon me'ayef?

❺ מה את קונה?
Mah `at qonah?

Targil sheni – Hashlem   תַּרְגִּיל שֵׁנִי – הַשְׁלֵם

❶ He is tired.
Hu 'ayef.
ה_א עָיֵ_.

❷ She is tired.
Hi 'ayefah.
הִי_ עֲיֵפָ_.

❸ My wife buys.
`Ishti qonah.
אִשְׁתִּ_ קוֹ_ה.

❹ The mall is tiring.
Haqanyon me'ayef.
הַקַּנ___ _עַיֵּף.

❺ I do not buy*(masc.)*.
`Ani lo qoneh.
_נִי לֹ_ קוֹ_ה.

Answers to Exercise 1

❶ I am tired. ❷ She is not tired. ❸ He buys, but she does not buy. ❹ Why is the mall tiring? ❺ What are you buying?

Answers to Exercise 2

❶ הוּא עָיֵף. ❷ הִיא עֲיֵפָה. ❸ אִשְׁתִּי קוֹנָה. ❹ הַקַּנְיוֹן מְעַיֵּף.
❺ אֲנִי לֹא קוֹנֶה.

You've just learned the Hebrew word for tired, *but this is no time to give in to learning-fatigue. Try to devote half an hour every day to your Hebrew studies. If you find something too hard, leave it for now and move on to something else. As you progress through the lessons, you'll find that everything falls into place.*

13 Thirteenth lesson (Shi'ur shlosh 'esreh)

Pitput, pitputim ①
Chit-chat

1 – **`Eyfoh Dan veYosef?**
where Dan and-Yoseph
Where [are] Dan and Joseph?

2 – **Hem medabrim betelefon `alchuti ②.**
they(masc.) talk(masc.) on-telephone wireless
They are talking on a cordless telephone.

3 – **`Eyfoh Leah veSarah?**
where Leah and-Sarah
Where are Leah and Sarah?

4 – **Hen medabrot betelefon nayad ③.**
they(fem.) speak(fem.) on-telephone mobile
They are speaking on a mobile phone.

5 – **Gam `ani rotzah telefon!**
also I want(fem.) telephone
I want a telephone, too!

6 – **`Eyn be'ayah ④. Yesh diburit ⑤ bamekhonit.**
there-is-no problem. there-is a-hands-free-set in-the-car
No problem. There is a hands-free set in the car.

Notes

① **pitput** פִּטְפּוּט, **pitputim** פִּטְפּוּטִים means *a chat* or *chit-chat* – you can use either the singular (**pitput**) or the plural (**pitputim**) form. Israelis are world-class chatterers and are particularly fond of their mobile phones.

② **`alchuti** אַלְחוּטִי is an adjective formed from two words. The second part, **chut** חוּט, means *wire*, while the **`al** אַל prefix means *not* or *non-*. In this case, the English translation is *wireless* or *cordless*. ▸

13 שִׁעוּר שְׁלוֹשׁ עֶשְׂרֵה

פִּטְפּוּט, פִּטְפּוּטִים

1 – אֵיפֹה דָן וְיוֹסֵף?

2 – הֵם מְדַבְּרִים בְּטֶלֶפוֹן אַלחוּטִי.

3 – אֵיפֹה לֵאָה וְשָׂרָה?

4 – הֵן מְדַבְּרוֹת בְּטֶלֶפוֹן נַיָּד.

5 – גַּם אֲנִי רוֹצָה טֶלֶפוֹן!

6 – אֵין בְּעָיָה. יֵשׁ דִּבּוּרִית בַּמְכוֹנִית.

③ **nayad** נַיָּד *mobile*. This adjective comes from the root ניד *to move*.

④ **`eyn be'ayah** אֵין בְּעָיָה *No problem*. Always a handy expression to know!

⑤ **diburit** דִּבּוּרִית is a recently created word for a hands-free telephone set designed to be installed in a car. Israelis love driving and chatting on the telephone, so to do both at once is a dream come true. This word ends in the suffix **-it** ית, and like all nouns with this ending, it is feminine (the same ending is also used for many feminine adjectives). The root of **diburit** is דבר *to speak*, *to talk*, which was introduced in lesson 8. The three root letters are 'broken' by the insertion of the **vav** ו, but can still be clearly identified.

←	פִּטְפּוּט	פִּטְפּוּטִים
	T U P T Pi	M I Ti U P T Pi
	pitput	**pitputim**

1	אֵיפֹה	דָן	וְיוֹסֵף
←	H Fo Y `e	N Da	F Se O Y Ve
	`eyfoh	**Dan**	**veYosef**

2	הֵם	מְדַבְּרִים
←	M He	M I Ri B Da Me
	hem	**medabrim**
	בְּטֶלֶפוֹן	אַלְחוּטִי
	N O F Le Te Be	I Ti U CH L `a
	betelefon	**`alchuti**

3	אֵיפֹה	לֵאָה	וְשָׂרָה
←	H Fo Y `e	H `a Le	H Ra Sa Ve
	`eyfoh	**Le`ah**	**veSarah**

Targil rishon – Targem — תַּרְגִּיל רִאשׁוֹן – תַּרְגֵּם

❶ הם מדברים בטלפון אלחוטי.
Hem medabrim betelefon `alchuti.

❷ אני רוצה דבורית במכונית.
`Ani rotzeh diburit bamekhonit.

❸ אין בעיה.
`Eyn be'ayah

4 הֵן מְדַבְּרוֹת בְּטֶלֶפוֹן נַיָּד
← N He T O R B Da Me N O F Le Te Be D Ya Na
hen medabrot betelefon nayad

5 גַּם אֲנִי רוֹצָה טֶלֶפוֹן
← M Ga I Ni `a H TZa O R N O F Le Te
gam `ani rotzah telefon

6 אֵין בְּעָיָה יֵשׁ דִּבּוּרִית בַּמְכוֹנִית
← N Y `e H Ya 'a Be SH Ye T I Ri U B Di
`eyn be'ayah yesh diburit

← T I Ni O KH Me Ba
bamekhonit

❹ הן מדברות בטלפון ניד.
Hen medabrot betelefon nayad.

❺ איפה יש טלפון?
`Eyfoh yesh telefon?

Answers to Exercise 1

❶ They are talking on a cordless telephone. ❷ I want a hands-free set in the car. ❸ No problem. ❹ They are talking on a mobile telephone. ❺ Where is there a telephone?

Targil sheni – Hashlem תַרְגִיל שֵׁנִי – הַשְׁלֵם

❶ Cordless telephone
Telefon `alchuti
_ לֶפוֹן _ _ ל _ וּטִ _

❷ There is a hands-free set in the car.
Yesh diburit bamekhonit.
_שׁ דִבּוּרִ_ _ בַּמְכוֹנִ_ _.

❸ Where is the car?
`Eyfoh hamekhonit?
אֵי _ ה _ _ מְ _ וֹנִית?

❹ Sarah is speaking on a mobile phone.
Sarah medaberet betelefon nayad.
_ רָה מְדַבֶּרֶ_ _טֶלֶפ_ _ נַ_ד.

❺ Joseph is also in the car.
Gam Yosef bamekhonit.
_ם יוֹסֵ_ _ _מְכוֹנִית.

Answers to Exercise 2

❶ טֶלֶפוֹן אַלְחוּטִי ❷ יֵשׁ דְבוּרִית בַּמְכוֹנִית. ❸ אֵיפֹה הַמְכוֹנִית? ❹ שָׂרָה מְדַבֶּרֶת בְּטֶלֶפוֹן נַיָד. ❺ גַם יוֹסֵף בַּמְכוֹנִית.

פטפוט, פטפוטים

You now know enough Hebrew to start chatting. All you need to worry about is your phone bill!

14 Fourteenth lesson (Shi'ur arba' 'esreh)

חֲזָרָה Chazarah – Review

Well done! You've reached the second review lesson. You're well and truly on your way to reading Hebrew!

1 Letters

The following table shows the Hebrew letters in alphabetical order, with their name and transliteration. The number refers to the lesson in which each letter appears for the first time.

א	**`alef**	`	1	מ	**mem**	**m**	3
בּ	**bet**	**b**	1	ם	final **mem**	**m**	2
ב	**vet**	**v**	1	נ	**nun**	**n**	5
ג	**gimel**	**g**	10	ן	final **nun**	**n**	5
ד	**dalet**	**d**	4	ס	**samekh**	**s**	6
ה	**hey**	**h**	3	ע	**'ayin**	**'**	5
ו	**vav**	**v**	1	פּ	**pe**	**p**	8
ז	**zayin**	**z**	11	פ	**fe**	**f**	10
ח	**chet**	**t**	6	ף	final **fe**	**f**	12
ט	**tet**	**t**	1	צ	**tsadi**	**tz**	9
י	**yod**	**y**	2	ץ	final **tsadi**	**tz**	11
כּ	**kaf**	**k**	3	ק	**qof**	**q**	1
כ	**khaf**	**kh**	3	ר	**resh**	**r**	1
ך	final **khaf**	**kh**	3	שׁ	**shin**	**sh**	2
ל	**lamed**	**l**	2	שׂ	**sin**	**s**	9
				ת	**tav**	**t**	4

14 שִׁעוּר אַרְבַּע עֶשְׂרֵה

2 Vowels

Here is a summary of the Hebrew vowel marks and their names.

• **a**: ַ **patach** פַּתָח is pronounced **a** as in *apple*. The root פתח means *to open*, perhaps because we open our mouths quite wide when we produce this sound.

• **a**: ָ **qamatz** קָמַץ is also pronounced **a** as in *apple*. In modern Israeli Hebrew, there is no difference between these two **a** sounds. Israeli high school students and Bible scholars need to understand the difference between the two, but you can treat them as identical.

• **e**: ֶ **segol** סֶגוֹל is pronounced **e** as in *met*.

• **e**: ֵ **tzereh** צֵרֶה is very similar to **segol**, though some speakers pronounce it like the **ay** in *day* (but shorter).

• **i**: **chiriq** חִירִיק (with or without a following **yod** ִי) is pronounced like **ee** in *meet* (but shorter).

• **o**: וֹ **cholam** חוֹלָם is pronounced **o** as in *dog*.

• **u**: וּ **shuruq** שׁוּרוּק is pronounced like **oo** in *moon* (but shorter). The name of this vowel mark comes from a root meaning *to whistle*, since the sound of the name resembles a short whistle.

• **u**: ֻ **qubutz** קֻבּוּץ is also pronounced like **oo** in *moon*.

• The last vowel mark, **shva`** ְ is slightly unusual.
– In some cases, this mark stands for a **shva` nach** שְׁוָא נָח – a 'resting' **shva`**; that is, one that is silent. Since it is silent, we do not transliterate the vowel mark in these cases. You can see an example of this in the name of this vowel mark itself – שְׁוָא – which we transliterate simply **shva`**, as it is pronounced.
– In other cases, this mark stands for a **shva` na'** שְׁוָא נָע – a 'moving' **shva`**; that is, one that is pronounced. In these cases, the vowel has a short, indeterminate 'uh' sound like the **a** in *about*, the **i** in *pencil* or the **u** in *supply*. An example of this type of **shva`** occurs in the word **bevaqashah** בְּבַקָּשָׁה *please*.

Don't worry too much about this! We'll show you when a vowel sound is needed.

3 Personal pronouns

Without even noticing, you have already encountered all the personal pronouns. Here they are again in an orderly fashion:

`ani	אֲנִי	*I* (masc./fem.)
`atah	אַתָּה	*you* (masc./sing.)
`at	אַתְּ	*you* (fem./sing.)
hu	הוּא	*he*
hi	הִיא	*she*
`anachnu	אֲנַחְנוּ	*we* (masc./fem.)
`atem	אַתֶּם	*you* (masc./plural)
`aten	אַתֶּן	*you* (fem./plural)
hem	הֵם	*they* (masc.)
hen	הֵן	*they* (fem.)

As you discovered in this set of lessons, Hebrew not only distinguishes between *you* when referring to a male or female, but also between *you* referring to one person or more than one person. So there are four personal pronouns for *you* in all.

Compare **`ani** אֲנִי and **`anachnu** אֲנַחְנוּ, **`atah** אַתָּה and **`atem** אַתֶּם, **`at** אַתְּ and **`aten** אַתֶּן : note the similarity between the singular and plural forms of the first-, second- and third-person. This should help you remember them.

4 Verbs

We have already learned several verbs in the present tense. As you have seen, present tense verbs have four different forms: masculine singular, masculine plural, feminine singular and feminine plural. Here is a full table showing the present tense forms from the root דבר *to speak* or *to talk*.

• root: דבר

<u>If the person/people doing the action is/are masculine:</u>

`ani medaber	אֲנִי מְדַבֵּר	*I speak*
`atah medaber	אַתָּה מְדַבֵּר	*you speak* (sing.)
hu medaber	הוּא מְדַבֵּר	*he speaks*
`anachnu medabrim	אֲנַחְנוּ מְדַבְּרִים	*we speak*
`atem medabrim	אַתֶּם מְדַבְּרִים	*you speak* (plural)
hem medabrim	הֵם מְדַבְּרִים	*they speak*

<u>If the person/people doing the action is/are feminine:</u>

`ani medaberet	אֲנִי מְדַבֶּרֶת	*I speak*
`at medaberet	אַתְּ מְדַבֶּרֶת	*you speak* (sing.)
hi medaberet	הִיא מְדַבֶּרֶת	*she speaks*
`anachnu medabrot	אֲנַחְנוּ מְדַבְּרוֹת	*we speak*
`aten medabrot	אַתֶּן מְדַבְּרוֹת	*you speak* (plural)
hen medabrot	הֵן מְדַבְּרוֹת	*they speak*

Notice that the feminine singular ends in **-et** ֶת, the masculine plural in **-im** ִים and the feminine plural verb in **-ot** וֹת. This is worth knowing, since the same is true of most verbs.

In our next example, however, the third root letter is ה. In verbs of this type, no letter is added to the masculine singular to form the feminine singular, but the vowel changes: **eh** ֶה in the masculine becomes **ah** ָה in the feminine. In the plural, the ה is dropped before adding the **-im** ים ending for the masculine or **-ot** וֹת for the feminine. Here is the table for the root רצה *to want.*

• root: רצה

<u>masculine</u>

`ani rotzeh	אֲנִי רוֹצֶה	*I want*
`atah rotzeh	אַתָּה רוֹצֶה	*you want* (sing.)
hu rotzeh	הוּא רוֹצֶה	*he wants*
`anachnu rotzim	אֲנַחְנוּ רוֹצִים	*we want*
`atem rotzim	אַתֶּם רוֹצִים	*you want* (plural)
hem rotzim	הֵם רוֹצִים	*they want*

<u>feminine</u>

`ani rotzah	אֲנִי רוֹצָה	*I want*
`at rotzah	אַתְּ רוֹצָה	*you want* (sing.)
hi rotzah	הִיא רוֹצָה	*she wants*
`anachnu rotzot	אֲנַחְנוּ רוֹצוֹת	*we want*
`aten rotzot	אַתֶּן רוֹצוֹת	*you want* (plural)
hen rotzot	הֵן רוֹצוֹת	*they want*

Now practice the forms for all the personal pronouns for the following two verbs (*to drink* and *to buy*):

shoteh	שׁוֹתֶה	**shotah**	שׁוֹתָה
shotim	שׁוֹתִים	**shotot**	שׁוֹתוֹת
qoneh	קוֹנֶה	**qonah**	קוֹנָה
qonim	קוֹנִים	**qonot**	קוֹנוֹת

So, it isn't too hard to conjugate verbs in the present tense!

1)	masc. sing.:	**tov**	טוֹב	*good*
	fem. sing.:	**tov**ah	טוֹבָה	
	masc. plural:	**tov**im	טוֹבִים	
	fem. plural:	**tov**ot	טוֹבוֹת	
2)	masc. sing.:	**'ayef**	עָיֵף	*tired*
	fem. sing.:	**'ayef**ah	עֲיֵפָה	
	masc. plural:	**'ayef**im	עֲיֵפִים	
	fem. plural:	**'ayef**ot	עֲיֵפוֹת	

In Hebrew, unlike in English, the ending of the adjective changes so it 'agrees' with the grammatical gender and quantity (singular

Review exercise

❶ שָׁלוֹם, בּוֹרִיס. ❷ שָׁלוֹם, רִנָה. ❸ גַם אַתָּה בַּקַנְיוֹן? ❹ אֲנִי קוֹנֶה מַחְשֵׁב לַבֵּן וְלַבַּת. ❺ אֲנִי קוֹנָה טֶלֶפוֹן נַיָד. ❻ בּוֹרִיס, אַתָּה מְדַבֵּר עִבְרִית? ❼ עִבְרִית שֶׁל אוּלְפָּן. ❽ אֲבָל אַתְּ, רִנָה, מְדַבֶּרֶת עִבְרִית שֶׁל שַׁבָּת. ❾ אֲנִי עֲיֵפָה. אַתָּה רוֹצֶה קָפֶה וְעוּגָה? ❿ אֵין בְּעָיָה. יֵשׁ בֵּית קָפֶה בַּקַנְיוֹן.

or plural) of the noun it describes. So an adjective can have four different forms, as shown in the table. But don't be discouraged, it's easy, really: to form the feminine singular form, take the masculine singular and add the suffix **-ah** ָה. To form the masculine plural, add **-im** ים to the masculine singular. To form the feminine plural, just add **-ot** וֹת.

6 A strange construction – *smikhut*

Hebrew nouns can appear in an isolated form, such as **'ugah** עוּגָה *cake*, or in association with a following noun: **'ugat shoqolad** עוּגַת שׁוֹקוֹלָד *chocolate cake*. The first instance, **'ugah** עוּגָה, is called the 'absolute state', while the second, עוּגַת **'ugat**, is referred to as the 'construct state' (because it forms part of a grammatical construction). In this case, the absolute form **'ugah** עוּגָה changes into **'ugat** עוּגַת in the construct. The construct form is known in Hebrew as **smikhut** סְמִיכוּת.

Answers

❶ Hello, Boris. *(peace Boris)* ❷ Hello, Rinah. *(peace Rinah)* ❸ Are you also in the mall? *(also you[masc. sing.] in-the-mall)* ❹ I am buying a computer for my son and daughter. *(I buy[masc.] computer for-the-son and-for-the-daughter)* ❺ I am buying a mobile telephone. *(I buy[fem.] telephone mobile)* ❻ Boris, do you speak Hebrew? *(Boris you speak[masc.] Hebrew)* ❼ Ulpan Hebrew. *(Hebrew of Ulpan)* ❽ But you, Rinah, speak Shabbat Hebrew. *(but you Rinah speak[fem.] Hebrew of Shabbat)* ❾ I am tired. Do you want coffee and cake? *(I tired[fem.]. you want[masc.] coffee and-cake)* ❿ No problem. There is a café in the mall. *(there-is-no problem. there-is house-of coffee in-the-mall)*

Congratulations! You're making excellent progress in Hebrew. Keep it up!

15 Fifteenth lesson (Shi'ur chamesh 'esreh)

Bayam
At the sea

1 – Me`ayin ① `atah ba ②?
from-where you(masc.) come(masc.)
Where are you coming from?

2 – `Ani ba michof ③ hayam.
I come(masc.) from-beach-of the-sea
I'm coming from the beach.

3 Baboqer `ani socheh bayam.
in-the-morning I swim(masc.) in-the-sea
In the morning I swim in the sea.

4 – Yesh 'chatikhot' ④ bechof hayam ⑤?
there-are 'bits' in-beach-of the-sea
Are there hot chicks at the beach?

Notes

① **Me`ayin?** ?מֵאַיִן *From where?* This word begins with the preposition **mi** מ *from*, and the answers to questions beginning with **me`ayin** מֵאַיִן also begin with **mi** מ.

② **ba** בָּא *I(masc.)/you(masc.) come, he comes*. This two-letter verb comes from the three-letter root בוא. Do not confuse this with the single-letter preposition **ba-** בַּ *in the*, which is attached to the word it comes in front of.

③ **michof** מֵחוֹף *from the beach*. Note that the answer to a question beginning with **me`ayin** מֵאַיִן *from where* begins with the same letter **m** מ meaning *from* – in this case, *from the beach*.

④ The plural word **chatikhot** חֲתִיכוֹת (sing. **chatikhah** חֲתִיכָה) means *pieces* or *bits*. **Chatikhot shoqolad** חֲתִיכוֹת שׁוֹקוֹלָד: ▸

15 שִׁעוּר חֲמֵשׁ עֶשְׂרֵה

בַּיָּם

1 – מֵאַיִן אַתָּה בָּא?

2 – אֲנִי בָּא מִחוֹף הַיָּם.

3 בַּבּוֹקֶר אֲנִי שׂוֹחֶה בַּיָּם.

4 – יֵשׁ "חֲתִיכוֹת" בְּחוֹף הַיָּם?

בים

pieces of chocolate. But the word has also come to be used to refer to attractive women ('hot chicks' is a rough equivalent). A masculine form, **chatikh** חֲתִיךְ, meaning 'hot guy', was invented from the feminine. By the way, the plural construct (**smikhut**) form **chatikhot** חֲתִיכוֹת is the same as the 'absolute' form, so that if we say **chatikhot shel shoqolad** (**shel** = *of*), the noun remains the same.

⑤ **bechof hayam** בְּחוֹף הַיָּם. It might seem unnecessary to specify 'the beach of the sea', but this is a common way of saying *beach* in Israel and is how it appears on road signs. However, you can also simply say **chof** חוֹף.

5 – Lo, baboqer `eyn sham 'chatikhot'.
no in-the-morning there-are-not there 'bits'
No, in the morning there aren't any hot chicks there.

6 – Lo? `Az lamah `atah bayam baboqer?
no? so why you(masc.) in-the-sea in-the-morning?
No? So why do you go to the sea in the morning?

Cursive script

Since the beginning of the book, we have used the printed Hebrew letters, which are known as square letters or block script. The letters also have a cursive form used in handwriting, and sometimes on signs. We will introduce you gradually to the cursive forms of the different letters. The cursive letters are not joined together, but written separately, like the square letters. Use a notebook to practice writing the letters, with your pen following the movement indicated by the arrows.

bet	ב	בּ	**qof**	ק	ק
vav	ו	ו	**resh**	ר	ר

boqer:
square letters: בּוֹקֶר cursive letters: בּוֹקֶר

5 – לֹא, בַּבּוֹקֶר אֵין שָׁם "חֲתִיכוֹת".

6 – לֹא? אָז לָמָּה אַתָּה בַּיָּם בַּבּוֹקֶר? □

Transliteration

בַּיָּם
M Ya Ba
bayam

1 מֵאַיִן אַתָּה בָּא
N Yi `a Me / H Ta `a / ` Ba
me`ayin** **`atah **ba**

2 אֲנִי בָּא מִחוֹף הַיָּם
I Ni `a / ` Ba / F O CH Mi / M Ya Ha
`ani **ba** **michof** **hayam**

3 בַּבּוֹקֶר אֲנִי שׂוֹחֶה בַּיָּם
R Qe O B Ba / I Ni `a / H CHe O S / M Ya Ba
baboqer **`ani** **socheh** **bayam**

4 יֵשׁ חֲתִיכוֹת בְּחוֹף הַיָּם
SH Ye / T O KH I Ti Ha / F O CH Be / M Ya Ha
yesh **chatikhot** **bechof** **hayam**

5 לֹא בַּבּוֹקֶר אֵין שָׁם חֲתִיכוֹת
` Lo / R Qe O B Ba / N Y `e / M SHa / T O KH I Ti CHa
lo **baboqer** **`eyn** **sham** **chatikhot**

6 לֹא אָז לָמָּה אַתָּה בַּיָּם בַּבּוֹקֶר
` Lo / Z `a / H Ma La / H Ta `a / M Ya Ba / R Qe O B Ba
lo **`az** **lamah** **`atah** **bayam** **baboqer**

Targil rishon – Targem תַּרְגִּיל רִאשׁוֹן – תַּרְגֵּם

❶ Me`ayin `atah ba baboqer? מאין אתה בא בבוקר?
❷ `Eyn ‘chatikhot’ bachof. אין "חתיכות" בחוף.
❸ `Ani socheh bayam. אני שוחה בים.
❹ `Ani lo bechof hayam. אני לֹא בחוף הים.
❺ `Ani ba mehayam. אני בא מהים.

Targil sheni – Hashlem תַּרְגִּיל שֵׁנִי – הַשְׁלֵם

❶ I’m coming *(masc.)*.
`Ani ba.
אֲנִ_ בָּ_.

❷ My wife and I [are] at the beach *(of the sea)*.
`Ani ve`ishti bechof hayam.
_נִי _אִשְׁתִּ_ _חוֹ_ _ _יָם.

❸ In the morning, I swim *(masc.)*.
Baboqer `ani socheh.
_בּוֹקֶר _נִי _וֹחֶה.

❹ There [are] hot chicks on the beach.
Yesh chatikhot bachof.
_שׁ _תִ_וֹת בַּ_וֹף.

❺ So, why [are] you *(masc. sing.)* in the sea?
`Az, lamah `atah bayam?
אָ_ לָמָּ_ _תָה בַּ_ם?

Exercise 3 – Write in cursive letters
boqer בּוֹקֶר

Israel’s hot climate and relaxed lifestyle mean that families and groups of friends often hang out together at the beach. You are never too far from the sea in Israel, a small and elongated country. Hebrew traditionally refers to four ‘seas’, although two are actually lakes. The Mediterranean Sea forms Israel’s western boundary; Eilat borders on the Red Sea, which offers coral, colourful fish, an underwater observatory and a carefree atmosphere; the Dead Sea is the lowest point on Earth (400 metres below sea level), and its water is so salty that you can study Hebrew while lying on the water like it was a couch. Last comes the Sea of Galilee, which in Hebrew

Answers to Exercise 1

❶ Where are you coming from this *(in the)* morning? ❷ There aren't any hot chicks on the beach. ❸ I swim in the sea. ❹ I am not at the beach. ❺ I'm coming from the sea.

Answers to Exercise 2

❶ אֲנִי בָּא. ❷ אֲנִי וְאִשְׁתִּי בְּחוֹף הַיָּם. ❸ בַּבּוֹקֶר אֲנִי שׂוֹחֶה. ❹ יֵשׁ חֲתִיכוֹת בַּחוֹף. ❺ אָז לָמָּה אַתָּה בַּיָּם?

Answer to Exercise 3 – Cursive letters

בּוֹקֶר

is called **Kineret** כִּנֶּרֶת *from the word* **kinor** כִּנּוֹר*, meaning* violin. *The Sea of Galilee is Israel's largest freshwater source. The River Jordan enters the Sea of Galilee from the north and leaves it to the south, eventually reaching the Dead Sea.*

You're continuing to make very good progress. You've already learned all the letters in the square script. In the coming lessons, you'll learn the cursive script, which you can use to write notes and letters to Hebrew-speaking friends – and to understand what they write back!

16 Sixteenth lesson (Shi'ur shesh 'esreh)

Bar Mitzvah

1 – **Mah chadash?**
what new
What's new?

2 – **Beqarov bar mitzvah liNetan`el** ① **bni** ②**. `Ani bedi`etah.**
soon son-of commandment to-Nethanel son-my. I in-diet
It's my son Nethanel's Bar Mitzvah soon. I'm on a diet.

3 – **Mazal tov!** ③
luck good
Congratulations!

4 **`Aval `ani lo mevinah. Lamah di`etah levar mitzvah?**
but I not understand(fem.). why diet for-boy-of commandment
But I don't understand. Why [go on a] diet for a Bar Mitzvah?

Notes

① **li** לִ is the preposition **le** לְ *for*, which we first came across in lesson 9, note 3. The constant feature of this preposition is the consonant ל. To understand the different forms it can take, let's look at the three instances where it appears in this lesson:

• line 2: **liNetan`el** לִנְתַנְאֵל *for Nethanel*. Here, the preposition **li** לִ is followed by **ne** נ. The **le** changes to **li** because Hebrew speakers find it difficult to begin a word with two consonants each followed by the **shva** vowel (i.e. לְנְ).
• line 4: **levar mitzvah** לְבַר מִצְוָה *for a Bar Mitzvah*. The form here (**le** לְ) is the usual form of the preposition. ▶

16 שְׁעוּר שֵׁשׁ עֶשְׂרֵה

בַּר מִצְוָה

1 – מַה חָדָשׁ?

2 – בְּקָרוֹב בַּר מִצְוָה לִנְתַנְאֵל בְּנִי. אֲנִי בְּדִיאֶטָה.

3 – מַזָּל טוֹב!

4 אֲבָל אֲנִי לֹא מְבִינָה. לָמָּה דִיאֶטָה לְבַר מִצְוָה?

• line 6: **labar mitzvah** לַבַּר מִצְוָה *for the Bar Mitzvah*. When the preposition **le** לְ is followed by the definite article **ha** הַ, the words are contracted to form **la** לַ *for the*.

② We have already seen the word **ben** בֵּן *son*. Here we have the form **bni** בְּנִי *my son*: the **-i** suffix carries the meaning of 'my'. The **e** vowel sound disappears due to Hebrew's tendency to prefer shorter sound patterns.

③ **mazal tov** מַזָּל טוֹב: **mazal** is an ancient Hebrew word for a sign of the zodiac, and has therefore come to mean *luck*. Although **mazal tov** literally means 'good luck', its actual meaning in Hebrew is much closer to the English 'congratulations'. If you wish a basketball player **mazal tov** as they go onto the court, it sounds as though you're a little surprised they were picked for the team. Wishing them **mazal tov** after they win the game is an appropriate use of the phrase.

5 – **Lamah `at lo mevinah?**
why you(fem.) not understand(fem.)
What don't you understand?

6 **`Ani bedi`etah ki `ani rotzah liqnot simlah yafah labar mitzvah shel Netan`el!**
I in-diet because I want(fem.) to-buy dress pretty for-the-son-of commandment of Nethanel
I'm on a diet because I want to buy a pretty dress for Nethanel's Bar Mitzvah!

Transliteration

מִצְוָה בַּר
H Va TZ Mi — R Ba
mitzvah **bar**

1
חָדָשׁ מַה
SH Da CHa — H Ma
chadash **mah**

2
מִצְוָה בַּר בְּקָרוֹב
H Va TZ Mi — R Ba — V O R Qa Be
mitzvah **bar** **beqarov**

בְּדִיאֶטָה אֲנִי בְּנִי לִנְתַנְאֵל
H Ta `e I Di Be — I Ni `a — I Ni B — L `e N Ta Ne Li
bedi`etah** **`ani **bni** **liNetan`el**

3
טוֹב מַזָּל
V O T — L Za Ma
tov **mazal**

5 – לָמָה אַת לֹא מְבִינָה?

6 אֲנִי בְּדִיאֶטָה כִּי אֲנִי רוֹצָה לִקְנוֹת שִׂמְלָה יָפָה לַבַּר מִצְוָה שֶׁל נְתַנְאֵל! □

מְ בִ י נָ ה	לֹא	אֲ נִ י	אֲבָל	4
H Na I Vi Me	` Lo	I Ni `a	L Va `a	
mevinah	**lo**	**`ani**	**`aval**	
מִ צְ וָ ה	לְ בַּ ר	דִ י אֶ טָ ה	לָ מָ ה	
H Va TZ Mi	R Ba Le	H Ta `e I Di	H Ma La	
mitzvah	**lebar**	**di`etah**	**lamah**	
מְ בִ י נָ ה	לֹא	אַת	לָמָה	5
H Na I Vi Me	` Lo	T `a	H Ma La	
mevinah	**lo**	**`at**	**lamah**	
אֲ נִ י	כִּ י	בְּ דִ י אֶ טָ ה	אֲנִי	6
I Ni `a	I Ki	H Ta `e I Di Be	I Ni `a	
`ani	**ki**	**bedi`etah**	**`ani**	
יָ פָ ה	שִׂמְלָה	לִקְנוֹת	רוֹצָה	
H Fa Ya	H La M Si	T O N Q Li	H TZa O R	
yafah	**simlah**	**liqnot**	**rotzah**	
נְ תַ נ אֵ ל	שֶׁ ל	מִ צְ וָ ה	לַ בַּ ר	
L `e N Ta Ne	L SHe	H Va TZ Mi	R Ba La	
Netan`el	**shel**	**mitzvah**	**labar**	

16 Cursive script

Here are five more cursive letters:

mem	מ	מ	**zayin**	ז	ז
lamed	ל	ל	**tet**	ט	ט
vet	ב	ב			

Look at the words **mazal tov** in square letters: מַזָּל טוֹב
in cursive letters: מַזָּל טוב

The letter **lamed** is written ל. Notice that in both the scripts, this letter is taller than all the others.

Targil rishon – Targem תַּרְגִּיל רִאשׁוֹן – תַּרְגֵּם

❶ יש בר מצוה לנתנאל. Yesh bar mitzvah liNetan`el.

❷ אני רוצה לקנות שמלה יפה לאשתי.
`Ani rotzeh liqnot simlah yafah le`ishti.

❸ אני בדיאטה. `Ani bedi`etah.

❹ מה? את לא מבינה? Mah? `At lo mevinah?

❺ מזל טוב! Mazal tov!

Targil sheni – Hashlem תַּרְגִּיל שֵׁנִי – הַשְׁלֵם

❶ Congratulations, Nethanel!
Mazal tov, Netan`el!
מַ _ ל _ וֹב נֵ _ נ _ ל!

❷ Do you *(fem. sing.)* want *(fem. sing.)* to buy a dress?
`At rotzah liqnot simlah?
אַ _ רוֹצָ _ _ קְנוֹת _ מְלָה?

❸ I do not understand *(fem.)*.
`Ani lo mevinah.
אֲנִ _ לֹ _ מְבִינָ _.

Answers to Exercise 1

❶ Nethanel has a Bar Mitzvah. ❷ I want to buy a pretty dress for my wife. ❸ I am on a diet. ❹ What? Don't you understand? ❺ Congratulations!

❹ Why are you *(fem. sing.)* on a diet?
Lamah `at bedietah?
לָמָ _ _ _ ת _ דִיאֶ _ ה?

❺ The Bar Mitzvah [is] soon!
Habar mitzvah beqarov!
הַ _ ר מִצ _ ה _ קָרוֹ _!

Answers to Exercise 2

❶ מַזָל טוֹב נֵתַנאֵל! ❷ אַת רוֹצָה לִקנוֹת שִׂמלָה? ❸ אֲנִי לֹא מְבִינָה. ❹ לָמָה אַת בְּדִיאֶטָה? ❺ הַבַּר מִצוָה בְּקָרוֹב!

Exercise 3 – Write in cursive letters

Mazal tov! מַזָל טוֹב!

Bar Mitzvah בַּר מִצְוָה son of commandment. *According to Jewish tradition, when boys reach the age of 13 and girls the age of 12, they take on the responsibility of observing the religious commandments. The celebration for girls is called a* **Bat Mitzvah** בַּת מִצְוָה daughter of commandment. *The following are some of the main customs often associated with this important event in the lives of young Jews:*

- *Putting on* **tfilin** תְּפִילִין. *Also known in English as phylacteries, these are two small leather boxes with leather straps. One box is attached to the forehead, and the other to the boy's left arm (or right arm, if he is left-handed). Each box contains tiny parchments bearing four texts from the Bible. The word* **tfilin** תְּפִילִין *comes from* **tfilah** תְּפִילָה prayer. *The* **Bar Mitzvah** *boy also receives a* **talit** טַלִּית *or prayer shawl.*
- *The synagogue ceremony includes a special service in which the* **Bar Mitzvah** *boy plays a role, often reading a section from the Bible. The ceremony may include a special* **qidush** קִדּוּשׁ blessing over wine.

Answer to Exercise 3 – Cursive letters

מַזָל טוֹב!

• *The occasion is usually marked by a large celebration, second only in elegance (and cost) to that of a wedding. A festive meal may be held in a large banqueting hall, with an accompanying band. In many less observant families, the party may be the main or only way to mark the event. The* **Bar Mitzvah** *boy appears in fine clothes, as does the whole family – particularly his mother. After all, this is her 'last' chance to be the focus of attention – at a wedding, all eyes are on the bride!*

Liberal and Reform Jews hold exactly the same ceremonies for girls as for boys. Other families mark the **Bat Mitzvah** *with a party and possibly a community celebration.*

Don't forget to wish the happy family מַזָל טוֹב *– perhaps you can even write them a note in cursive script!*

17 Seventeenth lesson (Shi'ur shva' 'esreh)

Habalaganist
The messy guy

1 – **Mah habalagan hazeh ① poh?**
what the-mess the-this here
What's this mess?

2 – **Zeh lo balagan, `ani mesader `et ② hacheder!**
this not mess, I arrange(masc.) [`**et**] *the-room*
This isn't a mess, I'm tidying my room!

3 – **Hamitah hazot sham …**
the-bed the-this there
That bed there …

4 **Hashulchan hazeh vehakis`ot ha`eleh poh …**
the-table the-this and-the-chairs the-those there
This table here and these chairs there …

5 **Zeh seder ③ zeh?**
this order this
Is this [what you call] order?

Notes

① **habalagan hazeh** הַבַּלָגָן הַזֶּה *this mess*. Notice that the definite article **ha** הַ appears both before the noun **balagan** and before the demonstrative adjective **zeh** זֶה (*this* is a demonstrative adjective here because it describes *which* mess). This is because an adjective accompanying a noun with a definite article also needs the definite article. But when **zeh** זֶה is used as a pronoun (to replace a noun), it does not take the article. For example, **zeh seder** זֶה סֵדֶר *this [is] order* (line 5). ▸

17 שְׁעוּר שְׁבַע עֶשְׂרֵה

הַבַּלְגָנִיסט

1 – מַה הַבַּלָגָן הַזֶּה פֹּה?

2 – זֶה לֹא בַּלָגָן, אֲנִי מְסַדֵּר אֶת הַחֶדֶר.

3 – הַמִּטָּה הַזֹּאת שָׁם...

4 הַשּׁוּלְחָן הַזֶּה וְהַכִּסְאוֹת הָאֵלֶּה פֹּה.

5 זֶה סֵדֶר זֶה?

② **`et** אֶת is an essential word for forming correct Hebrew sentences, even though it may seem superfluous to English speakers as it has no direct translation. Basically, this word must be placed before a direct object (the receiver of the action in a sentence) when it is definite (i.e. referring to something specific rather than general). So when we say sentences in Hebrew such as 'I see the boy', 'She wants the steak', 'They love America', in each case, the word **`et** אֶת must come before the object.

③ **seder** סֵדֶר *order.* In lesson 6, we learned the expression **beseder** בְּסֵדֶר *all right, okay,* literally, 'in order'. The masculine singular present tense verb form is **mesader** מְסַדֵּר *I(masc.)/you(masc.) order/arrange, he orders, arranges.* The Passover feast is called the **Seder** because it follows a ritual sequence or order.

הַ בַּ לַ גָ נִ י ס ט
T S I Ni Ga La Ba Ha
habalaganist

1	מַ ה	הַ בַּ לַ גָ ן	הַ זֶ ה	פֹּ ה
	H Ma	N Ga La Ba Ha	H Ze Ha	H Po
	mah	**habalagan**	**hazeh**	**poh**
2	זֶ ה	לֹא	בַּ לַ גָ ן	
	H Ze	` Lo	N Ga La Ba	
	zeh	**lo**	**balagan**	
	אֲ נִ י	מְ סַ דֵ ר	אֶ ת	הַ חֶ דֶ ר
	I Ni `a	R De Sa Me	T `e	R De CHe Ha
	`ani	**mesader**	**`et**	**hacheder**
3	הַ מִ טָ ה	הַ זֹ א ת	שָׁ ם	
	H Ta Mi Ha	T ` Zo Ha	M Sha	
	hamitah	**hazot**	**sham**	

Targil rishon – Targem — תַרגִיל רִאשׁוֹן – תַרגֵם

1. הבלגניסט מסדר את החדר.
Habalaganist mesader `et hacheder.
2. המטה הזאת פה.
Hamitah hazot poh.
3. הכסאות האלה שם.
Hakis`ot haeleh sham.
4. מה הבלגן הזה?
Mah habalagan hazeh?
5. זה סדר זה!?
Zeh seder zeh!?

4

וְהַכִּסָּאוֹת	הַזֶּה	הַשּׁוּלְחָן
T O ` S Ki Ha Ve	H Ze Ha	N CHa L U SH Ha
vehakis`ot	**hazeh**	**hashulchan**

פֹּה	הָאֵלֶּה
H Po	H Le `e Ha
poh	**ha`eleh**

5

זֶה	סֵדֶר	זֶה
H Ze	R De Se	H Ze
zeh	**seder**	**zeh**

Cursive script

he ה **samekh** ס **dalet** ד

Zeh seder zeh?

square: זֶה סֵדֶר זֶה?

cursive: זֶה סֵדֶר זֶה?

Answers to Exercise 1

❶ The messy guy clears up the room. ❷ This bed goes here. ❸ These chairs go there. ❹ What is this mess? ❺ You call this order?!

Targil sheni – Hashlem תַּרְגִּיל שֵׁנִי – הַשְׁלֵם

❶ You*(masc. sing.)* set *(arrange)* the table.
`Atah mesader `et hashulchan.
_תָּה מְ_דֵר אֶ_ _שׁוּל_ן.

❷ He does not make *(arrange)* his bed in the morning.
Hu lo mesader `et hamitah baboqer.
הו_ לֹ_ מְסַ_ר אֶת _מִ_ה _בּוֹ_ר.

❸ There's a mess in Lior's car.
Yesh balagan bamekhonit shel Li`or.
_שׁ בַּלַ_ן _מְ_וֹנִ_ _ שֶׁל לִי_וֹר.

❹ I am tired*(fem.)* of messy David.
`Ani 'ayefah miDavid habalaganist.
_נִי _יֵפָה מִדָ_ד _בַּלַגָנִי_ _.

❺ In the room there is a bed, a table and some chairs.
Bacheder yesh mitah, shulchan vekis`ot.
בַּ_דֶר יֵשׁ מִטָ_, שׁ_לְחָן _כִּסְ_ _ת.

Exercise 3 – Write in cursive letters

Zeh seder zeh? זֶה סֵדֶר זֶה?

Answers to Exercise 2

❶ אַתָּה מְסַדֵּר אֶת הַשּׁוּלְחָן. ❷ הוּא לֹא מְסַדֵּר אֶת הַמִּטָּה בַּבּוֹקֶר.
❸ יֵשׁ בַּלָּגָן בַּמְּכוֹנִית שֶׁל לִיאוֹר. ❹ אֲנִי עֲיֵפָה מִדָּוִד הַבַּלַּגָנִיסְט.
❺ בַּחֶדֶר יֵשׁ מִטָּה, שׁוּלְחָן וְכִסְאוֹת.

Answer to Exercise 3 – Cursive letters

זֶה סֵדֶר זֶה?

You are surely starting to make some **seder** סֵדֶר *out of your Hebrew, but don't worry if you sometimes feel things are still a bit of a* **balagan** בַּלָּגָן*. In any case, a little bit of* **balagan** *can have its charm!*

18 Eighteenth lesson (Shi'ur shmoneh 'esreh)

Chatunat Figaro ①
The Marriage of Figaro

1 – **`Atah lavush kmo chatan!**
you(masc.) dressed like groom
You're dressed up like a groom!

2 **Le`an** ② **`atah holekh?**
to-where you(masc.) go(masc.)
Where are you going?

3 – **Lechatunat Figaro ba`operah.**
to-wedding-of Figaro in-the-opera
To 'The Marriage of Figaro' at the opera.

4 – **'im mi** ③**?**
with who
Who with?

5 – **'im `Avivah** ④**.**
with Avivah
With Avivah.

6 – **Mi zot `Avivah** ⑤**?**
who this Avivah
Who is Avivah?

Notes

① **Chatunat Figaro** חֲתוּנַּת פִּיגָרוֹ *[The] Marriage of Figaro.* Unlike in English, there is no need in Hebrew for the definite article here. When the second word in a construct (**smikhut**) phrase is a proper noun (such as the name of a person or place), the whole phrase is considered definite, and **ha** הַ is not added. It would also be grammatically correct to say **hachatunah shel Figaro** הַחֲתוּנָּה שֶׁל פִּיגָרוֹ, but the construct form is a little more formal and elegant.

18 שִׁעוּר שְׁמוֹנֶה עֶשְׂרֵה

חֲתוּנַת פִּיגָרוֹ

1 – אַתָּה לָבוּשׁ כּמוֹ חָתָן.

2 לְאָן אַתָּה הוֹלֵךְ?

3 – לַחֲתוּנַת פִּיגָרוֹ בָּאוֹפֶּרָה.

4 – עִם מִי?

5 – עִם אֲבִיבָה.

6 – מִי זֹאת אֲבִיבָה?

▸ ② **Le`an?** לְאָן *To where?* The preposition **le** לְ often indicates direction or movement. **Le`an** is always an interrogative pronoun (it always forms a question). The answer will usually begin with **le** לְ (or **la** לַ or **li** לִ, as we discussed in lesson 16).

③ **mi?** מִי *who?* This is a two-letter word that is written on its own. Don't confuse it with the preposition **mi** מִ *from* (for example, **miPolanyah** מִפּוֹלָנְיָה *from Poland*, lesson 8), which has only one letter (**mem** מ) and is therefore connected to the word that follows it.

④ **`Avivah** אֲבִיבָה is the feminine form of **`aviv** אָבִיב *spring*, a word we find in the name of the city **Tel Aviv**, which literally means 'hill-of spring'.

⑤ **zot `Avivah** זֹאת אֲבִיבָה *this [is] Avivah.* You may have noticed that certain Hebrew sentences lack a verb. This is the case when the missing verb is understood to be a form of *to be*: that is, *is*, *am* or *are*. Although this construction is extremely rare in standard English, it is common in Hebrew and is called a nominal sentence.

7 – **Hi hasoprano ba`operah. `Ani haba'al ⑥ shel `Avivah.**
she the-soprano in-the-opera. I the-husband of Avivah
She is the soprano in the opera. I am Avivah's husband.

Notes

⑥ **ba'al** בַּעַל *husband.* This word also means *owner* or *master.* Some people dislike the implied superiority of the husband over the wife suggested by this term and so use alternatives, but for most Israelis this is the usual word. A related term is **ba'al bayit** בַּעַל בַּיִת *master of the house, landlord* (or the feminine **ba'alat bayit** בַּעֲלַת בַּיִת *mistress of the house, landlady*). In the Canaanite fertility cult, **Ba'al** was a male god, ruler of the Earth and partner of the goddess Astarte.

Transliteration

פִ י גָ ר וֹ	חֲ ת וּ נַ ת
O R Ga I Fi	T Na U T CHa
Figaro	**chatunat**

חָ תָ ן	כְּ מ וֹ	לָ ב וּ שׁ	אַ תָּ ה	1
N Ta CHa	O M K	SH U V La	H Ta `a	
chatan	**kmo**	**lavush**	**`atah**	

ה וֹ לֵ ךְ	אַ תָּ ה	לְ אָ ן	2
KH Le O H	H Ta `a	N `a Le	
holekh	**`atah**	**le`an**	

בָּ א וֹ פֶּ רָ ה	פִ י גָ ר וֹ	לַ חֲ ת וּ נַ ת	3
H Ra Pe O ` Ba	O R Ga I Fi	T Na U T CHa Le	
ba`operah	**Figaro**	**lechatunat**	

18

7 – הִיא הַסּוֹפְּרָנוֹ בָּאוֹפֶּרָה. אֲנִי הַבַּעַל שֶׁל אֲבִיבָה. □

4	עִם M 'i **'im**	מִי I Mi **mi**	
5	עִם M 'i **'im**	אֲבִיבָה H Va I Vi `a **`Avivah**	
6	מִי I Mi **mi**	זֹאת T ` Zo **zot**	אֲבִיבָה H Va I Vi `a **`Avivah**
7	הִיא ` I Hi **hi**	הַסּוֹפְּרָנוֹ O N Ra P O S Ha **hasoprano**	בָּאוֹפֶּרָה H Ra Pe O ` Ba **ba`operah**
	אֲנִי I Ni `a **`ani**	הַבַּעַל L 'a Ba Ha **haba'al**	שֶׁל L She **shel**	אֲבִיבָה H Va I Vi `a **`Avivah**

Cursive script

chet ח

kaf/khaf כ-כּ

final **nun** ן

shin/sin שׁ-שׂ

t̲av ת

lavush kmo chatan
in square letters: לָבוּשׁ כּמוֹ חָתָן
in cursive letters: לָבוּשׁ כּמוֹ חָתָן

Targil rishon – Targem תַּרְגִּיל רִאשׁוֹן – תַּרְגֵּם

❶ למה אתה לבוש כמו באופרה?
Lamah `atah lavush kmo ba`operah?

❷ זה החתן של יעל?
Zeh hachatan shel Yael?

❸ מה נשמע? לאן אתה הולך?
Mah nishma'? Le`an `atah holekh?

❹ עם מי הוא הולך לבית קפה?
'Im mi hu holekh leveyt qafeh?

❺ שלום, אני הבעל של אורית.
Shalom, `ani haba'al shel Orit.

Targil sheni – Hashlem תַּרְגִּיל שֵׁנִי – הַשְׁלֵם

❶ He [is] dressed like a groom.
Hu lavush kmo chatan.
הוּ _ לָ_וּשׁ _מוֹ _תָן.

❷ My wife has *(To-my-wife there-is)* a pretty dress for the opera.
Le`ishti yesh simlah yafah la`operah.
לְ_שְׁתִּ_ יֵ_ _ _מְלָה יָ_ה _אוֹ_רָה.

❸ This [is] Rinah from the Hebrew Ulpan.
Zot Rinah meha`ulpan le'ivrit.
זֹ_ת רִנָּ_ _הָ_ _לְפָּן _ _בְרִית.

Exercise 3 – Write in cursive letters

lavush kmo chatan לָבוּשׁ כְּמוֹ חָתָן

Answers to Exercise 1

❶ Why are you dressed up like at the opera? ❷ Is this Yael's fiancé *(groom)*? ❸ How are you? Where are you going? ❹ Who are you going to the café with? ❺ Hello, I'm Orit's husband.

❹ Where are you*(masc. sing.)* going*(masc. sing.)* this *(the)* morning?
Le`an atah holekh haboqer?
לְ_ן אַתָ_ הוֹלֵ_ _בּוֹ_ר?

❺ The wedding of Shirli and Lior is [coming up] soon!
Beqarov hachatunah shel Shirli veLi`or.
_קָרוֹ_ _חֲתוּנָ_ שֶׁל שִׁ_רלִ_ _לִ_א_ר.

Answers to Exercise 2

❶ הוּא לָבוּשׁ כְּמוֹ חָתָן. ❷ לְאִשְׁתִּי יֵשׁ שִׂמְלָה יָפָה לָאוֹפֶּרָה.
❸ זֹאת רִנָה מֵהָאוּלְפָּן לְעִבְרִית. ❹ לְאָן אַתָּה הוֹלֵךְ הַבֹּקֶר?
❺ בְּקָרוֹב הַחֲתוּנָה שֶׁל שִׁירְלִי וְלִיאוֹר.

Answer to Exercise 3 – Cursive letters

לָבוּשׁ כְּמוֹ חָתָן

19 Nineteenth lesson (Shi'ur tsha' 'esreh)

Mishpachah sportivit ①
A sporty family

1 – **Baboqer, `aba mesacheq kaduregel** ②**.**
in-morning dad plays(masc.) ball-foot
In the morning Dad plays football.

2 – **`Ima mesacheqet tenis bechof hayam.**
mom plays(fem.) tennis in-beach-of the-sea
Mom plays tennis on the beach.

3 – **`Achi hagadol** ③ **ve`achi haqatan mesachaqim kaduryad** ④**.**
brother-my the-big and-brother-my the-little play(masc.) ball-hand
My big brother and my little brother play handball.

4 – **`Achoti** ⑤ **hagdolah ve`achoti haqtanah mesachaqot kadursal** ⑥**.**
sister-my the-big and-sister-my the-little play(fem.) ball-basket
My big sister and my little sister play basketball.

Notes

① **sportivit** סְפּוֹרטִיבִית is the feminine form of the adjective **sportivi** סְפּוֹרטִיבִי. It is feminine here because **mishpachah** *family* is a feminine noun. Other examples of how to form masculine and feminine adjectives: from the noun **`aviv** אָבִיב *spring*, the masculine adjective **`avivi** אֲבִיבִי *springlike* is formed, as well as the feminine adjective **`avivit** אֲבִיבִית. The masculine adjective **`alchuti** אַלחוּטִי *wireless*, *cordless* becomes **`alchutit** אַלחוּטִית with a feminine noun. ▸

19 שִׁעוּר תֵּשַׁע עֶשְׂרֵה

מִשְׁפָּחָה ספּוֹרטִיבִית

1 – בַּבֹּקֶר אַבָּא מְשַׂחֵק כַּדּוּרֶגֶל.

2 – אִמָּא מְשַׂחֶקֶת טֶנִיס בְּחוֹף הַיָּם.

3 – אָחִי הַגָּדוֹל וְאָחִי הַקָּטָן מְשַׂחֲקִים כַּדּוּרְיָד.

4 – אֲחוֹתִי הַגְּדוֹלָה וַאֲחוֹתִי הַקְּטַנָּה מְשַׂחֲקוֹת כַּדּוּרְסַל.

② **kaduregel** כַּדּוּרֶגֶל *football* (i.e. soccer) is a contracted combination of **kadur** כַּדּוּר *ball* and **regel** רֶגֶל *foot.*

③ **`achi hagadol** אָחִי הַגָּדוֹל *my big brother.* Note that the adjective **gadol** גָּדוֹל *big* is preceded here by **ha** הַ, the definite article. There is no **ha** הַ before **`ach** אָח *brother*, because the suffix **-i** that makes it mean 'my brother' makes it definite (if you think of אָחִי as meaning 'the brother of me', it may help you remember that it does not need a definite article as well). The same is true of lines 3 and 4: **`achi haqatan** אָחִי הַקָּטָן *my litte brother*, **`achoti hagdolah** אֲחוֹתִי הַגְּדוֹלָה *my big sister.*

④ **kaduryad** כַּדּוּרְיָד *handball* comes from **kadur** כַּדּוּר *ball* and **yad** יָד *hand.*

⑤ **`achot** אָחוֹת *sister.* Watch out! This is a feminine singular noun, whereas the **ot** in **chatikhot** חֲתִיכוֹת (lesson 15) and **mesachaqot** מְשַׂחֲקוֹת (in this lesson), is a suffix that marks the feminine plural. The infinitive of many verbs also ends in **-ot** וֹת, as in **lehitra`ot** לְהִתְרָאוֹת *to see each other* (lesson 6, line 5) and **liqnot** לִקְנוֹת *to buy* (lesson 16, line 6). In fact, this unusual word, **achot** אָחוֹת, is an irregularity.

⑥ **kadursal** כַּדּוּרְסַל *basketball*, from **kadur** כַּדּוּר *ball* and **sal** סַל *basket.*

5 – `Ani mesacheq bemischaq video babayit ⑦.
I play(masc.) in-game-of video in-the-house
I play a video game at home.

Note

⑦ **bayit** בַּיִת *house*. Here, this word appears in its 'separate' or 'absolute' form. When it is in 'construct state' (**smikhut**) and connected to a following noun, it takes the form **beyt** בֵּית, as you learned in lesson 10.

Transliteration

ספּוֹרְטִיבִית	מִשְׁפָּחָה
T I Vi I Ti R O P S	H CHa Pa SH Mi
sportivit	**mishpachah**

כַּדּוּרֶגֶל	מְשַׂחֵק	אַבָּא	בַּבּוֹקֶר	1
L Ge Re U D Ka	Q CHe Sa Me	` Ba `a	R Qe O B Ba	
kaduregel	**mesacheq**	**`aba**	**baboqer**	

הַיָּם	בְּחוֹף	טֶנִיס	מְשַׂחֶקֶת	אִמָּא	2
M Ya Ha	F O CH Be	S I Ni Te	T Qe CHe Sa Me	` Ma `i	
hayam	**bechof**	**tenis**	**mesacheqet**	**`ima**	

הַקָּטָן	וְאַחִי	הַגָּדוֹל	אָחִי	3
N Ta Qa Ha	I CHi `a Ve	L O D Ga Ha	I CHi `a	
haqatan	**ve`achi**	**hagadol**	**`achi**	

כַּדּוּרְיָד	מְשַׂחֲקִים
D Ya R U D Ka	M I Qi CHa Sa Me
kaduryad	**mesachaqim**

5 – אֲנִי מְשַׂחֵק בְּמִשְׂחָק וִידֵאוֹ בַּבַּיִת.

---

4   אֲחוֹתִי   הַגְּדוֹלָה   וַאֲחוֹתִי

I Ti O CH `a    H La O D G Ha    I Ti O CH `a Ve

`achoti    hagdolah    ve`achoti

הַקְּטַנָּה   מְשַׂחֲקוֹת   כַּדּוּרְסַל

H Na Ta Q Ha   T O Q CHa Sa Me   L Sa R U D Ka

haqtanah   mesachaqot   kadursal

5   אֲנִי   מְשַׂחֵק   בְּמִשְׂחָק

I Ni `a   Q CHe Sa Me   Q CHa S Mi Be

`ani   mesacheq   bemischaq

וִידֵאוֹ   בַּבַּיִת

O ` De I Vi   T Yi Ba Ba

video   babayit

Cursive script

pe   ᗞ   פ   fe   ᗞ   פ   yod   ׳   י

Compare the title of this lesson in square script:

מִשְׂפָּחָה סְפּוֹרְטִיבִית

and in cursive letters:

מִשְׂפָּחָה סְפּוֹרְטִיבִית

19 Targil rishon – Targem תַּרְגִּיל רִאשׁוֹן – תַּרְגֵּם

❶ אמא ואבא משחקים טניס.
`Ima ve`aba mesachaqim tenis.

❷ אחותי הגדולה משחקת במשחק וידאו.
`Achoti hagdolah mesacheqet bemischaq video.

❸ האח הקטן משחק כדורגל.
Ha`ach haqatan mesacheq kaduregel.

❹ האחות הקטנה ואמא משחקות כדוריד.
Ha`achot haqtanah ve`ima mesachaqot kaduryad.

❺ האח הגדול משחק כדורסל.
Ha`ach hagadol mesacheq kadursal.

Targil sheni – Hashlem תַּרְגִּיל שֵׁנִי – הַשְׁלֵם

❶ Danny is playing tennis on the beach.
Dani mesacheq tenis bechof hayam.
_ נִי מְ _ חֵק _ נִיס בְּ _ וֹף _ יָם.

❷ Mom is playing a computer game.
`Ima mesacheqet bemischaq machshev.
_ מָ _ מְשַׂ _ קֶ _ _ מִ _ חָק מַחשֵׁ _.

❸ My little sister and my big brother are playing at home.
`Achoti haqtanah ve`achi hagadol mesachaqim babayit.
אַ _ וֹתִ _ הַק _ נָה _ אַחִי הַ _ _ _ ל _ שַׂחֲקִ _ _ _ _ יִת.

Exercise 3 – Write in cursive letters

מִשְׁפָּחָה ספּוֹרטִיבִית.

Answers to Exercise 1

❶ Mom and Dad play tennis. ❷ My big sister is playing a video game. ❸ The little brother plays football/soccer. ❹ The little sister and Mom play handball. ❺ The big brother plays basketball.

❹ Dad and my little brother are playing football.
`Aba ve`achi haqatan mesachaqim kaduregel.
_ בָּ _ וְאָחִ _ _ קָטָ _ מְשַׂחֲק _ _ כַּדוּרֶ _ _.

❺ Dad and Mom are playing basketball.
`Aba ve`ima mesachaqim kadursal.
אַ _ א וְאִ _ א מְ _ חֲק _ _ כַּדוּר _ _.

Answers to Exercise 2

❶ דָּנִי מְשַׂחֵק טֶנִיס בְּחוֹף הַיָּם. ❷ אִמָּא מְשַׂחֶקֶת בְּמִשְׂחָק מַחְשֵׁב. ❸ אֲחוֹתִי הַקְטַנָּה וְאָחִי הַגָּדוֹל מְשַׂחֲקִים בַּבַּיִת. ❹ אַבָּא וְאָחִי הַקָּטָן מְשַׂחֲקִים כַּדוּרֶגֶל. ❺ אַבָּא וְאִמָּא מְשַׂחֲקִים כַּדוּרְסַל.

Answer to Exercise 3 – Cursive letters

מִשְׁפָּחָה סְפּוֹרְטִיבִית.

20 Twentieth lesson (Shi'ur 'esrim)

Sof shavu'a ①
Weekend

1 – **Sof sof! Sof shavu'a!**
end end! end-of week
At last! The weekend!

2 – **Baboqer `anachnu sochim babrekhah.**
in-the-morning we swim(masc.) in-the-pool
In the morning we swim in the pool.

3 – **Ba'erev `anachnu holkhim lechaverim,**
in-the-evening we go(masc.) to-friends
In the evening we go to friends,

4 **Medabrim 'al politiqah,**
[we] speak(masc.) about politics
we talk politics,

Notes

① **shavu'a** שָׁבוּעַ *week*. This word comes from **sheva'** שֶׁבַע *seven*, since a week has seven days, like the seven days of creation, according to Genesis. *Seven* is sometimes considered a lucky or special number in Jewish tradition.

Transliteration

שָׁ ב וּ עַ	ס וֹ ף
'a U V SHa	F O S
shavu'a	**sof**

שָׁ ב וּ עַ	ס וֹ ף	ס וֹ ף	ס וֹ ף	1
'a U V SHa	F O S	F O S	F O S	
shavu'a	**sof**	**sof**	**sof**	

20 שִׁעוּר עֶשְׂרִים

סוֹף שָׁבוּעַ

1 – סוֹף סוֹף! סוֹף שָׁבוּעַ!

2 – בַּבּוֹקֶר אֲנַחנוּ שׂחִים בַּבְּרֵכָה.

3 – בָּעֶרֶב אֲנַחנוּ הולכִים לַחֲבֵרִים,

4 מְדַבּרִים עַל פּוֹלִיטִיקָה,

❦

2

שׂוֹחִים	אֲנַחנוּ	בַּבּוֹקֶר
M I CHi O S	U N CH Na `a	R Qe O B Ba
sochim	**`anachnu**	**baboqer**

בַּבְּרֵכָה
H KHa Re B Ba
babrekhah

3

הוֹלכִים	אֲנַחנוּ	בַּעֶרֶב
M I KHi L O H	U N CH Na `a	V Re 'e Ba
holkhim	**`anachnu**	**ba'erev**

לְחֲבֵרִים
M I Ri Ve CHa Le
lechaverim

4

פּוֹלִיטִיקָה	עַל	מְדַבּרִים
H Qa I Ti I Li O P	L 'a	M I Ri B Da Me
politiqah	**'al**	**medabrim**

5   **mefatpetim** ② **ve`okhlim ''al ha`esh'** …

[we] chat(masc.) and-eat(masc.) on the-fire

we chat and have a barbeque …

6 –   Sof shavu'a bekef!

end-of week in-fun

A fun weekend!

Notes

② **mefatpetim** מְפַטְפְּטִים *[we] chat* (masc.). We saw the word **pitput** פִּטְפּוּט **pitputim** פִּטְפּוּטִים *chit-chat* in the title of lesson 13. These words come from a four-letter root based on the repetition of the letters **pe** פ (or **fe** פ) and **tet** ט.

Cursive script

alef אֵC א   **ayin** 𝒳 ע   final **mem** 𝒫 ם

Compare the letters in their square and cursive forms:

`okhlim 'al ha`esh

square: אוֹכְלִים עַל הָאֵשׁ.

cursive: אוֹכ𝓁ים 𝒳ℓ הָאֵשׁ.

❦

Targil rishon – Targem   תַּרְגִּיל רִאשׁוֹן – תַּרְגֵּם

❶ בְּסוֹף שָׁבוּעַ אַתֶּם שׂוֹחִים בַּיָּם.

Besof shavu'a `atem sochim bayam.

❷ אֲנַחְנוּ הוֹלְכִים לַבְּרֵכָה עִם חֲבֵרִים.

`Anachnu holkhim labrekhah 'im chaverim.

❸ בָּעֶרֶב אֲנַחְנוּ אוֹכְלִים עַל הָאֵשׁ.

Ba'erev `anachnu `okhlim 'al ha`esh.

❹ לָמָה הֵם מְדַבְּרִים עַל פּוֹלִיטִיקָה?

Lamah hem medabrim 'al politiqah?

5 מְפַטְפְּטִים וְאוֹכְלִים "עַל הָאֵשׁ"

6 – סוֹף שָׁבוּעַ בְּכֵף!

5 מְ פַ ט פְּ טִ י ם — M I Ti Pe T Fa Me — **mefatpetim**
וְ א וֹ כ לִ י ם — M I Li KH O ` Ve — **ve`okhlim**
עַ ל — L 'a — **'al**
הָ אֵ שׁ — SH `e Ha — **ha`esh**

6 ס וֹ ף — F O S — **sof**
שָׁ ב וּ עַ — 'a U V SHa — **shavu'a**
בְּ כֵ ף — F Ke Be — **bekef**

⑤ בבוקר אנחנו מפטפטים בטלפון.
Baboqer `anachnu mefatpetim batelefon.

Answers to Exercise 1

❶ At the weekend you swim in the sea. ❷ We go to the swimming pool with friends. ❸ In the evening we have *(eat)* a barbecue. ❹ Why are they talking politics? ❺ In the morning we chat on the telephone.

Targil sheni – Hashlem תַּרְגִּיל שֵׁנִי – הַשְׁלֵם

❶ Weekend of fun.
Sof shavu'a bekef.
סו_ שָׁבוּ_ בְּכֵ_.

❷ In the morning they*(masc.)* swim*(masc.)* in the pool.
Baboqer hem sochim babrekhah.
_בּוֹקֶר _ם _ _חִים בַּבְּרֵ_ה.

❸ In the evening we chat*(masc.)* about politics.
Ba'erev `anachnu mefatpetim 'al politiqah.
בּ_רֶב אֲנַ_נוּ מְפַ_פֶּ_ים _ל פּוֹלִיטִי_ה.

❹ On Shabbat you*(masc. plural)* go*(masc. plural)* to the Levy's *(the Levy family)*.
Beshabat `atem holkhim lemishpachat Levy.
_שַׁבָּ_ אַ_ם _וֹל_ים _מִשְׁפַּ_ת לֵ_י.

❺ Ah! The weekend at last!
Oof! Sof, sof, sof shavu'a.
_וּף! סו_, ס_ף _וֹף שָׁ_וּעַ.

Sof shavu'a סוֹף שָׁבוּעַ weekend. *The Israeli weekend consists of Friday and Saturday. Some people work on Friday mornings, and post offices, banks and shops are open until at least 1 pm. So make sure to get your errands done in time! Later on Friday, the volume of traffic falls, and a calm, pleasant atmosphere takes over.*

Muslims and Christians in Israel keep their own days of rest (Friday and Sunday, respectively). In the Old City of Jerusalem, each community opens and closes it shops according to its own traditions. In Israel as a whole, Shabbat is a day to spend with family and friends. Israelis are sociable and informal, and impromptu gatherings often go on until late on Friday night.

Most Israelis take a strong interest in domestic and international politics. The weekend newspapers, which go on sale on Friday, are loaded with magazines and supplements. Israelis often read them

Answers to Exercise 2

❶ סוֹף שָׁבוּעַ בְּכֵף. ❷ בַּבּוֹקֶר הֵם שׂוֹחִים בַּבְּרֵכָה. ❸ בָּעֶרֶב אֲנַחְנוּ מְפַטְפְּטִים עַל פּוֹלִיטִיקָה. ❹ בְּשַׁבָּת אַתֶּם הוֹלְכִים לְמִשְׁפַּחַת לֵוִי. ❺ אוּף! סוֹף סוֹף, סוֹף שָׁבוּעַ.

Exercise 3 – Write in cursive letters

אוֹכְלִים עַל הָאֵשׁ.

Answer to Exercise 3 – Cursive letters

אוֹכְלִים עַל הָאֵשׁ

while crunching on **gar'inim** גַּרְעִינִים *(literally, 'seeds'), a term that refers to sunflower or pumpkin seeds, pistachios and other nuts, usually roasted and salted. In many kiosks, newspapers and* **gar'inim** *are sold in the same area.*

'al ha`esh עַל הָאֵשׁ *literally, 'on the fire', means barbecue, and is a popular way of referring to this style of dining, which is possible almost all year round thanks to the Israeli climate. The women send their husbands off to play with fire; it's the easiest way to make sure they stay out of the kitchen!*

Well done! After twenty lessons, you are well on your way to being able to chat **bekef** בְּכֵף *in Hebrew.*

21 Twenty-first lesson (Shi'ur 'esrim ve`achat)

חֲזָרָה Chazarah – Review

Mazal tov! *You've reached the third review section. You've learned how to read Hebrew script, and you have begun to speak some Hebrew. As of now, you know how to write most of the letters in their cursive form.*

1 Alphabet

This table reviews the alphabet, including the cursive letters we have learned so far. A slash (/) is used to indicate any cursive letters we have not yet encountered – we'll learn these in the following lessons.

`	**`alef**	א	א	m	**mem**	מ	מ
b	**bet**	בּ	ב	m	final **mem**	ם	ם
v	**vet**	ב	ב	n	**nun**	נ	/
g	**gimel**	ג	/	n	final **nun**	ן	ן
d	**dalet**	ד	ד	s	**samekh**	ס	ס
h	**hey**	ה	ה	'	**'ayin**	ע	ע
v	**vav**	ו	ו	p	**pe**	פּ	פ
z	**zayin**	ז	ז	f	**fe**	פ	פ
ch	**chet**	ח	ח	f	final **fe**	ף	/
t	**tet**	ט	ט	tz	**tsadi**	צ	/
y	**yod**	י	י	tz	final **tsadi**	ץ	/
k	**kaf**	כּ	כ	q	**qof**	ק	ק
kh	**khaf**	כ	/	r	**resh**	ר	ר
kh	final **khaf**	ך	/	sh	**shin**	שׁ	שׁ
l	**lamed**	ל	ל	s	**sin**	שׂ	שׂ
				t	**tav**	ת	ת

Take time to learn the cursive forms, particularly the ones that are quite different from their equivalent in the square script.

2 Demonstrative pronouns (‘this’, ‘that’, ‘those’)

- masculine singular: **zeh** זֶה *this*
- feminine singular: **zot** זֹאת *this*
- masculine and feminine plural: **`eleh** אֵלֶה *these, those*

In Hebrew, the demonstrative pronoun has to agree with the grammatical gender of the noun – **zeh** if the noun is masculine, and **zot** if the noun is feminine. There is just one demonstrative pronoun for plural nouns of either gender: **`eleh**.

Zeh shulchan gadol. זֶה שׁוּלְחָן גָדוֹל.
This [is] a big table (masc.).
Zot mitah yafah. זֹאת מִטָה יָפָה.
This [is] a pretty bed (fem.).
`Eleh chaverim tovim. אֵלֶה חֲבֵרִים טוֹבִים.
These [are] good friends (masc.).
`Eleh chaverot tovot. אֵלֶה חֲבֵרוֹת טוֹבוֹת.
These [are] good friends (fem.).

Did you notice that the adjective also has to agree with the grammatical gender and number of the noun? Don’t forget!

3 Interrogative pronouns (‘who’, ‘what’, ‘why’, etc.)

- **Mi?** מִי? *Who?*
- **Mah?** מַה? *What?*
- **Lamah?** לָמָה? *Why?*
- **`Eyfoh?** אֵיפֹה? *Where?*
- **Meayin?** מֵאַיִן? *From where?* (The reply will begin with **mi-**.)
- **Le`an?** לְאָן? *To where?* (The reply will begin with **le-**.)

Remember:
– *Who* is there? – מִי שָׁם?
– It’s Oleg. – זֶה אוֹלֶג.
– *What* is he eating? – מַה הוּא אוֹכֵל?
– Cheesecake. – עוּגַת גְבִינָה.

21

– *Why?*	– לָמָּה?
– There isn't any poppyseed cake.	– אֵין עוּגַת פֶּרֶג.
– *Where* is he this weekend?	– אֵיפֹה הוּא בְּסוֹף הַשָּׁבוּעַ?
– At the beach.	– בְּחוֹף הַיָּם.
– *From where* is he coming?	– מֵאַיִן הוּא בָּא?
– From the pool.	– מֵהַבְּרֵכָה.
– *Where* is he going?	– לְאָן הוּא הוֹלֵךְ?
– To friends'.	– לַחֲבֵרִים.

4 Adjectives

	masculine singular	masculine plural	feminine singular	feminine plural
big	**gadol** גָּדוֹל	**gdolim** גדוֹלִים	**gdolah** גדוֹלָה	**gdolot** גדוֹלוֹת
small	**qatan** קָטָן	**qtanim** קְטָנִים	**qtanah** קְטָנָה	**qtanot** קְטָנוֹת
good	**tov** טוֹב	**tovim** טוֹבִים	**tovah** טוֹבָה	**tovot** טוֹבוֹת

When an adjective qualifies a noun preceded by the definite article (**ha** הַ), the adjective also needs to take the definite article **ha**. For example: **ha`ach hagadol** הָאָח הַגָּדוֹל *the big brother*, or literally, 'the-brother the-big' (remember that in Hebrew, adjectives always come after the noun they describe). If a noun is obviously definite (for example, if it is a proper noun, such as the name of a person or country, or if it has a possessive suffix), then the definite article is not needed before the noun, but it must still be placed before any accompanying adjectives. For example: **`achi hagadol** אָחִי הַגָּדוֹל *my big brother*, literally, 'brother-my the-big'.

5 Verbs

Most verbs, and indeed most of the Hebrew language, are based on three-letter roots. By adding vowels and additional letters before, after and in between the root letters, a huge variety of verbs, nouns and adjectives can be made according to fairly predictable patterns. There are also some two- and four-letter roots.

Hebrew verbs have three main tenses – past, present and future. So far we have only seen the present tense.

• *to go* – root: הָלַךְ

<u>masc.</u>

`ani holekh	אֲנִי הוֹלֵךְ	*I go*
`atah holekh	אַתָּה הוֹלֵךְ	*you go* (sing.)
hu holekh	הוּא הוֹלֵךְ	*he goes*
`anachnu holkhim	אֲנַחְנוּ הוֹלְכִים	*we go*
`atem holkhim	אַתֶּם הוֹלְכִים	*you go* (pl.)
hem holkhim	הֵם הוֹלְכִים	*they go*

<u>fem.</u>

`ani holekhet	אֲנִי הוֹלֶכֶת	*I go*
`at holekhet	אַתְּ הוֹלֶכֶת	*you go* (sing.)
hi holekhet	הִיא הוֹלֶכֶת	*she goes*
`anachnu holkhot	אֲנַחְנוּ הוֹלְכוֹת	*we go*
`aten holkhot	אַתֶּן הוֹלְכוֹת	*you go* (pl.)
hen holkhot	הֵן הוֹלְכוֹת	*they go*

• *to eat* – root: אָכַל

<u>masc.</u>

`ani `okhel	אֲנִי אוֹכֵל	*I eat*
`atah `okhel	אַתָּה אוֹכֵל	*you eat* (sing.)
hu `okhel	הוּא אוֹכֵל	*he eats*
`anachnu `okhlim	אֲנַחְנוּ אוֹכְלִים	*we eat*
`atem `okhlim	אַתֶּם אוֹכְלִים	*you eat* (pl.)
hem `okhlim	הֵם אוֹכְלִים	*they eat*

<u>fem.</u>

`ani `okhelet	אֲנִי אוֹכֶלֶת	*I eat*
`at `okhelet	אַתְּ אוֹכֶלֶת	*you eat* (sing.)
hi `okhelet	הִיא אוֹכֶלֶת	*she eats*
`anachnu `okhlot	אֲנַחְנוּ אוֹכְלוֹת	*we eat*
`aten `okhlot	אַתֶּן אוֹכְלוֹת	*you eat* (pl.)
hen `okhlot	הֵן אוֹכְלוֹת	*they eat*

• *to play* – root: שִׂחֵק

<u>masc.</u>

`ani mesacheq	אֲנִי מְשַׂחֵק	*I play*
`atah mesacheq	אַתָּה מְשַׂחֵק	*you play* (sing.)
hu mesacheq	הוּא מְשַׂחֵק	*he plays*
`anachnu mesachaqim	אֲנַחְנוּ מְשַׂחֲקִים	*we play*
`atem mesachaqim	אַתֶּם מְשַׂחֲקִים	*you play* (pl.)
hem mesachaqim	הֵם מְשַׂחֲקִים	*they play*

fem.	`ani mesacheqet	אֲנִי מְשַׂחֶקֶת	*I play*
	`at mesacheqet	אַתְּ מְשַׂחֶקֶת	*you play* (sing.)
	hi mesacheqet	הִיא מְשַׂחֶקֶת	*she plays*
	`anachnu mesachaqot	אֲנַחְנוּ מְשַׂחֲקוֹת	*we play*
	`aten mesachaqot	אַתֶּן מְשַׂחֲקוֹת	*you play* (pl.)
	hen mesachaqot	הֵן מְשַׂחֲקוֹת	*they play*

6 Forming negative sentences

We have already seen two ways to make a statement negative:

• `eyn אֵין is the negative of yesh יֵשׁ. It is used with nouns, not verbs.

Yesh sukar baqafeh?   יֵשׁ סוּכָּר בַּקָּפֶה?
Is there sugar in the coffee?

Review exercise

❶ סוֹף שָׁבוּעַ בָּא. סוֹף סוֹף! ❷ בַּבּוֹקֶר אֲנַחְנוּ שׂוֹחִים בַּיָּם. ❸ אֲנַחְנוּ מְשַׂחֲקִים טֶנִיס בְּחוֹף הַיָּם. ❹ אֲנַחְנוּ אוֹכְלִים "עַל הָאֵשׁ" עִם הַמִּשְׁפָּחָה. ❺ בָּעֶרֶב, אַבָּא "לָבוּשׁ כְּמוֹ חָתָן" וְאִמָּא בְּשִׂמְלָה יָפָה הוֹלְכִים לָאוֹפֶּרָה. ❻ אֲחוֹתִי הַקְּטַנָּה וַאֲחוֹתִי הַגְּדוֹלָה הוֹלְכוֹת לַבַּר מִצְוָה שֶׁל נְתַנְאֵל. ❼ אִשְׁתִּי וַאֲנִי הוֹלְכִים לַחֲבֵרִים. מְדַבְּרִים עַל פּוֹלִיטִיקָה. ❽ אֲנִי בַּלָּגָנִיסְט, אֲבָל בָּעֶרֶב אֲנִי מְסַדֵּר אֶת הַבַּלָּגָן בַּחֶדֶר. ❾ אֲנִי מְסַדֵּר אֶת הַמִּטָּה וְגַם אֶת הַשּׁוּלְחָן. ❿ שָׁבוּעַ טוֹב!

You may be surprised to learn that you've already completed a quarter of our course. To celebrate this milestone, we're introducing two changes:
• The lessons will no longer include the colour-coded transliterations, since you are becoming more familiar with the

`Eyn. אֵין.
There isn't [any].

• **lo** לֹא is used before a verb.
`Ishti lo sochah. אִשְׁתִּי לֹא שׂוֹחָה.
My wife does not swim.
Ve`atah? וְאַתָּה?
And you?
Lo. `Ani lo sportivi. לֹא. אֲנִי לֹא סְפּוֹרְטִיבִי.
No. I am not sporty.
`Ani lo holekh labrekhah. אֲנִי לֹא הוֹלֵךְ לַבְּרֵכָה.
I do not go to the swimming pool.

Answers

❶ The weekend's here. At last! *(end-of week comes. end end)* ❷ In the morning we swim in the sea. *(in-the-morning we swim in-the-sea)* ❸ We play tennis on the beach. *(we play tennis in-beach-of the-sea)* ❹ We have a barbecue with the family. *(we eat on the-fire with the-family)* ❺ In the evening, Dad, dressed up like a groom, and Mom, in her pretty dress, go to the opera. *(in-the-evening dad dressed like groom and-Mom in-dress pretty go to-the-opera)* ❻ My little sister and my big sister are going to Nethanel's Bar Mitzvah. *(sister-my the-small and-sister-my the-big go to-son-of commandment of Netan`el)* ❼ My wife and I are going [over] to [our] friends'. We [will] talk politics. *(wife-my and-I go to-friends. [we] talk about politics.)* ❽ I am messy, but this evening I'm cleaning up the mess in my room. *(I messy but the-evening I arrange* [`**et**] *the-mess in-the-room)* ❾ I make the bed and clear the table. *(I arrange* [`**et**] *the-bed and-also* [`**et**] *the-table)* ❿ A good week! *(week good)* (the traditional greeting at the end of the Sabbath)

Hebrew script.
• Exercise 2 will now involve completing whole words rather than single letters.

22 Twenty-second lesson
(Shi'ur 'esrim ushtayim)

Do`ar `eleqtroni
Electronic mail

1 – **Shalom Rivqah, `ulay `at yekholah la'azor** ① **li** ②**?**
hello Rivqah perhaps you(fem.) can to-help me
Hello Rivka, can you possibly help me?

2 **Yesh lakh** ③ **`et haktovet ha`eleqtronit** ④ **shel mishpachat Kohen** ⑤**?**
there-is for-you(fem.) [**`et**] *the-address the-electronic of family-of Cohen*
Do you have the email address of the Cohen family?

Notes

① **`at yekholah la'azor** אַתְּ יְכוֹלָה לַעֲזוֹר *Can you help?* Literally, 'You can to-help?' In Hebrew, constructions with the verb *can* are followed by the infinitive. Here, **yekholah** *you* (fem.) *can* is conjugated, and **la'azor** is an infinitive. We'll come back to the subject of the infinitive in lesson 24.

② **li** לִי, **lakh** לָךְ *for/to me, for/to you* (fem.) In lesson 9 (note 3), we learned that the preposition לְ can imply movement and mean 'to'. Here, it means 'for' or 'for the benefit of' and is declined into two different words. These are formed by connecting the לְ to the endings for the first-person singular and the second-person feminine singular. Later we'll learn how to decline this preposition for the other persons. The phrase **todah lakh** תּוֹדָה לָךְ 'thanks to-you (fem.)' (in line 6) is common in Hebrew, and is slightly more formal than simply saying **todah** תּוֹדָה *thanks.*

③ **yesh lakh** יֵשׁ לָךְ literally, 'there-is for-you' means *you have.* Similarly, **yesh li** יֵשׁ לִי (line 3), 'there-is for-me' means *I have.* ▸

דוֹאַר אֶלֶקטרוֹנִי

1 – שָׁלוֹם רִבְקָה, אוּלַי אַת יְכוֹלָה לַעֲזוֹר לִי?

2 יֵשׁ לָךְ אֶת הַכּתוֹבֶת הָאֶלֶקטרוֹנִית שֶׁל מִשְׁפַּחַת כֹּהֵן?

▸ We learned the word **yesh** יֵשׁ *there is* in lesson 10, lines 3 and 4. Here, this word forms part of the construction used to express the meaning *to have*. The invariable word **yesh** יֵשׁ is combined with the appropriate form of the preposition **l** לְ in the first-, second- or third-person, singular or plural, masculine or feminine.

④ **haktovet ha`eleqtronit** הַכּתוֹבֶת הָאֶלֶקטרוֹנִית literally, 'the electronic address' = *email address*. As we've seen, both the noun and the adjective take the definite article **ha** הָ. The noun **ktovet** כּתוֹבֶת *address* and the verb **kotev** כּוֹתֵב *you* (masc.) *write* in line 5 both come from the same root: כתב. Once again, we see how Hebrew words are formed from three-letter roots. The English word *email* is also used in Hebrew and is written אימייל.

⑤ **mishpachat Kohen** מִשְׁפַּחַת כֹּהֵן *[the] Cohen family*. Since this phrase is in the construct form and *Cohen* is a proper noun, there is no need for the definite article **ha** הַ before **mishpachat** or **Kohen**. Note that the final **hey** ה in the word **mishpachah** מִשְׁפָּחָה changes to **tav** ת to make the construct form **mishpachat** מִשְׁפַּחַת. We learned about the construct form (**smikhut**) in lesson 10 (note 4) and lesson 14. It is used to associate two nouns without having to use 'of'.

3 – Ken, yesh li. Dalyah Kohen, shtrudel ⑥**…**
yes there-is for-me Dalyah Cohen strudel
Yes, I do. Dalya Cohen, 'strudel'…

4 – Mah? Ha'ugah? Ah! Zeh hashtrudel ha`eleqtroni!
what the-cake ah this the-strudel the-electronic
What? The cake?! Oh, you mean the email 'strudel'!

5 – Nu ⑦**? `Atah kotev? Dalyah Kohen, shtrudel, zahavnet nequdah il.**
well you(masc.) write? Dalyah Cohen strudel zahavnet dot il
Well, are you writing? Dalya Cohen at zahavnet dot 'I' 'L'.

6 – Beseder, todah lakh, Rivqah. Lehit ⑧**.**
in-order thank you Rivqah bye
Okay, thanks Rivka. Bye!

Notes

⑥ **shtrudel** שְׁטְרוּדֶל *strudel* = @ in the context of emails. The Israelis have decided that the @ sign reminds them of a curly strudel pastry, so don't be surprised when every email address seems to include a quick visit to the bakery! By the way, the '.il' in email addresses (see line 5) is the country code for Israel (like .uk for the UK or .ca for Canada).

⑦ **nu** נוּ does not have a direct English equivalent, although you may be familiar with it from Yiddish-influenced English. It often expresses impatience (as in 'Come on now, get on with it …') and encourages someone to move or speak a little faster.

⑧ **lehit** לְהִת is an abbreviation of **lehitra`ot** לְהִתְרָאוֹת (see lesson 6) – just as *bye* in English is an abbreviation of *goodbye*. This is an informal form, but is very widely used and not at all impolite.

3 – כֵּן, יֵשׁ לִי. דָלִיָה כֹּהֵן, שְׁטרוּדְל ...

4 – מַה? הָעוּגָה? אָה! זֶה הַשְׁטרוּדְל הָאֶלֶקטרוֹנִי!

5 – נוּ? אַתָה כּוֹתֵב? דָלִיָה כֹּהֵן, שְׁטרוּדְל, זָהָבנֶט נְקוּדָה יל.

6 – בְּסֵדֶר, תוֹדָה לָךְ, רִבקָה. לְהִת.

□

שרה, אולי יש לך עוגת גבינה?

Cursive script

Keep practicing writing the cursive script, because from lesson 29 all the exercises will be presented in these letters. Apart from that, any handwritten notes or letters you read or write will be written in the cursive script.

final **fe** ף nun נ final **khaf** ךְ

Shalom Yosef, yesh lekha `internet?
Square script: שָׁלוֹם יוֹסֵף, יֵשׁ לְךָ אִנטֶרנֶט?
Cursive script: שָׁלוֹם יוֹסֵף, יֵשׁ לְךָ אִנטֶרנֶט?

Targil rishon – Targem תַרגִיל רִאשׁוֹן – תַרגֵם

❶ שרה, אולי יש לך עוגת גבינה?
Sarah, `ulay yesh lakh 'ugat gvinah?

❷ שלום דליה, תודה לך, להת.
Shalom Dalyah, todah lakh, lehit.

❸ יוסף כותב כתובת אלקטרונית.
Yosef kotev ktovet `eleqtronit.

❹ דודלוין@זהבנט.יל
Davidlevin@zahavnet.il

❺ מרים יכולה לעזור לי בערב.
Miryam yekholah la'azor li ba'erev.

***

Targil sheni – Hashlem תַרגִיל שֵׁנִי – הַשלֵם

(Each line represents a letter and its vowel mark, if it has one.)

❶ I have a nice poppy strudel.
Yesh li shtrudel pereg tov.

_ _ לִי _ _ _ _ _ _ _ פֶּרֶג טוֹב.

❷ What is the address of the Levin family?
Mah haktovet shel mishpachat Levin?

מַה _ _ _ _ _ _ _ שֶׁל _ _ _ _ _ _ לֶוִין?

❸ I have a new email [address].
Yesh li do`ar `eleqtroni chadash.

יֵשׁ _ _ _ _ _ _ _ אֶלֶקטרוֹנִי _ _ _ _.

***

Exercise 3 – Write in cursive letters

שָׁלוֹם יוֹסֵף, יֵשׁ לְךָ אִנטֶרנֶט?

Answers to Exercise 1

❶ Sarah, do you happen to *(possibly)* have a cheesecake? ❷ Hello Dalya, thank you, bye. ❸ Yosef writes an email address. ❹ Davidlevin@zahavnet.il ❺ Miriam can help me this evening.

❹ I'm *(fem.)* tired, I can't help my sister.
`Ani 'ayefah, `ani lo yekholah la'azor le`achoti.

אֲנִי ____ אֲנִי לֹא ______ ______ לַאֲחוֹתִי.

❺ Yosef wants a new computer.
Yosef rotzeh machshev chadash.

____ ____ מַחְשֵׁב חָדָשׁ.

Answers to Exercise 2

❶ יֵשׁ – שְׁטְרוּדֶל – ❷ – הַכְּתוֹבֶת – מִשְׁפַּחַת – ❸ – לִי דּוֹאַר – חָדָשׁ ❹ – עֲיֵפָה – יְכוֹלָה לַעֲזוֹר – ❺ יוֹסֵף רוֹצֶה –

Answer to Exercise 3 – Cursive letters

שָׁלוֹם יוֹסֵף, יֵשׁ לְךָ אִינְטֶרְנֶט?

23 Twenty-third lesson
(Shi'ur 'esrim veshalosh)

Sdeh ① te'ufah ②
Airport

1 – **Slichah, poh hatisah leYisra`el?**
excuse(fem.), here the-flight to-Israel
Excuse me, is this the flight to Israel?

2 – **Ken. `Atah lo ro`eh `et hamizvadot hagdolot?**
yes. you(masc.) not see [`**et**] *the-suitcases the-big?*
Yes. Can't you see the big suitcases?

3 **Kamah mizvadot yesh lekha?**
how-many suitcases there-is for-you(masc.)
How many suitcases do you have?

4 – **Yesh li raq mizvadah `achat. Zeh lo beseder?**
there-is for-me only suitcase one. this not in-order?
I only have one suitcase. Isn't that okay?

5 – **Zeh beseder. `Aval `atah haben `adam ③ harishon shetas ④ leYisra`el 'im mizvadah `achat!**
this in-order. but you(masc.) the-son-of adam the-first that-flies to-Israel with suitcase one
That's fine. But you're the first person to fly to Israel with just one suitcase!

Notes

① **sdeh** שְׂדֵה literally, 'field-of'. This word appears here in the construct form, which as we have seen is used to connect two nouns without having to use 'of'. The absolute form of this word is **sadeh** שָׂדֶה *field.* ▶

שָׂדֶה תְּעוּפָה

1 – סְלִיחָה, פֹּה הַטִּיסָה לְיִשְׂרָאֵל?

2 – כֵּן. אַתָּה לֹא רוֹאֶה אֶת הַמִּזְוָדוֹת הַגְדוֹלוֹת?

3 כַּמָּה מִזְוָדוֹת יֵשׁ לְךָ?

4 – יֵשׁ לִי רַק מִזְוָדָה אַחַת. זֶה לֹא בְּסֵדֶר?

5 – זֶה בְּסֵדֶר. אֲבָל אַתָּה הַבֶּן אָדָם הָרִאשׁוֹן שֶׁטָּס לְיִשְׂרָאֵל עִם מִזְוָדָה אַחַת!

▶ ② **te'ufah** תְּעוּפָה *flight*. This word comes from the root עוף, which relates to the concept of flying. This root appears in the Bible referring to birds that fly, but is now also used to refer to modern inventions like air travel.

③ **ben `adam** בֶּן אָדָם literally, 'son-of Adam' = *person, human being*. This phrase is very common in modern Hebrew – further evidence of the influence of Biblical language on everyday speech.

④ **she-** שֶׁ is a very useful word that is always joined to the following word (remember that a single letter never stands on its own in Hebrew). שֶׁ means *that*, *which* or *who*, as here in line 5: 'the first person who …'. In formal grammatical terms, this word serves both as a relative pronoun and as a conjunction.

6 Lamah `atah tas leYisra`el?
why you(masc.) fly to-Israel
Why are you flying to Israel?

7 – Yesh li chaverah biYrushalayim.
there-is for-me friend(fem.) in-Jerusalem
I have a girlfriend in Jerusalem.

8 – Hi yafah? Hachatunah beqarov?
she pretty? the-wedding soon?
Is she pretty? Are you getting married soon?

9 – Yafah me`od. `At rotzah tmunah?
beautiful very. you(masc.) want photo?
Very pretty. Do you want a photo?

Targil rishon – Targem תַּרְגִּיל רִאשׁוֹן – תַּרְגֵּם

❶ יש לך מזודה אחת קטנה.
Yesh lekha mizvadah `achat qtanah.

❷ יש לי חברה יפה בירושלים.
Yesh li chaverah yafah biYrushalayim.

❸ אתה הבן אדם הראשון שאני רואה הבוקר.
`Atah haben `adam harishon she`ani ro`eh haboqer.

❹ סליחה. מה פה לא בסדר?
Slichah. Mah poh lo beseder?

❺ אתה טס לחתונה בישראל?
`Atah tas lechatunah beYisra`el?

6 לָמָּה אַתָּה טָס לְיִשְׂרָאֵל?
7 – יֵשׁ לִי חֲבֵרָה בִּירוּשָׁלַיִם.
8 – הִיא יָפָה? הַתְּמוּנָה בְּקָרוֹב?
9 – יָפָה מְאֹד. אַתְּ רוֹצָה תְּמוּנָה?

□

Cursive script

tsadi ʒ צ

Mah `at rotzah?

Square script: מַה אַתְּ רוֹצָה?

Cursive script: מַה אַת רוֹצָה?

Answers to Exercise 1

❶ You have one small suitcase. ❷ I have a beautiful girlfriend in Jerusalem. ❸ You are the first person I've seen this *(the)* morning. ❹ Excuse me. What's wrong here? ❺ Are you travelling to a wedding in Israel?

Targil sheni – Hashlem תַּרְגִּיל שֵׁנִי – הַשְׁלֵם

❶ What's wrong at the airport?
Mah lo beseder bisdeh hate'ufah?

מַה לֹא בְּסֵדֶר ____ ______?

❷ How many suitcases do you *(masc.)* have?
Kamah mizvadot yesh lekha?

כַּמָּה מִזְוָדוֹת __ __?

❸ I only have a mobile phone.
Yesh li raq telefon nayad.

__ __ רַק טֶלֶפוֹן נַיָּד.

❹ Do you *(masc.)* have a photo of Nethanel?
Yesh lekha tmunah shel Nethanel?

יֵשׁ לְךָ _____ __ נְתַנְאֵל?

❺ What's new in the family?
Mah chadash bamishpachah?

מַה חָדָשׁ ______?

Exercise 3 – Write in cursive letters

מַה אַתְּ רוֹצָה?

The conversation in this lesson presents some of the vocabulary heard at the airport when flying to or from Israel. The security procedures are extremely strict, and you may feel that some of the questions asked by the security staff are surprisingly intrusive. Remember that everyone wants to enjoy a safe flight and try to take it all with a smile.

Answers to Exercise 2

❶ – בְּשְׂדֵה הַתְעוּפָה ❷ – יֵשׁ לְךָ ❸ יֵשׁ לִי – ❹ – תמוּנָה שֶׁל – ❺ – בַּמִשְׁפָּחָה

Answer to Exercise 3 – Cursive letters

מַה אַת רוֹצָה?

While you're waiting in line, you may come to understand the comments in the dialogue about the number and size of the travellers' luggage. Israelis on the move sometimes look as though they are moving house, carrying suitcases bursting with presents for the whole family and clothes for every possible eventuality.

24 Twenty-fourth lesson
(Shi'ur 'esrim ve`arba'a)

Hazmanah ①
Invitation

1 – **Matay `atem yekholim lavo ② le`aruchat 'erev ③?**
when you(masc. plural) can to-come for-meal-of evening
When can you come for dinner?

2 **`Ulay `efshar ④ beyom rishon `o beyom sheni?**
perhaps possible in-day first or in-day second
Would Sunday or Monday be possible?

3 – **Lo, `i-`efshar. Gadi 'oved baGolan, `aval `efshar beyom shlishi.**
no impossible. Gadi works in-the-Golan, but possible on-day third
No, [that's] impossible. Gadi is working in the Golan, but it's possible on Tuesday.

4 – **Chaval, beyom shlishi `anachnu bechatunah. `Ulay beyom revi'i?**
pity, on-day third we at-wedding. perhaps on-day fourth
Pity, on Tuesday we're at a wedding. Maybe on Wednesday?

Notes

① **hazmanah** הַזְמָנָה *invitation*. This word contains the root letters **zayin** ז **mem** מ **nun** נ, which also appear in the word **zman** זְמַן *time* (as a general concept, not as in 'What time is it?'). What's the connection? An invitation is essentially fixing a time: asking someone to be somewhere at a particular point in time. ▸

24 שִׁעוּר עֶשְׂרִים וְאַרְבַּע

הַזְמָנָה

1 – מָתַי אַתֶּם יְכוֹלִים לָבוֹא לַאֲרוּחַת עֶרֶב?

2 אוּלַי אֶפְשָׁר בְּיוֹם רִאשׁוֹן אוֹ בְּיוֹם שֵׁנִי?

3 – לֹא, אִי-אֶפְשָׁר. גָּדִי עוֹבֵד בַּגּוֹלָן, אֲבָל אֶפְשָׁר בְּיוֹם שְׁלִישִׁי.

4 – חֲבָל, בְּיוֹם שְׁלִישִׁי אֲנַחְנוּ בַּחֲתוּנָּה. אוּלַי בְּיוֹם רְבִיעִי?

② **lavo** לָבוֹא *to come*. Virtually all Hebrew infinitives begin with an initial **lamed** ל, which will help you to spot them. When looking for a verb in a Hebrew dictionary, you search by the root rather than the infinitive.

③ **`aruchat 'erev** אֲרוּחַת עֶרֶב *dinner* (literally, 'meal-of evening'). Remember lesson 14?! Once again, we are dealing here with a noun in the construct form (**smikhut**).

④ **`efshar** אֶפְשָׁר *possible*; **`i-`efshar** אִי-אֶפְשָׁר *impossible*. **`i** אִי is one of several particles used to create negative forms of adjectives and nouns (just as in English we have *im-*, *non-*, *un-*, *dis-* and so forth).

5 – Lo. Gam lo beyom chamishi.
no. also not on-day fifth
No, not on Thursday, either.

6 – \`Az beyom shishi ba'erev, la\`aruchat shabat?
so on-day sixth in-the-evening for-the-meal-of shabat
So on Friday evening for the Shabbat meal?

7 – Bekef, todah rabah.
in-fun thanks great
Great, thanks very much.

Targil rishon – Targem   תַּרְגִּיל רִאשׁוֹן – תַּרְגֵּם

❶ מתי אתם יכולים לבוא?
Matay \`atem yekholim lavo?

❷ אי אפשר לבוא לארוחת שבת.
\`I \`efshar lavo la\`aruchat shabat.

❸ ביום ראשון גדי עובד בגולן.
Beyom rishon Gadi 'oved baGolan.

❹ ביום שבת אני לא עובד.
Beyom shabat \`ani lo 'oved.

❺ אולי אתם יכולים לבוא לארוחת ערב?
\`Ulay \`atem yekholim lavo le\`aruchat 'erev?

5 – לֹא. גַם לֹא בְּיוֹם חֲמִישִׁי.

6 – אָז בְּיוֹם שִׁישִׁי בָּעֶרֶב, לַאֲרוּחַת שַׁבָּת?

7 – בְּכֵף, תוֹדָה רַבָּה. □

Cursive script

gimel ג ג

Gadi 'oved baGolan.

Square script: גָּדִי עוֹבֵד בַּגּוֹלָן.

Cursive script: גָּדִי עוֹבֵד בַּגּוֹלָן.

Answers to Exercise 1

❶ When can you come? ❷ It's impossible to come for Shabbat dinner. ❸ On Sunday Gadi's working in the Golan. ❹ I don't work on Saturday. ❺ Perhaps you can come for dinner?

24 Targil sheni – Hashlem תַּרְגִּיל שֵׁנִי – הַשְׁלֵם

❶ Is it possible to come on Saturday?
`Efshar lavo beshabat?

____ לָבוֹא בְּשַׁבָּת?

❷ Tuesday, Wednesday, it's impossible.
Beyom shlishi, beyom revi'i, `i `efshar.

בְּיוֹם ______ , בְּיוֹם ______ , __אֶפְשָׁר.

❸ Shabbat dinner is on Friday night.
`Aruchat shabat beyom shishi ba'erev.

_____ ___ בְּיוֹם שִׁישִּׁי בָּעֶרֶב.

❹ Thanks [very] much, Sarah.
Todah rabah Sarah.

____ ___ שָׂרָה.

❺ We are at a wedding on Monday.
`Anachnu bechatunah beyom sheni.

אֲנַחְנוּ ______ בְּיוֹם ___.

Write in cursive letters

גָּדִי עוֹבֵד בַּגּוֹלָן.

Yom יוֹם day. *In Hebrew, the weekdays do not have individual names as such, but are numbered in order beginning after Shabbat (Friday evening to Saturday evening). Accordingly, Sunday is* **yom rishon** יוֹם רִאשׁוֹן *– the first day after Shabbat. The word*

Answers to Exercise 2

❶ אֶפְשָׁר– ❷ – שְׁלִישִׁי – רְבִיעִי אִי – ❸ אֲרוּחַת שַׁבָּת –
❹ תוֹדָה רַבָּה – ❺ – בְּחֲתוּנָה – שֵׁנִי

Answer to Exercise 3 – Cursive letters

דָּבִי עוֹבֵד בַּגּוֹלָן.

rishon רִאשׁוֹן *comes from the root* ראש, *as in* **rosh** רֹאשׁ head. *The sequence of the days of the week is taken from the story in the Book of Genesis about the creation of the world, ending with the Sabbath – the day of rest.*

25 Twenty-fifth lesson
(Shi'ur 'esrim vechamesh)

Bachanut tzilum ①
In the photo shop

1 – Shalom. Mah bishvilkha ②?
hello. what for-you(masc.)?
Hello. What can I do for you?

2 – \`Ani tzarikh ③ matzlemah tovah, ki \`anachnu tasim ④ lechutz la\`aretz ⑤.
I need camera good because we fly to-outside to-the-land
I need a good camera because we're flying abroad.

Notes

① **tzilum** צִלּוּם *photograph* is a modern word with a Biblical pedigree. The root צלם appears in the Book of Genesis when the text speaks of *God* creating man in 'his own image'. This root gives us an opportunity to see how an entire family of words can stem from a single base: **tzalam** צַלָּם (line 3) is a *photographer* (in the plural, line 4: **tzalamim** צַלָּמִים); a *camera* is **matzlemah** מַצְלֵמָה (line 2) (in the plural, line 5), using a common pattern to signify an object or device by placing מ before the root letters and adding the suffix ה to create a feminine noun. In line 3, **metzalem** מְצַלֵּם is the masculine singular form of the verb *to photograph* in the present tense.

② **bishvilkha** בִּשְׁבִילְךָ *for you* (masc. sing.). In this lesson, this word appears both in its basic form **bishvil** בִּשְׁבִיל *for* (line 5) and with possessive suffixes: **bishvilkha** בִּשְׁבִילְךָ *for you* (masc. sing.) (line 1) and **bishvilkhem** בִּשְׁבִילְכֶם *for you* (masc. plural) (line 6). In lesson 23, line 3 we learned **lekha** לְךָ *for you* (masc.). The difference between the two forms is that **bishvil** בִּשְׁבִיל has a stronger sense of doing something for someone's sake or as a favour to them.

25 שִׁעוּר עֶשְׂרִים וְחָמֵשׁ

בַּחֲנוּת צִילוּם

1 – שָׁלוֹם, מַה בִּשְׁבִילְךָ?

2 – אֲנִי צָרִיךְ מַצְלֵמָה טוֹבָה, כִּי אֲנַחְנוּ טָסִים לְחוּץ לָאָרֶץ.

③ **`ani tzarikh** אֲנִי צָרִיךְ *I need* (masc.); **`ani tzrikhah** אֲנִי צְרִיכָה *I need* (fem.). Here is another root to add to our collection – צרך, meaning *need*. We can't learn all the words formed from each root at this stage, but having gained a sense of the way roots work, you may not be too surprised to learn that the root צרך produces words meaning 'consumer', 'commodity' and 'require', among others.

④ **`anachnu tasim** אֲנַחְנוּ טָסִים *we fly/are flying.* Whereas in English we often use the general verb *to go* to talk about travelling somewhere, as in 'We're going to India' or 'I went to Israel', in Hebrew the verb must more specifically refer to the form of travel used – walking, flying, driving and so on. In slang Hebrew, אֲנַחְנוּ טָסִים can also mean 'We're going really fast'. A little joke may help to clarify this. An Israeli is driving along a side road at 120 mph. A policeman orders the driver to stop. The driver exclaims **'Mah qarah? `Ani nose'a maher?'** '*What's the matter, am I driving too fast?*' The policeman replies, **'Lo, `atah tas namukh.'** '*No, you're flying too low.*'

⑤ **lechutz la`aretz** לְחוּץ לָאָרֶץ *(to) abroad.* **chutz la`aretz** חוּץ לָאָרֶץ literally means 'outside from-the-land'. We will return to the meaning of the word 'land' here a little later. For now, though, notice that in Hebrew when we say we are going abroad, we actually say 'to abroad', which explains the ל prefixed to the expression in this example.

3 – **`Atah tzalam chovev? Mah `atah metzalem?**
you(masc.) photographer amateur? what you photograph?
Are you an amateur photographer? What do you take pictures of?

4 – **`Ani metzalem `et hamishpachah. `Aval hayeladim sheli ⑥ tzalamim metzuyanim.**
I photograph [`**et**] *the-family but the-children of-me photographers excellent*
I take pictures of the family, but my children are excellent photographers.

5 – **Nu, ken, machshevim, matzlemot, telefonim nayadim ... bishvil hayeladim `eleh mischaqim.**
well yes computers cameras telephones mobile ... for the-children these games
Well, yes, computers, cameras, mobile phones … for kids these are like toys.

6 **Yesh li bishvilkhem matzlemah metzuyenet.**
there-is for-me for-you(plural) camera excellent
I have an excellent camera for you.

Note

⑥ **sheli** שֶׁלִּי *of me, mine.* This preposition declines to indicate possession. Here it appears in the first-person singular: **shel + `ani = sheli** שֶׁלִּי = אֲנִי + שֶׁל

3 – אַתָּה צַלָּם חוֹבֵב? מַה אַתָּה מְצַלֵּם?

4 – אֲנִי מְצַלֵּם אֶת הַמִּשְׁפָּחָה. אֲבָל הַיְלָדִים שֶׁלִּי צַלָּמִים מְצוּיָּנִים.

5 – נוּ, כֵּן, מַחשֵׁבִים, מַצלֵמוֹת, טֶלֶפוֹנִים נַיָּדִים, בִּשׁבִיל הַיְלָדִים אֵלֶּה מִשׂחָקִים.

6 יֵשׁ לִי בִּשׁבִילכֶם מַצלֵמָה מְצוּיֶּנֶת. □

Cursive script

final **tsadi** ץ

Lechutz la`aretz

Square script: לְחוּץ לָאָרֶץ

Cursive script: לְחוּץ לָאָרֶץ

Targil rishon – Targem תַּרְגִּיל רִאשׁוֹן – תַּרְגֵּם

❶ בשביל מי אתה צריך מצלמה?
Bishvil mi `atah tzarikh matzlemah?

❷ מה יש בחנות בשבילך?
Mah yesh bachanut bishvilkha?

❸ יש בחנות מצלמה בשבילכם.
Yesh bachanut matzlemah bishvilkhem.

❹ הוא מצלם את המשפחה.
Hu metzalem `et hamishpachah.

❺ אנחנו טסים לחוץ לארץ.
`Anachnu tasim lechutz la`aretz.

Targil sheni – Hashlem תַּרְגִּיל שֵׁנִי – הַשְׁלֵם

❶ Who is the camera for?
Bishvil mi hamatzlemah?

_ _ _ _ _ מִי הַמַּצְלֵמָה?

❷ He is an amateur photographer, but Danny and David are excellent photographers.
Hu tzalam chovev, `aval Dani veDavid tzalamim metzuyanim.

הוּא _ _ _ _ _ _ _ _ אֲבָל דָּנִי וְדוִֹד _ _ _ _ _ מְצוּיָּנִים.

❸ Mom and Dad have a camera because they are travelling *(flying)* abroad.
Le`aba ve`ima yesh matzlemah ki hem tasim lechutz la`aretz.

לְאַבָּא וְאִמָּא _ _ _ _ _ _ _ _ כִּי הֵם טָסִים
_ _ _ _ _ _ _ _?

Answers to Exercise 1

❶ Who do you need a camera for? ❷ What is there in the shop for you? ❸ There is a camera for you *(pl.)* in the shop. ❹ He photographs his *(the)* family. ❺ We are flying abroad.

❹ For you*(plural)*, I have an excellent camera.
Bishvilkhem, yesh li matzlemah metzuyenet.
בִּשְׁבִילְכֶם _ _ _ _ מַצְלֵמָה מְצוּיֶּנֶת.

❺ I photograph the hot chicks on the beach.
\`Ani metzalem \`et hachatikhot bechof hayam.
אֲנִי _ _ _ _ אֶת _ _ _ _ _ _ _ _ בְּחוֹף הַיָּם.

Answers to Exercise 2

❶ בִּשְׁבִיל – ❷ – צַלָּם חוֹבֵב – צַלָּמִים – ❸ – יֵשׁ מַצְלֵמָה – לְחוּץ לָאָרֶץ ❹ – יֵשׁ לִי – ❺ – מְצַלֵּם – הַחֲתִיכוֹת –

Exercise 3 – Write in cursive letters

הוּא טָס לְחוּץ לָאָרֶץ

Lechutz la`aretz** לְחוּץ לָאָרֶץ: *this expression (which appears in Talmudic Hebrew) makes sense when you realize that* הארץ *can mean not only 'the land', but also 'the Land' – that is to say, Israel. An Israeli who is outside Israel speaks about returning* **la`aretz to the Land. *One of Israel's daily newspapers is called* **Ha`aretz** The Land הָאָרֶץ.

---

26 Twenty-sixth lesson
(Shi'ur 'esrim veshesh)

Hatarmilay ①
The backpacker

1 – **Darkon** ② **vekhartis tisah, bevaqasha.**
passport and-ticket-of flight by-request
Passport and flight ticket, please.

2 **`Atah tarmilay? Le`an `atah tas?**
you(masc.) backpacker? to-where you fly?
Are you a backpacker? Where are you flying to?

Notes

① **tarmilay** תַרְמִילַאי *backpacker.* The word **tarmil** תַרְמִיל means a *pod* (i.e. of peas or beans), but has also acquired the meaning of a bag, and particularly a knapsack or backpack. The form **tarmilay** includes the suffix אַי **-ay**, which indicates a person's profession or activity. For example, from **yam** יָם *sea*, we have the word **yamay** יַמַּאי *seaman.*

② **darkon** דַרכּוֹן *passport* comes from the word **derekh** דֶרֶך *way, route*. We saw an example of how the suffix **-on** וֹן is used to form nouns in lesson 12 when we learned the word **qanyon** קַניוֹן *mall.* Similarly, from the word **shabat** שַׁבָּת comes **shabaton** שַׁבָּתוֹן meaning *sabbatical*, or any period when we do not work.

Answer to Exercise 3 – Cursive letters

הוּא טָס לְחוּץ לָאָרֶץ

With this lesson, you have completely learned the cursive script. Well done! Now you can read and write like an Israeli!

---

26 שִׁעוּר עֶשְׂרִים וְשֵׁשׁ

הַתַּרְמִילַאי

1 – דַרְכּוֹן וְכַרְטִיס טִיסָה בְּבַקָּשָׁה.

2 אַתָּה תַרְמִילַאי? לְאָן אַתָּה טָס?

דוד בן עשרים ואחת ושרה בת עשרים.

3 – `Ani tas leHodu 'im chaverim lemasa' ③ tarmila`im 'ad `oqtober.
I fly(masc.) to-India with friends for-trek-of backpackers until October
I'm flying to India with friends on a backpacking trek until October.

4 – Ben kamah `atah ④?
son-of how-many you(masc.)
How old are you?

5 – Ben 'esrim. `Ani `acharey hatzava velifney ha`universitah.
son-of twenty. i [am] after the-army and-before the-university
I'm twenty. I've finished my military service and I'll be going to university.

6 – Mah `atah rotzeh lilmod?
what you(masc.) want to-study
What do you want to study?

7 – Ge`ografyah ⑤.
geography
Geography.

8 – Tisah ne'imah!
flight pleasant
Have a pleasant flight!

Notes

③ **lemasa'** לְמַסָּע *for a trek.* **Masa'** מַסָּע *trek* is a real journey, carrying overtones of adventure.

④ **Ben kamah `atah?** ?בֶּן כַּמָּה אַתָּה ('Son-of how-many you?') = *How old are you* (masc.)*?* This may seem a rather colourful way of asking a simple question, but in Hebrew it is the everyday formula used for this purpose. When talking about a woman, the form used is: **Bat kamah (Rut)?** ?(בַּת כַּמָּה (רוּת ('Daughter-of how-many (Ruth)?') *How old is (Ruth)?*

3 – אֲנִי טָס לְהוֹדוּ עִם חֲבֵרִים לְמַסָּע תַּרְמִילָאִים עַד אוֹקְטוֹבֶּר.

4 – בֶּן כַּמָּה אַתָּה?

5 – בֶּן עֶשְׂרִים. אֲנִי אַחֲרֵי הַצָּבָא וְלִפְנֵי הָאוּנִיבֶרְסִיטָה.

6 – מַה אַתָּה רוֹצֶה לִלְמוֹד?

7 – גֵיאוֹגְרַפְיָה.

8 – טִיסָה נְעִימָה!

□

Here are a few more examples:
Ben kamah Naty? בֶּן כַּמָּה נָתִי? *How old is Nati?*
Bat kamah `at? בַּת כַּמָּה אַתְּ? *How old are you* (fem.)*?*

And in the plural:
Bney kamah hem? בְּנֵי כַּמָּה הֵם? *How old are they* (masc.)*?*
Bnot kamah hen? בְּנוֹת כַּמָּה הֵן? *How old are they* (fem.)*?*

The replies to these questions will use the word **ben / bat / bney / bnot** followed by the appropriate number.

⑤ **ge`ografyah** גֵיאוֹגְרַפְיָה *geography*. In Hebrew, this familiar word is pronounced with a hard **g** at the beginning, as in 'good'.

Targil rishon – Targem   תַּרְגִּיל רִאשׁוֹן – תַּרְגֵּם

❶ יֵשׁ לְךָ דַרְכּוֹן וְכַרְטִיס טִיסָה?
Yesh lekha darkon vekhartis tisah?

❷ דָּוִד בֶּן עֶשְׂרִים וְאַחַת וְשָׂרָה בַּת עֶשְׂרִים.
David ben 'esrim ve`achat veSarah bat 'esrim.

❸ אַחֲרֵי הַצָּבָא הוּא טָס לְבְרָזִיל.
`Acharey hatzava hu tas liBrazil.

❹ הֵם בְּמַסָּע תַרְמִילָאִים בְּהוֹדוּ.
Hem bemasa' tarmila`im beHodu.

❺ הוּא רוֹצֶה לִלְמוֹד גֵּיאוֹגְרַפְיָה בָּאוּנִיבֶרְסִיטָה.
Hu rotzeh lilmod ge`ografyah ba`universitah.

✿

Targil sheni – Hashlem   תַּרְגִּיל שֵׁנִי – הַשְׁלֵם

❶ Danny is going to Brazil with his backpacking friends.
Dani tas liBrazil 'im chaverim tarmila`im.

דָּנִי _ _ לְבְרָזִיל _ _ חֲבֵרִים _ _ _ _ _ _ •

❷ Yosef is a backpacker in India.
Yosef tarmilay beHodu.

יוֹסֵף _ _ _ _ _ _ בְּהוֹדוּ.

❸ My son wants to study Hebrew at university.
Bni rotzeh lilmod 'ivrit ba`universitah.

_ _ _ רוֹצֶה _ _ _ _ _ עִבְרִית בָּאוּנִיבֶרְסִיטָה.

✿

Exercise 3 – Write in cursive letters
יֵשׁ לִי כַּרְטִיס טִיסָה וְדַרְכּוֹן.

Answers to Exercise 1

❶ Do you have a passport and a flight ticket? ❷ David is 21 and Sarah is 20. ❸ After the army, he's going to Brazil. ❹ They are on a backpacking trek in India. ❺ He wants to study geography at university.

❹ Sarah has finished the army and is going to start university.
Sarah `acharey hatzava velifney ha`universitah.
שָׂרָה _ _ _ _ הַצָּבָא _ _ _ _ _ הָאוּנִיבֶרְסִיטָה.

❺ The backpacker has a flight ticket and a passport.
Latarmilay yesh kartis tisah vedarkon.
לַתַּרְמִילָאִי יֵשׁ _ _ _ _ _ _ _ _ _ _ _ _ _ _ _ _.

Answers to Exercise 2

❶ – טָס – עִם – תַּרְמִילָאִים ❷ – תַּרְמִילַאי – ❸ בְּנִי – לִלְמוֹד – ❹ – אַחֲרֵי – וְלִפְנֵי – ❺ – כַּרְטִיס טִיסָה וְדַרְכּוֹן

Answer to Exercise 3 – Cursive letters

יֵשׁ לִי כַּרְטִיס טִיסָה וְדַרְכּוֹן.

Masa' tarmilaim **מַסָּע תַּרְמִילָאִים** backpacking trek. *After high school, most Israelis perform military service – two years for women and at least three for men. After completing this challenging period of their life, many young Israelis take time out to visit faraway lands. Israel is a tiny country (about 8,000 square miles, roughly the same as Wales or New Jersey). Israeli backpackers reach almost every point on the globe; particularly popular destinations include Australia, the Far East and Latin America. Special travel agencies cater for this market, balancing backpackers' dreams with financial constraints (the young travellers often work for a few months to cover at least part of their travel costs, but usually parents also contribute). Israeli consulates around the world spend much of their time dealing with various problems and requests for help from backpackers. In popular destinations, religious organizations even hold mass Passover Seder meals so that the backpackers can follow their traditions while on the move.*

The Hebrew calendar has its origins in the Bible. The calendar is basically lunar, but it is linked to the solar calendar by a complicated system of rules and calculations. In Israel, festivals and special days follow the Hebrew calendar. Everyday civil and commercial activities use the Gregorian calendar (the standard

27 Twenty-seventh lesson
(Shi'ur 'esrim vesheva')

Mikhtav me`Eylat
A letter from Eilat

1 – **Shalom `Ima ve`Aba hayeqarim,**
hello mom and-dad dear
Dear Mom and Dad

2 **Dani va`ani be`Eylat kvar yomayim** ①**.**
Dani and-I in-Eilat already two-days
Danny and I have already been in Eilat two days.

Notes

① **yomayim** יוֹמַיִים *two days*, **shvu'ayim** שְׁבוּעַיִים *two weeks* (line 7): Hebrew has a special form (called the 'dual') for ▶

Western calendar). Diaries and calendars include dates from both calendars. Some Israelis celebrate their birthday according to the Hebrew date, some according to the Gregorian date – and some both!

Note that the months do not usually coincide. Part of October may fall during the Hebrew month of **Tishrey** *and part during the month of* **Cheshvan**. *The years are also not synchronized. The Hebrew year begins in* **Tishrey** *(sometime during September, varying from year to year), while the Gregorian calendar begins, of course, in January. The Hebrew New Year is a religious festival and national holiday, whereas the first of January is a regular work day (although young people, in particular, may go to parties on New Year's Eve).*

The Hebrew years are counted from year 1, starting from 3,761 years before the beginning of the Common Era. The Gregorian year 2000, for example, coincides with the Hebrew year 5761, written in Hebrew letters as ה' תשס"ו.

The days of the Hebrew months are counted using the numerical value attached to the Hebrew letters (see lesson 28 for a full explanation of the use of the Hebrew letters to represent numbers). The second day of the month of **Tishrey**, *for example, is* **bet betishrey** ב' בְּתִשְׁרֵי.

27 שִׁעוּר עֶשְׂרִים וְשֶׁבַע

מִכְתָּב מֵאֵילַת

1 – שָׁלוֹם אִמָּא וְאַבָּא הַיְקָרִים.

2 דָּנִי וַאֲנִי בְּאֵילַת כְּבָר יוֹמַיִים.

some nouns that come in pairs in everyday speech. The dual is formed by adding the suffix _ַיִים **-ayim**. Although there are two י, the form is pronounced as if there were just one.

3 – Poh cham me`od gam bayom vegam ② balaylah,
here hot very also in-the-day and-also in-the-night
It's very hot here both day and night,

4 `Aval `eyn be'ayot mipney shekol ③ hayom ④ `anachnu bayam.
but there-are-no problems because that-all the-day we in-the-sea
but it's no problem because we are in the sea all day.

5 – Habalagan poh gadol, biglal ⑤ hafestival 'Jazz ⑥ bayam ha`Adom'.
the-disorder here big because-of the-festival-of 'jazz in-the-sea the-red'
It's wild here because of the Red Sea Jazz Festival.

6 `Anachnu `okhlim falafel, tchinah, chumus, salatim, veshotim harbeh mayim ⑦.
we eat falafel tahini hummus salads and-drink much water
We eat falafel, tahini, hummus and salads and drink lots of water.

7 – Lehitra`ot be'od shvu'ayim.
to-see-each-other in-more two-weeks
See you in two weeks.

Notes

② **gam …vegam …** ... גַּם ... וְגַם ... *both*. This construction is used to express the idea of *both*, *also* or *as well as*. In English, we would say 'I want falafel and also tahini', but in Hebrew the **gam** is repeated: אֲנִי רוֹצָה גַּם פָּלָאפֶל וְגַם טְחִינָה.

Another example: the English 'He is both eating and speaking' would be in Hebrew 'He also eats and also speaks':
הוּא גַּם אוֹכֵל וְגַם מְדַבֵּר.

③ **mipney she …** מִפְּנֵי שֶׁ *because ...* The **she** שֶׁ must be used and is attached to the following word.

④ **kol hayom** כָּל הַיּוֹם means *all day (long)*, whereas **kol yom** כָּל יוֹם means *every day.*

3 – פֹּה חַם מְאֹד גַּם בַּיּוֹם וְגַם בַּלַּיְלָה,

4 אֲבָל אֵין בְּעָיוֹת מִפְּנֵי שֶׁכֹּל הַיּוֹם אֲנַחְנוּ בַּיָּם.

5 – הַבַּלָגָן פֹּה גָּדוֹל, בִּגְלַל הַפֶסְטִיבָל "גַ'אז בַּיָּם הָאָדוֹם".

6 אֲנַחְנוּ אוֹכְלִים פָלָאפֶל, טְחִינָה, חוּמוּס, סָלָטִים וְשׁוֹתִים הַרְבֵּה מַיִם.

7 – לְהִתְרָאוֹת בְּעוֹד שְׁבוּעַיִם.

⑤ **biglal** בִּגְלַל *because of* is followed directly by a noun. This word can also be declined for different persons. For example: **biglalkha** בִּגְלָלְךָ *because of you* (masc.), **biglalekh** בִּגְלָלֵךְ *because of you* (fem.). We will return to this in later lessons.

⑥ **jazz** גַ'אז. The sound **j** as in *jazz* does not occur in 'native' Hebrew words. When it appears in a loanword, it is spelled ג' (the letter **gimel** ג followed by an apostrophe ').

⑦ **mayim** מַיִם *water*. Strange as it may seem to English speakers, this masculine word always appears in the plural. Since adjectives must agree with the noun in gender and number, *hot water* is **mayim hamim** מַיִם חַמִּים. A traditional play on words begins with the word **yam** יָם *sea*. Add on a **mem** מ at the beginning and you get **mayim** מַיִם *water*. Now add the word **sham** שָׁם *up there*, and the result is **shamayim** שָׁמַיִם *sky* (where water comes from and finds its way to the sea). Note that the word **sham** as in *there* is the opposite of **poh** פֹּה *here*, with the former signifying things that are farther away and the latter signifying things that are closer, depending on the context. By the way, the word **shamayim** שָׁמַיִם *sky* is another example of a noun that is plural in Hebrew but singular in English.

8 Be`ahavah.
in-love
With love.

9 – Ruti veDani.
Ruti and-Danny
Ruti and Danny.

Targil rishon – Targem תַּרְגִּיל רִאשׁוֹן – תַּרְגֵּם

❶ באילת יש פסטיבל "ג'אז בים האדום".
Be`Eylat yesh festival ‘jazz bayam ha`Adom’.

❷ דני ורותי שותים הרבה מים ואוכלים פלאפל.
Dani veRuti shotim harbeh mayim ve`okhlim falafel.

❸ אנחנו כבר שבועיים פה.
`Anachnu kvar shvu'ayim poh.

❹ להתראות בעוד יומיים.
Lehitra`ot be'od yomayim.

❺ הן אוכלות בקפטריה גם בבוקר וגם בערב.
Hen `okhlot baqafeteryah gam baboqer vegam ba'erev.

8 בְּאַהֲבָה.

9 – רוּתִי וְדָנִי. □

Answers to Exercise 1

❶ In Eilat there is a festival [called] 'Jazz in the Red Sea'. ❷ Danny and Ruti drink lots of water and eat falafel. ❸ We've already been here for two weeks. ❹ See you in two days. ❺ They eat in the cafeteria both in the morning and in the evening.

27 **Targil sheni – Hashlem** **תַרְגִּיל שֵׁנִי – הַשְׁלֵם**

❶ We eat both tahini and hummus.
`Anachnu `okhlim gam tchinah vegam chumus.
אֲנַחְנוּ אוֹכְלִים גַם _ _ _ _ _ _ וְגַם _ _ _ _ _ _.

❷ They*(masc.)* are in the sea all day [long], because it is hot here.
Hem kol hayom bayam, mipney shecham poh.
הֵם _ _ _ _ _ _ _ בַּיָם, _ _ _ _ _ _ _ פֹּה.

❸ It's wild here because of the festival.
Biglal hafestival yesh balagan gadol.
_ _ _ _ הַפֶסְטִיבָל יֵשׁ _ _ _ _ גָדוֹל.

Exercise 3 – Write in cursive letters
רוּתִי וְדָנִי כְּבָר שְׁבוּעַיִים בְּאֵילַת.

Situated on the shores of the Red Sea, **Eilat** *is Israel's southernmost city. The name of the city appears eight times in the Bible. The Book of Kings, for example, describes the activities at the port around the 10th century BCE: gold is loaded and unloaded, as well as sandalwood, precious stones, ivory, monkeys, peacocks, horses and much more. King Solomon's copper mines were not far away (and are now a popular tourist attraction). Today Eilat has a population of over 20,000, but during high season there can be four times as many tourists as residents in the city. Tourism is the lifeblood of Eilat, which offers hotels, restaurants, cabarets, diving in the Red Sea with its beautifully coloured fish, and water sports. The city is also an important port and a centre for Israel's commercial ties with its neighbours Jordan and Egypt.*

The origins of the name Red Sea are uncertain. Some claim the name refers to the colour of the corals in the area, while others suggest that it was named after the deposits of copper along its shores. In any case, the name dates back to the ancient Greeks.

❹ We've already been here two days. See you in two weeks.
`Anachnu poh kvar yomayim. Lehitra`ot be'od shvu'ayim.

אֲנַחְנוּ פֹּה ___ ________. לְהִתְרָאוֹת ____
________.

❺ Love, Mom and Dad.
Be`ahavah, `Ima ve`Aba.

______, אִמָּא וְאַבָּא.

Answers to Exercise 2

❶ – טְחִינָה – חוּמוּס ❷ – כֹּל הַיּוֹם – מִפְּנֵי שֶׁחַם – ❸ בִּגְלַל – בַּלָּגָן – ❹ – כְּבָר יוֹמַיִם – בְּעוֹד שְׁבוּעַיִם ❺ בְּאַהֲבָה –

Answer to Exercise 3 – Cursive letters

רוּתִי וְדָנִי כְּבָר שְׁבוּעַיִים בְּאֵילַת.

The Hebrew name of the sea is יָם סוּף *– 'the sea of reeds', so it is possible that 'Red Sea' is a corruption of 'Reed Sea'.*

The Red Sea Jazz Festival is an annual music festival held in Eilat at the end of August. Musicians from Israel and around the world gather in the city for concerts, clinics and jam sessions that can turn into musical marathons.

'Drink water!' Don't be surprised that the young vacationers reassure their parents that they are drinking plenty of water. Exhortations to drink are common in this hot country, and particularly in Eilat, where the summer is extremely hot and dry. Most of the water in Eilat comes from a desalination plant; it's safe to drink, but many people find the taste unpleasant and prefer bottled water.

You have now reached the end of another set of lessons – it's almost time for the review חֲזָרָה*. Before you start, why not take a quick break and have a falafel while listening to some jazz?*

28 Twenty-eighth lesson
(Shi'ur 'esrim ushmoneh)

חֲזָרָה Chazarah – Review

1 The whole alphabet, in square and cursive scripts

The following table shows all the letters in both the square and cursive scripts. (Note that the table reads from right to left, as is normal in Hebrew!) Make sure you are familiar with all the cursive forms. We also show the numerical value of each letter – we will discuss this subject later in this lesson, but for now we should explain that this numbering system is used for dates in the Hebrew calendar, as well as for various other purposes. In school, for example, the Hebrew for 'Year 1' or '1st grade' does not refer to the number 1, but its equivalent – the letter **alef** א. Similarly, Israeli children breathe a sigh of relief when they complete class **yod bet** י"ב – the equivalent of 'Year 12' or '12th grade'. Don't worry, it will all become clearer when you read the next section.

`	**`alef**	1	א	א
b	**bet**	2	בּ	בּ
v	**vet**	2	ב	ב
g	**gimel**	3	ג	ג
d	**dalet**	4	ד	ד
h	**hey**	5	ה	ה
v	**vav**	6	ו	ו
z	**zayin**	7	ז	ז
ch	**chet**	8	ח	ח
t	**tet**	9	ט	ט
y or i	**yod**	10	י	י
k	**kaf**	20	כּ	כּ
kh	**khaf**	20	כ	כ
kh	final **khaf**	20	ך	ך
l	**lamed**	30	ל	ל
m	**mem**	40	מ	מ
m	final **mem**	40	ם	ם
n	**nun**	50	נ	נ
n	final **nun**	50	ן	ן
s	**samekh**	60	ס	ס
'	**'ayin**	70	ע	ע
p	**pe**	80	פּ	פּ
f	**fe**	80	פ	פ
f	final **fe**	80	ף	ף
tz	**tsadi**	90	צ	צ
tz	final **tsadi**	90	ץ	ץ
q	**qof**	100	ק	ק
r	**resh**	200	ר	ר
sh	**shin**	300	שׁ	שׁ
s	**sin**	300	שׂ	שׂ
t	**tav**	400	ת	ת

1.1 Hebrew numerals

How does the Hebrew numerical system work? Up to 10, there is no problem – simply use the appropriate letter from **alef** א through **yod** י. But what happens when we get to 11? We write a **yod** י for 10, followed (in Hebrew order, to the left) by **alef** א for 1. A double apostrophe is used to separate the two letters and indicate that they are being used to represent numbers: י"א. When reading, we pronounce the names of the two letters in order: **yod alef** יוד אלף. (By the way, the double apostrophe is also used to indicate acronyms, of which there are many in Hebrew, but we'll come back to that another time.)

The same principle is used to form other numbers:
23 = 20 and 3, or in Hebrew letters: כ"ג
487 = 400 and 80 and 7, or in Hebrew letters: תפ"ז

As you can see from the alphabet table, the letter with the highest value is **tav** ת = 400. To represent numbers higher than 400, further combinations are needed. For example, 658 = 400 + 200 + 50 + 8, or in Hebrew letters: תרנ"ח. Of course, to write a number with the fewest letters, the highest possible numbers are used, in descending order.

When we get above 999, a letter followed by a single apostrophe is used to indicate thousands. So:
• numbers from 1,000 to 1,999 begin with א'
• numbers from 2,000 to 2,999 begin with ב'
• numbers from 3,000 to 3,999 begin with ג' etc.

The year 2000 in the Gregorian calendar is 5760 in the Hebrew calendar, or in Hebrew letters: ה' תש"ס.

The hey ה followed by an apostrophe represents 5,000.

Two exceptions may seem strange at first. For the numbers 15 and 16, you would expect that Hebrew would first use the letter **yod** י, equivalent to 10, and then the letter **hey** ה (5) or **vav** ו (6), respectively. However, this produces two letters that form part of the sacred four-letter name for God (**yod** – **hey** – **vav** – **hey**). To avoid this, Hebrew engages in some mathematical gymnastics and produces the forms ט״ו (9 + 6 = **15**) and ט״ז (9 + 7 = **16**).

2 Days of the week

The Hebrew word for week – **shavu'a** שָׁבוּעַ – comes from the root שבע, and is related to the word **sheva'** שֶׁבַע *seven*. In Jewish tradition, the day begins with sunset and ends just before sunset the next day. Accordingly, Jewish festivals begin in the evening, when three stars can be seen in the sky. This explains why an invitation to a 'Shabbat dinner' usually means that you are expected on Friday night!

Here is a review of the days of the week:

yom rishon	יוֹם רִאשׁוֹן	'day first'	*Sunday*
yom sheni	יוֹם שֵׁנִי	'day second'	*Monday*
yom shlishi	יוֹם שְׁלִישִׁי	'day third'	*Tuesday*
yom revi'i	יוֹם רְבִיעִי	'day fourth'	*Wednesday*
yom chamishi	יוֹם חֲמִישִׁי	'day fifth'	*Thursday*
yom shishi	יוֹם שִׁישִׁי	'day sixth'	*Friday*
shabat	שַׁבָּת	'Shabbat'	*Saturday*

3 The dual form

In Hebrew, a pair is not considered the same as other plurals. In some cases, when concepts or objects often come in a pair, a special form called the 'dual' is used, with the ending ַ־יִם **-ayim**.

The words for the number two also follow this pattern: **shnayim** שְׁנַיִם *two* is used with masculine nouns, and **shtayim** שְׁתַּיִם is used with feminine nouns.

The dual is used for several words relating to lengths of time:
yom = *1 day* יוֹם; **yomayim** = *2 days* יוֹמַיִים

shavu'a = *1 week* שָׁבוּעַ; **shvua'yim** = *2 weeks* שׁבוּעַיִים

As we will see, the dual is also used for many parts of the body.

4 Age

To ask someone's age, Hebrew uses the following construction:

Ben kamah `atah?	בֶּן כַּמָה אַתָּה?	'A-son-of how-many you?'
Bat kamah `at?	בַּת כַּמָה אַת?	'A-daughter-of how-many you?'
Ben kamah hu?	בֶּן כַּמָה הוּא?	'A-son-of how-many he?'
Bat kamah hi?	בַּת כַּמָה הִיא?	'A-daughter-of how-many she?'

The reply will take the following form:

`ani ben shloshim	אֲנִי בֶּן שלוֹשִׁים	'I son-of thirty'
		I'm (masc.) *thirty.*
`ani bat 'esrim	אֲנִי בַּת עֶשׂרִים	'I daughter-of twenty'
		I'm (fem.) *twenty.*
hu ben `arba'im	הוּא בֶּן אַרבָּעִים	'he son-of forty'
		He's forty.
hi bat 'eser	הִיא בַּת עֶשֶׂר	'she daughter-of ten'
		She's ten.

5 Gimatria – playing with numbers

The Hebrew term **gimatria** may come from the order of the Greek alphabet in which gamma is the third letter (gamma + tria) or from the same Greek source as the English word *geometry*. However, gimatria refers not to calculating shapes, but to arithmetical exercises using the numerical value of the Hebrew letters. If you look back at the alphabet table in section 1, you can see that it is quite easy to calculate the numerical value of any given word. The word **chay** חַי *alive*, for example, consists of **chet** ח (8) and **yod** י (10), so **chay** = 18. As a result, 18 is considered a lucky number, and people often give presents in multiples of 18. A guest at a Bar/ Bat Mitzvah might bring a cheque for 180 new shekels – **shqalim** שְׁקָלִים (the Israeli currency).

Gimatria is also used to convey moral or pedagogic messages. For example, there is a Hebrew proverb **nikhnas yayin, yatza sod** נִכְנָס יַיִן יָצָא סוֹד, which could be translated as 'When the wine goes in, the secret comes out'. As well as making sense in its own right, this proverb also relies on gematria. The word **yayin** יַיִן *wine* = 70: (10 = י) + (10 = י) + (50 = נ). And the word **sod** סוֹד *secret* also equals 70: (60 = ס) + (6 = ו) + (4 = ד).

Israelis making a toast at a wedding or a speech on some auspicious occasion sometimes use gimatria both to amuse the audience and to make serious points. Take a sheet of paper and try to calculate the value of your name in Hebrew letters and you'll soon see the appeal.

6 Questions

Why do Israelis ask so many questions? Why not?! To help you keep up with the natives, here is a review of three of the many words used to form questions:

- **Kamah?** כַּמָּה? *How many?*

Kamah yeladim yesh lekha? — כַּמָּה יְלָדִים יֵשׁ לְךָ?
How many children do you have?

- **Matay?** מָתַי? *When?*

Matay `atem yekholim lavo? — מָתַי אַתֶּם יְכוֹלִים לָבוֹא?
When can you come?

- **Le`an?** לְאָן? *Where to?*

Le`an hem holkhim ba'erev? — לְאָן הֵם הוֹלְכִים בָּעֶרֶב?
Where are they going this evening?

Note that whereas in English we often use *where* to mean 'to where', in Hebrew we must use **le`an** לְאָן if the question involves movement and could be replaced with 'where to'.

7 Three ways of saying 'because'

In almost every conversation, we need to explain that one thing happened because of another. Here are three ways of doing this in Hebrew that we've seen so far:

• **ki** כִּי *because, since*
Hu biYrushalayim ki cham be`Eylat.
הוּא בִּירוּשָׁלַיִם כִּי חַם בְּאֵילַת.
He is in Jerusalem because it is hot in Eilat.
• **mipney she-** מִפְּנֵי שֶׁ- *because*
Hi tzrikhah matzlemah mipney shehi tasah lechutz la`aretz.
הִיא צְרִיכָה מַצְלֵמָה מִפְּנֵי שֶׁהִיא טָסָה לְחוּץ לָאָרֶץ.
She needs a camera because she's going abroad.

What **ki** כִּי and **mipney she-** מִפְּנֵי שֶׁ- have in common is that they never come at the beginning of a sentence. As seen in the examples above, they are used in sentences with the structure 'x because of y'.

• **biglal** בִּגְלַל *because of, due to* comes at the beginning of the sentence or phrase – 'because of x, y'. Take the following sentence, for example:
Biglal festival hajazz yesh harbeh tarmila`im be`Eylat.
בִּגְלַל פֶסְטִיבָל הַגַּ'אז יֵשׁ הַרְבֵּה תַרְמִילָאִים בְּאֵילַת.
Due to the jazz festival, there are many backpackers in Eilat.

As in this example, **biglal** בִּגְלַל is often followed by a noun.

8 Verbs

Here is a review of two verbs we've learned that express possibility or obligation. Both these verbs are used frequently in combination with another verb (always in infinitive form) to make phrases such as 'I can swim', 'They can't come', 'She must study' and 'You must stop'.

• *to be able to* – root: יכל

masculine

`ani yakhol	אֲנִי יָכוֹל	*I can*
`atah yakhol	אַתָּה יָכוֹל	*you can*
hu yakhol	הוּא יָכוֹל	*he can*
`anachnu yekholim	אֲנַחְנוּ יְכוֹלִים	*we can*
`atem yekholim	אַתֶּם יְכוֹלִים	*you* (plural) *can*
hem yekholim	הֵם יְכוֹלִים	*they can*

28 <u>feminine</u>

`ani yekholah	אֲנִי יְכוֹלָה	*I can*
`at yekholah	אַת יְכוֹלָה	*you can*
hi yekholah	הִיא יְכוֹלָה	*she can*
`anachnu yekholot	אֲנַחנוּ יְכוֹלוֹת	*we can*
`aten yekholot	אַתֶן יְכוֹלוֹת	*you* (plural) *can*
hen yekholot	הֵן יְכוֹלוֹת	*they can*

• *to need* – root: צרך
<u>masculine</u>

`ani tzarikh	אֲנִי צָרִיךְ	*I need*
`atah tzarikh	אַתָה צָרִיךְ	*you need*
hu tzarikh	הוּא צָרִיךְ	*he needs*
`anachnu tzrikhim	אֲנַחנוּ צְרִיכִים	*we need*
`atem tzrikhim	אַתֶם צְרִיכִים	*you* (plural) *need*
hem tzrikhim	הֵם צְרִיכִים	*they need*

<u>feminine</u>

`ani tzrikhah	אֲנִי צְרִיכָה	*I need*
`at tzrikhah	אַת צְרִיכָה	*you need*
hi tzrikhah	הִיא צְרִיכָה	*she needs*
`anachnu tzrikhot	אֲנַחנוּ צְרִיכוֹת	*we need*
`aten tzrikhot	אַתֶן צְרִיכוֹת	*you* (plural) *need*
hen tzrikhot	הֵן צְרִיכוֹת	*they need*

9 Backpacks and backpackers

Remember that **tarmil** תַרמִיל means *pod* and **tarmil gav** תַרמִיל גַב is a *backpack*. From this, the Israelis formed the new word **tarmilay** תַרמִילַאי *backpacker* (**tarmila`it** תַרמִילָאִית in the feminine). The plural forms are **tarmila`im** תַרמִילָאִים and **tarmila`iyot** תַרמִילָאִיוֹת, respectively.

10 Possession: 'to have'

As we have seen, the sense of 'I have' is represented in Hebrew by a construction that literally means 'there-is for-me': **yesh li** יֵשׁ לִי. In a moment, we'll see the other forms, no matter who is speaking.

First, though, a word of warning: the **yesh li** יֵשׁ לִי construction is used for 'to have' only in the sense of *to possess* or *to own* ('I have a car', 'She has a brother', etc.). In English, we also use *to have* as an auxiliary verb to form one of our many past tenses – *I have seen, she has visited*, etc. Hebrew does not use this construction for the past tense, so be careful not to use **yesh li** in this way. However, if you can replace the 'have' with 'own' (even if it sounds a little strange!), then go ahead and use it. Having clarified that point, here is a full list of the **yesh li** יֵשׁ לִי construction.

yesh li	יֵשׁ לִי	*I have* ('there-is for-me' – masc./fem.)
yesh lekha	יֵשׁ לְךָ	*you have* ('there-is for-you' – masc.)
yesh lakh	יֵשׁ לָךְ	*you have* ('there-is for-you' – fem.)
yesh lo	יֵשׁ לוֹ	*he has* ('there-is for-him')
yesh lah	יֵשׁ לָהּ	*she has* ('there-is for-her')
yesh lanu	יֵשׁ לָנוּ	*we have* ('there-is for-us')
yesh lakhem	יֵשׁ לָכֶם	*you have* ('there-is for-you' – m. pl.)
yesh lakhen	יֵשׁ לָכֶן	*you have* ('there-is for-you' – f. pl.)
yesh lahem	יֵשׁ לָהֶם	*they have* ('there-is for-them' – masc.)
yesh lahen	יֵשׁ לָהֵן	*they have* ('there-is for-them' – fem.)

11 Declining a preposition

Let's come back now to the preposition **bishvil** בִּשְׁבִיל, which we first encountered in lesson 25. Remember that this means *for* or *for the sake of*, with a stronger sense of purpose than the preposition **le** לְ.

bishvili	בִּשְׁבִילִי	*for me* (masc./fem.)
bishvilkha	בִּשְׁבִילְךָ	*for you* (masc.)
bishvilekh	בִּשְׁבִילֵךְ	*for you* (fem.)
bishvilo	בִּשְׁבִילוֹ	*for him*
bishvilah	בִּשְׁבִילָהּ	*for her*
bishvilenu	בִּשְׁבִילֵנוּ	*for us* (masc./fem.)
bishvilkhem	בִּשְׁבִילְכֶם	*for you* (masc. plural)
bishvilkhen	בִּשְׁבִילְכֶן	*for you* (fem. plural)
bishvilam	בִּשְׁבִילָם	*for them* (masc.)
bishvilan	בִּשְׁבִילָן	*for them* (fem.)

28 You may notice that the last two forms in the previous list follow a slightly different pattern from the declension we saw above with **yesh li** יֵשׁ לִי. The main reason for this is that Hebrew tends to prefer the shortest possible form that can carry the required grammatical information.

Review exercise

❶ יְלָדִים יְקָרִים שֶׁלִּי, ❷ אֲנַחנוּ בִּירוּשָׁלַיִם מִיּוֹם שְׁלִישִׁי עַד שַׁבָּת. ❸ אַבָּא כּוֹתֵב בַּדוֹאַר הָאֶלֶקטרוֹנִי לַחֲבֵרִים וְלַמִשְׁפָּחָה גַם בָּאָרֶץ וְגַם בְּחוּץ לָאָרֶץ. ❹ אוּלַי אַתֶּם יְכוֹלִים לָבוֹא לִירוּשָׁלַיִם לְשַׁבָּת? ❺ יֵשׁ לָנוּ בִּשְׁבִילכֶם מַצלֵמָה מְצוּיֶנֶת וְגַם תמוּנָה יָפָה מֵהַחֲתוּנָּה שֶׁל דָוִד וְשָׂרָה. ❻ יֵשׁ לִי גַם דַרכּוֹן חָדָשׁ וְגַם כַּרטִיס טִיסָה. ❼ אֲנַחנוּ טָסִים בְּיוֹם רִאשׁוֹן. לְהִתרָאוֹת בְּשַׁבָּת. ❽ בְּאַהֲבָה. ❾ אִמָּא וְאַבָּא

Answers

❶ My dear children, *(children dear of-me)* ❷ We are spending Tuesday through Shabbat in Jerusalem. *(we in-Jerusalem from-day third until shabbat)* ❸ Dad is writing emails to our friends and relatives in Israel and abroad. *(dad writes in-the-mail the-electronic to-the-friends and-to-the-family also in-the-land and-also in-outside from-the-Land)* ❹ Perhaps you will be able to come to Jerusalem for Shabbat? *(perhaps you[masc.] can to-come to-Jerusalem for-shabbat)* ❺ We have an excellent camera for you, as well as a nice photograph from David and Sarah's wedding. *(there-is for-us for-you[masc.] camera excellent and-also picture beautiful from-the-wedding of David and-Sarah)* ❻ I have a new passport and also a flight ticket. *(there-is for-me also passport new and-also ticket flight)* ❼ We're flying on Sunday. See you on Shabbat. *(we fly on-day first. to-see-each other on-shabbat)* ❽ Love *(in-love)* ❾ Mom and Dad *(mom and-dad)*

Twenty-ninth lesson
(Shi'ur 'esrim vetesha')

Hanudniq ①
The pest

1 – **`Ani nofelet meharaglayim ②.**
I fall(fem.) from-the-feet
I'm dead on my feet.

2 – **Mah qarah ③, Tamar?**
what happened Tamar
What's wrong, Tamar?

Notes

① **nudniq** נוּדְנִיק means *pest* (masc.) – not in the literal sense, but in the sense of a person who may be very nice, but is a bit irritating or clingy. The ending **-niq** נִיק, and **-it** ית in the feminine, is used to form words describing people's characteristics or where they come from. For example, a **kibutzniq** קִבּוּצְנִיק is a *kibbutznik* or *kibbutz* resident; the feminine is **kibutzniqit** קִבּוּצְנִיקִית. The **-niq** נִיק ending originally comes from Yiddish and is colloquial rather than formal.

② **`Ani nofelet meharaglayim** אֲנִי נוֹפֶלֶת מֵהָרַגְלַיִים literally, 'I am falling from the feet', means *I am really tired.* The nearest English equivalent is 'I'm dead on my feet'. Many idiomatic expressions in Hebrew refer to various parts of the body – we'll learn more of these in later lessons. The **me** מֵ at the beginning of **meharaglayim** מֵהָרַגְלַיִים is a slightly different form of **mi** מִ meaning *of* (lesson 8) that is used depending on the following vowel or letter. Don't worry too much about this. Israelis are very unlikely to notice or correct you if you don't use the precise vowel (in fact, many Israelis themselves are not too strict about observing such fine grammatical points).

הַנוּדנִיק

1 – אֲנִי נוֹפֶלֶת מֵהָרַגלַיִים.

2 – מַה קָרָה, תָמָר?

הַנוּדנִיק

③ **Mah qarah?** מַה קָרָה? *What happened? What's wrong?* This phrase is used frequently in Hebrew as a way of asking someone to explain why they are acting or speaking in a particular way. For example, if a friend (male or female) is laughing or is angry for no obvious reason, you ask them **Mah qarah?** The verb **qarah** קָרָה is the third-person masculine singular past tense form of *to happen.* This is the first time we've seen a verb in the past tense, which we'll find out more about in this lesson.

3 – **Halakhti ④ kol haboqer vekha`asher bati lado`ar, ra`iti `et Vered veDavid `Oren.**
I-walked all the-morning and-when I-came to-the-post I-saw [`**et**] *Vered and-David Oren*
I walked all morning, and when I got to the post office I saw Vered and David Cohen.

4 **Hu nudniq lo normali, `aval ben `adam tov …**
he pest not normal but son-of Adam good
He's a first-class pest, but he's a good guy …

5 – **Gam Vered nudniqit?**
also Vered pest(fem.)
Is Vered a pest, too?

6 – **Lo. Hi chevremanit ⑤!**
no she cool
No. She's cool!

7 **Matay ra`it `otam ⑥?**
when you-saw(fem.) [`**et**]*-them*
When did you [last] see them?

8 – **Lifney chodshayim beGiv'atayim ⑦.**
before two-months in-Givatayim
Two months ago in Givatayim.

Notes

④ **halakhti** הָלַכְתִּי *I went/walked*, **bati** בָּאתִי *I came* (line 3), **ra`iti** רָאִיתִי *I saw* (line 7). Firstly, note that in the past tense, the first-person singular form is the same for both masculine and feminine (the same is true of the first-person plural, as we will learn shortly). Secondly, since these forms are specific to the first-person singular – unlike in the present tense, where the same form is used for *I*, *you* (m.) and *he*, for example – there is normally no need to add the pronoun as well. A Hebrew speaker will use the pronoun with the past tense only if they want to emphasize it. For example, they might say **`ani halakhti** אֲנִי הָלַכְתִּי in the context of 'Sarah didn't want to go to the beach, but I went there with Ruti'. The **-ti** תִי ending of ▸

3 – הָלַכְתִּי כֹּל הַבּוֹקֶר וְכַאֲשֶׁר בָּאתִי לַדּוֹאַר, רָאִיתִי אֶת וֶרֶד וְדָוִד אוֹרֶן.

4 הוּא נוּדְנִיק לֹא נוֹרמַלִי, אֲבָל בֶּן אָדָם טוֹב ...

5 – גַּם וֶרֶד נוּדְנִיקִית?

6 – לֹא. הִיא חֶבְרֶמָנִית!

7 מָתַי רָאִית אוֹתָם?

8 – לִפְנֵי חוֹדְשַׁיִים בְּגִבְעָתַיִים.

the verb is the marker for the first-person singular in the past tense (in every case, without any exception).

Line 7 includes another past tense form: **ra`it** רָאִית *you saw* (fem.). Second-person feminine singular verbs in the past always end in **-t** ת, while the masculine ends in **-ta** תָ. Once again, there are no irregular forms.

In line 2, **qarah** קָרָה *happened* is not a third-person singular feminine form, though it looks like it, but the third-person masculine singular form – the subject of the verb is **mah** מַה *what*. The **hey** ה at the end of **qarah** קָרָה comes from the root קרה meaning *to happen*.

⑤ **chevremanit** חֶבְרֶמָנִית is a slang word for someone who is 'cool' and sociable. This is the feminine form; the masculine is **chevreman** חֶבְרֶמָן. This word comes from the word **chaver** *friend*.

⑥ **`otam** אוֹתָם *them*. In lesson 17, note 2, we saw that **`et** אֶת is a particle that comes before a direct object (he sees the girl, they love Israel, or, as in line 7, you saw them). While **`et** אֶת is used as is before nouns, it changes form when combined with a pronoun. **`otam** אוֹתָם is the declension of this word for the third-person plural masculine pronoun *them* when used as a direct object.

⑦ **chodshayim** חוֹדְשַׁיִים *two months*. A month is **chodesh** חוֹדֶשׁ. Here, the word appears in the dual form, used for referring to two things. It is followed immediately by a place name that is also a dual form, **Giv'atayim** גִּבְעָתַיִים, a suburb of Tel Aviv. Its name literally means *two hills*. The singular form is **giv'ah** גִּבְעָה *hill*.

From this lesson on, all the exercises will be presented in the cursive script, since this is the form Israelis use for handwriting.

Targil rishon – Targem תַּרְגִּיל רִאשׁוֹן – תַּרְגֵּם

❶ ורד נודניקית לא נורמלית אבל אשה טובה.
Vered nudniqit lo normalit `aval `ishah tovah.

❷ הבוקר הלכתי לדואר.
Haboqer halakhti lado`ar.

❸ ראיתי אותם לפני חודשיים.
Ra`iti `otam lifney chodshayim.

❹ אני נופלת מהרגליים כי הלכתי כל היום.
`Ani nofelet meharaglayim ki halakhti kol hayom.

❺ הם חברים טובים של משפחת אורן.
Hem chaverim tovim shel mishpachat `Oren.

Targil sheni – Hashlem תַּרְגִּיל שֵׁנִי – הַשְׁלֵם

❶ I went to the post [office] and saw Sarah, the pest.
Halakhti lado`ar vera`iti `et Sarah hanudniqit.

_____ לַדֹּאַר וְ_____ אֶת שָׂרָה הַ________ .

❷ Two months ago I went to Vered and David's wedding.
Lifney chodshayim halakhti lachatunah shel Vered veDavid.

____ ______ הָלַכְתִּי לַ_____ שֶׁל וֶרֶד וְדָוִד.

❸ I came to the café, but I didn't see Vered there.
Ba`ti leveyt haqafeh `aval lo ra`iti sham `et Vered.

____ לְבֵית הַקָּפֶה אֲבָל לֹא _____ __ אֶת וֶרֶד.

❹ They are friends*(masc.)* of my son's girlfriend's mother.
Hem chaverim shel `ima shel hachaverah shel bni.

הֵם _____ שֶׁל ___ שֶׁל הַ____ שֶׁל ___ .

Answers to Exercise 1

❶ Vered is a first-class pest, but a good woman. ❷ This *(The)* morning I went to the post [office]. ❸ I saw them two months ago *(before two-months)*. ❹ I'm dead on my feet *(I am falling from the feet)* because I walked all day. ❺ They are good friends of the Oren family.

❺ I'm tired*(fem.)*, I'm dead on my feet *(I am falling from the feet)*.
`Ani 'ayefah, `ani nofelet meharaglayim.

אֲנִי ____, אֲנִי _____ ________ .

Answers to Exercise 2

❶ הָלַכְתִּי - רָאִיתִי - נוּדְנִיקִית ❷ לִפְנֵי חוֹדְשַׁיִים - חֲתוּנָה - ❸ בָּאתִי - רָאִיתִי
שָׁם - ❹ - חֲבֵרִים - אִמָּא - חֲבֵרָה - בְּנֵי ❺ - עֲיֵפָה - נוֹפֶלֶת מֵהָרַגְלַיִים

Tamar תָּמָר **Vered** וֶרֶד **Oren** אוֹרֶן. *These three names are all drawn from the world of botany.* **Tamar** תָּמָר *means* date *(both the fruit and the tree it comes from). The Bible associates the date with such qualities as majesty, beauty and softness. The* pine, **Oren** אוֹרֶן, *is praised for its permanent foliage.* **Vered** וֶרֶד *means* rose *(again, both the flower and the plant). This word does not appear in the Bible, but is regarded in Hebrew poetry as the queen of flowers.*

Ben `adam tov בֶּן אָדָם טוֹב *'good son of Adam'. This expression is the equivalent of saying someone is a 'good guy'.*

30 Thirtieth lesson (Shi'ur shloshim)

Saba tza'ir
A young grandfather

1 – **Nolad li nekhed ①, `ach lanekhdah shelanu ②.**
is-born for-me grandson, brother to-granddaughter our
I have a new grandson, a brother for our granddaughter.

2 – **Mazal tov! Matay haytah ③ brit hamilah?**
luck good! when was covenant-of the-circumcision?
Congratulations! When was the circumcision?

3 – **Habrit haytah lifney ④ shavu'a.**
the-covenant was before week
The circumcision was last week.

4 – **`Atah saba tza'ir. Ben kamah `atah?**
you grandfather young. son-of how-many you?
You're a young grandfather. How old are you?

5 – **Ben chamishim vechamesh ⑤.**
son-of fifty and-five
I'm fifty-five.

Notes

① **nekhed** נֶכֶד *grandson*, **nekhdah** נֶכְדָה *granddaughter*: note that the Hebrew words for these relationships are not derived from the words for *son* and *daughter*. Let's recap: in the first generation, we have **`aba** אַבָּא and **`ima** אִמָּא, in the second, **ben** בֵּן and **bat** בַּת, and in the third, **nekhed** נֶכֶד and **nekhdah** נֶכְדָה. Finally, in the fourth generation, we have **nin** נִין *great-grandson* and **ninah** נִינָה *great-granddaughter*.

② **shelanu** שֶׁלָנוּ *our*, *of us*. In the last review lesson, we learned **yesh lanu** יֵשׁ לָנוּ ('there-is for-us'), meaning *we have*. Here,

סַבָּא צָעִיר

1 – נוֹלַד לִי נֶכֶד, אָח לַנֶּכְדָה שֶׁלָּנוּ.

2 – מַזָּל טוֹב! מָתַי הָיְתָה בְּרִית הַמִּילָה?

3 – הַבְּרִית הָיְתָה לִפְנֵי שָׁבוּעַ.

4 – אַתָּה סַבָּא צָעִיר. בֶּן כַּמָּה אַתָּה?

5 – בֶּן חֲמִישִּׁים וְחָמֵשׁ.

the preposition **shel** שֶׁל *of* is placed before **lanu** לָנוּ, and the two **lameds** ל merge. So **shelanu** ('of-for-us') *our*.

③ **haytah** הָיְתָה *she was/has been*. English has a whole range of past tense forms – I walked, I was walking, I had walked and so on. You'll be pleased to hear that Hebrew, on the other hand, has one main past tense form. There is one other past tense used for constructions such as 'I used to walk' or 'I would walk' (in the past), but you don't need to worry about that for now. Here we have the third-person singular feminine past tense of the verb *to be*. In line 7, we see the first-person plural form, **hayinu** הָיִינוּ *we were* (remember, the first-person past tense forms are the same in the masculine and feminine).

④ **lifney** לִפְנֵי *before* is also used as the equivalent of the English *ago* in expressions of time such as 'three days ago', 'a long time ago' and so forth.

⑤ **chamishim vechamesh** חֲמִישִּׁים וְחָמֵשׁ *fifty-five*. Note that the word **chamishim** חֲמִישִּׁים is essentially a plural form of **chamesh** חָמֵשׁ *five* (as we've mentioned before, don't worry about the slight vowel changes that occur when Hebrew words fit into different patterns).

6 – Gam `ishtekha savta tze'irah veyafah. `Atem be`oto gil?
also wife-your grandmother young and-pretty. you in-same age?
Your wife is also a young and pretty grandmother. Are you both the same age?

7 – Ka`asher hayinu tze'irim, hayinu be`oto gil.
when we-were young we-were in-same age
When we were young, we were both the same age.

8 `Aval kvar chamesh shanim ⑥ hi `omeret shehi bat `arba'im ve'eser ⑦!
but already five years she says that-she daughter-of forty and-ten
But for five years now, she's been saying that she's 'forty-ten' years old!

Notes

⑥ **shanim** שָׁנִים *years*. From the **-im** ים ending on this word, you might assume that it is a masculine plural form. In fact, ▸

Targil rishon – Targem תַּרְגִּיל רִאשׁוֹן – תַּרְגֵּם

❶ נולד נכד לאשתי ולי.
Nolad nekhed le`ishti veli.

❷ אני רק בן חמישים וחמש אבל אני כבר סבא.
`Ani raq ben chamishim vechamesh `aval `ani kvar saba.

❸ ביום שישי בבוקר היתה ברית מילה לנכד של שרה ודני.
Beyom shishi baboqer haytah brit milah lanekhed shel Sarah veDani.

❹ דינה סבתא צעירה ויפה.
Dinah savta tze'irah veyafah.

❺ הנכד והנכדה שלי באותו גיל.
Hanekhed vehanekhdah sheli be`oto gil.

6 – גַּם אִשְׁתְּךָ סַבְתָא צְעִירָה וְיָפָה. אַתֶּם בְּאוֹתוֹ גִּיל?

7 – כַּאֲשֶׁר הָיִינוּ צְעִירִים, הָיִינוּ בְּאוֹתוֹ גִּיל.

8 אֲבָל כְּבָר חָמֵשׁ שָׁנִים הִיא אוֹמֶרֶת שֶׁהִיא בַּת אַרְבָּעִים וְעֶשֶׂר! □

the noun *year* is feminine. You have already seen the singular form in the greeting **shanah tovah** שָׁנָה טוֹבָה *Happy (New) Year* ('year good'). In the plural, we would say **shanim tovot** שָׁנִים טוֹבוֹת *good years, happy years.*

⑦ **`arba'im ve'eser** אַרְבָּעִים וְעֶשֶׂר 'forty and-ten'. Don't misunderstand here – 'forty and ten' isn't a real number. It sounds just as strange in Hebrew as it would in English. The speaker's wife has invented this amusing formula to try to make herself sound a bit younger …

Answers to Exercise 1

❶ My wife and I have just had a grandson. ❷ I'm only fifty-five, but I'm already a grandfather. ❸ Friday morning was the circumcision of Sarah and Danny's grandson. ❹ Dina is a young and pretty grandmother. ❺ My grandson and my granddaughter are the same age.

Targil sheni – Hashlem תַּרְגִּיל שֵׁנִי – הַשְׁלֵם

❶ Dina is a young grandmother and David is a young grandfather.
Dinah savta tze'irah veDavid saba tza'ir.

דִּינָה סַבְתָּא _____ וְדָוִד סַבָּא ____ .

❷ The circumcision was on Shabbat.
Brit hamilah haytah beshabat.

____ _____ הָיְתָה בְּשַׁבָּת.

❸ Congratulations! You are grandparents.
Mazal tov! `Atem saba vesavta.

מַזָּל טוֹב! אַתֶּם ___ וְ____ .

❹ When we were young, the family did not have a car.
Ka`asher hayinu tze'irim lo haytah lamishpachah mekhonit.

____ _____ צְעִירִים לֹא ____ לַמִּשְׁפָּחָה ______ .

❺ A week ago, we were at a circumcision in Israel.
Lifney shavu'a hayinu bevrit milah beYisra`el.

____ ____ הָיִינוּ בִּבְרִית מִילָה בְּ _____ .

Brit milah בְּרִית מִילָה circumcision. *Jewish boys are traditionally circumcised eight days after birth. The act of circumcision symbolizes the covenant between God and Abraham, and the word* **brit** בְּרִית *means* covenant. *The word* **milah** מִילָה cutting *comes from the root* מול *and is used solely in the context of circumcision. The same root also produces the word* **mohel** מוֹהֵל *– the* circumciser, *i.e. the person who performs this delicate task.*

Answers to Exercise 2

❶ - צְעִירָה - צָעִיר ❷ בְּרִית הַמִּילָה - ❸ - סַבָּא - סַבְתָא ❹ כַּאֲשֶׁר הָיִינוּ - הָיְתָה - מְכוֹנִית ❺ לִפְנֵי שָׁבוּעַ - יִשְׂרָאֵל

A boy's בְּרִית מִילָה *is attended by family and friends. The ceremony usually takes place in the morning and may be followed by a festive lunch with music and gifts. Newborn girls are welcomed with a party, and in religious families the girl may be presented to the community in front of the Torah in synagogue. These days, as many parents choose to know the sex of their baby before it is born, preparations can be made in advance.*

31 Thirty-first lesson
(Shi'ur shloshim ve`achat)

Baqolno'a ①
At the cinema

1 – **`Etmol halakhnu ② leqolno'a 'Gil' vera`inu qomedyah shoveret qupot ③.**
yesterday we-went to-cinema-of Gil and-we-saw comedy breaking cash-registers
Yesterday we went to the Gil cinema and saw a comedy blockbuster.

2 – **'Al mah haqomedyah?**
on what the-comedy
What was the comedy about?

Notes

① **qolno'a** קוֹלְנוֹעַ *cinema, movie theatre*. This modern Hebrew word is formed from two roots that date back to Biblical Hebrew: **qol** קוֹל *voice* and **no'a** נוֹעַ *movement*. In lesson 19 we saw **kaduregel** כַּדּוּרֶגֶל *football* and **kadursal** כַּדּוּרסַל *basketball*, which are formed in a similar way.

② **halakhnu** הָלַכְנוּ *we went*. This is an example of a plural past tense form, as is **halakhtem** הֲלַכְתֶּם *you* (m. pl.) *went* (line 4). Note the similarities between the endings of the personal pronouns and the endings of the verb forms in the past:
masculine
`anachnu halakhnu אֲנַחנוּ הָלַכְנוּ *we went*
`atem halakhtem אַתֶּם הֲלַכְתֶּם *you* (plural) *went*
hem halkhu הֵם הָלכוּ *they went*
feminine
`anachnu halakhnu אֲנַחנוּ הָלַכְנוּ *we went*
`aten halakhten אַתֶּן הֲלַכְתֶּן *you* (plural) *went*
hen halkhu הֵן הָלכוּ *they went*

31 שִׁעוּר שְׁלוֹשִׁים וְאַחַת

בַּקוֹלְנוֹעַ

1 – אֶתמוֹל הָלַכנוּ לְקוֹלְנוֹעַ "גִ'יל" וְרָאִינוּ קוֹמֶדיָה שׁוֹבֶרֶת קוּפּוֹת.

2 – עַל מַה הַקוֹמֶדיָה?

Since the personal pronoun is integrated in the past tense verb, it is not necessary to use the pronoun as well, unless special emphasis is intended. Don't worry, however – it's not considered an error to use it.

③ **shoveret qupot** שׁוֹבֶרֶת קוּפּוֹת ('breaks cash registers') *a sell-out success.* This expression is the equivalent of *blockbuster* (the idea being that the play or film is so popular that the cash registers break from excessive use). Remember the conjugation of verbs in the present tense: **shover** שׁוֹבֵר, **shoveret** שׁוֹבֶרֶת, **shovrim** שׁוֹבְרִים, **shovrot** שׁוֹברוֹת. If talking about a past big-screen success, the past tense is used: the film *Titanic* **shavar qupot** שָׁבַר קוּפּוֹת 'broke cash registers' = *it was a blockbuster.* As for how to express that a film will prove to be a future blockbuster, we'll have to wait until we study the future tense! Another term that uses the same verb is **shover galim** שׁוֹבֵר גַלִים, literally, 'breaks waves', the Hebrew for a *breakwater* in the sea.

3 – **Kmo kol ④ haqomedyot. Hem `ahavu, hem lo `ahavu, hem shuv `ohavim …**
like all the-comedies. they loved they not loved they again love
Like every comedy. They loved each other, then they didn't, then they love each other again …

4 – **Halakhtem 'im hayeladim?**
you(plural)-went with the-children
Did you go with the children?

5 – **Lo. Hem halkhu 'im chaverim leqolno'a 'Dan' vera`u `et James Bond ⑤ hachadash.**
no they went with friends to-the-cinema-of Dan and-they-saw [**`et**] *James Bond the-new*
No. They went with friends to the Dan cinema to see the new James Bond [film].

6 – **Ah, James Bond hayafeh! Hu shover qupot vegam shover levavot ⑥!**
ah James Bond the-beautiful! he breaks cash-registers and-also breaks hearts!
Ah, handsome James Bond! He's a blockbuster and also a heartbreaker!

Notes

④ **kol** כֹּל *all.* Note that the **o** sound is represented only by the vowel mark between the two letters, and not by a **vav** with a dot on top. Why? This is just the way it is with some words, particularly a number of monosyllabic words. We have already seen this in the words **lo** לֹא *no* in lesson 8 and **poh** פֹּה *here* in lesson 17.

⑤ **James Bond** גֶ'ימְס בּוֹנְד. In lesson 27, note 6, we learned that the **j** sound (as in *jazz* or *jeep*) is represented in Hebrew by ג'.

⑥ **shover levavot** שׁוֹבֵר לְבָבוֹת *breaks hearts.*

3 – כמוֹ כֹּל הַקוֹמֶדיוֹת. הֵם אָהֲבוּ, הֵם לֹא אָהֲבוּ, הֵם שׁוּב אוֹהֲבִים...

4 – הֲלַכתֶם עִם הַיְלָדִים?

5 – לֹא. הֵם הָלכוּ עִם חֲבֵרִים לְקוֹלנוֹעַ "דָן" וְרָאוּ אֶת גֶ'ימס בּוֹנד הֶחָדָשׁ.

6 – אָה, גֶ'ימס בּוֹנד הַיָפֶה! הוּא שׁוֹבֵר קוּפּוֹת וְגַם שׁוֹבֵר לְבָבוֹת!

בקולנוע

Targil rishon – Targem תַּרְגִּיל רִאשׁוֹן – תַּרְגֵּם

❶ אתמול הלכנו לקולנוע דן.
`Etmol halakhnu leqolno'a Dan.

❷ אנחנו ראינו קומדיה והילדים ראו ג'יימס בונד.
`Anachnu ra`inu qomedyah vehayeladim ra`u James Bond.

❸ אתם ראיתם קומדיה בקולנוע חדש.
`Atem re`item qomedyah beqolno'a chadash.

❹ ג'יימס בונד גם שובר קופות וגם שובר לבבות.
James Bond gam shover qupot vegam shover levavot.

❺ מתי הלכתם עם הילדים לקולנוע?
Matay halakhtem 'im hayeladim laqolno'a?

Targil sheni – Hashlem תַּרְגִּיל שֵׁנִי – הַשְׁלֵם

❶ Like all *(the)* comedies: they loved [each other], [now] they don't love [each other] …
Kmo kol haqomedyot: hem `ahavu, hem lo `ohavim…

___ ___ הַקּוֹמֶדְיוֹת : הֵם ____, הֵם __ אוֹהֲבִים...

❷ Yesterday we saw a comedy blockbuster.
`Etmol ra`inu qomedyah shoveret qupot.

_____ רָאִינוּ קוֹמֶדְיָה _____ _____ .

❸ James Bond is a heartbreaker *(breaks hearts)*.
James Bond shover levavot.

ג'יימס בּוֹנְד ____ _____ .

❹ The children saw a soccer game/match.
Hayeladim ra`u mischaq kaduregel.

הַיְלָדִים רָאוּ ____ ______ .

Answers to Exercise 1

❶ Yesterday we went to the Dan cinema. ❷ We saw a comedy and the children saw a James Bond [film]. ❸ You saw a comedy in a new cinema. ❹ James Bond is a blockbuster and also a heartbreaker. ❺ When did you go to the cinema with the children?

❺ They went with friends to buy falafel.
Hem halkhu 'im chaverim liqnot falafel.
הֵם ___ עִם חֲבֵרִים _____ _____ .

Answers to Exercise 2

❶ כאן כֹּל – כָּוֹהֲבוּ – לכו – ❷ כֶּתֶאוּלֹ – שׁוֹבֶרֶת קוּפּוֹת ❸ – שׁוֹבֵר לְבָבוֹת
❹ – מִשְׂחָק כַּדּוּרֶגֶל ❺ – הָלְכוּ – לִקְנוֹת פָלָאפֶל

32 **Qolno'a קוֹלְנוֹעַ** cinema. *We discovered the origin of this word in note 1. This is a good place to consider the general question of how an ancient language creates words for modern concepts, particularly in the field of technology. Two approaches can be found in Hebrew. The first is the creation of a new word from ancient roots; the second is the adoption of a foreign word and adapting it to Hebrew word patterns. Some examples of new words based on native Hebrew roots include:*
- **`ofanayim אוֹפַנַּיִם** *'two wheels' (notice the dual ending on this word) for bicycle;* **`ofan אוֹפָן** wheel *is found in the Bible.*
- **chalal חָלָל** space *(as in the* Final Frontier*) provided the inspiration for the new word* **chalalit חֲלָלִית** spaceship. *The feminine suffix* **-it** ית *is often used to form new words in modern Hebrew.*

---

32 Thirty-second lesson
(Shi'ur shloshim ushtayim)

Matanah ①
Present

1 – `Ornah hizminah ② `otanu ③ leyom huledet ④ hashloshim shel `Ori ⑤.
Ornah invited(fem.) [**`et**]*-us for-day-of birth the-thirty of Ori*
Orna has invited us to Ori's thirtieth birthday.

2 – Kvar qanita matanah?
already you-bought(masc.) present
Have you already bought a present?

Notes

① **matanah מַתָּנָה** *present*, *gift*. This word is associated with a number of Hebrew names that have common English equivalents, such as: **Matityahu מַתִּתְיָהוּ** *Matthew*, **Natan נָתָן** *Nathan*, **Netanel נְתַנְאֵל** *Nethanel* and **Yonatan יוֹנָתָן** *Jonathan*.

② **hizminah הִזְמִינָה** *she invited/has invited.* As we have seen, the third-person singular feminine form in the past tense always ends in **-ah** ָה.

• **diburit** דִּבּוּרִית hands-free set, *a term we saw in lesson 13.*
• **lavyan** לַוְיָן satellite *comes from the verb* **lelavot** לְלַווֹת to accompany.
• *And here is an example of the adoption of a foreign word:* **pyjama** פִּיגָ'מָה pyjamas. *The Academy of the Hebrew Language has made various suggestions for a native Hebrew word for this concept, but none have caught on, and some have provoked great amusement. For the moment, the loanword remains in use, unless you have any suggestions...*

Soon your Hebrew will be good enough to invent new words of your own!

---

32 שִׁעוּר שְׁלוֹשִׁים וּשְׁתַּיִם

מַתָּנָה

1 – אוֹרְנָה הִזְמִינָה אוֹתָנוּ לְיוֹם הוּלֶדֶת הַשְּׁלוֹשִׁים שֶׁל אוֹרִי.

2 – כְּבָר קָנִיתָ מַתָּנָה ?

③ **`otanu** אוֹתָנוּ *us*. In lesson 17, note 2 we saw that the direct-object particle **`et** אֶת declines depending on the personal pronoun that follows it – here we see it with **-nu** נוּ to form the first-person plural *us*. In lesson 29, note 6 we saw the form **`otam** אוֹתָם *they*.

④ **yom huledet** יוֹם הוּלֶדֶת *birthday* (literally, 'day-of birth').

⑤ **`Ori** אוֹרִי. Way back in lesson 1, we learned the word **`or**, אוֹר *light*. Here, the addition of **i** ִי creates a first name meaning 'My light'. In lesson 2, we saw a very similar name: **Li`or** לִיאוֹר 'I have light'. Another name is **`Orli** אוֹרְלִי, also meaning 'I have light'. There are many other first names that begin with **`or** אוֹר *light*.

3 – 'Od lo. Chashavti liqnot kartisim.
yet not. I-thought to-buy tickets.
Not yet. I was thinking of buying some tickets.

4 – Lemischaq kaduregel `o lemischaq kadursal?
for-game-of football or for-game-of basketball
For a soccer or basketball game?

5 – Lo zeh velo zeh.
not this and-not this
Neither.

6 – `Ulay kartisim leTe`atron Yerushalayim?
maybe tickets for-theatre-of Jerusalem
Perhaps tickets to the Jerusalem Theatre?

7 – Oof! Lo! Mah hamatanah hatovah beyoter ⑥?
oh no! what the-present the-good in-more?
Oh no! What's the best present?

8 – Kesef?
money
Money?

9 – Metzuyan! Bimzumanim ⑦ `o behamcha`ah?
excellent! in-cashes or in-cheque?
Excellent! In cash or by cheque?

10 – `Eyzeh nudniq!
what pest
What a pest!

Notes

⑥ **hatovah beyoter** הַטּוֹבָה בְּיוֹתֵר *the best* (literally, 'the-best in-more'). This is our first example of a superlative (best, biggest, youngest, etc.). Here it agrees with the feminine noun **matanah** מַתָּנָה *gift*. With a masculine noun, the form is **hatov beyoter** הַטּוֹב בְּיוֹתֵר.

3 – עוֹד לֹא. חָשַׁבְתִּי לִקְנוֹת כַּרְטִיסִים .

4 – לְמִשְׂחָק כַּדוּרֶגֶל אוֹ לְמִשְׂחָק כַּדוּרְסַל?

5 – לֹא זֶה וְלֹא זֶה.

6 – אוּלַי כַּרְטִיסִים לְתֵאַטְרוֹן יְרוּשָׁלַיִם?

7 – אוּף! לֹא! מַה הַמַּתָּנָה הַטּוֹבָה בְּיוֹתֵר?

8 – כֶּסֶף?

9 – מְצוּיָן. בִּמְזוּמָנִים אוֹ בְּהַמְחָאָה?

10 – אֵיזֶה נוּדְנִיק!

מתנה

▸ ⑦ **bimzumanim** בִּמְזוּמָנִים *in cash*. This is another word formed from the root **zman** זְמַן *time* (lesson 24, note 1). The connection is that cash is a form of money that is readily available at any time.

Targil rishon – Targem תַּרְגִּיל רִאשׁוֹן – תַּרְגֵּם

❶ היא הזמינה אותנו ליום ההולדת של אורנה.
Hi hizminah `otanu leyom hahuledet shel `Ornah.

❷ עוד לא קניתי מתנה.
'Od lo qaniti matanah.

❸ קנית כרטיסים למשחק כדורסל?
Qanita kartisim lemischaq kadursal?

❹ מה המתנה הטובה ביותר ליום הולדת?
Mah hamatanah hatovah beyoter leyom huledet?

❺ חשבתי לקנות כרטיסים לתיאטרון ירושלים.
Chashavti liqnot kartisim leTe`atron Yerushalayim.

Targil sheni – Hashlem תַּרְגִּיל שֵׁנִי – הַשְׁלֵם

❶ Money in cash or *(money in a)* cheque?
Kesef bimzumanim `o kesef behamcha`ah?

כֶּסֶף בְּ_______ או כֶּסֶף בְּ_____?

❷ Tickets for the *(a)* theatre or *(tickets)* for the *(a)* cinema?
Kartisim lete`atron `o kartisim leqolno'a?

_______ לְתֵיאַטְרוֹן או כַּרְטִיסִים לְ______?

❸ I haven't thought about a present for the children.
Lo chashavti 'al matanah leyeladim.

לא _____ עַל ____ לְ_____ .

❹ She invited us to Danny's thirtieth birthday party.
Hi hizminah `otanu leyom huledet hashloshim shel Dani.

הִיא ______ _____ לְיוֹם הוּלֶדֶת ה______ שֶׁל דָּנִי.

Answers to Exercise 1

❶ She invited us to Orna's birthday. ❷ I haven't bought a present yet. ❸ Did you buy tickets to the basketball game? ❹ What's the best present for a birthday? ❺ I was thinking of buying tickets for the Jerusalem Theatre.

❺ It's a problem to buy a good *(beautiful)* present for Ori.
Zot be'ayah liqnot matanah yafah le`Ori.
--- בְּעָיָה לִקְנוֹת ---- --- לְאוֹרִי.

Answers to Exercise 2

❶ - מְזֻמָּנִים - הַמַּחֲזֶה ❷ כַּרְטִיסִים - קוֹלְנוֹעַ ❸ - חָשַׁבְתִּי - מַתָּנָה - יְלָדִים ❹ - הִכְנִיסָה אוֹתָנוּ - שְׁלוֹשִׁים - ❺ זֹאת - מַתָּנָה יָפָה -

The Jerusalem Theatre תֵּאַטְרוֹן יְרוּשָׁלַיִם *opened in 1971. Situated in a central neighbourhood of the city and close to the President's House, the Jerusalem Theatre has become one of the liveliest centres of Israeli culture. The theatre's halls are used to stage plays and screen films, as well as for various cultural events.*

One of the most important of these events is the annual International Bible Quiz. The quiz is held each year on **yom ha'atzma'ut**, *Israel's Independence Day. David Ben Gurion, the first prime minister of Israel, developed the idea of the quiz together with professors who wanted to link the emergence of the new state to Biblical culture. To select the contestants, Jewish communities around the world organize national quizzes, which attract both Jewish and non-Jewish participants. Three winners from each country are treated to a free trip to Jerusalem so that they can participate in the final. The three finalists receive prestigious prizes.*

33 Thirty-third lesson
(Shi'ur shloshim veshalosh)

Shvitah ①
Strike

1 – `Eyfoh hayit? Ra`it mah hasha'ah?
where you-were(fem.)? you-saw what the-time?
Where have you been? Have you seen the time?

2 – Nasa`ti she'atayim ki hayu harbeh mekhoniyot biglal hashvitah.
I-travelled two-hours because there-were many cars because-of the-strike
I drove for two hours because there were [so] many cars due to the strike.

3 – `Eyzo shvitah?
what strike
What strike?

4 – Lo shama'ta chadashot? Hayom haytah shvitat ② `otobusim.
not you-heard(masc.) news? the-day it-was(fem.) strike-of buses
Didn't you hear the news? There was a bus strike today.

Notes

① **shvitah** שְׁבִיתָה *strike*; **shabat** שַׁבָּת *Saturday.* The play on words in line 7 of the Hebrew dialogue highlights the Biblical origins of the word **shvitah**. One of the Ten Commandments prohibits work on the day of Sabbath: שַׁבָּת. The root שבת, meaning *to cease from work*, provided the foundation for the modern word שְׁבִיתָה *strike*. Only Hebrew could move so quickly from Biblical serenity to modern labour conflicts!

② **shvitat** שְׁבִיתַת *strike-of.* This is the construct state of **shvitah**: the final **-ah** ָה becomes **-at** ת.

שְׁבִיתָה

1 – אֵיפֹה הָיִית? רָאִית מַה הַשָּׁעָה?

2 – נָסַעְתִּי שְׁעָתַיִם כִּי הָיוּ הַרְבֵּה מְכוֹנִיּוֹת בִּגְלַל הַשְּׁבִיתָה.

3 – אֵיזוֹ שְׁבִיתָה?

4 – לֹא שָׁמַעְתָּ חֲדָשׁוֹת? הַיּוֹם הָיְתָה שְׁבִיתַת אוֹטוֹבּוּסִים.

5 – **Shuv shvitah? Kvar shnatayim kol sheni vachamishi mishehu shovet.**

again strike? already two-years every Monday and-Thursday someone strikes.

Another strike? For the past two years there's been a strike every other day.

6 – **'Al ③ mah `atah medaber? Lifney chodshayim shavateta yomayim.**

about what you(masc.) speak? before two-months you-struck two-days.

What are you talking about? Two months ago you went on strike for two days.

7 – **Tov. Machar shabat! `Ani shuv shovet ④.**

well. tomorrow shabat! I again strike.

Good. Tomorrow is Shabbat [and] I['ll be on] strike again!

Notes

③ **'al** עַל *on, above, about.* This preposition translates as 'on' in the physical sense – **'al hakise** עַל הַכִּסֵּא *on the chair* – as well ▶

───── ✦ ─────

Targil rishon – Targem תַּרְגִּיל רִאשׁוֹן – תַּרְגֵּם

❶ נָסַעְתִּי שַׁעֲתַיִם בִּגְלַל שְׁבִיתַת אוֹטוֹבּוּסִים.

Nasa'ti she'atayim biglal shvitat `otobusim.

❷ לָמָּה לֹא שָׁמַעְתָּ חֲדָשׁוֹת?

Lamah lo shama'ta chadashot?

❸ כָּל שֵׁנִי וַחֲמִישִׁי הוּא הוֹלֵךְ לִקְנוֹת בַּקַּנְיוֹן.

Kol sheni vachamishi hu holekh liqnot baqanyon.

5 – שׁוּב שְׁבִיתָה? כְּבָר שְׁנָתַיִים כׇּל שֵׁנִי וַחֲמִישִׁי מִישֶׁהוּ שׁוֹבֵת.

6 – עַל מַה אַתָּה מְדַבֵּר? לִפְנֵי חוֹדְשַׁיִים שָׁבַתְתָּ יוֹמַיִים.

7 – טוֹב. מָחָר שַׁבָּת! אֲנִי שׁוּב שׁוֹבֵת. □

as in the sense of 'about' (a book *on* mathematics, a speech *on* the political situation). In lesson 32, exercise 3 we saw **lo chashavti 'al matanah** לֹא חָשַׁבְתִּי עַל מַתָּנָה *I haven't thought about a present*. Another example: **'Al mah `atah medaber?** עַל מַה אַתָּה מְדַבֵּר? *What are you talking about?*

④ **shovet** שׁוֹבֵת *I/you* (masc.)*/he rests from work, strikes*. As explained, this verb expresses both the meaning of 'resting from work' and 'striking'. In most cases, of course, the context makes it quite clear which meaning is intended.

❹ ראית מה קרה בבוקר בבריכה?
Ra`it mah qarah baboqer babrekhah?

❺ היו הרבה מכוניות בגלל הפסטיבל.
Hayu harbeh mekhoniyot biglal hafestival.

Answers to Exercise 1

❶ I drove for two hours because of a bus strike. ❷ Why didn't you hear the news? ❸ Every few days he goes shopping in the mall. ❹ Did you see what happened in the swimming pool this morning? ❺ There were lots of cars because of the festival.

Targil sheni – Hashlem תַּרְגִּיל שֵׁנִי – הַשְׁלֵם

❶ Didn't you*(masc.)* hear [the] news? Today there was a big strike.
Lo shama'ta chadashot? Hayom haytah shvitah gdolah.

לֹא ____ חֲדָשׁוֹת? הַיּוֹם ____ _____ גְּדוֹלָה.

❷ Where were you*(fem.)*? What did you see?
`Eyfoh hayit? Mah ra`it?

אֵיפֹה ____? מָה ____?

❸ Every few days *(second and fifth – i.e. Monday and Thursday)* there is a strike.
Kol sheni vachamishi yesh shvitah.

כֹּל ___ וַ_____ יֵשׁ שְׁבִיתָה.

❹ Two weeks ago you*(masc.)* went on strike *(struck)* for two days.
Lifney shvu'ayim shavateta yomayim.

לִפְנֵי _______ שָׁבַתְתָּ ______ .

❺ I travelled two hours from Givatayim to Jerusalem.
Nasa'ti she'atayim miGiv'atayim liYerushalayim.

נָסַעְתִּי ______ מִ_______ לִירוּשָׁלַיִם.

---

34 Thirty-fourth lesson
(Shi'ur shloshim ve`arba')

Yovel
Jubilee

1 – **Mesibat hahafta'ah hayafah beyoter shera`iti haytah likhvod Hanah veNatan.**
party-of the-surprise the-beautiful in-more that-I-saw was(fem.) to-honour-of Hannah and-Natan
The finest surprise party I've ever seen was in honour of Hannah and Nathan.

Answers to Exercise 2

❶ - שָׁמַעְתָּ - הָיְתָה שְׁבִיתָה - ❷ - הָיִית - רָאִית ❸ - שֵׁנִי - חֲמִישִׁי -
❹ - שְׁבוּעַיִם - יוֹמַיִם ❺ - שְׁעָתַיִם - גִּבְעָתַיִם

Kol sheni vachamishi כֹּל שֵׁנִי וַחֲמִישִׁי every Monday and Thursday. *This expression is used to mean 'very often' or 'every few days'. Since ancient times, Monday and Thursday have been market days in Jerusalem. Formerly, these were also the days when the courts convened, and when villagers visiting the city took the opportunity to read from the Torah in public. Ezra the Scribe introduced this custom in the 4th century CE so that not more than three days would pass between Torah readings (the Torah is also read on Saturday). This same custom is observed when the* **Bar Mitzvah** *boy reads from the Torah on these days, as discussed in the note at the end of lesson 16.*

34 שִׁעוּר שְׁלוֹשִׁים וְאַרְבַּע

יוֹבֵל

1 – מְסִיבַּת הַהַפְתָּעָה הַיָּפָה בְּיוֹתֵר שֶׁרָאִיתִי הַיְתָה לִכְבוֹד חַנָּה וְנָתָן.

2 – Haytah sibah lamesibah?
was(fem.) reason to-party?
Was there a reason for the party?

3 – Zot haytah mesibat hafta'ah leyovel hachamishim lanisu`im ① shel Hanah veNatan.
this was(fem.) party-of surprise to-jubilee the-fifty to-marriage of Hannah and-Natan
It was a surprise party for Hannah and Nathan's fiftieth wedding anniversary.

4 – Chatunat zahav! `Eyfoh hem hikiru ② zeh `et zo ③?
wedding-of gold! where they acquainted this(masc.) [**`et**] *this(fem.)?*
A golden wedding! Where did they meet each other?

5 – 'Al ha`oniyah 'Yetzi`at `Eyropah'.
on the-boat 'departure-of Europe'
On the boat 'Exodus'.

Notes

① **nisu`im** נִשׂוּאִים *marriage* is a plural masculine noun. The root is נשׂא, from which comes the verb **nasa** נָשָׂא *to take, to carry*. The word **nasi`** נָשִׂיא comes from the same root and means *president*: for example, the president of the State of Israel, or of a university, etc. **nasi`** נָשִׂיא contains the word **si`** שִׂיא *summit*, which, although the two words are not related, seems appropriate, since to be at the summit of a field is both an honour and a responsibility.

Line 4 includes the word **chatunah** חֲתוּנָה *wedding*, which refers to the ceremony itself, whereas **nisu`im** נִשׂוּאִים means *marriage* in the broader sense, as an institution and an ongoing relationship. In **lanisu`im** לַנִּשׂוּאִים *[to] the marriage*, notice that the definite article **ha** הַ has merged with the preposition **l** לְ at the beginning of the word to form **la** לַ *to the*. We have

2 – הָיְתָה סִיבָּה לַמְסִיבָּה?

3 – זֹאת הָיְתָה מְסִיבַּת הַפְתָּעָה לְיוֹבֵל הַחֲמִישִּׁים לַנִּשּׂוּאִים שֶׁל חַנָּה וְנָתָן.

4 – חֲתוּנַּת זָהָב! אֵיפֹה הֵם הִכִּירוּ זֶה אֶת זוֹ?

5 – עַל הָאוֹנִיָּה "יְצִיאַת אֵירוֹפָּה".

seen this several times in previous lessons (see lesson 16, note 1). In English we say 'for the fiftieth anniversary', but in Hebrew, **l** לְ *to* is used in this context.

② **hikiru** הִכִּירוּ *they became acquainted/met*. This is another example of a third-person plural form in the past tense. All such forms end in **u** וּ, without exception.

③ **zeh `et zo** זֶה אֶת זוֹ This idiom is used with a reciprocal sense – to 'do' something with each other or to one another. In this case, they became acquainted with each other: 'this-one (masc.) to this-one (fem.)'. If we were talking about two women who met each other, we would ask: **`Eyfoh hen hikiru zo `et zo?** אֵיפֹה הֵן הִכִּירוּ זוֹ אֶת זוֹ?

6 – Hem hitchatnu ④ 'al ha`oniyah?
they married-each-other on the-boat?
Did they get married on the boat?

7 – Lo, baqibutz, 'im hachaverim meha`oniyah. Zot chatunah historit!
no in-the-kibbutz with the-friends from-the-boat. this wedding historical!
No, in the kibbutz with their friends from the boat. It was a historic wedding!

Notes

④ **hitchatnu** הִתְחַתְּנוּ *they married/got married.* The **hit-** prefix at the beginning of this word is the sign of a reflexive verb in

Targil rishon – Targem תַּרְגִּיל רִאשׁוֹן – תַּרְגֵּם

❶ היינו בחתונת הזהב של חנה ונתן.
Hayinu bechatunat hazahav shel Hanah veNatan.

❷ זאת היתה מסיבת הפתעה יפה מאוד.
Zot haytah mesibat hafta'ah yafah me`od.

❸ איפה הם הכירו זה את זו?
`Eyfoh hem hikiru zeh `et zo?

❹ למה הם לא התחתנו על האוניה?
Lamah hem lo hitchatnu 'al ha`oniyah?

❺ מה הסיבה למסיבה?
Mah hasibah lamesibah?

6 – הֵם הִתחַתנוּ עַל הָאוֹנִיָה?

7 – לֹא, בַּקִיבּוּץ, עִם הַחֲבֵרִים מֵהָאוֹנִיָה. זֹאת חֲתוּנָה הִסטוֹרִית!

the past tense. Reflexive verbs indicate that the subject of the sentence has performed an action on itself or, as here, refer to a reciprocal action. Examples in English include 'to wash oneself', 'to dress oneself' or 'to help each other'. Sometimes Hebrew requires a reflexive verb where a regular verb is used in English, such as here.

Answers to Exercise 1

❶ We were at the golden wedding [anniversary] of Hannah and Nathan. ❷ It was a very nice surprise party. ❸ Where did they meet *(become acquainted)*? ❹ Why didn't they get married *(marry each other)* on the boat? ❺ What's the reason for the party?

Targil sheni – Hashlem תַּרְגִּיל שֵׁנִי – הַשְׁלֵם

1. Surprise party for the fiftieth wedding anniversary of Dina and Dan.
   Mesibat hafta'ah leyovel hanisu`im shel Dinah veDan.
   מְסִיבַּת הַפְתָּעָה _____ _______ שֶׁל דִּינָה וְדָן.

2. They met on the boat ‘Exodus’.
   Hem hikiru 'al ha`oniyah ‘Yetzi`at `Eyropah’.
   הֵם _____ עַל ______ "יְצִיאַת אֵירוֹפָּה".

3. Who was the birthday party for?
   Likhvod mi haytah mesibat yom hahuledet?
   לִכְבוֹד מִי ____ מְסִיבַּת יוֹם _____?

4. They got married in the kibbutz two years ago.
   Hem hitchatnu baqibutz lifney shnatayim.
   הֵם ______ בַּקִּבּוּץ ____, ______ .

5. What is the reason for the surprise party this evening?
   Mah hasibah limesibat hahafta'ah ba'erev?
   מַה _____ לִמְסִיבַּת ______ בָּעֶרֶב?

Yovel יוֹבֵל Jubilee. *This term originally referred to the year at the end of seven cycles of Sabbatical years (that is, 49 or 50 years). It was translated in English versions of the Bible as ‘jubilee’ (via the Latin jubilaeus), which is derived from the Hebrew* **yovel**. *What is Jubilee year? Biblical rules required that every 50 years, indentured slaves were to be freed. All financial debts were also cancelled in the Jubilee year (a custom that unfortunately is no longer observed). Today,* **yovel** יוֹבֵל *in Hebrew is used to refer generally to the fiftieth anniversary of an institution or event.*

Yetzi`at `Eyropah יְצִיאַת אֵירוֹפָּה Departure from Europe. *In 1947, Britain, which controlled the region under the British Mandate of Palestine (1917–48), continued to restrict Jewish*

Answers to Exercise 2

❶ - ליוֹבֵל הַנִּשׂוּאִים - ❷ - הִכִּירוּ - הָאוֹנִיָּה - ❸ - הָיְתָה - הָהוּלֶדֶת
❹ - הִתְחַתְּנוּ - לִפְנֵי שְׁנָתַיִם ❺ - הַסִּבָּה - הָהַפְתָּעָה -

immigration to the Land of Israel (remember the Hebrew word for such immigration is **'aliyah עֲלִיָּה** ascent*). However, Jewish organizations found creative ways to overcome these restrictions. In one famous example, they bought a boat in Baltimore and renovated it to make it suitable for carrying a large number of passengers. It then sailed to the Mediterranean, where it picked up 4,515 Jewish refugees from a port in southern France and departed for Palestine. The Hebrew name chosen for the boat,* יְצִיאַת אֵירוֹפָּה Departure from Europe *or* Exit from Europe*, is a reference to the Exodus – or the departure of the Israelites from ancient Egypt. This is reflected in the English name given to the boat: 'Exodus'. Today, the Exodus can be seen at the Naval Museum in Haifa.*

35 Thirty-fifth lesson
(Shi'ur shloshim vechamesh)

חֲזָרָה Chazarah – Review

1 Verbs

As we've explained, Hebrew has just one main past tense that is used in most cases. Note the different tenses we've used in English to translate the Hebrew forms. Here are two examples:

• **`ani hayiti** (masc./fem.) אֲנִי הָיִיתִי
I was, I have been, I was being, I had been, etc.

• **`aten halakhten** (fem. plural) אַתֶן הֲלַכְתֶן
you went, you have gone, you were going, you had gone, etc.

In the following list of conjugations, we've translated into the simple past (*I was*, *I went*, etc.) for the sake of simplicity.

Hebrew verbs are usually referred to not by the infinitive, which as we have learned virtually always begins with **lamed** ל, but by the third-person singular masculine in the past tense (*he was, he saw*, etc.) This form usually reflects the root of the verb, from which all the other forms are derived.

NB: Remember that there is no present tense of the verb *to be* in Hebrew. *He is big* is simply **hu gadol** הוּא גָדוֹל – literally, 'he big'.

• *to be* – root: היה

masculine

(`ani) hayiti	(אֲנִי) הָיִיתִי	*I was*
(`atah) hayita	(אַתָה) הָיִיתָ	*you were*
(hu) hayah	(הוּא) הָיָה	*he was*
(`anachnu) hayinu	(אֲנַחנוּ) הָיִינוּ	*we were*
(`atem) hayitem	(אַתֶם) הָיִיתֶם	*you* (plural) *were*
(hem) hayu	(הֵם) הָיוּ	*they were*

feminine

(`ani) hayiti	(אֲנִי) הָיִיתִי	*I was*
(`at) hayit	(אַתְּ) הָיִית	*you were*
(hi) haytah	(הִיא) הָיְתָה	*she was*
(`anachnu) hayinu	(אֲנַחְנוּ) הָיִינוּ	*we were*
(`aten) hayiten	(אַתֶּן) הֱיִיתֶן	*you* (plural) *were*
(hen) hayu	(הֵן) הָיוּ	*they were*

• *to see* – root: ראה

masculine

(`ani) ra`iti	(אֲנִי) רָאִיתִי	*I saw*
(`atah) ra`ita	(אַתָּה) רָאִיתָ	*you saw*
(hu) ra`ah	(הוּא) רָאָה	*he saw*
(`anachnu) ra`inu	(אֲנַחְנוּ) רָאִינוּ	*we saw*
(`atem) re`item	(אַתֶּם) רְאִיתֶם	*you* (plural) *saw*
(hem) ra`u	(הֵם) רָאוּ	*they saw*

feminine

(`ani) ra`iti	(אֲנִי) רָאִיתִי	*I saw*
(`at) ra`it	(אַתְּ) רָאִית	*you saw*
(hi) ra`atah	(הִיא) רָאֲתָה	*she saw*
(`anachnu) ra`inu	(אֲנַחְנוּ) רָאִינוּ	*we saw*
(`aten) re`iten	(אַתֶּן) רְאִיתֶן	*you* (plural) *saw*
(hen) ra`u	(הֵן) רָאוּ	*they saw*

• *to walk, to go* – root: הלך

masculine

(`ani) halakhti	(אֲנִי) הָלַכְתִּי	*I went*
(`ani) halakhti	(אַתָּה) הָלַכְתָּ	*you went*
(hu) halakh	(הוּא) הָלַךְ	*he went*
(`anachnu) halakhnu	(אֲנַחְנוּ) הָלַכְנוּ	*we went*
(`atem) halakhtem	(אַתֶּם) הֲלַכְתֶּם	*you* (plural) *went*
(hem) halkhu	(הֵם) הָלְכוּ	*they went*

feminine

(`ani) halakhti	(אֲנִי) הָלַכְתִּי	*I went*
(`at) halakht	(אַתְּ) הָלַכְתְּ	*you went*
(hi) halkhah	(הִיא) הָלְכָה	*she went*
(`anachnu) halakhnu	(אֲנַחְנוּ) הָלַכְנוּ	*we went*
(`aten) halakhten	(אַתֶּן) הֲלַכְתֶּן	*you* (plural) *went*
(hen) halkhu	(הֵן) הָלְכוּ	*they went*

2 Possessive adjectives

The following list shows the declension of the preposition שֶׁל *of*, which is used to make both possessive pronouns (e.g. *mine*, *yours*, etc.) and possessive adjectives (e.g. *my*, *your*). In fact, the same Hebrew word is used in both contexts: **sheli** שֶׁלִּי, literally 'of-me', means both *my* and *mine*:

zot hamekhonit sheli זֹאת הַמְּכוֹנִית שֶׁלִּי
this is my car ('this car of-me')
hamekhonit hazot sheli הַמְּכוֹנִית הַזֹּאת שֶׁלִּי
this car is mine ('car this-one of-me')

singular

sheli	שֶׁלִּי	(of me) *my, mine*
shelkha	שֶׁלְּךָ	(of you)(masc.) *your, yours*
shelakh	שֶׁלָּךְ	(of you)(fem.) *your, yours*
shelo	שֶׁלּוֹ	(of him) *his*
shelah	שֶׁלָּהּ	(of her) *her, hers*

plural

shelanu	שֶׁלָּנוּ	(of us) *our, ours*
shelakhem	שֶׁלָּכֶם	(of you)(masc.) *your, yours*
shelakhen	שֶׁלָּכֶן	(of you)(fem.) *your, yours*
shelahem	שֶׁלָּהֶם	(of them)(masc.) *their, theirs*
shelahen	שֶׁלָּהֶן	(of them)(fem.) *their, theirs*

3 Direct object pronouns

The direct object pronouns in English are *me, you, him, her, it, us* and *them.* We use these pronouns to show the direct object of an action: 'David kissed her', 'We thanked them', 'They thanked us', and so forth. As we've seen, in Hebrew the direct object of an action is marked with the untranslatable but essential particle **`et** אֶת. This particle declines (changes form) when used with different 'persons' to produce the Hebrew equivalents of *me*, *you*, etc. Note that the vowel **e** that begins **`et** אֶת is replaced by **`o** אוֹ in most of the persons, followed by the ending of the relevant pronoun.

singular

`oti	אוֹתִי	*me* (masc./fem.)
`otkha	אוֹתךָ	*you* (masc.)
`otakh	אוֹתָךְ	*you* (fem.)
`oto	אוֹתוֹ	*him**
`otah	אוֹתָה	*her*

* (not to be confused with **`oto** *same*, see lesson 30, which is written in the same way.)

plural

`otanu	אוֹתָנוּ	*us* (masc./fem.)
`etkhem	אֶתכֶם	*you* (masc.)
`etkhen	אֶתכֶן	*you* (fem.)
`otam	אוֹתָם	*they* (masc.)
`otan	אוֹתָן	*they* (fem.)

4 Duals

When referring to two of something, you'll see **-yim** at the end of the noun.

shnayim	שנַיִים	*two* (masc.)
shtayim	שתַיִים	*two* (fem.)
sha'ah	שָׁעָה	*1 hour*
she'atayim	שעָתַיִים	*2 hours*
yom	יוֹם	*1 day*
yomayim	יוֹמַיִים	*2 days*
shavu'a	שָׁבוּעַ	*1 week*

shvu'ayim	שְׁבוּעַיִם	*2 weeks*
chodesh	חוֹדֶשׁ	*1 month*
chodshayim	חוֹדְשַׁיִים	*2 months*
shanah	שָׁנָה	*1 year*
shnatayim	שְׁנָתַיִים	*2 years*

5 Family

mishpachah	מִשְׁפָּחָה	*family*
savta	סַבְתָא	*grandmother*
saba	סַבָּא	*grandfather*
`ima	אִמָא	*Mom, mother*
`aba	אַבָּא	*Dad, father*
bat	בַּת	*daughter*
ben	בֵּן	*son*
nekhdah	נֶכְדָה	*granddaughter*
nekhed	נֶכֶד	*grandson*
ninah	נִינָה	*great-granddaughter*
nin	נִין	*great-grandson*

6 Celebrations

brit milah	בְּרִית מִילָה	*circumcision* (both the practice and the accompanying celebration)
bar mitzvah (masc.)	בַּר מִצְוָה	*Bar Mitzvah* (both the celebration and the boy celebrating his entry into adulthood)
bat mitzvah (fem.)	בַּת מִצְוָה	*Bat Mitzvah* (both the celebration and the girl celebrating her entry into adulthood)
chatunah	חֲתוּנָה	*wedding, marriage* (the ceremony)

chatunat zahav	חֲתוּנַת זָהָב	*golden wedding anniversary*
nisu`im	נִשּׂוּאִים	*marriage* (the institution, married life)
yom huledet	יוֹם הוּלֶדֶת	*birthday*
mesibah	מְסִיבָּה	*party*
mesibat hafta'ah	מְסִיבַּת הַפְתָעָה	*surprise party*
yovel	יוֹבֵל	*jubilee*

7 Idiomatic expressions

• **nudniq** (masc.) נוּדנִיק
nudniqit (fem.) נוּדנִיקִית
pest, 'nudnik'

• **`ani nofel meharaglayim** (masc.) אֲנִי נוֹפֵל מֵהָרַגלַיִים
`ani nofelet meharaglayim (fem.) אֲנִי נוֹפֶלֶת מֵהָרַגלַיִים
I'm dead on my feet

• **`atah nofel meharaglayim** (masc.) אַתָּה נוֹפֵל מֵהָרַגלַיִים
`at nofelet meharaglayim (fem.) אַת נוֹפֶלֶת מֵהָרַגלַיִים
you're dead on your feet

• **Mah qarah?** מַה קָרָה?
What's up? What's wrong?

• **chevreman** (masc.) חֶברֶמַן
chevremanit (fem.) חֶברֶמָנִית
cool, sociable, outgoing

• **mazal tov** מַזָל טוֹב
congratulations

• **shover levavot** (masc.) שׁוֹבֵר לְבָבוֹת
shoveret levavot (fem.) שׁוֹבֶרֶת לְבָבוֹת
heartbreaker, good looker

• **shover qupot** (masc.) שׁוֹבֵר קוּפּוֹת
blockbuster, hit, sell-out success

• **kol sheni vachamishi** כֹּל שֵׁנִי וַחֲמִישִׁי
every few days (literally, 'every Monday and Thursday')

① אֲנִי נוֹפֵל מֵהָרַגְלַיִם. הָיָה לִי שָׁבוּעַ שֶׁל מְסִיבּוֹת. ② בְּיוֹם שִׁישִׁי בָּעֶרֶב הָיִינוּ עִם כֹּל הַמִּשְׁפָּחָה בְּאֲרוּחַת שַׁבָּת. ③ בְּשַׁבָּת בַּבּוֹקֶר הָלַכְנוּ לַבַּת מִצְוָה שֶׁל שָׂרָה. ④ בְּיוֹם רִאשׁוֹן הָיְתָה בְּרִית מִילָה לַנֶּכֶד שֶׁלָּנוּ. ⑤ בְּיוֹם שֵׁנִי הָיְתָה מְסִיבַּת הַפְתָּעָה לַנֶּכְדָה. הִיא בַּת שְׁמוֹנֶה. ⑥ בְּיוֹם שְׁלִישִׁי קָנִינוּ מַתָּנוֹת לְיוֹבֵל הַנִּישׂוּאִים שֶׁל סַבָּא וְסַבְתָּא. ⑦ בְּיוֹם רְבִיעִי בָּעֶרֶב רָאִינוּ קוֹמֶדְיָה שׁוֹבֶרֶת קוּפּוֹת בְּתֵיאַטְרוֹן יְרוּשָׁלַיִם. ⑧ בְּיוֹם חֲמִישִׁי קָנִיתִי כַּרְטִיסִים לְקוֹנְצֶרְט. ⑨ בְּיוֹם שִׁישִׁי וְשַׁבָּת אֲנַחְנוּ אֵצֶל אֲחוֹתִי בְּתֵל אָבִיב.

---

36 Thirty-sixth lesson
(Shi'ur shloshim veshesh)

Cham, chamot ①
Father-in-law, mother-in-law

1 – `Eykh ② **hachamot shelakh?**
how the-mother-in-law of-you(fem.)
What's your mother-in-law like?

Notes

① **cham** חָם *hot.* This adjective declines in a regular way: masculine singular, **cham** חָם; feminine singular, **chamah** חַמָּה; masucline plural, **chamim** חַמִּים; feminine plural, **chamot** חַמּוֹת. The related word **chamim** חָמִים means *warm*, both in the literal sense and in the sense of *friendly* or *hospitable*. This is a singular form, formed according to a pattern for creating diminutive or moderated versions of the original word. **Dan chamim** דָּן חָמִים *Dan is warm*, **Rinah chamimah** רִינָה חֲמִימָה *Rinah is warm*. The plural forms are

Answers

❶ I'm dead on my feet. I had a whole week of parties. *(I fall[masc.] from-the-feet. it-was for-me week of parties.)* ❷ On Friday night we had Shabbat dinner with the whole family. *(in-day sixth in-the-evening we-were with all the-family in-meal-of shabbat)* ❸ On Saturday morning we went to Sarah's Bat Mitzvah. *(in-shabbat in-the-morning we-went to-daughter-of commandment of Sarah)* ❹ On Sunday it was our grandson's circumcision. *(in-day first it-was covenant-of circumcision to-the-grandson of-us)* ❺ On Monday there was a surprise party for our granddaughter. She is eight. *(in-day second it-was party-of surprise for-the-granddaughter. she daughter-of eight.)* ❻ On Tuesday we bought presents for the fiftieth wedding anniversary of Grandfather and Grandmother. *(in-day third we-bought presents for-jubilee-of the-marriage of grandfather and-grandmother)* ❼ On Wednesday evening we saw a blockbuster comedy at the Jerusalem Theatre. *(in-day fourth in-the-evening we-saw comedy breaking-of cash-registers in-theatre-of Jerusalem)* ❽ On Thursday I bought tickets for a concert. *(in-day fifth I-bought tickets for-concert)* ❾ On Friday and Saturday we are at my sister's in Tel Aviv. *(in-day sixth and-shabat we at my-sister in-Tel Aviv)*

---

36 שִׁעוּר שְׁלוֹשִׁים וְשֵׁשׁ

חָם, חָמוֹת

1 – אֵיךְ הַחָמוֹת שֶׁלָּךְ?

chamimim חֲמִימִים and **chamimot** חֲמִימוֹת. This lesson also introduces the words **cham** חָם *father-in-law* and **chamot** חָמוֹת *mother-in-law*. Like the word **achot** אָחוֹת *sister*, which we learned in lesson 19, **chamot** חָמוֹת looks like a plural form, but is actually singular. The words for mother-in-law and father-in-law are not related etymologically to **cham** חַם, but the similarity creates many opportunities for puns. Be careful in using **cham** חַם *hot* to refer to people – as in English, it can have a sexual connotation that could be very offensive.

② In this phrase, **`eykh** אֵיךְ *how* is used to ask <u>what</u> something or someone is like. So here this sentence does not mean 'How is your mother-in-law?' but 'What is your mother-in-law like?'.

2 – **Mamash ne'imah vechamah.**
really pleasant(fem.) and-hot
Really pleasant and warm.

3 **Machar `elekh** ③ **lechamoti ulechami** ④ **le`aruchat chag.**
tomorrow I-will-go to-mother-in-law-my and-to-father-in-law-my for-meal-of festival
Tomorrow I will go to my parents-in-law's for the holiday meal.

4 **`Etzlam tamid na'im, chamim veta'im.**
at-them always pleasant warm and-tasty
It's always pleasant, warm and tasty at theirs.

5 **Ve`eykh `etzlekh?**
and-how by-you(fem.)
And how is it in your family?

6 – **Gam lechamoti veli yesh yechasim chamim me`od …**
also to-mother-in-law-my and-to-me there-is relations hot very
My mother-in-law and I also have a very 'heated' relationship …

7 **`Anachnu lo medabrot kvar shnatayim!**
we not speak(fem.) already two-years
We haven't spoken for two years now!

Notes

③ This is our first example of the future tense: **`elekh** אֵלֵךְ *I will go*. Hebrew has just one future tense, and it is formed according to a very regular pattern. The initial **`alef** א used to form the first-person singular seems natural when we recall that the first-person singular pronoun is **`ani** אֲנִי *I*. As we will see later, the other persons of the future tense have similarly logical forms. As we saw when we studied the past tense, it is not usually necessary to use a pronoun, since the verb form contains enough information to make this clear.

2 – מַמָּשׁ נְעִימָה וְחַמָּה.

3 מָחָר אֵלֵךְ לַחֲמוֹתִי וּלְחָמִי לַאֲרוּחַת חַג.

4 אֶצְלָם תָּמִיד נָעִים, חָמִים וְטָעִים.

5 וְאֵיךְ אֶצְלֵךְ?

6 – גַּם לַחֲמוֹתִי וְלִי יֵשׁ יְחָסִים חַמִּים מְאֹד...

7 אֲנַחְנוּ לֹא מְדַבְּרוֹת כְּבָר שְׁנָתַיִם! □

In the present tense, however, don't forget that the pronoun is always required: **`ani holekh** אֲנִי הוֹלֵךְ *I go.* Notice that the future tense retains two of the three root letters הלך. Although Hebrew verbs follow very regular patterns, as we've seen, sometimes one of the root letters drops out. Don't worry about this too much. The connection between **halakhti** הָלַכְתִּי *I went* and **`elekh** אֵלֵךְ *I will go* is still fairly obvious (unlike the English words 'went' and 'go', which don't share a single letter in common!).

④ **ulechami** וּלְחָמִי *and to my father-in-law's*, 'and-to-father-in-law-my'. In this instance, **ve** וְ *and* becomes **u** וּ. The reason is that otherwise the first two letters of this word would both have the vowel ְ, which is a sound pattern Hebrew dislikes. By the way, we have already seen a different modification of the conjunction וְ in **viYrushalayim** וִירוּשָׁלַיִם *and Jerusalem.* If you look back to the previous lesson, you'll also see that the lesson title is **shloshim vachamishah** שְׁלוֹשִׁים וַחֲמִישָּׁה *thirty-five*, where וְ **ve** has changed to **va** וַ. This may seem confusing, but as we've mentioned before, Israelis do not mind about these niceties. Many of them could not tell you which form should be used in some cases. Someone reading a prayer or official speech will be careful to get it right, but in everyday conversation this is unnecessary and might even seem pretentious. We teach the correct forms here, but please take our word for it that this is not something to lose any sleep over.

Targil rishon – Targem תַּרְגִּיל רִאשׁוֹן – תַּרְגֵּם

❶ תודה, אצלך תמיד נעים, חמים וטעים.
Todah, `etzlekh tamid na'im, chamim veta'im.

❷ חמותי חברמנית ונעימה.
Chamoti chevremanit une'imah.

❸ חמי בן אדם חמים ונעים.
Chami ben `adam chamim vena'im.

❹ מחר אלך ללמוד עברית באולפן.
Machar `elekh lilmod 'ivrit ba`ulpan.

❺ איך היתה ארוחת החג אצלם?
`Eykh haytah `aruchat hachag `etzlam?

Targil sheni – Hashlem תַּרְגִּיל שֵׁנִי – הַשְׁלֵם

❶ My mother-in-law is a good woman but chatty.
Chamoti `ishah tovah `aval patpetanit.
_____ אִשָּׁה טוֹבָה אֲבָל _______ .

❷ We like to barbecue for dinner *(We like meal evening on the fire)*.
`Anachnu `ohavim `aruchat 'erev 'al ha`esh.
אֲנַחְנוּ _____ אֲרוּחַת עֶרֶב __ ___ .

❸ We have a 'heated' relationship – we aren't speaking to each other *(this with this)*!
Yesh lanu yechasim chamim, `anachnu lo medabrim zeh 'im zeh!
יֵשׁ לָנוּ _____ חָמִים, אֲנַחְנוּ לֹא מְדַבְּרִים __ עִם __!

❹ How was the party at Grandfather and Grandmother's?
`Eykh haytah hamesibah `etzel saba vesavta?
___ ____ הַמְסִיבָּה ___ סַבָּא וְסַבְתָּא?

Answers to Exercise 1

❶ Thank you, it's always pleasant, warm and tasty at yours. ❷ My mother-in-law is a good sport and pleasant. ❸ My father-in-law is a warm and pleasant person. ❹ Tomorrow I'm going to study Hebrew at the Ulpan. ❺ How was the holiday dinner at theirs?

❺ I'm going to my parents-in-law's for a party tomorrow evening.
`Elekh lechami ulechamoti limesibah machar ba'erev.
___ לְ___ וּלְ_____ לִמְסִיבָּה ___ בָּעֶרֶב.

Answers to Exercise 2

❶ חֲמוֹתִי - פַּטְפְּטָנִית ❷ - אוֹהֲבִים - עַל הָאֵשׁ ❸ - יְחָסִים - כֵּה - כֵּה
❹ אֵיךְ הָיְתָה - אֵצֶל - ❺ אֵלֵךְ - חָמִי - חֲמוֹתִי - מָחָר -

`aruchat chag אֲרוּחַת חַג the holiday dinner, *like Shabbat dinner, is an important event in the lives of Israeli families, religious and secular alike. Each festival has its traditions and dishes – pomegranates and honey at the Jewish New Year, doughnuts and potato pancakes at Chanukah (which we'll learn more about in lesson 41), special dairy dishes at Shavuot, and so forth. As already noted, Jewish festivals begin in the evening, and holiday dinners may take place in the evening and/or at lunchtime on the day of the festival.*

We wish you, too, a pleasant and peaceful day!

37 Thirty-seventh lesson
(Shi'ur shloshim vesheva')

Dirah chadashah
A new apartment

1 – **Be'od `arba'ah chodashim yiheyeh lanu 'od ben.**
in-more four months there-will-be for-us more son
In four months we will have another son.

2 **Be'od chodesh na'avor ① ledirah gdolah vechadashah.**
in-more month we-will-pass to-apartment large and-new
In a month we will move to a big new apartment.

3 – **Mazal tov! `Aval mah ya'asu hayeladim?**
luck good! but what they-will-do the-children?
Congratulations! But what will the children do?

Notes

① Continuing our study of the future tense, almost every line in this dialogue introduces a new form. As you will see, the future is formed by adding a letter before the root letters and, in some persons, a letter after the root letters, too. We will continue to review these forms throughout the book, so don't worry – you have plenty of time to get the hang of it. The following list shows the full conjugation of the future tense for one of the verbs in the dialogue. We have highlighted in blue the letters added to the root, as well as the letters in the personal pronouns that appear in the corresponding verb form. This correspondence is not found in the third-person singular or plural.

(`ani) e'evor אֶעֱבוֹר (אֲנִי) *I will move*

(`atah) ta'avor תַּעֲבוֹר (אַתָּה) *you will move* (masc.)

37 שִׁעוּר שלוֹשִׁים וְשֶׁבַע

דִירָה חֲדָשָׁה

1 – בְּעוֹד אַרְבָּעָה חוֹדָשִׁים יִהְיֶה לָנוּ עוֹד בֵּן.

2 בְּעוֹד חוֹדֶשׁ נַעֲבוֹר לְדִירָה גדוֹלָה וַחֲדָשָׁה.

3 – מַזָל טוֹב! אֲבָל מַה יַעֲשׂוּ הַיְלָדִים?

(`at) ta'avri תַּעַבְרִי (אַתְּ) *you will move* (fem.)

(hu) ya'avor יַעֲבוֹר (הוּא) *he will move* (line 4)

(hi) ta'avor תַּעֲבוֹר (הִיא) *she will move* (line 4)

(`anachnu) na'avor נַעֲבוֹר (אֲנַחְנוּ) *we will move* (line 2)

(`atem) ta'avru תַּעַבְרוּ (אַתֶּם) *you will move* (masc. pl.)

(`aten) ta'avru תַּעַבְרוּ (אַתֶּן) *you will move* (fem. pl.)

(hem) ya'avru יַעַבְרוּ (הֵם) *they will move* (masc.)

(hen) ya'avru יַעַבְרוּ (הֵן) *they will move* (fem.)

As we've already mentioned, you do not usually have to use the personal pronoun with the future form. However, it is sometimes used for emphasis or clarity – see line 6 of the dialogue for two examples of this.

4 – Dinah ta'avor legan-yeladim chadash veDani ya'avor leveyt-sefer ② chadash.
Dinah she-will-pass to-garden-of-children new and-Dani he-will-pass to-house-of-book new
Dina will move to a new kindergarten and Danny will move to a new school.

5 – Mah ta'aseh `ishtekha?
what she-will-do wife-your
What will your wife do?

6 – Hi tisa' la'avodah bamekhonit va`ani esa' be`otobous.
she she-will-travel to-work in-the-car and-I I-will-travel in-bus
She will travel to work by car and I will travel by bus.

7 – `Atem makirim `et hashkhenim hachadashim?
you(masc. pl.) know [`**et**] *the-neighbours the-new*
Do you know the new neighbours?

8 – 'Od lo. Nazmin `et hashkhenim leqafeh ve'ugot. Yiheyeh beseder!
yet not. we-will-invite [`**et**] *the-neighbours for-coffee and-cakes. it-will-be in-order!*
Not yet. We'll invite the neighbours for coffee and cake. It will be okay!

Notes

② **beyt-sefer** בֵּית-סֵפֶר *school* – literally, 'house-of book'. Some constructs create a noun that has a distinctly different meaning to that of its two constituent nouns. There are hundreds of these in Hebrew. To give just a few examples: **beyt-kneset** בֵּית-כְּנֶסֶת 'house-of assembly' means *synagogue*; **beyt-mishpat** בֵּית-מִשְׁפָּט 'house-of judgement' means *court*; **beyt-qafeh** בֵּית-קָפֶה 'house-of coffee' means *café*; and **beyt-shimush** בֵּית-שִׁימּוּשׁ 'house-of utility' means *toilet*.

4 – דִּינָה תַּעֲבוֹר לְגַן-יְלָדִים חָדָשׁ וְדָנִי יַעֲבוֹר לְבֵית-סֵפֶר חָדָשׁ.

5 – מַה תַּעֲשֶׂה אִשְׁתְּךָ?

6 – הִיא תִּסַּע לַעֲבוֹדָה בַּמְּכוֹנִית וַאֲנִי אֶסַּע בְּאוֹטוֹבּוּס.

7 – אַתֶּם מַכִּירִים אֶת הַשְּׁכֵנִים הַחֲדָשִׁים?

8 – עוֹד לֹא. נַזְמִין אֶת הַשְּׁכֵנִים לְקָפֶה וְעוּגוֹת. יִהְיֶה בְּסֵדֶר! □

Targil rishon – Targem   תַּרְגִּיל רִאשׁוֹן – תַּרְגֵּם

❶ באוקטובר נעבור לדירה חדשה.
Be`oqtober na'avor ledirah chadashah.

❷ בעוד שבוע היא תסע לחברים באילת.
Be'od shavu'a hi tisa' lechaverim be`Eylat.

❸ מה היא תעשה שם אחרי העבודה?
Mah hi ta'aseh sham `acharey ha'avodah?

❹ אולי אתם מכירים את השכנים החדשים שלי?
`Ulay `atem makirim `et hashkhenim hachadashim sheli?

❺ נזמין את הילדים של השכנים למסיבה.
Nazmin `et hayeladim shel hashkhenim limesibah.

Targil sheni – Hashlem   תַּרְגִּיל שֵׁנִי – הַשְׁלֵם

❶ In two months the children will have a beautiful new school.
Be'od chodshayim yiheyeh layeladim beyt sefer chadash veyafeh.

בְּעוֹד _______ ____ לַיְלָדִים ___ ___ חָדָשׁ וְיָפֶה.

❷ In a month Dina will have another brother.
Be'od chodesh leDinah yiheyeh 'od `ach.

____ חוֹדֶשׁ לְדִינָה ____ ___ אָח.

❸ At theirs, everything's new: apartment, car, school, neighbours …
`Etzlam hakol chadash: dirah, mekhonit, beyt sefer, shkhenim …

____ הַכֹּל חָדָשׁ: ____ מְכוֹנִית, ___ סֵפֶר _____…

❹ He will move from Tel Aviv to Jerusalem.
Hu ya'avor miTel Aviv liYrushalayim.

הוּא _____ _תֵּל אָבִיב _יְרוּשָׁלַיִם.

Answers to Exercise 1

❶ In October we will move to a new apartment. ❷ In a week she will travel to [visit] friends in Eilat. ❸ What will she do there after work? ❹ Perhaps you know [`**et**] my new neighbours? ❺ We will invite the neighbours' children to a party.

❺ It will be okay with the new neighbours.
Yiheyeh beseder 'im hashkhenim hachadashim.
____ ____ עִם ______ הַחֲדָשִׁים.

Answers to Exercise 2

❶ - חוֹדְשַׁיִים יִהְיֶה - בֵּית סֵפֶר - ❷ בְּעוֹד - יִהְיֶה עוֹד - ❸ אֶצְלָם - דִּירָה - בֵּית - שְׁכֵנִים ❹ - יַעֲבוֹר אִ - לְ - ❺ יִהְיֶה בְּסֵדֶר - הַשְּׁכֵנִים -

38 **Chodesh** חוֹדֶשׁ month *comes from the same root as* **chadash** חָדָשׁ new. *To understand the connection, it is important to appreciate that the Hebrew calendar, which was already in use in the Biblical period, is essentially a lunar one. In other words, the passage of time is marked by the waxing and waning of the moon. In ancient times, when people observed a new moon, they knew that a new month had arrived. The religious authorities later created a more centralized system, based first on hilltop fires and later on official messengers, to spread the news that the new moon had been sighted. In a purely lunar system, festivals marking specific celebrations can rotate around the entire year. In the Islamic calendar, for example, the fasting month of Ramadan shifts from summer through winter and back, over a period of about 33 years. In Judaism, each festival is closely connected to a particular agricultural season – Sukkot (Feast of Tabernacles) must come in autumn or it would lose much of its meaning – so a way had to be found to reconcile the lunar*

---

38 Thirty-eighth lesson
(Shi'ur shloshim ushmoneh)

Rahitim chadishim ①
Modern furniture

1 – **Machar niqneh ② rahitim chadashim: sapah vekhursa`ot, shulchan vekhis`ot.**
tomorrow we-will-buy furniture(pl.) new: sofa and-armchairs table and-chairs
Tomorrow we will buy new furniture: a sofa and armchairs, a table and chairs.

2 – **Yofi! Matay tachgegu `et chanukat habayit?**
great! when you(masc. pl.)-will-celebrate [**`et**] *dedication-of the-house?*
Great! When will you celebrate the housewarming?

Notes

① **chadishim** חֲדִישִׁים *modern*, *latest*. This word is, of course, related to the more common **chadash** חָדָשׁ *new*. The word *character of the Hebrew calendar with the solar-based seasons. Since each lunar year is almost 11 days shorter than the solar year, the Jewish Sages devised a system whereby in seven out of every 19 years, an extra month is added. The additional month is added after the sixth month* **Adar** אֲדָר *and before the seventh month* **Nisan** נִיסָן *(falling in March or April according to the Gregorian calendar). This additional month is called* **Adar Bet** אֲדָר בֵּית *(***bet***, the second letter of the alphabet, is used here in a numerical sense to mean 'two' or 'second'). In English, the month is referred to as Adar II. The seven leap years are dispersed through each cycle of 19 years according to complex calculations, but the main point is the net result, which ensures consistency in the period when a celebration occurs. Although the Jewish festivals fall on different dates in the Gregorian calendar each year, the range is limited to no more than a month or so.*

---

38 שִׁעוּר שְׁלוֹשִׁים וּשְׁמוֹנֶה

רָהִיטִים חֲדִישִׁים

1 – מָחָר נִקְנֶה רָהִיטִים חֲדָשִׁים: סַפָּה וְכוּרְסָאוֹת, שׁוּלְחָן וְכִסְאוֹת.

2 – יוֹפִי! מָתַי תַּחגְגוּ אֶת חֲנוּכַּת הַבַּיִת?

'atiqim עתיקים *old* or *antique* in line 5 refers to anything that is very old, from furniture to ancient archaeological finds!

② This dialogue provides a further opportunity to study the future tense. In order of appearance, the forms that appear are:

('anachnu) niqneh (אֲנַחנוּ) נִקְנֶה *we will buy* (line 1)

('atem) tachgegu (אַתֶּם) תַּחגְגוּ *you* (masc. plural) *will celebrate* (line 2)

(hem) yagi'u (הֵם) יַגִּיעוּ *they* (masc.) *will arrive* (line 3)

(hu) yiheyeh (הוּא) יִהְיֶה *it* (masc.) *will be* (line 3)

3 – **Ka`asher harahitim yagi'u … sheyiheyeh 'al mah ③ lashevet!**
when the-furniture(pl.) they-will-arrive ... that-there-will-be on what to-sit
When the furniture arrives … so there'll be something to sit on!

4 – **`Eylu rahitim `atem `ohavim?**
which furniture(pl.) you like
What [kind of] furniture do you like?

5 – **Ba'ali `ohev rahitim 'atiqim ve`ani `ohevet rahitim chadishim.**
husband-my likes furniture(pl.) antique and-I like(fem.) furniture modern
My husband likes antique furniture and I like modern furniture.

6 **Yesh 'od be'ayah: kesef.**
there-is another problem: money
There's another problem: money.

7 **Mah shemotze chen be'eynay: yaqar. Mah shezol lo motze chen be'eynay ④.**
what that-finds grace in-eyes-my: expensive. what that-cheap not find grace in-eyes-my.
What I like is expensive. What's cheap – I don't like.

Notes

③ **'al mah lashevet** עַל מָה לָשֶׁבֶת *something to sit on* – literally, 'on what to-sit' ('something on which to sit' would be another way of expressing this in English). So far we have seen **mah** מָה used as an interrogative particle, but here it is used as a relative pronoun.

④ **motze chen be'eynay** מוֹצֵא חֵן בְּעֵינַי 'it finds grace in my eyes' – in other words: *I like it*. This picturesque turn of phrase appears 40 times in the Bible. The verb form **motze** מוֹצֵא can be changed into another tense as required. Similarly,

3 – כַּאֲשֶׁר הָרָהִיטִים יַגִּיעוּ... שֶׁיִּהְיֶה עַל מַה לָשֶׁבֶת!

4 – אֵילוּ רָהִיטִים אַתֶּם אוֹהֲבִים?

5 – בַּעֲלִי אוֹהֵב רָהִיטִים עַתִּיקִים וַאֲנִי אוֹהֶבֶת רָהִיטִים חֲדִישִׁים.

6 יֵשׁ עוֹד בְּעָיָה: כֶּסֶף.

7 מַה שֶּׁמּוֹצֵא חֵן בְּעֵינַי: יָקָר. מָה שֶׁזּוֹל לֹא מוֹצֵא חֵן בְּעֵינַי...

be'eynay בְּעֵינַי *in my eyes* can be adapted for any other grammatical person. Here is an example where both the tense and the person have been changed: **harahitim matzu chen be'eyneynu**. הָרָהִיטִים מָצְאוּ חֵן בְּעֵינֵינוּ 'the furniture found favour in our eyes', that is to say: *we liked the furniture*. Notice that what is the object in English is the subject in the Hebrew construction ('the furniture pleases me'), so since רָהִיטִים *furniture* is plural in Hebrew, the verb form also appears in the third-person plural.

Targil rishon – Targem תַּרְגִּיל רִאשׁוֹן – תַּרְגֵּם

❶ יש לכם רהיטים חדישים?
Yesh lakhem rahitim chadishim?

❷ יש לי בעיה. מה שמוצא חן בעיני: יקר.
Yesh li be'ayah. Mah shemotze chen be'eynay: yaqar.

❸ הרהיטים יגיעו בעוד חודש.
Harahitim yagi'u be'od chodesh.

❹ מתי תחגגו את חנוכת בית-הספר החדש?
Matay tachgegu `et chanukat beyt-hasefer hachadash?

❺ דליה אוהבת רק רהיטים עתיקים מאירופה.
Dalyah `ohevet raq rahitim 'atiqim me`Eyropah.

Targil sheni – Hashlem תַּרְגִּיל שֵׁנִי – הַשְׁלֵם

❶ Tomorrow we will buy a sofa and armchairs.
Machar niqneh sapah vekhursa`ot.

מָחָר נִקְנֶה ___ ________ .

❷ I don't like the old table any more.
Hashulchan ha'atiq lo motze chen be'eynay.

הַשּׁוּלְחָן הָעַתִּיק לֹא ____ __ _____ .

❸ The modern furniture will arrive at the new apartment.
Harahitim hachadishim yagi'u ladirah hachadashah.

הָרָהִיטִים הַ______ _____ לַדִּירָה הַ____ .

❹ The computer is a good buy *(cheap)*, but [it's] not the latest [model].
Hamachshev zol `aval lo chadish.

הַמַּחְשֵׁב ___ אֲבָל לֹא ____ .

Answers to Exercise 1

❶ Do you have the latest furniture? ❷ I have a problem. What I like is expensive. ❸ The furniture will arrive in a month. ❹ When will you celebrate the opening *(dedication)* of the new school? ❺ Dalya only likes antique furniture from Europe.

❺ When the armchairs and chairs *(will)* arrive, there'll be something to sit on.
Ka`asher hakhursa`ot vehakisot yagi'u, yiheyeh 'al mah lashevet.

____ הַכּוּרְסָאוֹת וְהַכִּסְאוֹת יַגִּיעוּ ____ עַל מַה ____ .

Answers to Exercise 2

❶ - סַפָּה וְכוּרְסָאוֹת ❷ - מוֹצֵא חֵן בְּעֵינַי ❸ - חֲדִישִׁים יַגִּיעוּ - חֲדָשָׁה
❹ - כּוֹל - חָדִישׁ ❺ כַּאֲשֶׁר - יִהְיֶה - לָשֶׁבֶת

Chanukat habayit חֲנוּכַּת הַבַּיִת housewarming *(literally, 'dedication-of the-house'). This expression is first seen in Psalm 30:1, referring to the Temple. In modern Hebrew, it is used to refer to a housewarming or to the inauguration of a school, hospital or other public institution.*

39 Thirty-ninth lesson
(Shi'ur shloshim vetesha')

Dirat nofesh
A vacation apartment

1 – **Haqayitz niskor** ① **dirat nofesh, bikhfar** ② **nofesh.**
the-summer we-will-rent apartment-of holiday in-village-of holiday
This summer we will rent a vacation apartment in a holiday village.

2 – **`Atem mishpachah gdolah, hadirah maspiq gdolah bishvilkhem?**
you(masc. pl.) family big the-apartment enough big for-you
You're a large family, will the apartment be big enough for you?

3 – **Ken. Yesh bah `arba'ah chadarim, mitbach gadol vegam mirpeset yafah.**
yes there-is in-it four rooms kitchen large and-also balcony pretty
Yes. It has four rooms, a large kitchen and also a pretty balcony.

4 – **`Atem tihyu bechof hayam?**
you you(masc. pl.)-will-be on-coast-of the-sea
Will you be on the beach?

5 – **Ken. `Anachnu `ohavim yam vechol.**
yes we like sea and-sand
Yes. We like the sea and sand.

דִּירַת נוֹפֶשׁ

1 – הַקַּיִץ נִשְׂכּוֹר דִּירַת נוֹפֶשׁ, בִּכְפַר נוֹפֶשׁ.

2 – אַתֶּם מִשְׁפָּחָה גְּדוֹלָה, הַדִּירָה מַסְפִּיק גְּדוֹלָה בִּשְׁבִילְכֶם?

3 – כֵּן. יֵשׁ בָּהּ אַרְבָּעָה חֲדָרִים, מִטְבָּח גָּדוֹל וְגַם מִרְפֶּסֶת יָפָה.

4 – אַתֶּם תִּהְיוּ בְּחוֹף הַיָּם?

5 – כֵּן. אֲנַחְנוּ אוֹהֲבִים יָם וְחוֹל.

Notes

① We continue our exploration of the future tense. Hopefully it's getting easier as we progress.

('anachnu) niskor (אֲנַחְנוּ) נִשְׂכּוֹר *we will rent* (line 1)

('atem) tihyu (אַתֶּם) תִּהְיוּ *you* (m. pl.) *will be* (line 4)

('atem) tevalu (אַתֶּם) תְּבַלּוּ *you* (m. pl.) *will spend [time]* (line 7)

② **bikhfar** בִּכְפָר *in a village*. Notice that the **be** בְּ becomes **bi** בִּ when the following consonant is not followed by a vowel (i.e. is marked with the ְ symbol, known as the **shva'**). The first letter **k** כּ of the word **kfar** כְּפָר *village* becomes **kh** כ when it follows the preposition בְּ.

6 Yesh sham gam `oniyot vetzolelet zekhukhit latayarim.
there-are there also ships and-submarine glass for-the-tourists
There are also ships there and a glass-domed submarine for the tourists.

7 – Tevalu ③ bane'imim!
you(masc. pl.)-will-spend-time in-pleasantness
Have a good time!

8 – Todah. Gam `atem.
thanks. also you(masc.pl.)
Thanks. You too.

Notes

③ **tevalu** תְּבַלּוּ *Have a good time!* Literally, 'you (pl.)-will-spend-time'. The root בלה can mean *to wear out*, but it also means ▸

Targil rishon – Targem תַּרְגִּיל רִאשׁוֹן – תַּרְגֵּם

❶ בקיץ נשכור מכונית בנתניה.
Baqayitz niskor mekhonit biNetanyah.

❷ באילת יש צוללת זכוכית לתיירים.
Be`Eylat yesh tzolelet zekhukhit latayarim.

❸ תבלו בנעימים בחוף הים!
Tevalu bane'imim bechof hayam!

❹ איפה אתם תהיו בקיץ?
`Eyfoh `atem tihyu baqayitz?

❺ בדירה ארבעה חדרים, מטבח ומרפסת.
Badirah `arba'ah chadarim, mitbach umirpeset.

6 יֵשׁ שָׁם גַּם אוֹנִיּוֹת וְצוֹלֶלֶת זְכוּכִית לַתַּיָּרִים.

7 – תְּבַלּוּ בַּנְּעִימִים!

8 – תּוֹדָה. גַּם אַתֶּם.

□

to spend time, almost always with the positive connotation of having a good time. In line 7, even if the speaker had just said **tevalu** תְּבַלּוּ, this meaning would still be clear. By the way, notice that in English we use the imperative in this context, whereas Hebrew uses the future. The future tense in Hebrew can convey a sense of a wish or hope, but the imperative is only used for commands.

Answers to Exercise 1

❶ In the summer, we will rent a car in Netanya. ❷ In Eilat there is a glass submarine for the tourists. ❸ Have a good time at the beach! ❹ Where will you be *(in)* this summer? ❺ In the apartment [there are] four rooms, a kitchen and a balcony.

Targil sheni – Hashlem תַּרְגִּיל שֵׁנִי – הַשְׁלֵם

❶ Will you be in a holiday village in the summer?
`Atem tihyu bikhfar nofesh baqayitz?

אַתֶּם תִּהְיוּ ____ ____ בַּקַּיִץ?

❷ The apartment isn't [too] small for you*(masc. pl.)*?
Hadirah lo qtanah bishvilkhem?

____ לֹא קְטַנָּה _______?

❸ Have *(You[masc. pl.]-will-have)* a good time on holiday!
Tevalu bane'imim bachofesh!

____ _______ בַּחוֹפֶשׁ!

❹ In the summer I like to sit on the balcony.
Baqayitz `ani `ohevet lashevet bamirpeset.

____ אֲנִי אוֹהֶבֶת ____ בַּ____ בְּ_____ .

❺ He needs a large kitchen because he has four children.
Hu tzarikh mitbach gadol ki yesh lo `arba'ah yeladim.

הוּא צָרִיךְ ____ גָּדוֹל כִּי יֵשׁ לוֹ _____ _____ .

Kfar nofesh **כְּפָר נוֹפֶשׁ** holiday village. *The term 'holiday village' conjures up images of palm trees, bronzed men and pretty girls in bikinis, but let's see if we can add a little soul to the mixture.* **Nofesh** **נוֹפֶשׁ** *means* holiday *or* vacation *in modern Hebrew. It is related to the word* **nefesh** **נֶפֶשׁ** soul*; the root of both of these words conveys the sense of breathing – including getting your breath back. In the Bible (Exodus 31:17), we read that God* **nafash** **נָפַשׁ** rested *on the seventh day of Creation. The root letters* **נפשׁ** *can be seen in all three words, and certainly a vacation is an ideal way to take a breather and maybe even do some soulsearching.*

Answers to Exercise 2

❶ - בִּכְפָר נוֹפֶשׁ - ❷ הַדִּירָה - בִּשְׁבִילְכֶם ❸ תְּבַלּוּ בַּנְּעִימִים - ❹ בַּקַּיִץ - לָשֶׁבֶת - מִרְפֶּסֶת ❺ - מִטְבָּח - אַרְבָּעָה יְלָדִים

Shall we take a break? You've certainly earned yourself a little **nofesh** נוֹפֶשׁ.

40 Fortieth lesson (Shi'ur arba'im)

Bashanah haba`ah ①
Next year

1 – **Mah shlom ② hayeladim shelakhem?**
what peace-of the-children of-you(pl.)
How are your children?

2 – **Hayeladim shelanu? Hem kvar lo yeladim!**
the-children of-us? they already not children!
Our children? They aren't children anymore!

3 **Dani ben shloshim. Bashanah haba`ah, hu yelamed ③ handasat machshevim baTekhniyon beCheyfah.**
Dani son-of thirty. in-the-year the-coming he he-will-teach engineering-of computers in-the-Technion in-Haifa.
Danny is thirty. Next year he will teach computer engineering at the Technion in Haifa.

4 **Shiri bat 'esrim vechamesh. Hi tilmad shanah revi'it refu`ah ba`universitah ha'ivrit biYrushalayim.**
Shiri daughter-of twenty and-five. she she-will-study year fourth medicine in-university the-Hebrew in-Jerusalem.
Shiri is twenty-five. She will be in her fourth year of medical school at the Hebrew University of Jerusalem.

Notes

① **bashanah haba`ah** בַּשָּׁנָה הַבָּאָה *next year* (literally, 'the year coming'). **Haba`ah** is in the feminine singular because **shanah** is a feminine singular noun. The plural is **bashanim haba`ot** בַּשָּׁנִים הַבָּאוֹת *the coming years* (**shanim** is a feminine plural, even though it has what looks like a masculine plural ▸

40 שִׁעוּר אַרְבָּעִים

בַּשָּׁנָה הַבָּאָה

1 – מַה שְׁלוֹם הַיְלָדִים שֶׁלָּכֶם?

2 – הַיְלָדִים שֶׁלָּנוּ? הֵם כְּבָר לֹא יְלָדִים!

3 דָּנִי בֶּן שְׁלוֹשִׁים. בַּשָּׁנָה הַבָּאָה הוּא יְלַמֵּד הַנְדָּסַת מַחְשְׁבִים בַּטֶּכְנִיּוֹן בְּחֵיפָה.

4 שִׁירִי בַּת עֶשְׂרִים וְחָמֵשׁ. הִיא תִּלְמַד שָׁנָה רְבִיעִית רְפוּאָה בָּאוּנִיבֶרְסִיטָה הָעִבְרִית בִּירוּשָׁלַיִם.

ending; there are a handful of nouns that follow this pattern). Further examples: **bachodesh haba** בַּחוֹדֶשׁ הַבָּא *next month*; **bachodashim habaim** בַּחוֹדָשִׁים הַבָּאִים *the coming months.*

② **Mah shlom … ? …** מַה שְׁלוֹם *How is/are …?* (literally, 'What peace-of …'). **Shalom** שָׁלוֹם appears here in a shortened form, as is often the case when a word shifts from the absolute state to the construct state (**smikhut**). **Shlom** may be followed by a personal pronoun suffix, as in lesson 3, or by a noun, as here.

③ Some more future forms (the characteristic consonants of each grammatical person are in blue: lesson 37, note 1.

(hu) yelamed יְלַמֵּד (הוּא) *he will teach* (line 3)

(hi) tilmad תִּלְמַד (הִיא) *she will study* (line 4)

(hu) yilmad יִלְמַד (הוּא) *he will study* (line 5)

(hem) yavo`u יָבוֹאוּ (הֵם) *they* (masc.) *will come* (line 7)

5 Roni ben 'esrim. Hu yilmad shanah rishonah mishpatim be`universitat Be`er Sheva'.
Roni son-of twenty. he he-will-study year first law in-university-of Beersheva.
Ronnie is twenty. He will be in his first year of law school at Beersheva University.

6 – Nitpardah hachavilah.
fell-apart the-package
The family has broken up.

7 – Nakhon, `aval hem yavo`u habaytah ④ lesof shavu'a.
correct, but they they(masc.)-will-come the-house-to for-end-of week
That's right, but they'll come home for the weekend.

Targil rishon – Targem תַּרְגִּיל רִאשׁוֹן – תַּרְגֵּם

❶ בשנה הבאה, היא תלמד רפואה.
Bashanah haba`ah, hi tilmad refu`ah.

❷ בשנה הבאה, נתי ילמד משפטים.
Bashanah haba`ah, Nati yilmad mishpatim.

❸ מה שלום שירי ורוני?
Mah shlom Shiri veRoni?

❹ הוא ילמד ג׳יאוגרפיה בבית-ספר.
Hu yelamed ge`ografyah beveyt-sefer.

❺ בסוף השבוע, ליאור ושירי יבואו הביתה.
Besof hashavu'a, Li`or veShiri yavo`u habaytah.

5 רוֹנִי בֶּן עֶשְׂרִים. הוּא יִלְמַד שָׁנָה רִאשׁוֹנָה מִשְׁפָּטִים בְּאוּנִיבֶרְסִיטַת בְּאֵר שֶׁבַע.

6 – נִתְפָּרְדָה הַחֲבִילָה.

7 – נָכוֹן, אֲבָל הֵם יָבוֹאוּ הַבַּיְתָה לְסוֹף שָׁבוּעַ. □

Notes

④ **habaytah** הַבַּיְתָה *home*. The word **bayit** בַּיִת *house* here appears with a **he** ה both at the beginning and the end. The first is the definite article, because we are speaking not of any house, but the person's specific home. The second is a suffix used to indicate movement towards a place. Similarly, **Yerushalaymah** יְרוּשָׁלַיְמָה means *to Jerusalem* or *towards Jerusalem*.

Answers to Exercise 1

❶ Next year, she will study medicine. ❷ Next year, Nati will study law. ❸ How are Shiri and Ronnie? ❹ He will teach geography in a school. ❺ At the weekend, Lior and Shiri will come home.

Targil sheni – Hashlem תַּרְגִּיל שֵׁנִי – הַשְׁלֵם

❶ Tel Aviv University is the largest in the country *(in Israel)*.
`Universitat Tel Aviv hagdolah beyoter ba`aretz.

_________ תֵּל אָבִיב ______ _____ בָּאָרֶץ.

❷ This is the fourth year that he will teach law at Beersheva.
Zot hashanah harevi'it shehu yelamed mishpatim beBeer Sheva'.

___ הַשָּׁנָה _______ שֶׁהוּא ____ מִשְׁפָּטִים ____ ___ .

❸ Gadi will study at the university and Nitza will study at the Technion.
Gadi yilmad ba`universitah veNitzah tilmad baTekhnyion.

גָּדִי ____ בַּ_________ וְנִיצָה ____ בַּ______ .

❹ Well, I see that your children aren't children anymore.
Nu, ani ro`eh shehayeladim shelakhem kvar lo yeladim.

__ אֲנִי ____ שֶׁהַיְּלָדִים ____ ___ __ יְלָדִים.

❺ The family broke up *(The package fell apart)*, what a pity!
Hachivalah nitpardah, chaval!

______ ______, חֲבָל!

In 1913, a group of German Jews envisioned the opening of a technological institute in Haifa. They assumed that the teaching would be conducted in German, as they didn't think that Hebrew was capable of conveying technical subjects. The future teachers and students strongly disagreed, and when the Technion opened ten years later, the courses were given in Hebrew. When necessary, new words for modern scientific and technological concepts were formed from Hebrew roots.

In 1925, when Chaim Weizmann (who later became Israel's first president) opened the Hebrew University of Jerusalem, he declared:

Answers to Exercise 2

❶ אוּנִיבֶרְסִיטַת - הַגְּדוֹלָה בְּיוֹתֵר - ❷ כִּתּוֹת - הָרְבִיעִית - יְלַמֵּד - בַּבֹּקֶר
שֶׁבַע ❸ - יְלַמֵּד - אוּנִיבֶרְסִיטָה - תְּלַמֵּד - טֶכְנִיּוֹן ❹ נוּ - רוֹצֶה - שֶׁלָּכֶם כְּבָר
לָכֵן - ❺ הַחֲבִילָה נִתְפָּרְדָה -

'Inside these halls, all religions and races will, I hope, be united in the grand task of the search for truth ...' Among the distinguished guests at the inaugural ceremony were Freud, Einstein and the poet Bialik. In this case, however, the founders were in no doubt that the courses, even on scientific subjects, should be in Hebrew, as reflected in the name of the institution.

Chaim Weizmann served as the President of Israel from the nation's independence in 1948 until his death in 1952. His name is perpetuated in the Chaim Weizmann Institute in Rehovot, which specializes in teaching chemistry and biology.

Ben Gurion University of the Negev in Beersheva was founded in 1968 to help advance the development of Israel's arid southern region. Its precursor, the Institute for Arid Zone Research, was established in 1957, focusing in particular on the methods used by the ancient Nabataeans 2,000 years earlier to cultivate the desert. The institute soon extended its interest to such subjects as the desalination of saltwater, the conservation of rainwater, solar energy, and even the influence of the desert on the human psyche.

41 Forty-first lesson
(Shi'ur arba'im ve`achat)

Hame'il ①
The coat

1 – **`Ani `atus** ② ③ **bachoref liYrushalayim.**
I I-will-fly in-the-winter to-Jerusalem
I will fly to Jerusalem this winter.

2 – **Nehedar! `At tatusi liYrushalayim lechag hamolad** ④**?**
wonderful! you you(fem.)-will-fly to-Jerusalem for-festival-of the-birth?
Wonderful! Will you go to Jerusalem for Christmas?

3 – **Lo, leChanukah.**
no for-Chanukah
No, for Chanukah.

Notes

① **me'il** מְעִיל *coat*. A coat is something we put over our clothes, and inside this word you may be able to identfiy **'al** עַל *on, over* (as in the English word 'overcoat'). The מ is a prefix used to form words for various objects, such as **ma'alit** מַעֲלִית *lift, elevator* and **ma'alah** מַעֲלָה *step* (in a staircase). In previous lessons, we've seen **machshev** מַחְשֵׁב *computer*, **mikhtav** מִכְתָב *letter* (the kind you send in the mail), **mischaq** מִשְׂחָק *game* and **mitbach** מִטְבָּח *kitchen*.

② Back to the future again, so let's make the most of it! Here are the examples of the future tense that appear in this dialogue, organized according to grammatical person:

(`ani) `atus אָטוּס (אֲנִי) *I will fly* (line 1)

(`ani) `eqah אֶקַח (אֲנִי) *I will take* (line 6)

(`at) tatusi תָטוּסִי (אַת) *you* (fem.) *will fly* (line 2)

הַמְּעִיל

1 – אֲנִי אָטוּס בַּחוֹרֶף לִירוּשָׁלַיִם.

2 – נֶהְדָר! אַת תָּטוּסִי לִירוּשָׁלַיִם לְחַג הַמּוֹלָד?

3 – לֹא. לַחֲנוּכָּה.

(`at) tiqchi (אַתְּ) תִּקְחִי *you* (fem.) *will take* (line 8)

(hu) yiheyeh (הוּא) יִהְיֶה *it* (masc.) *will be* (line 4)

Lines 6 and 7 together provide examples of all three basic tenses: present, **rotzeh** רוֹצֶה; future, **`eqah** אֶקַח; past, **hishtaga'ta** הִשְׁתַּגַּעְתָּ. In line 6, note that while in English we say 'You want me to take a coat?' the Hebrew construction is 'You want that I will take a coat?', mixing the present and future tense. Line 8 includes three verb forms: present tense, **yoda'at** יוֹדַעַת; future, **tiqchi** תִּקְחִי and a feminine singular imperative, **qchi** קְחִי.

③ **`atus** אָטוּס *I will fly*. In English, we do not always use a specific verb to describe the form of transport we are using to get from one place to another. We may simply say 'I'm going to Israel for Chanukah'. Hebrew tends to be more precise:

`esa' אֶסַּע *I will travel* (e.g. by bus, car, train or bicycle)

`elekh אֵלֵךְ *I will walk* (go on foot)

`atus אָטוּס *I will fly*

④ **molad** מוֹלָד *birth*. In lesson 32, we learned **huledet** הוּלֶדֶת *birth*. Both words come from the same root, ילד. However, **huledet** is the word used more often, whereas **molad** appears only in very specific contexts, such as **chag hamolad** חַג הַמּוֹלָד *festival-of the-birth*, i.e. *Christmas*.

4 – Chag hamolad `o Chanukah, bechodesh detzember yiheyeh qar me`od biYrushalayim!
Christmas or Chanukah, in-month-of December it(masc.)-will-be cold very in-Jerusalem
Christmas or Chanukah, in December it will be very cold in Jerusalem!

5 Qchi ⑤ me'il choref, `afilu parvah.
take coat-of winter even fur
Take a winter coat, even a fur coat.

6 – `Atah rotzeh she`eqah parvah?
you want that-I-will-take fur
You want me to take a fur coat?

7 Hishtaga'ta ⑥? Yisrael `eretz ⑦ chamah.
you(masc.)-have-gone-crazy? Israel land hot.
Have you gone crazy? Israel is a hot country.

8 – `At yoda'at mah? `Im lo tiqchi me'il, qchi kesef liqnot sham me'il ...
you know what? if not you(fem.)-will-take coat take money to-buy there coat
You know what? If you won't take a coat, take money to buy one there …

Notes

⑤ **qchi** קְחִי *take*. Here is our first imperative (i.e. command). The three imperative forms of this verb are **qach** קַח (masc. sing.), **qchi** קְחִי (fem. sing.) and **qchu** קְחוּ (pl.), all of which translate into English as *Take!*

⑥ **hishtaga'ta** הִשְׁתַּגַּעְתָּ *you have gone crazy*. This single Hebrew verb represents the whole phrase 'to go crazy'.

⑦ **`eretz** אֶרֶץ *land, earth, country*. In lesson 25 we learned the phrase **la`aretz** לָאָרֶץ *to the Land, to Israel*. The difference in the vowel under the א is due to the presence of the article **ha** ה in the latter instance.

4 – חַג הַמּוֹלָד אוֹ חֲנוּכָּה, בְּחוֹדֶשׁ דֶּצֶמְבֶּר יִהְיֶה קַר מְאֹד בִּירוּשָׁלַיִם!

5 קְחִי מְעִיל חוֹרֶף, אֲפִילוּ פַּרְוָה.

6 – אַתָּה רוֹצֶה שֶׁאֶקַּח פַּרְוָה?

7 הִשְׁתַּגַּעְתָּ? יִשְׂרָאֵל אֶרֶץ חַמָּה.

8 – אַתְּ יוֹדַעַת מַה? אִם לֹא תִקְחִי מְעִיל, קְחִי כֶּסֶף לִקְנוֹת שָׁם מְעִיל... □

Targil rishon – Targem תַּרְגִּיל רִאשׁוֹן – תַּרְגֵּם

❶ בחנוכה אטוס עם בעלי לנופש.
BeChanukah `atus 'im ba'ali lenofesh.

❷ שם קר מאוד בחורף וחם מאוד בקיץ.
Sham qar me`od bachoref vecham me`od baqayitz.

❸ השתגעת? אתה רוצה שאקח מעיל חורף לאילת?
Hishtaga'ta? `Atah rotzeh she`eqah me'il choref leEylat?

❹ בחבילה הזאת יש הפתעה: מתנה יקרה.
Bachavilah hazot yesh hafta'ah: matanah yeqarah.

❺ אם תטוסי לחוץ לארץ, קחי את הפרוה.
`Im tatusi lechutz la`aretz, qchi `et haparvah.

Targil sheni – Hashlem תַּרְגִּיל שֵׁנִי – הַשְׁלֵם

❶ Many tourists will come from abroad to Jerusalem for Christmas.
Harbeh tayarim michutz la`aretz yavo`u liYrushalayim lechag hamolad.

הַרְבֵּה תַּיָּרִים ____ ____ _____ לִירוּשָׁלַיִם לְ__ _____ .

❷ There's a strike at the airport. When will I leave *(fly)*?
Yesh shvitah bisdeh hate'ufah. Matay `atus?

יֵשׁ _____ בְּ___ ______. מָתַי ____?

❸ Take*(fem. sing.)* money to buy hummus, tahini, falafel and coffee.
Qchi kesef liqnot chumus, tchinah, falafel veqafeh.

___ כֶּסֶף לִקְנוֹת _____, _____, _____ וְקָפֶה.

❹ She doesn't know what's in the package.
Hi lo yoda'at mah yesh bachavilah.

הִיא __ _____ מַה יֵּשׁ בַּ_____ .

Answers to Exercise 1

❶ At Chanukah I will go *(fly)* on holiday with my husband. ❷ It is very cold there in winter and very hot in summer. ❸ Have you gone crazy? You want me to take a winter coat to Eilat? ❹ There is a surprise in this package: an expensive present. ❺ If you go *(fly)* abroad, take the fur coat.

❺ Nethanel really likes the festival of Chanukah.
Netanel `ohev me`od `et chag haChanukah.

נְתַנְאֵל אוֹהֵב מְאוֹד אֶת __ ______ .

Answers to Exercise 2

❶ - מִחוּץ לָאָרֶץ יָבוֹאוּ - חַג הַמּוֹלָד ❷ - שְׁבִיתָה - שְׂדֵה הַתְּעוּפָה - אָטוּס
❸ קְחִי - חוּמוּס טְחִינָה פָּלָאפֶל - ❹ - לֹא יוֹדַעַת - חֲבִילָה ❺ - חַג הַחֲנוּכָּה

42 **Chanukah** חֲנוּכָּה dedication. *This festival (which is also spelled* Hannukah *in English) falls in December and lasts eight days. Chanukah commemorates the victory of the Maccabee family over the Syrian King Antiochus IV in 165 BCE. Antiochus sought to impose paganism on the Jews, turning the Temple into a place of worship for his gods and defiling the sacred oil used to light the seven-branch* **menorah** מְנוֹרָה candelabrum. *The story goes that after this desecrecation, the Jews found only a single small container of oil that remained pure. Although there was only enough for one day, miraculously it lasted for eight days – enough to keep the* **menorah** burning.

Today, families gather around a nine-branched candelabrum called a **hanukiyah** חֲנוּכִּיָּה *(many people outside of Israel speak*

---

42 Forty-second lesson
(Shi'ur arba'im ushtayim)

חֲזָרָה Chazarah – Review

You've reached the halfway point of your studies. Now that you've seen the present, past and future tense, your communication possibilities in Hebrew are three-dimensional!

1 The future tense

This review should help reinforce your grasp of the future tense. Before we start, remember that when conjugating Hebrew verbs, we usually begin from the root (generally consisting of three letters), rather than the infinitive. The basic principle for forming the future tense involves adding a letter before the root, and in some cases after the root, representing the different persons. The following shows the pattern (the three dashes represent the three root letters).

Singular

1st pers. masc./fem.	א - - -	אֲנִי
2nd pers. masc.	ת - - -	אַתָּה
2nd pers. fem.	ת - - - י	אַתְּ
3rd pers. masc.	י - - -	הוּא
3rd pers. fem.	ת - - -	הִיא

of 'lighting the menorah', but this is inaccurate). Eight branches each hold a candle commemorating one of the eight days of the miracle, while the ninth carries the **shamash** שַׁמָשׁ servant, *which is used to light the others. One candle (and the* shamash*) is lit on the first night, another on the next, and so on, until on the last night all nine candles burn in the windows of homes throughout Israel. In recent years, large electric* **hanukiyot** *have become popular in towns around Israel (and abroad).*

The story behind the conversation in this lesson is not unusual. Many tourists imagine that all of Israel is hot all year round. In reality, it can be very cold in winter, particularly in Jerusalem and other hilly areas. Occasionally, it even snows in the hills.

---

42 שִׁעוּר אַרְבָּעִים וּשְׁתַּיִם

Plural

1st pers. masc./fem.	נ - - -	אֲנַחְנוּ
2nd pers. masc.	ת - - - וּ	אַתֶּם
2nd pers. fem.	ת - - - וּ	אַתֶּן
3rd pers. masc.	י - - - וּ	הֵם
3rd pers. fem.	י - - - וּ	הֵן

• Now let's apply this pattern to the root למד *to learn* (an appropriate example!):

(`ani) `elmad	אֶלְמַד	(אֲנִי)	*I will learn*
(`atah) tilmad	תִּלְמַד	(אַתָּה)	*you will learn* (masc. sing.)
(`at) tilmedi	תִּלְמְדִי	(אַתְּ)	*you will learn* (fem. sing.)
(hu) yilmad	יִלְמַד	(הוּא)	*he will learn*
(hi) tilmad	תִּלְמַד	(הִיא)	*she will learn*
(`anachnu) nilmad	נִלְמַד	(אֲנַחְנוּ)	*we will learn*
(`atem) tilmedu	תִּלְמְדוּ	(אַתֶּם)	*you will learn* (masc. pl.)
(`aten) tilmedu	תִּלְמְדוּ	(אַתֶּן)	*you will learn* (fem. pl.)

(hem) yilmedu יִלְמְדוּ (הֵם) *they will learn* (masc.)
(hen) yilmedu יִלְמְדוּ (הֵן) *they will learn* (fem.)

Note that the letters used are the same for each person, even when there are distinct masculine and feminine forms: א for *I*, ת for *you*, י for *he*, *she*, *it* and *they*, and נ for *we*.

However, the vowels that accompany these letters vary from one verb to another. For example: in **`atah telekh** אַתָּה תֵּלֵךְ *you will go* (masc. sing.), the vowel under the ת of the verb is **e** ֵ , whereas in **`atah tilmad** אַתָּה תִּלְמַד *you will learn*, the vowel is **i**, and in **`atah ta'aseh** אַתָּה תַּעֲשֶׂה *you will do*, the vowel is **a**. The best way to learn which vowel is used is simply through practice.

• Another example, this time using the root עשה *to do*, which ends in the letter ה. In the future tense, the ה remains, except in those persons where י or וּ is added after the root. In these cases, leaving the ה would produce a very difficult combination to pronounce.

(`ani) `e'eseh אֶעֱשֶׂה (אֲנִי) *I will do*
(`atah) ta'aseh תַּעֲשֶׂה (אַתָּה) *you will do* (masc. sing.)
(`at) ta'asi תַּעֲשִׂי (אַתְּ) *you will do* (fem. sing.)
(hu) ya'aseh יַעֲשֶׂה (הוּא) *he will do*
(hi) ta'aseh תַּעֲשֶׂה (הִיא) *she will do*
(`anachnu) na'aseh נַעֲשֶׂה (אֲנַחְנוּ) *we will do*
(`atem) ta'asu תַּעֲשׂוּ (אַתֶּם) *you will do* (masc. pl.)
(`aten) ta'asu תַּעֲשׂוּ (אַתֶּן) *you will do* (fem. pl.)
(hem) ya'asu יַעֲשׂוּ (הֵם) *they will do* (masc.)
(hen) ya'asu יַעֲשׂוּ (הֵן) *they will do* (fem.)

• Let's take the opportunity to conjugate the verb היה *to be*. This verb, which also has ה as its third root letter, follows the same pattern as עשה *to do*:

(`ani) `ehyeh אֶהְיֶה (אֲנִי) *I will be*
(`atah) tihyeh תִּהְיֶה (אַתָּה) *you will be* (masc. sing.)

(`at) tihyi	תִּהְיִי	(אַתְּ)	*you will be* (fem. sing.)
(hu) yihyeh	יִהְיֶה	(הוּא)	*he will be*
(hi) tihyeh	תִּהְיֶה	(הִיא)	*she will be*
(`anachnu) nihyeh	נִהְיֶה	(אֲנַחְנוּ)	*we will be*
(`atem) tihyu	תִּהְיוּ	(אַתֶּם)	*you will be* (masc. pl.)
(`aten) tihyu	תִּהְיוּ	(אַתֶּן)	*you will be* (fem. pl.)
(hem) yihyu	יִהְיוּ	(הֵם)	*they will be* (masc.)
(hen) yihyu	יִהְיוּ	(הֵן)	*they will be* (fem.)

• Our final example, *to travel*, root נסע, loses the נ in all the future tense forms, as do many other verbs beginning with this letter.

(`ani) `esa'	אֶסַּע	(אֲנִי)	*I will travel*
(`atah) tisa'	תִּסַּע	(אַתָּה)	*you will travel* (masc. sing.)
(`at) tis'i	תִּסְעִי	(אַתְּ)	*you will travel* (fem. sing.)
(hu) yisa'	יִסַּע	(הוּא)	*he will travel*
(hi) tisa'	תִּסַּע	(הִיא)	*she will travel*
(`anachnu) nisa'	נִסַּע	(אֲנַחְנוּ)	*we will travel*
(`atem) tis'u	תִּסְעוּ	(אַתֶּם)	*you will travel* (masc. pl.)
(`aten) tis'u	תִּסְעוּ	(אַתֶּן)	*you will travel* (fem. pl.)
(hem) yis'u	יִסְעוּ	(הֵם)	*they will travel* (masc.)
(hen) yis'u	יִסְעוּ	(הֵן)	*they will travel* (fem.)

2 The imperative

The imperative is the shortest form of the verb. This makes sense, because when you're telling someone to do something, you want to do so as snappily as possible. We will learn three forms of the imperative – masculine singular when addressing a male, feminine singular when addressing a female, and a plural form (the same for both genders) when addressing more than one person. To form the imperative, take the appropriate second-person form of the future tense and remove the **t** ת prefix. Let's see how it works.

tiqach	תִקַח	*you will take* (masc.)	→	**qach**	קַח	*Take!* (masc.)
tiqchi	תִקְחִי	*you will take* (fem.)		**qchi**	קְחִי	*Take!* (fem.)
tiqchu	תִקְחוּ	*you will take* (pl.)		**qchu**	קְחוּ	*Take!* (pl.)

tiqneh	תִקְנֶה	*you will buy* (masc.)	→	**qneh**	קְנֵה	*Buy!* (masc.)
tiqni	תִקְנִי	*you will buy* (fem.)		**qni**	קְנִי	*Buy!* (fem.)
tiqnu	תִקְנוּ	*you will buy* (pl.)		**qnu**	קְנוּ	*Buy!* (pl.)

In some cases, it is difficult to predict what vowel will appear in the imperative. We will indicate the vowels whenever an imperative appears, and over time you'll pick them up.

3 Question words

We've already learned quite a few words used to form questions:

\`Eyzeh?	אֵיזֶה?	*Which?* (masc.)
\`Eyzo?	אֵיזוֹ?	*Which?* (fem.)
\`Eykh?	אֵיךְ?	*How?*
\`Eyfoh?	אֵיפֹה?	*Where?*
Kamah?	כַּמָּה?	*How many?*
Ben kamah?	בֶּן כַּמָּה?	*How old?* (masc.)
Bat kamah?	בַּת כַּמָּה?	*How old?* (fem.)
Le\`an?	לְאָן?	*Where to?*
Me\`ayin?	מֵאַיִן?	*From where?*
Mi?	מִי?	*Who?*
Mah?	מַה?	*What?*
Matay?	מָתַי?	*When?*

4 Prepositions

The three prepositions reviewed here are sometimes referred to in Hebrew as 'letters of usage', since each of them consists of just one letter, which is attached to a word as a prefix. The vowel under each of these letters varies depending on the vowel accompanying the first letter of the word it attaches to, and it also changes if the 'letter of usage' is combined with the definite pronoun. As we have mentioned before, this shouldn't worry you too much. Here are the 'letters of usage' we've already learned:

• **b...** בּ *in*. Examples: **beveyt hasefer** בְּבֵית הַסֵּפֶר *in the school*; **beveyt sefer** בְּבֵית סֵפֶר *in a school*; **biYrushalayim** בִּירוּשָׁלַיִם *in Jerusalem*; **be`otobous** בְּאוֹטוֹבּוּס *in a bus*; **ba`otobous** בָּאוֹטוֹבּוּס *in the bus* (the definite article **ha** loses the **h** ה here, and only its vowel remains).

• **l...** ל *to*. Examples: **leYisra`el** לְיִשְׂרָאֵל *to Israel*; **la`aretz** לָאָרֶץ *to the Land* (again, the definite **ha** loses its **h** ה); **liYrushalayim** לִירוּשָׁלַיִם *to Jerusalem*.

• **m...** מ *of, from* (origin). Examples: **mehabayit** מֵהַבַּיִת *from the house*; **meha'avodah** מֵהָעֲבוֹדָה *from work*; **miTel Aviv** מִתֵּל אָבִיב *from Tel Aviv*. Note that when מ appears before the definite article, the article does not contract: **mehabayit** and **meha'avodah**.

5 Useful expressions

Yiheyeh beseder!	יִהְיֶה בְּסֵדֶר!	*It'll be okay/all right!*
... motze chen be'eynay	...מוֹצֵא חֵן בְּעֵינַי	*I like ...* ('... pleases me')
Tevalu bane'imim!	תְּבַלּוּ בַּנְּעִימִים!	*Have a good time!* (plural)
Hishtaga'ta!	הִשְׁתַּגַּעְתָּ!	*You've gone crazy!* (masc.)

❶ בַּקַּיִץ נִסַע עִם הַיְלָדִים לְדִירַת נוֹפֶשׁ בִּכְפַר נוֹפֶשׁ. ❷ בַּשָּׁנָה הַבָּאָה נְתַנאֵל יְלַמֵּד רְפוּאָה בָּאוּנִיבֶרְסִיטָה הָעִבְרִית בִּירוּשָׁלַיִם. ❸ דוֹרִית תִּלְמַד הַנְדָסַת מַחְשְׁבִים בַּטֶכְנִיוֹן בְּחֵיפָה. ❹ בַּחֲנוּכָּה נִהְיֶה אֵצֶל חֲמוֹתִי וְחָמִי בִּירוּשָׁלַיִם. ❺ יִהְיֶה שָׁם קַר מְאוֹד. אֲבָל נִקְנֶה פַּרְוָה חַמָּה וְיִהְיֶה בְּסֵדֶר. ❻ בְּעוֹד אַרְבָּעָה חוֹדָשִׁים נַעֲבוֹר לְדִירָה גדוֹלָה וַחֲדָשָׁה. ❼ אֲנַחְנוּ עוֹד לֹא מַכִּירִים אֶת הַשְּׁכֵנִים הַחֲדָשִׁים, אֲבָל נַזְמִין אוֹתָם לְקָפֶה וְעוּגוֹת. ❽ נִקְנֶה גַּם רָהִיטִים חֲדָשִׁים לַדִּירָה, ❾ אִם נִמְצָא רָהִיטִים שֶׁיִּמְצְאוּ חֵן בְּעֵינֵינוּ וְלֹא יִהְיוּ יְקָרִים. ❿ נַזְמִין אֶת הַמִּשְׁפָּחָה וְהַחֲבֵרִים לַחֲנוּכַּת הַבַּיִת.

Answers

❶ This summer we are going with the children to a vacation apartment in a holiday village. *(in-the-summer we-will-travel with the-children to-apartment-of holiday in-village-of holiday)* ❷ Next year, Nethanel will teach medicine at the Hebrew University of Jerusalem. *(in-the-year the-coming Netanel he-will-teach medicine in-the-university the-Hebrew in-Jerusalem)* ❸ Dorit will study computer engineering at the Technion in Haifa. *(Dorit she-will-study engineering-of computers in-Technion in-Haifa)* ❹ At Chanukah, we will be at my parents-in-law's in Jerusalem. *(in-Chanukah we-will-be at mother-in-law-my and-father-in-law-my in-Jerusalem)* ❺ It will be very cold there. But we'll buy a warm fur coat and it will be okay. *(it-will-be there cold very but we-will-buy fur hot and-it-will-be in-order)* ❻ In four months we will move to a big new apartment. *(in-more four months we-will-move to-apartment big and-new)* ❼ We do not know the new neighbours yet, but we'll invite them for coffee and cake. *(we yet not know* [`**et**] *the-neighbours the-new but we-will-invite* [`**et**]*-them for-coffee and-cakes)* ❽ We will also buy new furniture for the apartment, *(we-will-buy also furniture[pl.] new for-the-apartment)* ❾ if we find furniture that we like and it isn't expensive. *(if we-will-find furniture[pl.] that-they-will-find grace in-eyes-our and-not they-will-be expensive)* ❿ We will invite our family and friends to the housewarming party. *(we-will-invite* [`**et**] *the-family and-the-friends to-the-dedication-of the-house)*

That's the end of this set of lessons! Until the next one: תְּבַלּוּ בַּנְּעִימִים!

43 Forty-third lesson
(Shi'ur arba'im veshalosh)

Fiziqah
Physics

1 **Beshi'ur fiziqah beveyt hasefer, shama'** ① **Yoni mehamoreh shegufim mitrachavim bachom umitkavtzim baqor** ②**.**
in-lesson-of physics in-school-of the-book heard Yoni from-the-teacher that-bodies expand in-the-heat and-contract in-the-cold
In a physics lesson at school, Yoni heard from the teacher that objects expand in heat and contract in cold.

2 **Yoni ratzah** ③ **lihiyot batuach** ④ **shehevin.**
Yoni wanted to-be sure that-he-understood
Yoni wanted to be sure that he had understood.

Notes

① Let's take a look at all the past tense (**'avar** עָבָר *past*) verbs that appear in this lesson:

shama' שָׁמַע *he heard* (line 1)

ratzah רָצָה *he wanted* (line 2)

hevin הֵבִין *he understood* (line 2)

sha`al שָׁאַל *he asked* (line 3)

'anah עָנָה *he replied* (line 3)

Four of these verbs share the same form – the triliteral root letters have the vowel **a** under each of the first two letters. This is the third-person masculine singular of the past tense; it is the usual form in which verbs are presented in dictionaries.

② **mitrachavim** מִתרַחֲבִים *they expand*; **mitkavtzim** מִתכַּוצִים *they contract*: these are examples of reflexive verbs, which are

43 שִׁעוּר אַרְבָּעִים וְשָׁלוֹשׁ

פִיזִיקָה

1 בְּשִׁיעוּר פִיזִיקָה בְּבֵית הַסֵפֶר, שָׁמַע יוֹנִי מֵהַמוֹרֶה שֶׁגוּפִים מִתְרַחֲבִים בַּחוֹם וּמִתְכַּוּצִים בַּקוֹר.

2 יוֹנִי רָצָה לִהְיוֹת בָּטוּחַ שֶׁהֵבִין.

verbs that indicate that the subject performs the action on itself (an idea expressed in English with *myself*, *yourself*, *itself*, etc.) or that the action is reciprocal (expressed in English with *each other*). The reflexive sense in English is often implied rather than included explicitly: for example, we don't need to say *they expand/contract themselves*. In Hebrew, the present tense of reflexive verbs begins with מִת:
mitrachev (masc.) מִתְרַחֵב *(I/you/he) expand(s)*
mitrachevet (fem.) מִתְרַחֶבֶת *(I/you/she) expand(s)*
The complete conjugation of reflexive verbs is given in review lesson 49.

③ **ratzah** רָצָה *he wanted*. Here, the final **h** ה is not the third-person feminine singular past tense ending, but the third root letter of this verb: רצה. In verbs of this type, the **h** also appears in the present tense singular (masculine and feminine): **rotzeh** רוֹצֶה *he wants*, **rotzah** רוֹצָה *she wants*. The feminine singular past tense is **ratztah** רָצְתָה *she wanted*. The verb **'anah** עָנָה *he replied* follows the same pattern.

④ **batuach** בָּטוּחַ *sure*, *certain*. Notice that the חַ at the end of this word is pronounced **ach** and not **cha**, as you might expect. The vowel marks on Hebrew letters are almost always pronounced after the letter, but whenever חַ appears at the end of a word, it is pronounced **ach**.

3 Hu sha`al `et `Oren, `Oren 'anah:
he asked [`**et**] *Oren, Oren replied*
He asked Oren, and Oren replied:

4 – Nakhon me`od. `Eten ⑤ lekha `et hadugmah hatovah beyoter:
correct very. I-will-give you [`**et**] *the-example the-good in-more*
Quite right. I'll give you the best example:

5 Baqayitz cham, hayamim `arukim. Bachoref qar, hayamim qtzarim.
in-the-summer hot the-days long. in-the-winter cold the-days short
In summer it's hot and the days are long. In winter it's cold and the days are short.

Notes

⑤ Note the future tense form: **`eten** אֶתֵּן *I will give.*

Targil rishon – Targem תַּרְגִּיל רִאשׁוֹן – תַּרְגֵּם

❶ מי אמר שגופים מתרחבים בחום ומתכווצים בקור?
Mi `amar shegufim mitrachavim bachom umitkavtzim baqor?

❷ דני לא בטוח שהבין את השעור.
Dani lo batuach shehevin `et hashi'ur.

❸ זאת דוגמה מצוינת.
Zot dugmah metzuyenet.

❹ באיזה חודש הימים הארוכים ביותר?
Be`eyzeh chodesh hayamim ha`arukim beyoter?

❺ בחורף הימים קצרים וקרים.
Bachoref hayamim qtzarim veqarim.

3 הוּא שָׁאַל אֶת אוֹרֶן. אוֹרֶן עָנָה:

4 – נָכוֹן מְאֹד. אֶתֵּן לְךָ אֶת הַדּוּגְמָה הַטּוֹבָה בְּיוֹתֵר:

5 בַּקַּיִץ חַם, הַיָּמִים אֲרוּכִּים. בַּחוֹרֶף קַר, הַיָּמִים קְצָרִים.

פיזיקה

Answers to Exercise 1

❶ Who said that bodies expand in heat and contract in cold? ❷ Danny is not sure that he understood the lesson. ❸ That's an excellent example. ❹ In which month are the longest days? ❺ In winter, the days are short and cold.

Targil sheni – Hashlem תַּרְגִּיל שֵׁנִי – הַשְׁלֵם

❶ The teacher asked Yoni if he had understood the example.
Hamoreh sha`al `et Yoni `im hu hevin `et hadugmah.

_____ ___ אֶת יוֹנִי אִם הוּא ____ אֶת הַ_____ .

❷ You can't be sure that it will be hot tomorrow.
`Atah lo yakhol lihiyot batuach shemachar yiheyeh cham.

אַתָּה __ ____ לִהְיוֹת ____ שֶׁמָּחָר ____ ___ .

❸ In December the days are the shortest in the year.
Bechodesh detzember hayamim haqtzarim beyoter bashanah.

בְּחוֹדֶשׁ _____ הַיָּמִים הַ_____ בְּיוֹתֵר ____ .

❹ He wanted to be a physics teacher at the university.
Hu ratzah lihiyot moreh lefisiqah ba`universitah.

הוּא רָצָה _____ ____ לְפִיסִיקָה בָּאוּנִיבֶרְסִיטָה.

Hamoreh הַמּוֹרֶה, **hamorah** הַמּוֹרָה the teacher *(masc./fem.). Education in Israel is compulsory from ages 5 to 16, and is free up to the age of 18. Israel's multicultural character is reflected in its education system. In the Jewish sector, the state system includes 'state' (non-religious) and 'state-religious' schools, while most ultra-Orthodox children attend separate schools that are also recognized and funded by the state. Israel's Arab, Druze and Bedouin communities have their own state schools, and there are also private schools, mainly affiliated to the Christian communities.*

*All schools teach Hebrew, but in Arab schools the main language of instruction is Arabic, which is an official language alongside Hebrew. New immigrant children (***'olim hadashim** עוֹלִים חֲדָשִׁים new immigrants*) receive intensive instruction in Hebrew in order to enable them to integrate in regular classes. All Jewish schoolchildren study the Bible. However, in non-religious schools the studies focus on the historical and cultural importance*

❺ He writes long letters to a friend in Israel.
Hu kotev mikhtavim `arukim lechaverah ba`aretz.
הוּא כּוֹתֵב ______ ______ לְ____ בַּ___ .

Answers to Exercise 2

❶ הַמּוֹרֶה שָׁאַל - הֵבִין - דּוּגְמָה ❷ - לֹא יָכוֹל - בָּטוּחַ - יִהְיֶה חַם ❸ - דֶּצֶמְבֶּר - קְצָרִים - בַּשָּׁנָה ❹ - לִהְיוֹת מוֹרֶה - ❺ - מִכְתָּבִים אֲרוּכִּים - חֲבֵרָה - אָרֶץ

of the Bible, whereas religious schools examine the Bible as the basis of Jewish faith and religious law.

Israel also has a rich variety of schools concentrating on specific subjects (such as music, the arts or agriculture), as well as schools for children with physical and/or intellectual disabilities, gifted children, and so forth.

After kindergarten, Israeli children begin class **`alef א***, and each subsequent class or grade is named according to the Hebrew letters, as we saw in an earlier lesson. From class* **zayin ז** *through* **tet ט***, children attend junior high school, before moving onto senior high school in class* **yod י***. Junior and senior high schools often operate as separate sections on the same physical premises. At the end of 12th grade (***yod bet י"ב***), Israeli schoolchildren take their matriculation examinations, and many of them also begin to prepare for a gruelling period of military service.*

44 Forty-fourth lesson
(Shi'ur `arba'im ve`arba')

Bdichah `arkhe`ologit
An archaeological joke

1 **`Arkhe`olog yisra`eli vearkhe`olog ① yevani nifgeshu ② bekhenes beynle`umi ③ le`arkhe`ologyah.**
archaeologist Israeli and-archaelogist Greek met at-conference international for-archaeology
An Israeli archaeologist and a Greek archaeologist met at an international archaeology conference.

2 **Ha`arkhe`olog hayevani `amar la`arkhe`olog hayisra`eli:**
the-archaeologist the-Greek said to-the-archaeologist the-Israeli
The Greek archaeologist said to the Israeli archaeologist:

Notes

① **`arkhe`olog** אַרְכֵיאוֹלוֹג. This word shouldn't be too hard to understand, but notice the Hebrew pronunciation – the 'ch' in the English word is pronounced **kh** in Hebrew, and the **g** at the end is hard, as in 'log' and not as in 'lodge'.

By the way, another Hebrew word relating to old things is **'atiq** עַתִּיק *ancient*, which we've already learned. This word is related to the English words *antique* and *ancient* (all these words share a common Latin root: *antiquus*). The Hebrew word **'atiq** עַתִּיק is used both to refer to things that are literally ancient, and also to things that are just very old.

בְּדִיחָה אַרְכֵיאוֹלוֹגִית

1 אַרְכֵיאוֹלוֹג יִשְׂרְאֵלִי וְאַרְכֵיאוֹלוֹג יְוָנִי נִפְגְּשׁוּ בְּכֶנֶס בֵּינְלְאוּמִי לְאַרְכֵיאוֹלוֹגְיָה.

2 הָאַרְכֵיאוֹלוֹג הַיְּוָנִי אָמַר לָאַרְכֵיאוֹלוֹג הַיִּשְׂרְאֵלִי:

② Here is a summary of the past tense forms in this lesson:

nifgeshu נִפְגְּשׁוּ *they met (each other)* (line 1)

`amar אָמַר *he said* (lines 2 and 4)

matzanu מָצָאנוּ *we found* (lines 3 and 7)

lemadetem לְמַדְתֶּם *you learned* (plural) (lines 5 and 8)

lamadnu לָמַדנוּ *we learned* (lines 6 and 9)

hayu הָיוּ *they were* (lines 6 and 9)

③ **beynle`umi** בֵּינלְאוּמִי *international.* This is an interesting example of how modern Hebrew forms new words: **beyn** בֵּין *between*, **le`umi** לְאוּמִי *national.* The latter word comes from **le`om** לְאוֹם *nation.*

3 – Bachafirot be`Atunah ha'atiqah matzanu ④ **harbeh chutim.**
in-the-excavations in-Athens the-ancient we-found many wires
In the excavations in ancient Athens we found lots of wires.

4 Ha`arkhe`olog hayisra`eli `amar:
the-archaeologist the-Israeli said
The Israeli archaeologist said:

5 – Mah lemadetem mehem?
what you-learned from-them
What did you learn from them?

6 – Lamadnu mehachutim shebe`Atunah ha'atiqah kvar hayu telefonim.
we-learned from-the-wires that-in-Athens the-ancient already were telephones
We learned from the wires that there were already telephones in ancient Athens.

7 – Me'anyen me`od! `Etzlenu bachafirot haKotel biYrushalayim lo matzanu chutim.
interesting very! at-ours in-excavations-of the-wall in-Jerusalem not we-found wires
Very interesting! At our excavations at the Western Wall in Jerusalem, we didn't find any wires.

8 – Mah lemadetem mehachafirot shelakhem?
what you-learned from-the-excavations of-you
What did you learn from your excavations?

9 – Lamadnu shebiYrushalayim ha'atiqah kvar hayu telefonim nayadim bitqufat Bayit Rishon.
we-learned that-in-Jerusalem the-ancient already were telephones mobile in-period-of house first
We learned that in ancient Jerusalem there were already mobile phones in the First Temple period.

3 – בַּחֲפִירוֹת בְּאַתּוּנָה הָעַתִּיקָה מָצָאנוּ הַרְבֵּה חוּטִים.

4 הָאַרְכֵיאוֹלוֹג הַיִּשְׂרְאֵלִי אָמַר:

5 – מַה לְמַדְתֶּם מֵהֶם?

6 – לָמַדְנוּ מֵהַחוּטִים שֶׁבְּאַתּוּנָה הָעַתִּיקָה כְּבָר הָיוּ טֶלֶפוֹנִים.

7 – מְעַנְיֵן מְאֹד! אֶצְלֵנוּ בַּחֲפִירוֹת הַכּוֹתֶל בִּירוּשָׁלַיִם לֹא מָצָאנוּ חוּטִים.

8 – מַה לְמַדְתֶּם מֵהַחֲפִירוֹת שֶׁלָּכֶם?

9 – לָמַדְנוּ שֶׁבִּירוּשָׁלַיִם הָעַתִּיקָה כְּבָר הָיוּ טֶלֶפוֹנִים נַיָּדִים בִּתְקוּפַת בַּיִת רִאשׁוֹן. □

Notes

④ **matzanu** מָצָאנוּ *we found.* The א is silent here, since it does not have an accompanying vowel mark. It appears because it is the third root letter of this verb.

Targil rishon – Targem תַּרְגִּיל רִאשׁוֹן – תַּרְגֵּם

1. הם נפגשו בכנס בינלאומי לארכיאולוגיה.
Hem nifgeshu bekhenes beynle`umi le`arkhe`ologyah.

2. בחפירות באתונה העתיקה מצאנו הרבה חוטים.
Bachafirot be`Atunah ha'atiqah matzanu harbeh chutim.

3. בחפירות הכותל מצאנו זכוכית עתיקה.
Bachafirot haKotel matzanu zekhukhit 'atiqah.

4. כל ישראלי הוא ארכיאולוג חובב.
Kol yisra`eli hu `arkhe`olog chovev.

5. למדתן בבית הספר על תקופת בית ראשון?
Lemadeten beveyt hasefer 'al tqufat bayit rishon?

Targil sheni – Hashlem תַּרְגִּיל שֵׁנִי – הַשְׁלֵם

1. An Israeli archaeologist and a Greek archaeologist met at a party.
`Arkhe`olog Yisra`eli ve`arkhe`olog yevani nifgeshu bimesibah.

אַרְכֵיאוֹלוֹג _____ וְאַרְכֵיאוֹלוֹג ____ _____ בִּמְסִיבָּה.

2. We studied the archaeology of ancient Athens.
Lamadnu `et ha`arkhe`ologyah shel `Atunah ha'atiqah.

_____ אֶת ___________ שֶׁל אַתּוּנָה הָ_____ .

3. We will invite the family to the Bar Mitzvah at the Western Wall excavations.
Nazmin `et hamishpachah labar mitzvah bachafirot haKotel.

_____ __ הַמִּשְׁפָּחָה לְבַר מִצְוָה _______ _____ .

4. What did you learn from your excavations?
Mah lemadetem mehachafirot `etzlekhem?

מַה _____ מֵהַחֲפִירוֹת _____?

Answers to Exercise 1

❶ They met at an international archaeology conference. ❷ In the excavations in ancient Athens, we found many wires. ❸ In the Western Wall excavations, we found ancient glass. ❹ Every Israeli is an amateur archaeologist. ❺ Did you*(fem. pl.)* study the First Temple period at school?

❺ In the Old City of Jerusalem there are many tourists who like archaeology.
BiYrushalayim ha'atiqah yesh harbeh tayarim she`ohavim `arkhe`ologyah.

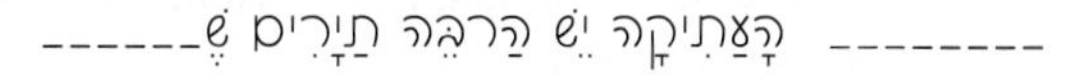
________ הָעַתִּיקָה יֵשׁ הַרְבֵּה תַּיָּרִים שֶׁ______
__________ .

Answers to Exercise 2

❶ – יִשְׂרְאֵלִי – יְוָנִי נִפְגְּשׁוּ – ❷ לָמַדְנוּ – הָאַרְכֵיאוֹלוֹגְיָה – עַתִּיקָה ❸ מָצָאנוּ אֶת – בַּחֲפִירוֹת הַכּוֹתֶל ❹ – לְמַדְתֶּם – אֶצְלְכֶם ❺ בִּירוּשָׁלַיִם – אוֹהֲבִים אַרְכֵיאוֹלוֹגְיָה

45 **Chafirot haKotel** חֲפִירוֹת הַכּוֹתֶל *excavations of the 'Wall'. The* **Kotel** *or Western Wall was the supporting wall of the Temple renovated by Herod the Great. In English, it used to be referred to as the 'Wailing Wall', but this term is not used these days. With a length of 485 metres, the Western Wall delineates one side of the rectangle that formed the heart of the Temple. If you're looking for the site in Jerusalem, watch out for signs pointing to* **HaKotel hama'aravi** הַכּוֹתֶל הַמַּעֲרָבִי the Western Wall. *The famous sections most visitors go to first actually represent just a small part of the wall, most of which can only be observed from a neighbouring*

---

45 Forty-fifth lesson
(Shi'ur arba'im vechamesh)

Bachamam ①
At the Turkish bath

1 **Chaverim tze'irim, 'ashirim chadashim yashvu bachamam.**
friends young rich new sat in-the-Turkish-bath
Some young friends, newly rich, were sitting in the Turkish bath.

2 **Pelefon** ② **tziltzel. `Echad mehachaverim 'anah. `Ishah `amrah:**
mobile-phone rang. one of-the-friends answered. woman said
A mobile phone rang. One of the friends answered and a woman said:

Notes

① **chamam** חָמָאם *hammam.* This is actually an Arabic word, but Arabic and Hebrew are closely related, and you may be able to guess its connection to a Hebrew word we've already learned: **cham** חָם *hot.* A hammam is a Turkish bath or hot steam bath.

underground gallery. Since the destruction of the Second Temple by the Romans in 70 CE, the Western Wall has been the most sacred site of Judaism.

Bayit rishon בַּיִת רִאשׁוֹן First Temple *(literally, 'first house'). Note that Hebrew uses the ordinary word 'house' to refer to this special building. The First Temple was built by King Solomon in the 10th century BCE. The Second Temple was constructed around 520 BCE after the Jews returned from Exile, and was later renovated and extended by Herod the Great around 20 BCE.*

---

45 שִׁעוּר אַרְבָּעִים וְחָמֵשׁ

בַּחֲמָאם

1 חֲבֵרִים צְעִירִים, עֲשִׁירִים חֲדָשִׁים יָשְׁבוּ בַּחֲמָאם.

2 פֶּלֶאפוֹן צִלְצֵל. אֶחָד מֵהַחֲבֵרִים עָנָה.

אִשָּׁה אָמְרָה:

② **pelefon** פֶּלֶאפוֹן *mobile phone, cell phone*. Formed from **pele** פֶּלֶא *miracle* and **telefon** טֶלֶפוֹן, this word was chosen by the first company in Israel that marketed mobile phones. Although it is a proprietary name, it has often been used as a generic word for mobile phone, although as the number of companies in this field grows, it is less common today than in the past.

3 – Shalom chamudi, yesh li she`elah qtanah. Ra`iti taba'at yahalomim zolah. Raq 'aseret `alafim shqalim. Liqnot ③?
hello my-cute-one there-is for-me question small. I-saw ring-of diamonds cheap. only ten thousands shekels. to-buy?
Hello darling, I've got a little question. I saw a cheap diamond ring – only ten thousand shekels. Should I buy [it]?

4 – Bevaqashah, qni ④.
by-request buy
By all means, buy [it].

5 – Yesh li 'od she`elah. Ra`iti gam parvah yafah. Raq 'esrim `elef ⑤ shqalim. Liqnot?
there-is for-me another question. I-saw also fur pretty. only twenty thousand shekels. to-buy?
I have another question. I also saw a pretty fur [coat]. Only twenty thousand shekels. Should I buy [it]?

6 – `Eyn be'ayot, qni.
there-are-no problems buy
No problem – buy [it].

7 – Ushe`elah `acharonah. Ra`iti mertzedes nehederet. Raq me`ah vachamishim `elef shqalim. Mah `atah `omer?
and-question last. I-saw Mercedes wonderful. only hundred and-fifty thousand shekels. what you say?
And one last question. I saw a wonderful Mercedes – only one hundred and fifty thousand shekels. What do you say?

Notes

③ **liqnot** לִקְנוֹת *to buy.* This infinitive, appearing here on its own followed by a question mark, conveys the meaning *Should I buy it?*

3 – שָׁלוֹם חֲמוּדִי. יֵשׁ לִי שְׁאֵלָה קְטַנָּה. רָאִיתִי טַבַּעַת יַהֲלוֹמִים זוֹלָה. רַק עֲשֶׂרֶת אֲלָפִים שְׁקָלִים. לִקְנוֹת?

4 – בְּבַקָּשָׁה. קְנִי.

5 – יֵשׁ לִי עוֹד שְׁאֵלָה. רָאִיתִי גַּם פַּרְוָה יָפָה. רַק עֶשְׂרִים אֶלֶף שְׁקָלִים. לִקְנוֹת?

6 – אֵין בְּעָיוֹת. קְנִי.

7 – וּשְׁאֵלָה אַחֲרוֹנָה. רָאִיתִי מֶרְצֶדֶס נֶהְדֶּרֶת. רַק מֵאָה וַחֲמִישִּׁים אֶלֶף שְׁקָלִים. מָה אַתָּה אוֹמֵר?

④ **qni** קְנִי *buy* (fem.). As we learned in lesson 42, the other imperative forms of this verb are **qneh** קְנֵה (masc.) and **qnu** קְנוּ (masc./fem. plural). Note that the **h** ה from the root of this verb appears in the masculine singular form, but for phonetic reasons disappears in the other two forms, which end with a vowel. In lesson 42, we saw that the verb עשה *to do* is conjugated in a similar way in the future tense – those forms that end in the vowels **i** ִי and **u** וּ lose the **h** ה.

⑤ **'aseret `alafim** עֲשֶׂרֶת אֲלָפִים *ten thousands* (line 3), but **'esrim `elef** עֶשְׂרִים אֶלֶף *twenty thousand* (line 5). Here we see the plural (**`alafim**) and the singular (**`elef**) for *thousand*. In English, *thousand* is always singular in numbers, whether it refers to one thousand, two thousand, ten thousand, etc. But in Hebrew, it's a bit more complicated. The singular is used for one thousand and then for numbers over ten thousand, but the plural is used for numbers between three thousand and ten thousand. Two thousand has its own special form (the dual)! Confused? The correct use of Hebrew numbers and the nouns they accompany is a fairly tricky subject. We'll come back to this in lesson 49.

8 – Mertzedes nehederet? Lamah lo? Qni.
Mercedes wonderful? why not? buy
A wonderful Mercedes? Why not? Buy [it].

9 – Todah rabah chamudi. Lehitra`ot.
thanks very darling. to-see-oneself
Thanks very much, darling. Bye.

10 Hu kibah `et hapelefon vesha`al:
he turned-off [`**et**] *the-mobile-phone and-asked*
He turned off the mobile phone and asked:

11 – Shel mi hatelefon hazeh?
of who the-telephone the-this
Whose telephone is this?

Targil rishon – Targem תַּרְגִּיל רִאשׁוֹן – תַּרְגֵּם

❶ יש לי שאלה: אפשר לקנות את הפרוה הזאת?
Yesh li she`elah: `efshar liqnot `et haparvah hazot?

❷ חמודי יש לי מתנה בשבילך: מרצדס נהדרת.
Chamudi, yesh li matanah bishvilkha: mertzedes nehederet.

❸ של מי הפלאפון החדש?
Shel mi hapelefon hachadash?

❹ אם יש לך כסף, אין בעיות, קני את המכונית.
`Im yesh lakh kesef, `eyn be'ayot, qni `et hamekhonit.

❺ השתגעת? לקנות טבעת יהלומים בעשרים אלף שקלים!
Hishtaga'ta? Liqnot taba'`at yahalomim be'esrim `elef shqalim!

8 – מֶרצֶדֶס נֶהֱדֶרֶת? לָמָּה לֹא? קְנִי.

9 – תוֹדָה רַבָּה חֲמוּדִי. לְהִתרָאוֹת.

10 הוּא כִּבָּה אֶת הַפֶּלֶאפוֹן וְשָׁאַל:

11 – שֶׁל מִי הַטֶּלֶפוֹן הַזֶּה? □

Answers to Exercise 1

❶ I have a question: is it possible to buy this fur coat? ❷ Darling, I have a present for you: a wonderful Mercedes. ❸ Whose is the new mobile phone? ❹ If you have money, there's no problem: buy the car. ❺ Have you gone crazy? Buying a diamond ring for twenty thousand shekels!

Targil sheni – Hashlem תַרְגִיל שֵׁנִי – הַשְׁלֵם

❶ They are rich, young and beautiful.
Hem 'ashirim, tze'irim veyafim.

הֵם ______ , ______ וְיָפִים.

❷ At my daughter's, the mobile phone rang all day.
\`Etzel biti hapelefon tziltzel kol hayom.

___ בִּתִּי _______ ____ כָּל הַיּוֹם.

❸ My darling, how are you*(masc.)* this morning?
Chamudi, mah shlomkha haboqer?

_____ מַה ______ הַבֹּקֶר?

❹ Dina is lucky: [she has] good friends, a fur [coat] and diamonds.
Yesh leDinah mazal: chaverim tovim, parvah veyahalomim.

יֵשׁ לְדִינָה ___ : _____ טוֹבִים ____ ! _______ .

❺ At night, he turned off the light in the apartment.
Balaylah, hu kibah \`et ha\`or badirah.

בַּלַּיְלָה, הוּא ___ אֶת ____ בַּדִּירָה.

Answers to Exercise 2

❶ - עֲשִׁירִים צְעִירִים - ❷ אֵצֶל - הַפֶּלֶאפוֹן צִלְצֵל - ❸ חֲמוּדִי - שְׁלוֹמֵךְ -
❹ - מַגָּל - חֲבֵרִים - פַּרְוָה - יַהֲלוֹמִים ❺ - כִּבָּה - הָאוֹר -

Sheqel שֶׁקֶל shekel *(the Israeli currency). 'Abraham ... weighed out the price: four hundred shekels of silver, according to the weight current among the merchants' (Genesis 23:16). The root* שקל *means to weigh – the shekel was originally a measure of weight. Coins from the Hasmonean dynasty (2nd century BCE) bear the legend 'shekel Israel' on one side and 'Holy Jerusalem' on the other. Since 1980, the shekel has been Israel's official currency. It is divided into one hundred* אֲגוֹרוֹת **agorot** *(plural)* – אֲגוֹרָה **agora** *(sing.) – a term that comes from an Akkadian word meaning 'grain'.*

After a period of hyperinflation, the Israeli currency was devalued in 1985, and the shekel was replaced by the שֶׁקֶל חָדָשׁ new shekel. *Each new shekel was the equivalent of 1000* שְׁקָלִים shekels *under the old system. The new shekel is also divided into 100 agorot. Israeli coins and banknotes bear inscriptions in Hebrew, Arabic and English. Prices often use the abbreviation* ש"ח*, short for* **sheqel chadash** שֶׁקֶל חָדָשׁ new shekel*, and the rather fetching form* ₪ *is now the international symbol for the currency (in this form, the middle 'leg' of the letter* **shin** ש *also serves as the first part of the letter* **chet** ח*).*

46 Forty-sixth lesson
(Shi'ur `arba'im veshesh)

Harav vehanehag
The rabbi and the driver

1 **Rav venehag `otobus metu be`oto yom.**
rabbi and-driver-of bus died in-same day
A rabbi and a bus driver died on the same day.

2 **Shtey ① haneshamot higi'u ledelet Gan 'Eden.**
two the-souls(fem.) arrived to-door-of garden-of Eden
Both souls arrived at the door of paradise.

3 **Nishmat hanehag nikhnesah leGan 'Eden.**
soul-of the-driver entered to-garden-of Eden
The driver's soul went into paradise.

4 **Nishmat harav `amrah:**
soul-of the-rabbi said
The rabbi's soul said:

5 – **`Ani lo mevinah. Hanehag hazeh lo hayah dati. `Ani limadeti Talmud ② kol yom.**
I not understand(fem.). the-driver the-this not was religious. I taught Talmud every day
I don't understand. This driver wasn't religious. Me, I taught Talmud every day.

6 **Hamal`akh `amar:**
the-angel said
The angel said:

Notes

① **shtey** שְׁתֵּי *two* (fem.). When the number shtayim שְׁתַּיִים *two* appears directly before a feminine noun, it appears in this shortened version, which is an example of the construct form. (More on this in lesson 55.)

הָרַב וְהַנֶּהָג

1 רַב וְנֶהָג אוֹטוֹבּוּס מֵתוּ בְּאוֹתוֹ יוֹם.

2 שְׁתֵּי הַנְּשָׁמוֹת הִגִּיעוּ לְדֶלֶת גַּן עֵדֶן.

3 נִשְׁמַת הַנֶּהָג נִכְנְסָה לְגַן עֵדֶן.

4 נִשְׁמַת הָרַב אָמְרָה:

5 – אֲנִי לֹא מְבִינָה. הַנֶּהָג הַזֶּה לֹא הָיָה דָּתִי. אֲנִי לִמַּדְתִּי תַּלְמוּד כֹּל יוֹם.

6 הַמַּלְאָךְ אָמַר:

② **limadeti Talmud** לִמַּדְתִּי תַּלְמוּד *I taught Talmud.*
Look at the following two examples:
`ani lamadeti Talmud אֲנִי לָמַדְתִּי תַּלְמוּד *I studied Talmud*
`ani limadeti Talmud אֲנִי לִמַּדְתִּי תַּלְמוּד *I taught Talmud*
Both these verbs come from the root למד. The first – from **lamad** לָמַד *to learn* – is the basic verb formed from this root. The second – from **limed** לִמֵּד *to teach* – is a verb form based on a pattern that conveys a causative or intensive meaning of the basic verb; here, from 'to study' to 'to teach'.

This is an example of how each Hebrew root can be used to form a number of different verbs according to fixed patterns. As you progress in your Hebrew studies, you'll find that these patterns help you understand new verbs you encounter. And not just verbs – other words are also formed from the root: the noun **talmidim** תַּלְמִידִים *pupils, students* in line 9 also comes from the root למד, as does the noun **Talmud**, which is borrowed from Aramaic.

7 – Nakhon me`od. Gam `at tikansi ③ leGan 'Eden, `aval machar.
correct very. also you you-will-enter to-garden-of Eden, but tomorrow
That's quite right. You will also enter paradise, but tomorrow.

8 – 'Lamah?' sha`alah nishmat harav.
why? asked soul-of the-rabbi
'Why?' asked the rabbi's soul.

9 – 'Ka`asher harav limed Talmud, kol hatalmidim yashnu.
when the-rabbi taught Talmud all the-students slept
'When the rabbi taught Talmud, all the students slept.

10 Ka`asher hanehag nahag ba`otobus, kol hanos'im hitpalelu …'
when the-driver drove in-the-bus all the-passengers prayed
When the driver drove the bus, all the passengers prayed …'

Targil rishon – Targem תַּרְגִּיל רִאשׁוֹן – תַּרְגֵּם

❶ הרב למד תלמוד כל יום.
Harav limed Talmud kol yom.

❷ אני לא מבינה את השעור הזה.
`Ani lo mevinah `et hashi'ur hazeh.

❸ מחר תכנסי לדירה חדשה.
Machar tikansi ledirah chadashah.

❹ אחרי המסיבה כל הילדים ישנו אצלנו.
`Acharey hamesibah kol hayeladim yashnu `etzlenu.

❺ כל בוקר אנחנו נוסעים לעבודה באותו אוטובוס.
Kol boqer `anachnu nos'im la'avodah be`oto `otobus.

7 – נָכוֹן מְאֹד, גַּם אַתְּ תִּכָּנְסִי לְגַן עֵדֶן, אֲבָל מָחָר.

8 – 'לָמָּה?' שָׁאֲלָה נִשְׁמַת הָרַב.

9 – 'כַּאֲשֶׁר הָרַב לִמֵּד תַּלְמוּד, כֹּל הַתַּלְמִידִים יָשְׁנוּ.

10 כַּאֲשֶׁר הַנֶּהָג נָהַג בָּאוֹטוֹבּוּס, כֹּל הַנּוֹסְעִים הִתְפַּלְּלוּ...'

□

Notes

③ **tikansi** תִּכָּנְסִי *you will enter* is in the feminine because this comment is addressed to **nishmat harav** נִשְׁמַת הָרַב *the rabbi's soul*, and נְשָׁמָה *soul* is a feminine noun.

Answers to Exercise 1

❶ The rabbi taught Talmud every day. ❷ I don't understand this lesson. ❸ Tomorrow you*(fem.)* will enter the new apartment. ❹ After the party, all the children slept at our place. ❺ Every morning we travel to work on the same bus.

Targil sheni – Hashlem תַּרְגִּיל שֵׁנִי – הַשְׁלֵם

❶ It's a joke about a rabbi and a driver.
Zot bdichah 'al rav venehag.

זֹאת _____ עַל רַב וְ___ .

❷ Two good souls arrived in paradise.
Shtey neshamot tovot higi'u leGan 'Eden.

___ _____ טוֹבוֹת _____ לְגַן עֵדֶן.

❸ The teacher didn't understand why all the students were sleeping in the lesson.
Hamoreh lo hevin lamah kol hatalmidim yashnu bashi'ur.

הַמּוֹרֶה __ ____ לָמָּה כֹּל ________ ____ בַּשִּׁעוּר.

❹ Are you sure that the passengers prayed in the bus? Isn't that a joke?
`Atah batuach shehanos'im hitpalelu ba`otobus? Zot lo bdichah?

אַתָּה ____ שֶׁהַנּוֹסְעִים ______ בָּאוֹטוֹבּוּס? ___ __ בְּדִיחָה?

Secular or religious? The joke in this lesson touches on a sensitive subject in modern-day Israel – the relations between secular and religious Jews. Of course, everyone can behave as they like in their own home. The problems arise in the public domain. Should the Jewish commandments as interpreted by some Jews determine the rules of public behaviour?

An anecdote may help to illustrate the dilemma. A new synagogue opened in a mainly religious area of Jerusalem. The residents asked the municipality to close the road to traffic on Shabbat, the Jewish Sabbath, because Orthodox Judaism prohibits the use of motor vehicles on the holy day of rest. Secular residents of the city objected, pointing out that this would force them to make a long detour. After the municipality failed to act, the religious residents decided to stage a protest on the Sabbath. They closed

❺ Come in *(Enter[fem.])*, please, all the friends have already arrived.
Tikansi, bevaqashah, kol hachaverim kvar higi'u.
_____ בְּבַקָּשָׁה, כֹּל ______ כְּבָר _____ .

כל בוקר אנחנו נוסעים לעבודה באותו אוטובוס.

Answers to Exercise 2

❶ - בְּדִיחָה - נֶהָג ❷ שְׁתֵּי נְשָׁמוֹת - הִגִּיעוּ - ❸ - לֹא הֵבִין - הַתַּלְמִידִים
יָשְׁנוּ - ❹ - בָּטוּחַ - הִתְפַּלְּלוּ - כּוֹת לֹא - ❺ תִּכָּנְסִי - הַחֲבֵרִים - הִגִּיעוּ

off the road and came out of the synagogue carrying prayer books and a Torah scroll. When the time came to read from the Torah, they turned to one of the policemen: 'What is your name?' He replied, 'Avner.' 'And your father's name?' The policeman replied, 'Moshe.' 'Avner son of Moshe will now come up to the podium,' the prayer leader chanted in the traditional style. All those present, demonstrators and police officers, listened as the policeman recited the prayer before a portion was read from the Torah.

How was the conflict resolved? Both sides were able to claim victory. The municipality dug a tunnel under the road. The road itself is now closed on Sabbath so the religious residents are not troubled by vehicles, while secular Jerusalemites can drive through the tunnel under the area without having to go around it.

Forty-seventh lesson
(Shi'ur arba'im vesheva')

Ha`ishah hayechidah ba'olam ①
The only woman in the world

1 **`Adam hayah bebar beGan 'Eden. Hu chazar habaytah balaylah.**
Adam was in-bar in-garden-of Eden. he returned home at-the-night
Adam was in a bar in the Garden of Eden. He came home at night.

2 **Chavah `amrah lo ②:**
Chavah said to-him
Eve said to him:

3 – **`Adam, `ani betuchah sheyesh lekha `ishah `acheret.**
Adam I sure that-there-is for-you woman other
Adam, I'm sure that you have another woman.

4 – **Chavahleh ③, `al ④ tedabri shtuyot. `At ha`ishah hayechidah ba'olam.**
Chavah-my-dear not you-will-talk nonsense. you the-woman the-only in-the-world
My dear Eve, don't talk nonsense. You are the only woman in the world.

Notes

① The Biblical story of Adam and Eve appears in Genesis 2:20–24.

② **lo** לוֹ *to him* is formed, as you already know, from the preposition **le-** לְ and the ending for the third-person masculine singular (see lesson 28). Don't confuse this word with **lo** לֹא *no, not*, which is spelled differently in Hebrew. The feminine form is **lah** לָהּ *to her.*

הָאִשָּׁה הַיְחִידָה בָּעוֹלָם

1 אָדָם הָיָה בְּבַר בְּגַן עֵדֶן. הוּא חָזַר הַבַּיְתָה בַּלַּיְלָה.

2 חַוָּה אָמְרָה לוֹ:

3 – אָדָם, אֲנִי בְּטוּחָה שֶׁיֵּשׁ לְךָ אִשָּׁה אַחֶרֶת.

4 – חַוָּה'לֶה, אַל תְּדַבְּרִי שְׁטוּיוֹת. אַתְּ הָאִשָּׁה הַיְחִידָה בָּעוֹלָם.

③ **Chavahleh** חַוָּה'לֶה *my dear Eve.* Eve is the modern Anglicization (from the Latin Eva) of the original Hebrew name Chavah in Genesis. The **-leh** suffix is used to make affectionate nicknames or diminutives. Note the apostrophe in the Hebrew between the original form of the name and the suffix. Other examples include **Danileh** דָּנִי'לֶה for **Dani** דָּנִי, **Lealeh** לֵאָה'לֶה for **Leah** לֵאָה, and **Zeevaleh** זְאֵב'לֶה for **Zeev** זְאֵב.

④ **`al** אַל *do not.* The negative imperative (prohibiting someone from doing something) is formed by combining אַל with the appropriate form of the future tense: **`al tedabri** אַל תְּדַבְּרִי *Don't talk!* (feminine – i.e. addressed to a woman). Compare this with the affirmative imperative: **dabri** דַּבְּרִי *Talk!* Or, from lesson 45, **qni** קְנִי *Buy!* becomes **`al tiqni** אַל תִּקְנִי *Don't buy!* (fem.) in the negative. Note that the negative form אַל contains the same letters as לֹא **lo**, but in reverse order. אַל is also used as a suffix to form words such as **`alchuti** אַלְחוּטִי *wireless* (lesson 13, note 2).

5 `Adam halakh lishon. Balaylah hu hirgish sheChavah litfah `oto ⑤.
Adam went to-sleep. in-the-night he felt that-Chavah caressed [`**et**]-*him*
Adam went to sleep. In the night, he felt Eve caressing him.

6 – Mah `at 'osah?
what you do?
What are you doing?

7 – `Ani soferet `et hatzla'ot shelkha.
I count [`**et**] *the-ribs of-you*
I'm counting your ribs.

Notes

⑤ **`oto** אוֹתוֹ *him*. This word is the combination of the particle **`et** and the ending for the third-person masculine singular. It has a homonym that means *same* (see lesson 30).

Targil rishon – Targem תַּרְגִּיל רִאשׁוֹן – תַּרְגֵּם

❶ חוה היתה האשה היחידה בעולם.
Chavah haytah ha`ishah hayechidah ba'olam.

❷ שאלה: כמה צלעות היו לאדם הראשון?
She`elah: kamah tzla'ot hayu la`adam harishon?

❸ הוא שותה בבר ומדבר שטויות כל הערב.
Hu shoteh babar umedaber shtuyot kol ha'erev.

❹ דוד חזר הביתה עיף מאוד והלך לישון.
David chazar habaytah 'ayef me`od vehalakh lishon.

❺ אנחנו רוצים לקנות מכונית אחרת.
`Anachnu rotzim liqnot mekhonit `acheret.

5 אָדָם הָלַךְ לִישׁוֹן. בַּלַּיְלָה הוּא הִרְגִּישׁ שֶׁחַוָּה לִטְפָּה אוֹתוֹ.

6 – מַה אַתְּ עוֹשָׂה?

7 – אֲנִי סוֹפֶרֶת אֶת הַצְּלָעוֹת שֶׁלְּךָ. □

Answers to Exercise 1

❶ Eve was the only woman in the world. ❷ Question: how many ribs did the first man have? ❸ He drinks in a bar and talks nonsense all evening. ❹ David came home very tired and went to sleep. ❺ We want to buy another car.

Targil sheni – Hashlem תַּרְגִּיל שֵׁנִי – הַשְׁלֵם

❶ Mom caressed Nati and told him, 'Good night, darling!'
`Ima litfah `et Naty ve`amrah lo: 'Laylah tov, chamudi!'

אִמָּא ____ אֶת נָתִי וְ____ לוֹ: "____ ___ חֲמוּדִי!"

❷ Eve counts Adam's ribs.
Chavah soferet `et hatzla'ot shel `Adam.

חַוָּה _____ אֶת ______ שֶׁל אָדָם.

❸ Don't be silly *(do nonsense)* in front of our *(the)* friends!
`Al ta'aseh shtuyot lifney hachaverim!

__ ____ שְׁטֻיוֹת ____ הַחֲבֵרִים!

❹ Sarah's husband has another woman!
Laba'al shel Sarah yesh `ishah `acheret.

____ שֶׁל שָׂרָה יֵשׁ ___ ____!

---

48 Forty-eighth lesson
(Shi'ur arba'im ushmoneh)

Ha'anivah
The tie

1 **David Ben Guryon hayah bimesibah rishmit baKneset, beyom qayitz cham me`od.**
David Ben Gurion was in-party official in-the-Knesset on-day-of summer hot very
David Ben Gurion was at an official reception at the Knesset on a very hot summer day.

2 **Hu hesir `et ha'anivah veqipel `et hasharvulim.**
he removed [`**et**] *the-tie and-folded* [`**et**] *the-sleeves*
He took off his tie and rolled up his sleeves.

⑤ He felt unwell and went to sleep.
Hu hirgish lo tov vehalakh lishon.

הוּא _____ לֹא טוֹב _ _ _ ! _ _ _ _ .

Answers to Exercise 2

❶ - לִטְפָּה - עָמְרָה - לַיְלָה טוֹב - ❷ - סוֹפֶרֶת - הַבְּלָצוֹת - ❸ אַל תַּעֲשֶׂה - לְפָנַי - ❹ לְבַטֵּל - אִשָּׁה אַחֶרֶת ❺ הִרְגִּישׁ - הָלַךְ לִישׁוֹן

Adam veChavah אָדָם וְחַוָּה Adam and Eve. *As we mentioned in lesson 43, all Israeli schoolchildren study the Bible, whether they come from religious or secular families. As a result, biblical figures such as Adam and Eve, Moses or Solomon often crop up in anecdotes and jokes, and everyone understands the references to these legendary characters.*

---

48 שִׁעוּר אַרְבָּעִים וּשְׁמוֹנֶה

הָעֲנִיבָה

1 דָּוִד בֶּן גּוּרְיוֹן הָיָה בִּמְסִיבָּה רִשְׁמִית בַּכְּנֶסֶת בְּיוֹם קַיִץ חַם מְאֹד.

2 הוּא הֵסִיר אֶת הָעֲנִיבָה וְקִפֵּל אֶת הַשַּׁרְווּלִים.

3 **Sar `amar lo:**
minister said to-him
A minister said to him:

4 – **David, `al ta'aseh `et zeh. `Anachnu bimesibah rishmit.**
David not you-will-do [`**et**] *this. we in-party official*
David, don't do that. We're at an official reception.

5 – **`Aval, Churchill** ① **`amar li …**
but Churchill told me
But Churchill told me …

6 – **Churchill? Ha`Angli?**
Churchill the Englishman
Churchill? The Englishman?

7 – **Ken. Hayiti 'im Churchill bimesibah rishmit beLondon …**
yes. I-was with Churchill at-party official in-London
Yes, I was with Churchill at an official reception in London …

8 **… hayah sham qayitz cham me`od. Hesarti `et ha'anivah veqipalti `et hasharvulim. Churchill `amar li:**
was there summer hot very. I-removed [`**et**] *the-tie and-folded* [`**et**] *the-sleeves. Churchill said to-me*
… it was a very hot summer there. I removed my tie and rolled up my sleeves. Churchill said to me:

9 **David, `et zeh ta'aseh beYisra`el.**
David [`**et**] *this you-will-do in-Israel*
David, you can do that in Israel.

Notes

① **Churchill** צֶ'רְצִ'יל. An apostrophe is added to the left of certain Hebrew letters in order to represent foreign sounds used in names or loanwords: for example, the 'ch' in *Churchill*

3 שָׂר אָמַר לוֹ:

4 – דָוִד, אַל תַּעֲשֶׂה אֶת זֶה. אֲנַחְנוּ בִּמְסִיבָּה רִשְׁמִית.

5 – אֲבָל, צָ׳רְצִ׳יל אָמַר לִי...

6 – צָ׳רצִ׳יל? הָאַנְגְּלִי?

7 כֵּן. הָיִיתִי עִם צָ׳רְצִ׳יל בִּמְסִיבָּה רִשְׁמִית בְּלוֹנְדוֹן ...

8 ... הָיָה שָׁם קַיִץ חַם מְאֹד. הֵסַרְתִּי אֶת הָעֲנִיבָה וְקִפַּלְתִּי אֶת הַשַּׁרְווּלִים. צָ׳רְצִ׳יל אָמַר לִי:

9 דָוִד, אֶת זֶה תַּעֲשֶׂה בְּיִשְׂרָאֵל.

העניבה

is represented by 'צָ. In lesson 27, we saw that the 'j' sound in *jazz* is written 'ג.

Targil rishon – Targem תַּרְגִּיל רִאשׁוֹן – תַּרְגֵּם

❶ נזמין את השר למסיבה רשמית בכנסת.
Nazmin `et hasar limesibah rishmit baKneset.

❷ ביום חם הוא הסיר את העניבה.
Beyom cham hu hesir `et ha'anivah.

❸ אתמול היתה מסיבת גן יפה מאוד.
`Etmol haytah mesibat gan yafah me`od.

❹ קפלתי את השרוולים והלכתי למטבח.
Qipalti `et hasharvulim vehalakhti lamitbach.

❺ בישראל לא צריך עניבה בקיץ.
BeYisra`el lo tzarikh 'anivah baqayitz.

Targil sheni – Hashlem תַּרְגִּיל שֵׁנִי – הַשְׁלֵם

❶ I removed the food from the heat *(fire)*.
Hesarti `et ha`okhel meha`esh.

_____ אֶת הָאוֹכֶל ____ .

❷ Don't do anything silly *(do nonsense)* at the official reception.
`Al ta'aseh shtuyot bimesibah rishmit.

-- ____ שְׁטוּיוֹת בִּמְסִיבָּה _____ .

❸ On Wednesday we are going to dinner at the minister's.
Beyom revi'i `anachnu holkhim la`aruchat 'erev `etzel hasar.

____ _____ אֲנַחְנוּ ______ לַאֲרוּחַת עֶרֶב ___ ___ ___ .

❹ Which bus will we take *(By which bus will we travel)* to the Knesset?
Be`eyzeh `otobus nisa' laKneset?

בְּאֵיזֶה אוֹטוֹבּוּס ___ לַ____ .

Answers to Exercise 1

❶ We will invite the minister to an official reception at the Knesset. ❷ On a hot day, he took off his tie. ❸ Yesterday, there was a very nice garden party. ❹ I rolled up my *(the)* sleeves and went to the kitchen. ❺ In Israel, a tie is not required in summer.

❺ At the Jerusalem Theatre, I was the only person with *(only for-me was)* a tie.
Bete`atron Yerushalayim, raq li haytah 'anivah.
עֲנִיבָה. ---- -- רַק יְרוּשָׁלַיִם ------

Answers to Exercise 2

❶ הֵסַרְתִּי - מֵהָכּוּשׁ ❷ אַל תַּעֲשֶׂה - רִשְׁמִית ❸ בְּיוֹם רְבִיעִי - הוֹלְכִים - אֵצֶל הַשַּׂר ❹ - נִסַּע - כְּנֶסֶת ❺ בְּתֵאַטְרוֹן - לִי הָיְתָה -

49 *The Knesset is the Israeli Parliament. It has just a single chamber, unlike the Senate and House of Representatives in the United States, or the House of Lords and House of Commons in the United Kingdom. The Knesset is situated in a modern, green area of Jerusalem. Each of the 120 representatives is known as a* **chaver kneset** חֲבֵר כְּנֶסֶת *(masc.) or* **chavrat kneset** חֲבֶרֶת כְּנֶסֶת *(fem.). We've seen the word* **chaver** חָבֵר *meaning* friend, *but it also means a member of a club, organization or institution, as in this case.*

The word **Kneset** Assembly *comes from the term* **Kneset hagdolah** כְּנֶסֶת הַגְּדוֹלָה, the Great Assembly, *a body that operated during the Second Temple period, after the Jews returned from Exile in Babylon (536 BCE), and which also had 120 members. The*

---

49 Forty-ninth lesson
(Shi'ur arba'im vetesha')

חֲזָרָה Chazarah – Review

You've already made your way through 49 lessons! Think of the progress you've made in so little time! You can now read and understand short stories in Hebrew, and maybe you've even started to tell some yourself. Let's take a few minutes to review the past six lessons.

1 The negative imperative

To tell someone not to do something, use **`al** אַל *do not*, followed by the appropriate future tense form.
`Al tedabri shtu'yot! !אַל תְּדַבְּרִי שְׁטוּיוֹת *Don't talk* (fem. sing.) *nonsense!*
`Al ta'aseh `et zeh! !אַל תַּעֲשֶׂה אֶת זֶה *Don't do* (masc. sing.) *that!*

Plural forms can also be used, of course, if you are telling more than one person not to do something:

`Al tedabru! !אַל תְּדַבְּרוּ *Don't talk!*

`Al ta'asu! !אַל תַּעֲשׂוּ *Don't do [that]!*

It may help you to remember this word if you bear in mind that **`al** אַל is the reverse form of the other main word of negation, **lo** לֹא.

Great Assembly presided over national life, just as the Knesset does in modern-day Israel.

Today's Members of Knesset are elected for a four-year term, which is often shortened if the government falls. The Knesset is situated in a park that features a five-metre-high bronze **menorah** candelabra – *a gift from the British Government. The* **menorah** *features pictorial depictions of 29 events from Jewish history. A huge tapestry by the artist Marc Chagall hangs in the entrance hall.*

The word **kneset** *also appears in* **beyt kneset** בֵּית כְּנֶסֶת synagogue *('house of assembly'). The word for a church is* **knesiyah**, *from the same root.*

---

49 שִׁעוּר אַרְבָּעִים וְתֵשַׁע

2 The superlative

Hadugmah hatovah beyoter הַדּוּגְמָה הַטּוֹבָה בְּיוֹתֵר *the best example*, or literally, 'the-example the-good in-more'. This is how the superlative is formed in Hebrew. Note the underlying structure: [article + noun] + [article + adjective in the appropriate gender and number] + the invariable form **beyoter** בְּיוֹתֵר *in more.*

3 Numbers: thousands

Although in English 'thousand' in a number is always singular, in Hebrew it changes in the dual and certain plural forms. The number 2,000 takes the dual ending. Numbers from 3,000 to 10,000 use the plural **`alafim** *thousands*, but for numbers above 10,000, **`elef** אֶלֶף *thousand* usually appears in the singular.

`elef	אֶלֶף	*thousand*
`alpayim	אַלְפַּיִם	*two thousand* (dual form)
shloshet `alafim	שְׁלוֹשֶׁת אֲלָפִים	*three thousand* (pl.)
'aseret `alafim	עֲשֶׂרֶת אֲלָפִים	*ten thousand* (pl.)
'esrim `elef	עֶשְׂרִים אֶלֶף	*twenty thousand*
me`ah `elef	מֵאָה אֶלֶף	*one hundred thousand*

4 Expressing 'two'

The masculine and feminine forms for *two* appear in a shortened construct form when they come before a noun. We've seen two examples of this:

• The feminine form **shtayim** שְׁתַּיִים becomes **shtey** שְׁתֵּי in the construct: **shtey neshamot** שְׁתֵּי נְשָׁמוֹת *two souls.*

• The masculine form **shnayim** שְׁנַיִים becomes **shney** שְׁנֵי in the construct: **shney chaverim** שְׁנֵי חֲבֵרִים *two friends.*

5 Writing foreign sounds in Hebrew

To represent sounds that do not occur in 'native' Hebrew words but may be needed to write foreign names or loanwords, Hebrew places an apostrophe after the closest equivalent letter. Here are some examples:
ch as in *Churchill* is written צ'
j as in *jazz* → גָ'
g as in *giraffe* → גִ'
j as in *Jacques* → זָ'

Or, as in the following example, two Hebrew letters are combined to represent a foreign sound:
x as in *Alexander* → אַלֶכְּסַנְדֶר

6 Reflexive verbs

The reflexive verbal pattern in Hebrew is known as **hitpa'el** הִתְפַּעֵל. This form can have a reflexive sense (e.g. *they wash themselves*) or a reciprocal meaning (e.g. *they write to each other*). Sometimes, a reflexive verb in Hebrew is used when the equivalent in English has no reflexive meaning (e.g. הִתְפַּלֵל *to pray*, lesson 46). Even in cases in which the English verb could be followed by a reflexive or reciprocal word, as in the examples in the previous sentence, these are often left out in English as they're understood implicitly. Let's look at the reflexive verbs we've seen so far.

In the present tense, reflexive verbs usually begin with **mit -מִת**:

mitrachev (masc.)	מִתרַחֵב	*(I/you/he/it) expands/ enlarges/widens*
mitrachevet (fem.)	מִתרַחֶבֶת	*(I/you/she/it) expands*
mitrachavim (masc.)	מִתרַחֲבִים	*(we/you/they) expand* (lesson 43)
mitrachavot (fem.)	מִתרַחֲבוֹת	*(we/you/they) expand*

mitkavetz (masc.)	מִתכַּוֵץ	*(I/you/he/it) contracts/shrinks*
mitkavetzet (fem.)	מִתכַּוֶצֶת	*(I/you/she/it) contracts*
mitkavtzim (masc.)	מִתכַּוצִים	*(we/you/they) contract*
mitkavtzot (fem.)	מִתכַּוצוֹת	*(we/you/they) contract*

In the past tense, reflexive verbs usually begin with **hit -הִת**:

hitchatnu	הִתחַתנוּ	*they got married* (lesson 34)
hitpalelu	הִתפַּלְלוּ	*they prayed* (lesson 46)
hishtaga'ta	הִשתַגַעתָ	*you have gone crazy* (lesson 41: notice that the first root letter, שׁ, has swapped places with the **tav** ת of the **hit-** prefix of the verb. Some other letters also result in similar changes when they appear at the beginning of reflexive verbs.)

7 When one verb follows another …

… the second verb often appears in the infinitive. This is sometimes the case in English (e.g. 'he wanted to buy'), but not always (e.g. 'she can help', and not 'she can to help'!). In Hebrew, the infinitive is used in both cases:

hu ratzah liqnot	הוּא רָצָה לִקנוֹת	*he wanted to buy*
tzarikh lilmod	צָרִיך לִלמוֹד	*it is necessary to study*
hu halakh lishon	הוּא הָלַך לִישׁוֹן	*he went to sleep*
hi yekholah la'azor	הִיא יְכוֹלָה לַעֲזוֹר	*she can help*

8 Quadriliteral roots

In lesson 45, we saw **pelefon tziltzel** פֶּלֶאפוֹן צִלְצֵל *a mobile phone rang*. The verb here has the particularity of having four, instead of the usual three, root letters: צלצל. Quadriliteral roots are fairly common in Hebrew, though much less so than triliteral ones. Actually, this verb belongs to a specific category of quadriliteral roots in which the first two root letters are repeated to form the base. Another example of this is the root נדנד *to balance*.

Review exercise

1 אֲנִי פֹּה בְּכֶנֶס לְהַנְדָּסַת מַחְשֵׁבִים וְאַרְכֵיאוֹלוֹגְיָה בַּטֶכְנִיוֹן בְּחֵיפָה. 2 אֵיךְ הַכֶּנֶס? 3 מְעַנְיֵן מְאֹד. הַטֶכְנִיוֹן יָפֶה מְאֹד וְגַם חֵיפָה יָפָה מְאֹד. 4 הַקַּיִץ חַם, הַיָּמִים אֲרוּכִּים, אֲבָל בַּבּוֹקֶר אֲנִי בַּבְּרֵכָה אוֹ בַּיָּם, גַּם בַּחַמָּאם. 5 בַּחַמָּאם? בַּחוֹם הַזֶּה? 6 אֶתְמוֹל בָּעֶרֶב הָיִיתִי בִּמְסִיבָּה רִשְׁמִית עִם שָׂר. 7 הָיִיתִי גַּם בִּמְסִיבַּת גַּן נֶהְדֶּרֶת אֵצֶל חַוָּה'לֶה. 8 הִיא שָׁאֲלָה: 'חֲמוּדִי, אַתָּה מַכִּיר אֶת הַבְּדִיחָה עַל הַצַּלָּעוֹת שֶׁל אָדָם?' 9 אָמַרְתִּי לָהּ: 'כֵּן, זֹאת בְּדִיחָה עַתִּיקָה כְּמוֹ הָעוֹלָם. מָצָאת אוֹתָהּ בַּחֲפִירוֹת?'

9 'To learn' – 'to teach'

As we mentioned in lesson 46, each Hebrew root can produce a number of verbs (and other words) with different but related meanings. Here are two verbs derived from the root למד, whose basic meaning is *to learn*:

lamad לָמַד *he studied*

limed לִמֵּד *he taught*

Answers

❶ I'm here at a conference of computer engineering and archaeology at the Technion in Haifa. *(I here at-conference for-engineering-of computers and-archaeology at-the-Technion in-Haifa)* ❷ How is the conference? *(how the-conference)* ❸ Very interesting! The Technion is very beautiful, and Haifa is also very beautiful. *(interesting very. the-Technion beautiful very and-also Haifa beautiful very)* ❹ The summer is hot, the days are long, but in the morning I'm at the swimming pool or the sea, or at the Turkish bath. *(the-summer hot the-days long but in-the-morning I at-the-swimming-pool or at-the-sea also at-the-hammam)* ❺ At the Turkish bath? In this heat?! *(at-the-hammam in-the-heat the-this)* ❻ Yesterday evening, I was at an official reception with a [government] minister. *(yesterday in-the-evening I-was at-party official with minister)* ❼ I also went to a wonderful garden party at Chavale's. *(I-was also at-party-of garden wonderful at Chavale)* ❽ She asked: 'Darling, do you know the joke about Adam's ribs?' *(she asked my-darling you know* [**`et**] *the-joke about the-ribs of Adam)* ❾ I told her, 'Yes, that joke's as old as the world. Did you find it in the excavations?' *(I-said to-her yes this joke ancient like the-world. you-found it[f.] in-the-excavations?)*

Congratulations! You've finished the first part of your studies. From now on, you'll begin the 'active phase' or 'second wave' to consolidate your learning ... Don't worry, you'll find out what we're talking about in the next lesson!

From now on, we won't always provide literal translations unless the Hebrew requires a more explicit explanation. Words that do not appear in the Hebrew but are needed in English are enclosed in

50 Fiftieth lesson (Shi'ur chamishim)

Mah qarah leMosheh?
What happened to Moses?

1 – **Mah ta'aseh naheget sheto'ah baderekh?**
What will a woman driver who takes the wrong road do?

2 – **Hi tikanes letachanat deleq vetish`al `eykh lehagi'a.**
She will go into a petrol station and *(will)* ask how to get there *(how to arrive)*.

3 – **Mah ya'aseh nehag?**
What will a man driver do?

4 – **Gever lo yish`al `eykh lehagi'a! Hu lo yeled qatan! Hu ya'adif linso'a sha'ot ulechapes.**
A man will not ask how to get there. He isn't a little boy! He will prefer to drive [for] hours looking [for the way].

5 – **'Akhshav `ani mevinah mah qarah leMosheh.**
Now I understand what happened to Moses.

square brackets [ ]. If you're not sure of the gender of a noun, you can look it up in the glossary at the back of the book.

---

50 שִׁעוּר חֲמִישִּׁים

מַה קָּרָה לְמֹשֶׁה?

1 – מַה תַּעֲשֶׂה נָהֶגֶת שֶׁטּוֹעָה בַּדֶּרֶךְ?

2 – הִיא תִּכָּנֵס לְתַחֲנַת דֶּלֶק וְתִשְׁאַל אֵיךְ לְהַגִּיעַ.

3 – מַה יַּעֲשֶׂה נֶהָג?

4 – גֶּבֶר לֹא יִשְׁאַל אֵיךְ לְהַגִּיעַ! הוּא לֹא יֶלֶד קָטָן! הוּא יַעֲדִיף לִנְסוֹעַ שָׁעוֹת וּלְחַפֵּשׂ.

5 – עַכְשָׁיו אֲנִי מְבִינָה מַה קָּרָה לְמֹשֶׁה.

הוא הסתובב שעות עד שמצא תחנת דלק.

6 **Lamah Mosheh rabenu histovev ① 'im bney Yisra`el `arba'im shanah ② bamidbar?**
Why did Moses our master wander with the Children of Israel [for] forty years *(year)* in the desert?

7 – **`Eykh zeh qarah shehem yatzu miMitzrayim, mima'arav ③ leYisra`el vehigi'u laYarden ④ mimizrach ⑤ leYisra`el?**
How did it happen that they left Egypt, to the west of Israel, and arrived at the [River] Jordan, to the east of Israel?

8 – **Ki, kmo kol gever, Mosheh lo ratzah lish`ol `eykh lehagi'a …**
Because, like every man, Moses didn't want to ask how to get there …

Notes

① **histovev** הִסְתוֹבֵב *he wandered, he turned around.* In this past tense reflexive verb, the first letter ס of the root סבב appears in between the letters הִ and ת (the characteristic prefix of the past tense in reflexive verbs). The reason is that it is easier to pronounce. We saw the same phenomenon in a previous lesson in **hishtaga'ta** הִשְׁתַּגַּעְתָּ *you have gone crazy.*

② **`arba'im shanah** אַרְבָּעִים שָׁנָה *forty years* ('forty year'). In lesson 45 (note 5), we learned that in **'esrim `elef** עֶשְׂרִים אֶלֶף *twenty thousand*, the **`elef** is singular, despite the fact that we are talking about many thousands (the same is true in English, of course – we say 'twenty thousand' and not 'twenty thousands'). Here, we see that the word *year* is also in the singular, although we are speaking of more than one year. The rule is that with numbers twenty and above, it is preferable to use the singular form of the noun being counted. However, if you were to say **`arba'im shanim**, no one would have any trouble understanding you.

6 לָמָּה מֹשֶׁה רַבֵּנוּ הִסְתּוֹבֵב עִם בְּנֵי יִשְׂרָאֵל אַרְבָּעִים שָׁנָה בַּמִּדְבָּר?

7 – אֵיךְ זֶה קָרָה שֶׁהֵם יָצְאוּ מִמִּצְרַיִם, מִמַּעֲרָב לְיִשְׂרָאֵל וְהִגִּיעוּ לַיַּרְדֵּן מִמִּזְרָח לְיִשְׂרָאֵל?

8 – כִּי כְּמוֹ כֹּל גֶּבֶר, מֹשֶׁה לֹא רָצָה לִשְׁאוֹל אֵיךְ לְהַגִּיעַ ... □

③ **ma'arav** מַעֲרָב *west*. This word is related to עֶרֶב *evening* – in the evening, the sun sets in the west.

④ **yarden** יַרְדֵּן *Jordan*. The Hebrew name for the River Jordan is also used for the country Jordan. As in English, this can also be a first name, and it is given to both boys and girls (see the end of lesson 54).

⑤ **mizrach** מִזְרָח *east*. The root of this word is זרח, which is also found in the verb **lizroach** לִזְרוֹחַ *to shine*. The shining sun appears each day from the east.

Targil rishon – Targem תַּרְגִּיל רִאשׁוֹן – תַּרְגֵּם

❶ סליחה, איך אני יכול להגיע לתל-אביב?
Slichah, `eykh `ani yakhol lehagi'a leTel-Aviv?

❷ הוא הסתובב שעות עד שמצא תחנת דלק.
Hu histovev sha'ot 'ad shematza tachanat deleq.

❸ בני ישראל היו ארבעים שנה במדבר.
Bney Yisra`el hayu `arba'im shanah bamidbar.

❹ הנהגת טועה בדרך ושואלת נהג איפה הקניון החדש.
Hanaheget to'ah baderekh vesho`elet nehag `eyfoh haqanyon hachadash.

Targil sheni – Hashlem תַּרְגִּיל שֵׁנִי – הַשְׁלֵם

Let's try something new! In this exercise, the missing words you need to find in the Hebrew are also missing from the transliteration. Look back to the lesson text if you can't remember which word belongs in the blank.

❶ You*(fem.)* have got the wrong address. You need to look next to the post office.
`At [...] baktovet. `At tzrikhah [...] 'al yad ha[...].
אַת ____ בַּכְּתוֹבֶת. אַת צְרִיכָה ____ עַל יַד הַ_____.

❷ A man will not ask how to get to the beach.
[...] lo [...] `eykh [...] lechof hayam.
___ לֹא ____ אֵיךְ _____ לְחוֹף הַיָּם.

❸ The Jordan is to the east of Israel and the sea is to the west.
HaYarden mi[...] leYisra`el vehayam mi[...].
הַיַּרְדֵּן מִ____ לְיִשְׂרָאֵל וְהַיָּם מִ____.

⑤ הם רצו לנסוע לים במערב תל-אביב, אבל הם הגיעו למזרח.

Hem ratzu linso'a layam bema'arav Tel-Aviv, `aval hem higi'u lamizrach.

Answers to Exercise 1

❶ Excuse me, how do I get to Tel Aviv? ❷ He wandered [around] for hours before he found a petrol station. ❸ The Children of Israel spent *(were)* forty years in the desert. ❹ The woman driver takes the wrong road and asks a *(male)* driver where the new mall is. ❺ They wanted to travel to the sea in the west of Tel Aviv, but they arrived in the east.

❹ Do you have another joke about our master Moses?

Yesh lakhem [...] bdichah 'al [...] [...]?

יֵשׁ לָכֶם ___ בְּדִיחָה עַל ___ _____?

❺ He does not take the plane *(fly)* because he likes to drive *(travel)* through the desert to *(until)* Eilat.

Hu lo [...] ki hu `ohev linso'a ba[...] 'ad Eylat.

הוּא לֹא __ כִּי הוּא אוֹהֵב לִנְסוֹעַ בַּ____ עַד אֵילַת.

Answers to Exercise 2

The missing words from the exercise are given here both in Hebrew script (from right to left), and in transliteration (from left to right).

❶ – **to'ah – lechapes – do`ar** — ❶ - טוֹעָה - לְחַפֵּשׂ - דּוֹאַר

❷ **Gever – yish`al – lehagi'a –** — ❷ גֶּבֶר - יִשְׁאַל - לְהַגִּיעַ -

❸ – **mizrach – ma'arav** — ❸ - מִזְרָח - מַעֲרָב

❹ – **'od – Mosheh rabenu** — ❹ - עוֹד - משֶׁה רַבֵּנוּ

❺ – **tas – midbar –** — ❺ - טָס - מִדְבָּר -

50 **Midbar** מִדְבָּר desert. *Deserts account for over half of Israel's area. The* נֶגֶב **Negev** *extends from north of Beersheva all the way to Eilat, while the Judaean Desert* מִדְבָּר יְהוּדָה **Midbar Yehuda** *lies east of Jerusalem and descends to the Dead Sea. The deserts in Israel are not endless vistas of sand dunes, but diverse environments that include rocky mountains, dry river beds and sandy expanses. It is said that* מֹשֶׁה **Mosheh** *received the* **'aseret hadibrot** עֲשֶׂרֶת הַדִּבְּרוֹת Ten Commandments *on Mount Sinai in the Sinai Desert in Egypt.*

Mitzrayim מִצְרַיִם Egypt. *The Hebrew name of this country has the appearance of a dual noun.*

Mosheh rabenu מֹשֶׁה רַבֵּנוּ Our master (or rabbi) Moses. *The word* **rabenu** רַבֵּנוּ *is related to* **rav** רַב great, *suggesting the high level of knowledge and prestige embodied in the rabbi's vocation (the English word rabbi comes from the Hebrew source). The same root appears in* **harbeh** הַרְבֵּה many, much. **rav** רַב *has been used as an honorific title since the Second Temple period.*

Consolidation: the 'second wave'

Well done – you've just completed lesson 50! At this stage, it's time to take the next step, ensuring that you retain what you've already learned as you continue to progress.

From now on, at the end of each lesson, you'll go back to a lesson you've already done (beginning with lesson 1). In the previous lesson, hide the Hebrew on the right-hand side, as well as the transliteration. Then try to translate the English into Hebrew – first, by speaking out loud, and then in writing (in Hebrew letters, of course). When you've finished, compare your translation to the actual text and correct any mistakes. Next, complete the same process with exercise 1 of the same lesson: translate the English into Hebrew first by speaking out loud, and then in writing, and finally compare your translation to the original text of the exercise.

So each lesson from now on will include two stages: discovering new material (the comprehension phase) and then consolidating what you've already learned (the 'active' phase). This combination will ensure that you're both building on and reinforcing your skills.

Second wave: lesson 1

51 Fifty-first lesson
(Shi'ur chamishim ve`achat)

HaKarmel
The Carmel

1 – **Slichah gvirti, `ani lo makir `et Cheyfah. `Eyfoh tachanat 'hakarmelit' ①?**
Excuse me, madam *(Pardon my-lady)*, I don't know Haifa. Where [is the] Carmelit station?

2 – **Lekh ② qadimah ③ 'al hamidrakhah hahi ④. Baramzor ⑤ harishon pneh smolah ⑥.**
Go forward along that sidewalk *(the-sidewalk that-one[fem.])*. At the first traffic light *(At-the-traffic-light the-first)*, turn left *(to-left)*.

Notes

① **karmelit** כַּרְמֶלִית. The Carmelit is the name of an underground funicular railway line in Haifa. Constructed by a French company, the Carmelit begins at Paris Square in downtown Haifa and ascends through four stations to the top of Mount Carmel.

② **lekh** לֵךְ *go*; **pneh** פְּנֵה *turn* (in the next sentence). Note these two imperative forms.

③ Lines 2 and 3 include three adverbs of direction or movement:

qadimah קָדִימָה *forwards*

smolah שְׂמֹאלָה *left, to the left*

yaminah יָמִינָה *right, to the right*

This same suffix, **-ah** ָה, can be added to nouns and place names, as we saw in lesson 40: **habaytah** הַבַּיְתָה *home, homewards*, and **Yerushalaymah** יְרוּשָׁלַיְמָה *to Jerusalem*. This suffix is known as 'the **hey** ה of direction'.

④ **hahi** הַהִיא (line 2), **hahu** הַהוּא (line 3) *that, that one* (fem., masc.). These demonstratives, used to indicate something at

51 שִׁעוּר חֲמִישִּׁים וְאַחַת

הַכַּרְמֶל

1 – סלִיחָה גבִירתִי, אֲנִי לֹא מַכִּיר אֶת חֵיפָה. אֵיפֹה תַחֲנַת "הַכַּרמֶלִית"?

2 – לֵךְ קָדִימָה עַל הַמִדרָכָה הָהִיא. בָּרַמזוֹר הָרִאשׁוֹן פּנֵה שׂמֹאלָה.

a certain distance, are formed from the definite article **ha** הָ followed by the personal pronoun **hu** הוּא, **hi** הִיא, **hem** הֵם or **hen** הֵן. So the plural forms are **hahem** הָהֵם and **hahen** הָהֵן *those, those ones* (masc., fem.).

⑤ **ramzor** רַמזוֹר *traffic light*. This modern Hebrew word combines the root רמז *to indicate, hint* and the noun אוֹר *light*.

⑥ **smolah** שׂמֹאלָה *to the left*. The associated adjectives are **smali** שׂמָאלִי (masc. sing.), **smalit** שׂמָאלִית (fem. sing.), **smaliyim** שׂמָאלִיִים (masc. pl.) and **smaliyot** שׂמָאלִיוֹת (fem. pl). Note that the **alef** א is completely silent and is never pronounced.

3 Barechov hahu, lekh me`ah metrim 'ad hamidrachov ⑦. Batamrur 'atzor pneh yaminah.
On that road *(At-road the-it[masc.])*, go a hundred metres until the pedestrianized street. At the stop sign *(At-sign-of the-stop)*, turn right.

4 `Atah rotzeh lehagi'a lechof haKarmel?
Do you want to get to Carmel Beach?

5 – Lo. Lemerkaz haKarmel. `Ani gar bemalon 'Dan Karmel'.
No. To Central Carmel *(To-centre-of the-Carmel)*. I'm staying *(I live)* at Hotel Dan Carmel.

6 – `Atah tayar?
[Are] you a tourist?

7 – Lo. `Ani gar beKharmi`el ⑧. Bati levaqer chaver miDalyat El Karmel. Hu rofe beveyt hacholim 'Karmel'.
No. I live in Carmiel. I've come to visit a friend from Dalyat el-Carmel. He [is] a doctor at the Carmel Hospital *(house-of the-sick)*.

8 Ba li litzchoq. Poh hakol Karmel. Hayom `akhalti `avoqado 'Karmel' va`afilu qrem qaramel.
I feel like laughing *(It-comes for-me to-laugh)*. Here everything [is] Carmel. Today I ate a 'Carmel' avocado and even a crème caramel.

Notes

⑦ **midrachov** מִדְרָחוֹב *pedestrian street.* Like רַמְזוֹר above, this is another good example of how modern Hebrew forms new words by combining existing words to deal with new concepts. This is a combination of **midrakhah** מִדְרָכָה *sidewalk*

3 בָּרְחוֹב הָהוּא, לֵךְ מֵאָה מֶטְרִים עַד הַמִּדְרָחוֹב. בַּתַּמְרוּר עָצוֹר פְּנֵה יָמִינָה.

4 אַתָּה רוֹצֶה לְהַגִּיעַ לְחוֹף הַכַּרְמֶל?

5 – לֹא. לְמֶרְכָּז הַכַּרְמֶל. אֲנִי גָּר בְּמָלוֹן "דָּן כַּרְמֶל".

6 – אַתָּה תַּיָּר?

7 – לֹא. אֲנִי גָּר בְּכַרְמִיאֵל. בָּאתִי לְבַקֵּר חָבֵר מִדָּלִיַּת אֶל כַּרְמֶל. הוּא רוֹפֵא בְּבֵית הַחוֹלִים "כַּרְמֶל".

8 בָּא לִי לִצְחוֹק. פֹּה הַכֹּל כַּרְמֶל. הַיּוֹם אָכַלְתִּי אֲבוֹקָדוֹ "כַּרְמֶל" וַאֲפִילוּ קְרֶם קָרָמֶל.

pavement (in which you may be able to detect **derekh** דֶּרֶךְ *way*) and **rechov** רְחוֹב *road.*

⑧ **Karmi`el** is a new town to the east of Acre. The name can be interpreted as *vineyard of God*, from **kerem** כֶּרֶם *vineyard* and **`el** אֵל *God.*

**51   9   Hayah li na'im lehakir `otakh. Shmi ⑨
`Eliyahu. Mah shmekh?**

It was a pleasure to get to meet you *(It-was
for-me pleasant to-be-acquainted [`et]-you)*. My
name [is] Eliyahu. What's your name?

10 –   Karmela.

Carmela.

Notes

⑨ **shmi** שְׁמִי *my name* is the short form of **hashem sheli**
הַשֵּׁם שֶׁלִּי 'the-name of-me'. In the same way, the form

Targil rishon – Targem   תַּרְגִּיל רִאשׁוֹן – תַּרְגֵּם

❶ הַתַּיָּרִים רוֹצִים לִנְסֹעַ בְּכַרְמְלִית מִמֶּרְכַּז הַכַּרְמֶל לַיָּם.
Hatayarim rotzim linso'a bakarmelit mimerkaz
haKarmel layam.

❷ הוּא רוֹפֵא יְלָדִים בְּבֵית הַחוֹלִים "כַּרְמֶל".
Hu rofe yeladim beveyt hacholim 'Karmel'.

❸ לֵךְ שְׂמֹאלָה עַל הַמִּדְרָכָה הַהִיא עַד תַּמְרוּר הֶעָצֹר.
Lekh smolah 'al hamidrakhah hahi 'ad tamrur he'atzor.

❹ בָּרְחוֹב הַהוּא יֵשׁ רַמְזוֹר כָּל עֲשָׂרָה מֶטֶר.
Barechov hahu yesh ramzor kol 'asarah meter.

❺ שְׁמִי אֵלִיָּהוּ, נָעִים לִי לְהַכִּיר אוֹתָךְ.
Shmi `Eliyahu, na'im li lehakir `otakh.

9 הָיָה לִי נָעִים לְהַכִּיר אוֹתָךְ. שְׁמִי אֵלִיָּהוּ. מַה שְּׁמֵךְ?

10 – כַּרְמֶלָה.

shmekh שְׁמֵךְ *your name* is a shorter version of **hashem shelakh** הַשֵּׁם שֶׁלָּךְ 'the-name of-you (fem.)'. Similar forms can be formed for all persons and genders.

Answers to Exercise 1

❶ The tourists want to travel by the Carmelit from the centre of Carmel to the sea. ❷ He is a paediatrician *(doctor-of children)* at the Carmel Hospital. ❸ Go to the left along *(on)* that sidewalk up to the stop sign. ❹ On that road there is a traffic light every ten metre[s]. ❺ My name is Eliyahu, nice *(pleasant)* to meet *(to get to know)* you.

Targil sheni – Hashlem — תַּרְגִּיל שֵׁנִי – הַשְׁלֵם

❶ He is staying in a wonderful hotel in Central Carmel *(centre-of the-Carmel).*
Hu [...] [...] nehedar be[...] ha[...].
הוּא __ _____ נֶהְדָר בְּ____ הַ____ .

❷ I feel like laughing about all the stupid things I*(masc.)* hear.
[...] [...] litzchoq mikol [...] sheani shome'a.
__ __ לִצְחוֹק מִכָּל _______ שֶׁאֲנִי שׁוֹמֵעַ.

❸ From the pedestrian street on the Carmel, you can see *(they-see)* a beautiful beach.
Meha[...] 'al haKarmel [...] chof [...].
מֵהַ______ עַל הַכַּרְמֶל _____ חוֹף ___ .

❹ I ate an avocado with orange cream. Very tasty!
`Akhalti qrem [...] 'im tapuzim. [...] me`od!
אָכַלְתִּי קְרֶם ______ עִם תַּפּוּזִים. ____ מְאוֹד!

Dalyat el-Carmel *is a Druze village on Mount Carmel, approximately 20 kilometres from Haifa. The village is popular with tourists thanks to its artisanal crafts and popular restaurants, but it also bears witness to an enigmatic religious minority. The Egyptian ruler Caliph Al-Hakim was a Shiite Muslim at the end of the 11th century. Towards the end of his life, he claimed to be of divine origin. His vizier, Al-Daruzi, became the founder of a new faith that bears his name. Today, some 350,000 Druze live in Syria, and roughly the same number in Lebanon. In Israel, the Druze population is about 60,000 (fewer than in the United States, where some 100,000 Druze live). The Druze speak Arabic, but jealously preserve their unique religious and cultural identity. In the past, the Druze faced attacks from the surrounding Muslim population, and, as a result, Druze villages were usually established on hilltops in order to provide a measure of security. Druze men in Israel are drafted into the army just like their Jewish peers, and many Druze continue to serve in the army, police and prison service after completing the mandatory military service.*

❺ She is taking the wrong road, but she knows that the sea is always to the west. Phew!
Hi [...] baderekh `aval hi [...] shehayam tamid [...]. Oof!

הִיא ____ בַּדֶּרֶךְ אֲבָל הִיא _____ שֶׁהַיָּם תָּמִיד _____ . אוּף!

Answers to Exercise 2

❶ – **gar bemalon** – **merkaz** – **Karmel** — גָּר בְּמָלוֹן - מֶרְכָּז - כַּרְמֶל - ❶
❷ **Ba li** – **hashtuyot** – — בָּאוּ לִי - הַשְּׁטוּיוֹת - ❷
❸ – **midrachov** – **ro`im** – **yafeh** — מִדְרָחוֹב - רוֹאִים - יָפֶה - ❸
❹ – **`avoqado** – **Ta'im** – — אֲבוֹקָדוֹ - טָעִים - ❹
❺ – **to'ah** – **yoda'at** – **bama'arav** – — טוֹעָה - יוֹדַעַת - בַּמַּעֲרָב - ❺

The **Carmel** *is a hilly plateau some 25-kilometres long and reaching a height of 546 meters above sea level. The Carmel has religious significance as the place where the Prophet Elijah forcefully challenged the prophets of Baal (see Kings I, Chapter 18). Christian hermits maintained a monastic lifestyle on the site until the rise of Islam. Their traditions are perpetuated today in the Carmelite order of monks and nuns.*

Now that you've finished lesson 51, go back to lesson 2 and follow the instructions described in the previous lesson. You're gradually mastering this fascinating language. Keep it up!

Second wave: lesson 2

52 Fifty-second lesson
(Shi'ur chamishim ushtayim)

'Iton ① mashmin
A fattening newspaper

1 – **Shalom `adoni. `Ani mevaqeshet levatel `et haminuy ② lashevu'on ③ shelakhem.**
Hello, sir. I [would] like to cancel my *(the)* subscription to your weekly *(weekly your)*.

2 – **Gvirti, `at menuyah ④ kvar 'eser shanim. Mah lo motze chen be'eynayikh bashevu'on shelanu?**
Madam, you [have been] subscribing [for] *(already)* ten years. What don't you like *(What not finds grace in-your-eyes)* about *(in)* our weekly?

3 – **Hashevu'on metzuyan. Hayiti menuyah 'al ha'iton 'od keshehayah yarchon ⑤.**
The weekly [is] excellent. I was a subscriber to the journal when it was still a monthly.

4 – **Ve`at rotzah levatel `et haminuy?**
And you want to cancel the subscription?

Notes

① **'iton** עִתּוֹן *newspaper* comes from the word **'et** עֵת *time, epoch*. The suffix **-on** וֹן indicates a noun.

② **minuy** מִינּוּי *subscription*. The root of this word is מנה *to count*.

③ **shevu'on** שְׁבוּעוֹן *weekly* comes from **shavu'a** שָׁבוּעַ *week*, with the same suffix **-on** וֹן as we saw in note 1.

④ **`at menuyah** אַתְּ מְנוּיָה *you have been subscribing*. Note that Hebrew uses the present tense for the equivalent of 'I/you/he etc. have been …-ing'. This construction often appears with a

עִתּוֹן מַשְׁמִין

1 – שָׁלוֹם אֲדוֹנִי. אֲנִי מְבַקֶּשֶׁת לְבַטֵּל אֶת הַמִּינּוּי לַשְּׁבוּעוֹן שֶׁלָּכֶם.

2 – גְּבִירְתִּי, אַתְּ מְנוּיָה כְּבָר עֶשֶׂר שָׁנִים. מַה לֹּא מוֹצֵא חֵן בְּעֵינַיִךְ בַּשְּׁבוּעוֹן שֶׁלָּנוּ?

3 – הַשְּׁבוּעוֹן מְצוּיָּן. הָיִיתִי מְנוּיָה עַל הָעִתּוֹן עוֹד כְּשֶׁהָיָה יַרְחוֹן.

4 – וְאַתְּ רוֹצָה לְבַטֵּל אֶת הַמִּינּוּי?

measure of time – 'for one week', 'for six years', and so forth. The exercises include other examples of this.

⑤ **yarchon** יַרְחוֹן *monthly*. Once again, the **-on** וֹן suffix is used to form a noun. The root ירח is related to the words for both month and moon, since the Hebrew calendar is lunar.

5 – `Agid lekha `et ha`emet. `Ani `ohevet `et
hamador 'Mehamitbach ⑥ be`ahavah'...
I'll tell you the truth. I like the column 'From
the Kitchen with Love'...

6 – `Anachnu be`emet me`od ge`im ⑦ bamador
hazeh.
We are really very proud of that column *(We in-
truth very proud in-column that).*

7 – Zot bediyuq hasibah. Medor hamitbach ⑧
mashmin ⑨: 'eser shanim, 'asarah qilo!
That [is] exactly the reason. The kitchen
column is fattening: ten years – ten kilo[s]!

Notes

⑥ **mehamitbach** מֵהַמִּטְבָּח *from the kitchen.* **Me-** מֵ *from*
indicates origin.

⑦ `**anachnu ge`im** אֲנַחְנוּ גֵּאִים *we are proud.* This is the present
tense. In the past and the future, the verb is used in a reflexive
form: **hitga`enu** הִתְגָּאֵנוּ *we were proud*; **nitga`eh beSarah**
נִתְגָּאֶה בְּשָׂרָה *we will be proud of Sarah.*

❧

Targil rishon – Targem   תַּרְגִּיל רִאשׁוֹן – תַּרְגֵּם

❶ לְשִׁירִי יֵשׁ מִינּוּי לְיַרְחוֹן יְלָדִים.
LeShiri yesh minuy leyarchon yeladim.

❷ כְּבָר שְׁנָתַיִם דַּלְיָה מְנוּיָה לְבִרְכַת הַכְּפָר.
Kvar shnatayim Dalyah menuyah livrekhat hakfar.

❸ אֶסַּע לַמְּסִיבָה אֵצֶל מִשְׁפַּחַת אוֹרֶן, אֲבָל הָאוֹכֶל שָׁם מַשְׁמִין
מְאוֹד.
`Esa' lamesibah `etzel mishpachat `Oren, `aval ha`okhel
sham mashmin me`od.

❹ הֵם גֵּאִים בְּבֵן הֶחָמוּד שֶׁלָּהֶם.
Hem ge`im baben hachamud shelahem.

5 – אָגִיד לְךָ אֶת הָאֱמֶת. אֲנִי אוֹהֶבֶת אֶת הַמָּדוֹר "מֵהַמִּטְבָּח בְּאַהֲבָה"...

6 – אֲנַחְנוּ בֶּאֱמֶת מְאֹד גֵּאִים בַּמָּדוֹר הַזֶּה.

7 – זֹאת בְּדִיּוּק הַסִּיבָּה. מְדוֹר הַמִּטְבָּח מַשְׁמִין: עֶשֶׂר שָׁנִים, עֲשָׂרָה קִילוֹ! □

⑧ **medor hamitbach** מְדוֹר הַמִּטְבָּח *the kitchen column*. As we've seen, the first word in a construct state often changes form slightly. The absolute state of the word *column* is **mador** מָדוֹר. Note that when written without vowel marks (as is usual), this difference cannot be seen. The context enables you to read the word correctly.

⑨ **mashmin** מַשְׁמִין *fattening*. This comes from the word **shemen** שֶׁמֶן *oil*.

❺ לכל אשה בישראל יש הספר "מהמטבח באהבה".
Lekhol `ishah beYisra`el yesh hasefer 'Mehamitbach be`ahavah'.

Answers to Exercise 1

❶ Shiri has a subscription to a children's monthly. ❷ For two years, Dalya has been a member at *(has been subscribing to)* the village swimming pool. ❸ I'll go the party at the Orens', but the food there is very fattening. ❹ They are proud of their cute son. ❺ Every woman in Israel has the book 'From the Kitchen with Love'.

Targil sheni – Hashlem   תַּרְגִּיל שֵׁנִי – הַשְׁלֵם

❶ Every Friday, he buys this weekly because of the sport column.
Kol [...] [...] hu qoneh `et [...] hazeh biglal [...] hasport.

כֹּל __ ____ הוּא קוֹנֶה אֶת _______ הַזֶּה בִּגְלַל ____ הַסְּפּוֹרְט.

❷ Do you*(fem.)* really want me to tell you the truth about the idiocies there are in your book?
`At [...] rotzah [...] lakh `et [...] 'al [...] sheyesh basefer [...]?

אַתְּ ____ רוֹצָה _____ לָךְ אֶת ____ עַל _______ שֶׁיֵּשׁ בַּסֵּפֶר ___?

❸ Sorry. That's all talk, talk. What exactly is the price of this car?
Slichah. Hakol [...] [...]. Mah [...] hamechir shel hamekhonit [...]?

סְלִיחָה. הַכֹּל _______ ________. מַה _____ הַמְּחִיר שֶׁל הַמְּכוֹנִית ____?

❹ This coat makes me [look] fat *(is fattening)*. Do you have anything nicer?
Hame'il [...] [...] `oti. Yesh lakhem [...] yoter yafeh?

הַמְּעִיל ___ _____ אוֹתִי. יֵשׁ לָכֶם ____ יוֹתֵר יָפֶה?

❺ [Is it] possible to cancel the flight ticket? I [have been] in hospital for a week.
[...] levatel `et kartis hatisah? `ani [...] [...] kvar shavu'a.

___ לְבַטֵּל אֶת כַּרְטִיס הַטִּיסָה? אֲנִי ____ _____ כְּבָר שָׁבוּעַ.

Answers to Exercise 2

❶ – **yom shishi** – **hashevu'on** – **medor** –

❶ - יוֹם שִׁישִׁי - הַשְּׁבוּעוֹן - מְדוֹר -

❷ – **be`emet** – **she`agid** – **ha`emet** – **hashtuyot** – **shelakh**

❷ - בֶּאֱמֶת - שֶׁאָגִיד - הָאֱמֶת - הַשְּׁטוּיוֹת - שֶׁלָּךְ

❸ – **diburim diburim** – **bediyuq** – **hazot**

❸ - דִּיבּוּרִים דִּיבּוּרִים - בְּדִיּוּק - הַזֹּאת

❹ – **hazeh mashmin** – **mashehu** –

❹ - הַזֶּה מַשְׁמִין - מַשֶּׁהוּ -

❺ **`Efshar** – **beveyt cholim** –

❺ אֶפְשָׁר- בְּבֵית חוֹלִים -

In this lesson, the man and woman refer to each other as **gvirti** גְבִירְתִי my lady, *i.e.* madam, *and* **`adoni** אֲדוֹנִי my master, *i.e.* sir. *This is as formal as it gets in Hebrew. Israelis are usually very informal. Children call their teachers by their first names, as do bosses and workers, however senior or junior. Whenever you meet someone new in Israel, you should always exchange names as soon as possible and then move straight onto first-name terms. If you're asking someone you don't know for information, you can use* **gvirti** גְבִירְתִי *or* **`adoni** אֲדוֹנִי *for an adult,* **bachur** בָּחוּר young man *or* **bachurah** בָּחוּרָה young woman *for someone in their teens or twenties, and* **yeled** יֶלֶד boy *or* **yaldah** יַלְדָה girl *for a child.*

Mehamitbach be`ahavah מֵהַמִּטְבָּח בְּאַהֲבָה *is a well-known Israeli cookbook. Written by Ruth Sirkis, the first edition appeared in 1975. It is so popular that people sometimes jokingly talk about Israeli cuisine 'before' and 'after' Ruth Sirkis!*

Second wave: lesson 3

53 Fifty-third lesson
(Shi'ur chamishim veshalosh)

Keday ① lirzot!
It pays to lose weight!

1 **Mahapekhah be'olam hatayarut ② beYisra`el.**
A revolution in the world of tourism in Israel.

2 **Sokhnut hanesi'ot 'Nofesh Yashir' mokheret kartisey tisah ③ le`Eyropah ule`artzot hayam haTikhon ④ lefi mishqal hanose'a.**
The travel agency Direct Vacation[s] is selling plane *(flight)* tickets to Europe and to countries [around] the Mediterranean *(Sea)* according to the weight of the traveller.

3 **Hamechir: midolar vachetzi 'ad chamishah dolarim leqilo.**
The price [ranges] from one dollar fifty to five dollars a kilogram.

4 **Dugma`ot: kartis tisah leLondon `o leRoma shloshah dolarim leqilo.**
[Some] examples: a flight ticket to London or Rome [costs] three dollars a kilogram.

5 **LeParis qtzat yoter yaqar: shloshah vachetzi dolarim leqilo.**
To Paris [it's a] little more expensive: three and a half dollars a kilogram.

Notes

① **keday** כְּדַאי *it is worth*, *it pays* (followed by an infinitive). Do not confuse **keday** כְּדַאי (rhymes with *reply*) with כְּדֵי **kedey** (rhymes with *today*), which means *in order to*, *for*.

② **tayarut** תַּיָּרוּת *tourism*. The **-ut** וּת suffix usually forms feminine abstract nouns from another noun, as in the following examples:

כְּדָאִי לִרזוֹת

1 מַהֲפֵּכָה בְּעוֹלָם הַתַּיָּרוּת בְּיִשְׂרָאֵל.

2 סוֹכנוּת הַנְסִיעוֹת "נוֹפֶשׁ יָשִׁיר" מוֹכֶרֶת כַּרטִיסֵי טִיסָה לְאֵירוֹפָּה וּלְאַרצוֹת הַיָּם הַתִיכוֹן, לְפִי מִשקָל הַנוֹסֵעַ.

3 הַמְחִיר: מִדוֹלָר וַחֵצִי עַד חֲמִישָּׁה דוֹלָרִים לְקִילוֹ.

4 דוּגמָאוֹת: כַּרטִיס טִיסָה לְלוֹנדוֹן אוֹ לְרוֹמָא שְׁלוֹשָׁה דוֹלָרִים לְקִילוֹ.

5 לְפָּרִיס קְצָת יוֹתֵר יָקָר: שְׁלוֹשָׁה וַחֵצִי דוֹלָרִים לְקִילוֹ.

tayar תַּיָּר *tourist*; **tayarut** תַּיָּרוּת *tourism*
sokhen סוֹכֵן *agent*; **sokhnut** סוֹכנוּת *agency*
'iton עִתוֹן *newspaper, journal*; **'itonut** עִתוֹנוּת *journalism*
`efshar** אֶפשָׁר *possible*; **`efsharut אֶפשָׁרוּת *possibility.*

③ **kartisey tisah** כַּרטִיסֵי טִיסָה *flight tickets, plane tickets.* The final **yod** י of the construct form **kartisey** is all that remains of the normal masculine plural ending of the absolute form **kartisim** כַּרטִיסִים. The longer form **kartisim shel tisah** would not be incorrect, but sounds strange to an Israeli ear.

④ **`artzot hayam haTikhon** אַרצוֹת הַיָּם הַתִיכוֹן *Mediterranean countries* ('countries-of the-sea-of the-Mediterranean'). The singular **`eretz** אֶרֶץ *country* is **`aratzot** אֲרָצוֹת in the plural absolute and **`artzot** אַרצוֹת in the plural construct (as here).

6 **Menahel sokhnut hanesi'ot hodi'a sheyesh mishqal bamisrad.**
The manager of the travel agency announced that there are scales in the office.

7 **Kol nose'a tzarikh lehishaqel lifney shehu qoneh kartis tisah.**
Every passenger must be weighed before buying *(that he-buys)* a flight ticket.

8 **Tzarikh lehosif me`ah ve'esrim dolar le`agrat sdeh te'ufah vesidurey bitachon ⑤.**
[You] must add one hundred and twenty dollars for the airport tax and security arrangements *(for-right-of field-of aviation and-arrangements-of security)*.

9 **`Az tihiyu razim veyafim. Tisah zolah une'imah!**
So be *(you-will-be)* thin and beautiful! [Have a] cheap and pleasant flight!

Targil rishon – Targem תַּרְגִּיל רִאשׁוֹן – תַּרְגֵּם

❶ אנחנו כבר שנים קונים כרטיסי טיסה באותה סוכנות נסיעות.
`Anachnu kvar shanim qonim kartisey tisah be`otah sokhnut nesi'ot.

❷ בשיעור גאוגרפיה למדנו על הים התיכון.
Beshi'ur geografyah lamadnu 'al hayam hatikhon.

❸ סידורי הביטחון בשדה התעופה מצוינים.
Sidurey habitachon bisdeh hate'ufah metzuyanim.

❹ איפה הנוסעים צריכים להשקל לפני שהם קונים כרטיסים?
`Eyfoh hanos'im tzrikhim lehishaqel lifney shehem qonim kartisim?

6 מְנַהֵל סוכנוּת הַנְּסִיעוֹת הוֹדִיעַ שֶׁיֵּשׁ מִשְׁקָל בַּמִּשְׂרָד.

7 כֹּל נוֹסֵעַ צָרִיךְ לְהִשָּׁקֵל לִפְנֵי שֶׁהוּא קוֹנֶה כַּרְטִיס טִיסָה.

8 צָרִיךְ לְהוֹסִיף מֵאָה וְעֶשְׂרִים דוֹלָר לְאַגְרַת שְׂדֵה תְּעוּפָה וְסִידּוּרֵי בִּטָּחוֹן.

9 אָז תִּהְיוּ רָזִים וְיָפִים. טִיסָה זוֹלָה וּנְעִימָה! □

Notes

⑤ **sidurey bitachon** סִידּוּרֵי בִּטָּחוֹן *security arrangements, security measures*. In grammatical terms, this construction is the same as **kartisey tisah** in note 3.

❺ כדאי לך לקנות את הטבעת, היא גם יפה וגם זולה.
Keday lakh liqnot `et hataba'at, hi gam yafah vegam zolah.

Answers to Exercise 1

❶ For years, we have been buying flight tickets from the same travel agency. ❷ In the geography lesson, we studied the Mediterranean Sea. ❸ The security arrangements at the airport are excellent. ❹ Where do the passengers have to be weighed before they buy tickets? ❺ It's worth buying the ring, it's both beautiful and cheap.

Targil sheni – Hashlem תַּרְגִּיל שֵׁנִי – הַשְׁלֵם

❶ To lose weight *(get thin)*, I swim every day [for] an hour in the pool.
[...] lirzot `ani [...] [...] [...] sha'ah babrekhah.

___ לִרְזוֹת אֲנִי ____ __ __ שָׁעָה בַּבְּרֵכָה.

❷ The office manager announced the new working arrangement.
[...] [...] hodi'a 'al [...] [...] chadashim.

____ _____ הוֹדִיעַ עַל ______ _____ חֲדָשִׁים.

❸ The agency Direct Vacations sells the cheapest tickets.
[...] ‘Nofesh yashir’ [...] `et hakartisim [...] [...].

______ "נוֹפֶשׁ יָשִׁיר" _____ אֶת הַכַּרְטִיסִים ______ _____.

❹ At the mall it is possible to buy hummus and tahini by weight.
[...] `efshar [...] chumus vetchinah [...].

______ אֶפְשָׁר _____ חוּמוּס וּטְחִינָה _____.

❺ The tourists travel to Europe in the summer and to the Mediterranean countries in the winter.
Hatayarim nos'im [...] baqayitz ule`artzot [...] [...] bachoref.

הַתַּיָּרִים נוֹסְעִים ______ בַּקַּיִץ וּלְאַרְצוֹת ___ ______ בַּחוֹרֶף.

Sokhnut hanesi'ot סוֹכְנוּת הַנְּסִיעוֹת travel agency. *There are two main reasons why Israelis are so fond of medium- and long-distance travel: Israel's often tense relations with its immediate neighbours, and the influence of the Jewish Diaspora. The Greek word 'diaspora' (dispersion) is used to refer to the Jewish communities outside the Land of Israel. Most Israeli Jews come from families with a personal story of immigration as recent as their parents or grandparents. Sometimes the ways in which they came to Israel are*

Answers to Exercise 2

❶ **Kedey – sochah kol yom –** ❶ כְּדַי - שׁוֹחָה כֹּל יוֹם -
❷ **Menahel hamisrad – sidurey 'avodah –**
❷ מְנַהֵל הַמִּשְׂרָד - סִידּוּרֵי עֲבוֹדָה -
❸ **Sokhnut – mokheret – hazolim beyoter**
❸ סוֹכְנוּת - מוֹכֶרֶת - הַזּוֹלִים בְּיוֹתֵר
❹ **Baqanyon – liqnot – bemishqal** ❹ בַּקַּנְיוֹן - לִקְנוֹת - בְּמִשְׁקָל
❺ **– le`Eyropah – hayam hatikhon –** ❺ - לְאֵירוֹפָּה - הַיָּם הַתִּיכוֹן -

amazing and moving. As a result, the younger generation also has a sense of adventure, sometimes tinged by an element of rivalry: who will manage to find the most exotic destination for their next foreign trip? Travel agencies make a good living from this Israeli trait. The anecdote in this lesson is based on a humoristic advertisement that appeared in the press.

Second wave: lesson 4

Fifty-fourth lesson
(Shi'ur chamishim ve`arba')

Hakhanot ①
Preparations

1 **'Adi shalach mikhtav `eleqtroni le`achiv hagadol.**
Adi sent an email to his big brother *(to-brother-his the-big)*.

2 – **"`Achi hayaqar. Raq `atah yakhol la'azor li.**
"My dear brother. Only you can help me *(help for-me)*.

3 **Nikhshalti bamekhinah la`universitah. Takhin ② `et Aba. Todah, 'Adi."**
I failed *(in)* the preparatory course for the university. Prepare *(You-will-prepare)* Dad. Thanks, Adi."

4 **`Acharey shloshah yamim, hu qibel tshuvah `eleqtronit:**
Three days later, he received an email reply:

5 – **"Shalom `achi haqatan. 'Asiti mah shebiqashta mimeni.**
Greetings, my little brother. I did what you asked me to *(of me)*.

Notes

① **hakhanot** הֲכָנוֹת *preparations* (note that with the definite article, this would be **hahakhanot** הַהֲכָנוֹת *the preparations*). The singular form is **hakhanah** הֲכָנָה. This noun is feminine, like almost all those with the ending **-ah**. The root is כון, which appears several times in this lesson in different forms. It is an example of a so-called 'hollow' root, since the middle letter is **vav** ו. In this type of verb, the **vav** sometimes disappears, as in ▸

הֲכָנוֹת

1 עֲדִי שָׁלַח מִכתָב אֶלֶקטרוֹנִי לְאָחִיו הַגָּדוֹל.

2 – "אָחִי הַיָּקָר. רַק אַתָּה יָכוֹל לַעֲזוֹר לִי.

3 נִכשַׁלתִּי בַּמְּכִינָה לָאוּנִיבֶרסִיטָה. תָּכִין אֶת אַבָּא. תוֹדָה. עֲדִי."

4 אַחֲרֵי שלוֹשָׁה יָמִים הוּא קִבֵּל תשׁוּבָה אֶלֶקטרוֹנִית:

5 – "שָׁלוֹם אָחִי הַקָּטָן. עָשִׂיתִי מַה שֶּׁבִּקַּשׁתָּ מִמֶּנִּי.

hakhanot הֲכָנוֹת, only to reappear elsewhere, as in the word **titkonen** תִּתכּוֹנֵן *you will get ready, prepare yourself* (line 6).

The related noun **mekhinah** מְכִינָה (line 3) refers to a special preparatory course at university before students begin their regular classes. The same word can also be the present tense feminine singular of *to prepare*, as in **hi mekhinah shi'ur** הִיא מְכִינָה שִׁיעוּר *she prepares a lesson.*

② **takhin** תָּכִין *prepare* ('you [masc.] will prepare'). The future tense here is used with the sense of an imperative. This is very common in Hebrew – more common, in fact, than the specific imperative forms we've learned, which sound a bit impolite.

6 **`Aba mukhan. Titkonen ③!**
Dad [is] ready. Prepare yourself *(You-will-prepare-yourself)*!

7 **`Ometz! Shelkha, Roni."**
Courage! Yours, Roni."

Notes

③ **titkonen** תִּתְכּוֹנֵן *prepare yourself, get yourself ready*. As we will discuss later, this is a reflexive verb. For the moment, note that the triliteral root we discussed in note 1 appears here in its

Targil rishon – Targem תַּרְגִּיל רִאשׁוֹן – תַּרְגֵּם

❶ הוא שלח מתנה בדואר, אבל קבל מכתב תודה אלקטרוני.
Hu shalach matanah bado`ar, `aval qibel mikhtav todah `eleqtroni.

❷ יש להם אומץ לנסוע למדבר בקיץ.
Yesh lahem `ometz linso'a lamidbar baqayitz.

❸ מתי תהיה מוכן להכיר חברה חדשה?
Matay tiheyeh mukhan lehakir chaverah chadashah?

❹ תתכונן טוב לפני שאתה מדבר עם מנהל המשרד.
Titkonen tov lifney she`atah medaber 'im menahel hamisrad.

❺ לסוכנות הנסיעות יש הרבה הכנות לכנס במרכז התירות באילת.
Lesokhnut hanesi'ot yesh harbeh hakhanot lakenes bemerkaz hatayarut be`Eylat.

6 אַבָּא מוּכָן. תִתכּוֹנֵן!

7 אוֹמֶץ! שֶׁלְּךָ, רוֹנִי.“

☐

complete form, with the ו. It's also worth noting that the first root letter sometimes appears as **k** and sometimes as **kh**, but this is the same letter.

Answers to Exercise 1

❶ He sent a present by post, but received a thank you letter by email. ❷ They have the courage to travel to the desert in the summer. ❸ When will you be ready to get to know a new *(female)* friend? ❹ Prepare yourself well before you speak to the office manager. ❺ The travel agency has a lot of preparations for the conference at the tourist centre in Eilat.

יש להם אומץ לנסוע
למדבר בקיץ.

Targil sheni – Hashlem — תַּרְגִּיל שֵׁנִי – הַשְׁלֵם

❶ I didn't do what you asked me because I haven't been at home all day.
Lo [...] mah [...] ki lo [...] babayit kol hayom.
לֹא _____ מַה _____ _____ כִּי לֹא _____ בַּבַּיִת כָּל הַיּוֹם.

❷ Prepare yourself for a revolution in the security measures at the airport.
[...] besidurey [...] bisdeh hate'ufah.
______ ______ בְּסִידּוּרֵי ______ בִּשְׂדֵה הַתְּעוּפָה.

❸ If you aren't ready now, when will you be ready?
[...] `atah lo [...] 'akhshav, matay [...] mukhan?
__ אַתָּה לֹא ____ עַכְשָׁו, מָתַי ____ מוּכָן?

❹ Because of the preparations for the party, I was tired and went to sleep.
Biglal [...] lamesibah hayiti [...] ve[...] lishon.
בִּגְלַל ______ לַמְּסִיבָּה הָיִיתִי ____ וְ____ לִישׁוֹן.

❺ I don't have the courage to study medicine for seven years *(to study seven years medicine).*
`Eyn li [...] lilmod [...] shanim [...].
אֵין לִי ____ לִלְמוֹד ___ שָׁנִים _____ .

Answers to Exercise 2

❶ – **'asiti – shebiqashta mimeni – hayiti –**

❶ - עָשִׂיתִי - שֶׁבִּקַּשְׁתָּ מִמֶּנִּי - הָיִיתִי -

❷ **Titkonen lemahapekhah – habitachon –**

❷ תִּתְכּוֹנֵן לְמַהְפֵּכָה - הַבִּטָּחוֹן -

❸ **`Im – mukhan – tiheyeh –**

❸ עִם - מוּכָן - תִּהְיֶה -

❹ – **hahakhanot – 'ayefah – halakhti –**

❹ - הַהֲכָנוֹת - אֵיפֹה - הָלַכְתִּי -

❺ – **`ometz – sheva' – refu`ah**

❺ - אוֹמֶץ - שֶׁבַע - רְפוּאָה

First names: The brothers in this lesson's text both have short names – **'Adi** עֲדִי *and* **Roni** רוֹנִי*. Like many modern Israeli names, these can be given to either boys or girls. Their meaning has no gender connotation:* **Ron** רוֹן joy*;* **Roni** רוֹנִי my joy*;* **'Adi** עֲדִי jewel. *The nicknames formed from these short names are actually longer than the names themselves –* **Ronileh**, **'Adileh**, *following the pattern we saw in lesson 47, with* **Chavaleh** *as the 'diminutive' of* **Chavah** חַוָּה Eve.

Second wave: lesson 5

55 Fifty-fifth lesson
(Shi'ur chamishim vechamesh)

Tchinah yisra`elit ①
Israeli tahini

1 **Kos `achat ② tchinah ③ golmit.**
One cup *(Cup one)* of raw tahini.

2 **Shney shlishim ④ kos mayim.**
Two-thirds of a cup of water.

3 **Shlish ⑤ kos mitz limon.**
One-third of a cup of lemon juice.

4 **Le'arbev. ⑥**
Mix *(To-mix)*.

5 **Lehosif shtey shiney shum ⑦ me'ukhot, kapit melach, qtzat pilpel.**
Add *(To-add)* two cloves *(teeth)* of garlic, crushed, a teaspoon of salt [and] a little pepper.

Notes

① **Yisra`elit** יִשְׂרְאֵלִית *Israeli* (fem.); **Yisra`eli** יִשְׂרְאֵלִי *Israeli* (masc.). Similarly, the noun **gelem** גֶּלֶם *raw (material)* produces the adjectives **golmit** גּוֹלְמִית (fem.) (line 1) and **golmi** גּוֹלְמִי (masc.) meaning *raw*, *crude* or *gross*.

② **kos `achat** כּוֹס אַחַת *one cup*. This could just as easily have simply been **kos tchinah** כּוֹס טְחִינָה *a cup of tahini*, without specifying the number **`achat** אַחַת *one*. However, including the number is more usual in recipes, where precise measurements are given.

③ **tchinah** טְחִינָה *tahini* is a thick paste made from ground sesame seeds.

④ **shney shlishim** שְׁנֵי שְׁלִישִׁים *two-thirds*. In its absolute state (when it is not part of a construct), the masculine form of the word for *two* is **shnayim**. In the construct state, as here, the

טחִינָה יִשׂרְאֵלִית

1 כּוס אַחַת טחִינָה גולמִית.

2 שׁנֵי שׁלִישִׁים כּוס מַיִם.

3 שׁלִישׁ כּוס מִיץ לִימון.

4 לְעַרבֵּב.

5 לְהוסִיף שׁתֵי שִׁינֵי שׁוּם מְעוּכות, כַּפִּית מֶלַח, קְצָת פִּלפֵּל.

shorter form **shney** is used. Similarly, the feminine **shtayim** שׁתַּיִם becomes **shtey**: for example, **shtey kosot** שׁתֵי כּוסות *two cups* or **shtey shiney** שׁתֵי שִׁינֵי *two cloves* as in line 5.

⑤ **shlish** שׁלִישׁ *one-third* comes from **shalosh** שָׁלוֹשׁ *three*. The plural is required for *two-thirds* – so **shlish** becomes **shlishim**, as in line 2.

⑥ **le'arbev** לְעַרבֵּב *to mix*. Note that Hebrew uses the infinitive to give recipe instructions – 'to mix', 'to add' – whereas in English we use the imperative – 'mix', 'add', etc.

⑦ **shtey shiney shum** שׁתֵי שִׁנֵי שׁוּם *two cloves* ('teeth') *of garlic*. Notice that the first two words in this phrase are both in the construct state ('two-of teeth-of garlic'): **shen** שֵׁן *tooth*, **shinayim** שִׁנַיִם *teeth* (absolute state), **shiney** שִׁנֵי *teeth* (construct state).

6 **Le'arbev hakol. Lehosif 'al hatchinah kaf petrozilyah qtzutzah, chatzi kapit pilpel `adom.**
Mix it all. Add to the tahini a tablespoon of chopped parsley [and] a half-teaspoon of paprika *(pepper red)*.

7 **`Okhlim ⑧ 'im pitah `o 'im lechem.**
Eat*(impers. subj.)* with pita or with bread.

8 **Bete`avon!**
Bon appétit *(In-appetite)*!

Notes

⑧ Note that **`okhlim** – the masculine plural of 'eat' – appears here without a subject. This is a very common way in Hebrew ▸

Targil rishon – Targem תַּרְגִּיל רִאשׁוֹן – תַּרְגֵּם

❶ לטחינה טובה צריך להוסיף מיץ לימון, שום, מלח ופלפל.
Letchinah tovah tzarikh lehosif mitz limon, shum, melach ufilpel*.

❷ אפשר לערבב חומוס וטחינה. משמין אבל טעים.
`Efshar le'arbev chumus vetchinah. Mashmin `aval ta'im.

❸ תתכונן טוב לשעור בבית הספר בשבוע הבא.
Titkonen tov lashi'ur beveyt hasefer bashavu'a haba.

❹ במדרחוב אוכלים פלאפל בפיתה ושותים מיץ.
Bamidrachov `okhlim falafel bepitah veshotim mitz.

❺ בכל אוניברסיטה בישראל יש מכינה לעברית לעולים חדשים.
Bekhol `universitah beYisra`el yesh mekhinah le'ivrit le'olim chadashim.

* **pilpel** becomes **filpel** here, but it's the same word and the same letter.

6 לְעַרְבֵּב הַכֹּל. לְהוֹסִיף עַל הַטְחִינָה כַּף פֶּטרוֹזִילְיָה קְצוּצָה, חֲצִי כַּפִּית פִּלְפֵּל אָדוֹם.

7 אוֹכְלִים עִם פִּיתָה אוֹ עִם לֶחֶם.

8 בְּתֵאָבוֹן!

to form sentences similar to the English 'you eat it with pita', 'people eat it with pita' (or 'one eats it with pita', if you're a member of the British royal family). This form is known as the impersonal subject, abbreviated to 'impers. subj.' in our translations.

Answers to Exercise 1

❶ For good tahini, you need to add lemon juice, garlic, salt and pepper. ❷ You can *(It is possible to)* mix hummus and tahini. Fattening, but tasty! ❸ Prepare yourself well for the lesson at school next week. ❹ In the pedestrianized street, you can eat *(impers. subj.)* falafel in pita and drink juice. ❺ In every university in Israel there is a preparatory course in Hebrew for new immigrants.

55 **Targil sheni – Hashlem** **תַּרְגִּיל שֵׁנִי – הַשְׁלֵם**

1. For a good coffee, you need *(it is necessary)* a cup of water, a tablespoon of coffee and two teaspoons of sugar.
   Leqafeh tov tzarikh [...] mayim, [...] qafeh ushtey [...] sukar.
   לְקָפֶה טוֹב צָרִיךְ ___ מַיִם, __ קָפֶה וּשְׁתֵי _____ סוּכָּר.

2. Do you know how much one-half and two-thirds are?
   `At yoda'at [...] hem, chetzi ve'od [...]?
   אַתְּ יוֹדַעַת ___ הֵם, חֵצִי וְעוֹד ___ ______?

3. In the Mediterranean countries *(In-countries-of the-sea-of the-Mediterranean)*, they eat lots of garlic and parsley.
   [...] hayam haTikhon [...] harbeh shum ufetrozilyah.
   ______ הַיָּם הַתִּיכוֹן ______ הַרְבֵּה שׁוּם וּפֶטְרוֹזִילְיָה.

4. How can one *(How is it possible to)* lose weight *(get thin)* with an appetite like his?
   [...] `efshar [...] 'im [...] kmo shelo?
   ___ אֶפְשָׁר _____ עִם _____ כְּמוֹ שֶׁלָּה?

5. In every Ulpan [they] talk*(impers. subj.)* about Israeli cheesecake.
   Bekhol [...] 'al 'ugat hagvinah [...].
   בְּכָל _____ ______ עַל עוּגַת הַגְּבִינָה ________ .

Answers to Exercise 2

❶ – **kos – kaf – kapiyot –** ❶ - כּוֹס - כַּף - כַּפִּיּוֹת -
❷ – **kamah – shney shlishim** ❷ - כַּמָּה - שְׁנֵי שְׁלִישִׁים
❸ **Be`artzot – `okhlim –** ❸ בְּאַרְצוֹת - אוֹכְלִים -
❹ **`Eykh – lirzot – te`avon –** ❹ אֵיךְ - לִרְצוֹת - תֵּאָבוֹן -
❺ – **`ulpan medabrim – hayisra`elit**
❺ - אוּלְפָּן מְדַבְּרִים - הַיִּשְׂרְאֵלִית

If you ask for a **falafel** פָּלָאפֶל *in a restaurant in Israel, you will usually receive the following combination: a hot* **pitah** פִּתָּה pita bread *containing three or four* **kadurey falafel** כַּדּוּרֵי פָּלָאפֶל falafel balls. *These are made of ground* **chumus** חוּמוּס chickpeas, *generously spiced and fried. The* **pitah** *also contains various salad items, such as chopped cabbage, cucumber, and so forth (in many restaurants, you can choose which additions you want, or even add them yourself at an open counter). The whole ensemble may be topped with* **tchinah** טְחִינָה, *tahini paste flavoured with chopped parsley.* !בְּתֵאָבוֹן **Bete`avon!** Bon appétit!

Second wave: lesson 6

56 Fifty-sixth lesson
(Shi'ur chamishim veshesh)

חֲזָרָה Chazarah – Review

You're coping with a lot of new material in each lesson, so let's recap the main points you've learned.

1 Location and direction words

yamin (adv.)	יָמִין	*right*
yemani / yemanit	יְמָנִי / יְמָנִית	*right, right-hand, right-handed* (m./f.)
yaminah (adv.)	יָמִינָה	*to the right*
smol (adv.)	שׂמֹאל	*left*
smali / smalit	שׂמָאלִי / שׂמָאלִית	*left, left-hand, left-handed* (m./f.)
smolah (adv.)	שׂמֹאלָה	*to the left*
merkaz (masc.)	מֶרְכָּז	*centre*
merkazi / merkazit	מֶרְכָּזִי / מֶרְכָּזִית	*central* (m./f.)

The final **he** הָ in **yaminah** and **smolah** indicates a direction. This suffix is known as the '**hey** ה of direction'. Here are some more examples:

qadimah	קָדִימָה	*forwards*
`achorah	אֲחוֹרָה	*backwards*
Yerushalaymah	יְרוּשָׁלַיְמָה	*to/towards Jerusalem*
habaytah	הַבַּיְתָה	*home, homewards*
tzafonah	צָפוֹנָה	*to the north, northwards*
daromah	דָרוֹמָה	*to the south, southwards*
ma'aravah	מַעֲרָבָה	*to the west, westwards*
mizrachah	מִזְרָחָה	*to the east, eastwards*

Note: To refer, for example, to a woman from the north, south, west or east, we use the feminine adjectives **tzfonit** צְפוֹנִית, **dromit** דְרוֹמִית, **ma'aravit** מַעֲרָבִית, **mizrachit** מִזְרָחִית. Don't confuse these with the directional adverbs, which have a 'feminine' appearance due to the **-ah** suffix.

2 Time words

yom (masc.)	יוֹם	*day*
yomi / yomit	יוֹמִי / יוֹמִית	*daily* (m./f.)
yomon	יוֹמוֹן	*daily paper*
shavu'a (masc.)	שָׁבוּעַ	*week*
shevu'i / shvu'it	שְׁבוּעִי / שְׁבוּעִית	*weekly* (m./f.)
shevu'on (masc.)	שְׁבוּעוֹן	*weekly paper*
yerach (masc.)	יֶרַח	*month* (literary term)
yarchon (masc.)	יַרְחוֹן	*monthly publication*
chodesh (masc.)	חוֹדֶשׁ	*month* (everyday term)
chodshi / chodshit	חוֹדְשִׁי / חוֹדְשִׁית	*monthly* (m./f.)
shanah (fem.)	שָׁנָה	*year*
shnaton (masc.)	שְׁנָתוֹן	*annual publication*
shnati / shnatit	שְׁנָתִי / שְׁנָתִית	*annual* (m./f.)

As you can see, Hebrew has two words for *month*: **yerach** יֶרַח is a literary term that also means *moon*, while **chodesh** חוֹדֶשׁ, the everyday word for *month*, comes from the root חדשׁ, as does the word **chadash** חָדָשׁ *new*. The link is that the Hebrew month changes with each new moon. **Shanah** שָׁנָה *year* comes from the root שׁנה, meaning *to repeat* or *to change*.

3 About 'this' and 'that' ...

Just as 'look at this' refers to something near, and 'look at that' to something farther away, so Hebrew has two sets of demonstratives:

Nearby objects or people			Distant objects or people		
zeh	זֶה	*this* (m. sing.)	**hahu**	הָהוּא	*that* (masc.)
zot	זֹאת	*this* (fem. sing.)	**hahi**	הָהִיא	*that* (fem.)
`eleh	אֵלֶּה	*these* (pl.)	**hahem**	הָהֵם	*those* (masc. pl.)
			hahen	הָהֵן	*those* (fem. pl.)

As you can see, the demonstratives that indicate distance (*that/those*) are formed with the definite article **ha** הַ followed by the appropriate third-person pronoun – masculine or feminine, singular or plural.

4 Singular possessive adjectives

Possessive adjectives are used to indicate who something belongs to. In English, they are *my, your, his, her, our* and *their*. One way Hebrew indicates this is to add an ending to the noun (the thing possessed) to form a single word. The ending changes depending on who the possessor is, and depending on whether what is possessed is singular or plural. For the moment, here are the singular endings with the singular word *brother*:

`achi	אָחִי	*my brother*
`achikha	אָחִיךָ	*your brother* (when speaking to a male)
`achikh	אָחִיךְ	*your brother* (when speaking to a female)
`achiv	אָחִיו	*his brother*
`achiha	אָחִיהָ	*her brother*
`achinu	אָחִינוּ	*our brother*
`achikhem	אֲחִיכֶם	*your brother* (when speaking to more than one male)
`achikhen	אֲחִיכֶן	*your brother* (when speaking to more than one female)
`achihem	אֲחִיהֶם	*their brother* (referring to more than one male)
`achihen	אֲחִיהֶן	*their brother* (referring to more than one female)

As you can see, apart from *my* and *our*, the possessive adjective specifies if the possessor is masculine or feminine.

5 The future tense

The future tense of *to enter*, from the root כנס, is conjugated as follows (note that the prefixes often recall the pronouns):

(`ani) `ekanes	אֲנִי אֶכָּנֵס	*I will enter*
(`atah) tikanes	אַתָּה תִּכָּנֵס	*you will enter* (masc. sing.)
(`at) tikansi	אַתְּ תִּכָּנְסִי	*you will enter* (fem. sing.)

(hu) yikanes	הוּא יִכָּנֵס	*he will enter*
(hi) tikanes	הִיא תִּכָּנֵס	*she will enter*
(`anachnu) nikanes	אֲנַחְנוּ נִכָּנֵס	*we will enter*
(`atem) tikansu	אַתֶּם תִּכָּנְסוּ	*you will enter* (masc. pl.)
(`aten) tikansu	אַתֶּן תִּכָּנְסוּ	*you will enter* (fem. pl.)
(hem) yikansu	הֵם יִכָּנְסוּ	*they will enter* (masc.)
(hen) yikansu	הֵן יִכָּנְסוּ	*they will enter* (fem.)

6 The construct state: *smikhut*

You should now be getting more familiar with this form. It's very common in Hebrew and appears in every lesson in one form or another. The Hebrew term for the construct state is **smikhut** סְמִיכוּת, which means *proximity*. As the name implies, the construct state consists of two nouns placed next to each other to form a phrase. The first noun is called the **nismakh** נִסְמָךְ *supported*, while the second is the **somekh** סוֹמֵךְ *supporter*. **Smikhut** can be used freely, or in fixed, set phrases.

6.1 The free construct

In a free construct, both words retain their original sense. For example, in **'ugat shoqolad** עוּגַת שׁוֹקוֹלָד *chocolate cake* we can understand the literal meaning, 'cake-of chocolate'. Each of the two words retains its ordinary meaning, and either could be removed and still make sense. Sometimes you can replace a free construct with a phrase using **shel** שֶׁל *of*: **'ugah shel shoqolad** עוּגָה שֶׁל שׁוֹקוֹלָד *cake of chocolate*. Although unidiomatic, it means the same as the construct form. Note that the first word **'ugah** *cake* changes to **'ugat** *cake-of* in the construct state. The **nismakh** (the first of the two nouns) often has a distinct construct form. Other examples of the free construct are **`aruchat 'erev** אֲרוּחַת עֶרֶב *dinner* ('meal-of evening'), **medor sport** מְדוֹר סְפּוֹרְט *sports column*, **mitz limon** מִיץ לִימוֹן *lemon juice* and **shney shlish** שְׁנֵי שְׁלִישׁ *two-thirds*.

6.2 The fixed construct

Many fixed phrases in the construct state are different from the free construct in that they combine to mean something quite different from the original nouns. For example, **beyt sefer** בֵּית סֵפֶר means *school*, although literally it would appear to mean 'house-of book'. Other examples of fixed constructs include **sdeh te'ufah**

שְׂדֵה תְעוּפָה *airport* (literally, 'field-of flight'), **gan 'eden** גַּן עֵדֶן *Garden of Eden* or *paradise*, and **ben `adam** בֶּן אָדָם *man, human* (masc.) (literally, 'son-of man'). In three of these four constructs, the **nismakh** appears in a distinct construct form. In one case (**gan 'eden** גַּן עֵדֶן) the **nismakh** is so short that there is no real change. The best way to learn the construct forms is simply through practice and repetition.

7 The utility letter 'm'

We've already seen the utility letter **m** מ *from*, indicating origin. This useful form is used as the base for prepositional pronouns meaning *from me/you/him*, etc. For example: **hatshuvah higi'ah mimenah velo mimenu** הַתְּשׁוּבָה הִגִּיעָה מִמֶּנָּה וְלֹא מִמֶּנּוּ *the reply came from her and not from him*. Note that the first-person plural form is completely different from the others. The first-person plural of **m** מ is in fact **mimenu** מִמֶּנּוּ. But because this is identical to the third-person masculine singular, modern Hebrew usually avoids this form for the first-person plural and uses **me`itanu** מֵאִתָּנוּ, which is formed from **m** מ and the first-person plural form of the particle **`et** אֶת.

Review exercise

❶ עֲדִי שָׁלַח מִכְתָּב אֶלֶקְטרוֹנִי לַשְּׁבוּעוֹן "הַגֶּבֶר". ❷ אַחֲרֵי יוֹמַיִים קִבֵּל תְשׁוּבָה: ❸ שָׁלוֹם לְךָ. יֵשׁ לָנוּ עֲבוֹדָה בִּשְׁבִילְךָ בַּמָּדוֹר "הַמִּטְבָּח לַגֶּבֶר הַסְּפּוֹרְטִיבִי". ❹ עֲדִי רָצָה עֲבוֹדָה בַּמָּדוֹר "עוֹלָם הַתַּיָּרוּת הַסְּפּוֹרְטִיבִית", כִּי הוּא אוֹהֵב סְפּוֹרְט וּנְסִיעוֹת לַאֲרָצוֹת חַמּוֹת. ❺ לִפְנֵי שָׁבוּעַ הוּא נָסַע עִם חֲבֵרִים לַמִּדְבָּר. הֵם הִסְתּוֹבְבוּ שָׁעוֹת וְהָיוּ גֵּאִים כַּאֲשֶׁר סוֹף הִגִּיעוּ לְאֵילַת. ❻ מֵאֵילַת עֲדִי שָׁלַח תְשׁוּבָה לָעִתּוֹן ❼ "תּוֹדָה, אֲנִי מוּכָן". ❽ בָּא לוֹ לִצְחוֹק. הוּא וּמִטְבָּח! אֲבָל הוּא צָרִיךְ עֲבוֹדָה וְיֵשׁ לוֹ אוֹמֶץ! ❾ הָאֱמֶת? אִמּוֹ יְכוֹלָה לַעֲזוֹר לוֹ. ❿ כְּבָר אֲכַלְתֶּם אֶצְלָהּ?

Here is the full declension:

mimeni	מִמֶּנִּי	*from me*	**me`itanu**	מֵאִתָּנוּ	*from us*
mimkha	מִמְּךָ	*from you* (masc. sing.)	**mikem**	מִכֶּם	*from you* (masc. pl.)
mimekh	מִמֵּךְ	*from you* (fem. sing.)	**miken**	מִכֶּן	*from you* (fem. pl.)
mimenu	מִמֶּנּוּ	*from him*	**mehem**	מֵהֶם	*from them* (masc.)
mimenah	מִמֶּנָּה	*from her*	**mehen**	מֵהֶן	*from them* (fem.)

Answers

❶ Adi sent an email to the weekly *The Man. (Adi sent letter electronic to-weekly-of The-Man)* ❷ Two days later, he got a reply: *(after two-days he-received reply)* ❸ Hello. We have work for you on the column 'The Kitchen for the Sporty Man'. *(hello to-you there-is for-us work for-you in-column-of 'the-kitchen for-the-man the-sporty')* ❹ Adi wanted a job on the column 'The World of Sport Tourism', because he likes sport and trips to hot countries. *(Adi wanted work in-column-of 'world-of the-tourism the-sporty' because he likes sport and-trips to-countries hot)* ❺ A week ago, he travelled to the desert with friends. They drove around for hours and were proud when they finally reached Eilat. *(ago week he drove with friends to-the-desert they-went-around hours and-they-were proud when end-end they-arrived to-Eilat)* ❻ From Eilat, Adi sent a reply to the newspaper: *(from-Eilat Adi sent reply to-the-newspaper)* ❼ "Thanks, I'm ready." *(thanks I ready)* ❽ He wanted to laugh. Him and kitchens! But he needs work and he is courageous! *(comes to-him to-laugh. he and-kitchen! but he needs work and-there-is to-him courage)* ❾ The truth? His mother can help him. *(the-truth? mother-his can to-help for-him)* ❿ Have you eaten at her place yet? *(already you-ate by-her?)*

You've now completed the first set of lessons in the second phase of your learning. You've proved that you've already acquired a large enough vocabulary and a good enough grasp of Hebrew syntax to enjoy some humorous banter!

Second wave: lesson 7

57 Fifty-seventh lesson
(Shi'ur chamishim vesheva')

Mikhtav ①
A letter

1 **Shalom lekha, qore` yaqar; shalom lakh, qor`ah yeqarah.**
Hello to you, dear reader*(masc.)*; hello to you, dear reader*(fem.)*.

2 **Na'im lanu me`od likhtov lakhem be'ivrit.**
We are very pleased *(Pleasant for-us very)* to write to you in Hebrew.

3 **`Anachnu mevarkhim `etkhem 'al hatzlachatkhem ② belimud 'ivrit.**
We congratulate *(bless)* you on your success in learning Hebrew.

4 **`Anachnu betuchim shetatzlichu gam be'atid.**
We [are] sure that you will also be successful in the future *(will-be-successful also in-the-future)*.

Notes

① **mikhtav** מִכְתָּב *letter*. This word is formed from the root כתב *to write*, plus the prefix מ, which is used to form words for many objects. Other examples we have already encountered include **machshev** מַחְשֵׁב *computer* (from the root חשב *to think*); **mischaq** מִשְׂחָק *game* (שׂחק *to play*); and **merkaz** מֶרְכָּז *centre* (רכז *to centre, concentrate*). (Just a reminder that for the purposes of clarity we've used English infinitives to give the meanings of roots, however, a Hebrew root is not an infinitive.)

② **hatzlachatkhem** הַצְלָחַתְכֶם *your success*. This word began life as **hatzlachah** הַצְלָחָה *success*, which in the construct state becomes **hatzlachat** הַצְלָחַת *success-of*. To this, we add

57 שִׁעוּר חֲמִישִּׁים וְשֶׁבַע

מִכְתָּב

1 שָׁלוֹם לְךָ קוֹרֵא יָקָר; שָׁלוֹם לָךְ קוֹרְאָה יְקָרָה.

2 נָעִים לָנוּ מְאֹד לִכְתּוֹב לָכֶם בְּעִבְרִית.

3 אֲנַחְנוּ מְבָרְכִים אֶתְכֶם עַל הַצְלָחַתְכֶם בְּלִמּוּד עִבְרִית.

4 אֲנַחְנוּ בְּטוּחִים שֶׁתַּצְלִיחוּ גַּם בֶּעָתִיד.

מכתב

the second-person masculine plural possessive suffix (*your*). You can think of this suffix as consisting of **shelakhem** שֶׁלָּכֶם *of-you* in an abridged form that retains only the part specifying that we are dealing with the second-person masculine plural, i.e. **khem** כֶם.

5 **Tihyu ge'im, she`atem kvar yod'im liqro` `otiyot dfus ③ velikhtov `otiyot ktav ④.**
Be *(You-will-be)* proud that you already know [how] to read printed letters *(letters-of print)* and to write cursive letters *(letters-of writing)*.

6 **`Atem `afilu qor`im vekhotvim bli niqud ⑤.**
You [are] even reading and writing without vowel points.

7 **Bashi'ur haba, yiheyeh chidush: sefer mehaTanakh ⑥ be'ivrit tanakhit.**
In the next lesson *(In the-lesson the-next)*, there will be something new *(an innovation)*: a story *(book)* from the Bible in Biblical Hebrew.

8 **Todah' al hama`amatz she'asitem vesheta'asu be'atid.**
Thank you for the effort you have made and that you will be making in the future.

9 **Kol hakavod ⑦ lakhem. Behatzlachah!**
Well done *(All the-honour)* to you. Good luck *(With-success)*!

Notes

③ **`otiyot dfus** אוֹתִיּוֹת דפוּס *printed letters*. This is the term used for the square script in which almost all printed material appears. An official form may ask citizens to fill in their details in **`otiyot dfus** אוֹתִיּוֹת דפוּס. This doesn't mean that they are expected to print their replies, but that they should write using the square rather than the cursive script. A printing works is a **beyt dfus** בֵּית דפוּס.

④ **ktav** כְּתָב *writing*. Here, the term is used to refer to cursive script as opposed to the square script. **Ktav yad** כְּתַב יָד 'writing-of hand' means *handwriting*.

⑤ **niqud** נִיקוּד *vowel mark*. The root of this word is נקד, which is also the root of **nequdah** נְקוּדָה *point*, *dot*, *period*.

5 תִּהְיוּ גֵּאִים, שֶׁאַתֶּם כְּבָר יוֹדְעִים לִקְרוֹא אוֹתִיּוֹת דְּפוּס וְלִכְתּוֹב אוֹתִיּוֹת כְּתָב.

6 אַתֶּם אֲפִילוּ קוֹרְאִים וְכוֹתְבִים בְּלִי נִקּוּד.

7 בַּשִּׁיעוּר הַבָּא יִהְיֶה חִדּוּשׁ: סֵפֶר מֵהַתַּנַ"ךְ בְּעִבְרִית תַּנָכִית.

8 תּוֹדָה עַל הַמַּאֲמָץ שֶׁעֲשִׂיתֶם וְשֶׁתַּעֲשׂוּ בֶּעָתִיד.

9 כֹּל הַכָּבוֹד לָכֶם. בְּהַצְלָחָה! □

Niqud, literally 'applying points', refers to the system of using diacritical marks to indicate vowels. Apart from the two diacritical marks for *a*, all the Hebrew vowel marks are composed of dots.

⑥ **Tanakh** תַּנַ"ךְ *Bible*. Acronyms and most abbreviations in Hebrew are indicated by a double quotation mark before the final letter. Here are three common examples: **Tel-`Aviv** ת"א; **beyt sefer** בי"ס *school*; **'al yad** ע"י *by*, *next to*. As mentioned, the upcoming lessons contain Biblical Hebrew vocabulary, but the syntax remains in modern Hebrew – otherwise it would be too confusing!

⑦ **kavod** כָּבוֹד *honour*. The root כבד produces the adjective **kaved** כָּבֵד *heavy*, **kvedah** כְּבֵדָה (m./f.). The Hebrew word for *liver* is **kaved** כָּבֵד, possibly because this is considered the heaviest organ in the body. The connection with *honour* is presumably that someone who is honoured is 'weighty' or substantial. The expression **kol hakavod** כֹּל הַכָּבוֹד 'all honour' means *congratulations*, and is similar in tone to the American expression 'Way to go!'

57

Targil rishon – Targem תַּרְגִּיל רִאשׁוֹן – תַּרְגֵּם

❶ במאמץ גדול אני קוראת עתון בעברית בלי ניקוד.
Bema`amatz gadol `ani qor`et 'iton be'ivrit bli niqud.

❷ דניאל מנהל בית דפוס.
Daniel menahel beyt dfus.

❸ כל הכבוד לכם על הצלחתכם.
Kol hakavod lakhem 'al hatzlachatkhem.

❹ בעברית קוראים וכותבים עם ניקוד או בלי ניקוד.
Be'ivrit qor`im vekhotvim 'im niqud `o bli niqud.

❺ אפשר לכתוב עוד חידושים על העברית התנכית?
`Efshar likhtov 'od chidushim 'al ha'ivrit hatanakhit?

Targil sheni – Hashlem תַּרְגִּיל שֵׁנִי – הַשְׁלֵם

❶ Printed letters, cursive letters, after half a year of study, we know them all *(the-all)*!
`otiyot [...], `otiyot [...], `acharey [...] shnat limudim `anachnu [...] hakol!

אוֹתִיּוֹת ____, אוֹתִיּוֹת ___, אַחֲרֵי ___ שְׁנַת לִמּוּדִים
אֲנַחְנוּ ______ הַכֹּל!

❷ The teachers congratulate *(bless)* the students at the end of the school year *(year-of studies)*.
Hamorim [...] `et [...] besof [...] [...].

הַמּוֹרִים ______ אֶת ________ בְּסוֹף ___ ________.

❸ This will be an interesting innovation.
Zeh yiheyeh [...] [...].

זֶה יִהְיֶה ____ _____.

❹ Which book of the Bible are you studying now?
`Eyzeh sefer [...] `atem lomdim [...]?

אֵיזֶה סֵפֶר ______ אַתֶּם לוֹמְדִים ____?

Answers to Exercise 1

❶ With a big effort, I read a newspaper in Hebrew without vowel marks. ❷ Daniel is the manager of a printing firm. ❸ Congratulations to you on your success. ❹ In Hebrew you*(impers. subj.)* read with or without vowel marks. ❺ Is it still possible to write something new about Biblical Hebrew?

❺ Congratulations *(All honour)* to you*(fem. pl.)* for the effort you have made.
[...] [...] lakhen 'al [...] she'asiten.
-- ----- לָכֶן עַל ----- שֶׁעֲשִׂיתֶן.

Answers to Exercise 2

❶ **– dfus – ktav – chetzi – yod'im** -- ❶ - דְּפוּס - כְּתָב - חֲצִי - יוֹדְעִים --
❷ **– mevarkhim – hatalmidim – shnat halimudim**
❷ - מְבָרְכִים - הַתַּלְמִידִים - שְׁנַת הַלִּימּוּדִים
❸ **– chidush me'anyen** ❸ - חִדּוּשׁ מְעַנְיֵן
❹ **– mehatanakh – 'akhshav** ❹ - מֵהַתַּנַ״ךְ - עַכְשָׁו
❺ **Kol hakavod – hama`amatz –** ❺ כָּל הַכָּבוֹד - הַמַּאֲמָץ -

58 *As we mentioned, the Hebrew word for the Bible,* **Tanakh** תנ"ך, *is an acronym, as indicated by the double quotation mark before the last letter. The abbreviation stands for the different parts of the Hebrew Bible:*

t ת: **Torah** תּוֹרָה teaching, law
n נ: **Nevi`im** נְבִיאִים prophets
k ך (כ): **Ktuvim** כְּתוּבִים writings.

• *The* **Torah** *consists of five books (which is the meaning of its Greek name,* Pentateuch*). The names of the books in Hebrew are completely different from the English names. In Jewish tradition, each book (as well as each weekly portion read in the synagogue) is named after the first word or two in that section.*

---

58 Fifty-eighth lesson
(Shi'ur chamishim ushmoneh)

Migdal ① Bavel ② – cheleq rishon
The Tower of Babel – part one

1 **Pa'am ③ kol ha`aretz haytah safah ④ `achat udvarim `achadim.**
Once all the Earth used *(was)* one language and few words *(words ones)*.

Notes

① **migdal** מִגְדָּל *tower.* This word comes from the root גדל, as does the word **gadol** גָּדוֹל *big.* As we've seen in previous lessons, the prefix מְ is often used to transform a root into a noun to describe an object: כתב *write* + מְ = מִכְתָּב **mikhtav** *letter.*

② **bavel** בָּבֶל *Babel.* Babel, or Babylon, was situated in modern-day Iraq. To this day, some Jewish communities from this region refer to themselves as **yehudey bavel** יְהוּדֵי בָּבֶל *Jews of Babylon.*

Bereshit בְּרֵאשִׁית *'In the beginning'* – Genesis
Shmot שְׁמוֹת *'Names'* – Exodus
Vayiqra וַיִּקְרָא *'He called'* – Leviticus
Bamidbar בְּמִדְבָּר *'In the desert'* – Numbers
Dvarim דְּבָרִים *'Words'* – Deuteronomy

• **Nevi`im** נְבִיאִים *is divided into two subsections: the Early Prophets (Joshua, Judges, Samuel and Kings) and the Late Prophets (Isaiah, Jeremiah, Ezekiel and the Twelve Prophets).*

• **Ktuvim** כְּתוּבִים Writings *(also known by the Greek name Hagiographa, 'writings about saints') includes the Psalms, Proverbs, Job, Song of Songs, Ruth, Lamentations, Ecclesiastes, Esther, Daniel, Ezra-Nehemiah and Chronicles.*

Second wave: lesson 8

58 שִׁעוּר חֲמִישִּׁים וּשְׁמוֹנֶה

מִגְדָּל בָּבֶל: חֵלֶק רִאשׁוֹן

1 פַּעַם כֹּל הָאָרֶץ הָיְתָה שָׂפָה אַחַת וּדְבָרִים אֲחָדִים.

③ **pa'am** פַּעַם is a noun meaning *time* (as in one time – once – three times, etc.). When used in the dual form, **pa'amayim** פַּעֲמַיִים, it means *twice*. It is also often used, as here, as an adverb meaning *once*, i.e. in the past.

④ **safah** שָׂפָה *lip*, *language*. When used to mean *lips*, this word often appears in the dual **sfatayim** שְׂפָתַיִים. In the singular it means *language*, in which case the plural is **safot** שָׂפוֹת. A second word for language comes from another part of the body used to produce speech: **lashon** לָשׁוֹן *tongue*, *language* (think of the English expressions 'mother tongue' and 'speaking in tongues').

2 **Ha`anashim nas'u ⑤ miQedem le`eretz Shin'ar ⑥ lagur sham.**
The people had travelled from the east to the land of Shinar to live there.

3 **Hem `amru `echad ⑦ lasheni:**
They said to each other *(one to-the-second)*:

4 **"Nivneh lanu 'ir. Ba'ir nivneh migdal verosho ⑧ bashamayim ⑨.**
"Let us build ourselves *(for-us)* a city. In the city, we will build a tower with its top *(and-its-head)* in the heavens.

5 **Na'aseh lanu shem,**
We will make ourselves *(for-us)* a name,

6 **velo nafutz 'al pney ⑩ kol ha`aretz."**
and we will not be scattered all over the face of the Earth *(on the-face-of all the-land)*."

Notes

⑤ **nas'u** נָסעוּ *they had travelled*. Remember that Hebrew has one main past tense, so depending on the context this could mean *they travelled, they were travelling, they have travelled, they had travelled* and so on. Here, it is the equivalent of *they had travelled.*

⑥ **Shin'ar** שִׁנְעָר is the name used for southern Mesopotamia in the Book of Genesis. The Hebrew Bible states that Babel (Babylon) was located in the *Land of Shinar*, while English translations of the Bible call it the *Plain of Shinar.*

⑦ **`echad** אֶחָד *one* is the masculine form of the cardinal numeral. The feminine form is **`achat** אַחַת (see lesson 23).

⑧ **rosho** רֹאשׁוֹ *its head*. The masculine singular possessive (*his head*, or here *its head*, since **migdal** מִגְדָּל *tower* is a masculine noun) is indicated by the suffix **o**, written וֹ. In modern Hebrew you can also say **harosh shelo** הָרֹאשׁ שֶׁלּוֹ ('the-head of-him'), but this construction is not usual in Biblical Hebrew. This

2 הָאֲנָשִׁים נָסעוּ מִקֶּדֶם לְאֶרֶץ שִׁנעָר לָגוּר שָׁם.

3 הֵם אָמרוּ אֶחָד לַשֵּׁנִי:

4 "נִבנֶה לָנוּ עִיר. בָּעִיר נִבנֶה מִגדָל וְרֹאשׁוֹ בַּשָּׁמַיִם.

5 נַעֲשֶׂה לָנוּ שֵׁם.

6 וְלֹא נָפוּץ עַל פְּנֵי כֹּל הָאָרֶץ."

masculine possessive suffix can be attached to nouns of either gender: **`achot** אָחוֹת *sister*; **`achoto** אֲחוֹתוֹ *his sister.*

⑨ **shamayim** שָׁמַיִם *sky, skies, heavens.* Note that the Hebrew word is a dual form (there is no equivalent singular form of this word). The ancient Jewish Sages suggested that this word could be understood as a combination of **sham** שָׁם *there* and **mayim** מַיִם *water*, since the sky is the source of water. Don't misunderstand these pearls of wisdom from the Jewish sources: the rabbis weren't actually suggesting that this was the origin of the word. They were less interested in etymology than in making moral or educational points. They also wanted to help people remember the Hebrew words. Don't forget that throughout most of history, Jews have learned Hebrew as their second or third language – alongside Aramaic or Greek in early times, and alongside Arabic, Yiddish, English and countless other languages ever since. We hope these imaginative commentaries will help you remember the Hebrew words, just as they have helped people over the centuries.

⑩ **'al pney** עַל פְּנֵי *on the face of.* **Pney** is the construct state of **panim** פָּנִים *face.* Note that the Hebrew word for *face* is a plural noun. This word also means *surface*, for example, in the expression **pney hayam** פְּנֵי הַיָּם 'face-of the-sea' – *sea level.*

Targil rishon – Targem תַּרְגִּיל רִאשׁוֹן – תַּרְגֵּם

❶ הוא כתב ספר מצוין ועשה לו שם בארץ.
Hu katav sefer metzuyan ve'asah lo shem ba`aretz.

❷ בכל הספרים לתיירים יש תמונה של מגדל דוד בירושלים.
Bekhol hasfarim latayarim yesh tmunah shel migdal David biYerushalayim.

❸ פעם האנשים נסעו מארץ לארץ באוניה.
Pa'am ha`anashim nas'u me`eretz le`eretz be`oniyah.

❹ הרבה משפחות באות לגור בעיר החדשה.
Harbeh mishpachot ba`ot lagur ba'ir hachadashah.

❺ אם לא נגור בעיר אחת, נפוץ בארץ.
`Im lo nagur be'ir `achat, nafutz ba`aretz.

Targil sheni – Hashlem תַּרְגִּיל שֵׁנִי – הַשְׁלֵם

❶ At school she studies three languages.
[...] [...], hi lomedet shalosh [...].
____ ____, הִיא לוֹמֶדֶת שָׁלוֹשׁ ____ .

❷ In this letter I wrote *(to)* you*(fem. sing.)* several things *(words ones)* before my trip *(I travel)* abroad.
[...] hazeh `ani [...] lakh [...] [...] lifney she`ani nose'a [...] [...].
____ הַזֶּה אֲנִי ____ לָךְ ____ ____ לִפְנֵי שֶׁאֲנִי נוֹסֵעַ
____ ____ .

❸ When we *(will)* have lots of money, we will build ourselves *(for-us)* a big and beautiful house.
[...] lanu harbeh kesef [...] [...] bayit gadol veyafeh.
____ ____ לָנוּ הַרְבֵּה כֶּסֶף ____ ___ בַּיִת גָּדוֹל וְיָפֶה.

Answers to Exercise 1

❶ He wrote an excellent book and made a name for himself in Israel *(in the Land)*. ❷ In all the tourist guidebooks there is a picture of the Tower of David in Jerusalem. ❸ Once people travelled from country to country by ship. ❹ Many families come to live in the new city. ❺ If we do not live in one city, we will be scattered around the country.

הוא כתב ספר מצוין
ועשה לו שם בארץ.

❹ My sister bought a magnificent apartment in a tower in the centre of the city.
[...] qantah dirah nehederet [...] bemerkaz ha'ir.
_____ קָנְתָה דִּירָה נֶהֱדֶּרֶת _____ בְּמֶרְכַּז הָעִיר.

❺ They are real chatterboxes *(chatterers big)*: what do they say to each other *(one to-the-second)* all evening?
Hem [...] gdolim. Mah hem `omrim [...] [...] kol ha'erev?
הֵם _______ גְּדוֹלִים. מַה הֵם אוֹמְרִים ___ ____
כֹּל הָעֶרֶב?

Answers to Exercise 2

❶ **Beveyt hasefer – safot** ❶ בְּבֵית הַסֵּפֶר - שָׂפוֹת
❷ **Bamikhtav – kotev – dvarim `achadim – lechutz la`aretz**
❷ בַּמִּכְתָּב - כּוֹתֵב -דְּבָרִים אֲחָדִים - לְחוּץ לָאָרֶץ
❸ **Ka`asher yiheyeh – nivneh lanu –** ❸ כַּאֲשֶׁר יִהְיֶה -נִבְנֶה לָנוּ -
❹ **`Achoti – bemigdal –** ❹ אֲחוֹתִי - בְּמִגְדָּל -
❺ **– patpetanim – `echad lasheni –** ❺ - פַּטְפְּטָנִים - אֶחָד לַשֵּׁנִי -

Second wave: lesson 9

59 Fifty-ninth lesson
(Shi'ur chamishim vetesha')

Migdal Bavel: cheleq sheni
The Tower of Babel – part two

1 **`Elohim ① ra`ah `et ha'ir ve`et hamigdal. Hu `amar:**
God saw the city and the tower. He said:

2 – **"Hem 'am `echad vesafah ② `achat lekhulam ③.**
"They [are] one people and [there is] one language for them all.

3 **Hem yekholim la'asot mah shehem rotzim."**
They can do whatever they want *(what that-they want)*."

4 **`Elohim balal `et sfatam.**
God mixed up *(jumbled)* their language.

5 **Hem lo hevinu `echad `et hasheni ④.**
They did not understand each other *(one* [**`et**] *the-second)*.

Notes

① **`Elohim** אֱלֹהִים *God.* Although this looks like a plural noun, it is used as a singular (which has given theologians something to think about for centuries). You may notice that the **`alef** א at the beginning of this word has five points underneath [ֱ] – a **sheva** [ְ] and a **segol** [ֶ]. This combination is used under certain letters, but you needn't worry about it too much. The pronunciation is **e**, as if it was a normal **segol**.

② **safah** שָׂפָה *lip, language.* As we saw in the previous lesson this word has two possible plurals. Used in the sense of *lips*, it has a dual plural form similar to those we've learned for

מִגְדָּל בָּבֶל: חֵלֶק שֵׁנִי

1 אֱלֹהִים רָאָה אֶת הָעִיר וְאֶת הַמִּגְדָּל.
הוּא אָמַר:

2 – ״הֵם עַם אֶחָד וְשָׂפָה אַחַת לְכוּלָם.

3 הֵם יְכוֹלִים לַעֲשׂוֹת מַה שֶּׁהֵם רוֹצִים.״

4 אֱלֹהִים בָּלַל אֶת שְׂפָתָם.

5 הֵם לֹא הֵבִינוּ אֶחָד אֶת הַשֵּׁנִי.

many body parts: **sfatayim** שְׂפָתַיִים. When used to mean *languages*, it forms its plural like most feminine nouns that end in **-ah**: **safot** שָׂפוֹת (line 9). In line 4, **sfatam** שְׂפָתָם *their language* consists of the singular noun with the addition of the possessive suffix for the third-person masculine plural.

③ **lekhulam** לְכוּלָם *for them all*. You already know the word כֹּל meaning *all* or *each*. Personal suffixes can be added to this word, so that כּוּלָם, for example, means *all of them*. Similarly, in line 8 we have **lekhol** לְכֹל *for each* or *for all the*. Here, the initial **k** כּ in **kol** כֹּל changes to **kh** כ due to the preceding **shva** ` [ְ] under the ל.

④ **`echad `et hasheni** אֶחָד אֶת הַשֵּׁנִי 'one [`**et**] the second'. This is how to say *each other* in Hebrew. If we were talking about two women, we would say **hen lo hevinu `achat `et hashniyah** הֵן לֹא הֵבִינוּ אַחַת אֶת הַשְּׁנִיָּה *they didn't understand each other.*

6 **Velo yakhlu livnot `et hamigdal.**
And they could not build the tower.

7 **Ha`anashim** ⑤ **nafotzu bekhol ha'olam.**
The people dispersed throughout the whole world *(in-all the-world)*.

8 **Me`az** ⑥ **lekhol 'am safah ve`eretz.**
Since then, each people [has had its own] language and country.

9 **Me`az `anachnu lomdim safot ve`Assimil 'oseh 'asaqim.**
Since then, we have been learning *(we study)* languages and Assimil has been doing *(does)* [good] business.

Notes

⑤ **`anashim** אֲנָשִׁים *men, people*. Be careful not to confuse the following two nouns:

singular	plural
`ish אִישׁ *man*	**`anashim** אֲנָשִׁים *men, people*
`ishah אִשָּׁה *woman*	**nashim** נָשִׁים *women*

It is particularly easy to confuse the two plurals when they are preceded by the definite article: **ha`anashim** הָאֲנָשִׁים *the people, the men*, but **hanashim** הַנָּשִׁים *the women*. As you can see, **nashim** *women* has the ending that usually appears on masculine nouns, although – needless to say – it is feminine. Any adjectives used with the word take the usual feminine form: **nashim yafot** נָשִׁים יָפוֹת *beautiful women.*

⑥ **me`az** מֵאָז *since* – this useful adverb combines **me** מֵ *from* and **`az** אָז *then*. But be careful! **me`az** only means 'since' in the temporal sense – 'since he started to play golf, he always comes home late', 'since the war, he has been unhappy'. When

6 וְלֹא יָכְלוּ לִבְנוֹת אֶת הַמִּגְדָּל.

7 הָאֲנָשִׁים נָפוֹצוּ בְּכֹל הָעוֹלָם.

8 מֵאָז לְכֹל עַם שָׂפָה וְאֶרֶץ.

9 מֵאָז אֲנַחְנוּ לוֹמְדִים שָׂפוֹת וְאַסִימִיל עוֹשֶׂה עֲסָקִים.

□

שתי הנשים לא הבינו אחת את השניה.

since in English can be replaced with *because* ('since you refuse to listen', 'since there is no point talking about this'), you must use one of the words for *because*: **ki** כִּי, **biglal she-** בִּגְלַל שֶׁ or **mipnay she-** מִפְּנֵי שֶׁ.

Targil rishon – Targem תַּרְגִּיל רִאשׁוֹן – תַּרְגֵּם

❶ שתי הנשים לא הבינו אחת את השניה.
Shtey hanashim lo hevinu `achat `et hashniyah.

❷ בחלק השני של המסע כולם הלכו לבקר בעיר העתיקה.
Bacheleq hasheni shel hamasa' kulam halkhu levaqer ba'ir ha'atiqah.

❸ איש העסקים הסתובב בהרבה ארצות כדי לחפש מכוניות זולות.
`Ish ha'asaqim histovev beharbeh `aratzot kedey lechapes mekhoniyot zolot.

❹ מאז מגדל בבל, בכל עיר גדולה רוצים לבנות מגדלים.
Me`az migdal Bavel, bekhol 'ir gdolah rotzim livnot migdalim.

Targil sheni – Hashlem תַּרְגִּיל שֵׁנִי – הַשְׁלֵם

❶ Once all the people had only one language.
[...] lekhol ha`anashim haytah raq [...] [...].
___ לְכֹל הָאֲנָשִׁים הָיְתָה רַק ___ ___ .

❷ The Tower of Babel is an illustration *(example)* of people who do not understand each other.
[...] [...] hu dugmah le'anashim shelo mevinim [...] `et [...].
_____ _____ הוּא דּוּגְמָה לַאֲנָשִׁים שֶׁלֹּא מְבִינִים ___ אֶת ____ .

❸ In the first part of the lesson, you*(masc. pl.)* read *(in)* printed letters.
[...] [...] shel hashi'ur `atem qor`im [...] [...].
____ ______ שֶׁל הַשִּׁעוּר אַתֶּם קוֹרְאִים _______ ____ .

❺ הם חברים טובים, הם מבינים מצוין אחד את השני.
Hem chaverim tovim, hem mevinim metzuyan `echad `et hasheni.

Answers to Exercise 1

❶ The two women didn't understand each other. ❷ In the second part of the journey, they all went to visit the old city. ❸ The businessman wandered around many countries in order to search for cheap cars. ❹ Since the Tower of Babel, in every big city, people*(impers. subj.)* want to build towers. ❺ They are good friends, they understand each other perfectly.

❹ In the second part of the lesson, you*(fem. pl.)* write in cursive *(written)* letters.
[...] [...] shel hash'iur `aten [...] be`otiyot [...].
____ ____ שֶׁל הַשִּׁעוּר אַתֶּן ______ בְּאוֹתִיּוֹת ___ .

❺ God mixed up *(jumbled)* the language of the people of Babel.
[...] [...] `et sfat [...] bebavel.
_____ ___ אֶת שְׂפַת ______ בְּבָבֶל.

Answers to Exercise 2

❶ **Pa'am – safah `achat** ❶ פַּעַם - שָׂפָה אַחַת
❷ **Migdal Bavel – `echad – hasheni** ❷ מִגְדַּל בָּבֶל - אֶחָד - הַשֵּׁנִי
❸ **Bacheleq harishon – be`otiyot dfus** ❸ בַּחֵלֶק הָרִאשׁוֹן - בְּאוֹתִיּוֹת דְּפוּס
❹ **Bacheleq hasheni – kotvot – ktav** ❹ בַּחֵלֶק הַשֵּׁנִי - כּוֹתְבוֹת - כְּתָב
❺ **`Elohim balal – ha`anashim –** ❺ אֱלֹהִים בָּלַל - הָאֲנָשִׁים -

60 *The Tower of Babel: This story in the Bible (Genesis 11.1–9) sought to explain the proliferation of different languages (and by extension, cultures) in the world. The word 'babel' in English is still used to describe a confused noise or scene, and perhaps there is a link with the verb 'babble', although there are other possible sources for this word as well. Why would God want to prevent the people of Babel from understanding each other by making them speak in different tongues? One interpretation claims it was punishment for the hubris of planning such a massive building project. Other more recent interpretations suggest that it was to avoid cultural homogeneity and the concentration of power by scattering people all over the Earth.*

---

60 Sixtieth lesson (Shi'ur shishim)

Vekhulam beyachad! (moda'ah ① ba'iton)
All together now! (newspaper announcement)

1 **Leyl shirah ② betzibur**
Singalong night *(Night-of song in-public)*

2 **'im Sarah'leh**
with Sarahleh

Notes

① **moda'ah** מוֹדָעָה *announcement*, *advertisement* comes from the root ידע meaning *to know*.

② **leyl shirah** לֵיל שִׁירָה *night of song*. In the absolute state, the word for *night* is **laylah** לַיְלָה. In construct forms, however, the form **leyl** לֵיל is used, as in the following examples:

• **leyl haseder** לֵיל הַסֵּדֶר *Seder night* (the special meal that begins the festival of Passover)

• **leyl shabat** לֵיל שַׁבָּת *Shabbat night* (Friday night – remember that Shabbat begins before sunset on Friday, so 'Shabbat night' means Friday night, not Saturday night!)

Babylon was the capital of the Babylonian Kingdom in ancient Mesopotamia. The remains of the city are located on the Euphrates River, south of Baghdad in modern-day Iraq. It was a very rich and important city, considered as one of the wonders of the ancient world. The Babylonians were a polytheistic people, and this, combined with its power and wealth at the time, as well as the fact that Babylonians laid siege to Jerusalem, destroying it in 587 BC, have given it connotations that have survived to the present day of a luxurious, pleasure-seeking and even immoral way of life.

Second wave: lesson 10

60 שִׁעוּר שִׁשִּׁים

וְכוּלָם בְּיַחַד! (מוֹדָעָה בָּעִתוֹן)

1 לֵיל שִׁירָה בְּצִבּוּר

2 עִם שָׂרָה'לֶה

• **leyl menuchah** לֵיל מְנוּחָה *night of rest* (This is a slightly formal way of saying 'good night'. **Laylah tov** לַיְלָה טוֹב is the more usual expression – **laylah** is a masculine noun, despite its appearance.)

• **leyl choref** לֵיל חוֹרֶף *a winter night*

• **leyl qayitz** לֵיל קַיִץ *a summer night* (Shakespeare's *A Midsummer Night's Dream* is called **chalom leyl qayitz** חֲלוֹם לֵיל קַיִץ in Hebrew – note that the first two words are both in the construct state).

3 **beshirey** ③ **'Zug mehashamayim'** ④**,**
[and her] songs from 'A couple from heaven'

4 **mo'adon** ⑤ **'Tzavta', Tel-`Aviv,**
Tzavta Club, Tel Aviv

5 **beyom vav** ⑥**, 'esrim veshishah (26) be`april be'esrim veshalosh efes efes (23).**
on Friday *(day vav=6)*, April 26 *(twenty and-six in-April)* at 11 pm *(in-twenty and-three=23:00)*

6 **Pratim vehazmanat kartisim: 03-524 73 73 (`efes, shalosh – chamesh, shtayim, `arba'– sheva', shalosh – sheva', shalosh).**
Details and reservation *(ordering)* of tickets: 03-5247373.

7 **Pratim nosafim be`atar hamo'adon: Tzavta shtrudel zahavnet nequdah il.**
Further details on the club website: Tzavta@zahavnet.il.

8 **Chanayah beshefa'.**
Plenty of parking *(Parking in-abundance)*.

9 **`Avtachah mele`ah.**
Full security *(Security full)*.

Notes

③ **shirey** שִׁירֵי *songs-of* is the construct form of the plural **shirim**.

④ **zug mehashamayim** זוּג מֵהַשָּׁמַיִם 'couple from the sky'. The closest English equivalent of this expression is *a match made in heaven*. **Zug** זוּג means *couple*, and also *pair*: **zug na'alayim** זוּג נַעֲלַיִים is *a pair of shoes*.

⑤ **mo'adon** מוֹעֲדוֹן *club*. The root of this word is יעד; **ya'ad** יַעַד means *target* or *destination* – the members of a club have a common aim. For example: **mo'adon sport** מוֹעֲדוֹן ספּוֹרט *sport club*, **mo'adon sefarim** מוֹעֲדוֹן סְפָרִים *book club*.

⑥ **yom vav** יוֹם ו' *Friday*. In lesson 28, we learned that the days of the week do not have special names in Hebrew (except

3 בְּשִׁירֵי ״זוּג מֵהַשָּׁמַיִם״.

4 מוֹעֲדוֹן ״צַוְתָּא״, תֵּל אָבִיב.

5 בְּיוֹם ו׳, עֶשְׂרִים וְשִׁשָּׁה בְּאַפְּרִיל, בְּ- 23:00 (עֶשְׂרִים וְשָׁלוֹשׁ).

6 פְּרָטִים וְהַזְמָנַת כַּרְטִיסִים: 03-5247373 (אֶפֶס שָׁלוֹשׁ - חָמֵשׁ, שְׁתַּיִם, אַרְבַּע, שֶׁבַע, שָׁלוֹשׁ, שֶׁבַע, שָׁלוֹשׁ).

7 פְּרָטִים נוֹסָפִים בְּאֲתָר הַמוֹעֲדוֹן: צַוְתָּא@זָהָבנֶט.יל.

8 חֲנָיָה בְּשֶׁפַע.

9 אַבטָחָה מְלֵאָה.

for Shabbat), and are named according to their sequence, beginning with **yom rishon** יוֹם רִאשׁוֹן *Sunday*. In writing, the days can also be referred to simply by the Hebrew letter that corresponds with their numerical order, beginning with **`alef** א for Sunday. When reading the days out loud, they can be read either as **yom `alef** יוֹם אָלֶף or as **yom rishon** יוֹם רִאשׁוֹן. Here are the days of the week again using the Hebrew letters rather than the full ordinal numbers:

yom `alef יוֹם א׳ *Sunday*
yom bet יוֹם ב׳ *Monday*
yom gimel יוֹם ג׳ *Tuesday*
yom dalet יוֹם ד׳ *Wednesday*
yom hey יוֹם ה׳ *Thursday*
yom vav יוֹם ו׳ *Friday*
shabat שַׁבָּת *Saturday*

Targil rishon – Targem תַּרְגִּיל רִאשׁוֹן – תַּרְגֵּם

❶ כל יום שישי בבוקר אני הולכת עם חברה למועדון התאטרון.

Kol yom shishi baboqer `ani holekhet 'im chaverah lemo'adon hate`atron.

❷ הזמנת כרטיסים רק באתר המועדון.

Hazmanat kartisim raq be`atar hamo'adon.

❸ אחרי עשרים שנה הם זוג מהשמים. כל הכבוד להם!

`Acharey 'esrim shanah hem zug mehashamayim. Kol hakavod lahem!

❹ אנחנו קונים בקניון, כי יש שם חניה בשפע.

`Anachnu qonim baqanyon, ki yesh sham chanayah beshefa'.

Targil sheni – Hashlem תַּרְגִּיל שֵׁנִי – הַשְׁלֵם

❶ Once a month *(One-time in-month)*, the friends come to sing with us at home.

[...] [...] hachaverim ba`im [...] `etzlenu [...].

___ _____ הַחֲבֵרִים בָּאִים ____ אֶצְלֵנוּ ____ .

❷ Everyone *(All together)* congratulates *(blesses)* the young couple with Mazal Tov.

[...] [...] mevarkhim `et [...] hatza'ir be[...] [...].

____ ____ מְבָרְכִים אֶת ____ הַצָּעִיר בְּ___ ___ .

❸ I'm*(fem.)* reading an *(in)* advertisement in the newspaper [with] details about a concert at the Tzavta Club.

`Ani qore`t [...] ba'iton [...] 'al qontzert [...] ‘Tzavta’.

אֲנִי קוֹרֵאת ______ בָּעִתּוֹן _____ עַל קוֹנְצֶרְט ______ "צַוְתָּא".

❺ שלום. אני רוצה פרטים נוספים על מרכז העסקים החדש.

Shalom. `Ani rotzah pratim nosafim 'al merkaz ha'asaqim hachadash.

Answers to Exercise 1

❶ Every Friday *(day sixth)* morning I go with a friend to the theatre club. ❷ Reservation *(booking)* of tickets [is] only on the club website. ❸ After twenty years, they [are still] a match made in heaven. Congratulations to them! ❹ We shop in the mall, because there is plenty of parking there. ❺ Hello. I'd like *(want)* further details about the new business centre.

❹ On Tuesday at 7 pm *(19:00)* [it's the] Seder night dinner at grandfather and grandmother's.

[...] [...] betsha' 'esreh `aruchat [...] [...] `etzel saba vesavta.

____ _ בְּתֵשַׁע עֶשְׂרֵה אֲרוּחַת ___ ____ אֵצֶל סַבָּא וְסַבְתָּא.

❺ Full security at The Tower tourist centre.

[...] mele`ah [...] hatayarut '[...]'.

_____ מְלֵאָה _____ הַתַּיָּרוּת "_____".

Answers to Exercise 2

❶ **Pa'am bechodesh – lashir – babayit**

❶ פַּעַם בְּחוֹדֶשׁ - לָשִׁיר - בַּבַּיִת

❷ **Kulam beyachad – hazug – mazal tov**

❷ כּוּלָּם בְּיַחַד - הַזּוּג - מַזָּל טוֹב

❸ **– bamoda'ah – pratim – bemo'adon –**

❸ - בַּמּוֹדָעָה - פְּרָטִים - בְּמוֹעֲדוֹן -

❹ **Beyom gimel – leyl haseder –** ❹ בְּיוֹם ג׳ - לֵיל הַסֵּדֶר -

❺ **`Avtachah – bemerkaz – hamigdal** ❺ אַבְטָחָה - בְּמֶרְכָּז - הַמִּגְדָּל

Shirah betzibur שִׁירָה בְּצִבּוּר singing in public, group singing. *The 'singalong' has been an important part of Hebrew and Israeli culture since before the State of Israel was established. Many Israelis enjoy getting together at home or in pubs and clubs to sing songs, which range from traditional Hebrew songs of yesteryear to Oriental favourites and more recent pop songs. The words appear on screens or in booklets distributed to the audience. Every so often the MC will cry out* **Vekhulam beyachad!** !וְכוּלָּם בְּיַחַד – All together now! *(literally, 'And-all-of-them together!').*

61 Sixty-first lesson (Shi'ur shishim ve`achat)

Shem
A name

1 **Shir shel Zeldah: "Lekhol `ish yesh shem**
A poem by Zeldah: "Every person has a name

2 **shenatan lo `Elohim**
that God gave him *(that-he-gave to-him God)*

3 **venatnu lo `aviv ve`imo ①."**
and [that] his father and mother gave him *(and-that-gave to-him his-father and-his-mother)*."

Notes

① **`aviv ve`imo** אָבִיו וְאִמּוֹ *his father and his mother.* Although both these possessive forms end in a **vav** ו, the first is a consonant pronounced **v** ו, while the second carries the vowel sound **o** וֹ. In both cases, this is the third-person masculine singular suffix (*his* father, *his* mother). The different pronunciation is due to the fact that in **`aviv** אָבִיו, the **vav** ו is

Second wave: lesson 11

61 שִׁעוּר שִׁשִּׁים וְאַחַת

שֵׁם

1 שִׁיר שֶׁל זֶלְדָה: "לְכֹל אִישׁ יֵשׁ שֵׁם

2 שֶׁנָּתַן לוֹ אֱלֹהִים

3 וְנָתְנוּ לוֹ אָבִיו וְאִמּוֹ."

preceded by a **yod** ׳, which changes the final sound from **o** וֹ to **v** ו. The **vav** ו in **`imo** אִמּוֹ *his mother* is the same vowel that appears in **shelo** *of-him*. Other examples of words in which the ו **vav** of the third-person masculine singular possessive suffix is pronounced **v** include: **`achiv** אָחִיו *his brother* and **piv** פִּיו *his mouth*.

4 – Yofi shel shir! `Anachnu kvar bachodesh hashvi'i,
What a beautiful poem *(Beautiful of poem)*! We are already in the seventh month.

5 `aval 'od lo matzanu shem latinoq `o latinoqet shelanu.
but we still haven't found a name for our baby boy or girl *(for-the-baby-boy or for-the-baby-girl of-us)*.

6 `Anachnu rotzim shem yisra`eli ②, qatzar, `ofnati ③, tanakhi, 'im tzlil na'im.
We want an Israeli name, short, fashionable, Biblical [and] with a nice *(pleasant)* sound.

7 – Mah `atem `omrim 'al hashemot ha`eleh:
What do you say about *(on)* these names:

8 Chen, Noy, Gal, Tal, Gili, Sharon ④, 'Adi, Shani, Gali, Tali, 'Eden, Qeren, `Ortal?
Grace, Beauty, Wave, Dew, My joy, Sharon, Jewel, Scarlet, My wave, My dew, Delight, Ray, Dew-light *(light-of-dew)*?

9 – Tov. `Aval mah poh shem shel yeled umah shem shel yaldah?
Good. But which *(what)* here is a boy's name and which is a girl's name?

10 – Zot ha`ofnah hayom: `oto shem, `oto jins!
That's the fashion today: same name, same jeans!

Notes

② **yisra`eli** יִשְׂרְאֵלִי *Israeli* is the masculine singular form of the adjective. The other forms are **yisra`elit** יִשְׂרְאֵלִית (fem. sing.); **yisra`eliyot** יִשְׂרְאֵלִיוֹת (fem. pl.); **yisra`eliyim** יִשְׂרְאֵלִיִּים (masc. pl.). The masculine plural ends in two **yods** because the masculine plural suffix ים. **yim** is added to the singular form ▸

4 – יוֹפִי שֶׁל שִׁיר! אֲנַחנוּ כְּבָר בַּחוֹדֶשׁ הַשְּׁבִיעִי.

5 אֲבָל עוֹד לֹא מָצָאנוּ שֵׁם לַתִּינוֹק אוֹ לַתִּינוֹקֶת שֶׁלָּנוּ.

6 אֲנַחנוּ רוֹצִים שֵׁם יִשְׂרְאֵלִי, קָצָר, אוֹפנָתִי, תַּנָכִי, עִם צְלִיל נָעִים.

7 – מַה אַתֶּם אוֹמרִים עַל הַשֵּׁמוֹת הָאֵלֶּה:

8 חֵן, נוֹי, גַּל, טַל, גִּילִי, שָׁרוֹן, עֲדִי, שָׁנִי, גָּלִי, טָלִי, עֵדֶן, קֶרֶן, אוֹרטָל?

9 – טוֹב. אֲבָל מַה פֹּה שֵׁם שֶׁל יֶלֶד וּמַה שֵׁם שֶׁל יַלדָּה?

10 – זֹאת הָאוֹפנָה הַיּוֹם: אוֹתוֹ שֵׁם, אוֹתוֹ גִּ'ינס!

yisra`eli, which already ends in a **yod**. The same is true of the adjective **tanakhi** תַּנָכִי *Biblical*: **tanakhit** תַּנָכִית, **tanakhiyot** תַּנָכִיּוֹת, **tanakhiyim** תַּנָכִיִּים.

③ **`ofnati** אוֹפנָתִי *fashionable* comes from **`ofnah** אוֹפנָה *fashion*. Note that the **hey** at the end of **`ofnah** is replaced by a **tav**: **`ofnatit** אוֹפנָתִית, **`ofnatiyot** אוֹפנָתִיּוֹת, **`ofnatiyim** אוֹפנָתִיִּים.

④ **Sharon** שָׁרוֹן *Sharon* is the name of the fertile coastal plain to the north of Tel Aviv. There is no direct translation for this place name, but the Hebrew word has also been adopted as a female first name in English.

Targil rishon – Targem תַּרְגִּיל רִאשׁוֹן – תַּרְגֵּם

❶ הג'ינס באופנה אצל הצעירים בכל העולם.
Hajins ba`ofnah `etzel hatze'irim bekhol ha'olam.

❷ אביו ואמו נתנו לתינוק שם אופנתי קצר: דן.
`Aviv ve`imo natnu latinoq shem `ofnati qatzar: Dan.

❸ המורה קורא כל יום שיר תנכי לתלמידים.
Hamoreh qore` kol yom shir tanakhi latalmidim.

❹ זה פלאפון אופנתי ויש לו גם צליל נעים מאוד.
Zeh pelefon `ofnati veyesh lo gam tzlil na'im me`od.

❺ מה הם אומרים על הרהיטים העתיקים האלה?
Mah hem `omrim 'al harahitim ha'atiqim ha`eleh?

Targil sheni – Hashlem תַּרְגִּיל שֵׁנִי – הַשְׁלֵם

❶ We do not tell the children what they should do.
`Anachnu [...] [...] layeladim mah hem [...] [...].
אֲנַחְנוּ __ ______ לַיְּלָדִים מַה הֵם ______ _____ .

❷ Now [it is] very fashionable to live in a tower.
[...] [...] me`od [...] bemigdal.
____ ______ מְאוֹד ____ בְּמִגְדָּל.

❸ Zeldah has a beautiful poem about people's names.
LeZeldah yesh [...] yafeh 'al [...] shel [...].
לְזֶלְדָּה יֵשׁ ___ יָפֶה עַל ____ שֶׁל _____ .

❹ Do you*(fem.)* like your name?
`At `ohevet `et [...] [...]?
אַתְּ אוֹהֶבֶת אֶת ___ ___?

❺ What is the surname/last name *(name the-family)* of Yossi, the new manager?
Mah [...] [...] shel Yosi, [...] hachadash?
מַה __ ______ שֶׁל יוֹסִי, _____ הֶחָדָשׁ?

Answers to Exercise 1

❶ Jeans are in fashion among young people across *(in all)* the world. ❷ His father and his mother gave the baby boy a short, fashionable name: Dan. ❸ Every day the teacher reads a Biblical poem to the students. ❹ This is a fashionable cell/mobile phone and it also has a very pleasant sound. ❺ What do they say about this old/antique furniture *(the-furnitures ancient these)*?

Answers to Exercise 2

❶ – **lo `omrim – tzrikhim la'asot** ❶ - לֹא אוֹמְרִים - צְרִיכִים לַעֲשׂוֹת

❷ **'Akhshav `ofnati – lagur –** ❷ עַכְשָׁו אוֹפְנָתִי - לָגוּר -

❸ – **shir – shemot – `anashim** ❸ - שִׁיר - שֵׁמוֹת - אֲנָשִׁים

❹ – **hashem shelakh** ❹ - הַשֵּׁם שֶׁלָּךְ

❺ – **shem hamishpachah – hamenahel –** ❺ - שֵׁם הַמִּשְׁפָּחָה - הַמְנַהֵל -

62 *What's in a name? Ask an Israeli of any age what their name is, and they will reply by telling you their first name, or perhaps even their nickname. If you want to know someone's family name, you need to ask:* **Mah shem hamishpachah shelkha/shelakh?**
מַה שֵׁם הַמִּשְׁפָּחָה שֶׁלְּךָ / שֶׁלָּךְ?

Biblical yet modern: Many religious families give their children traditional Biblical names: **`Avraham** אַבְרָהָם; **Rivqah** רִבְקָה; **Mosheh** מֹשֶׁה; **Miryam** מִרְיָם, *and so on. Others aim to be both traditional and with-it at the same time:* **Sarah** שָׂרָה *becomes* **Sari** שָׂרִי *or* **Sarit** שָׂרִית; **Miryam** מִרְיָם *becomes* **Miry** מִירִי; **Yosef** יוֹסֵף **Yosi** יוֹסִי; **Ya'aqov** יַעֲקֹב **Qobi** קוֹבִּי *and so on. Many parents are particularly fond of short names such as* **Tal** טַל dew, *which is a*

---

62 Sixty-second lesson
(Shi'ur shishim ushtayim)

Pnay ①
Leisure

1 – **Mah `atah 'oseh bish'ot hapnay shelkha?**
What do you do in your leisure time *(in-hours-of the-leisure of-you)*?

2 – **Bemeshekh hashavu'a `eyn li pnay.**
During the week I don't have any leisure [time] *(there-is-not to-me leisure)*.

3 **Yesh li pnay raq beyom shishi `acharey hatzohorayim** ② **uveshabat.**
I only have leisure [time] on Friday afternoon *(after the-noon)* and Shabbat.

Notes

① **pnay** פְּנַאי *leisure, free time* comes from the adjective **panuy** פָּנוּי *vacant, unoccupied.* The English word 'vacation' is based on the same association with time that is 'empty' or free.

Biblical word (though it was not used as a name until modern times), and is also short, pleasant-sounding and unisex. Some parents opt for Hebrew names that also have an international sound to them. For example, **Guy** גַּיְא *sounds just like the English name Guy, but is also a Hebrew word for* valley *or* vale, *with Biblical and pastoral overtones.*

The poet **Zeldah Mishkowski** *(1914–84), born into a very religious family, worked throughout her life with disabled children. Her fame, illustrated by the fact that she is referred to by her first name only, is due to her simple, precise and direct poetical style.*

Second wave: lesson 12

62 שִׁעוּר שִׁשִּׁים וּשְׁתַּיִם

פְּנַאי

1 – מַה אַתָּה עוֹשֶׂה בִּשְׁעוֹת הַפְּנַאי שֶׁלְּךָ?

2 – בְּמֶשֶׁךְ הַשָּׁבוּעַ אֵין לִי פְּנַאי.

3 יֵשׁ לִי פְּנַאי רַק בְּיוֹם שִׁישִּׁי אַחֲרֵי הַצָּהֳרַיִם וּבְשַׁבָּת.

② **tzohorayim** צָהֳרַיִם *noon* (the Hebrew word is in the dual form); **`acharey hatzohorayim** אַחֲרֵי הַצָּהֳרַיִם *afternoon*, which you will also see in abbreviated form as אחה"צ. Although the vowel points suggest that this word should be pronounced **tzaharayim**, it is actually pronounced **tzohorayim** due to complicated grammatical rules. Just remember the correct pronunciation and you'll do fine!

4 **`Ani chaver bemo'adon shachmat ③.**
I [am a] member of *(in)* a chess club.

5 **`Ani qore` `et kol 'itoney ④ hashabat,**
I read all the Shabbat newspapers,

6 **poter tashbetzim ⑤ vetashchetzim ⑥ ba'itonim.**
[and] solve crosswords and arrow word puzzles in the newspapers.

7 – **`Atah du-leshoni `o tlat-leshoni ⑦? Be`eyzo safah `atah poter tashbetzim?**
Are you bilingual or trilingual? In what language do you solve crosswords?

8 – **`Ani choshev she`efshar liftor tashbetzim raq bisfat `em ⑧.**
I think that it is only possible to solve crosswords in [your] mother tongue *(in-tongue-of mother)*.

9 – **Mah hamiqtzo'a shelkha?**
What is your profession?

10 – **Balshan ⑨.**
Linguist.

Notes

③ **shachmat** שַׁחְמָט *chess*. This word is borrowed from Persian. The first part, **shach**, means *king* (as in the Shah of Iran). In Hebrew, **mat** מָט means *lean over* or *be about to fall*. Checkmate!

④ **'itoney** עִתּוֹנֵי *newspapers-of* – this is a plural construct form. In the absolute state, the plural of **'iton** עִתּוֹן is **'itonim** עִתּוֹנִים (see line 6). For *sports newspapers*, you can choose between **'itonim shel sport** עִתּוֹנִים שֶׁל ספּוֹרט and the construct **'itoney sport** עִתּוֹנֵי ספּוֹרט. Note that in the construct state of masculine plural nouns, the final **mem** ם disappears, and the preceding **i** becomes **ey**.

⑤ **tashbetzim** תַּשְׁבֵּצִים *crosswords*. The root שבץ can also be seen in **mishbetzet** מִשְׁבֶּצֶת *square, slot*.

4 אֲנִי חָבֵר בְּמוֹעֲדוֹן שַׁחְמָט.

5 אֲנִי קוֹרֵא אֶת כֹּל עִתּוֹנֵי הַשַּׁבָּת.

6 פּוֹתֵר תַּשְׁבְּצִים וְתַשְׁחֵצִים בָּעִתּוֹנִים.

7 – אַתָּה דוּ-לְשׁוֹנִי אוֹ תְּלַת-לְשׁוֹנִי? בְּאֵיזוֹ שָׂפָה אַתָּה פּוֹתֵר תַּשְׁבְּצִים?

8 – אֲנִי חוֹשֵׁב שֶׁאֶפְשָׁר לִפְתּוֹר תַּשְׁבְּצִים רַק בִּשְׂפַת אֵם.

9 – מַה הַמִּקְצוֹעַ שֶׁלְּךָ?

10 – בַּלְשָׁן. □

⑥ **tashchetzim** תַּשְׁחֵצִים *arrow word puzzles*. This word was formed by taking the first part of **tashbetz** and combining it with the word **chetz** חֵץ *arrow*.

⑦ **tlat-** תְּלַת *tri-* or *three*; **du-** דוּ *bi-* or *two*. These two Aramaic words are used to form a large number of compound words. For example, a *tricycle* is **tlat-`ofan** תְּלַת-אוֹפָן 'tri-wheel', and an *amphibian* is **du-chay** דוּ-חַי 'two-lives' ('amphibian' comes from the Greek for 'both lives', referring to the fact that these animals can live on land or in water).

⑧ **`em** אֵם *mother*. In lesson 61, we saw this word with the third-person masculine possessive suffix: **`imo** אִמּוֹ *his mother*.

⑨ **balshan** בַּלְשָׁן *linguist*. This modern word has an interesting Talmudic origin. In a discussion of the exiles who returned from Babylon, a certain Mordechai Balshan is mentioned. The Talmud comments that his name was appropriate, as he knew many languages. Like the Talmud, you may enjoy the idea that the name came from a combination of **ba'al** בַּעַל, which we've already seen with the meaning *husband*, but which here means *master* or *owner*, and **lashon** לָשׁוֹן *language*.

Targil rishon – Targem תַּרְגִּיל רִאשׁוֹן – תַּרְגֵּם

❶ הוא קורא את עתוני הבוקר בארוחת הצהריים בקפטריה של המשרד.
Hu qore` `et 'itoney haboqer ba`aruchat hatzohorayim baqafeteryah shel hamisrad.

❷ ישראל כותב במדור השחמט בעתון בכל יום ו.
Yisra`el kotev bimdor hashachmat ba'iton bekhol yom vav.

❸ היא אוהבת מאוד לפתור תשבצים, אבל רק בעברית.
Hi `ohevet me`od liftor tashbetzim, `aval raq be'ivrit.

❹ יש לו מקצוע מעייף והרבה שעות עבודה.
Yesh lo miqtzo'a me'ayef veharbeh she'ot 'avodah.

Targil sheni – Hashlem תַּרְגִּיל שֵׁנִי – הַשְׁלֵם

❶ You are trilingual, but what is your mother tongue *(tongue the-mother of-you)*?
`Atah [...]-[...], `aval mah [...] [...] shelkha?
אַתָּה ___ - _____, אֲבָל מָה ___ ___ שֶׁלְּךָ ?

❷ Do you*(masc. pl.)* think it is possible to solve physics problems *(problems in-physics)* in this mess?
`Atem choshvim [...] [...] be'ayot befisiqah [...] [...]?
אַתֶּם חוֹשְׁבִים _____ _____ בְּעָיוֹת בְּפִיסִיקָה _____ ___?

❸ On Tuesday at noon there is a street theatre in the city centre *(in-centre-of the-city)*.
Beyom [...] [...] yesh te`atron rechov [...] [...].
בְּיוֹם _ ______ יֵשׁ תֵּאַטְרוֹן רְחוֹב _____ ____ .

❹ The linguist speaks many languages.
[...] medaber harbeh [...].
_____ מְדַבֵּר הַרְבֵּה _____ .

❺ במשך השבוע אין לי פנאי למשחקים כמו תשחצים.
Bemeshekh hashavu'a `eyn li pnay lemischaqim kmo tashchetzim.

Answers to Exercise 1

❶ He reads the morning newspapers at lunch *(at-meal-of noon)* in the office cafeteria *(in-the-cafeteria of the-office)*. ❷ Yisrael writes the chess column in the newspaper every Friday. ❸ She very much likes *(likes very)* to solve crosswords, but only in Hebrew. ❹ He has a tiring profession and many hours of work. ❺ During the week I do not have leisure [time] for games like arrow word puzzles.

❺ During the year, he solves work problems in the hospital.
[...] [...] hu poter `et be'ayot ha'avodah [...] [...].
____ ____ הוּא פּוֹתֵר אֵת בְּעָיוֹת הָעֲבוֹדָה ____ ______.

Answers to Exercise 2

❶ – **tlat-leshoni** – **sfat ha`em** – ❶ - תְּלַת-לְשׁוֹנִי - שְׂפַת הָאֵם -

❷ – **she`efshar liftor** – **babalagan hazeh**

❷ - שֶׁאֶפְשָׁר לִפְתּוֹר - בַּבַּלָגָן הַזֶּה

❸ – **gimel batzohorayim** – **bemerkaz ha'ir**

❸ - ג' בַּצָּהֳרַיִם - בְּמֶרְכַּז הָעִיר

❹ **Habalshan** – **safot** ❹ הַבַּלְשָׁן - שָׂפוֹת

❺ **Bemeshekh hashanah** – **beveyt hacholim**

❺ בְּמֶשֶׁךְ הַשָּׁנָה - בְּבֵית הַחוֹלִים

Aramaic: The historical land of Aram lies in the north of modern-day Syria. Around the 10th century BCE, the population in the area continuously migrated to the east, to Mesopotamia. The genealogy presented in Genesis 11:28 defines the Arameans as related to the Hebrews. They spoke a Semitic language closely related to Hebrew and Phoenician. The earliest documents in Aramaic date back to the 10th century BCE. Aramaic was used as a religious and political language, and from an early stage also developed literary forms. Although Aramaic was spoken in various dialects, a common form enabled it to function as an international language for many centuries, not unlike the role played in later periods by Greek and Latin. Although Aramaic eventually lost its influence, it continued to be used in various forms by different groups of people, including the Nabataeans and the Samaritans. A number of Eastern Christian rites use Aramaic as a religious language to this day, and Aramaic is still spoken in varying forms by certain communities, mainly in Syria and Iraq. The inaugural mass of the Second Vatican Council (1962) was celebrated in Aramaic.

---

63 Sixty-third lesson
(Shi'ur shishim veshalosh)

חֲזָרָה Chazarah – Review

1 A head start

Bereshit בְּרֵאשִׁית 'In the beginning' is the Hebrew name for the first book of the Bible – Genesis. You may recognize that this word comes from the same root as **rosh** רֹאשׁ *head*. The same root appears in **rishon** רִאשׁוֹן *first*.

rosh רֹאשׁ appears in numerous constructions, all with the sense of either 'the top' or 'the beginning' of something:

rosh hashanah	רֹאשׁ הַשָּׁנָה	'head of the year' – *New Year* (the Hebrew festival of Rosh Hashanah usually falls in September)

Second wave: lesson 13

63 שִׁעוּר שִׁשִּׁים וְשָׁלוֹשׁ

rosh chodesh	רֹאשׁ חוֹדֶשׁ	'head of the month' – *first of the month* (that is, the Hebrew month)
rosh 'ir	רֹאשׁ עִיר	'head of city' – *mayor*
rosh memshalah	רֹאשׁ מֶמְשָׁלָה	'head of government' – *prime minister, president*
yoshev rosh	יוֹשֵׁב רֹאשׁ	'sitting [at the] head' – *chairman* (the person presiding)
berosh uvarishonah	בְּרֹאשׁ וּבָרִאשׁוֹנָה	'in head and firstly' – *first and foremost*

63 2 A possessive family

The possessive adjectives (*my, your, his, her, its, our, their*) in Hebrew are suffixes that are added to the end of the thing possessed. Let's review the full declensions of three words for important relatives:

Masculine possessor(s)		Feminine possessor(s)		
\`achot אָחוֹת *sister*				
\`achoti	אֲחוֹתִי	**\`achoti**	אֲחוֹתִי	*my sister*
\`achotkha	אֲחוֹתְךָ	**\`achotekh**	אֲחוֹתֵךְ	*your sister* (sing.)
\`achoto	אֲחוֹתוֹ	**\`achotah**	אֲחוֹתָהּ	*his/her sister*
\`achotenu	אֲחוֹתֵנוּ	**\`achotenu**	אֲחוֹתֵנוּ	*our sister*
\`achotkhem	אֲחוֹתְכֶם	**\`achotkhen**	אֲחוֹתְכֶן	*your sister* (pl.)
\`achotam	אֲחוֹתָם	**\`achotan**	אֲחוֹתָן	*their sister*
\`av אָב *father*				
\`avi	אָבִי	**\`avi**	אָבִי	*my father*
\`avikha	אָבִיךָ	**\`avikh**	אָבִיךְ	*your father* (sing.)
\`aviv	אָבִיו	**\`aviha**	אָבִיהָ	*his/her father*
\`avinu	אָבִינוּ	**\`avinu**	אָבִינוּ	*our father*
\`avikhem	אֲבִיכֶם	**\`avikhen**	אֲבִיכֶן	*your father* (pl.)
\`avihem	אֲבִיהֶם	**\`avihen**	אֲבִיהֶן	*their father*
\`em אֵם *mother*				
\`imi	אִמִּי	**\`imi**	אִמִּי	*my mother*
\`imkha	אִמְּךָ	**\`imekh**	אִמֵּךְ	*your mother* (sing.)
\`imo	אִמּוֹ	**\`imah**	אִמָּהּ	*his/her mother*
\`imenu	אִמֵּנוּ	**\`imenu**	אִמֵּנוּ	*our mother*
\`imkhem	אִמְּכֶם	**\`imkhen**	אִמְּכֶן	*your mother* (pl.)
\`imam	אִמָּם	**\`iman**	אִמָּן	*their mother*

3 'To have'

To express *I have*, *you have*, and so on, use **yesh** יֵשׁ *there is* followed by the preposition **l-** לְ *to, for* with the appropriate ending for the person in question, for example: **yesh lah shem qatzar** יֵשׁ לָהֶן שֵׁם קָצָר *she has a short name.*

yesh li	יֵשׁ לִי	*I have*
yesh lekha	יֵשׁ לְךָ	*you have* (masc. sing.)
yesh lakh	יֵשׁ לָךְ	*you have* (fem. sing.)
yesh lo	יֵשׁ לוֹ	*he has*
yesh lah	יֵשׁ לָהּ	*she has*
yesh lanu	יֵשׁ לָנוּ	*we have*
yesh lakhem	יֵשׁ לָכֶם	*you have* (masc. pl.)
yesh lakhen	יֵשׁ לָכֶן	*you have* (fem. pl.)
yesh lahem	יֵשׁ לָהֶם	*they have* (masc.)
yesh lahen	יֵשׁ לָהֶן	*they have* (fem.)

4 Occupations and character traits

In the last lesson, we saw the word **balshan** בַּלְשָׁן *linguist*. The suffix **-an** ָן is often used to form words for occupations or character traits. For example, from the root שחק *to play, to act* comes the noun **sachqan** שַׂחְקָן (m.), **sachqanit** שַׂחְקָנִית (f.), which means *actor* or *player* (e.g. basketball or chess player).

pitput פִּטְפּוּט *chatter* produces:
patpetan / patpetanit פַּטְפְּטָנִית / פַּטְפְּטָן *a chatty person*

sefer סֵפֶר *book*:
safran / safranit סַפְרָנִית / סַפְרָן *librarian*

seder סֵדֶר *order*:
sadran / sadranit סַדְרָנִית / סַדְרָן *orderly, usher*

yahalom יַהֲלוֹם *diamond*:
yahaloman / yahalomanit יַהֲלוֹמָנִית / יַהֲלוֹמָן *diamond dealer*

chadash חָדָשׁ *new*:
chadshan / chadshanit חַדְשָׁנִית / חַדְשָׁן *innovator, pioneer*

`ofnah אוֹפְנָה *fashion*:
`ofnati / `ofnatit *fashionable* (m./f. sing.) אוֹפְנָתִי / אוֹפְנָתִית
`ofnatiyim / `ofnatiyot (m./f. pl.) אוֹפְנָתִיִים / אוֹפְנָתִיוֹת

bayit בַּיִת *house*, *home*:
beyti / beytit *homely*, *domestic* (m./f. sing.) בֵּיתִי / בֵּיתִית
beytiyim / beytiyot (m./f. pl.) בֵּיתִיִים / בֵּיתִיוֹת

dat דָּת *religion*:
dati / datit *religious* (m./f. sing.) דָּתִי / דָּתִית
datiyim / datiyot (m./f. pl.) דָּתִיִים / דָּתִיוֹת

choref חוֹרֶף *winter*:
chorpi / chorpit *wintry* (m./f. sing.) חוֹרְפִּי / חוֹרְפִּית
chorpiyim / chorpiyot (m./f. pl.) חוֹרְפִּיִים / חוֹרְפִּיוֹת

kfar כְּפָר *village*:
kafri / kafrit *rural*, *rustic* (m./f. sing.) כַּפְרִי / כַּפְרִית
kafriyim / kafriyot (m./f. pl.) כַּפְרִיִים / כַּפְרִיוֹת

chag חַג *festival*:
chagigi / chagigit *festive* (m./f. sing.) חֲגִיגִי / חֲגִיגִית
chagigiyim / chagigiyot (m./f. pl.) חֲגִיגִיִים / חֲגִיגִיּוֹת

6 *Shva` na'* (mobile) and *shva` nach* (immobile)

You have now progressed far enough in your study of Hebrew for us to discuss a more advanced point concerning one of the vowel marks. There are actually two different types of **shva`** [ְ]. There is no difference in the way they are written, but they reflect different pronunciations.

• The first type is called **shva` na'** שְׁוָא נָע *mobile shva*, since it is voiced in pronunciation. We transcribe this type of **shva`** with [**e**]. The **shva` na'** appears:
• At the beginning of a word: **shevu'on** שְׁבוּעוֹן *weekly (newspaper)*; **medor** מְדוֹר *column-of*; **me`od** מְאוֹד *very*.
• Immediately <u>after</u> another **shva`** (the first being a **shva` nach** – see following section): **beynle`umi** בֵּינְלְאוּמִי *international*; **nikhnesah** נִכְנְסָה *she entered*.
• When it appears under the first of two identical, successive letters: **hineni** הִנְנִי *here I am*.

When a **shva`** appears under one of the letters א/ה/ח/ע, it is combined with one of the other vowel marks, and the pronunciation in modern Hebrew is the same as the mark: **`anashim** אֲנָשִׁים *people*; **`ahavah** אַהֲבָה *love*; **chatunah** חֲתוּנָּה *wedding*; **ya'asu** יַעֲשׂוּ *they will do*; **`elohim** אֱלֹהִים *God.*

• The second type is called **shva` nach** שְׁוָא נָח *immobile shva*, in other words – silent. This type appears:
• Under the last letter of a syllable, e.g. **shulchan** שׁוּלְחָן *table.*
• Immediately before another **shva`** (the second one must therefore be a **shva` na'**): **nikhnesah** נִכְנְסָה *she entered.*
• At the end of a word: **`at** אַתְּ *you* (fem.), **lakh** לָךְ *for you* (fem.).

In this book, we have decided not to show the **shva` nach** throughout the lessons, in order to guide you in the usual pronunciation of the words in modern Israeli Hebrew. However, in this section we've included all the **shva`** signs, so that you can see how the words appear in fully pointed text. As we've mentioned before when discussing detailed points of Hebrew grammar: we really don't want you to lose sleep over this kind of thing. Many Israelis learn these rules at school and promptly forget them after they matriculate. In casual speech you may well hear someone pronounce a **shva`** where the rules say it should be silent, or leave it out where it 'should' be voiced.

63 Review exercise

❶ סָבִי לֹא הָיָה בַּלשָׁן, אֲבָל הוּא דִבֵּר חָמֵשׁ שָׂפוֹת. ❷ סַבתָא שֶׁלִי הָיתָה תלַת-לְשׁוֹנִית וּבַלשָׁנִית חוֹבֶבֶת. ❸ אֲנִי דוּ-לְשׁוֹנִית וּשׂפַת הָאֵם שָׁלִי עִברִית. ❹ הַיְלָדִים שָׁלִי מְדַבּרִים רַק עִברִית, אֲבָל הֵם לוֹמדִים אַנגלִית בְּבֵית הַסֵפֶר. ❺ פֹּה לֹא מִגדָל בָּבֶל, אֲבָל בָּאָרֶץ הַרבֵּה אֲנָשִׁים מְדַבּרִים הַרבֵּה שָׂפוֹת. ❻ לְבַלשָׁנִים יְכוֹלָה לִהְיוֹת פֹּה עֲבוֹדָה מְעַניֶנֶת. ❼ אֲנִי אוֹהֶבֶת לִקרוֹא תַנָ"ך, שִׁירִים וְגַם לִפתוֹר תַשבְּצִים וְתַשחֵצִים בְּעִתוֹנִים. ❽ לַיְלָדִים בָּאָרֶץ יֵשׁ שֵׁמוֹת תַנָכִיִים, אוֹפנָתִיִים וּקצָרִים.

Answers

❶ My grandfather wasn't a linguist, but he spoke five languages. *(grandfather-my not was linguist but he spoke five languages)* ❷ My grandmother was trilingual and an amateur linguist. *(grandmother of-me was tri-lingual and-linguist amateur)* ❸ I'm bilingual and my mother tongue is Hebrew. *(I bi-lingual and language-of the-mother of-me Hebrew)* ❹ My children speak only Hebrew, but they are studying English at school. *(the-children of-me speak only Hebrew but they study English at-house-of the-book)* ❺ It isn't the Tower of Babel here, but many people in the country speak many languages. *(here not tower-of Babel but in-the-Land many people speak many languages)* ❻ Linguists can have interesting work here. *(for-linguists can to-be here work interesting)* ❼ I like to read the Bible [and] poems and also to solve crosswords and arrow word puzzles in newspapers. *(I like to-read Bible, poems and-also to-solve crosswords and-arrow-word-puzzles in-newspapers)* ❽ Children in Israel have Biblical, fashionable, short names. *(to-the-children in-the-Land there-are names Biblical, fashionable and-short)*

Second wave: lesson 14

64 Sixty-fourth lesson
(Shi'ur shishim ve`arba')

Tzva'im uvgadim bacharuzim
Colours and clothes in rhymes

1 **Yeruqim ① hamikhnasayim ②.**
Green [are] the trousers.

2 **Kchulim ③ hamagafayim ④.**
Blue [are] the boots.

3 **`Adumah ⑤ ha'anivah.**
Red [is] the tie.

4 **`Aforah ⑥ hachultzah.**
Grey [is] the shirt.

5 **Shchorot ⑦ hana'alayim.**
Black [are] the shoes.

Notes

① **yeruqim** יְרוּקִּים *green*: like any other adjective, adjectives of colour must 'agree' in gender and number with the noun they describe. Since **mikhnasayim** מִכְנָסַיִים *trousers* is a masculine dual noun in Hebrew, the adjective **yaroq** יָרוֹק *green* (masc. sing.) appears in the masculine plural form (there is no separate dual form of adjectives, only singular and plural). Note that the first six lines in this text are written in poetic style, with the normal word order inverted, as in the English translation. The normal way to say 'the trousers are green' is **hamikhnasayim yeruqim** הַמִּכְנָסַיִים יְרוּקִּים. Review lesson 70 includes a list of the main adjectives of colour in all four forms (masculine and feminine singular and masculine and feminine plural). **yaroq** יָרוֹק *green* shares the same root ירק as **yereq** יֶרֶק *greenery, vegetable* and **Yarqon** יַרְקוֹן, the name of the river with rich vegetation on its banks that runs through Tel Aviv to the sea.

צְבָעִים וּבְגָדִים בַּחֲרוּזִים

1 יְרוּקִים הַמִּכְנָסַיִים.

2 כְּחוּלִים הַמַּגָּפַיִים.

3 אֲדוּמָה הָעֲנִיבָה.

4 אֲפוֹרָה הַחוּלְצָה.

5 שְׁחוֹרוֹת הַנַּעֲלַיִים.

② **mikhnasayim** מִכְנָסַיִים *trousers*. This word is in the dual form, which is reasonable enough given that trousers have two legs (in English, the dual nature is reflected in the phrase 'a pair of trousers'). The root כנס means *to enter*. As we've seen in many words now, the initial מ is used to form a noun referring to an object.

③ **kchulim** כְּחוּלִים *blue* (masc. pl.) (masc. sing.: **kachol** כָּחוֹל).

④ **magafayim** מַגָּפַיִים *boots* (another dual form). This word is related to **guf** גּוּף *body*.

⑤ **`adumah** אֲדוּמָה *red* (fem. sing.); **`adom** אָדֹם *red* (masc. sing.). From the same root comes **ma`adim** מַאְדִּים *Mars* (the 'Red Planet').

⑥ **`aforah** אֲפוֹרָה *grey* comes from the root אפר, as does the word **`efer** אֵפֶר *ash*.

⑦ **shchorot** שְׁחוֹרוֹת *black, dark* (fem. pl.). Interestingly, the similar word **shachar** שַׁחַר means *dawn*!

6 **Levanot hagarbayim ⑧.**
White [are] the socks.

7 **Ve`eyfoh hame'ilim?**
And where [are] the coats?

8 **Mah zeh? Bgadim lePurim?**
What is this *(What this)*? Clothes for Purim?

Notes

⑧ **garbayim** גַּרְבַּיִם *socks*, **mikhnasayim** מִכְנָסַיִם *trousers*, **na'alayim** נַעֲלַיִם *shoes*, **magafayim** מַגָּפַיִם *boots* are all dual nouns, referring to 'pairs'. Nouns with the dual ending may be

Targil rishon – Targem תַּרְגִּיל רִאשׁוֹן – תַּרְגֵּם

❶ הבגדים האופנתיים ביותר הם גם היקרים ביותר.
Habgadim ha`ofnatiyim beyoter hem gam hayeqarim beyoter.

❷ הוא צעיר אבל הוא לבוש בבגדים שחורים.
Hu tza'ir `aval hu lavush bivgadim shchorim.

❸ קניתי לי שמלת ערב אדומה ארוכה למסיבה הרשמית.
Qaniti li simlat 'erev `adumah `arukah lamesibah harishmit.

❹ בחורף היא אוהבת מגפיים שחורים ומעיל אפור.
Bachoref hi `ohevet magafayim shchorim ume'il `afor.

❺ מכנסיים אדומים, חולצה כחולה, עניבה ירוקה: בגדים ממש לפורים.
Mikhnasayim `adumim, chultzah kchulah, 'anivah yeruqah: bgadim mamash lePurim!

6 לְבָנוֹת הַגַּרְבַּיִים.

7 וְאֵיפֹה הַמְּעִילִים?

8 מַה זֶה? בְּגָדִים לְפּוּרִים? □

either feminine or masculine. You can look up these nouns in the glossary at the end of the book to check their gender.

Answers to Exercise 1

❶ The most fashionable clothes are also the most expensive. ❷ He is young, but he is dressed in black clothes. ❸ I bought myself *(for-me)* a long red evening dress for the formal party. ❹ In winter she likes [to wear] black boots and a grey raincoat. ❺ Red trousers, blue shirt, green tie: truly *(really)* clothes for Purim!

Targil sheni – Hashlem תַּרְגִּיל שֵׁנִי – הַשְׁלֵם

❶ When I was a little girl, I had red shoes and white socks.
Ka`asher [...] yaldah qtanah, [...] li [...] `adumot [...] levanot.

כַּאֲשֶׁר ______ יַלְדָּה קְטַנָּה, ___ לִי ______ אֲדוּמּוֹת ______ לְבָנוֹת.

❷ Where is the blue shirt and the white tie?
`Eyfoh [...] [...] veha[...] halevanah?

אֵיפֹה ______ ______ וְהַ______ הַלְּבָנָה?

❸ At this party, the children are dressed [in] white and blue clothes.
[...] hazot hayeladim levushim [...] [...] u[...].

______ הַזֹּאת הַיְּלָדִים לְבוּשִׁים ______ ______ וּ______.

❹ We saw at the cinema 'The Big Blond [Man] with the Black Shoe'.
Ra`inu [...] `et 'Hablondini hagadol 'im [...] [...]'.

רָאִינוּ ______ אֶת "הַבְּלוֹנְדִינִי הַגָּדוֹל עִם ____ ______".

❺ Grandfather writes rhyming songs *(songs in-rhymes)* for the birthday of each of his grandchildren.
[...] kotev [...] [...] leyom hahuledet shel kol `echad mi[...].

___ כּוֹתֵב ______ ______ לְיוֹם הַהוּלֶּדֶת שֶׁל כָּל אֶחָד מִ____.

Answers to Exercise 2

❶ – **hayiti** – **hayu** – **na'alayim** – **vegarbayim** –

❶ - הָיִיתִי - הָיוּ - נַעֲלַיִים - וְגַרְבַּיִים -

❷ – **hachultzah hakchulah** – **'anivah** –

❷ - הָחוּלְצָה הַכְּחוּלָה - עֲנִיבָה -

❸ **Bamesibah** – **bivgadim levanim** – **kchulim**

❸ בַּמְסִיבָּה - בִּבְגָדִים לְבָנִים - כְּחוּלִים

❹ – **baqolno'a** – **hana'al hashchorah** –

❹ - בַּקוֹלְנוֹעַ - הַנַּעַל הַשְּׁחוֹרָה

❺ **Saba** – **shirim bacharuzim** – **nekhadav**

❺ סַבָּא - שִׁירִים בַּחֲרוּזִים - נְכָדָיו

Purim: *'In the first month, that is the month Nisan, in the twelfth year of King Ahasuerus, they cast the pur (that is, the lot) before Haman from day to day, and from month to month, to the twelfth month, that is, the month of Adar.' (Esther 3:7)*

The Bible relates that the Persian King Ahasuerus (or Xerxes) was persuaded by his minister Haman to plan a massacre of the Jewish exiles in Mesopotamia. Haman cast lots to determine the date of the slaughter. The king's wife, Esther, niece of the wise Mordechai, revealed her Jewish origins and intervened to save her fellow Jews. Thanks to her intelligence and beauty, Esther convinced her husband to reverse the plans: Haman and his ten sons were executed, and Mordechai took his place.

*The festival of Purim, commemorating the deliverance of the Jewish people from Haman's plot, falls at the end of February or in March. In the synagogue, the reading of the 'Scroll of Esther' (***megilat Ester** מְגִילַת אֶסְתֵּר*) is interrupted by catcalls and the noise of rattles every time Haman's name is mentioned. Children dress up in costumes and there is a carnival atmosphere in the streets. A popular treat during the festival are small pastry triangles filled with dates, poppy seeds or chocolate, known as 'Haman's ears' (***`ozney Haman** אוֹזְנֵי הָמָן*).*

Second wave: lesson 15

65 Sixty-fifth lesson
(Shi'ur shishim vechamesh)

Haqirqas ①
The circus

1 **Yitzchaq ② haqatan `ahav me`od litzchoq.**
Little Yitzhak liked to laugh a lot *(liked very to-laugh)*.

2 **Lakhen hu ratzah lalekhet lisratim ③ matzchiqim uleqirqasim.**
That's why *(Therefore)* he wanted to go to funny films and to the circus *(to-circuses)*.

3 **Be'iqar, hitlahev ④ mehaleytzan babgadim hatziv'oniyim:**
In particular, he was excited *(he-became-excited)* about the clown *(from-the-clown)* with the colourful clothes:

4 **Sharvul `echad katom, sharvul `echad kachol.**
One orange sleeve, one blue sleeve.

5 **Panim ⑤ levanim ve`af `adom.**
White face and red nose.

Notes

① **qirqas** קִרְקָס *circus*. The Hebrew and English words both have their origins in the Greek word 'kirkos' *circle*, which was romanized to the Latin 'circus'.

② **yitzchaq** יִצְחָק *he will laugh* is also a man's name (Isaac, in English). From the root צחק we find **litzchoq** לִצחוֹק *to laugh* (line 1) (masculine singular third-person present tense **tzocheq** צוֹחֵק *he laughs*, and past tense **tzachaq** צָחַק *he laughed*), as well as the noun **tzchoq** צחוֹק *laughter* and the adjective **matzchiq** מַצחִיק *funny* (line 2).

③ **sratim** סרָטִים *films*. The singular is **seret** סֶרֶט *film*. As well as 'movie', this word also retains its original meaning of *ribbon, band*

הַקִּרְקָס

1 יִצְחָק הַקָּטָן אָהַב מְאוֹד לִצְחוֹק.

2 לָכֵן הוּא רָצָה לָלֶכֶת לִסְרָטִים מַצְחִיקִים וּלְקִרְקָסִים.

3 בְּעִקָּר הִתְלַהֵב מֵהַלֵּיצָן בַּבְּגָדִים הַצִּבְעוֹנִיִּים.

4 שַׁרְווּל אֶחָד כָּתוֹם, שַׁרְווּל אֶחָד כָּחוֹל.

5 פָּנִים לְבָנִים וְאַף אָדוֹם.

④ **hitlahev me** הִתְלַהֵב מ *he became excited about, enthusiastic about.* This verb comes from the root להב, as does **lehavah** לֶהָבָה *flame.* Note that the thing causing the excitement is introduced in Hebrew by **me** מֵ *from, of,* as in 'to himself be on fire from …'. The same root is found in **lahav** לַהַב *blade* (of a knife). The connection between *flame* and *blade* is an example of the fascinating and sometimes poetic associations that underlie the development of Hebrew vocabulary. This verb, with the **hit-** prefix, belongs to the form we refer to as 'reflexive', although in this case the meaning is 'to become excited' rather than 'to excite oneself'.

⑤ **panim** פָּנִים *face.* When referring to the part of the body, this word is always used in the plural. The singular noun **pan** פָּן means *side* or *aspect.* Like the words for other body parts, **panim** appears in various expressions: **qabalat panim** קַבָּלַת פָּנִים *reception, welcome* ('receipt-of face'), **hadrat panim** הַדְרַת פָּנִים *dignified appearance* ('splendour-of face').

6 **Hu ra`ah qirqasim sheba`u michutz la`aretz, mipney she'od lo hayu qirqasim yisra`eliyim.**

He saw circuses that came from abroad *(from-out-of the-Land)*, because there were not yet *(because-yet not were)* [any] Israeli circuses.

7 **Lamrot shehayom Yitzchaq kvar `adam mevugar, hu holekh leqirqasim, `aval 'im yeladav ⑥ unekhadav ⑦.**

Although today Yitzhak is a grown man *(already man adult)*, he [still] goes to circuses, but with his children and his grandchildren.

Notes

⑥ **yeladav** יְלָדָיו *his children*. This could also have been expressed as **hayeladim shelo** הַיְלָדִים שֶׁלוֹ *the-children*

Targil rishon – Targem   תַּרְגִּיל רִאשׁוֹן – תַּרְגֵּם

❶ יְלָדִים אוֹהֲבִים לֵיצָנִים צִבְעוֹנִיִּים, לָכֵן הֵם רוֹצִים לָלֶכֶת לְקִרְקָס.

Yeladim `ohavim leytzanim tziv'oniyim, lakhen hem rotzim lalekhet laqirqas.

❷ לַמְרוֹת גִּילוֹ, הוּא הַגֶּבֶר הֵיָפֶה בְּיוֹתֵר בְּמִשְׁפַּחְתּוֹ.

Lamrot gilo, hu hagever hayafeh beyoter bemishpachto.

❸ לַמְרוֹת שֶׁהֵם לֹא נִפְגְּשׁוּ הַרְבֵּה שָׁנִים, הֵם הִכִּירוּ אֶחָד אֶת הַשֵּׁנִי בַּכֶּנֶס.

Lamrot shehem lo nifgeshu harbeh shanim, hem hekiru `echad `et hasheni bakenes.

❹ נָתִי הִתְלַהֵב בְּעִיקָר מִמִּשְׂחֲקֵי הַכַּדּוּרֶגֶל הַבֵּינְלְאוּמִיִּים שֶׁהָיוּ בַּקַּיִץ.

Naty hitlahev be'iqar memischaqey hakaduregel habeynle`umiyim shehayu baqayitz.

6 הוּא רָאָה קִרְקָסִים שֶׁבָּאוּ מִחוּץ לָאָרֶץ, מִפְּנֵי שֶׁעוֹד לֹא הָיוּ קִרְקָסִים יִשְׂרְאֵלִיִּים.

7 לַמְרוֹת שֶׁהַיּוֹם יִצְחָק כְּבָר אָדָם מְבוּגָר, הוּא הוֹלֵךְ לְקִרְקָסִים, אֲבָל עִם יְלָדָיו וּנְכָדָיו. □

of-his. The suffix **-av** יו means *his*, when the possessed item is plural ('several children'). Note that the **yod** is silent, but helps the reader identify the possessive suffix.

⑦ **nekhadav** נְכָדָיו *his grandchildren*. As in the previous note, this could also be expressed as **hanekhadim shelo**.

❺ הוא סבא נהדר שנוסע לנופש בחוץ לארץ עם נכדיו.
Hu saba nehedar shenose'a lenofesh bechutz la`aretz 'im nekhadav.

Answers to Exercise 1

❶ Children like colourful clowns, so *(therefore)* they want to go to the circus. ❷ Despite his age, he is the most handsome man in his family. ❸ Although they had not met *(not they-met)* for many years, they recognized each other *(one* [**`et**] *the-second)* at the conference. ❹ Nati was particularly excited about the international soccer games that took place *(were)* in the summer. ❺ He is a wonderful grandfather who goes *(travels)* on holiday abroad with his grandchildren.

Targil sheni – Hashlem תַּרְגִּיל שֵׁנִי – הַשְׁלֵם

❶ I think she is sick because her face is white and her nose is very red.
`Ani [...] shehi [...] mipney she[...] shelah levanim veha[...] shelah [...] me`od.
אֲנִי _____ שֶׁהִיא ____ מִפְּנֵי שֶׁ_____ שֶׁלָּהּ לְבָנִים וְהַ___
שֶׁלָּהּ ____ מְאוֹד.

❷ Although he is only sixteen, he thinks he is already an adult.
[...] shehu raq ben [...] [...], hu choshev shehu kvar [...].
_____ שֶׁהוּא רַק בֶּן __ ____, הוּא חוֹשֵׁב שֶׁהוּא כְּבָר
_____.

❸ The clown's shirt has *(For-the-shirt of clown there-is)* one short black sleeve and one long green sleeve.
[...] shel [...] yesh [...] `echad [...] veshachor vesharvul `echad `arokh [...].
______ שֶׁל _____ יֵשׁ _____ אֶחָד ___ וְשָׁחוֹר
וְשַׁרְווּל אֶחָד אָרוֹךְ _____.

❹ When he was a little boy, he was already enthusiastic about funny films.
[...] hayah yeled qatan, [...] kvar misratim [...].
___ הָיָה יֶלֶד קָטָן, _____ כְּבָר מִסְרָטִים _______.

❺ You cannot sing in front of your friends, because you have not yet learned the new song.
`Atem lo yekholim [...] lifney hachaverim [...] she'od lo [...] `et [...] hachadash.
אַתֶּם לֹא יְכוֹלִים ____ לִפְנֵי הַחֲבֵרִים ____ שֶׁעוֹד לֹא
_____ אֶת ____ הַחָדָשׁ.

Answers to Exercise 2

❶ **– choshevet – cholah – hapanim – `af – `adom –**

❶ - חוֹשֶׁבֶת - חוֹלָה - הַפָּנִים - אַף - אָדוֹם -

❷ **Lamrot – shesh 'esreh – mevugar**

❷ לַמְרוֹת - שֵׁשׁ עֶשְׂרֵה - מְבוּגָּר

❸ **Lachultzah – haleytzan – sharvul – qatzar – veyaroq**

❸ לַחוּלְצָה - הַלֵּיצָן - שַׁרווּל - קָצָר - וְיָרוֹק

❹ **Ka`asher – hitlahev – matzchiqim**

❹ כַּאֲשֶׁר - הִתְלַהֵב - מַצְחִיקִים

❺ **– lashir – mipney – lemadtem – hashir –**

❺ - לָשִׁיר - מִפְּנֵי - לְמַדְתֶּם - הַשִּׁיר -

הקרקס

As an elderly couple, Abraham and Sarah found it difficult to believe the promise of a son. The Bible relates (Genesis 17:17) that 'Abraham fell face down; he laughed and said to himself, "Will a son be born to a man a hundred years old? Will Sarah bear a child at the age of ninety?"' But the incredulous laughter that is commemorated in the name **yitzchaq** יִצְחָק *he will laugh also represents happiness. Sarah, too, laughs when she hears the news: 'After I am worn out and my lord is old, will I now have this pleasure?' (Genesis 18:12). After God reproaches her for laughing, she says: 'I did not laugh,' to which God replies: 'Yes, you did laugh.' The unexpected child seems to have a jolly future: he hasn't even been born yet, but he's made everyone around him conjugate the verb 'to laugh' in every tense!*

Second wave: lesson 16

Mischaq qlafim
A game of cards

1 **Shotrim ba`u lemaqom tziburi shehamischaq biqlafim `asur ① bo.**
Policemen came to a public place where card playing is forbidden *(that-the-playing in-cards forbidden in-it)*.

2 **Hem ra`u Yehudi, Polani veRusi yoshvim ② sviv shulchan ve'alav qlafim.**
They saw a Jew, a Pole and a Russian sitting around a table with cards on it *(and-on-it cards)*.

3 **Rosh hashotrim ratzah le`esor `otam.**
The chief *(head)* of the policemen wanted to arrest *(imprison)* them.

4 **Hashloshah `amru:**
The three [men] said:

5 – **'Haqlafim hayu 'al hashulchan, `aval lo sichaqnu bahem. Zeh mutar ③!'**
'The cards were on the table, but we were not playing with them. That [is] permitted!'

6 **Hashotrim `amru:**
The policemen said:

7 – **'`Im tishav'u shelo sichaqtem, neshachrer `etkhem.'**
'If you swear *(you-will-swear)* that you were not playing *(that-not you-played)*, we will free you.'

Notes

① **`asur** אסוּר *prohibited, forbidden* (feminine: **`asurah** אֲסוּרָה)
It is interesting to note that this word comes from the same

66 שִׁעוּר שִׁשִּׁים וְשֵׁשׁ

מִשְׂחַק קְלָפִים

1 שׁוֹטְרִים בָּאוּ לְמָקוֹם צִבּוּרִי שֶׁהַמִּשְׂחָק בִּקְלָפִים אָסוּר בּוֹ.

2 הֵם רָאוּ יְהוּדִי, פּוֹלָנִי וְרוּסִי יוֹשְׁבִים סְבִיב שׁוּלְחָן וְעָלָיו קְלָפִים.

3 רֹאשׁ הַשּׁוֹטְרִים רָצָה לֶאֱסוֹר אוֹתָם.

4 הַשְּׁלוֹשָׁה אָמְרוּ:

5 – "הַקְּלָפִים הָיוּ עַל הַשּׁוּלְחָן, אֲבָל לֹא שִׂחַקְנוּ בָּהֶם. זֶה מוּתָּר!"

6 הַשּׁוֹטְרִים אָמְרוּ:

7 – "אִם תִּשָּׁבְעוּ שֶׁלֹּא שִׂחַקְתֶּם, נְשַׁחְרֵר אֶתְכֶם."

root as **le`esor** לֶאֱסוֹר *to imprison* in line 3. The word in line 1 is a passive past participle from the root אסר, while in line 3 we see a verb from the same root. The early meaning of the verb was *to tie* or *bind*, which led to the meaning *to imprison*, and also *to forbid* (to put metaphorical shackles on someone).

② **yoshvim** יוֹשְׁבִים *sitting*, literally, '[they] sit'.

③ **mutar** מוּתָּר *permitted* (the opposite of **`asur** אסור) has the same root (יתר) as התיר **hitir** *untied* and also *allowed.*

8 **HaRusi nishba' vehishtachrer.**
The Russian swore and was freed.

9 **HaPolani nishba' vehishtachrer.**
The Pole swore and was freed.

10 – **'Ve`atah ?' `amar hashoter laYehudi.**
'And you?' said the policeman to the Jew.

11 – **'Lamah lehishava'? Shneyhem ④ lo sichaqu.
`Atah lo yode'a shebilti-`efshari ⑤ lesacheq
poqer levad?'**
'Why swear? These two *(They both)* were not
playing. Don't you know *(You not know)* that [it
is] impossible to play poker alone?'

Notes

④ **shneyhem** שְׁנֵיהֶם *they both*, *both of them*. Once again, we see
how Hebrew uses suffixes to refer to different grammatical
persons: **shneynu** שְׁנֵינוּ *us both*, *both of us*; **shneykhem**

৯৫৯৫৯

Targil rishon – Targem   תַּרְגִּיל רִאשׁוֹן – תַּרְגֵּם

① אָסוּר לְשַׂחֵק בִּקְלָפִים עַל כֶּסֶף.
`Asur lesacheq biqlafim 'al kesef.

② שְׁנֵיהֶם יוֹשְׁבִים סְבִיב הַשֻּׁלְחָן כְּדֵי לְשַׂחֵק שַׁחְמָט.
Shneyhem yoshvim sviv hashulchan kedey lesacheq
shachmat.

③ הַשּׁוֹטְרִים בָּאוּ לֶאֱסוֹר אֶת הָאִישׁ עַל יַד תַּחֲנַת הַדֶּלֶק.
Hashotrim ba`u le`esor `et ha`ish 'al yad tachanat
hadeleq.

④ אָסוּר לִנְסוֹעַ כַּאֲשֶׁר יֵשׁ אוֹר אָדוֹם בָּרַמְזוֹר.
`Asur linso'a ka`asher yesh `or `adom baramzor.

⑤ בִּלְתִּי אֶפְשָׁרִי לִקְנוֹת בְּגָדִים בְּלִי כֶּסֶף.
Bilti `efshari liqnot bgadim bli kesef.

8 הָרוּסִי נִשְׁבַּע וְהִשְׁתַּחְרֵר.

9 הַפּוֹלָנִי נִשְׁבַּע וְהִשְׁתַּחְרֵר.

10 – "וְאַתָּה?" אָמַר הַשּׁוֹטֵר לַיְּהוּדִי.

11 – "לָמָּה לְהִשָּׁבַע? שְׁנֵיהֶם לֹא שִׂחֲקוּ. אַתָּה לֹא יוֹדֵעַ שֶׁבִּלְתִּי אֶפְשָׁרִי לְשַׂחֵק פּוֹקֶר לְבַד?" □

שְׁנֵיכֶם *you both, both of you* (masc.), **shteykhen** שְׁתֵּיכֶן *you both, both of you* (fem.).

⑤ **bilti-`efshari** בִּלְתִּי אֶפְשָׁרִי *impossible* (fem.: **bilti-`efsharit** בִּלְתִּי אֶפְשָׁרִית). **Bilti** is a word of negation similar to the English prefixes *not, non-, un-, im-*, etc. Here it modifies the adjective **`efshari** אֶפְשָׁרִי *possible*. We've already seen another way of saying *impossible* using a different expression: **`i `efshar** אִי אֶפְשָׁר *it is impossible* (lesson 24).

Answers to Exercise 1

❶ It is forbidden to play cards for *(on)* money. ❷ They both sit around the table to play chess. ❸ The policemen came to arrest the man by the petrol station. ❹ It is forbidden to drive when the traffic light is red *(when there-is light red at-the-traffic-light)*. ❺ It is impossible to buy clothes without money.

בלתי אפשרי לקנות בגדים בלי כסף.

66 **Targil sheni – Hashlem** **תַּרְגִּיל שֵׁנִי – הַשְׁלֵם**

❶ He freed himself from the policemen and drove home.
Hu [...] [...] venasa' [...].

הוּא ______ ________ וְנָסַע _____ .

❷ I [can]not find my mobile phone, so *(therefore)* I am calling *(speaking)* from a public telephone.
`Ani lo [...] `et ha[...] sheli, [...] `ani medaber mitelefon [...].

אֲנִי לֹא ____ אֶת הַ______ שֶׁלִּי, ___ אֲנִי מְדַבֵּר מִטֶּלֶפוֹן _____ .

❸ After David was released *(freed himself)* from the army, he travelled for a year around the world.
`Acharey sheDavid [...] mehatzava hu nasa' shanah [...] [...].

אַחֲרֵי שֶׁדָּוִד ______ מֵהַצָּבָא הוּא נָסַע שָׁנָה ____ _____ .

❹ Although this is a new and beautiful chair, I don't like to sit on it.
[...] shezeh [...] chadash veyafeh, `ani lo `ohevet [...] [...].

_____ שֶׁזֶּה ___ חָדָשׁ וְיָפֶה, אֲנִי לֹא אוֹהֶבֶת ____ ____ .

❺ Abraham says that he is religious, that's why *(therefore)* he does not want to make an oath *(to swear)*.
[...] `omer shehu [...], [...] hu lo rotzeh [...].

_____ אוֹמֵר שֶׁהוּא ___, ___ הוּא לֹא רוֹצֶה _____ .

Answers to Exercise 2

❶ – **hishtachrer mehashotrim – habaytah**

❶ - הִשְׁתַּחְרֵר מֵהַשּׁוֹטְרִים - הַבַּיְתָה

❷ – **motze – pelefon – lakhen – tziburi**

❷ - מוֹצֵא - פֶּלֶאפוֹן - לָכֵן - צִבּוּרִי

❸ – **hishtachrer – sviv ha'olam** ❸ - הִשְׁתַּחְרֵר - סְבִיב הָעוֹלָם

❹ **Lamrot – kise – lashevet 'alav** ❹ לַמְרוֹת - כִּסֵּא - לָשֶׁבֶת עָלָיו

❺ **`Avraham – dati – lakhen – lehishava'**

❺ אַבְרָהָם - דָּתִי - לָכֵן - לְהִשָּׁבַע

Yehudi יְהוּדִי Jew. **Yehudah** יְהוּדָה Judah, *the son of* **Ya'aqov** יַעֲקֹב Jacob *and* **Leah** לֵאָה Leah. **Yehudah** יְהוּדָה *is also the name of a region of the Land of Israel, extending to the south of Jerusalem beyond* **Chevron** חֶבְרוֹן Hebron. *The name Judea is used in English to refer to this region, whose inhabitants are therefore known as* **Yehudim** יְהוּדִים – Judeans, *or simply* Jews.

In 930 BCE, following King Solomon's death, his kingdom split into two. In the north, ten tribes formed the Kingdom of Israel. The two remaining tribes – Judah and Benjamin – formed the Kingdom of Judea in the south, with Jerusalem as its capital. The two kingdoms fought each other incessantly. In 720 BCE, the Assyrians conquered the Kingdom of Israel and many of the inhabitants were exiled. In 586 BCE, Judea in turn fell to the Babylonians. The exile continued until 538 BCE, when the Persian King Cyrus allowed the Judeans to go back to their land. Psalm 126 offers a moving and poetic account of their return.

It is interesting to note that today, the Jews as a people and a religion preserve the name of one of the two kingdoms (Judea), while the name of their state preserves the other (Israel).

Second wave: lesson 17

67 Sixty-seventh lesson
(Shi'ur shishim vesheva')

`Eykh lomdim Talmud?
How does one study Talmud?

1 – **Lo qasheh lilmod Talmud?**
‘Isn’t it difficult *(Not difficult)* to study Talmud?’

2 **sha`al talmid chadash `et rav hayeshivah ①.**
a new student asked the rabbi of the Yeshiva.

3 – **Harav `amar:**
The rabbi said:

4 – **Tzarikh liqro harbeh, lizkor, `akh ② be'iqar lachashov.**
‘It is necessary to read a lot, to remember, but in particular to think.

5 **Hineh dugmah metzuyenet:**
Here is an excellent example:

6 **Shney `anashim 'alu 'al gag bayit lenaqot `arubah.**
Two men went up *(ascended)* on the roof of a house to clean a chimney.

7 **`Echad mehem ③ yatza naqi veha`acher melukhlakh. Mi tzarikh lehitrachetz?**
One of them came out clean and the other dirty. Who needed *(needs)* to wash himself?’

8 – **Hamelukhlakh!**
‘The dirty [one]!’

Notes

① **rav hayeshivah** רַב הַיְשִׁיבָה *the rabbi of the Yeshiva.* This could also be expressed as **harav shel hayeshivah**

אֵיךְ לוֹמְדִים תַּלְמוּד?

1 – לֹא קָשֶׁה לִלְמוֹד תַּלְמוּד?

2 שָׁאַל תַּלְמִיד חָדָשׁ אֶת רַב הַיְּשִׁיבָה.

3 – הָרַב אָמַר.

4 – צָרִיךְ לִקְרוֹא הַרְבֵּה, לִזְכּוֹר, אַךְ בְּעִקָּר לַחֲשׁוֹב.

5 הִנֵּה דוּגְמָה מְצוּיֶּנֶת:

6 שְׁנֵי אֲנָשִׁים עָלוּ עַל גַּג בַּיִת לְנַקּוֹת אֲרוּבָּה.

7 אֶחָד מֵהֶם יָצָא נָקִי וְהָאַחֵר מְלוּכְלָךְ. מִי צָרִיךְ לְהִתְרַחֵץ?

8 – הַמְלוּכְלָךְ!

הָרַב שֶׁל הַיְשִׁיבָה. Note that **yeshiva** can also refer to a *session*, *workshop* or *meeting* in a workplace or organization.

② **`akh** אַךְ *but* – this word is more literary than **`aval**.

③ **mehem** מֵהֶם *of them*. It is not difficult to understand how this word is formed: **me** מֵ indicating origin (*from*), followed by the masculine third-person plural ending **hem** הֵם *them*.

9 – **`Aval hamelukhlakh ro`eh shechavero ④ naqi ⑤ vechoshev shegam hu naqi.**
'But the dirty one sees that his friend is clean and thinks that he is also clean *(that-also he clean)*.'

10 – **`Im kakh, hanaqi tzarikh lehitrachetz.**
'So *(If so)* the clean [one] needs to wash himself.'

11 – **Lamah lehitrachetz? Hu naqi!**
'Why wash himself? He [is] clean!'

12 – **Lefi mah she`atah `omer, hu ro`eh shechavero melukhlakh vechoshev shegam hu melukhlakh …**
'According to what you say, he sees that his friend is dirty and thinks that he is also dirty ...'

13 – **`Aval hu naqi!**
'But he [is] clean!'

14 – **Lefi mah she`atah masbir li …**
'According to what you are explaining to me ...'

15 – **Shma', ish tza'ir: ha`im ⑥ `efshar sheshney `anashim yikansu le`arubah ve`echad mehem yetze naqi?**
'Listen, young man: is it possible for two people to enter *(that two people will-enter)* a chimney and one of them will come out clean?

16 **HaTalmud melamed shetalmid chakham tzarikh lachshov be'atzmo ⑦!**
The Talmud teaches that a wise student must think for himself!'

Notes

④ **shechavero** שֶׁחֲבֵרוֹ *that his friend.* Again, the construction is logical if we take a moment to analyze it: **she** שֶׁ *that*, **chaver** חָבֵר *friend*, **o** וֹ *his.*

9 – אֲבָל הַמְּלוּכְלָךְ רוֹאֶה שֶׁחֲבֵרוֹ נָקִי וְחוֹשֵׁב שֶׁגַּם הוּא נָקִי.

10 – אִם כָּךְ, הַנָּקִי צָרִיךְ לְהִתְרַחֵץ.

11 – לָמָה לְהִתְרַחֵץ? הוּא נָקִי!

12 – לְפִי מַה שֶׁאַתָּה אוֹמֵר הוּא רוֹאֶה שֶׁחֲבֵרוֹ מְלוּכְלָךְ וְחוֹשֵׁב שֶׁגַּם הוּא מְלוּכְלָךְ...

13 – אֲבָל הוּא נָקִי!

14 – לְפִי מַה שֶׁאַתָּה מַסְבִּיר לִי...

15 – שְׁמַע, אִישׁ צָעִיר: הַאִם אֶפְשָׁר שֶׁשְּׁנֵי אֲנָשִׁים יִכָּנְסוּ לַאֲרוּבָּה וְאֶחָד מֵהֶם יֵצֵא נָקִי?

16 הַתַּלְמוּד מְלַמֵּד שֶׁתַּלְמִיד חָכָם צָרִיךְ לַחְשׁוֹב בְּעַצְמוֹ!

⑤ **naqi** נָקִי *clean*, from the root נקה.

⑥ **ha`im?** הַאִם? turns a statement into a yes/no question. It has the advantage of being invariable – it doesn't need to change for tense or number: **`ata ra'ev** אַתָּה רָעֵב *you are hungry*, **Ha`im `ata ra'ev?** הַאִם אַתָּה רָעֵב? *Are you hungry?*; **hem ratzu glidah** הֵם רָצוּ גְּלִידָה *they wanted ice cream*, **Ha`im hem ratzu glidah?** הַאִם הֵם רָצוּ גְּלִידָה? *Did they want ice cream?* and so forth.

⑦ **be'atzmo** בְּעַצְמוֹ *by himself*. **'etzem** עֶצֶם means *bone*, and by extension, *essence*.

Targil rishon – Targem תַּרְגִּיל רִאשׁוֹן – תַּרְגֵּם

❶ נתנאל הקטן רק בן ארבע, אבל הוא רוצה להתרחץ בעצמו.

Netanel haqatan raq ben `arba', `aval hu rotzeh lehitrachetz be'atzmo.

❷ אמרו על שלמה שהוא היה האיש החכם ביותר בתקופה העתיקה.

`Amru 'al Shlomoh* shehu hayah ha`ish hachakham beyoter batqufah ha'atiqah.

❸ דוד יצא מהבית נקי וחזר מלוכלך כמו איש שהיה בארובה.

David yatza mehabayit naqi vechazar melukhlakh kmo `ish shehayah be`arubah.

❹ הצלם מצלם את העיר מגג מלון "דן כרמל".

Hatzalam metzalem `et ha'ir migag malon ‘Dan Karmel’.

❺ בישיבה לומדים בעיקר תלמוד ותנ"ך.

Bayeshivah lomdim be'iqar Talmud veTanakh.

Answers to Exercise 1

❶ Little Nathaniel is only four, but he wants to bathe *(wash himself)* by himself. ❷ They said of Solomon that he was the wisest man of ancient times *(in-the-period the-ancient)*. ❸ David left home clean and returned [as] dirty as *(like)* someone who has been in a chimney. ❹ The photographer photographs the city from the roof of Dan Carmel Hotel. ❺ At the Yeshiva, they*(impers. subj.)* study mainly Talmud and Bible.

* **Shlomoh** שלמה = Solomon

נתנאל הקטן רק בן ארבע, אבל הוא רוצה להתרחץ בעצמו.

Targil sheni – Hashlem תַּרְגִּיל שֵׁנִי – הַשְׁלֵם

❶ Now you *(already)* know that it is not difficult to study Hebrew.
[...] `atem kvar [...] shelo [...] lilmod 'ivrit.
____ אַתֶּם כְּבָר ______ שֶׁלֹּא ___ לִלְמוֹד עִבְרִית.

❷ This morning, I was at a work meeting with several *(how many)* people from the office.
Haboqer hayiti [...] [...] 'im [...] [...] mehamisrad.
הַבּוֹקֶר הָיִיתִי ______ _____ עִם ___ _____ מֵהַמִּשְׂרָד.

❸ On the internet, he mainly reads the news about Israel *(in-the-Land)* and about *(in)* [the] world.
Ba`internet hu qore`h [...] `et hachadashot ba[...] uva[...].
בָּאִינְטֶרְנֶט הוּא קוֹרֵא ____ אֶת הַחֲדָשׁוֹת בָּ___ וּבַ____.

❹ Are you able to remember who your first girlfriend was *(was the-girlfriend the-first of-you)*?
Ha`im `atah [...] [...] mi [...] hachaverah [...] shelkha?
הַאִם אַתָּה ____ _____ מִי ____ הַחֲבֵרָה _______ שֶׁלְּךָ?

❺ According to what she has seen, he thinks mainly about himself.
[...] mah shehi [...] hu choshev [...] 'al [...].
___ מַה שֶּׁהִיא ____ הוּא חוֹשֵׁב ____ עַל ____.

Answers to Exercise 2

❶ **'Akhshav – yod'im – qasheh –** ❶ עַכְשָׁו - יוֹדְעִים - קָשֶׁה -

❷ **– biyshivat 'avodah – kamah `anashim –**
❷ - בִּישִׁיבַת עֲבוֹדָה - כַּמָּה אֲנָשִׁים -

❸ **– be'iqar – `aretz – 'olam** ❸ - בְּעִקָּר - אֶרֶץ - עוֹלָם

❹ **– yakhol lizkor – haytah – harishonah –**
❹ - יָכוֹל לִזְכּוֹר - הָיְתָה - הָרִאשׁוֹנָה -

❺ **Lefi – ra`atah – be'iqar – 'atzmo**
❺ לְפִי - רַעֲתָהּ - בְּעִקָּר - עַצְמוֹ

Yeshivah יְשִׁיבָה *is a school specializing in the study of Jewish religious texts, particularly the Talmud. The word comes from the root* ישב *meaning to sit (the same idea can be seen in the English expression 'seat of learning').*

Another word from the same root, **yishuv** יִשּׁוּב*, means a place of settlement, but is used in a specific sense to refer to the Jewish community in the Land of Israel, particularly during the period before independence. Two other words from the same root also have their place in the Zionist lexicon:* **moshav** מוֹשָׁב village *(specifically a cooperative agricultural settlement with more private ownership than a kibbutz) and* **moshavah** מוֹשָׁבָה colony.

Lizkor לִזְכּוֹר to remember. *The Jewish memorial prayer for the dead is called* **yizkor** יִזְכּוֹר He will remember *(that is, God, or in a civil and national context – the people). When mentioning a dead person, Israelis often add the phrase* **zikhrono** *(masc.)*/**zikhronah** *(fem.)* **livrakhah** זִכרוֹנוֹ\זִכרוֹנָה לִבְרָכָה *'his/her memory for a blessing' after the person's name. This phrase is abbreviated as* ז"ל*, in which form it appears on gravestones and in print.*

Second wave: lesson 18

68 Sixty-eighth lesson
(Shi'ur shishim ushmoneh)

Mis'adah memuzeget
An air-conditioned restaurant

1 – **Tzohorayim tovim ①!**
Good afternoon! *(Noon good!)*

2 **`Eyfoh `atem rotzim lashevet? Bamirpeset? 'Al yad hachalon mul hanof shelanu?**
Where do you want to sit? On the balcony? By the window facing our view?

3 – **Lo chashuv `eyfoh. Ha'iqar sheyiheyeh mizug `avir ②!**
[It is] not important where. The main [thing] is that there will be air-conditioning!

4 – **`Etzli yesh mizug bekhol maqom.**
At my place *(By-me)* there is air-conditioning everywhere *(in-all place)*.

5 **Mah `atem choshvim? Bli mizug `avir, lo hayiti poh!**
What do you think?! Without air-conditioning, I wouldn't be *(not I-was)* here!

Notes

① **Tzohorayim tovim!** !צָהֳרַיִם טוֹבִים This greeting is used at lunchtime, and literally means 'Good noon!' The word for *noon, midday*, **tzohorayim** צָהֳרַיִם, is a masculine dual noun (see lesson 62, note 2), so the accompanying adjective is in the masculine plural.

② **mizug `avir** מִזּוּג אֲוִיר *air-conditioning* (or often simply **mizug** on its own). The verb **lemazeg** לְמַזֵּג *to mix* produces

68 שִׁעוּר שִׁשִּׁים וּשְׁמוֹנֶה

מְסעָדָה מְמוּזֶגֶת

1 – צָהֳרַיִם טוֹבִים!

2 אֵיפֹה אַתֶּם רוֹצִים לָשֶׁבֶת? בַּמִּרְפֶּסֶת? עַל יַד הָחַלּוֹן מוּל הַנּוֹף שֶׁלָּנוּ?

3 – לֹא חָשׁוּב אֵיפֹה. הָעִקָּר שֶׁיִּהְיֶה מִזּוּג אֲוִיר!

4 – אֶצְלִי יֵשׁ מִזּוּג בְּכֹל מָקוֹם.

5 מַה אַתֶּם חוֹשְׁבִים? בְּלִי מִזּוּג אֲוִיר לֹא הָיִיתִי פֹּה!

the adjective **memuzag** מְמוּזָג / **memuzeget** מְמוּזֶגֶת *mixed, conditioned*. The root מזג also conveys the meanings *to moderate, to amalgamate*. The 'melting pot' blending of Jewish communities from around the world is referred to as **mizug galuyot** מִזּוּג גָּלֻיּוֹת *the ingathering of the dispersions* (or *the Diasporas*). **mezeg** מֶזֶג means *temperament*, and **mezeg `avir** מֶזֶג אֲוִיר (line 6) is *weather, climate* (literally, 'temper of air'). An air-conditioner is **mazgan** (masc.) מַזְגָן (line 8): the ןָ suffix is used to form a noun for a machine or device.

6 – **Bemezeg `avir kazeh ③ gam `anachnu lo zazim bli mizug.**
In weather like this, we do not move without air-conditioning either.

7 – **`Atah yakhol limzog ④ lanu mayim qarim velatet ⑤ lanu `et hatafrit?**
Can you pour us some cold water and give us the menu?

8 – **Batem le`ekhol bamis'adah? Chashavti shebatem letaqen `et hamazgan sheli.**
You've come to eat in the restaurant? I thought you'd come to fix my air-conditioner.

9 **Davqa ⑥ hayom hu mequlqal!**
Just today, it's broken!

Notes

③ **kazeh** כָּזֶה *such, like this.* The prefix **k-** כּ is used for comparisons.

④ **limzog** לִמזוֹג *to pour* (liquids only). Once again we see the root מזג.

⑤ **latet** לָתֵת *to give*. The root of this verb is נתן, but the infinitive is highly irregular. The past and future forms also need to be studied carefully: **natan** נָתַן *he gave*, **yiten** יִתֵּן *he will give*. The present tense is more predictable: **noten** נוֹתֵן *I give, you give, he gives*.

⑥ **davqa** דַוקָא *precisely, rather.* This Aramaic word, which is frequently used in colloquial conversation, is difficult to translate into a single English word or phrase. English speakers who move to Israel often find themselves peppering their English with it. According to context, it can mean 'exactly', 'ironically', 'rather', 'just to spite', as well as various other shades of meaning. **davqa** is related to **bediyuq** בְּדִיוּק *precisely* (lesson 52), but with an additional sense of contrariness or irony.

6 – בְּמֶזֶג אֲוִיר כַּזֶה גַם אֲנַחנוּ לֹא זָזִים בּלִי מִזוּג.

7 – אַתָה יָכוֹל לִמזוֹג לָנוּ מַיִם קָרִים וְלָתֵת לָנוּ אֶת הַתַפרִיט?

8 – בָּאתֶם לֶאֱכוֹל בַּמִסעָדָה? חָשַבתִי שֶבָּאתֶם לְתַקֵן אֶת הַמַזגָן שֶלִי.

9 דַוקָא הַיוֹם הוּא מְקוּלקָל!

מסעדה ממוזגת

Targil rishon – Targem תַּרְגִּיל רִאשׁוֹן – תַּרְגֵּם

❶ בחום הקיץ יותר טוב להיות בבית על יד המזגן.
Bechom haqayitz yoter tov lihyot babayit 'al yad hamazgan.

❷ מה למזוג לכם? בירה קרה? מיץ? אולי תה קר?
Mah limzog lakhem? Birah qarah? Mitz? `Ulay teh qar?

❸ יש לי הרבה עבודה ודוקא היום המחשב שלי מקולקל.
Yesh li harbeh 'avodah vedavqa hayom hamachshev sheli mequlqal.

❹ הדירה שלנו ממוזגת ונעימה מאוד בקיץ.
Hadirah shelanu memuzeget une'imah me`od baqayitz.

Targil sheni – Hashlem תַּרְגִּיל שֵׁנִי – הַשְׁלֵם

❶ Do you want [something] to drink? What [shall I] *(to)* pour for you?
`Atem [...] lishtot? Mah [...] lakhem?
אַתֶּם _____ לִשְׁתּוֹת? מַה _____ לָכֶם?

❷ Every morning, I watch the weather news on the television.
Kol [...] `ani ro`ah `et hachadashot 'al [...] [...] batelevizyah.
כֹּל ____ אֲנִי רוֹאָה אֶת הַחֲדָשׁוֹת עַל ___ _____ בַּטֶּלֶוִיזְיָה.

❸ Before the journey for the holidays, we must repair [`**et**] the car.
Lifney [...] lenofesh, `anachnu tzrikhim [...] `et [...].
לִפְנֵי _____ לְנוֹפֶשׁ, אֲנַחְנוּ צְרִיכִים _____ אֶת _______.

❹ What gift is it possible to give to someone who already has everything?
`Eyzo [...] `efshar [...] lemi sheyesh kvar hakol?
אֵיזוֹ ____ אֶפְשָׁר ____ לְמִי שֶׁיֵּשׁ כְּבָר הַכֹּל?

❺ התפריט של המסעדה הזאת ממש מצוין.
Hatafrit shel hamis'adah hazot mamash metzuyan.

Answers to Exercise 1

❶ In the heat of the summer, it's better to be at home by the air-conditioner. ❷ What [shall I] *(to)* pour for you? A cold beer? Juice? Perhaps [some] cold tea? ❸ I have a lot of work, and precisely today my computer is broken. ❹ Our apartment is air-conditioned and very pleasant in the summer. ❺ The menu of this restaurant is really excellent.

❺ The children play in the public park and move from game to game.
Hayeladim mesachqim ba[...] ha[...] ve[...] mimischaq lemischaq.
הַיְּלָדִים מְשַׂחֲקִים בַּ__ הַ______ וְ____ מִמִּשְׂחָק לְמִשְׂחָק.

Answers to Exercise 2

❶ – **rotzim** – **limzog** –
❶ - רוֹצִים - לִמְזוֹג -
❷ – **boqer** – **mezeg ha`avir** –
❷ - בּוֹקֶר - מֶזֶג הָאֲוִויר -
❸ – **hanesi'ah** – **letaqen** – **hamekhonit**
❸ - הַנְּסִיעָה - לְתַקֵּן - הַמְּכוֹנִית
❹ – **matanah** – **latet** –
❹ - מַתָּנָה - לָתֵת -
❺ – **gan** – **tziburi** – **zazim** –
❺ - גַּן - צִיבּוּרִי - זָזִים -

The Israeli climate is characterized by a hot, dry summer and a mild, wetter winter of roughly equal lengths. The transitional seasons (spring and autumn) are short and bring mixed weather conditions. Although Israel is a very small country, the climate varies considerably from one part to another. **Tzfat** צְפַת Safed *in Galilee has an annual rainfall of 718 mm (including occasional snow in winter), but the annual rainfall in* **Eilat** אֵילַת *on the Red Sea averages just 25 mm! While the hilly inland areas and the*

69 Sixty-ninth lesson
(Shi'ur shishim vetesha')

Cheleq ha`ari ①
The lion's share

1 **`Izopos hayevani katav 'al hatzedeq.**
Aesop the Greek wrote about justice.

2 **`Aryeh, chamor veshu'al yatzu latzayid ②. Hem `amru:**
A lion, a donkey and a fox went hunting *(went-out to-the-hunt)*. They said:

3 – **‘`Im natzud chayah ③ nechaleq `otah beyneynu ④.’**
‘If we *(will)* hunt an animal, we will share it between us.’

Notes

① **`ari** אֲרִי *lion*. In lines 2 and 4, we find a slightly different word for the same animal: **`aryeh** אַרְיֵה. There is no difference in meaning between the two words, but the shorter version is usually used in compounds: **`ari hayam** אֲרִי הַיָּם *sea lion*; **lo'a ha`ari** לֹעַ הָאֲרִי *lion's throat* (the Hebrew name for the flower called *snapdragon* or *dragon flower* in English). Another usage is in the expression **ha`ari shebachavurah** הָאֲרִי שֶׁבַּחֲבוּרָה, literally ‘the lion of the gang’, which refers to the dominant member of a given group or circle.

Negev Desert are known for their dry heat in summer, the coastal areas can be unpleasantly humid during the summer months.

Wherever they live, many Israelis have **mizug `avir** air-conditioning *in their homes, and this is also the norm in shopping malls and public buildings. By law, all cars in Israel must be equipped with air-conditioning.*

Second wave: lesson 19

---

69 שִׁעוּר שִׁשִּׁים וְתֵשַׁע

חֵלֶק הָאֲרִי

1 אִיזוֹפּוֹס הַיְּוָנִי כָּתַב עַל הַצֶּדֶק.

2 אַרְיֵה, חֲמוֹר וְשׁוּעָל יָצְאוּ לַצַּיִד. הֵם אָמְרוּ:

3 – "אִם נָצוּד חַיָּה נְחַלֵּק אוֹתָהּ בֵּינֵינוּ."

② **tzayid** צַיִד *hunt*. Other words from the same root include לְצַיֵּד *to equip* and צִיּוּד *equipment*, the connection being to get supplies or provisions.

③ **chayah** חַיָּה *animal*. This noun comes from the word **chay** חַי *living*. **Hachayim** הַחַיִּים means *life* – note the use of a masculine plural form to refer to a singular concept. You may already be familiar with the Hebrew toast **Lechayim!** !לְחַיִּים *To life!*, which is the equivalent of *Cheers!* The plural of **chayah** חַיָּה animal is **chayot** חַיּוֹת.

④ **beyneynu** בֵּינֵינוּ *between us*. By now, you're probably getting used to the way Hebrew adds personal suffixes onto prepositions to create useful words. Here, **beyn** בֵּין *between*, *among* is followed by a first-person plural suffix (the **nu** should remind you of **`anachnu** *we*). Another example is **beyneykhen** בֵּינֵיכֶן *between you, among you* (fem. pl.).

4 **`Acharey hatzayid `amar ha`aryeh lachamor:**
After the hunt, the lion said to the donkey:

5 – **'`Atah techaleq `et hachayah beyn shloshtenu ⑤.'**
'You will divide *(share)* the animal between the three of us.'

6 **Hachamor chileq `otah lishloshah chalaqim shavim ⑥.**
The donkey divided it into three equal parts.

7 **Ha`aryeh ka'as me`od vetaraf `et hachamor. `Achar kakh, hu `amar lashu'al:**
The lion was very angry and devoured the donkey. Then *(After that)* he said to the fox:

8 – **''Akhshav `atah techaleq `et hachayah.'**
'Now, you *(will)* divide the animal.'

9 **Hashu'al laqach le'atzmo ⑦ cheleq qatan me`od venatan `et hacheleq hagadol la`aryeh.**
The fox took for himself a very small piece and gave the large piece to the lion.

10 – **'Mi limed ⑧ `otkha `et hachaluqah hatzodeqet ⑨ hazot?'**
'Who taught you this fair division *(the-division the-just the-this)*?'

11 – **'Hachamor!'**
'The donkey!'

Notes

⑤ **shloshtenu** שְׁלוֹשְׁתֵּנוּ *the three of us, we three*. Let's break this word down to its components: **shloshah** שְׁלוֹשָׁה *three* (masc.) and **[`anach]nu** אֲנַחְנוּ *we*, with a **t** ת added in to link the two. To give another example, *you three* is **shloshtekhem** שְׁלוֹשְׁתְּכֶם (masc.) or **shloshtan** שְׁלוֹשְׁתָּן (fem.).

By the way, regarding masculine and feminine forms in the plural, you may have wondered what happens if you're speaking to (or about) a mixed group of males and females.

4 אַחֲרֵי הַצַּיִד אָמַר הָאַרְיֵה לַחֲמוֹר:

5 – "אַתָּה תְּחַלֵּק אֶת הַחַיָּה בֵּין שְׁלוֹשְׁתֵּנוּ."

6 הַחֲמוֹר חִלֵּק אוֹתָהּ לִשְׁלוֹשָׁה חֲלָקִים שָׁוִים.

7 הָאַרְיֵה כָּעַס מְאֹד וְטָרַף אֶת הַחֲמוֹר. אַחַר כָּךְ הוּא אָמַר לַשּׁוּעָל:

8 – "עַכְשָׁו אַתָּה תְּחַלֵּק אֶת הַחַיָּה."

9 הַשּׁוּעָל לָקַח לְעַצְמוֹ חֵלֶק קָטָן מְאֹד וְנָתַן אֶת הַחֵלֶק הַגָּדוֹל לָאַרְיֵה.

10 – "מִי לִמֵּד אוֹתְךָ אֶת הַחֲלוּקָה הַצּוֹדֶקֶת הַזֹּאת?"

11 – "הַחֲמוֹר!"

☐

Although the answer may seem sexist, the accepted rule in Hebrew is to use the masculine form, even if there is only one male present among a group of females!

⑥ **shavim** שָׁוִים *equal* (masc. pl.). The other forms of this adjective are **shaveh** שָׁוֶה (masc. sing.); **shavah** שָׁוָה (fem. sing.) and **shavot** שָׁווֹת (fem. pl.). The word also means *to be worth*: הַחוּלְצָה שָׁוָה שִׁשִּׁים שְׁקָלִים. **Hachultzah shavah shishim shqalim**. *The shirt is worth sixty shekels.*

⑦ **le'atzmo** לְעַצְמוֹ *for himself* (see lesson 67, note 7): **'atzmo** עַצְמוֹ *himself*; **be'atzmo** בְּעַצְמוֹ *by himself.*

⑧ **limed** לִמֵּד *he taught*. It is important to note both the similarity and the difference between this form and **lamad** לָמַד *he learned, he studied*. Both verbs come from the root למד. We discussed this aspect of Hebrew verbs and this particular example in lesson 46.

⑨ **tzodeqet** צוֹדֶקֶת (fem. sing.), **tzodeq** (masc. sing.) צוֹדֵק is the adjective *fair, just, legitimate, right*. The masculine noun **tzedeq** צֶדֶק means *justice* (line 1).

Targil rishon – Targem תַּרְגִּיל רִאשׁוֹן – תַּרְגֵּם

❶ אם אתם בירושלים, לכו לגן החיות התנכי.
`Im `atem biYrushalayim, lekhu legan hachayot hatanakhi.

❷ היא תחלק את העוגה לשמונה חלקים שווים.
Hi techaleq `et ha'ugah lishmonah chalaqim shavim.

❸ כמה שווה מכונית בת חמש שנים?
Kamah shavah mekhonit bat chamesh shanim?

❹ בישראל אנשים לא הולכים לציד.
BeYisra`el `anashim lo holkhim letzayid.

❺ אחרי המסיבה נחלק את המתנות בין שלושתנו.
`Acharey hamesibah nechaleq `et hamatanot beyn shloshtenu.

Targil sheni – Hashlem תַּרְגִּיל שֵׁנִי – הַשְׁלֵם

❶ He was angry because the division of the money was not fair.
Hu [...] ki [...] shel hakesef lo haytah [...].
הוּא ___ כִּי ______ שֶׁל הַכֶּסֶף לֹא הָיְתָה _____ .

❷ At night, the lion devoured the small animals.
Balaylah ha[...] [...] chayot [...].
בַּלַּיְלָה הַ____ ___ חַיּוֹת _____ .

❸ What [shall we] *(to)* do so that there is more justice in the world?
Mah [...] [...] sheyiheyeh yoter [...] ba'olam?
מַה _____ ___ שֶׁיִּהְיֶה יוֹתֵר ___ בָּעוֹלָם.

❹ He took for himself the lion's share in the games.
Hu [...] [...] `et [...] [...] mehamischaqim.
הוּא ___ _____ אֶת ___ ____ מֵהַמִּשְׂחָקִים.

Answers to Exercise 1

❶ If you are in Jerusalem, go to the Biblical Zoo *(garden-of animals biblical)*. ❷ She will divide the cake into eight equal parts. ❸ How much is a five-year-old car worth? ❹ In Israel, people don't go hunting. ❺ After the party, we will divide the presents between the three of us.

❺ Who these days has *(For-who is-there today)* a donkey in the house?

[...] yesh hayom [...] babayit?

___ יֵשׁ הַיּוֹם ____ בַּבַּיִת?

Answers to Exercise 2

❶ – **ka'as – hachaluqah – tzodeqet** ❶ - כָּעַס - הַחֲלוּקָה - צוֹדֶקֶת

❷ – **`aryeh taraf – qtanot** ❷ - אַרְיֵה טָרַף - קְטַנּוֹת

❸ – **la'asot kedey – tzedeq –** ❸ - לַעֲשׂוֹת כְּדֵי - צֶדֶק -

❹ – **laqach le'atzmo – cheleq ha`ari –** ❹ - לָקַח לְעַצְמוֹ - חֵלֶק הָאֲרִי -

❺ **Lemi – chamor –** ❺ לְמִי - חֲמוֹר -

The Jerusalem Biblical Zoo: The Bible is a work rooted in the life of an agricultural people. The animals mentioned in its pages were a feature of daily life in ancient times – even city dwellers were never too far from rural concerns and the sometimes harsh realities of nature. At the Biblical Zoo in Jerusalem, animals that are mentioned in the Bible are accompanied by signs quoting relevant verses. Situated in the **Malchah** מַלְחָה *neighbourhood, the zoo attracts visitors from all sections of the Jerusalem public, as well as tourists from Israel and around the world. The* **'Eyn ya'el** עֵין יָעֵל *'spring of the ibex' living museum, on the site of an ancient*

70 Seventieth lesson (Shi'ur shiv'im)

חֲזָרָה Chazarah – Review

1 Vocabulary

Here are some more useful words to add to your growing Hebrew vocabulary:

pa'am (fem.)	פַּעַם	*once*
pa'amayim (dual)	פַּעֲמַיִים	*twice*
shalosh pe'amim	שָׁלוֹשׁ פְּעָמִים	*three times*
`af pa'am	אַף פַּעַם	*never, not once,* (the particle **`af** אַף is used to form some negative expressions).

Examples:
Pa'am beshavu'a hem lomdim 'ivrit be`ulpan.
פַּעַם בְּשָׁבוּעַ הֵם לוֹמְדִים עִבְרִית בְּאוּלְפָּן.
Once a week they study Hebrew in an Ulpan.

Pa'amayim beshanah hem nos'im lefestival qirqasim bechutz la`aretz.
פַּעֲמַיִים בְּשָׁנָה הֵם נוֹסעִים לְפֶסְטִיבַל קִרְקָסִים בְּחוּץ לָאָרֶץ .
Twice a year they travel to a circus festival ('festival-of circuses') *abroad* ('in-outside-of the-Land').

spring not far from the zoo, preserves the crafts and agricultural techniques of ancient times.

Many names of animals are used as first names in modern Hebrew: **Dvorah** דבוֹרָה bee*;* **'Ofrah** עוֹפְרָה young doe*;* **Rachel** רָחֵל ewe*;* **Tziporah** צִפּוֹרָה bird*;* **Ya'el** יָעֵל ibex*;* **Yonah** יוֹנָה dove*;* **`Ari, `Aryeh** אֲרִי, אַרְיֵה lion*;* **Dov** דֹב bear*;* **Tzvi** צְבִי buck, stag, hart*;* **Ze`ev** זְאֵב wolf.

Second wave: lesson 20

---

70 שִׁעוּר שִׁבְעִים

Hu `af pa'am lo ratzah lagur bemerkaz ha'ir.
הוּא אַף פַּעַם לֹא רָצָה לָגוּר בְּמֶרְכַּז הָעִיר.
He never wanted to live in the city centre.

`af אַף also has other uses, as we'll see in later lessons.

Let's move on to some other useful words:

mul	מוּל	*opposite, facing*
'iqar	עִקָּר	*essential, main, principal*
be'iqar	בְּעִקָּר	*mainly, principally, in particular*
ha'iqar	הָעִקָּר	*the main thing*
lakhen	לָכֵן	*therefore, so, that's why*
lamrot	לַמְרוֹת	*despite*
lamrot she	לַמְרוֹת שֶׁ	*although*
mipney she	מִפְּנֵי שׁ	*because*
'od	עוֹד	*more, yet*
'od lo	עוֹד לֹא	*not yet*
`akh	אַךְ	*but*
`efshar	אֶפְשָׁר	*possible*
`i efshar	אִי אֶפְשָׁר	*it is impossible*
bilti `efshari	בִּלְתִּי אֶפְשָׁרִי	*impossible*
davqa	דַוְקָא	*precisely, rather*
ki	כִּי	*because, since*

2 'By myself', 'by yourself' ...

To say *by myself, by yourself* and so forth, Hebrew uses the word **'etzem** עֶצֶם *self, bone, essence* with the appropriate suffix:

be'atzmi	בְּעַצְמִי	*by myself*
be'atzmekha	בְּעַצְמְךָ	*by yourself* (masc. sing.)
be'atzmekh	בְּעַצְמֵךְ	*by yourself* (fem. sing.)
be'atzmo	בְּעַצְמוֹ	*by himself, by itself*
be'atzmah	בְּעַצְמָהּ	*by herself, by itself*
be'atzmenu	בְּעַצְמֵנוּ	*by ourselves*
be'atzmekhem	בְּעַצְמְכֶם	*by yourselves* (masc. pl.)
be'atzmekhen	בְּעַצְמְכֶן	*by yourselves* (fem. pl.)
be'atzmam	בְּעַצְמָם	*by themselves* (masc.)
be'atzman	בְּעַצְמָן	*by themselves* (masc.)

Hu yode'a la'asot hakol be'atzmo, gam letaqen `et hamekhonit shelo.
הוּא יוֹדֵעַ לַעֲשׂוֹת הַכֹּל בְּעַצְמוֹ, גַּם לְתַקֵּן אֶת הַמְּכוֹנִית שֶׁלּוֹ.
He knows [how] to do everything by himself, even (also) *fix his car.*

3 Possessive forms of plural nouns

Let's use the example of the masculine plural noun **nekhadim** נְכָדִים *grandchildren* (the singular is **nekhed** נֶכֶד *grandchild*). Its possessive forms are:

nekhaday	נְכָדַי	*my grandchildren*
nekhadekha	נְכָדֶיךָ	*your grandchildren* (speaking to a man – the grandfather)
nekhadayikh	נְכָדַיִךְ	*your grandchildren* (speaking to a woman – the grandmother)
nekhadav	נְכָדָיו	*his grandchildren*
nekhadeha	נְכָדֶיהָ	*her grandchildren*
nekhadeynu	נְכָדֵינוּ	*our grandchildren*
nekhdeykhem	נֶכְדֵיכֶם	*your grandchildren* (speaking to men)
nekhdeykhen	נֶכְדֵיכֶן	*your grandchildren* (speaking to women)
nekhdeyhem	נֶכְדֵיהֶם	*their grandchildren* (speaking about men)
nekhdeyhen	נֶכְדֵיהֶן	*their grandchildren* (speaking about women)

As you can see, the vowels change between the different persons. Detailing the complicated rules behind these changes would probably only make the whole thing seem more confusing. Our advice is to simply learn the different forms: over time, and with practice, they will become second nature.

To take another example, the following is the declension of **yeladim** יְלָדִים *children*, *boys* (the plural of **yeled** יֶלֶד *child*, *boy*):

yeladay	יְלָדַי	*my children*
yeladeykha	יְלָדֶיךָ	*your children* (to a man)
yeladayikh	יְלָדַיִךְ	*your children* (to a woman)
yeladav	יְלָדָיו	*his children*
yeladeyha	יְלָדֶיהָ	*her children*
yeladeynu	יְלָדֵינוּ	*our children*
yaldeykhem	יַלְדֵיכֶם	*your children* (to men)
yaldeykhen	יַלְדֵיכֶן	*your children* (to women)
yaldeyhem	יַלְדֵיהֶם	*their children* (speaking of men)
yaldeyhen	יַלְדֵיהֶן	*their children* (" of women)

4 Reflexive verbs

The reflexive form of Hebrew verbs (known as **hitpa'el** הִתְפַּעֵל) is used to describe reflexive or reciprocal actions (*I wash myself, we see each other*, etc.). In some cases, a concept that English speakers do not consider to be reflexive is expressed reflexively in Hebrew, in the sense of to 'become' (e.g. הִתְלַהֵב *he was excited, he was enthusiastic*; literally, 'he became fiery').

In the infinitive, these verbs begin with a **lamed**, as all infinitives do, followed by **hit**: **le-hit-rachetz** לְהִתְרַחֵץ *to wash oneself*; **le-hit-lahev** לְהִתְלַהֵב *to be excited.*

The past tense is as follows:

(`ani) hitrachatzti	הִתְרַחַצְתִּי	*I washed myself*
(`atah) hitrachatzta	הִתְרַחַצְתָּ	*you* (masc.) *washed yourself*
(`at) hitrachatzt	הִתְרַחַצְת	*you* (fem.) *washed yourself*
(hu) hitrachetz	הִתְרַחֵץ	*he washed himself*

(hi) hitrachatzah	הִתְרַחֲצָה	*she washed herself*
(`anachnu) hitrachatznu	הִתְרַחַצְנוּ	*we washed ourselves*
(`atem) hitrachatztem	הִתְרַחַצְתֶּם	*you* (masc.) *washed yourselves*
(`aten) hitrachatzten	הִתְרַחַצְתֶּן	*you* (fem.) *washed yourselves*
(hem) hitrachatzu	הִתְרַחֲצוּ	*they* (masc.) *washed themselves*
(hen) hitrachatzu	הִתְרַחֲצוּ	*they* (fem.) *washed themselves*

Note that the suffixes are the same as those for other types of verbs; only the **hit-** prefix marks the reflexive nature of the verb.

5 Adjectives

5.1 Adjectives beginning with a מ

Here are some adjectives that feature a מ before the root letters. They change form according to gender and number.

From the root מזג (*to mix, moderate*):

memuzag *air-conditioned*	מְמוּזָג	(masc. sing.)
memuzeget	מְמוּזֶגֶת	(fem. sing.)
memuzagim	מְמוּזָגִים	(masc. pl.)
memuzagot	מְמוּזָגוֹת	(fem. pl.)

Hamisrad shelanu memuzag baqayitz ubachoref.
הַמִּשְׂרָד שֶׁלָּנוּ מְמוּזָג בַּקַּיִץ וּבַחוֹרֶף.
Our office is air-conditioned in summer and in winter.

From the root צחק (*to laugh*):

matzchiq *funny*	מַצְחִיק	(masc. sing.)
matzchiqah	מַצְחִיקָה	(fem. sing.)
matzchiqim	מַצְחִיקִים	(masc. pl.)
matzchiqot	מַצְחִיקוֹת	(fem. pl.)

Two other adjectives we've seen also have an initial מ. These two both come from quadriliteral roots (roots with four letters, rather than the usual three). Note that in both these cases, the four root letters consist of the same two letters repeated twice.

From the root לכלך (*to dirty*):

melukhlakh *dirty*	מְלוּכְלָךְ	(masc. sing.)
melukhlekhet	מְלוּכְלֶכֶת	(fem. sing.)
melukhlakhim	מְלוּכְלָכִים	(masc. pl.)
melukhlakhot	מְלוּכְלָכוֹת	(fem. pl.)

Hu chazar habaytah melukhlakh vehalakh lehitrachetz.

הוּא חָזַר הַבַּיְתָה מְלוּכְלָךְ וְהָלַךְ לְהִתְרַחֵץ.

He came back home dirty and went to wash himself.

From the root קלקל (*to spoil, become broken*):

mequlqal *broken, spoiled*	מְקוּלְקָל	(masc. sing.)
mequlqelet	מְקוּלְקֶלֶת	(fem. sing.)
mequqalim	מְקוּלְקָלִים	(masc. pl.)
mequlqalot	מְקוּלְקָלוֹת	(fem. pl.)

Hamekhonit mequlqelet, tzarikh letaqen `otah.

הַמְכוֹנִית מְקוּלְקֶלֶת, צָרִיךְ לְתַקֵּן אוֹתָהּ.

The car has broken down, it needs to be repaired. ('The car is broken, it is necessary to repair it.')

5.2 Adjectives of colour

Here are some of the commonest colours (first line, masculine and feminine singular; second line, masculine and feminine plural):

Green			
yaroq	יָרוֹק	yeruqah	יְרוּקָה
yeruqim	יְרוּקִים	yeruqot	יְרוּקוֹת
Blue			
kachol	כָּחוֹל	kchulah	כְּחוּלָה
kchulim	כְּחוּלִים	kchulot	כְּחוּלוֹת
Red			
`adom	אָדוֹם	`adumah	אֲדוּמָה
`adumim	אֲדוּמִים	`adumot	אֲדוּמוֹת
Grey			
`afor	אָפוֹר	`aforah	אֲפוֹרָה
`aforim	אֲפוֹרִים	`aforot	אֲפוֹרוֹת

Black			
shachor	שָׁחוֹר	**shchorah**	שְׁחוֹרָה
shchorim	שְׁחוֹרִים	**shchorot**	שְׁחוֹרוֹת
White			
lavan	לָבָן	**levanah**	לְבָנָה
levanim	לְבָנִים	**levanot**	לְבָנוֹת

Review exercise

❶ בַּקַּיִץ עָבַדְתִּי הַרְבֵּה, מִפְּנֵי שֶׁאֲנִי יוֹדֵעַ לְתַקֵּן בְּעַצְמִי כֹּל מַזְגָן. ❷ אֲבָל הַמַּזְגָנִים בַּמְּכוֹנִיּוֹת הֵם חֵלֶק הָאֲרִי מֵהָעֲבוֹדָה שֶׁלִּי. ❸ בְּמֶזֶג הָאֲוִיר הַיִּשְׂרְאֵלִי, הָאֲנָשִׁים לֹא זָזִים בְּלִי מַזְגָן. ❹ בַּבַּיִת יֵשׁ לָהֶם מִזּוּג אֲוִיר. מֵהַדִּירָה הֵם יוֹצְאִים לִמְכוֹנִית מְמוּזֶּגֶת וְנִכְנָסִים לְמִשְׂרָד מְמוּזָּג. ❺ מִשָּׁם הֵם הוֹלְכִים לֶאֱכוֹל בְּמִסְעָדָה מְמוּזֶּגֶת. ❻ אִם הַמַּזְגָן מְקוּלְקָל זֶה סוֹף הָעוֹלָם! ❼ אֲבָל אֲנִי אוֹהֵב אֶת הַקַּיִץ: סַנְדָּלִים בְּלִי גַּרְבַּיִם, בְּגָדִים צִבְעוֹנִיִּים, ❽ תַּפְרִיטִים שֶׁל קַיִץ בְּמִסְעָדוֹת עַל יַד הַיָּם, ❾ סְרָטִים מַצְחִיקִים אוֹ שִׁירָה בְּצִבּוּר בְּגַן צִבּוּרִי. ❿ נוּ, אָז הָעִקָּר שֶׁיִּהְיֶה גַּם לָכֶם קַיִץ נָעִים וּמְמוּזָּג!

Answers

❶ In the summer I worked a lot because I know how to fix any air-conditioner by myself. *(in-the-summer I-worked much because that-I know to-fix by-myself all air-conditioner)* ❷ ... but car air-conditioners are the lion's share of my work. *(but the-air-conditioners in-cars they share-of the-lion of-the-work of-me)* ❸ In the Israeli climate, people do not move without an air-conditioner. *(in-weather-of the-air the-Israeli, the-people not move without air-conditioner)* ❹ At home they have air-conditioning. From the apartment they go to an air-conditioned car and then into an air-conditioned office. *(in-the-house there-is to-them mixture-of air. from-the-apartment they go-out to-a-car air-conditioned and-enter to-an-office air-conditioned)* ❺ From there, they go to eat in an air-conditioned restaurant. *(from-there they-go to-eat in-restaurant air-conditioned)* ❻ If the air-conditioner is broken, it's the end of the world! *(if the-air-conditioner broken this end-of the-world)* ❼ But I like the summer: sandals without socks, colourful clothes, *(but I like* [`**et**] *the-summer: sandals without socks clothes colourful)* ❽ summer menus in restaurants by the sea, *(menus of summer in-restaurants by the-sea)* ❾ funny films or outdoor singing in a public park *(films funny or singing in-public in-park public)* ❿ Well then, the main thing is that you also have a pleasant and air-conditioned summer! *(well then the-principal that-there-will-be also for-you summer pleasant and-air-conditioned)*

Second wave: lesson 21

71 Seventy-first lesson
(Shi'ur shiv'im ve`achat)

Mitologyah ve'ivrit
Mythology and Hebrew

1 **`Im `atem choshvim shelekhol milah chadashah ba'ivrit ha'akhshavit ① yesh shoresh ② raq batanakh `o batalmud, `atem to'im!**
If you think that every word in modern Hebrew *(word new in-the-Hebrew the-contemporary)* has its root only in the Bible or Talmud, you're wrong!

2 **Leharbeh milim yisre`eliyot yesh shorashim bamitologyah hayevanit `o haromit. Zeh lo paradoqs!**
Many Hebrew *(Israeli)* words have roots in Greek or Roman mythology. This is no paradox!

3 **Mah da'atkhem ③ 'al hamilah Muzah? Likhvodah ④ `anachnu shom'im musiqah veholkhim lemuze`on.**
What do you think *(What your-opinion)* about the word 'muse'? In her honour we listen to music and go to the museum.

Notes

① **'akhshavit** עַכְשָׁוִית *contemporary*. This adjective comes from the adverb **'akhshav** עַכְשָׁו *now*, which you should be familiar with by now.

② **shoresh** שֹׁרֶשׁ *root*, and in the plural (line 2): **shorashim** שָׁרָשִׁים. As in English, the original meaning of this word was the root of a plant or tree, which was later extended to refer to the root of a verb, a square root and other meanings.

מִיתוֹלוֹגְיָה וְעִבְרִית

1 אִם אַתֶּם חוֹשְׁבִים שֶׁלְּכֹל מִלָּה חֲדָשָׁה בָּעִבְרִית הָעַכְשָׁוִית יֵשׁ שׁוֹרֶשׁ רַק בַּתַּנַ"ךְ אוֹ בַּתַּלְמוּד, אַתֶּם טוֹעִים!

2 לְהַרְבֵּה מִלִּים יִשְׂרְאֵלִיּוֹת יֵשׁ שָׁרָשִׁים בַּמִּתוֹלוֹגְיָה הַיְּוָנִית אוֹ הָרוֹמִית. זֶה לֹא פָּרָדוֹקס!

3 מַה דַּעַתְכֶם עַל הַמִּלָּה מוּזָה? לִכְבוֹדָהּ אֲנַחְנוּ שׁוֹמְעִים מוּסִיקָה וְהוֹלְכִים לְמוּזֵיאוֹן.

Related verbs include **lehashrish** לְהַשְׁרִישׁ *to set down roots*; **lesharesh** לְשָׁרֵשׁ *to uproot.*

③ **da'atkhem** דַּעַתְכֶם *your opinion.* **de'ah** דֵּעָה *opinion* comes from the root ידע *to know.* The suffix ־כֶם is, of course, the second-person masculine plural possessive form.

④ **likhvodah** לִכְבוֹדָהּ *in her honour.* The word **kavod** כָּבוֹד *honour* is preceded by the preposition ל *for*, *to*, and the final ־ָהּ is the third-person feminine singular possessive suffix. If it was referring to a man, it would be **likhvodo** לִכְבוֹדוֹ *in his honour.*

4 **Ha`im `atem makirim `et hame`amen hamitologi shel qvutzat hakadursal, `alufat ⑤ `Eyropah?**
Do you know the mythological trainer of the basketball team [that is] champion of Europe?

5 **Hu lo raq me`amen tov, bekosher ⑥ `olimpi, hu gam yefeyfeh ⑦ kmo `Apolo.**
He's not only a good trainer, in Olympian fitness – he's also as handsome as Apollo.

6 **Hu mit'anyen behipnozah uvepsikhologyah kedey leyatzer giborey `itztadyon.**
He is interested in hypnosis and *(in)* psychology in order to produce *(create)* heroes of the stadium.

7 **Yoter `eqologi me`asher ⑧ trufot!**
[It's] more environmentally friendly *(ecological)* than medicines!

8 **Vehakol beshalvah `olimpit!**
And all [this] with Olympian tranquillity!

Notes

⑤ **`alufat** אַלּוּפַת *champion of.* The absolute state of this noun is **`alufah** אַלּוּפָה in the feminine and **`aluf** אַלּוּף in the masculine. This word is related to **`alef** א, the first letter of the Hebrew alphabet.

⑥ **kosher** כּוֹשֶׁר *fitness, form.* This word comes from the same root as כשר *kosher*; that is, ritually fit for consumption. **kashrut** כַּשְׁרוּת refers to the system of Jewish religious laws relating to food.

⑦ **yefeyfeh** יְפֵהפֶה *very handsome*; **yefeyfiyah** יְפֵהפִיָּה *very beautiful.* This adjective is derived from **yafeh** יָפֶה *handsome, beautiful* by doubling the final syllable. The meaning is an

4 הַאִם אַתֶּם מַכִּירִים אֶת הַמְאַמֵּן הַמִּתוֹלוֹגִי שֶׁל קְבוּצַת הַכַּדּוּרסַל, אַלוּפַת אֵירוֹפָּה?

5 הוּא לֹא רַק מְאַמֵּן טוֹב, בְּכוֹשֶׁר אוֹלִימפִּי, הוּא גַם יְפֵהפֶה כּמוֹ אַפּוֹלוֹ.

6 הוּא מִתעַנֵיֵן בְּהִפּנוֹזָה וּבְפּסִיכוֹלוֹגיָה, כְּדֵי לְיַצֵר גִבּוֹרֵי אִצטָדיוֹן.

7 יוֹתֵר אֶקוֹלוֹגִי מֵאֲשֶׁר תרוּפוֹת!

8 וְהַכֹּל בְּשַׁלוָה אוֹלִימפִּית!

אופנת הבגדים העכשוית יפה רק לצעירים או לצעירות.

intensive version of the original adjective: **nashim yefehfiyot** נָשִׁים יְפֵהפִיוֹת *very beautiful women.*

⑧ **me`asher** מֵאֲשֶׁר *than*. This word is used to form comparisons, following the pattern **yoter** + adjective + **me`asher** + second term of comparison.

9 **'Od milim? Pitchu `et hamilon ⑨, `aval `al ta'ezu liftoach `et tevat ⑩ Pandorah!**
More words? Open the dictionary, but don't dare *(not you-will-dare)* to open Pandora's Box!

Notes

⑨ **milon** מִלּוֹן *dictionary*. As discussed at the end of this lesson, this modern Hebrew term comes from מִלָּה *word*, with the ending וֹן, which is often used to form the names of objects: **'iton** עִתּוֹן *newspaper*; **chalon** חַלּוֹן *window*, etc.

Targil rishon – Targem   תַּרְגִּיל רִאשׁוֹן – תַּרְגֵּם

❶ כאשר למדתי בבית הספר, אהבתי לקרוא ספרים על המתולוגיה היונית.
Ka`asher lamadeti beveyt hasefer, `ahavti liqro` sfarim 'al hamitologyah hayevanit.

❷ אופנת הבגדים העכשוית יפה רק לצעירים או לצעירות.
`Ofnat habgadim ha'akhshavit yafah raq litz'irim `o litz'irot.

❸ אחרי שבוע במרכז הספורט, אני ממש בכושר אולימפי.
`Acharey shavu'a bemerkaz hasport, `ani mamash bekhosher `olimpy.

❹ איזו קבוצה אלופת העולם בכדורגל?
`Eyzo qvutzah `alufat ha'olam bekhaduregel?

❺ אם אתם יודעים מה השורש של המלה, אתם יכולים לחפש אותה במילון.
`Im `atem yod'im mah hashoresh shel hamilah, `atem yekholim lechapes `otah bamilon.

9 עוֹד מִלִּים? פִּתְחוּ אֶת הַמִּילוֹן, אֲבָל אַל תָּעֵזּוּ לִפְתּוֹחַ אֶת תֵּבַת פַּנְדוֹרָה!

⑩ **tevah** תֵּבָה *box, chest*; **tevat do`ar** תֵּבַת דּוֹאַר *post box, mailbox*; **tevat tza'atzu'im** תֵּבַת צַעֲצוּעִים *toy chest*. The same word appears in two well-known Biblical stories, in reference to Noah's Ark (Genesis 6:14) and the basket in which the baby Moses was placed in the Nile (Exodus 2:3).

Answers to Exercise 1

❶ When I studied at school, I liked to read books about Greek mythology. ❷ Contemporary fashion only looks good on *(Style of clothes contemporary beautiful only for)* young men or young women. ❸ After a week at the sports centre, I'm really in Olympian form. ❹ Which team is world champion in soccer? ❺ If you know what the root of the word is, you can look it up *(search it)* in the dictionary.

Targil sheni – Hashlem תַּרְגִּיל שֵׁנִי – הַשְׁלֵם

From this lesson on, start writing the Hebrew words in the exercises without vowel points. After all, it's easier that way! Note that in some words written without their vowel points, a **yod** *or a* **vav** *is added to hint at the vowel sound. For example,* **shi'ur** שִׁעוּר lesson *appears without points as* שיעור. *Similarly,* **`ometz** אוֹמֶץ courage *may also be written without the* **vav**: אֹמֶץ. *Don't worry about this, we're just letting you know in case you notice this discrepancy.*

❶ Shirly was the only muse of the fashion photographer.
Shirly haytah [...] hayechidah shel [...] ha`ofnah.
שירלי היתה _____ היחידה של ___ האופנה.

❷ The physician gives him medicines for his back problems *(for-the-problems the-back of-him).*
Ha[...] noten lo [...] live'ayot ha[...] shelo.
ה____ נותן לו ______ לבעיות ה__ שלו.

❸ After the hypnosis at the psychologist, she enters *(is in)* Olympian tranquillity.
[...] [...] `etzel hapsikholog hi be[...] `olimpit.
____ _______ אצל הפסיכולוג היא ב____ אולימפית.

❹ When we were children, we learned about Noah's Ark in the Bible lesson.
[...] hayinu yeladim lamadnu 'al [...] Noach be[...] Tanakh.
____ היינו ילדים למדנו על ___ נוח ב____ תנ"ך.

❺ Don't dare break Mom and Dad's hearts!
[...] [...] lishbor `et ha[...] shel `aba ve`ima.
__ ____ לשבור את ה_____ של אבא ואמא.

When **`Eli'ezer Ben Yehudah** אֱלִיעֶזֶר בֶּן יְהוּדָה *(born Eliezer Yitzhak Perlman in 1858) began to write the first modern Hebrew dictionary, the language did not have a word for the work he*

Answers to Exercise 2

❶ – **hamuzah – tzalam –** — ❶ - המוזה - צלם -
❷ – **rofe – trufot – gav –** — ❷ - רופא - תרופות - גב -
❸ **`Acharey hipnozah – shalvah –** — ❸ - אחרי היפנוזה - שלוה
❹ **Ka`asher – tevat – sh'iur –** — ❹ כאשר - תבת - שעור -
❺ **`Al ta'ezu – levavot –** — ❺ אל תעזו - לבבות -

wanted to produce. Accordingly, he created the word **milon** מִלוֹן dictionary *from* **milah** מִלָה word.

At this time, in the late 19th century, Hebrew was used for religious and literary purposes, but was ill-suited for colloquial conversation or academic writing. Perlman, a young Russian Jew, arrived in Paris in 1878 to study medicine. There he met other Jewish immigrants from Eastern Europe, and he and his friends started to speak to each other in Hebrew in a café on the Boulevard Montmartre. Their imaginations ran wild: if Jews were to move to Palestine, Hebrew could serve as the common language. Perlman adopted the Hebrew name Ben Yehudah and began to compile a Hebrew dictionary. In the course of his endeavour, he drew on 40,000 works, extracted 20,000 words and copied 500,000 quotes. To make the language more practical, he replaced compound terms with new, simpler nouns: **beyt `okhel** בֵּית אוֹכֶל house of food *was replaced by* **mis'adah** מִסעָדָה restaurant, **`ish milchamah** אִישׁ מִלחָמָה man of war *gave way to* **chayal** חַיָל soldier, *and so forth. He was thorough and systematic in his approach. First of all, he turned to Hebrew and Aramaic roots to find inspiration for new words. If this failed, he adapted Arabic roots and forms. He only drew on European words when there was no alternative – examples include* **sabon** סַבּוֹן soap *('savon' in French) and* **birah** בִּירָה beer. *Some of his inventions have since been replaced by European words. For example, Hebrew speakers have preferred to adopt the word* **demoqratyah** דֶמוֹקרָטיַה *rather than use* **`amanah** אֲמָנָה, *a word Ben Yehudah suggested on the basis of* **`emun** אֵמוּן confidence, trust.

Less than 20 years after the linguistic discussions in the Paris café, another Eastern European Jew, Theodor Herzl, wrote his work The Jewish State *while staying in a hotel in the city. The work (written in German) was published in 1896. The complete set of volumes of Ben Yehudah's Hebrew dictionary would not be published until after his death in 1922.*

Second wave: lesson 22

72 Seventy-second lesson
(Shi'ur shiv'im ushtayim)

Heykhal ① hasefer biYrushalayim
The Shrine of the Book in Jerusalem

1 **Heykhal hasefer hu ② mivneh lavan betzurat mikhseh shel qanqan.**
The Shrine *(Palace)* of the Book *(it)* is a white building in the shape of a pot lid.

2 **Hu mesamel `et haqanqan shebo ③ nimtze`u cheleq mehamegilot hagnuzot ④ bime'arot Qumran.**
It symbolizes the pot in which some of the hidden scrolls were found in the Qumran caves.

3 **Sviv hamivneh hazeh, yesh brekhat mayim kchulah ⑤.**
Around this building, there is a blue[-bottomed] water pool.

Notes

① **heykhal** הֵיכָל *shrine, palace.* This word can have a secular or sacred meaning, depending on the context. It originally referred to the Temple in Jerusalem, but in modern Israel, **heykhal hasport** הֵיכַל הַספּוֹרט *sports palace* and **heykhal hatarbut** הֵיכַל הַתַרבּוּת *Palace of Culture* are examples of its use to refer to secular institutions.

② **hu** הוּא *it.* Including a third-person pronoun to link two nouns in phrases that do not have a verb is common in Hebrew (remember that there is no present tense of the verb *to be* in Hebrew). Here, the masculine **hu** is used because it refers back to **heykhal hasefer** הֵיכַל הַסֵפֶר *Shrine of the Book*, which is masculine.

הֵיכַל הַסֵּפֶר בִּירוּשָׁלַיִם

1 הֵיכַל הַסֵּפֶר הוּא מִבְנֶה לָבָן בְּצוּרַת מִכְסֶה שֶׁל קַנְקַן.

2 הוּא מְסַמֵּל אֶת הַקַּנְקַן שֶׁבּוֹ נִמְצְאוּ חֵלֶק מֵהַמְגִילוֹת הַגְּנוּזוֹת בִּמְעָרוֹת קוּמְרָאן.

3 סְבִיב הַמִּבְנֶה הַזֶּה, יֵשׁ בְּרֵכַת מַיִם כְּחוּלָה.

③ **shebo** שֶׁבּוֹ *in which* (literally, 'that-in-it') consists of the relative particle **she-** שֶׁ, followed by the preposition **b-** בּ with the third-person masculine singular suffix **o** וֹ.

④ **gnuzot** גְנוּזוֹת comes from the root גנז, which means *to hide, to archive*. **ganzakh** גַּנְזַךְ means *archives*. See the end of this lesson for a discussion of the related word **gnizah** גְנִיזָה.

⑤ **brekhat mayim kchulah** בְּרֵכַת מַיִם כְּחוּלָה *blue water pool*. The form of the adjective **kchulah** shows that it refers to the colour of the pool, not the water. If the latter had been the intention, the adjective would have taken the form **kchulim** כְּחוּלִים, since **mayim** is a masculine plural noun.

4 **'Al yad hamivneh halavan yesh qir shachor.**
Alongside the white building there is a black wall.

5 **Shneyhem mesamlim `et milchemet ⑥ bney `or bivney ⑦ choshekh,**
Both of them *(The-two-of-them)* symbolize the war between the 'Sons of Light' and the 'Sons of Darkness',

6 **kmo hashem shel `achat mehamegilot.**
like the name of one of the scrolls.

7 **Yordim laheykhal umagi'im likhnisah shemazkirah me'arah `arukah.**
You go down *(They[impers. subj.] descend)* to the shrine and arrive at an entrance that recalls a long cave.

8 **Yesh bah ⑧ mikhtavim shel Bar ⑨ Kokhva ute'udot ⑩ shel `ishah beshem Bavta.**
It contains *(There-is in-it)* letters of Bar Kokhva and documents of a woman by the name of Bavta.

Notes

⑥ **milchemet** מִלְחֶמֶת *war-of* is the construct state of **milchamah** מִלְחָמָה.

⑦ **bivney** בִּבְנֵי *against sons-of.* This word consists of the preposition **b-** בּ followed by **bney**, whose initial **bet** בּ changes to **vet** ב in this position. You've already seen the form **bney** בְּנֵי *sons-of* as the construct state of **banim** בָּנִים. By the way, note that the preposition **b-** בּ *in* here means *against*, as in a war against something or someone.

⑧ **bah** בָּהּ *in it/her* (fem.). In note 3, we saw the equivalent masculine form **bo** בּוֹ *in it/him.*

4 עַל יַד הַמִּבְנֶה הַלָּבָן יֵשׁ קִיר שָׁחוֹר.

5 שְׁנֵיהֶם מְסַמְּלִים אֶת מִלְחֶמֶת בְּנֵי אוֹר בִּבְנֵי חוֹשֶׁךְ,

6 כְּמוֹ הַשֵּׁם שֶׁל אַחַת מֵהַמְּגִילוֹת.

7 יוֹרְדִים לָהֵיכָל וּמַגִּיעִים לִכְנִיסָה שֶׁמַּזְכִּירָה מְעָרָה אֲרוּכָּה.

8 יֵשׁ בָּהּ מִכְתָּבִים שֶׁל בַּר כּוֹכְבָא ⑨ וּתְעוּדוֹת ⑩ שֶׁל אִשָּׁה בְּשֵׁם בָּבְתָא.

בהיכל הספורט יהיה בשבוע הבא משחק כדורגל בינלאומי.

⑨ **bar** בַּר *son-of.* This is an Aramaic word, equivalent to the Hebrew **ben**. We've already encountered it in the phrase **Bar Mitzvah** בַּר מִצְוָה 'son-of commandment'.

⑩ **te'udot** תְּעוּדוֹת *documents*, *certificates*. The same root is seen in the word **'edut** עֵדוּת *evidence*, *testimony*.

9 **Ba`ulam hamerkazi nimtza`ot hamegilot hagnuzot.**
In the central hall there are *(are-found)* the hidden scrolls.

10 **Hen yedu'ot gam bashem megilot yam hamelach.**
They are also known as the Dead Sea Scrolls *(scrolls-of sea-of the-salt)*

11 **Bemerkaz ha`ulam hazeh, nimtzet gam megilah `arukah me`od shel kol sefer Yesha'eyahu.**
In the centre of this hall, there is *(is-found)* also a very long scroll of the entire Book of Isaiah.

12 **Zeh ktav hayad haqadum ⑪ beyoter shel sefer tanakhi shalem.**
This is the oldest manuscript *(writing-of the-hand ancient)* of an entire Biblical Book.

Targil rishon – Targem תַּרְגִּיל רִאשׁוֹן – תַּרְגֵּם

❶ בלשנים מכל העולם התלהבו מהמגילות הגנוזות.
Balshanim mikol ha'olam hitlahavu mehamegilot hagnuzot.

❷ איפה המכסה של קנקן הקפה?
`Eyfoh hamikhseh shel qanqan haqafeh?

❸ בהיכל הספורט יהיה בשבוע הבא משחק כדורגל בינלאומי.
Beheykhal hasport yiheyeh bashavu'a haba mischaq kaduregel beynle`umi.

❹ קניתי שלוש כורסאות כחולות ושולחן זכוכית קטן.
Qaniti shalosh kursa`ot kchulot veshulchan zekhukhit qatan.

9 בָּאוּלָם הַמֶּרְכָּזִי נִמְצָאוֹת הַמְּגִילוֹת הַגְּנוּזוֹת.

10 הֵן יְדוּעוֹת גַּם בַּשֵּׁם מְגִילוֹת יַם הַמֶּלַח.

11 בְּמֶרְכָּז הָאוּלָם הַזֶּה, נִמְצֵאת גַּם מְגִילָה אֲרוּכָּה מְאֹד שֶׁל כֹּל סֵפֶר יְשַׁעְיָהוּ.

12 זֶה כְּתַב הַיָּד הַקָּדוּם בְּיוֹתֵר שֶׁל סֵפֶר תַּנָ"כִי שָׁלֵם. □

Notes

⑪ **qadum** קָדוּם *old, ancient*; the feminine singular form is **qdumah** קְדוּמָה. The root קדם is found in a large number of words, such as **qodem** קוֹדֶם *before*, **qadimah** קָדִימָה *forwards* and **muqdam** מֻקְדָּם *early*.

⑤ במשרד בית הספר נמצאות התעודות של התלמידים.
Bemisrad beyt hasefer nimtza`ot hate'udot shel hatalmidim.

Answers to Exercise 1

❶ Linguists from all over the *(the whole)* world were excited by the hidden scrolls. ❷ Where is the lid of the coffee pot? ❸ At the sports palace there will be an international soccer match next week. ❹ I bought three blue armchairs and a small glass table. ❺ The students' certificates are found in the school office.

Targil sheni – Hashlem   תַּרְגִּיל שֵׁנִי – הַשְׁלֵם

① What a surprise! We met at the entrance to the cinema.
 [...] [...]! Nifgashnu [...] laqolno'a.

‏_____ _____ ! נפגשנו _____ לְקוֹלנוֹעַ.

② Do we know each other? You remind me of Ruti Cohen. Is that you?
 `Anachnu [...]? `At [...] [...] `et Ruti Kohen. [...] [...]?

‏אנחנו _____? אַתְּ _____ _____ אֶת רותי כהן. _____ __?

③ What does the black wall by the white palace symbolize?
 Mah [...] [...] hashachor 'al yad [...] halavan?

‏מה _____ _____ הַשחור עַל יָ _____ הַלָבָן?

④ That is a very beautiful pot, but what is inside it?
 [...] [...] yafeh me'od, `aval mah yesh [...]?

‏__ _____ יָפֶה מְאוֹד, אֲבָל מה יש __?

⑤ If there is no light at night, the Israelis say: 'Really, [it is the] darkness of Egypt'.
 `Im `eyn [...] [...] haYisre'elim `omrim: '[...] [...] Mitzrayim'.

‏אִם אֵין _____ _____ הישראֵלִים אוֹמרים: "_____ _____ מִצְרַיִם".

✿

Heykhal hasefer הֵיכַל הַסֵּפֶר Shrine of the Book. *Situated on a hill in West Jerusalem, close to the Knesset, the Israel Museum includes impressive collections of Judaica, art and archaeological finds. The Shrine of the Book, which was constructed in 1965, is perhaps the most unique feature of the museum. Designed by two American Jewish architects, Frederic Kiesler and Armand Bartos, its shape recalls the lids of the pots in which the Dead Sea Scrolls were found in 1947. The building houses a complete scroll of the Book of Isaiah, dating back to the 1st century CE. The contrast*

Answers to Exercise 2

❶ **`Eyzo hafta'ah – baknisah –** ❶ איזו הפתעה - בכניסה -

❷ **– makirim – mazkirah li – zot `at** ❷ - מכירים - מזכירה לי - זאת את

❸ **– mesamel haqir – haheykhal –** ❸ - מסמל הקיר - ההיכל -

❹ **Zeh qanqan – bo** ❹ זה קנקן - בו

❺ **– `or balaylah – mamash choshekh –** ❺ - אור בלילה - ממש חושך -

between the white shrine and the black facing wall symbolizes the battle between the Sons of Light and the Sons of Darkness recounted in one of the Dead Sea Scrolls. The 'War Scroll' presents the apocalyptic vision of the Essenes, an ascetic Jewish sect that lived by the Dead Sea. They believed themselves to be the Sons of Light and accused the priests in Jerusalem of compromising with idol worship.

The Cairo **gnizah גְנִיזָה***: In 1896, thousands of documents were discovered in the* **gnizah** *of a synagogue in the Old City of Cairo. The findings included fragments and longer documents in Hebrew, Aramaic and Greek, some dating back to the 7th century CE. A* **gnizah** *is an archive in a synagogue used to store religious documents that cannot be destroyed since they include the name of God and are therefore sacred. The Cairo Genizah has provided valuable historical and linguistic information covering centuries of Jewish religious, commercial and social life.*

Second wave: lesson 23

73 Seventy-third lesson
(Shi'ur shiv'im veshalosh)

Kaduregel
Soccer

1 **Zeh sipur 'al qvutzat kaduregel shekhunatit ①.**
This is the story of a neighbourhood soccer team.

2 **Mitachtit haligah hi ② zinqah hashanah, kemete`or, `el pisgat ligat hakaduregel hale`umit.**
From the bottom of the league, it soared this year like a meteor to the top of the national soccer league.

3 **Bemeshekh hashanim hayu laqvutzah 'aliyot unefilot, `ibdu yadayim veraglayim ③ venikhnesu 'im harosh baqir ④.**
Over *(During)* the years, the team has had [its] ups and downs, lost its footing *(lost hands and-legs)* and banged its head against the wall *(entered with the-head in-the-wall)*.

4 **Hashanah, hem menatzchim mischaq ve'od mischaq 'aqev betzad `agudal ⑤.**
This year, they are winning match after match *(match and-another match)*, step by step *(heel by toe)*.

Notes

① **shekhunatit** שְׁכוּנָתִית *neighbourhood* (adjective). This adjective (which appears here in the feminine singular) comes from the noun **shekhunah** שְׁכוּנָה *neighbourhood.*

② **hi zinqah** הִיא זָנְקָה *it soared, leapt*. The feminine third-person pronoun **hi** הִיא *it, she* refers to the team; it could have

כַּדּוּרֶגֶל

1 זֶה סִפּוּר עַל קְבוּצַת כַּדּוּרֶגֶל שְׁכוּנָתִית.

2 מִתַּחְתִּית הַלִּיגָה הִיא זִנְּקָה הַשָּׁנָה, כְּמֶטָאוֹר, אֶל פִּסְגַּת לִיגַת הַכַּדּוּרֶגֶל הַלְּאוּמִית.

3 בְּמֶשֶׁךְ הַשָּׁנִים הָיוּ לַקְּבוּצָה עֲלִיּוֹת וּנְפִילוֹת, אִבְּדוּ יָדַיִם וְרַגְלַיִם וְנִכְנְסוּ עִם הָרֹאשׁ בַּקִּיר.

4 הַשָּׁנָה, הֵם מְנַצְּחִים מִשְׂחָק וְעוֹד מִשְׂחָק עָקֵב בְּצַד אֲגוּדָל.

been left out, but its inclusion makes the subject of the verb clearer.

③ **`ibdu yadayim veraglayim** אִבְּדוּ יָדַיִם וְרַגְלַיִם (literally, 'they lost hands and legs') is used here in the figurative sense of *they lost their way*. This expression, which comes from the Talmud, means 'they didn't know what they were doing'.

④ **nikhnesu 'im harosh baqir** נִכְנְסוּ עִם הָרֹאשׁ בַּקִּיר literally, 'they entered with the head into the wall'. The closest English expression is 'they were banging their heads against a brick wall'. Note that **qir** קִיר is more common in everyday use than **kotel** כּוֹתֶל *wall* (lesson 44).

⑤ **'aqev betzad `agudal** עָקֵב בְּצַד אֲגוּדָל literally, 'heel by the side of toe'. Although **`agudal** usually means *thumb*, it can also refer to the *large toe*. This expression thus means to advance carefully, placing one foot just a little in front of the other to move forward step by step.

5 **Ha`asimon nafal ⑥ vehem bashpitz ⑦ shel haligah.**
The penny dropped *(The-token fell)* and they are at the summit *(at-the-point)* of the league.

6 **Lesachqaney hakaduregel niftach chalon hahizdamnuyot ⑧,**
The window of opportunity opened for the soccer players *(For-players-of the-soccer opened window-of the-opportunity)*

7 **ka`asher higi'a me`amen tza'ir shedoresh mehasachqanim metzuyanut bachayim ⑨ uvamigrash `aval lelo ⑩ qitzurey derekh.**
when a young coach arrived who demands excellence of the players in life and on *(in)* the field, but without shortcuts *(of-path)*.

8 **Hu be'ad ha'arakhah 'atzmit umenahel du-siach begovah ha'eynayim.**
He is in favour of self-esteem *(the-consideration personal)* and engages in *(manages)* dialogue as equals *(at-level-of the-eyes)*.

9 **Me`amen shaqet veya'il she'asah `et hamahapakh ⑪ hagadol.**
A calm and effective coach who has led *(made)* a *(the)* major transformation.

Notes

⑥ **ha`asimon nafal** הָאֲסִימוֹן נָפַל (literally, 'the token fell') is an expression that comes from the fact that for many years, public telephones in Israel were operated using tokens – the idea being that the token dropping results in the desired outcome. The English expression 'the penny dropped' uses a similar reference (but to old penny slot machines). The connotation of both the Hebrew and the English expression is to do with a connection finally being made and an idea becoming clear. The word **`asimon** *token* is of Greek origin.

5 הָאֲסִימוֹן נָפַל וְהֵם בַּשְּׁפִּיץ שֶׁל הַלִּיגָה.

6 לְשַׂחְקָנֵי הַכַּדּוּרֶגֶל נִפְתַּח חַלּוֹן הַהִזְדַּמְנוּיוֹת,

7 כַּאֲשֶׁר הִגִּיעַ מְאַמֵּן צָעִיר שֶׁדּוֹרֵשׁ מֵהַשַּׂחְקָנִים מְצוּיָּנוּת בַּחַיִּים וּבַמִּגְרָשׁ אֲבָל לְלֹא קִצּוּרֵי דֶּרֶךְ.

8 הוּא בְּעַד הַעֲרָכָה עַצְמִית וּמְנַהֵל דּוּ-שִׂיחַ בְּגוֹבַה הָעֵינַיִים.

9 מְאַמֵּן שָׁקֵט וְיָעִיל שֶׁעָשָׂה אֶת הַמַּהְפָּךְ הַגָּדוֹל.

⑦ **shpitz** שְׁפִּיץ *point* – this is a slang word originally introduced to Hebrew by German-speaking Jewish immigrants in the 1930s.

⑧ **chalon hahizdamnuyot** חַלּוֹן הַהִזְדַּמְנוּיוֹת *window of opportunity.* This modern Hebrew expression means the same as its English equivalent.

⑨ **chayim** חַיִּים *life.* Note that this noun only exists in plural form. Any accompanying verb or adjective must also be in the masculine plural.

⑩ **lelo** לְלֹא *without.* This word has the same meaning as **bli** בְּלִי *without* (see lesson 57).

⑪ **mahapakh** מַהְפָּךְ *upheaval, transformation.* The root הפך means *to turn, to turn over.* A related noun is **mahapekhah** מַהְפֵּכָה *revolution.* Both these terms are often used in a political context – **mahapakh** usually refers to a change of government (e.g. from left-wing to right-wing), while the second has a more radical connotation: **hamahapekhah hatzarfatit** *the French Revolution.*

10 **Herim `et haqvutzah miklum venatan lasachqanim bitachon 'atzmi.**
He raised the team from nothing and gave the players self-confidence.

11 **Ve'od davar chashuv: `ish 'asaqim, 'ashir me`od, milyoner, qanah `et haqvutzah.**
And another important thing: a very rich businessman, a millionaire, bought the team.

12 **Hu gever tza'ir venimratz. Peh gadol ve`ego 'od yoter gadol.**
He is a young and dynamic man [with] a big mouth and an even bigger ego.

13 **Hahatzlachah lo mesachreret `oto. Rega' `atah lema'elah verega' `atah lematah. Tzarikh la'avod, la'avod vela'avod!**
Success does not faze him *(not make him dizzy)*. One moment you are on top and one moment you are at the bottom. You*(impers. subj.)* have to work, work and work!

14 **Hamotiv shelo: tzarikh mazal bachayim, `aval `asur lismokh 'al hamazal ve`asur lihiyot frayer** ⑫**.**
His motto: you need luck in life, but it is forbidden to rely on luck and it is forbidden to be a sucker.

15 **Ve'akhshav kulanu beyachad: 'Lanu hanitzachon!** ⑬
And now all *(all-of-us)* together: 'Victory is ours!

Notes

⑫ **frayer** פְרַאיֶר *sucker, dupe*. This slang word is commonly used by Israelis. If you insist on paying the full price when you

10 הֵרִים אֶת הַקְבוּצָה מִכְּלוּם וְנָתַן לַשַּׂחְקָנִים בִּטָּחוֹן עַצְמִי.

11 וְעוֹד דָּבָר חָשׁוּב: אִישׁ עֲסָקִים, עָשִׁיר מְאֹד, מִילְיוֹנֶר, קָנָה אֶת הַקְבוּצָה.

12 הוּא גֶּבֶר צָעִיר וְנִמְרָץ. פֶּה גָּדוֹל וְאֶגוֹ עוֹד יוֹתֵר גָּדוֹל.

13 הַהַצְלָחָה לֹא מְסַחְרֶרֶת אוֹתוֹ. רֶגַע אַתָּה לְמַעְלָה וְרֶגַע אַתָּה לְמַטָּה. צָרִיךְ לַעֲבוֹד, לַעֲבוֹד וְלַעֲבוֹד!

14 הַמּוֹטִיב שֶׁלוֹ: צָרִיךְ מַזָּל בַּחַיִּים, אֲבָל אָסוּר לִסְמוֹךְ עַל הַמַּזָּל וְאָסוּר לִהְיוֹת פְרַאיֶר!

15 וְעַכְשָׁו כּוּלָנוּ בְּיַחַד: "לָנוּ הַנִּצָּחוֹן!

could get a discount, or wait patiently in line while others skip to the front, someone may well say to you **`al tihyeh frayer** אַל תִּהְיֶה פְרַאיֶר *don't be a sucker*, or, if you are a woman: **`al tihyi frayerit** אַל תִּהְיִי פְרַאיֶרִית (plural: **frayerim** פְרַאיֶרִים and **frayeriyot** פְרַאיֶרִיּוֹת). Note that the first letter of this word does not have a point and is pronounced *f*. This can only occur in words borrowed from other languages (in this case, Russian via Yiddish).

⑬ **Lanu hanitzachon!** לָנוּ הַנִּצָּחוֹן! *Victory is ours!* This slogan was made famous by the Hebrew translation of Handel's oratorio **Yehudah hamakabi** יְהוּדָה הַמַּכַּבִּי *Judas Maccabeus*.

16 **Hagavi'a hu shelanu!’** ⑭
The cup is ours!’

Notes

⑭ **Hagavi'a hu shelanu!** !הַגָּבִיעַ הוּא שֶׁלָּנוּ *The cup is ours!* The pronoun **hu** הוּא *it*, *he* refers back to the masculine noun

Targil rishon – Targem תַּרְגִּיל רִאשׁוֹן – תַּרְגֵּם

❶ מי הוא המורה הטוב? זה שנותן ביטחון עצמי לתלמידים.
Mi hu hamoreh hatov? Zeh shenoten bitachon 'atzmi latalmidim.

❷ לטלפונים העכשוויים אין חוטים ואין אסימונים.
Latelefonim ha'akhshaviyim `eyn chutim ve`eyn `asimonim.

❸ מאז שיש לה תעודה מהטכניון, נפתח לה חלון ההזדמנויות.
Me`az sheyesh lah te'udah mehatekhniyon, niftach lah chalon hahizdamnuyot.

❹ כל הכבוד! בלי מהפך, עקב בצד אגודל הצלחתם להגיע לפסגת הליגה.
Kol hakavod! Bli mahapakh, 'aqev betzad `agudal hitzlachtem lehagi'a lefisgat haligah.

❺ הוא מאמן נמרץ ואפשר לסמוך עליו.
Hu me`amen nimratz ve`efshar lismokh 'alav.

gavi'a *cup.* This phrase would make sense even if the **hu** were left out, but this form is more emphatic and poetic.

Answers to Exercise 1

❶ Who is the good teacher? The one *(this)* who gives the students self-confidence. ❷ Contemporary telephones do not have wires and do not have tokens. ❸ Since she has a certificate from the Technion, a window of opportunity has opened for her. ❹ Well done *(All the-honour)*! Without an upheaval, step by step *(heel by toe)*, you succeeded in reaching the top of the league. ❺ He is a dynamic coach and he can be relied on *(possible to-rely on-him)*.

לטלפונים העכשויים אין חוטים ואין אסימונים.

Targil sheni – Hashlem   תַּרְגִּיל שֵׁנִי – הַשְׁלֵם

❶ The beautiful woman dazed him *(makes-dizzy the-head).*
[...], hayefefiyah, [...] lo `et ha[...].

____ , היפיפיה, ______ לו את ה___ .

❷ The director demands excellence at work, but talks to the workers as equals *(at-level the-eyes).*
Hamankalit [...] [...] ba'avodah, `aval medaberet 'im ha'ovdim [...] [...].

המנכלית _____ _______ בעבודה, אבל מדברת עם העובדים _____ ______ .

❸ After the victory in the European championship *(championship-of Europe)*, we walked with the cup through *(in)* the streets of the city.
`Acharey [...] ba`alifut `Eyropah, halakhnu 'im ha[...] birechovot ha[...].

אחרי ______ באליפות אירופה, הלכנו עם ה____ ברחובות ה___ .

❹ It takes *(It[impers. subj.] needs)* courage to ride *(to-travel)* with this driver, because he always takes *(travels in-)* shortcuts *(of path).*
[...] [...] linso'a 'im hanehag hazeh, ki hu nose'a be[...] [...].

____ ____ לנסוע עם הנהג הזה, כי הוא נוסע ב_____ ___ .

❺ He has high self-esteem and a big mouth; he's no *(not)* sucker.
Yesh lo [...] [...] gvohah ufeh gadol; hu lo [...].

יש לו _____ _____ גבוהה ופה גדול; הוא לא _____ .

Answers to Exercise 2

❶ **Ha`ishah – mesachreret – rosh** האשה - מסחררת - ראש ❶

❷ **– doreshet metzuyanut – begovah ha'eynayim**
- דורשת מצוינות - בגובה העיניים ❷

❸ **– hanitzachon – gavi'a – 'ir** - הנצחון - גביע - עיר ❸

❹ **Tzarikh `ometz – qitzurey derekh** צריך אומץ - קיצורי דרך ❹

❺ **– ha'arakhah 'atzmit – frayer** - הערכה עצמית - פראייר ❺

Makhon Vingeyt מַכוֹן וִינגֵייט Wingate Institute. *The Wingate Institute, Israel's National Centre for Physical Education and Sport, is situated close to the sea, just a few miles south of Netanya, near the coastal highway from Tel Aviv to Haifa. The large campus includes gymnasiums, swimming pools, tennis courts, sports fields, laboratories and libraries. Top-notch Israeli athletes train here ahead of international competitions. The institute also trains coaches, physiotherapists and sports teachers for schools, and specializes in sport psychology. Founded in 1957, the institute is named after a British army officer who spent three years in Palestine a few years before Israel's independence. He introduced new training methods in sport and was a strong supporter of the Zionist cause. He became known by the nickname* **Hayadid** הַיָּדִיד the friend. *Wingate died in an airplane accident in India in 1944.*

Second wave: lesson 24

74 Seventy-fourth lesson
(Shi'ur shiv'im ve`arba')

`Ima yeqarah li ...
Dear Mother *(Mother dear to-me)*

1 – **Halo, `ima? Shalom `ima! `Ani yekholah lehavi `elayikh ① `et hayeladim? `Ani yotzet ha'erev.**
Hello, Mom? Hi, Mom! Can I bring the children to you? I'm going out this evening *(the-evening)*.

2 – **`At shuv yotzet? 'Im chaver chadash? 'Od batlan ②?**
You're going out again? With a new boyfriend? Another layabout?

3 – **Nakhon. Yesh li chaver chadash, `aval hu lo batlan.**
Correct. I do have a new boyfriend, but he isn't a layabout.

4 – **`Ani lo mevinah lamah hitgarasht ③ miba'alekh. Hu `adam metzuyan.**
I don't understand why you divorced your husband *(from-your-husband)*. He's an excellent person.

Notes

① **`elayikh** אֵלַיִךְ *to you, toward you* (fem. sing). The preposition **`el** אֶל *to, toward* appears here with the second-person feminine singular suffix. In the next review lesson we'll present the full declension of this preposition.

אִמָּא יְקָרָה לִי

1 – הַלּוֹ, אִמָּא? שָׁלוֹם אִמָּא! אֲנִי יְכוֹלָה לְהָבִיא אֵלַיִךְ אֶת הַיְלָדִים? אֲנִי יוֹצֵאת הָעֶרֶב.

2 – אַתְּ שׁוּב יוֹצֵאת? עִם חָבֵר חָדָשׁ? עוֹד בַּטְלָן?

3 – נָכוֹן. יֵשׁ לִי חָבֵר חָדָשׁ, אֲבָל הוּא לֹא בַּטְלָן.

4 – אֲנִי לֹא מְבִינָה לָמָּה הִתְגָּרַשְׁתְּ מִבַּעֲלֵךְ. הוּא אָדָם מְצוּיָּן.

② **batlan** בַּטְלָן *layabout*, *bum*. The root is בטל, and we've already learned quite a few words with the suffix ָן, which indicates a person or object that serves a particular function (or in this case, no function!). Some examples are **mazgan** מַזְגָן *air-conditioner* (lesson 68) and **balyan** בַּלְיָן *socialite* (see note 4).

③ **hitgarasht** הִתְגָּרַשְׁתְּ *you got divorced* (fem.). The prefix **hit** הִת signifies the reciprocal nature of the action – to divorce each other. In line 5, the infinitive form of the verb is used, still with the reciprocal **hit** הִת prefix.

5 – Zeh hu sheratzah lehitgaresh. `At yoda'at shehu balyan ④ yadu'a.
He's the one who wanted *(This he that-wanted)* to get divorced. You know that he's a well-known socialite.

6 – Ve`at lo balyanit? Yotzet 'im hashlumiel ⑤ hazeh!
And you're not a socialite? Going out with this bungler!

7 – `Ima, `eykh `at medaberet! `At `afilu lo makirah `oto.
Mom, how can you say that *(how you speak)*! You don't even know him.

8 – Gever sheyotze 'im grushah, `ima liyeladim, hu lo-yutzlach ⑥ vetinoq megudal ⑦ shemechapes `ima!
A man who goes out with a divorced woman, a mother of children, is a good-for-nothing and an overgrown baby looking for a mother!

9 – `Ima, `ani lo `avi `et hayeladim. `Ani lo `etze ha'erev! Lehishtame'a ⑧!
Mom, I won't bring the children. I won't go out this evening! Speak to you soon *(To-hear-each-other)*!

Notes

④ **balyan** בַּלְיָן *socialite, party-goer* (**balyanit** in the feminine). From the root בלה, the verb **levalot** לְבַלּוֹת means *to wear out*, but also *to spend time* or *to have a good time*. In lesson 39, we saw the expression **tevalu bane'imim** תְּבַלּוּ בַּנְּעִימִים *Have a good time!* A related word from the same root is **biluy** בִּלּוּי *pastime, entertainment*.

⑤ **shlumi`el** שְׁלוּמִיאֵל *idler*. This uncomplimentary word is of Yiddish origin.

5 – זֶה הוּא שֶׁרָצָה לְהִתְגָּרֵשׁ. אַתְּ יוֹדַעַת שֶׁהוּא בַּלְיָן יָדוּעַ.

6 – וְאַתְּ לֹא בַּלְיָנִית? יוֹצֵאת עִם הַשְּׁלוּמִיאֵל הַזֶּה!

7 – אִמָּא, אֵיךְ אַתְּ מְדַבֶּרֶת! אַתְּ אֲפִילוּ לֹא מַכִּירָה אוֹתוֹ.

8 – גֶּבֶר שֶׁיּוֹצֵא עִם גְּרוּשָׁה, אִמָּא לִילָדִים, הוּא לֹא יוּצְלַח וְתִינוֹק מְגוּדָל שֶׁמְּחַפֵּשׂ אִמָּא!

9 – אִמָּא אֲנִי לֹא אָבִיא אֶת הַיְלָדִים. אֲנִי לֹא אֵצֵא הָעֶרֶב! לְהִשְׁתַּמֵּעַ!

⑥ **lo-yutzlach** לֹא יוּצְלַח *good-for-nothing.* The Hebrew literally means 'not he-will-be-a-success' and comes from the Bible (Jeremiah 22:30). In lesson 57, we learned the word **hatzlachah** הַצְלָחָה *success.* Signs on the way out of towns wish drivers **derekh tzlechah** דֶּרֶךְ צְלֵחָה 'successful way', i.e. *bon voyage* or *have a safe trip.*

⑦ **megudal** מְגֻדָּל *overgrown.* Hopefully you're getting used to identifying the roots in new words. This word, of course, comes from the root גדל, as does **gadol** גָּדוֹל *big.*

⑧ **lehishtame'a** לְהִשְׁתַּמֵּעַ 'to hear each other'. This is the less common version of the greeting **lehitra`ot** לְהִתְרָאוֹת 'to see each other' (*See you!*). It is mainly used to end a telephone conversation. Since people talking on the phone do not see each other (unless it's a video call), Israelis feel it makes more sense to end the conversation with the wish that they will hear each other again. In English we'd probably say 'Speak to you soon' or 'Hope to hear from you again soon'. Here we see another reciprocal prefix – **hish**: **lishmo'a** לִשְׁמוֹעַ *to hear*; **lehishtame'a** לְהִשְׁתַּמֵּעַ *to hear each other.*

10 – **Chaki, `al tenatqi! Mah yihyeh? `At `af-pa'am ⑨ lo yotzet! `Im lo tetz`i, lo titchatni pa'am shniyah!**

Wait, don't hang up *(not you-will-disconnect)*!
What will happen? You never go out! If you don't *(will not)* go out, you won't get married again *(time second)*!

Notes

⑨ `af-pa'am אַף פַּעַם *never* consists of the negative particle `af אַף and the noun pa'am פַּעַם *time*, so the expression means

תַּרְגִּיל רִאשׁוֹן – תַּרְגֵּם   Targil rishon – Targem

❶ אֵיזוֹ מַתָּנָה אֶפְשָׁר לְהָבִיא לְמִי שֶׁיֵּשׁ לוֹ כְּבָר הַכֹּל?
`Eyzo matanah `efshar lehavi lemi sheyesh lo kvar hakol?

❷ אָבִיא אֵלַיִךְ אֶת הַבָּנִים מָחָר אַחֲרֵי הַצָּהֳרַיִם.
`Avi `elayikh `et habanim machar `acharey hatzohorayim.

❸ הוּא מַמָּשׁ תִּינוֹק מְגֻדָּל עִם מִשְׂחֲקֵי הַוִּידֵאוֹ שֶׁלּוֹ.
Hu mamash tinoq megudal 'im mischaqey havide'o shelo.

❹ הוּא שְׁלוּמִיאֵל יָדוּעַ: יֵשׁ לוֹ שְׁתֵּי יָדַיִם שְׂמָאלִיּוֹת.
Hu shlumi`el yadu'a: yesh lo shtey yadayim smaliyot.

❺ אַתְּ יוֹצֵאת עִם הַבַּלְיָן הֶחָתִיךְ הַזֶּה? תִּבְלִי בְּנַעֲלַיִם!
`At yotzet 'im habalyan hachatikh hazeh? Tevali bane'imim!

10 – חֲכִּי, אַל תְּנַתְּקִי! מַה יִּהְיֶה? אַתְּ אַף פַּעַם לֹא יוֹצֵאת! אִם לֹא תֵּצְאִי, לֹא תִּתְחַתְּנִי פַּעַם שְׁנִיָּה! □

'no time' or 'not even one time'. A similar construction is **`af `echad** אַף אֶחָד *no one*. The word **pa'am** פַּעַם comes from the same root as **lif'om** לִפְעוֹם *to beat* (only in the sense of the heart beating).

Answers to Exercise 1

❶ What present is it possible to bring to someone who already has everything *(that-there-is already the-all)*? ❷ I will bring the boys to you tomorrow afternoon. ❸ He is really an overgrown baby with his video games. ❹ He's a well-known bungler: he has two left hands. ❺ You're going out with this hunky socialite? Have a good time!

אביא אליך את הבנים מחר
אחרי הצהרים.

Targil sheni – Hashlem — תַּרְגִּיל שֵׁנִי – הַשְׁלֵם

❶ You are already thirty-four. When will you get married?
`At kvar bat [...] [...]. Matay [...]?

את כבר בת ______ ______ . מתי ______?

❷ It is not true *(correct)* that every socialite is also a layabout.
Zeh [...] shekol [...] hu gam [...].

זה __ ____ שכל ____ הוא גם ____.

❸ They do not know how to solve the work problems of their son, the good-for-nothing.
Hem lo yod'im `eykh [...] `et be'ayot [...] shel bnam [...] [...].

הם לא יודעים איך _____ את בעיות ______ של בנם ___ _____.

❹ Even if you have divorced your husband, do not cut off *(you will-not-cut-off)* the children from their father.
[...] `im hitgarasht miba'alekh, [...] [...] `et hayeladim [...] shelahem.

_____ אם התגרשת מבעלך, __ _____ את הילדים ____ שלהם.

❺ Do you know Ruty, the beautiful socialite? The one they write about *(That-they[impers. subj.]-write about-her)* in the newspapers?
`At [...] `et Ruti, [...] [...]? Shekotvim [...] [...]?

את _____ את רותי, _______ ____? שכותבים ____ - _______?

Answers to Exercise 2

❶ – **shloshim ve`arba' – titchatni** ❶ - שלושים וארבע - תתחתני

❷ – **lo nakhon – balyan – batlan** ❷ - לא נכון - בליין - בטלן

❸ – **liftor – ha'avodah – halo-yutzlach**
❸ - לפתור - העבודה - הלא-יוצלח

❹ **`Afilu – `al tenatqi – me`aba –** ❹ אפילו - אל תנתקי - מאבא -

❺ – **makirah – habalyanit hayafah – 'aleyha ba'itonim**
❺ - מכירה - הבליינית היפה - עליה בעתונים

In Israel, the only weddings recognized by the state are religious ceremonies, according to the religious community to which the individuals belong. In the case of Jewish Israelis, only Orthodox ceremonies are recognized. However, any marriage approved by the authorities of another country will be recognized by the civil authorities in Israel for the purpose of economic and legal rights. Each religious community in Israel (Jews, Muslims, Druze and several different Christian denominations) has its own religious court that holds exclusive powers in the field of marriage and divorce. However, under Israeli law, polygamy is not permitted in any religious community.

The following are some terms related to Jewish weddings. By the way, weddings in Israel usually take place in banqueting halls or other indoor or outdoor settings, and only rarely in the synagogue. The rabbi comes to the venue to perform the religious part of the ceremony.

• **Miqveh** מִקְוֶה ritual bath. *The groom comes to the* **miqveh** *on the day before the wedding. The* **miqveh** *is a pool of free-flowing water from a natural source, such as a river, rainwater, or even seawater. Women may also visit the* **miqveh** *as part of the Jewish laws of ritual purity. For people who choose to convert to Judaism, the visit to the* **miqveh** *forms an important part of the ritual.*

• **Qidushin** קִידוּשִׁין marriage, *literally, 'sanctifications' (*ין *is the Aramaic equivalent of the Hebrew masculine plural ending* ים*). From the root* קדש*, which carries meanings of* sacred, holy, *this word emphasizes the sacred and serious nature of marriage, before the wining and dining begin.*

• **Chupah** חוּפָּה wedding canopy. *During the short religious ceremony, the couple stand under a canopy consisting of four poles supporting a spread-out* **talit** prayer shawl. *It has been suggested that this frail structure carries the message that it is up to the couple to build a stable and lasting union.*
• **Taba'at nisu`im** טַבַּעַת נִשּׂוּאִים wedding ring. *The groom places a ring on the bride's finger and recites the following words:* **Harey `at mequdeshet li betaba'at zo kedat Mosheh veYisra`el** הֲרֵי אַתְּ מְקוּדֶּשֶׁת לִי בְּטַבַּעַת זוֹ כְּדַת מֹשֶׁה וְיִשְׂרָאֵל You are

75 Seventy-fifth lesson
(Shi'ur shiv'im vechamesh)

Re`ayon baradyo
Interview on the radio

1 **Hamera`ayenet ①: Tzohorayim tovim! Hayom yesh lanu `orachat meyuchedet, hadugmanit ② Yafit Noy.**
The interviewer: Good day *(Noon good)*! Today we have a special guest, the model Yafit Noy.

2 **`Anachnu baradyo, lakhen `ani `omeret lakhem: Yafit, kishmah ken hi ③!**
We [are] on *(in)* the radio, so I am telling you: Yafit is as her name [implies]!

Notes

① **mera`ayenet** מְרַאֲיֶינֶת *interviewer* (feminine). Like the English word 'view', the Hebrew is related to the idea of seeing, and comes from the root ראה.

② **dugmanit** דוּגמָנִית *model* (feminine). The masculine form is **dugman** דוּגמָן. Other words from the root דגם include **dugmah** דוּגמָה *example* and **degem** דֶּגֶם *model* (i.e. a reproduction of something).

consecrated to me by this ring, according to the Law of Moses and Israel. *Jewish tradition does not require the bride to give the groom a ring, but there is no prohibition against this.*

• **Ketubah** כְּתוּבָּה wedding contract. *This document, traditionally decorated and illuminated, is handed to the newly wed woman at the end of the ceremony. The* **Ketubah** *guarantees the woman's financial rights in the event of divorce. As you may have recognized, this word comes from the root* כתב to write.

Second wave: lesson 25

---

75 שִׁעוּר שִׁבְעִים וְחָמֵשׁ

רְאָיוֹן בְּבַרְדִיו

1 הַמְרַאֲיֶנֶת – צָהֳרַיִם טוֹבִים! הַיּוֹם יֵשׁ לָנוּ אוֹרַחַת מְיוּחֶדֶת: הַדּוּגְמָנִית יָפִית נוֹי.

2 אֲנַחְנוּ בְּבַרְדִיו, לָכֵן אֲנִי אוֹמֶרֶת לָכֶם: יָפִית, כִּשְׁמָהּ כֵּן הִיא!

③ **kishmah ken hi** כִּשְׁמָהּ כֵּן הִיא literally, 'like-her-name so she [is]'. The interviewer makes this comment because the root of the name **Yafit** is **yafah** יָפָה *beautiful*. In English we might say 'Yafit by name, yafit by nature'. The first word in this construction consists of **k-** כְּ *like*, followed by **shem** שֵׁם *name* with the third-person feminine singular possessive suffix **ah** ־ָהּ, then **ken** כֵּן, which here means *so*, and finally **hi** הִיא *she* – i.e. *she is*. In case you need reminding that the interviewee is beautiful, her family name, **Noy** נוֹי, means *beauty*, *ornament*.

3 **Yafit va`ani makirot zo `et zo ke`ilu hayinu chaverot le`oto qrem lachut miyamim yamimah ④.**
Yafit and I know each other as if we were friends [using] the same moisturizing cream since way back.

4 **Hi dugmanit tzameret, yefeyfiyah 'im qabalot ⑤, figurah teflonit ⑥.**
She is a top-ranking model, a certified beauty *(beautiful with receipts)* [with] a Teflon figure.

5 **Todah lakh, Yafit, shematzat zman lavo `eleynu beyn shney `avironim.**
Thank you, Yafit, for finding *(that-you-have-found)* time to come to us 'between two airplanes'.

6 **Mah hadavar she`at hakhi ⑦ `ohevet ba'avodatekh?**
What is the thing *(that-)* you most like about *(in)* your work?

7 – **Linso'a, lehakir `anashim chadashim, lilmod safot.**
To travel, to meet new people, to learn languages.

8 – **`Aval be'etzem ⑧, mi at? Mah `at `ohevet?**
But actually *(in-essence)*, who are you? What do you like?

Notes

④ **miyamim yamimah** מִיָּמִים יָמִימָה *for ever* – a poetic turn of phrase that is usually used in a positive sense to talk about the way something has always been.

⑤ **qabalot** קַבָּלוֹת *receipts*, from the verb **leqabel** לְקַבֵּל *to receive*. The colloquial expression **'im qabalot** ('with

3 יָפִית וַאֲנִי מַכִּירוֹת זוֹ אֶת זוֹ כְּאִילוּ הָיִינוּ חֲבֵרוֹת לְאוֹתוֹ קֶרֶם לַחוּת מִיָּמִים יָמִימָה.

4 הִיא דוּגמָנִית צַמֶּרֶת, יְפֵהפִיָּה עִם קַבָּלוֹת, פִיגוּרָה טֶפלוֹנִית.

5 תוֹדָה לָךְ, יָפִית, שֶׁמָּצָאת זמַן לָבוֹא אֵלֵינוּ בֵּין שְׁנֵי אֲוִירוֹנִים.

6 מַה הַדָּבָר שֶׁאַת הֲכִי אוֹהֶבֶת בַּעֲבוֹדָתֵךְ?

7 – לִנסוֹעַ, לְהַכִּיר אֲנָשִׁים חֲדָשִׁים, לִלמוֹד שָׂפוֹת.

8 – אֲבָל בְּעֶצֶם, מִי אַת? מַה אַת אוֹהֶבֶת?

receipts') is used to emphasize an adjective or epithet – a 'certified' beauty, a beauty with the receipts to prove it ...

⑥ **teflonit** טֶפלוֹנִית *Teflon*, *made of Teflon* – the interviewer creatively uses this expression to refer to someone who is slim (because, like Teflon, fat doesn't stick to them!).

⑦ **hakhi** הֲכִי *the most*, a more colloquial alternative for **beyoter**, which we saw in lesson 32.

⑧ **be'etzem** בְּעֶצֶם *in essence*, *in fact* (**'etzem** עֶצֶם *bone*). In lessons 67 and 70, we saw **be'atzmo** בְּעַצמוֹ *by himself* ('by-bone-of-himself') – this idea of self-reliance can also be seen in **Yom ha'atzma`ut** יוֹם הָעַצמָאוּת *Independence Day*. The Hebrew word for *noun* is **shem 'etzem**, literally, 'name-of bone' or 'name-of essence'.

9 – **Mah `ani `ohevet? `Ani metorefet** ⑨ **'al shoqolad, mishtaga'at 'al `okhel sini,**
What do I like? I'm crazy about chocolate, mad about Chinese food,

10 **mekhurah** ⑩ **lejins, me`ohevet** ⑪ **bemusiqat pop, qshurah lahorim sheli, ve …**
addicted to jeans, in love with pop music, close *(attached)* to my parents, and ...

11 – **Mah hadavar shehakhi metaskel `otakh?**
What is the thing that most frustrates you?

12 – **`Ani lo mechuberet** ⑫ **leshum maqom** ⑬**, tasah mikan** ⑭ **lesham umisham lekhan,**
I am not connected to any place, [I] fly from here to there and from there to here,

13 **`ani rotzah lihiyot mequba'at** ⑮ **bemaqom echad.**
I want to be fixed in one place.

Notes

⑨ **metorefet** מְטוֹרֶפֶת *crazy* (fem.). The masculine form of this adjective is **metoraf** מְטוֹרָף. A verb from the same root is **litrof** לִטרוֹף *to mix*, *to beat* (eggs), *to shuffle* (cards).

⑩ **mekhurah** מְכוּרָה *addicted*: the feminine singular form of the past participle of the verb לְמַכֵּר *to addict* or *to be addictive*.

⑪ **me`ohevet be …** מְאוֹהֶבֶת בְּ … *in love with*. Note the preposition that is used with this adjective, as it isn't the one we would use in English.

⑫ **mechuberet** מְחוּבֶּרֶת *connected*, *linked*, *joined*. The root חבר also gives us the words **chaver** חָבֵר *friend* and **mechaber** מְחַבֵּר *author*. The connection is that a friend is someone to whom we are linked, while an author joins words together to form longer texts. Three other useful nouns from this root are **machberet** מַחבֶּרֶת *exercise book*, **choveret** חוֹבֶרֶת *booklet*, and חֶבְרָה **chevra** *company*.

9 – מַה אֲנִי אוֹהֶבֶת? אֲנִי מְטוֹרֶפֶת עַל שׁוֹקוֹלָד, מִשְׁתַּגַּעַת עַל אוֹכֶל סִינִי,

10 מְכוּרָה לְג'ינס, מְאוֹהֶבֶת בְּמוּסִיקַת פּוֹפּ, קְשׁוּרָה לָהוֹרִים שֶׁלִּי, וְ...

11 – מַה הַדָּבָר שֶׁהֲכִי מְתַסכֵּל אוֹתָךְ?

12 – אֲנִי לֹא מְחוּבֶּרֶת לְשׁוּם מָקוֹם, טָסָה מִכָּאן לְשָׁם וּמִשָּׁם לְכָאן,

13 אֲנִי רוֹצָה לִהְיוֹת מְקוּבַּעַת בְּמָקוֹם אֶחָד.

⑬ **leshum maqom** לְשׁוּם מָקוֹם *to any place* – literally, 'to no place'. Unlike English, Hebrew uses double negatives, so Yafit's comment literally translates to 'I am not connected to no place'. **shum** שׁוּם is an invariable particle used to form negative expressions: **shum davar** שׁוּם דָּבָר *nothing*, **shum maqom** שׁוּם מָקוֹם *nowhere*. We've already learned a similar particle, **`af** אַף. **`af maqom** אַף מָקוֹם also means *nowhere*, while **`af `echad** אַף אֶחָד is *no one*.

⑭ **mikan** מִכָּאן *from here*. **kan** כָּאן *here* is of Talmudic origin. Another word for *here* is **poh** פֹּה, which comes from Biblical Hebrew. Both words are used more or less interchangeably.

⑮ **mequba'at** מְקוּבַּעַת *attached*, *fixed*, *settled*: a feminine singular adjective from the verb **liqbo'a** לִקְבּוֹעַ *to fix*, as in to affix something in place. The adjective can also mean *fixated*. The Hebrew phrase for *tenure* is **qvi'ut ba'avodah** קְבִיעוּת בַּעֲבוֹדָה.

14 – `Ani mevinah, `at bodedah batzameret.
I understand, you are lonely at the top.

15 – Ken, vesham yesh lif'amim scharchoret.
Yes, and sometimes it gets dizzy there *(and-there there-is sometimes dizziness)*.

Targil rishon – Targem תַּרְגִּיל רִאשׁוֹן – תַּרְגֵּם

❶ הוא חולה ולפעמים יש לו סחרחורת.
Hu choleh velif'amim yesh lo scharchoret.

❷ סדר היום של רותי מתסכל את בעלה, כי היא מכורה לעבודה.
Seder hayom shel Ruti metaskel `et ba'alah, ki hi mekhurah la'avodah.

❸ את קשורה אליו או את מאוהבת בו? זה לא אותו דבר.
`At qshurah `elav `o `at me`uhevet bo? Zeh lo `oto davar.

❹ היא מראיינת הצמרת של תחנת הרדיו.
Hi mera`ayenet hatzameret shel tachanat haradyo.

❺ מה שמה של היפהפיה שם? זאת עם הפיגורה הטלפונית!
Mah shmah shel hayefehfiyah sham? Zot 'im hafigurah hateflonit!

14 – אֲנִי מְבִינָה, אַת בּוֹדְדָה בַּצַּמֶּרֶת.

15 – כֵּן, וְשָׁם יֵשׁ לִפְעָמִים סחַרחוֹרֶת. □

Answers to Exercise 1

❶ He is ill and sometimes he is dizzy *(has dizziness).* ❷ Ruti's daily routine frustrates her husband, because she is addicted to work. ❸ Are you attached to him or are you in love with him? It's not the same thing. ❹ She is the top interviewer at the radio station. ❺ What is the name of that beautiful [woman] there? The one with the Teflon figure!

סדר היום של רותי מתסכל את בעלה, כי היא מכורה לעבודה.

Targil sheni – Hashlem   תַּרְגִּיל שֵׁנִי – הַשְׁלֵם

❶ The humidity in the summer in Tel Aviv is very tiring.
Ha[...] ba[...] beTel-Aviv me'ayefet [...].

ה____ ב___ בתל אביב מעיפת ____ .

❷ What is all this nonsense *(all nonsenses these)*? What are they actually talking about *(About what in-essence they speak)* in this interview?
Mah kol [...] ha`eleh? 'Al mah [...] hem medabrim [...] hazeh?

מה כל _______ האלה? על מה ____ הם מדברים
______ הזה?

❸ A guest came *(to us)* for a weekend, but she has been with us *(is at ours)* now *(already)* [for] two weeks!
Ba`ah [...] `orachat lesof [...] `aval hi [...] kvar shvu'ayim!

באה _____ אורחת לסוף ____ אבל היא _____ כבר
שבועיים!

❹ The fashion photographer photographs the model *(fem.)* on the beach in Netanya.
[...] ha[...] metzalem `et ha[...] bechof hayam biNetanyah.

___ ה_____ מצלם את ה_______ בחוף הים בנתניה.

❺ Yael is a real *(big)* socialite, not tied to any place, and actually very lonely.
Yael [...] gdolah, lo [...] be`af maqom, uve'etzem hi [...] me`od.

יעל ______ גדולה, לא ______ באף מקום, ובעצם היא
_____ מאוד.

Answers to Exercise 2

❶ – **lachut – qayitz – me`od** ❶ - לחות - קיץ - מאוד

❷ – **hashtuyot – be'etzem – bare`ayon –** ❷ - השטויות - בעצם - בראיון -

❸ – **`eleynu – shvu'a – `etzlenu –** ❸ - עלינו - שבוע - אצלנו -

❹ **Tzalam – `ofnah – dugmanit –** ❹ צלם - אופנה - דוגמנית -

❺ – **balyanit – mequba'at – bodedah –** ❺ - בלינית - מקובעת - בודדה

Most Israelis are avid media consumers, listening to hourly radio news broadcasts and watching news and current affairs programs on television in the evenings. The main daily newspapers are **Yedi'ot `Aharonot** יְדִיעוֹת אַחֲרוֹנוֹת Latest News, **Ha`aretz** הָאָרֶץ The Land, *and* **Ma'ariv** מַעֲרִיב Evening Prayer. *The English-language* **Jerusalem Post** *is popular with visitors and English-speaking immigrants.*

Qol Israel קוֹל יִשְׂרָאֵל The Voice of Israel *provides a number of radio stations, broadcasting news, music and other programs. The Israel Defense Forces broadcasts* **Galey Tzahal** גַּלֵּי צַהַ"ל, *which is popular with many Israelis, not only those serving in the army. There are also radio stations in Arabic, Russian and other languages, as well as a large number of private stations, including many broadcasting to the religious and ultra-Orthodox Jewish populations. A large number of television stations are available, using* cable **kevel** כֶּבֶל *or satellite technology. The wide choice of* **'arutzim** עֲרוּצִים channels *(singular,* **'arutz** עָרוּץ channel*) broadcast programs made in Israel for every possible taste and audience, as well as imported programs, mainly from the US and Britain.*

Second wave: lesson 26

76 Seventy-sixth lesson
(Shi'ur shiv'im veshesh)

Salat yeraqot ①
Vegetable salad

1 **`Afilu `im `eynkhem ② tzimchonim, tehanu ③ mehasalat shelanu.**
Even if you are not vegetarians, you will enjoy *(from)* our salad.

2 **Hu ta'im, tziv'oni, veha'iqar, qal ④ lehakhanah.**
It is tasty, colourful and, above all *(and-the-main-thing)*, easy to prepare *(easy for-preparation)*.

3 **`Im yesh lakhem qe'arah gdolah, qeresh chitukh vesakin, `atem me`urganim.**
If you have a large bowl, a chopping board and a knife, you are ready *(organized)*.

4 **Shloshah gzarim mequlafim umegurarim,**
Three carrots, peeled and grated,

5 **'aley chasah chatukhim liretzu'ot daqot,**
lettuce leaves chopped into thin strips,

6 **melafefonim, 'agvaniyot ufilpelim chatukhim lequbiyot,**
cucumbers, tomatoes and peppers chopped into cubes,

Notes

① **yeraqot** יְרָקוֹת *vegetables*; the singular is **yereq**. This noun is related to the adjective **yaroq** יָרוֹק *green* (like the English word 'greens' for vegetables), but it refers to vegetables of any colour.

סָלָט יְרָקוֹת

1 אֲפִילוּ אִם אֵינְכֶם צִמְחוֹנִים, תֵּהָנוּ מֵהַסָּלָט שֶׁלָּנוּ.

2 הוּא טָעִים, צִבְעוֹנִי, וְהָעִקָּר, קַל לַהֲכָנָה.

3 אִם יֵשׁ לָכֶם קְעָרָה גדולָה, קֶרֶשׁ חִתּוּךְ וְסַכִּין, אַתֶּם מְאוּרְגָּנִים.

4 שְׁלוֹשָׁה גְזָרִים מְקוּלָּפִים וּמְגוּרָרִים,

5 עֲלֵי חַסָּה חֲתוּכִים לִרְצוּעוֹת דַּקּוֹת,

6 מְלָפְפוֹנִים, עַגְבָנִיּוֹת וּפִלְפְּלִים חֲתוּכִים לְקוּבִּיּוֹת,

② **`eynkhem** אֵינְכֶם *you are not* (masc. pl.). The negative particle **`eyn** אֵין appears here with the second-person masculine plural suffix **khem** כֶם- (because the speaker is addressing a mixed group of people). For the full declension of this particle, see lesson 77.

③ **tehanu** תֵּהָנוּ *you will enjoy* (masc. pl.). The root הנה also appears in the nouns **hana`ah** הֲנָאָה *pleasure* and **nehenatan** נֶהֱנְתָן *hedonist*, among other words.

④ **qal** קַל means both *easy*, as here, and *light* (in weight).

7 **tznoniyot prusot, 'aley batzal yaroq, melafefonim chamutzim ⑤,**
radishes sliced [into rounds], *(leaves-of)* spring onion, pickled cucumbers,

8 **`avoqado bequbiyot, zeytim shchorim viyeruqim megul'anim ⑥.**
avocado in cubes, [and] black and green pitted olives.

9 **Rotev ⑦: mitz limon, shemen ⑧ zayit, melach, pilpel.**
Dressing: lemon juice, olive oil, salt, pepper.

10 **Hosifu yeraqot triyim ⑨ lefi ta'amkhem.**
Add fresh vegetables according to your taste.

11 **Lifney hahagashah, hosifu reychan qatzutz `o shamir qatzutz ufetrozilyah qtzutzah.**
Before serving *(the-serving)*, add chopped basil or chopped dill and chopped parsley.

Notes

⑤ **chamutzim** חֲמוּצִים *pickles, gherkins*, the plural of the masculine singular noun **chamutz**. The nouns **chametz** חָמֵץ *leavened dough* and **chometz** חוֹמֶץ *vinegar* both come from the same root, which is associated with the idea of fermentation in various forms. At **Pessach** פֶּסַח *Passover*, observant Jews remove every trace of **chametz** from the home, in a ritual known as **bediqat chametz** בְּדִיקַת חָמֵץ 'examination-of chametz'. The children have great fun hunting for the last crumbs of bread, some of which have been deliberately placed by their parents to make sure the household is alert.

⑥ **megul'anim** מְגוּלְעָנִים *pitted, stoned* (of olives or other fruit), from the noun **gal'in** גַּלְעִין *pit, stone*. The initial מ indicates a passive form (as in 'has been pitted').

⑦ **rotev** רוֹטֶב *sauce, (salad) dressing*. Other words from the root רטב include **lehartiv** לְהַרְטִיב *to moisten* and **ratuv** רָטוּב *wet*.

7 צְנוֹנִיּוֹת פְּרוּסוֹת, עֲלֵי בָּצָל יָרוֹק, מְלָפְפוֹנִים חֲמוּצִים,

8 אֲבוֹקָדוֹ בְּקוּבִּיּוֹת, זֵיתִים שְׁחוֹרִים וִירוּקִים מְגוּלְעָנִים.

9 רוֹטֶב: מִיץ לִימוֹן, שֶׁמֶן זַיִת, מֶלַח, פִּלְפֵּל.

10 הוֹסִיפוּ יְרָקוֹת טְרִיִּים לְפִי טַעַמְכֶם.

11 לִפְנֵי הַהַגָּשָׁה, הוֹסִיפוּ רֵיחָן קָצוּץ אוֹ שָׁמִיר קָצוּץ וּפֶטְרוֹזִילְיָה קְצוּצָה.

⑧ **shemen** שֶׁמֶן *oil*. Many related words share this root. Some examples include **shamen** שָׁמֵן / **shmenah** שְׁמֵנָה *fat* (m./f. adjective), **shamenet** שַׁמֶּנֶת *cream*, and the verbs **leshamen** לְשַׁמֵּן *to oil, to grease* and **lehashmin** לְהַשְׁמִין *to get fat*.

⑨ **triyim** טְרִיִּים *fresh* (masc. pl.). The singular forms of this adjective are **tari** (masc.) טָרִי and **triyah** (fem.) טְרִיָּה.

12 **Lehagish** ⑩ **`et hasalat 'al yad chumus, tchinah, gvinot.**
Serve the salad alongside hummus, tahini [and] cheeses.

13 **Bete`avon, labri`ut** ⑪**.**
Enjoy, eat in good health! *(In-appetite, to-health!)*

Notes

⑩ **lehagish** לְהָגִּישׁ *to serve* (e.g. food – or a lawsuit!). The root נגש means *to approach, access*. It appears in the verb **lageshet** לָגֶשֶׁת *to approach* and in the adjective **nagish** (masc.) נָגִישׁ / **negishah** (fem.) נְגִישָׁה *accessible, approachable*. A **magash** מַגָּשׁ is a *serving dish*.

Targil rishon – Targem תַּרְגִּיל רִאשׁוֹן – תַּרְגֵּם

❶ אני אוכלת ארוחת צהרים עם חברות מהמשרד במסעדה צמחונית.
`Ani `okhelet `aruchat tzohorayim 'im chaverot mehamisrad bemis'adah tzimchonit.

❷ האם אתם כבר מאורגנים לאליפות השחמט הבינלאומית?
Ha`im `atem kvar me`urganim la`alifut hashachmat habeynle`umit?

❸ עוגת הגזר טעימה, קלה להכנה ומצוינת על יד תה בלימון.
'Ugat hagezer te'imah, qalah lehakhanah umetzuyenet 'al yad teh belimon.

❹ לגבינה לבנה הוסיפו מלפפון חתוך לקוביות ושמיר קצוץ.
Ligvinah levanah hosifu melafefon chatukh lequbiyot veshamir qatzutz.

❺ הוא קנה קרש חיתוך וסכינים כדי לעשות סלטים.
Hu qanah qeresh chitukh vesakinim kedey la'asot salatim.

12 לְהַגִּישׁ אֶת הַסָלָט עַל יָד חוּמוּס, טחִינָה, גבִינוֹת.

□ **13** בְּתֵאָבוֹן, לַבּרִיאוּת.

⑪ **labri`ut** לַבּרִיאוּת literally, 'to [your] health'. If you present food to someone and they thank you, you can reply with **labri`ut**. This phrase is most commonly used as the equivalent of *Bless you* when someone sneezes. The adjective **bari`** בָּרִיא (masc.) and **bri`ah** בְּרִיאָה (fem.) is *healthy*.

Answers to Exercise 1

❶ I eat lunch *(meal-of noon)* with friends from the office at a vegetarian restaurant. ❷ Are you ready *(already organized)* for the international chess championship? ❸ The carrot cake is tasty, easy to prepare and excellent with *(alongside)* lemon tea *(tea in-lemon)*. ❹ To white cheese, add diced cucumber *(cucumber chopped in-cubes)* and chopped dill. ❺ He bought a chopping board and knives to make salads.

Targil sheni – Hashlem תַּרְגִּיל שֵׁנִי – הַשְׁלֵם

❶ This is a tasty and light sauce with fresh tomatoes peeled and chopped into cubes.
Hineh [...] ta'im veqal me[...] triyot [...] vechatukhot le[...].

הנה ___ טעים וקל מ_______ טריות _______ וחתוכות ל______ .

❷ Be daring *(You-will-dare)* [enough] to add grated carrots, fresh orange juice, chopped basil, clementines, salt [and] pepper.
Ta'izu [...] ligzarim [...], mitz [...] tari, [...] qatzutz, qlemantinot, [...] pilpel.

תעיזו ______ לגזרים _______ מיץ ______ טרי, ____ קצוץ, קלמנטינות, ___, פלפל.

❸ You will enjoy eating *(to-eat)* slices of red onion, olive oil *(and)* balsamic vinegar and parsley.
`Atem [...] le`ekhol [...] [...] `adom, [...] zayit ve[...] balzami ufetrozilyah.

אתם ___ לאכול ______ ___ אדום, ___ זית ו____ בלסמי ופטרוזיליה.

❹ At last *(End-end)* you have come out of the hospital: the main thing is [keeping one's] health!
Sof-sof yatzat mi[...] [...]: ha'iqar [...]!

סוף סוף יצאת מ___ ______ : העקר _______!

❺ Perhaps [I can] serve you [some] pickled cucumbers and radish with *(alongside)* lettuce?
`Ulay [...] lakhem melafefonim [...] ve[...] 'al yad ha[...].

אולי _____ לכם מלפפונים ______ ו_______ על יד ה___?

Answers to Exercise 2

❶ – **rotev – 'agvanyot – mequlafot – qubiyot**

❶ - רוטב - אגבניות - מקולפות - קוביות

❷ – **lehosif – megurarim – tapuzim – reychan – melach –**

❷ - להוסיף - מגוררים - תפוזים - ריחן - מלח -

❸ – **tehanu – prusot batzal – shemen – chometz –**

❸ - תהנו - פרוסות בצל - שמן - חומץ -

❹ – **beyt hacholim – habri`ut**

❹ - בית החולים - הבריאות

❺ – **lehagish – chamutzim – tznoniyot – chasah**

❺ - להגיש - חמוצים - צנוניות - חסה

Hachaqla`ut hayisre`elit הַחַקְלָאוּת הַיִשְׂרְאֵלִית Israeli agriculture
Israel suffers from a chronic shortage of water, and arable land is a precious commodity: just 20% of the country is suitable for farming. In 1964, Israel completed the expensive **movil hamayim ha`artzi** מוֹבִיל הַמַיִם הָאַרְצִי national water carrier, *which takes water from sources in the north of the country (from the River Jordan and the* **Kineret** כִּנֶרֶת Sea of Galilee*) south as far as the* **Negev** נֶגֶב. *Researchers at Israeli universities have developed creative techniques for encouraging agriculture in Israel's often difficult conditions, and many of these inventions are now in use around the world.*

Israeli agriculture is also influenced by the dramatic differences in terrain between various parts of the country, despite its small size. **'Emeq Izre`el** עֵמֶק יִזְרְעֶאל the Jezreel Valley *(around the small city of* **'Afulah** עֲפוּלָה*) is known for its rich, fertile soil. Just to the north, the hills of* Galilee, **Galil** גָלִיל, *are green for most of the year. But less than 300 kilometres to the south lies the dramatic crater* **Makhtesh Ramon** מַכתֵשׁ רָמוֹן Ramon Crater *and the* **Negev** *desert. It is difficult to imagine a more hostile setting for agricultural efforts, but an experimental farm in this region takes advantage of the almost endless sunshine to cultivate flowers, fruit and vegetables.*

Second wave: lesson 27

77 Seventy-seventh lesson
(Shi'ur shiv'im vesheva')

חֲזָרָה Chazarah – Review

You've reached the next-to-last review lesson – you've come a long way! The next set of lessons will mark the end of this book, though not, hopefully, the end of your progress in the Hebrew language!

1 Comparative forms

1.1 As ... as ...

In Hebrew, just one *as* is required to form this type of comparison. The preposition **k-** כְּ *as*, *like* is placed before the second part of the comparison:
Hakham kiShlomoh. חָכָם כִּשְׁלֹמֹה. *[As] wise as Solomon.*

In literary Hebrew, sometimes the preposition appears twice in a comparison: **ka'av kaben** כָּאָב כַּבֵּן *like father, like son*. However, this construction is relatively rare.

1.2 More ... than ...

In a similar construction to English, Hebrew uses **yoter** יוֹתֵר *more* before the adjective, and **m-** מ *than* before the second item being compared:
Naty yoter yafeh miDavid. נָתִי יוֹתֵר יָפֶה מִדָּוִד.
Nati [is] more handsome than David.

The **yoter** can sometimes be left out:
Hi tovah mimeni bematematiqah. הִיא טוֹבָה מִמֶּנִּי בְּמָתֵמָטִיקָה.
She is better than I at mathematics. ('She good than-me in-mathematics.')

1.3 Less ... than ...

The construction is the same as the previous one, but instead of **yoter, pachot** פָּחוֹת *less* is used:
Habayit shel hashkhenim pachot gadol mishelanu.
הַבַּיִת שֶׁל הַשְּׁכֵנִים פָּחוֹת גָּדוֹל מִשֶּׁלָּנוּ.
The neighbours' house is smaller than ours. ('The-house of the-neighbours less small than-ours.')

2 Superlative

This form uses the adverb **beyoter** בְּיוֹתֵר *most*, which comes after the adjective:

Hu hatalmid hatov beyoter beveyt hasefer.
הוּא הַתַּלְמִיד הַטּוֹב בְּיוֹתֵר בְּבֵית הַסֵּפֶר.
He is the best student in the school. ('He the-student the-good most in-house-of the-book.')

In colloquial Hebrew, **hakhi** הֲכִי *the most* is often used instead of **beyoter** בְּיוֹתֵר. Sometimes, a construction is used without **beyoter** בְּיוֹתֵר or **hakhi** הֲכִי:

Hi hayafah mikulan. הִיא הַיָּפָה מִכּוּלָּן.
She is the most beautiful of them all. ('She the-beautiful from-all-of-them.')
Hi hachamudah bakitah. הִיא הַחֲמוּדָה בַּכִּתָּה.
She is the cutest in the class. ('She the-cute in-the-class.')

Some adjectives can also be intensified with a particular construction:

yafeh יָפֶה *handsome* → **yefeyfeh** יְפֵהפֶה *very handsome*
yafah יָפָה *beautiful* → **yefeyfiyah** יְפֵהפִיָּה *very beautiful.*

3 Declined propositions

As you know by now, in Hebrew, verbs, nouns and prepositions can all be modified to refer to different persons (masculine/feminine, singular/plural, first-/second-/third-person). Here are the declensions of two very common prepositions:

• **`el** אֶל *to, toward*

`elay	אֵלַי	*toward me*
`eleykha	אֵלֶיךָ	*toward you* (masc. sing.)
`elayikh	אֵלַיִךְ	*toward you* (fem. sing.)
`elav	אֵלָיו	*toward him/it*
`eleyha	אֵלֶיהָ	*toward her/it*

\`eleynu	אֵלֵינוּ	*toward us*
\`aleykhem	אֲלֵיכֶם	*toward you* (masc. pl.)
\`aleykhen	אֲלֵיכֶן	*toward you* (fem. pl.)
\`aleyhem	אֲלֵיהֶם	*toward them* (masc.)
\`aleyhen	אֲלֵיהֶן	*toward them* (fem.)

Note the variations in the initial vowel. Although many Israelis keep the **e** vowel throughout the declension, this is considered incorrect. If you use the 'correct' forms, you may impress your Hebrew-speaking friends!

• **'al** עַל *on*

'alay	עָלַי	*on me*
'aleykha	עָלֶיךָ	*on you* (masc. sing.)
'alayikh	עָלַיִךְ	*on you* (fem. sing.)
'alav	עָלָיו	*on him/it*
'aleyha	עָלֶיהָ	*on her/it*
'aleynu	עָלֵינוּ	*on us*
'aleykhem	עֲלֵיכֶם	*on you* (masc. pl.)
'aleykhen	עֲלֵיכֶן	*on you* (fem. pl.)
'aleyhem	עֲלֵיהֶם	*on them* (masc.)
'aleyhen	עֲלֵיהֶן	*on them* (fem.)

4 The negative particle *\`eyn*

This particle is used to negate verbs in the present tense only. It is also used on its own to form negative sentences that in English use a present-tense form of *to be*: *I am not thin, They are not at home*, etc. Before looking at some more examples of how this form is used, let's see how it declines for the different persons:

\`eyni*	אֵינִי	*I am not / do not*
\`eynkha	אֵינְךָ	*you are not / do not* (masc.)
\`eynekh	אֵינֵךְ	*you are not / do not* (fem.)
\`eyno	אֵינוֹ	*he/it is not / does not*
\`eynah**	אֵינָהּ	*she/it is not / does not*
\`eynenu	אֵינֶנּוּ	*we are not / do not*
\`eynkhem	אֵינְכֶם	*you are not / do not* (masc. pl.)

`eynkhen	אֵינְכֶן	*you are not / do not* (fem. pl.)
`eynam	אֵינָם	*they are not / do not* (masc.)
`eynan	אֵינָן	*they are not / do not* (fem.)

* The form **`eyneni** אֵינֶנִּי is also used.
** The form **`eynenah** אֵינֶנָּה is also used.

Here is an example of this particle used together with a verb:
`Eyneni (`eyni) yekholah lavo 'akhshav.
I (fem.) *cannot come now.* אֵינֶנִּי יְכוֹלָה לָבוֹא עַכְשָׁו.

And an example without a verb:
Haboqer hu `eyno ba'avodah. הַבּוֹקֶר הוּא אֵינוֹ בַּעֲבוֹדָה.
This morning he isn't at work.

For both these examples, you could use the simple negative particle לֹא instead of the declined form of **`eyn**. For example:
`Ani lo yekholah lavo 'akhshav. אֲנִי לֹא יְכוֹלָה לָבוֹא עַכְשָׁו.

In fact, in casual speech that is what most Israelis would say. But in formal conversation and in writing, the forms with **`eyn** אֵין are considered more correct.

5 Honour all round ...

To continue our theme of the flexible (or 'synthetic', to use linguistic jargon) way that words are declined in Hebrew, let's take a look at the construction **likhvod** לִכְבוֹד *in honour of.* For example, **likhvodkha** לִכְבוֹדְךָ *in your honour* (masc. sing.) is composed of the following elements:
• the preposition **l-** לְ, which here means *to* or *for* (though in English we say 'in your honour')
• the word **kavod** כָּבוֹד *honour*, from the root כבד
• the second-person masculine singular suffix **kha-** ךָ.

According to the same principle, here is the full declension of this construction:

likhvodi	לִכְבוֹדִי	*in my honour*
likhvodkha	לִכְבוֹדְךָ	*in your honour* (masc. sing.)
likhvodekh	לִכְבוֹדֵךְ	*in your honour* (fem. sing.)
likhvodo	לִכְבוֹדוֹ	*in his honour*

likhvodah לִכְבוֹדָהּ *in her honour*
likhvodenu לִכְבוֹדֵנוּ *in our honour*
likhvodkhem לִכְבוֹדְכֶם *in your honour* (masc. pl.)
likhvodkhen לִכְבוֹדְכֶן *in your honour* (fem. pl.)
likhvodam לִכְבוֹדָם *in their honour* (masc.)
likhvodan לִכְבוֹדָן *in their honour* (fem.)

Among other uses, this construction is used for addresses on envelopes and at the head of letters. For example, an envelope addressed to Chaim Cohen will begin:

לִכְבוֹד
חַיִּים כֹּהֵן

... followed, of course, by the address.

6 An adjective derived from an adverb

The adjective **'akhshavi** עַכְשָׁוִי *contemporary* is derived from the adverb **'akhshav** עַכְשָׁו *now*:

'akhshavi עַכְשָׁוִי masc. sing.
'akhshaviyim עַכְשָׁוִיִּים masc. pl.
'akhshavit עַכְשָׁוִית fem. sing.
'akhshaviyot עַכְשָׁוִיּוֹת fem. pl.

7 'In which'

In lesson 72, we saw the phrase **Hu mesamel `et haqanqan shebo ...** הוּא מְסַמֵּל אֶת הַקַּנְקַן שֶׁבּוֹ *It symbolizes the pot in which* (that-in-it) ... Let's look for a moment at the way Hebrew expresses the idea of 'in which'.

Shebo שֶׁבּוֹ consists of **she** שֶׁ *that, which* followed by the preposition **b-** בּ *in* with the personal suffix. In the example above, the masculine singular suffix is used, since it refers back to the noun **qanqan** קַנְקַן. If the reference was to a feminine noun, the construction would be as follows: **Hu mesamel `et hatevah shebah** הוּא מְסַמֵּל אֶת הַתֵּבָה שֶׁבָּהּ *it symbolizes the box in which* ('that-in-it')... In this case, the personal suffix **-ah** ָהּ is used to refer back to **tevah** *box*, a feminine singular noun.

The following shows the full declension of the preposition **b-** בְּ *in*:

bi	בִּי	*in me*
bekha	בְּךָ	*in you* (masc. sing.)
bakh	בָּךְ	*in you* (fem. sing.)
bo	בּוֹ	*in him/it*
bah	בָּהּ	*in her/it*
banu	בָּנוּ	*in us*
bakhem	בָּכֶם	*in you* (masc. pl.)
bakhen	בָּכֶן	*in you* (fem. pl.)
bahem	בָּהֶם	*in them* (masc.)
bahen	בָּהֶן	*in them* (fem.)

8 Idiomatic expressions

Here are some colloquial expressions we've seen in this set of lessons. Use them when you can!

kosher `olimpi כּוֹשֶׁר אוֹלִימְפִּי
Olympian form/fitness (lesson 71)
shalvah `olimpit שַׁלְוָה אוֹלִימְפִּית
Olympian calm/tranquillity (71)
le`abed yadayim veraglayim לְאַבֵּד יָדַיִים וְרַגלַיִים
to lose one's footing, to lose one's way (73)
lehikanes 'im harosh baqir לְהִכָּנֵס עִם הָרֹאשׁ בַּקִּיר
to bang one's head against the wall (73)
'aqev betzad `agudal עָקֵב בְּצַד אֲגוּדָל
step by step (73)
ha`asimon nafal הָאֲסִימוֹן נָפַל
the penny dropped (73)
lelo qitzurey derekh לְלֹא קִצוּרֵי דֶרֶךְ
without shortcuts (73)
begovah ha'eynayim בְּגוֹבַה הָעֵינַיִים
as equals (73)
frayer פרַאיֶר
sucker (73)
tinoq megudal תִינוֹק מְגוּדָל
overgrown baby (74)
yefehfiyah 'im qabalot יְפֵהפִיָה עִם קַבָּלוֹת
certified beauty (75)

① הַשָּׁבוּעַ רָאִיתִי אֶת שָׂרִית. מֵאָז שֶׁהִיא הִתְגָּרְשָׁה הִיא לֹא מְאוֹהֶבֶת בְּאַף אֶחָד, אֲבָל הִיא לֹא בּוֹדְדָה. ② יֵשׁ לָהּ הַרְבֵּה פְּנַאי, וְהִיא יוֹצֵאת לְבַלּוֹת עִם הַמְּאַמֵּן הַמִּיתוֹלוֹגִי שֶׁל הַשְּׁכוּנָה. ③ הִיא אֲפִילּוּ הָלְכָה לִרְאוֹת מִשְׂחָקִים בָּאִיצְטַדְיוֹן. ④ הִיא מִשְׁתַּגַּעַת עַל מוֹעֲדוֹן הַלַּיְלָה הַיָּדוּעַ בְּיָפוֹ. ⑤ הִיא מַכִּירָה שָׁם הַרְבֵּה בַּלְיָנִים, בַּלְיָנִיּוֹת וְדוּגְמָנִיּוֹת. ⑥ הִיא עָשְׂתָה דִּיאֶטָה וְהַיּוֹם הִיא יְפֵהפִיָּה עִם פִיגוּרָה טֶפְלוֹנִית, וּבְגָדִים אוֹפְנָתִיִּים. ⑦ הִיא מְרַאֲיֶנֶת זַמֶּרֶת בְּתַחֲנַת רַדְיוֹ. עִם הַפֶּה הַגָּדוֹל שֶׁלָּהּ זֶה בְּדִיּוּק בִּשְׁבִילָהּ. ⑧ הָלַכְנוּ לְתַעֲרוּכָה שֶׁל הַמְּגִילּוֹת הַגְּנוּזוֹת בַּמּוּזֵיאוֹן הָאַרְכֵיאוֹלוֹגִי. ⑨ רָאִינוּ גַּם תְּעוּדוֹת עַתִּיקוֹת, סֵפֶר תַּנָ"ךְ קָדוּם וְקַנְקַנִּים מִמְּעָרוֹת קוּמְרָאן. ⑩ מִשָּׁם הָלַכְנוּ לְמִסְעָדָה עַל חוֹף הַיָּם. ⑪ יָשַׁבְנוּ בַּמִּרְפֶּסֶת, מַמָּשׁ שַׁלְוָה אוֹלִימְפִּית. ⑫ זֹאת בָּחוּרָה מְיוּחֶדֶת. רַק דָּבָר אֶחָד מְתַסְכֵּל אוֹתִי: הִיא לֹא מְדַבֶּרֶת עִם אֲנָשִׁים בְּגוֹבַהּ הָעֵינַיִים. ⑬ עַל כֹּל גֶּבֶר הִיא אוֹמֶרֶת שֶׁהוּא תִּינוֹק מְגוּדָל וְלֹא יוּצְלַח. מַה יִּהְיֶה אִתָּהּ? ⑭ אֶצְלֵנוּ הַכֹּל בְּסֵדֶר. לְהִשְׁתַּמֵּעַ וּלְהִת' בְּקָרוֹב. ⑮ שֶׁלָּכֶם רוֹנִי.

Answers

❶ This week I saw Sarit. Since she got divorced, she hasn't been in love *(she not in-love)* with anyone, but she is not lonely. ❷ She has lots of free time, and she goes out to enjoy herself with the 'mythical' coach of the neighbourhood. ❸ She has even gone to see games at the stadium. ❹ She is crazy about the well-known night club in Jaffa. ❺ She knows lots of socialites *(socialites[masc.] and-socialites[fem.])* and models *(fem.)* there. ❻ She went on *(did)* a diet and today she is beautiful, with a Teflon figure and fashionable clothes. ❼ She is a top interviewer for a radio station. With her big mouth, that is just [the job] for her. ❽ We went to an exhibition of the hidden scrolls in the archaeology museum. ❾ We also saw ancient documents, an old *(book-of)* Bible and pots from the Qumran Caves. ❿ From there, we went to a restaurant on the beach. ⓫ We sat on the balcony – real Olympian calm! ⓬ She's a special young woman. Only one thing frustrates me: she doesn't talk to people as equals *(at-level the-eyes).* ⓭ About every man, she says that he is an overgrown baby and a good-for-nothing. What will become of her *(it-will-be with-her)*? ⓮ Everything is fine with us. [Hope to] hear [from] you and see you soon! ⓯ Yours, Ronnie.

Second wave: lesson 28

78 Seventy-eighth lesson
(Shi'ur shiv'im ushmoneh)

`Im lo yo`il, lo yaziq! ①
If it doesn't help, it won't hurt!

1 – **Todah lekha, todah lakh, 'al hahatmadah** ②**.**
Thank you *(masc.)*, thank you *(fem.)* for your *(the)* perseverance.

2 **Zot sidrat hashi'urim ha`acharonah.**
This is the last series of lessons.

3 **Qasheh lekha(/lakh), lehitrakez? Nim`as** ③ **lekha(/lakh) lashevet 'al hakise velilmod?**
[Is it] difficult for you *(masc./fem.)* to concentrate? Are you *(masc./fem.)* fed up with sitting *(to-sit)* on your *(the)* chair and studying?

4 **`Anachnu matzi'im lakhem `et "shitat hachizuqim"** ④**.**
We suggest *(to-you)* the 'reinforcement method'.

Notes

① **`Im lo yo'il, lo yaziq!** !אִם לֹא יוֹעִיל, לֹא יַזִּיק *If it does not* ('will not') *help, it will not hurt!* This expression has a similar meaning to 'No harm in trying' in English. Notice the use of the future tense in the conditional statement starting with **`im** אִם *if* (more on this in review lesson 84). The verb **leho'il** לְהוֹעִיל means *to be useful*. The noun **ye'ilut** יְעִילוּת *efficiency* comes from the same root and has the **-ut** וּת suffix, which is used to form abstract nouns. The present tense **maziq** מַזִּיק *it harms, it damages* comes from the root נזק – the **nun** is missing in some forms of the verb, but can be seen in the noun **nezeq** נֶזֶק *damage*.

② **hatmadah** הַתְמָדָה *perseverance*. You may see a connection between this noun and the adverb **tamid** תָּמִיד *always*. The same root also appears in **lehatmid** לְהַתְמִיד *to persevere* and

אִם לֹא יוֹעִיל, לֹא יַזִּיק!

1 – תּוֹדָה לְךָ, תּוֹדָה לָךְ, עַל הַהַתְמָדָה.

2 זֹאת סִדְרַת הַשִּׁעוּרִים הָאַחֲרוֹנָה.

3 קָשֶׁה לְךָ (לָךְ) לְהִתְרַכֵּז? נִמְאַס לְךָ (לָךְ) לָשֶׁבֶת עַל הַכִּסֵּא וְלִלְמוֹד?

4 אֲנַחְנוּ מַצִּיעִים לָכֶם אֶת "שִׁיטַת הַחִזּוּקִים".

the expression **`achat uletamid** אַחַת וּלְתָמִיד *for once and all* (literally, 'one and-for-always'). In the Temple, the **ner tamid** נֵר תָּמִיד *perpetual candle* burned constantly in a golden candlestick. Today, the same term is used to refer to an electric lamp that is constantly lit under the 'Holy Ark' containing the Torah scrolls.

③ **nim`as lekha** נִמְאַס לְךָ *you are fed up, you've had enough.* This expression can be adapted for the appropriate person:

nim`as li** נִמְאַס לִי *I am fed up*; **nim`as lo נִמְאַס לוֹ *he is fed up*, etc. If the expression is followed by a verb, this appears in the infinitive. **Nim`as li lishmo'a `oto shir baradyo.** נִמְאַס לִי לִשְׁמוֹעַ אוֹתוֹ שִׁיר בְּרַדְיוֹ.
I'm fed up of hearing the same song on the radio.
When followed by a noun, the preposition מ is used:
Nim`as li mehachaver shelo. נִמְאַס לִי מֵהֶחָבֵר שֶׁלּוֹ.
I'm fed up of his friend.

④ **shitat hachizuqim** שִׁיטַת הַחִיזּוּקִים *the reinforcements/ rewards method*, which is based on positive reinforcement rather than threats or punishment. The term is from the field of psychology, but is tongue-in-cheek here.

5 – Klomar ⑤**, `atah(/`at) mavtiach/mavtichah le'atzmekha(/le'atzmekh) mashehu tov `acharey hama`amatz.**
That's to say, you *(masc./fem.)* promise yourself something good after the effort.

6 Lemashal ⑥**, `im `elmad `et hashi'ur hazeh mehahatchalah 'ad hasof, `elekh ba'erev leseret.**
For example, if I learn *(I-will-learn)* this lesson from *(the)* beginning to *(the)* end, I will go to a film in the evening.

7 – Hineh 'od 'etzah tovah, lehit'amel ⑦**, lefi hashitah hazot: magi'a lekha/lakh** ⑧ **qafeh ve'ugat shoqolad `acharey hahit'amlut.**
Here's another good [piece of] advice – work out according to this method *(the-method the-this)*: you['ll] deserve coffee and chocolate cake after the workout.

8 – Bevaqashah la'amod ⑨ **zaquf, haraglayim befisuq qal, hayadayim chofshiyot letzad haguf,**
Please stand up straight, legs slightly apart, arms free by the side of the body,

Notes

⑤ **klomar** כְּלוֹמַר *that is to say* is formed by combining **k** כּ *as like* and **lomar** לוֹמַר *to say.*

⑥ **lemashal** לְמָשָׁל *for example.* **mashal** has a wide range of meanings, including *fable* and *example.*

⑦ **lehit'amel** לְהִתְעַמֵּל *to work out, do exercises*; **hit'amlut** הִתְעַמְּלוּת *workout, gymnastics.* The root of these words is **'amal** עָמָל *labour, work.*

5 – כלוֹמַר, אַתָּה מַבטיחַ (אַת מַבטיחָה) לְעַצמֶךָ (לְעַצמֵך) מַשֶהוּ טוב אַחֲרֵי הַמַאֲמָץ.

6 לְמָשָל, אם אֶלמַד אֶת הַשִיעוּר הַזֶה מֵהַהַתחָלָה עַד הַסוֹף, אֵלֵך בַּעֶרֶב לְסֶרֶט.

7 – הִנֵה עוֹד עֵצָה טוֹבָה, לְהִתעַמֵל, לְפִי הַשִיטָה הַזֹאת מַגִיעַ לְךָ (לָך) קָפֶה וְעוּגַת שוֹקוֹלָד אַחֲרֵי הַהִתעַמלוּת.

8 – בְּבַקָשָה לַעֲמוֹד זָקוּף. הָרַגלַיִים בְּפִסוּק קַל, הַיָדַיִים חוֹפשִיוֹת לְצַד הַגוּף.

⑧ **magi'a lekha/lakh** (לָך) מַגִיעַ לְךָ *you deserve* (literally, ‘arrives to-you’). Here are two examples of this construction, the first with a positive connotation and the second in a negative context:

Chamudi, yesh lekha te'udah tovah, magi'ot lekha matanot.
חֲמוּדִי, יֵש לְךָ תְעוּדָה טוֹבָה, מַגִיעוֹת לְךָ מַתָנוֹת.
Darling, you got a good report, you deserve presents.

Hu ganav kesef mitayarim, magi'a lo 'onesh.
הוּא גָנַב כֶּסֶף מִתַיָרִים, מַגִיעַ לוֹ עוֹנֶש.
He stole money from tourists, he deserves punishment.

⑨ **la'amod** לַעֲמוֹד *to stand.* The noun **'amidah** עֲמִידָה means *standing position*; it is also the name of the central prayer in the synagogue service. The same root appears in **'amud** עַמוּד *column* (architectural), *page.*

9 **habeten mukhneset pnimah ⑩, hayashvan ⑪ mekhuvatz,**
stomach held in *(entered inwards)*, buttocks contracted,

10 **le`at, le`at, letzayer ma'galim 'im harosh,**
slowly, slowly, trace *(to-draw)* circles with the head,

11 **miyamin lismol umismol leyamin.**
from right to left and *(from)* left to right.

12 – **Targil sheni: laredet liyshivah mizrachit, gav zaquf,**
Second exercise: sit down legs crossed *(go-down to-sitting oriental)*, back straight,

13 **lehorid `et harosh le`at, pa'am lakatef hayemanit ufa'am lakatef hasmalit.**
lower the head slowly, once to the right shoulder and once to the left shoulder.

14 **Lachazor 'al hatargilim 'eser pe'amim.**
Repeat *(To-repeat)* the exercises ten times.

15 – **Kol hakavod! Ve`al tishkach/tishkechi `et "hachizuq" hamuvtach!**
Way to go! And don't forget *(masc./fem.)* the promised 'reinforcement'!

Notes

⑩ **pnimah** פְּנִימָה *inwards*. The word **pnim** פְּנִים *inside* is followed by the suffix ָה indicating movement, which we've already learned. A related word is **bifnim** בִּפְנִים *inside, on the inside*.

⑪ **yashvan** יַשְׁבָן *backside, buttocks*. You may recognize the root ישב *to sit* (**lashevet** לָשֶׁבֶת *to sit down*) in this word (the word 'seat' was also used in English in the past to refer to this part of

9 הַבֶּטֶן מוּכְנֶסֶת פְּנִימָה, הַיַּשְׁבָן מְכוּוָץ,

10 לְאַט, לְאַט, לְצַיֵּר מַעֲגָלִים עִם הָרֹאשׁ,

11 מִיָּמִין לִשְׂמֹאל וּמִשְּׂמֹאל לְיָמִין.

12 – תַּרְגִּיל שֵׁנִי! לָרֶדֶת לִישִׁיבָה מִזְרָחִית, גַּב זָקוּף.

13 לְהוֹרִיד אֶת הָרֹאשׁ לְאַט. פַּעַם לַכָּתֵף הַיְמָנִית וּפַעַם לַכָּתֵף הַשְּׂמָאלִית.

14 לַחֲזוֹר עַל הַתַּרְגִּילִים עֶשֶׂר פְּעָמִים.

15 – כֹּל הַכָּבוֹד! וְאַל תִּשְׁכַּח (תִּשְׁכְּחִי) אֶת הַחִיזּוּק הַמּוּבְטָח.

שיטת ההתעמלות של מועדון הספורט מצוינת לנשים.

the body). Like most languages, Hebrew also has some slang words for *backside*, not all of which are acceptable in polite company. **tusiq** טוּסִיק *bottom* is an inoffensive word that is often used when speaking to small children.

Targil rishon – Targem תַּרְגִּיל רִאשׁוֹן – תַּרְגֵּם

❶ שיטת ההתעמלות של מועדון הספורט מצוינת לנשים.
Shitat hahit'amlut shel mo'adon hasport metzuyenet lenashim.

❷ נמאס לכם לצייר נופים? אנחנו מציעים לכם לצייר אחד את השני!
Nim`as lakhem letzayer nofim? `Anachnu matzi'im lakhem letzayer `echad `et hasheni.

❸ מנהל שדורש מצוינות צריך לתת חיזוקים לעובדים.
Menahel shedoresh metzuyanut tzarikh latet chizuqim la'ovdim.

Targil sheni – Hashlem תַּרְגִּיל שֵׁנִי – הַשְׁלֵם

❶ [It is] known that sugar will be damaging for your health.
[...] shehasukar [...] la[...] shelkha.
____ שהסוכר ____ ל______ שלך.

❷ It is worth you thinking at some point *(to-think one-time)* about Dad's advice.
Keday lekha [...] pa'am 'al ha[...] shel `aba.
כדאי לך _____ פעם על ה___ של אבא.

❸ In order to concentrate and study, he listens [to] *(hears)* classical music.
Kedey [...] ve[...], hu shome'a [...] qlasit.
כדי ______ ו_____, הוא שומע ______ קלסית.

❹ When we *(fem.)* are free in the afternoon, we go to work out at the gym *(hall-of fitness)*.
Ka`asher `anachnu [...] `acharey ha[...] `anachnu holkhot [...] be[...] hakosher.

❹ הנה תרגיל טוב לכתפיים ולגב זקוף.
Hineh targil tov laktefayim ulegav zaquf.

❺ מי אומר שכל ההתחלות קשות?
Mi `omer shekol hahatchalot qashot?

Answers to Exercise 1

❶ The workout method of the sport club is excellent for women. ❷ Are you fed up with drawing landscapes? We suggest you draw each other. ❸ A manager who demands excellence must give the workers rewards *(reinforcements)*. ❹ Here is a good exercise for the shoulders and for a straight back. ❺ Who says that all beginnings are difficult?

***

כאשר אנחנו ______ אחרי ה______ אנחנו הולכות
______ ב____ הכושר.

❺ On television there is a film series about Israeli archaeology.
Batelevizyah yesh [...] [...] 'al `arkhe`ologyah [...].
בטלביזיה יש ____ _____ על ארכיאולוגיה _______ .

Answers to Exercise 2

❶ **Yadu'a – yaziq – bri`ut –** ❶ ידוע - יזיק - בריאות -

❷ **– lachshov – 'etzah –** ❷ - לחשוב - עצה -

❸ **– lehitrakez – lilmod – musiqah –**
❸ - להתרכז - ללמוד - מוסיקה -

❹ **– chofshiyot – tzohorayim – lehit'amel – `ulam –**
❹ - חופשיות - צהריים - להתעמל - אולם -

❺ **– sidrat sratim – yisra`elit** ❺ - סדרת סרטים - ישראלית

79 *If you have a mental picture of Israel as a country of constant sunshine and high temperatures, you might like to head for Mount* **Hermon** חֶרְמוֹן. *If you go during the winter, make sure to take your skis with you (or you can hire equipment there). Although the summit of this mountain lies over the border in Syria, the highest peak in Israel soars to an impressive 2224 metres above sea level, at a point known as* **Mitzpeh Hashlagim** מִצְפֵּה הַשְּׁלָגִים *'observatory of-the-snows'. You could stay in* **Neveh Ativ** נְוֵה אֲטִי"ב the Oasis of Ativ, *a picturesque* **moshav** מוֹשָׁב settlement *at the foot of the mountain, established in 1971 by young Israeli ski enthusiasts. The difference in climate and vegetation at different points on the*

---

79 Seventy-ninth lesson
(Shi'ur shiv'im vetesha')

'Ugat gvinah
Cheesecake

1 – **Beshalav zeh `atem `ulay metakhnenim nesi'ah leYisra`el, ledaber sham 'ivrit.**
By this stage, you may be planning a visit to Israel [in order] to speak Hebrew there.

2 **Beharbeh meqomot yatzi'u lakhem lishtot qafeh `o teh vele`ekhol 'ugah.**
In many places, they will offer that you drink *(to-drink)* coffee or tea and eat *(to-eat)* cake.

3 **Le'itim qrovot** ① **timtze`u batafrit 'ugat gvinah, lif'amim** ② **gvinah ufeyrot.**
You will often find on the menu cheesecake, [and] sometimes cheese and fruit.

Notes

① **le'itim qrovot** לְעִתִּים קְרוֹבוֹת *often* (literally, 'to-times near'); as well as **le'itim rechoqot** לְעִתִּים רְחוֹקוֹת *rarely* (literally,

mountain is striking – in the moshav, orchards of fruit trees and mushrooms grow. To get up to the ski area, take the **rakevel** רַכֶּבֶל ski lift. On a clear day, you can enjoy spectacular views of Syria and Israel. By the way, the word **rakevel** רַכֶּבֶל was created by combining **rakevet** רַכֶּבֶת train and **kevel** כֶּבֶל cable. Neve Ativ is named after four young soldiers who fell in action in the area: **Abraham** אַבְרָהָם, **Tuvyah** טוּבְיָה, **Ya`ir** יָאִיר and **Binyamin** בִּנְיָמִין. This explains why the Hebrew name has a double quotation mark, to indicate that it is an acronym.

Second wave: lesson 29

---

79 שִׁעוּר שִׁבְעִים וְתִשְׁעָ

עוּגַת גְבִינָה

1 – בְּשָׁלָב זֶה אַתֶּם אוּלַי מִתְכַּנְנִים נְסִיעָה לְיִשְׂרָאֵל לְדַבֵּר שָׁם עִבְרִית.

2 בְּהַרְבֵּה מְקוֹמוֹת יָצִיעוּ לָכֶם לִשְׁתוֹת קָפֶה אוֹ תֵה וְלֶאֱכוֹל עוּגָה.

3 לְעִתִּים קְרוֹבוֹת תִמְצְאוּ בַּתַפְרִיט עוּגַת גְבִינָה, לִפְעָמִים גְבִינָה וּפֵירוֹת.

'to-times far'). These expressions use the word **'et** עֵת *time, period.*

② **lif'amim** לִפְעָמִים *sometimes* is formed from לְ *to* and **pe'amim** פְּעָמִים, the plural of **pa'am** פַּעַם *time* (as in 'one time/once', 'four times', etc.).

4 – Kedey lehit`amen babayit, hineh matkon besisi ③.
In order to practice *(train)* at home, here is a basic recipe:

5 – Lishtoach batzeq parikh 'al tavnit `afiyah ④. Le`efot chamesh 'esreh daqot beme`ah shmonim ma'alot ⑤.
Roll out *(Flatten)* shortcrust pastry in a baking pan. Bake [for] fifteen minutes at one hundred and eighty degrees [Celsius].

6 – Beyntayim ⑥ lehakhin `et ta'arovet hagvinah.
In the meantime, prepare the cheese mixture.

7 – Lehaqtzif `arba'ah chelmonim ⑦ ume`ah vechamishim gram sukar.
Whip four egg yolks and one hundred and fifty grams of sugar.

8 – Lehosif shesh me'ot gram gvinah levanah mesunenet, 'esrim gram qrem samikh,
Add six hundred grams of strained white cheese, twenty grams of thick cream,

Notes

③ **besisi** בְּסִיסִי *basic*. The noun is **basis** בָּסִיס *base*, *basis*.

④ **`afiyah** אֲפִיָּה *baking*. Other words from the root אפה include **`ofeh** אוֹפֶה *baker* (feminine: **`ofah** אוֹפָה), **ma`afiyah** מַאֲפִיָּה *bakery*, and **ma`afeh** מַאֲפֶה, which means any kind of baked product.

⑤ **ma'alot** מַעֲלוֹת *degrees*; the singular is **ma'alah** מַעֲלָה. The root עלה also appears in **'aliyah** עֲלִיָּה *ascent*, which is used to refer to Jews immigrating to Israel, and also to people 'going up'

4 – כְּדֵי לְהִתְאַמֵּן בַּבַּיִת, הִנֵּה מַתְכּוֹן בְּסִיסִי.

5 – לִשְׁטוֹחַ בָּצֵק פָּרִיךְ עַל תַּבְנִית אֲפִיָּה. לֶאֱפוֹת חֲמֵשׁ עֶשְׂרֵה דַּקּוֹת בְּמֵאָה שְׁמוֹנִים מַעֲלוֹת.

6 – בֵּינְתַיִם לְהָכִין אֶת תַּעֲרוֹבֶת הַגְּבִינָה.

7 – לְהַקְצִיף אַרְבָּעָה חֶלְמוֹנִים וּמֵאָה וַחֲמִישִּׁים גְּרַם סוּכָּר.

8 – לְהוֹסִיף שֵׁשׁ מֵאוֹת גְּרַם גְּבִינָה לְבָנָה מְסוּנֶּנֶת, עֶשְׂרִים גְּרַם קֶרֶם סָמִיךְ.

to the podium for the Torah reading in the synagogue. Another useful word from the same root is **ma'alit** מַעֲלִית *lift*, *elevator*. When stating temperatures, the word **ma'alot** normally refers to the Celsius scale, which is the only system used in Israel (we've added the word 'Celsius' in the translations to prevent disappointments in the kitchen).

⑥ **beyntayim** בֵּינְתַיִם *meantime*. Note that this word has the characteristic dual ending, implying something like 'between two times'.

⑦ **chelmonim** חֶלְמוֹנִים *egg yolks*, and also the name of a flower from the daffodil family known in Hebrew as **chelmonit** חֶלְמוֹנִית. In line 11, we see the word **chelbon** חֶלְבּוֹן *egg white*, which comes from **chalav** חָלָב *milk*.

9 **saqit vanil, shesh kapot ⑧ qemach, mitz mechatzi limon,**
a packet of vanilla, six tablespoons of flour, [the] juice of half a lemon,

10 **shloshim gram chem`ah `o margarinah, chofen tzimuqim ⑨, kaf liqer matoq (`im rotzim).**
thirty grams of butter or margarine, a handful of raisins [and] a tablespoon of sweet liqueur (if [you] like).

11 – **Le'arbev hakol be'adinut. Lehaqtzif `arba'ah chelbonim leqetzef chazaq.**
Mix it all *(the-all)* gently. Beat four egg whites until stiff *(into-foam stiff)*.

12 – **Lehosif `et haqetzef lagvinah. Lehotzi `et habatzeq mehatanur. Lishtoach 'alav `et hata'arovet.**
Add the egg whites *(the-foam)* to the cheese. Remove the pastry from the oven. Spread the mixture on it.

13 – **Le`efot sha'ah beme`ah shishim ma'alot. Ka`asher ha'ugah mukhanah, lekhabot `et hatanur, `aval lehash`ir `otah bifnim, shetitqarer batanur.**
Bake [for one] hour at one hundred and sixty degrees [Celsius]. When the cake is ready, turn off the oven, but leave it inside to cool down in the oven.

Notes

⑧ **kapot** כַּפּוֹת *tablespoons* is the plural of **kaf** כַּף (see lesson 55).

⑨ **tzimuqim** צִמּוּקִים *raisins*. The root צמק also appears in the verb **lehitztameq** לְהִצְטַמֵּק *to shrivel*.

9 שְׂקִית וָנִיל, שֵׁשׁ כַּפּוֹת קֶמַח, מִיץ מֵחֲצִי לִימוֹן.

10 שלושים גרַם חֶמאָה או מַרגָרִינָה, חוֹפֶן צִימוּקִים, כַּף לִיקֶר מָתוֹק (אִם רוֹצִים).

11 – לְעַרבֵּב הַכֹּל בְּעֲדִינוּת. לְהַקצִיף אַרבָּעָה חֶלבּוֹנִים לְקֶצֶף חָזָק.

12 – לְהוֹסִיף אֶת הַקֶצֶף לַגבִינָה. לְהוֹצִיא אֶת הַבָּצֵק מֵהַתַנוּר. לִשטוֹחַ עָלָיו אֶת הַתַעֲרוֹבֶת.

13 – לֶאֱפוֹת שָׁעָה בְּמֵאָה שִׁשִּׁים מַעֲלוֹת. כַּאֲשֶׁר הָעוּגָה מוּכָנָה, לְכַבּוֹת אֶת הַתַנוּר, אֲבָל לְהַשׁאִיר אוֹתָה בִּפנִים, שֶׁתִתקָרֵר בַּתַנוּר.

בעוד עשר דקות יבואו האורחים, אתם צריכים לכבות את הטלביזיה.

14 – `Efshar le`ekhol `et ha'ugah 'im qatzefet ⑩ vetutim.
You can eat *(It-is-possible to-eat)* the cake with whipped cream and strawberries.

Notes

⑩ **qatzefet** קַצֶּפֶת *whipped cream* (literally, 'that-which-has-been-whipped-into-foam') from the verb **lehaqtzif** לְהַקְצִיף (line 7). The related word **qetzef** קֶצֶף can refer to the foam

Targil rishon – Targem תַּרְגִּיל רִאשׁוֹן – תַּרְגֵּם

❶ באיזה שלב אתם נמצאים בסידורים למסיבת היובל?
Be`eyzeh shalav `atem nimtza`im basidurim limesibat hayovel?

❷ בעוד עשר דקות יבואו האורחים, אתם צריכים לכבות את הטלביזיה.
Be'od 'eser daqot yavo`u ha`orchim, `atem tzrikhim lekhabot `et hatelevizyah.

❸ לפי המתכון שבספר, למוס שוקולד צריך להקציף ארבעה חלבונים וארבעה חלמונים.
Lefi hamatkon shebasefer, lemus shoqolad tzarikh lehaqtzif `arba'ah chelbonim ve`arba'ah chelmonim.

❹ בתפריט בית הקפה יש עוגת תותים וקצפת.
Betafrit beyt haqafeh yesh 'ugat tutim veqatzefet.

❺ לפעמים נמאס לי ללכת לעבודה ולראות את אותם האנשים.
Lif'amim nim`as li lalekhet la'avodah velir`ot `et `otam ha`anashim.

14 – אֶפְשָׁר לֶאֱכוֹל אֶת הָעוּגָה עִם קַצֶּפֶת וְתוּתִים. □

on the sea, and in literary Hebrew it is used to mean *anger* ('foaming mad').

Answers to Exercise 1

❶ What stage are you at in the arrangements for the jubilee party? ❷ In ten minutes the guests will come – you need to turn off the television. ❸ According to the recipe in the book, for chocolate mousse you *(impers. subj.)* must beat four egg whites and four egg yolks. ❹ On the menu at the café there is strawberry cake with whipped cream. ❺ Sometimes I get fed up with going to work and seeing the same people.

Targil sheni – Hashlem תַּרְגִּיל שֵׁנִי – הַשְׁלֵם

❶ During the festival of Passover, one does not eat cakes [made] from flour.

Be[...] hapesach, lo [...] 'ugot me[...].

ב__ הפסח, לא ______ עוגות מ___ .

❷ Before the Olympic Games, the basketball team will go to train *(practice)* at the Wingate Institute.

Lifney ha[...] ha`olimpiyim [...] hakadursal tisa'a [...] beMakhon Vingeyt.

לפני ה______ האולימפיים _____ הכדורסל תסע ______
במכון וינגייט.

❸ For dinner *(meal-of evening)*, I want to prepare a tomato salad, Tzfat cheese, basil and strained black olives.

Le[...] [...] `ani rotzah [...] salat [...], gvinah tzfatit, reychan vezeytim [...] mesunanim.

ל_____ ___ אני רוצה _____ סלט _______ , גבינה
צפתית, ריחן וזיתים ______ מסוננים.

❹ At breakfast *(meal-of morning)* I eat white cheese and a handful of raisins.

Ba[...] boqer, `ani `okhelet [...] [...] vechofen [...].

ב_____ בוקר, אני אוכלת _____ ____ וחופן _______ .

❺ On summer evenings, they often go to the beach to see the foam on the surface of the sea.

Be'arvey ha[...] hem holkhim [...] [...] lechof hayam lir`ot `et ha[...] 'al pney ha[...].

בערבי ה___ הם הולכים _____ ______ לחוף הים לראות
את ה___ על פני ה__ .

Answers to Exercise 2

❶ – **chag – `okhlim – qemach**
❶ - חג - אוכלים - קמח

❷ – **mischaqim – qvutzat – lehit`amen –**
❷ -משחקים - קבוצת - להתאמן -

❸ – **`aruchat 'erev – lehakhin – 'agvanyot – shchorim –**
❸ -ארוחת ערב - להכין - עגבניות - שחורים -

❹ – **`aruchat – gvinah levanah – tzimuqim**
❹ - ארוחת - גבינה לבנה - צימוקים

❺ – **qayitz – le'itim qrovot – qetzef – yam**
❺ -קיץ - לעתים קרובות - קצף - ים

Israelis are very fond of dairy foods, particularly various forms of soft white or cream cheese. A wide range of lower-calorie products is also available, labelled with the percentage of fat they contain (3, 5, 9 percent and so forth). Many Israelis try to watch their weight and choose their dairy products accordingly.

One of the most popular cheeses is **qotej קוֹטֶג'** *(cottage cheese). This is considered a staple food in Israel, and in 2011, a scandal surrounding the price of cottage cheese sparked massive demonstrations and protests.*

Tzfatit צְפָתִית *cheese is named after the historic city of* **Tzfat צְפָת** *in Galilee. This white cheese is sold in dense white blocks floating in brine or oil.* **Bulgarit בּוּלְגָרִית** Bulgarian *is similar.*

Ashkenazi cuisine features cakes (for example, cheesecake) made with cream cheese, sprinkled with sugar or mixed with fruit, nuts or poppy seeds.

Believe it or not, cows and dairies can even be found in Israel's desert regions. In the Arava, 40 kilometres north of Eilat, the oasis kibbutz **Yotvatah יוֹטְבָתָה** *is famous for its dairy products, which are now sold throughout the country.*

Second wave: lesson 30

80 Eightieth lesson (Shi'ur shmonim)

Pitgamim ①
Proverbs

1 – **`Al tistakel ② baqanqan `ela ③ bemah sheyesh bo.**
Don't look at the jug but at what it contains *(at-what there-is in-it)*.

2 – **`Al tiftach peh lasatan ④ ... hu lo rofe shinayim.**
Don't open [your] mouth to the devil ... he isn't a dentist *(doctor-of teeth)*.

3 – **`Eyzehu ⑤ hechakham ⑥? – Halomed ⑦ mikol `adam.**
Who is wise *(the-wise-one)*? The one who learns from every person.

Notes

① **pitgamim** פִּתְגָמִים *proverbs*. This word of Persian origin appears in the Bible (Esther 1:2), which makes sense, since the events described in the Book of Esther took place in Persia. In modern Hebrew it means proverbs, aphorisms or sayings.

② Remember that to tell someone not to do something (the negative imperative), **`al** אַל *do not* is followed by the appropriate future tense form (lesson 49).

③ **`ela** אֶלָּא is a more literary alternative for **`aval** אֲבָל *but*. It is used in particular to indicate which of two alternatives is intended ('not x but y').

④ **satan** שָׂטָן *satan, the devil.*

⑤ **`Eyzehu?** ?אֵיזֶהוּ *Which one/Who [is] ...?* This literary word also has a feminine equivalent: **`eyzohi** אֵיזוֹהִי. These words

פִּתְגָמִים

1 – אַל תִסתַכֵּל בַּקַנקַן אֶלָא בְּמַה שֶׁיֵּשׁ בּוֹ.

2 – אַל תִפתַח פֶּה לַשָׂטָן... הוּא לֹא רוֹפֵא שִׁינַיִים.

3 – אֵיזֶהוּ הֶחָכָם? – הַלוֹמֵד מִכֹּל אָדָם.

are formed by combining **`ey** אֵי *Where?*, **zeh** זֶה *this* (masc.) or **zo** זוֹ *this* (fem.) and **hu** הוּא *he* or **hi** הִיא *she*.

⑥ **hechakham** הֶחָכָם *the wise one, the sage*. Note that the definite article **ha** הַ takes the form הֶ here, because of the following חָ. This saying often appears without the **ha**.

⑦ **halomed** הַלוֹמֵד *the one who studies*. In literary Hebrew, the article **ha** הַ is used to form expressions referring to someone who or something that does a particular activity. In line 5, we have **hasameach** הַשָׂמֵחַ *the one who is happy*; in line 6, **hayotz`im** הַיוֹצְאִים *the ones that leave*; in line 7, **hamekhabed** הַמְכַבֵּד *the one who respects*. In the feminine, these forms would be **halomedet** הַלוֹמֶדֶת, **hasmechah** הַשְׂמֵחָה, **hayotz`ot** הַיוֹצאוֹת, **hamekhabedet** הַמְכַבֶּדֶת.

4 – **Lo midivshekh ⑧ velo me'uqtzekh.**
Neither of your honey, nor of your sting.

5 – **`Eyzehu 'ashir? – Hasameach bechelqo.**
Who is rich? The one who is happy with his lot.

6 – **Dvarim hayotz`im min halev, nikhnasim `el halev.**
Words coming *(the-leaving)* from the heart, enter the heart.

7 – **`Eyzehu mekhubad ⑨? – Hamekhabed `et habriyot.**
Who is respected? The one who respects people.

8 – **Mi shelibo ⑩ tzar, leshono rachav.**
The one whose heart is narrow has a wide tongue *(Who that-his-heart narrow his-tongue wide)*.

9 – **Bishloshah dvarim `adam nikar: bekhoso, bekhis`o uvekha'aso.**
By three things a person is distinguished: by his *(drinking)* glass, by his pocket and by his temper *(anger)*.

10 – **Lifney 'iver `al titen mikhshol.**
Before a blind person, do not place *(give)* an obstacle.

11 – **Lo mikol `oren ye'aseh toren.**
Not every pine will become a ship's mast *(Not from-every pine will-be-made mast)*.

12 – **`Im `eyn qemach, `eyn Torah.**
If there is no flour, there is no Torah.

Notes

⑧ **midivshekh** מִדִּבְשֵׁךְ *of your honey.* The 'your' here in 'neither of your honey nor of your sting' refers to the honey bee, indicated by the feminine singular ending ךְ since **dvorah**

4 – לֹא מִדבשֵׁך וְלֹא מֵעוּקצֵך.

5 – אֵיזֶהוּ עָשִׁיר? – הַשָּׂמֵחַ בְּחֶלקוֹ.

6 – דבָרִים הַיוֹצאִים מִן הַלֵב, נִכנָסִים אֶל הַלֵב.

7 – אֵיזֶהוּ מְכוּבָּד? – הַמְכַבֵּד אֶת הַבּרִיוֹת.

8 – מִי שֶׁלִבּוֹ צַר, לְשׁוֹנוֹ רָחָב.

9 – בִּשלוֹשָׁה דבָרִים אָדָם נִכָּר: בְּכוֹסוֹ, בְּכִיסוֹ וּבְכַעֲסוֹ.

10 – לִפנֵי עִוֵר אַל תִתֵן מִכשׁוֹל.

11 – לֹא מִכֹּל אוֹרֶן יֵעָשֶׂה תוֹרֶן.

12 – אִם אֵין קֶמַח, אֵין תוֹרָה.

☐

דבוֹרָה *bee* is a feminine noun. The modern word for *honey* is **dvash** דבַשׁ.

⑨ **mekhubad** מְכוּבָּד *respected.* This passive past participle has an active present equivalent: **mekhabed** מְכַבֵּד *respecting, respectful.* These words come from the same root as **kavod** כָּבוֹד *honour* (see lesson 57, note 7).

⑩ **shelibo** שֶׁלִבּוֹ *whose heart* (literally, 'that the heart of his'). Note the flexibility of the pronoun **she** שֶׁ, which can mean not only *that* but also *which*, *where* and *who*, depending on the context. Here, this particle is followed by the noun **lev** לֵב *heart*, which in turn appears with the third-person masculine singular possessive suffix **o** וֹ.

Targil rishon – Targem תַרְגִיל רִאשׁוֹן – תַרְגֵם

1 אם אין קמח, אין עוגות.
`Im `eyn qemach, `eyn 'ugot.

2 תסתכלי לאן את הולכת, יש מכשול במדרחוב.
Tistakli le`an `at holekhet, yesh mikhshol bamidrachov.

3 למרות שהוא עיוור, הוא התחתן והוא שמח בחלקו.
Lamrot shehu 'iver, hu hitchaten vehu sameach bechelqo.

4 סוף סוף היה לי אומץ ללכת לרופא שיניים.
Sof sof hayah li `ometz lalekhet lerofe shinayim.

5 יש לו תמיד הרבה דברים בכיסים.
Yesh lo tamid harbeh dvarim bakisim.

Targil sheni – Hashlem תַרְגִיל שֵׁנִי – הַשְׁלֵם

1 At night I drink [a] cup of hot milk with honey.
Balaylah `ani shotah [...] [...] cham 'im [...].

בלילה אני שותה ___ ___ חם עם ___ .

2 He likes to perform *(play)* in *(before the)* public, it is clear *(is-known about-him)* that he will have a nice career in the theatre.
Hu `ohev [...] lifney [...], [...] 'alav shetiheyeh lo qarierah [...] bate`atron.

הוא אוהב ___ לפני ____, ____ עליו שתהיה לו קריירה
___ בתאטרון.

3 Sayings are *(The-proverbs they)* the soul of the language.
Ha[...] hem ha[...] shel [...].

ה______ הם ה____ של ____ .

Answers to Exercise 1

❶ If there is no flour, there are no cakes. ❷ Look where you *(fem.)* are going, there is an obstacle on the pedestrianized street. ❸ Although he is blind, he has married and is happy with his lot. ❹ At last I had the courage to go to the dentist. ❺ He always has lots of things in his pockets.

❹ From the beach, we saw the mast of a ship in the middle *(in-heart)* of the sea.

Me[...] ra`inu `et ha[...] shel [...] belev ha[...].

מ____ ראינו את ה____ של _____ בלב ה__.

❺ He is a respected doctor. He was successful because he respects the patients.

Hu [...] [...]. Hu hitzliach ki hu [...] `et hacholim.

הוא ____ _____ . הוא הצליח כי הוא ____ את החולים.

Answers to Exercise 2

❶ – **kos chalav – dvash** ❶ - כוס חלב - דבש

❷ – **lesacheq – tzibur, nikar – yafah –**

❷ - לשחק - צבור - ניכר - יפה -

❸ – **pitgamim – neshamah – hasafah**

❸ - פתגמים - נשמה - השפה

❹ – **hachof – toren – `oniyah – yam** ❹ - החוף - תורן - אוניה - ים

❺ – **rofe mekhubad – mekhabed –** ❺ - רופא מכובד - מכבד -

Some of these proverbs have their roots in Jewish and Hebrew culture. The following are some of the more interesting origins:
• *No. 2* **`Al tiftach peh lasatan**. אַל תִּפתַח פֶּה לַשָּׂטָן
Do not open [your] mouth to the Devil.
This expression is used to mean something similar to the English saying 'Don't tempt fate'. It reflects the superstitious belief that merely saying a word or expressing a thought can make something undesirable happen.
• *No. 3* **`Eyzehu hechakham?** ?אֵיזֶהוּ הֶחָכָם
*This saying and the others that follow the same formula (*who is x – the one who y*) are taken from* **pirkey 'avot** פִּרקֵי אָבוֹת *the Ethics of the Fathers, a collection of ethical sayings that forms part of the Mishna.*
• *No. 4* **Lo midivshekh velo me'uqtzekh.** לֹא מִדִּבשֵׁךְ וְלֹא מֵעוּקצֵךְ
This saying has something of the flavour of the English 'Don't do me any favours'. The idea is that we don't want someone's help or advice. While **dvash** דְּבַש *means* honey *in modern Hebrew, in Biblical times the word was also used for date syrup (which is still popular in Israel).*
• *No. 10* **Lifney 'iver al titen mikhshol.** לִפנֵי עִוֵּר אַל תִּתֵּן מִכשׁוֹל
This proverb appears in Leviticus 19:14.
• *No. 11* **Lo mikol `oren ye'aseh toren.** לֹא מִכָּל אוֹרֶן יֵעָשֶׂה תּוֹרֶן
The idea behind this saying is that not everyone can be a leader or hero. It was coined by Yehuda Halevy, one of the greatest Jewish poets of medieval Spain (12th century CE).

81 Eighty-first lesson
(Shi'ur shmonim ve`achat)

Ha`entziqlopedyah ha'ivrit
Encyclopedia Hebraica

1 – `Entziqlopedyah miqir leqir ①? Lo bishvil hador hatza'ir shelanu!
A wall-to-wall encyclopedia? Not for our young generation!

Notes

① **miqir leqir** מִקִּיר לְקִיר *from wall to wall*: here the expression is used to refer to the numerous volumes of a traditional

• *No. 12* **`Im `eyn qemach, `eyn Torah.** אִם אֵין קֶמַח, אֵין תוֹרָה *Without attending to our basic needs, we will be unable to study or turn to higher matters – this is the idea behind this saying, which also comes from the Ethics of the Fathers (see No. 3).*

סוף סוף היה לי אומץ ללכת
לרופא שיניים.

Second wave: lesson 31

81 שִׁעוּר שְׁמוֹנִים וְאַחַת

הָאֶנְצִיקְלוֹפֶּדְיָה הָעִבְרִית

1 – אֶנְצִיקְלוֹפֶּדְיָה מִקִּיר לְקִיר? לֹא בִּשְׁבִיל הַדּוֹר הַצָּעִיר שֶׁלָּנוּ!

encyclopedia. This expression is used as in English – **shatiach miqir leqir** שָׁטִיחַ מִקִּיר לְקִיר *wall-to-wall carpet.*

2 **Mehayom ha`Entziqlopedyah ha'ivrit ba`internet.**
From today – the Encyclopedia Hebraica [is] on the internet.

3 – **Day lehaqlid ② `et hamilah `o hamusag hamevuqash ③.**
[It is] enough to type in the desired word or concept.

4 **`Acharey kamah shniyot hameyda' ④ mofi'a 'al hatzag ve`im `atem rotzim 'al hamadpeset.**
After a few seconds, the information appears on the screen and, if you want, on the printer.

5 – **`Atem yekholim lehaqlit ⑤ 'al hadisq haqashiach ulehadpis bekhamah 'otaqim she`atem rotzim.**
You can save it *(record)* on the hard disk and print as many copies as you want.

6 – **Tzevet mumchim me'adken ⑥ `et kol hanetunim bizman `emet.**
A team of experts updates all the data in real time.

Notes

② **lehaqlid** לְהַקְלִיד *to type*. The word **miqledet** מִקְלֶדֶת *keyboard* comes from the same root. The original meaning of this verb is to play a percussion instrument, particularly a piano.

③ **mevuqash** מְבוּקָּשׁ *desired.* The feminine form of this adjective is **mevuqeshet** מְבוּקֶּשֶׁת. We've already seen the active form of the verb: **biqashti** בִּקַּשְׁתִּי *I requested, desired.* The root בקש is also found in **bevaqashah** בְּבַקָּשָׁה *please, by request.*

④ **meyda'** מֵידַע *information*. The verb **lada'at** לָדַעַת *to know* also comes from the root ידע. Another noun from the same root is **mada'** מַדָּע *science.*

2 מֵהַיּוֹם הָאֶנְצִיקְלוֹפֶּדְיָה הָעִבְרִית בְּאִינְטֶרְנֶט.

3 – דַּי לְהַקְלִיד אֶת הַמִּלָּה אוֹ הַמּוּשָּׂג הַמְבוּקָּשׁ.

4 אַחֲרֵי כַּמָּה שְׁנִיּוֹת הַמֵּידָע מוֹפִיעַ עַל הַצָּג וְאִם אַתֶּם רוֹצִים, עַל הַמַּדְפֶּסֶת.

5 – אַתֶּם יְכוֹלִים לְהַקְלִיט עַל הַדִּיסְק הַקָּשִׁיחַ וּלְהַדְפִּיס בְּכַמָּה עוֹתָקִים שֶׁאַתֶּם רוֹצִים.

6 – צֶוֶת מוּמְחִים מְעַדְכֵּן אֶת כֹּל הַנְּתוּנִים בִּזְמַן אֱמֶת.

⑤ This is an unusual use of the verb **lehaqlit** לְהַקְלִיט, which usually refers to recording audio or video material. The usual word for saving a computer file is **lishmor** לִשְׁמוֹר *to save.*

⑥ **me'adken** מְעַדְכֵּן *update.* This verb is formed from **'ad** עַד *until* and **kan** כָּאן *here.* The reflexive form is also used:
`Ani rotzah lehit'adken bachadashot ha`acharonot.
אֲנִי רוֹצָה לְהִתְעַדְכֵּן בַּחֲדָשׁוֹת הָאַחֲרוֹנוֹת.
I (fem.) *want to update myself on the latest news.*

7 – **Bekhol haqladah ⑦ teqablu qishurim ⑧ nosafim, sheyashlimu `et hameyda' shelakhem.**
With each keystroke *(typing)* you *(will)* receive additional links that will supplement your information.

8 – **Hayitron ⑨ hagadol beyoter shel ha`Entziqlopedyah ba`internet, hu ma`agar hameyda' ha`eyn-sofi.**
The great advantage of the Encyclopedia on the internet [is that] it [is] an infinite database.

9 – **Benosaf, tehanu mimatzagot ⑩ multi-medyah, klomar, sirtey video, qivtzey qol.**
In addition, you will enjoy multimedia presentations, that is, videos *(films video)* [and] sound files.

10 – **Mi `amar she`Entziqlopedyah lo yekholah liheyot chavayah ⑪?**
Who said that an Encyclopedia cannot be an experience?

11 – **Nu… timtze`u `oti 'al yad hamiqledet, mul hatzag 'im ha'akhbar bayad.**
Well ... you'll find me by the keyboard, in front of the screen, with mouse in hand *(the-mouse in-the-hand)*.

Notes

⑦ **haqladah** הַקְלָדָה *typing* (see note 2) – here in reference to entering information during a search.

⑧ **qishurim** קִשּׁוּרִים *connections* – in this case, links to other information. The root קשר means *to connect, to tie*.

⑨ **yitaron** יִתְרוֹן *advantage*. You may be able to see the connection between this word and **yoter** יוֹתֵר *more*.

7 – בְּכֹל הַקְלָדָה תְּקַבְּלוּ קִשּׁוּרִים נוֹסָפִים, שֶׁיַּשְׁלִימוּ אֶת הַמֵּידַע שֶׁלָּכֶם.

8 – הַיִּתְרוֹן הַגָּדוֹל בְּיוֹתֵר שֶׁל הָאֶנְצִיקְלוֹפֶּדְיָה בָּאִינְטֶרְנֶט, הוּא מַאֲגַר הַמֵּידַע הָאֵין-סוֹפִי.

9 – בְּנוֹסָף, תֵּהָנוּ מִמַּצָּגוֹת מוּלְטִימֶדְיָה, כְּלוֹמַר, סִרְטֵי וִידֵאוֹ, קִבְצֵי קוֹל.

10 – מִי אָמַר שֶׁאֶנְצִיקְלוֹפֶּדְיָה לֹא יְכוֹלָה לִהְיוֹת חֲוָיָה?

11 – נוּ... תִּמְצְאוּ אוֹתִי עַל יַד הַמִּקְלֶדֶת, מוּל הַצָּג, עִם הָעַכְבָּר בַּיָּד. □

⑩ **matzagot** מַצָּגוֹת *presentations.* The singular is **matzeget** מַצֶּגֶת. This relatively new word is related to the noun **hatzagah** הַצָּגָה *show, performance.* **tzag** צָג means *screen* (on a computer or a telephone).

⑪ **chavayah** חֲוָיָה *experience*, related to the verbs **chayah** חָיָה *to live* and **chavah** חָוָה *to experience.* Unless negative adjectives are added, this noun almost always has a positive connotation, implying a wonderful or enjoyable experience.

Targil rishon – Targem תַּרְגִּיל רִאשׁוֹן – תַּרְגֵּם

❶ מידע בזמן אמת על ארועי התיירות בעיר נמצא באתר שלנו.
Meyda' bizman `emet 'al `eru'ey* hatayarut ba'ir nimtza ba`atar shelanu.

❷ היא מלמדת היסטוריה בבית ספר ויש לה בבית ספרים מקיר לקיר.
Hi melamedet historyah beveyt sefer veyesh lah babayit sfarim miqir leqir.

❸ בבית החולים יש צוות רופאים מומחים לבעיות עיניים.
Beveyt hacholim yesh tzevet rof`im mumchim live'ayot 'eynayim.

❹ המקלדת הישראלית דו-לשונית ואפשר להקליד בעברית ובאנגלית.
Hamiqledet hayisra`elit du-leshonit ve`efshar lehaqlid be'ivrit uve`anglit.

❺ לכבוד חג הפסח, התלמידים ראו מצגות מולטימדיה על יציאת מצרים.
Likhvod chag haPesach, hatalmidim ra`u matzagot multimedyah 'al yetzi`at Mitzrayim.

* **`eru'ey אֵרוּעֵי** = *events-of* (construct state)

Answers to Exercise 1

❶ Real-time information about tourism events in the city is found on our website. ❷ She teaches history at school and at home she has wall-to-wall books. ❸ At the hospital, there is a team of specialist doctors for eye problems. ❹ The Israeli keyboard is bilingual and it is possible to type in Hebrew and in English. ❺ In honour of the festival of Passover, the pupils watched multimedia presentations about the Exodus from Egypt.

בבית החולים יש צוות רופאים מומחים לבעיות עיניים.

Targil sheni – Hashlem תַּרְגִּיל שֵׁנִי – הַשְׁלֵם

❶ Where is he? What a question! Between the computer screen and the telephone screen!
[...] hu? – [...] she`elah! [...] ha[...] shel hamachshev ve[...] hatelefon!

____ הוא? ____ שאלה! ___ ה__ של המחשב ו___ הטלפון.

❷ Every day the manager updates the data on the hard disk.
Kol yom ha[...] me'adken `et ha[...] badisq ha[...].

כל יום ה____ מעדכן את ה______ בדיסק ה____.

❸ For [someone] who likes opera, sound files *(they)* [are a wonderful] musical experience.
Lemi she`ohev `operah, [...] hem [...] musiqalit.

למי שאוהב אופרה ____ ___ הם ____ מוסיקלית.

❹ The biggest advantage of the computer [is that] it [is] possible to correspond with people from all over the world.
[...] hagadol [...] shel hamachshev hu she`efshar lehitkatev 'im [...] mikol [...].

______ הגדול _____ של המחשב הוא שאפשר להתכתב
עם _____ מכל _____.

❺ A good doctor must update himself all the time about the latest innovations.
[...] tov tzarikh [...] kol hazman ba[...] ha`acharonim.

___ טוב צריך _______ כל הזמן ב_______ האחרונים.

Answers to Exercise 2

❶ **`Eyfoh – `Eyzo – Beyn – tzag – tzag –**

❶ איפה - איזו - בין - צג - צג -

❷ **– menahel – netunim – qashiach**

❷ - מנהל - נתונים - קשיח

❸ **– qivtzey qol – chavayah –**

❸ - קבצי קול - חויה -

❹ **Hayitaron – beyoter – `anashim – ha'olam**

❹ היתרון - ביותר - אנשים - העולם

❺ **Rofe – lehit'adken – chidushim –**

❺ רופא - להתעדכן - חידושים -

Ha`entziqlopedyah ha'ivrit הָאֶנְצִיקְלוֹפֶּדְיָה הָעִבְרִית The Encyclopedia Hebraica. *In July 1949, less than a year after the State of Israel declared its independence, Professor* **Brodetzqy** בְּרוֹדֶצְקִי*, President of the Hebrew University of Jerusalem, presented the first volume of this monumental work, which now comprises 32 volumes and sundry appendices. The encyclopedia places a special emphasis on Jewish and Israeli subjects, but also provides thorough information about all fields of human knowledge and history.*

Second wave: lesson 32

82 Eighty-second lesson
(Shi'ur shmonim ushtayim)

Bchirot ①
Elections

1 – **Be'od chatzi shanah yiheyu bchirot. Hayiti rotzeh ② livchor.**
In six months *(In-another half year)* there will be elections. I would like to vote *(I-was I-want to choose)*.

2 **`Ani 'oleh chadash velo yode'a mah la'asot.**
I am a new immigrant and [I] don't know what to do.

3 – **Davar rishon, `atah tzarikh levaqesh `ezrachut yisra`elit.**
Firstly *(Thing first)*, you need to request Israeli citizenship.

4 – **`Ani kvar `ezrach yisra`eli, yesh li te'udat zehut.**
I am already an Israeli citizen; I have an identity card *(certificate-of identity)*.

5 – **Yofi! Lekh lemisrad hapnim, sham teqabel kartis bocher.**
Wonderful! Go to the Interior Ministry, there you will receive a voter's card.

Notes

① **bchirot** בְּחִירוֹת *elections, choices.* The singular is **bchirah** בְּחִירָה *choice.*

② **hayiti rotzeh** הָיִיתִי רוֹצֶה *I would like.* As you know by now, Hebrew has three basic tenses – past, present and future. There is also a useful tense form that consists of a past form of the

בְּחִירוֹת

1 – בְּעוֹד חֲצִי שָׁנָה יִהְיוּ בְּחִירוֹת. הָיִיתִי רוֹצֶה לִבְחוֹר.

2 אֲנִי עוֹלֶה חָדָשׁ וְלֹא יוֹדֵעַ מַה לַעֲשׂוֹת.

3 – דָּבָר רִאשׁוֹן, אַתָּה צָרִיךְ לְבַקֵּשׁ אֶזְרָחוּת יִשְׂרְאֵלִית.

4 – אֲנִי כְּבָר אֶזְרָח יִשְׂרְאֵלִי, יֵשׁ לִי תְּעוּדַת זֶהוּת.

5 – יוֹפִי! לֵךְ לְמִשְׂרַד הַפְּנִים, שָׁם תְּקַבֵּל כַּרְטִיס בּוֹחֵר.

verb *to be* with a present tense verb. This has two main uses:
• to form the present conditional tense ('I would like to vote') as well as past conditional sentences ('he would have given you a present if he had any money'). See review lesson 84 for more details about this use.
• to express the 'habitual' past ('I used to drink beer', 'the children used to play in the garden'):
`Aba sheli hayah shoteh qafeh kol boqer.
אַבָּא שֶׁלִּי הָיָה שׁוֹתֶה קָפֶה כֹּל בֹּקֶר.
My dad used to drink coffee every morning.

6 – **'Akhshav `ani tzarikh lilmod `et shitat habchirot, kedey lehachlit le`eyzo miflagah lehatzbi'a ③.**
Now I need to study the electoral system *(method-of the-elections)* in order to decide which party to vote for.

7 – **`Eyn be'ayot! Yesh mivchar ④ gadol shel miflagot mikol hatzdadim: yamin, smol, merkaz …**
No problems! There is a big choice of parties on all sides: right, left, centre ...

8 – **Nu, zeh qlasi!**
Well, that's nothing unusual *(that's classical)*!

9 – **Zeh lo hakol. Yekholim limnot ⑤ 'od: mifleget 'olim chadashim, dovrey rusit, sfaradim ⑥,**
That's not all. More can be mentioned *(One-may count more)*: a new immigrants' party, Russian speakers, Sephardim,

Notes

③ **lehatzbi'a** לְהַצְבִּיעַ *to vote*. This verb comes from the word **`etzba'** אֶצְבַּע *finger*, since a finger or hand is raised to vote for or against something. The same verb is used for raising a hand to respond to a question – for example, in a classroom.

④ **mivchar** מִבְחָר *choice*, *selection*. Like **bchirah** (note 1), this noun comes from the root בחר. It also means *choice*, particularly in the sense of *selection* – picking something one wants from a range of items (clothes, food, etc.).

⑤ **limnot** לִמְנוֹת *to count*. Some other words from the root מנה include **moneh** מוֹנֶה *meter* (such as a taxi meter or gas meter); **monit** מוֹנִית *taxi* (because a **monit** has a **moneh**!); **manah** מָנָה *portion*, *ration*; **menayah** מְנָיָה *share* (in the stock market).

6 – עַכְשָׁו אֲנִי צָרִיךְ לִלְמוֹד אֶת שִׁיטַת הַבְּחִירוֹת, כְּדֵי לְהַחְלִיט לְאֵיזוֹ מִפְלָגָה לְהַצְבִּיעַ.

7 – אֵין בְּעָיוֹת! יֵשׁ מִבְחָר גָּדוֹל שֶׁל מִפְלָגוֹת מִכֹּל הַצְּדָדִים: יָמִין, שְׂמֹאל, מֶרְכָּז ...

8 – נוּ, זֶה קְלַסִּי!

9 – זֶה לֹא הַכֹּל. יְכוֹלִים לִמְנוֹת עוֹד: מִפְלֶגֶת עוֹלִים חֲדָשִׁים, דּוֹבְרֵי רוּסִית, סְפָרַדִּים,

⑥ **sfaradim** סְפָרַדִּים *Sephardim.* This term refers to Jews of Spanish origin, even if their families lived for centuries in the Balkans, Turkey, Morocco or elsewhere after the Jews were expelled from Spain in 1492 CE. It is sometimes used less precisely to refer to non-Ashkenazi Jews, including those from Muslim or Arab countries, such as Iran and Iraq. The term **mizrachim** מִזְרָחִים *Orientals* is preferred in this broader sense. **Sfarad** סְפָרַד is a place name that occurs once in the Bible, and has come to be associated with Spain. Similarly, the Biblical place name **Tzarfat** צָרְפַת has come to be used to refer to France.

82 **10** **datiyim, chiloniyim ⑦, vatiqim, miflagot 'arviyot, miflagah lema'an ⑧ `eykhut hasvivah ...**
religious *(ones)*, secular *(ones)*, senior citizens, Arab parties, an ecological party *(party for quality-of the-environment)*...

11 – Kamah?
How many?

12 – 'Al hashe`elah hazot `eyn li karega' tshuvah.
For that question, I don't have an answer at the moment *(as-the-moment answer)*.

13 Bekhol ma'arekhet bchirot qamot miflagot chadashot vene'elamot yeshanot.
In every election campaign, new parties appear *(rise up)* and old ones disappear.

14 – Kamah nivcharim ⑨?
How many are elected *(How-many elected-ones)*?

15 – Me`ah 'esrim chavrey kneset ⑩ nivcharim bivchirot yeshirot le`arba' shanim.
One hundred and twenty Members of Knesset are elected in direct elections for four years.

Notes

⑦ **chiloniyim** חִילוֹנִיִּים 'seculars' (plural noun), *secular people*. **chol** חוֹל means *common*, *secular* or *profane* as opposed to holy or consecrated. **yom chol** יוֹם חוֹל is a *weekday* – a regular working day that is not Shabbat or a festival.

⑧ **lema'an** לְמַעַן means *for* or *for the sake of*.

10 דָתִיִּים, חִילוֹנִיִּים, וָתִיקִים, מִפלָגוֹת עַרבִיוֹת, מִפלָגָה לְמַעַן אֵיכוּת הַסבִיבָה ...

11 – כַּמָה?

12 – עַל הַשְׁאֵלָה הַזֹּאת אֵין לִי כַּרֶגַע תשׁוּבָה.

13 בְּכֹל מַעֲרֶכֶת בּחִירוֹת קָמוֹת מִפלָגוֹת חֲדָשׁוֹת וְנֶעֱלָמוֹת יְשָׁנוֹת.

14 – כָּמָה נִבחָרִים?

15 – מֵאָה עֶשׂרִים חַבְרֵי כְּנֶסֶת נִבחָרִים בִּבחִירוֹת יְשִׁירוֹת לְאַרבַּע שָׁנִים.

⑨ **nivcharim** נִבחָרִים *elected ones, representatives.* This is another word from the root בחר. A **nivchar** נִבחָר is a man who has been elected or chosen for a particular position. The feminine form is **nivcheret** נִבחֶרֶת (singular) and **nivcharot** נִבחָרוֹת (plural). **livchor** לִבחוֹר is *to choose, to elect.*

⑩ **chavrey kneset** חַבְרֵי כְּנֶסֶת *Members of Knesset.* The construct state is used here, since the construction **chaverim shel hakneset** חֲבֵרִים שֶׁל הַכְּנֶסֶת would sound as if it meant 'friends of the Knesset'.

16 Tilmad `et hanose, lo yiheyeh lekha zman lehishta'amem! Tatzbi'a lefi matzpunkha ⑪**.**
Study *(You-will-study)* the subject, you won't have time to get bored! Vote *(You-will-vote)* according to your conscience.

Notes

⑪ **matzpunkha** מַצְפּוּנְךָ *your conscience*. Hopefully you will recognize the second-person masculine singular possessive suffix attached to this noun: **matzpun** מַצְפּוּן. A related word

Targil rishon – Targem תַּרְגִּיל רִאשׁוֹן – תַּרְגֵּם

❶ החלטתם בעד איזו מפלגה להצביע?
Hechlatetem be'ad `eyzo miflagah lehatzbi'a?

❷ היא קבלה תעודת זהות ממשרד הפנים.
Hi qiblah te'udat zehut mimisrad hapnim.

❸ באיזו שעה אתן קמות בבוקר?
Be`eyzo sha'ah `aten qamot baboqer?

❹ מספיק עם הפטפוטים! בקצור, מה אתם רוצים?
Maspiq 'im hapitputim! Beqitzur, mah `atem rotzim?

❺ בעולם המערבי אופנתי מאוד להיות חבר במפלגה לאיכות הסביבה.
Ba'olam hama'aravi `ofnati me`od lihiyot chaver bemiflagah le`eykhut hasvivah.

16 תִּלְמַד אֶת הַנּוֹשֵׂא, לֹא יִהְיֶה לְךָ זְמַן לְהִשְׁתַּעֲמֵם! תַּצְבִּיעַ לְפִי מַצְפּוּנְךָ. □

is **matzpen** מַצְפֵּן *compass* – our conscience is our internal guidance system that tells us in which direction we should go.

Answers to Exercise 1

❶ Have you decided which party to vote for? ❷ She received an identity card from the Interior Ministry. ❸ At what time do you get up in the morning? ❹ Enough chatting! Get to the point! *(In-brief)*, what do you want? ❺ In the Western world, it is very fashionable to be a member of an ecological party.

בחירות

Targil sheni – Hashlem תַּרְגִּיל שֵׁנִי – הַשְׁלֵם

❶ He's a man of the *(big)* world, he has Israeli citizenship, French citizenship and American citizenship.
Hu `ish [...] hagadol, yesh lo [...] yisra`elit, `ezrachut [...], ve`ezrachut `ameriqanit.

הוא איש _____ הגדול, יש לו ______ ישראלית, אזרחות
______ ואזרחות אמריקנית.

❷ Shabbat and the festivals are also important for secular people.
Hashabat [...] [...] gam le`anashim [...].

השבת ______ ______ גם לאנשים ________.

❸ In the election, everyone must vote according to their conscience.
[...] kol `echad tzarikh [...] lefi [...].

______ כל אחד צריך ______ לפי ______.

❹ I would have been happy *(I-was I-am-happy)* to arrive on time for your birthday!
[...] [...] lehagi'a ba[...] leyom huladetekh!

_____ ___ להגיע ב___ ליום הולדתך.

❺ Among the Members of Knesset, there are Russian speakers [and] Arabic speakers, but they all speak Hebrew.
Beyn [...] [...] yesh [...] russit, [...] 'aravit, `aval kulam [...] 'ivrit.

בין ____ _____ יש _____ רוסית, _____ ערבית, אבל
כולם ______ עברית.

Answers to Exercise 2

❶ – **ha'olam** – **`ezrachut** – **tzarfatit** –

❶ - העולם - אזרחות - צרפתית -

❷ – **vehachagim chashuvim** – **chiloniyim**

❷ - והחגים חשובים - חילוניים

❸ **Babchirot** – **lehatzbi'a** – **matzpuno**

❸ בבחירות - להצביע - מצפונו

❹ **Hayiti sameach** – **zman** –

❹ הייתי שמח - זמן -

❺ – **chavrey hakneset** – **dovrey** – **dovrey** – **medabrim** –

❺ - חברי הכנסת - דוברי - דוברי - מדברים -

Israel is a Western-style democracy, although (like the United Kingdom) it lacks a written constitution. Israel's Declaration of Independence serves as a statement of underlying values, while a series of 'basic laws' define the workings of the Knesset and guarantee human and civil rights.

The state president is called **nasi** נָשִׂיא*, a title that was once used for the head of the* **sanhedrin** סַנְהֶדְרִין*, the governing body of the Jews in the Land of Israel after the return from Exile in Babylon. The president of the modern State of Israel is elected for a seven-year term by the Knesset, and may serve for no more than two consecutive terms of office. The president's function is mainly ceremonial – signing laws and treaties, endorsing the credentials of foreign ambassadors, and so forth.*

The **memshalah** מֶמְשָׁלָה government *of Israel consists of a cabinet that includes the* **rosh hamemshalah** רֹאשׁ הַמֶּמְשָׁלָה prime minister *and the* **sarim** שָׂרִים ministers *that he or she has chosen.*

Second wave: lesson 33

83 Eighty-third lesson
(Shi'ur shmonim veshalosh)

`Eruach kafri ①
Rural hospitality

1 – **Lemi sherotzeh leshadreg** ② **`et ramat** ③ **chufshato** ④ **hineh hatza'ah le`eruach kafri, bli lifshot `et haregel** ⑤**.**
For who[ever] wants to upgrade the standard of his holiday, here is a suggestion for rural hospitality without going bankrupt *(without stretching the-leg)*.

2 **Sokhnuyot hanesi'ot matzi'ot 'isqot chavilah** ⑥ **mefatot beta`arikhim mesuyamim.**
Travel agencies offer tempting package deals on certain dates.

Notes

① **kafri** כַּפְרִי *rural*. This adjective comes from the noun **kfar** כְּפָר *village*. A 'village' may not always be what it seems – some Israeli communities that have the word **kfar** in their names are now large towns. **Kfar Sava** כְּפַר סָבָא to the north of Tel Aviv today has a population of tens of thousands.

② **leshadreg** לְשַׁדְרֵג *to upgrade*. This word is used particularly in the field of computers. Many other nouns are formed from the root דרג, including **dereg** דֶּרֶג *echelon*, *grade* and **madregah** מַדְרֵגָה *step* (on a staircase). Note that the letter **shin** has been added to the root – this sometimes occurs when the word contains the idea of doing something again or more intensively.

אֲרוּחַ כָּפְרִי

1 – לְמִי שֶׁרוֹצֶה לְשַׁדְרֵג אֶת רָמַת חוּפְשָׁתוֹ, הִנֵּה הַצָּעָה לְאֵרוּחַ כָּפְרִי, בְּלִי לִפְשׁוֹט אֶת הָרֶגֶל.

2 סוֹכְנוּיוֹת הַנְּסִיעוֹת מַצִּיעוֹת עִסְקוֹת חֲבִילָה מְפַתּוֹת בְּתַאֲרִיכִים מְסוּיָּמִים.

③ **ramah** רָמָה *level*, *height* can refer to a physical level (low, high, etc.) or to the level or standard of a course and such like. The expression **ramat chayim** is *standard of living*. In the construct state, the ה is replaced by ת: **Ramat haGolan** רָמַת הַגּוֹלָן *the Golan Heights*.

④ **chufshato** חוּפְשָׁתוֹ *his holiday*. **chufshah** חוּפְשָׁה appears here with the third-person masculine singular possessive suffix. Note that the final ה is replaced by a ת before the characteristic וֹ suffix for the masculine singular. If we were discussing a woman's holiday, the form would be **chufshatah** חוּפְשָׁתָהּ *her holiday*.

⑤ **lifshot `et haregel** לִפְשׁוֹט אֶת הָרֶגֶל *to go bankrupt*. Literally, 'to stretch the leg'. The noun *bankruptcy* is **pshitat regel** פְּשִׁיטַת רֶגֶל. The verb **lifshot** לִפְשׁוֹט also means *to undress*, *to take off* (an item of clothing).

⑥ **'isqat chavilah** עִסְקַת חֲבִילָה *package deal*. This Hebrew expression is a straightforward translation of the English.

3 – Zeh hamaqom lehitpaneq velitpos shalvah ⑦ mul nof 'otzer neshimah.
This is the place to spoil yourself and find *(catch)* some calm with a breathtaking view *(opposite landscape stopping breath)*.

4 – Biqtot 'etz yefeyfiyot beharey haGalil:
Beautiful wooden cabins in the Galilee mountains:

5 – habiqtah kolelet chadar megurim, chadar-sheynah, `ambatyah, sherutim vegaleryah lechadar yeladim.
[each] cabin includes a living room, bedroom, bath, toilet and a gallery as *(for)* a children's room.

6 – Mitbach me`uvzar: miqrogal, meqarer, tanur, kirayim, mediach-kelim.
A [well-]equipped kitchen: microwave, fridge, oven, stove top [and] dishwasher.

7 – Babiqtah mizug `avir baqayitz ve`ach bachoref.
The cabin [has] air-conditioning for *(in)* summer and a fireplace for *(in)* winter.

8 – Midsha`ot ⑧ gdolot, mitqanim liyeladim, brekhah, jaquzi.
Large lawns, children's play area *(facilities for-children)*, pool [and] jacuzzi.

Notes

⑦ **litpos shalvah** לִתְפּוֹס שַׁלְוָה *to find* ('grab') *calm, to hang out.*

3 – זֶה הַמָּקוֹם לְהִתְפַּנֵּק וְלִתְפּוֹס שַׁלְוָה מוּל נוֹף עוֹצֵר נְשִׁימָה.

4 – בִּקְתוֹת עֵץ יְפֵהפִיּוֹת בְּהָרֵי הַגָּלִיל:

5 – הַבִּקְתָה כּוֹלֶלֶת חֲדַר מְגוּרִים, חֲדַר שֵׁינָה, אַמְבַּטְיָה, שֵׁרוּתִים וְגָלֶרְיָה לַחֲדַר יְלָדִים.

6 – מִטְבָּח מְאוּבְזָר: מִיקְרוֹגַל, מְקָרֵר, תַּנּוּר, כִּירַיִים, מְדִיחַ-כֵּלִים.

7 – בַּבִּקְתָה מִזּוּג אֲוִיר בַּקַּיִץ וְאָח בַּחוֹרֶף.

8 – מִדְשָׁאוֹת גְּדוֹלוֹת, מִתְקָנִים לִיְלָדִים, בְּרֵכָה, גָ׳קוּזִי.

בחופשה הילדים אוהבים להתפנק אצל סבא וסבתא.

⑧ **midsha`ot** מִדְשָׁאוֹת *lawns*. The singular is **midsha`ah** מִדְשָׁאָה. This word is formed from the noun **deshe** דֶשֶׁא *grass*, with the מ prefix we have encountered countless times.

9 – **Yesh gam mis'adah, beyt qafeh, vechanut kolbo ⑨ qtanah.**
There is also a restaurant, a café and a small minimarket.

10 – **Bemerchaq shel shloshah kilometrim nimtzet shmurat teva' ⑩.**
Three kilometres away *(At-distance of three kilometres)* there is a nature reserve *(is-found a-conservation-of nature)*.

11 **Tukhlu letayel bishvilim nochim vela'alot lamitzpeh ⑪ `o lamitzpor ⑫.**
You will be able to walk along comfortable paths and climb up to a vantage point or bird's-eye lookout.

12 – **Bashmurah pinat chay-bar ⑬ liyeladim va`afilu brekhat dagim.**
The reserve [has] a wild animals' corner for children and even a fish pond *(pool-of fish)*.

Notes

⑨ **kolbo** כָּלְבּוֹ *minimarket* (literally, 'all in it'). This word was originally used to designate a *department store*, but it is now slightly old-fashioned and refers to a smaller shop offering a selection of food and household items.

⑩ **shmurat teva'** שְׁמוּרַת טֶבַע *nature reserve*. Israel has an extensive network of nature reserves and national parks, managed by **reshut hateva vehaganim** רְשׁוּת הַטֶּבַע וְהַגַּנִּים *Israel Nature and Parks Authority*. We've mentioned Hebrew's love of abbreviations and acronyms several times, so you probably won't be surprised to hear that this body is usually referred to by the acronym **ratag** רט"ג.

9 – יֵשׁ גַּם מִסְעָדָה, בֵּית קָפֶה וַחֲנוּת כּלבּוֹ קְטַנָּה.

10 – בְּמֶרְחָק שֶׁל שְׁלוֹשָׁה קִילוֹמֶטְרִים נִמְצֵאת שְׁמוּרַת טֶבַע.

11 תוּכלוּ לְטַיֵּל בִּשְׁבִילִים נוֹחִים, וְלַעֲלוֹת לַמִּצְפֶּה אוֹ לַמִּצְפּוֹר.

12 – בַּשְּׁמוּרָה פִּנַּת חַי-בַּר לִילָדִים וַאֲפִילוּ בְּרֵכַת דָּגִים.

⑪ **mitzpeh** מִצְפֶּה *observatory, lookout point*. The root צפה means *to observe, to expect*. One of the most beautiful views of Jerusalem can be enjoyed from **har hatzofim** הַר הַצּוֹפִים *Mount Scopus*.

⑫ **mitzpor** מִצְפּוֹר *bird's-eye lookout, vantage point*. This fairly recent word is used to refer either to a bird observation tower or to a point offering an impressive view, usually with shade and benches, and often with a map or plaque providing information about the landscape.

⑬ **chay-bar** חַי-בַּר – literally, 'living-wild'. This term usually refers to a large enclosure where wild animals can roam relatively freely. Here, the reference is to a small petting corner for young children. This is also known as **pinat chay** פִּינַּת חַי 'corner of-life'.

13 – Hasaqranim shebeynekhem yukhlu lehitnasot bimelakhot-yad mitqufat haTanakh.
The curious among you will be able to try *(to-gain-experience-in)* handicrafts from the Biblical period.

14 – Chufshah ne'imah vedabru 'ivrit!
[Have a] pleasant holiday – and speak Hebrew!

Targil rishon – Targem תַּרְגִּיל רִאשׁוֹן – תַּרְגֵּם

❶ עסקת החבילה כוללת כרטיס טיסה, בקתה כפרית ומכונית.
'Isqat hachavilah kolelet kartis tisah, biqtah kafrit umekhonit.

❷ בחופשה הילדים אוהבים להתפנק אצל סבא וסבתא.
Bachufshah hayeladim `ohavim lehitpaneq `etzel saba vesavta.

❸ אני ממש לא יודעת מה הייתי עושה בלי מיקרוגל ומדיח-כלים.
`Ani mamash lo yoda'at mah hayiti 'osah bli miqrogal umediach-kelim.

❹ מצוללת הזכוכית בים האדום רואים נוף ימי עוצר נשימה.
Mitzolelet hazkhukhit bayam ha`adom ro`im nof yami 'otzer neshimah.

❺ לבעלי יש חדר עבודה מאובזר בכל החידושים העכשוויים.
Leva'ali yesh chadar 'avodah me`uvzar bekhol hachidushim ha'akhshaviyim.

13 – הַסַקרָנִים שֶׁבֵּינֵיכֶם יוּכלוּ לְהִתנַסוֹת בִּמלָאכוֹת-יָד מִתקוּפַת הַתַנָ"ך.

14 – חוּפשָׁה נְעִימָה וְדַבּרוּ עִברִית.

Answers to Exercise 1

❶ The package deal includes a plane *(flight)* ticket, a rural cabin and a car. ❷ During *(In)* the holidays, the children like to get spoiled at Grandpa and Grandma's. ❸ I really don't know what I would do without a microwave and dishwasher. ❹ From the glass submarine in the Red Sea, you *(impers. subj.)* can see a breathtaking marine landscape. ❺ My husband has a study *(room-of work)* equipped with all the latest *(contemporary)* innovations.

83 Targil sheni – Hashlem תַּרְגִּיל שֵׁנִי – הַשְׁלֵם

❶ The teachers prepare interesting information in order to upgrade the level of the studies.
[...] mekhinim [...] me'anyen kedey [...] `et [...] halimudim.

_____ מכינים ____ מעניין כדי _____ את ___ הלימודים.

❷ A bath full of bubbles *(foam)*, music and coffee – what more does a person need in order to find [some] calm?
[...] mele`ah [...], musiqah veqafeh, mah 'od tzarikh haben `adam kedey [...] [...]?

______ מלאה ___, מוסיקה וקפה, מה עוד צריך הבן אדם
כדי _____ ____?

❸ At the end of the summer, there are tempting offers in all the clothes shops.
Besof haqayitz, yesh [...] [...] bekhol chanuyot ha[...].

בסוף הקיץ יש _____ _____ בכל חנויות ה_____ .

❹ Every two years, on a specific date, there is an international conference on medicine in the Bible.
Kol shnatayim be[...] yesh [...] beynle`umi 'al ha[...] baTanakh.

כל שנתיים ב_____ _____ יש ___ בינלאומי על
ה_____ בתנ"ך.

❺ They go *(travel)* every winter to ski [and stay] at the same hotel, because the hospitality there *(in-it)* is excellent.
Hem nos'im kol [...] lesqi le`oto [...] ki ha[...] bo [...].

הם נוסעים כל ____ לסקי לאותו ____, כי ה____ בו _____ .

Answers to Exercise 2

❶ **Hamorim – meyda' – leshadreg – ramat –**

❶ המורים - מידע - לשדרג - רמת -

❷ **`Ambatyah – qetzef – litpos shalvah**

❷ אמבטיה - קצף - לתפוס שלוה

❸ **– hatza'ot mefatot – bgadim**

❸ - הצעות מפתות - בגדים

❹ **– ta`arikh mesuyam – kenes – refu`ah –**

❹ - תאריך מסוים - כנס - רפואה -

❺ **– choref – malon – `eruach – metzuyan**

❺ - חורף - מלון - ארוח - מצוין

Galil גָּלִיל Galilee*: Wetter and greener than the rest of Israel, the Galilee has always been a fertile and attractive region. The Talmud refers to the Galilee as Israel's 'bread basket'.*

Reaching a height of 1208 metres above sea level, Mount Meron **Har Meron** הַר מֵרוֹן *offers spectacular views of the Sea of Galilee, which lies 200 metres below sea level. A few kilometres away, the ancient city of* **Tzfat** צְפַת Safed *is renowned for its old synagogues, picturesque alleyways and its association with the mystical and Kabbalistic side of Jewish tradition.*

The Prophet Isaiah and Matthew of the Christian Gospel both referred to the Galilee as a 'district of the nations', since it was populated by non-Jews of diverse origins. Today, too, the majority of the residents of the Galilee are not Jewish. They include Muslim and Christian Arabs, Druze and small communities of Circassians (a Muslim people originating from the Caucuses).

The city of **Tveryah** טְבֶרְיָה *on the Western shore of the Sea of Galilee is named after the Roman Emperor Tiberius. Not far away, at* **Qarnei Hittim** קַרְנֵי חִיטִּים The Horns of Hittim, *Salah ad-Din (Saladin) routed the Crusader army in 1187 CE.*

Second wave: lesson 34

84 Eighty-fourth lesson
(Shi'ur shmonim ve`arba')

חֲזָרָה Chazarah – Review

This is our final review lesson. What a long way you've come since the first lesson, when you learned only three or four words in short, basic sentences! To conclude the course, we offer some final additional vocabulary and grammatical points. In presenting the verb forms, in some cases we've just provided a sample of the harder forms rather than all the different persons. By now, you should be able to conjugate the different persons according to the regular patterns you've learned.

1 Vocabulary

• **me`uvzar** מְאוּבְזָר *equipped, accessorized.* **`avizar** אֲבִיזָר *accessory* (the form **`avzar** is also correct) is an Aramaic word that has acquired a modern meaning. Two phrases using this word are:

chanut le`avzarey `ofnah חֲנוּת לְאַבְזָרֵי אוֹפְנָה
fashion accessories shop
`avizarim limekhoniyot אֲבִיזָרִים לִמְכוֹנִיּוֹת
car accessories

• In the heat of the kitchen, don't mix up the different words we've seen for types of cooking:

le`adot	לְאַדּוֹת	*to steam*
le`efot	לֶאֱפוֹת	*to bake*
levashel	לְבַשֵּׁל	*to cook, boil*
letagen	לְטַגֵּן	*to fry*
litzlot	לִצְלוֹת	*to roast*
liqlot	לִקְלוֹת	*to grill* (**'al ha`esh** עַל הָאֵשׁ *over a flame*)

2 Adverbs of time

`achar kakh	אַחַר כָּךְ	*afterwards*
`af pa'am	אַף פַּעַם	*never*

84 שִׁעוּר שְׁמוֹנִים וְאַרְבַּע

`etmol	אֶתמוֹל	*yesterday*
haboqer	הַבּוֹקֶר	*this morning*
hayom	הַיּוֹם	*today*
ha'erev	הָעֶרֶב	*this evening*
le'itim qrovot	לְעִתִּים קרוֹבוֹת	*often*
le'itim rechoqot	לְעִתִּים רְחוֹקוֹת	*rarely*
le'olam lo	לְעוֹלָם לֹא	*never* (with future verbs)
lif'amim	לִפְעָמִים	*sometimes*
machar	מָחָר	*tomorrow*
me'olam lo	מֵעוֹלָם לֹא	*never* (with past verbs)
matay?	מָתַי?	*when?*
'ad matay?	עַד מָתַי?	*until when?*
'adayin	עֲדַיִן	*still*
'akhshav	עַכְשָׁו	*now*
pa'am	פַּעַם	*once, one time*
tamid	תָּמִיד	*always*

3 Some new verb conjugations

3.1 *lehaqlid* לְהַקְלִיד 'to type'

This verb comes from the root קלד, which is also found in **miqledet** מִקְלֶדֶת *keyboard*, **qaldan** קַלְדָן / **qaldanit** קַלְדָנִית *typist* (m./f.), and **haqladah** הַקְלָדָה *typing*, among other words.

• Present tense:
Masculine: **(`ani, `atah, hu) maqlid** מַקְלִיד *I, you type / he types*
Feminine: **(`ani, `at, hi) maqlidah** מַקְלִידָה *I, you type / she types*

• Past tense:
(`ani) hiqladeti הִקְלַדְתִּי *I typed*

• Future tense:
(`ani) `aqlid אַקְלִיד *I will type*

3.2 *la'amod* לַעֲמוֹד 'to stand'

The root is עמד.

- Present tense:

Masculine: **(`ani, `atah, hu) 'omed** עוֹמֵד *I, you stand / he stands*
Feminine: **(`ani, `at, hi) 'omedet** עוֹמֶדֶת *I, you stand / she stands*

- Past tense:

(`ani) 'amadeti עָמַדְתִּי *I stood*

- Future tense:

(`ani) `e'emod אֶעֱמוֹד *I will stand*

3.3 *lehagi'a* לְהַגִּיעַ 'to arrive'

The root is נגע, but the **nun** does not appear in any of the conjugations of this verb.

- Present tense:

(`ani, `atah, hu) magi'a	מַגִּיעַ	*I arrive, you arrive, he arrives* (masc.)
(`ani, `at, hi) magi'ah	מַגִּיעָה	*I arrive, you arrive, she arrives* (fem.)
(`anachnu, `atem, hem) magi'im	מַגִּיעִים	*we, you, they arrive* (masc.)
(`anachnu, `aten, hen) magi'ot	מַגִּיעוֹת	*we, you, they arrive* (fem.)

- Past tense:

(`ani) higa'ti	הִגַּעְתִּי	*I arrived*
(`atah) higa'ta/(`at) higa't	הִגַּעְתָּ, הִגַּעַת	*you arrived* (m./f.)
(hu) higi'a/(hi) higi'ah	הִגִּיעַ, הִגִּיעָה	*he/she arrived*
(`anachnu) higa'nu	הִגַּעְנוּ	*we arrived*
(`atem) higa'tem/ (`aten) higa'ten	הִגַּעְתֶּם, הִגַּעְתֶּן	*you arrived* (m./f. pl.)
(hem) higi'u/(hen) higi'u	הִגִּיעוּ	*they arrived* (m./f.)

- Future tense:

(`ani) agi'a	אַגִּיעַ	*I will arrive*
(`atah) tagia'/(`at) tagi'i	תַּגִּיעַ, תַּגִּיעִי	*you will arrive* (m./f.)
(hu) yagi'a/(hi) tagi'a	יַגִּיעַ, תַּגִּיעַ	*he/she will arrive*

(`anachnu) nagi'a	נַגִּיעַ	*we will arrive*
(`atem) tagi'u/(`aten) tagi'u	תַּגִּיעוּ	*you will arrive* (m./f. pl.)
(hem) yagi'u/(hen) yagi'u	יַגִּיעוּ	*they will arrive* (m./f.)

The verb **lehagi'a** לְהַגִּיעַ is also used to convey the idea of *deserving* something. Here are two examples:

• **magi'a li machshev chadash** מַגִּיעַ לִי מַחְשֵׁב חָדָשׁ (literally, 'arrives for me a new computer') *I deserve a new computer.* In the Hebrew expression, the subject of the verb is the thing that is being deserved, not the person who deserves it. Accordingly, the verb appears in the masculine singular, since **machshev** is a masculine noun.

• **magi'ot lakhen matanot** מַגִּיעוֹת לָכֶן מַתָּנוֹת (literally, 'arrive for you presents') *You deserve presents.* The 'you' in this case is the feminine plural – a father of three girls, for example, might say this to them if they had behaved well. The verb is in the feminine plural – not because of the girls who deserve the presents, but because **matanot** is a feminine plural noun.

3.4 *lehit'amel* לְהִתְעַמֵּל 'to work out', 'to exercise'

The root is עמל.

• Present tense:
Masculine: **(`ani, `atah, hu) mit'amel** מִתְעַמֵּל
I, you exercise, he exercises
Feminine: **(`ani, `at, hi) mit'amelet** מִתְעַמֶּלֶת
I, you exercise, she exercises
Masc. plural: **(`anachnu, `atem, hem) mit'amlim** מִתְעַמְּלִים
we, you, they exercise
Fem. plural: **(`anachnu, `aten, hen) mit'amlot** מִתְעַמְּלוֹת
we, you, they exercise

• Past tense:
(`ani) hit'amalti הִתְעַמַּלְתִּי
I exercised
(hu) hit'amel/(hi) hit'amlah הִתְעַמֵּל, הִתְעַמְּלָה
he/she exercised
(hem) hit'amlu/(hen) hit'amlu הִתְעַמְּלוּ
they exercised

• Future tense:
(`ani) `et'amel אֶתְעַמֵּל
I will exercise

84 **(`atah) tit'amel/(`at) tit'amli** תִּתְעַמֵּל, תִּתְעַמְּלִי
you will exercise (masc. sing./fem. sing.)

3.5 *likh'os* לִכְעוֹס 'to be angry'

Root כעס:
- Present tense:

Masculine: **(`ani, `atah, hu) ko'es** כּוֹעֵס
I am angry, you are angry, he is angry
Feminine: **(`ani, `at, hi) ko'eset** כּוֹעֶסֶת
I am angry, you are angry, she is angry
Masc. plural: **(`anachnu, `atem, hem) ko'asim** כּוֹעֲסִים
we, you, they are angry
Fem. plural: **(`anachnu, `aten, hen) ko'asot** כּוֹעֲסוֹת
we, you, they are angry

- Past tense:

(`ani) ka'asti כָּעַסְתִּי *I was angry*
(hu) ka'as כָּעַס *he was angry*
(hi) ka'asah כָּעֲסָה *she was angry*

- Future tense:

(`ani) `ekh'as אֶכְעַס *I will be angry*

3.6 *lifshot regel* לִפְשׁוֹט רֶגֶל 'to go bankrupt'

- Present tense:

Masculine: **(`ani, `atah, hu) poshet regel** פּוֹשֵׁט רֶגֶל
I, you go bankrupt, he goes bankrupt
Feminine: **(`ani, `at, hi) poshetet regel** פּוֹשֶׁטֶת רֶגֶל
I, you go bankrupt, she goes bankrupt
Masc. plural: **(`anachnu, `atem, hem) poshtim regel** פּוֹשְׁטִים רֶגֶל
we, you, they go bankrupt
Fem. plural: **(`anachnu, `aten, hen) poshtot regel** פּוֹשְׁטוֹת רֶגֶל
we, you, they go bankrupt

- Past tense:

(`ani) pashateti regel פָּשַׁטְתִּי רֶגֶל *I went bankrupt*
(`atem) peshatetem... פְּשַׁטְתֶּם... *you went bankrupt* (m. pl.)
(`aten) peshateten... פְּשַׁטְתֶּן... *you went bankrupt* (f. pl.)

(hem) pashtu…	פָּשְׁטוּ...	*they went bankrupt* (m.)
(hen) pashtu…	פָּשְׁטוּ...	*they went bankrupt* (f.)

• Future tense:

(`ani) `efshot regel	אֶפשׁוֹט רֶגֶל	*I will go bankrupt*
(`atem) tifshetu…	תִּפשְׁטוּ	*you will go bankrupt* (m. pl.)
(`aten) tifshetu	תִּפשְׁטוּ	*you will go bankrupt* (f. pl.)
(hem) yifshetu…	יִפשְׁטוּ	*they will go bankrupt* (m.)
(hen) yifshetu	יִפשְׁטוּ	*they will go bankrupt* (f.)

4 Conditional sentences

When making a statement that includes a condition (introduced by 'if'), the basic rule is that in Hebrew the future tense is used to refer to something that will or might happen in the future, whereas English tends to use the present tense to give the condition: 'If you come to Israel, I will take you to Jerusalem' (although the meaning is really if you will come). There are two basic types of conditional sentences. The future conditional is used to indicate that if a certain thing might potentially happen in the future, something else will happen as a result. The past conditional is used to indicate that if something had happened in the past (but didn't), then something else would have followed. Pay attention to the tenses used in Hebrew to form these different types of conditional sentences.

4.1 Future conditional sentences – it might hypothetically happen

Note that in Hebrew, the verbs in both clauses are in the future: condition: 'if our … will …' (future) / result: 'we will …' (future)

Im hayeladim shelanu yavo`u, nakhin lahem hafta'ah.

אִם הַיְלָדִים שֶׁלָּנוּ יָבוֹאוּ, נָכִין לָהֶם הַפתָּעָה.

If our children come ('will come')*, we will prepare a surprise for them.*

Im chavereynu yavo`u, nakhin lahem mesibah.

אִם חֲבֵרֵינוּ יָבוֹאוּ, נָכִין לָהֶם מְסִיבָּה.

If our friends come ('will come')*, we will prepare a party for them.*

`Im eheyeh bocher, `atzbi'a be'ad ishti.
אִם אֶהְיֶה בּוֹחֵר, אַצְבִּיעַ בְּעַד אִשְׁתִּי.
If I vote, I will vote for my wife. ('If I will be a voter, I will vote for my wife.')

4.2 Past conditional sentences – it could have happened, but it didn't

In sentences expressing a condition in the past, the verbs in both clauses use a construction formed with the past tense of the verb *to be* followed by the present tense (see lesson 82, note 2).

condition: past tense *to be* + present tense verb / result: past tense *to be* + present tense verb
`Ilu hayiti bocheret, hayiti matzbi'ah be'ad ba'ali.
אִילוּ הָיִיתִי בּוֹחֶרֶת, הָיִיתִי מַצְבִּיעָה בְּעַד בַּעֲלִי.
If I had voted ('I-was I-choose'), *I would have voted* ('I-was I-vote') *for my husband.*
`Ilu hayiti bocher otah, hayiti sameach.
אִילוּ הָיִיתִי בּוֹחֵר אוֹתָהּ, הָיִיתִי שָׂמֵחַ.
If I had chosen ('I-was I-choose') *her, I would have been happy* ('I-was I-am-happy').

Tip: What's the difference between **`im** אִם and **`ilu** אִילוּ? Both mean *if*, but the former indicates that the condition may happen, whereas the latter is used when the condition is unlikely or impossible.

4.3 The conditional tense

The conditional tense (both present and past – e.g. 'I would choose' or 'I would have chosen') are also formed in Hebrew using the past tense of *to be* followed by the present tense:
Hayiti rotzeh liqnot bayit gadol, `aval `eyn li kesef.
הָיִיתִי רוֹצֶה לִקְנוֹת בַּיִת גָּדוֹל, אֲבָל אֵין לִי כֶּסֶף.
I would like ('I-was I-like') *to buy a big house, but I don't have money.*
Hu lo yode'a mah hu hayah 'oseh bli `aba shelo.
הוּא לֹא יוֹדֵעַ מָה הוּא הָיָה עוֹשֶׂה בְּלִי אַבָּא שֶׁלּוֹ.
He doesn't know what he would have done ('he-was he-do') *without his dad.*

`Im lo yo'il, lo yaziq.	אִם לֹא יוֹעִיל, לֹא יַזִּיק.	*If it doesn't help, it won't hurt.* (lesson 78)
nim`as li/ lekha/lakh	נִמְאַס לִי, לְךָ, לָךְ ...	*I/you* (masc. sing./fem. sing.) *have had enough* ... (78)
magi'a li/ lekha/lakh ...	מַגִּיעַ לִי, לְךָ, לָךְ	*I/you* (masc. sing./fem. sing.) *deserve* (78)
miqir leqir	מִקִּיר לְקִיר	*wall to wall* (81)
`eyn sofi	אֵין סוֹפִי	*endless, infinite* (81)
Zot chavayah!	זֹאת חֲוָיָה!	*That's a [wonderful] experience!* (81)
`ekhut hasvivah	אֵכוּת הַסְבִיבָה	*environment, quality of the environment* (82)
leshadreg	לְשַׁדְרֵג	*to upgrade* (83)
lifshot `et haregel	לִפְשׁוֹט אֶת הָרֶגֶל	*to go bankrupt* (83)
'isqat chavilah	עִסְקַת חֲבִילָה	*package deal* (83)
litpos shalvah	לִתְפּוֹס שַׁלְוָה	*to find some calm* (83)
'otzer neshimah	עוֹצֵר נְשִׁימָה	*breathtaking* (83)
me`uvzar, me`uvzeret	מְאוּבְזָר, מְאוּבְזֶרֶת	*equipped* (masc./fem.) (83)

❶ זֹאת הַחֲזָרָה הָאַחֲרוֹנָה שֶׁלָּנוּ. תִּרְאֶה אֶת הַמִּלִּים הַחֲדָשׁוֹת שֶׁלָּמַדְתָּ. ❷ אַתָּה אוֹמֵר: עוֹד פַּעַם? ❸ לָמָּה לֹא? אִם לֹא יוֹעִיל, לֹא יַזִּיק. ❹ בַּשָּׁלָב הַזֶּה אַתָּה עֲדַיִן לֹא בְּרָמָה שֶׁל הָאֶנְצִיקְלוֹפֶּדְיָה הָעִבְרִית. ❺ אֲבָל אַתָּה יָכוֹל לְשַׁדְרֵג אֶת רָמַת הָעִבְרִית שֶׁלְּךָ. ❻ הַתַּלְמוּד אוֹמֵר: אִם לָמַדְתָּ פַּעַם אַחַת, תִּלְמַד פַּעֲמַיִם. ❼ אִם לָמַדְתָּ פַּעֲמַיִם, תִּלְמַד שָׁלוֹשׁ פְּעָמִים. ❽ כִּי מִי הוּא הֶחָכָם? הַלּוֹמֵד מִכֹּל אָדָם. ❾ אוּלַי תֵּלֵךְ לִרְאוֹת סֶרֶט קוֹלְנוֹעַ בְּעִבְרִית? ❿ וְאַל תִּשְׁכַּח אֶת הַחִיזּוּקִים אַחֲרֵי הַמַּאֲמָצִים.

---

85 Eighty-fifth lesson
(Shi'ur shmonim vechamesh)

Predah
Farewell

1 **Sababah ①! Zeh hashi'ur ha`acharon!**
Great! It's the last lesson!

2 **Mitz'ad echad `anachnu smechim, umitzad sheni `anachnu 'atzuvim.**
On [the] one hand we are happy, and on the other *(second)* hand we are sad.

Notes

① **sababah** סַבָּבָּה *great*, *wonderful*, *cool*. This popular slang word (which can also be written סַבָּאבָּה) comes from Arabic. It can be used as an adjective (it does not decline for number or

Answers

❶ This is our last review [lesson]. You'll see the new words you've learned. ❷ You [may] say: 'What, again?!' ❸ Why not? If it doesn't help, it won't hurt! ❹ At this stage, you're not yet on the level of the Encyclopedia Hebraica. ❺ But you can improve the level *(standard)* of your Hebrew. ❻ The Talmud says: If you've learned [it] once, learn [it] again! ❼ If you've learned [it] twice – learn [it] a third time! ❽ Because who is wise? He who learns from everyone. ❾ Perhaps you will go to see a film *(film-of cinema)* in Hebrew? ❿ And don't forget the rewards *(reinforcements)* after [your] efforts.

Second wave: lesson 35

שִׁעוּר שְׁמוֹנִים וְחָמֵשׁ 85

פְּרֵדָה

1 סַבָּבָּה! זֶה הַשִּׁעוּר הָאַחֲרוֹן!

2 מִצַּד אֶחָד אֲנַחְנוּ שְׂמֵחִים, וּמִצַּד שֵׁנִי אֲנַחְנוּ עֲצוּבִים.

gender), **mesibah sababah** מְסִיבָּה סַבָּבָּה *a great party*, or it can be used as an adverb, **Mah shlomkha?** מָה שְׁלוֹמְךָ? *How are you?* **Sababah!** סַבָּבָּה! *Great!*

3 Shmonim ve`arba'ah shi'urim, kim'at shloshah chodashim she`anachnu beyachad vehitragalnu ② zeh lazeh.
Eighty-four lessons – almost three months we've been together *(that-we together)* and we've become accustomed to each other *(this to-this)*.

4 Kol yom bilinu yachad chatzi sha'ah lefachot.
Every day we spent at least half an hour together.

5 Gam `im hayu yamim shelo nifgashnu, biglal 'avodah, limudim, hitchayvuyot ③ mishpachtiyot `o chevratiyot, haqesher beynenu tamid nishmar.
Even if there were days when we didn't meet because of work, studies, family or social commitments, the connection between us was always maintained.

6 Pitpatnu, qara`nu, katavnu targilim 'al nesi'ot, mis'adot, dirot, qniyot va`afilu siparnu bdichot vedibarnu besleng.
We chatted, we read, we did *(wrote)* exercises about trips, restaurants, apartments [and] shopping, and we even told jokes and spoke in slang.

Notes

② **hitragalnu** הִתְרַגַּלְנוּ *we got used to, we became accustomed to*. The infinitive is **lehitragel** לְהִתְרַגֵּל *to get used to*, from the same root as רֶגֶל *leg, foot*. Other words from the root רגל include **hergel** הֶרְגֵּל *habit* and **targil** תַּרְגִּיל *exercise*. **Lekhol sh'iur yesh shney targilim.** לְכֹל שִׁעוּר יֵשׁ שְׁנֵי תַּרְגִּילִים. *Every lesson has two exercises.*

3 שמונים וְאַרבָּעָה שִׁעוּרִים, כִּמעַט שלוֹשָׁה חוֹדָשִׁים שֶׁאֲנַחנוּ בְּיַחַד וְהִתרַגַלנוּ זֶה לַזֶה.

4 כֹּל יוֹם בִּילִינוּ יַחַד חֲצִי שָׁעָה לְפָחוֹת.

5 גַם אִם הָיוּ יָמִים שֶׁלֹא נִפגַשנוּ, בִּגלַל עֲבוֹדָה, לִמוּדִים, הִתחַיבוּיוֹת מִשפַּחתִיוֹת אוֹ חֶברַתִיוֹת, הַקֶשֶׁר בֵּינֵינוּ תָמִיד נִשמַר.

6 פִּטפַּטנוּ, קָרָאנוּ, כָּתַבנוּ תַרגִילִים עַל נְסִיעוֹת, מִסעָדוֹת, דִירוֹת, קְנִיוֹת וַאֲפִילוּ סִפַּרנוּ בְּדִיחוֹת, וְדִבַּרנוּ בְּסלֶנג.

③ **hitchayvuyot** הִתחַיבוּיוֹת *obligations*, *commitments*. This is a noun even though it looks like a reflexive verb. The root חוב **chov** means *debt* and **chovah** חוֹבָה means *duty*. **Hu chayav kesef labanq.** הוּא חָיָב כֶּסֶף לַבַּנק *He owes money to the bank.*

7 **Hishtadalnu laredet leshorshey hasafah ha'ivrit, limeqoroteyha ④ ha'atiqim beyoter.**
We tried to get down to the roots of the Hebrew language, to its most ancient sources.

8 **Samachnu she`atah(/she`at) shutaf(/shutafah) shelanu laharpatqah hamerateqet shel limud 'ivrit.**
We were pleased that you *(masc./fem.)* were our partner in the fascinating adventure of studying Hebrew.

9 **Hayom `anachnu bashi'ur hasofi, `aval sof hu tamid hatchalah shel mashehu `acher.**
Today we've reached *(we in)* the last lesson, but an end is always a beginning of something else.

10 **Besha'ah tovah umutzlachat higa'ta(/higa't) larega' shetzarikh liqpotz lamayim velischot be'atzmekha(/be'atzmekh).**
Congratulations! *(In-hour good and-successful)* you *(masc./fem.)* have reached the moment where you *(impers. subj.)* must jump into the water and swim by yourself.

11 **Ha'etzah hatovah beyoter shelanu: 'im qtzat chutzpah, ledaber 'ivrit `afilu bishgi`ot.**
Our best advice: with a little 'chutzpah', speak Hebrew even with mistakes.

Notes

④ **meqoroteha** מְקוֹרוֹתֶיהָ *its sources* is the plural of **maqor** מָקוֹר *source* with the feminine singular possessive suffix ֶיהָ. Israel's national water company is called **Meqorot** מְקוֹרוֹת *sources.*

7 הִשְׁתַּדַּלְנוּ לָרֶדֶת לְשׁוֹרָשֵׁי הַשָּׂפָה הָעִבְרִית, לִמְקוֹרוֹתֶיהָ הָעַתִּיקִים בְּיוֹתֵר.

8 שָׂמַחְנוּ שֶׁאַתָּה (שֶׁאַתְּ) שׁוּתָף (שׁוּתָפָה) שֶׁלָּנוּ לַהַרְפַּתְקָה הַמְרַתֶּקֶת שֶׁל לִמּוּד עִבְרִית.

9 הַיּוֹם אֲנַחְנוּ בַּשִּׁעוּר הַסּוֹפִי, אֲבָל סוֹף הוּא תָּמִיד הַתְחָלָה שֶׁל מַשֶּׁהוּ אַחֵר.

10 בְּשָׁעָה טוֹבָה וּמוּצְלַחַת הִגַּעְתָּ (הִגַּעַתְּ) לָרֶגַע שֶׁצָּרִיךְ לִקְפּוֹץ לַמַּיִם וְלִשְׂחוֹת בְּעַצְמְךָ (בְּעַצְמֵךְ).

11 הָעֵצָה הַטּוֹבָה בְּיוֹתֵר שֶׁלָּנוּ: עִם קְצָת חוּצְפָּה, לְדַבֵּר עִבְרִית אֲפִילוּ בִּשְׁגִיאוֹת.

12 Chaserah lekha(/lakh) milah? Pashut lishol: `eykh `omrim be'ivrit …?
Are you missing a word *(It-lacking to-you [masc./fem.] word)*? Simply ask: 'How do you *(impers. subj.)* say in Hebrew …?'

13 Kedey letargel `et ha'ivrit bechayey yom-yom `efshar latus le`Yisra`el lechufshah.
To practice Hebrew in everyday life, it is possible to fly to Israel for [a] holiday.

14 `Aval gam michutz leYisra`el yesh harbeh meqomot lelimud 'ivrit, kegon `ulpanim `o mo'adoney 'ivrit, va`afilu ba`internet.
But even outside Israel there are many places to learn Hebrew, such as Ulpans or Hebrew clubs, or even on *(in)* the internet.

15 Keday ⑤ liheyot manuy la'iton be'ivrit qalah, "Sha'ar lamatchil" ⑥.
It's worth subscribing *(to-be subscribed)* to the newspaper in easy Hebrew, 'Sha'ar lamatchil' *(Gate for-the-beginner)*.

16 Yesh gam sfarim yisra`eliyim me'ubadim ⑦ be'ivrit qalah.
There are also Israeli books adapted in easy Hebrew.

17 Na'im lilmod 'ivrit mishirim yisra`eliyim.
It is [also] very pleasant to learn Hebrew from Israeli songs.

Notes

⑤ **keday** כְּדַאי *it is worth*. Don't confuse this with **kedey** כְּדֵי *for, in order to*, which appears in line 13.

12 חֲסֵרָה לְךָ (לָךְ) מִלָּה? פָּשׁוּט לִשְׁאוֹל: אֵיךְ אוֹמְרִים בְּעִבְרִית...?

13 כְּדֵי לְתַרְגֵל אֶת הָעִבְרִית בְּחַיֵּי יוֹם-יוֹם אֶפְשָׁר לָטוּס לְיִשְׂרָאֵל לְחוּפְשָׁה.

14 אֲבָל גַּם מִחוּץ לְיִשְׂרָאֵל יֵשׁ הַרְבֵּה מְקוֹמוֹת לִלְמוֹד עִבְרִית, כְּגוֹן אוּלְפָּנִים אוֹ מוֹעֲדוֹנֵי עִבְרִית, וַאֲפִילוּ בְּאִינְטֶרְנֶט.

15 כְּדַאי לִהְיוֹת מָנוּי לָעִתּוֹן בְּעִבְרִית קַלָּה, "שַׁעַר לַמַּתְחִיל".

16 יֵשׁ גַּם סְפָרִים יִשְׂרְאֵלִיִּים מְעוּבָּדִים, בְּעִבְרִית קַלָּה.

17 נָעִים לִלְמוֹד עִבְרִית מִשִּׁירִים יִשְׂרְאֵלִיִּים.

⑥ **sha'ar lamatchil** שַׁעַר לַמַּתְחִיל 'Gate for-the-Beginner' was a useful newspaper written in easy Hebrew, but unfortunately it is no longer published.

⑦ **me'ubadim** מְעוּבָּדִים *adapted.* This is a passive form from the root עבד: **sadot me'ubadim** שָׂדוֹת מְעוּבָּדִים *cultivated* or *farmed fields.*

85

18 Berega' hapredah lo nagid shalom, nagid raq lehitra`ot.
At the moment of farewell, we [will] not say goodbye – but *(we say)* only see you soon!

19 Behatzlachah, biyedidut.
Good luck. In friendship.

20 Lehitra`ot. Shifrah, Roger.
See you! Shifra, Roger.

Targil rishon – Targem תַּרְגִּיל רִאשׁוֹן – תַּרְגֵּם

1 הוא מדבר עברית טובה, אבל הוא לא מבין את הסלנג העכשווי.
Hu medaber 'ivrit tovah, `aval hu lo mevin `et hasleng ha'akhshavi.

2 אני לא אוהבת פרדות בשדה התעופה.
`Ani lo `ohevet predot bisdeh hate'ufah.

3 היא התרגלה ללמוד עברית חצי שעה בכל בוקר.
Hi hitraglah lilmod 'ivrit chatzi sha'ah bekhol boqer.

4 הם לא רק חברים, הם גם שותפים לעסק.
Hem lo raq chaverim, hem gam shutafim la'eseq.

5 במשפחה הזאת הקשרים בין אבא, אמא והילדים ממש נהדרים.
Bamishpachah hazot haqsharim beyn `aba, `ima vehayeladim mamash nehedarim.

18 בְּרֶגַע הַפְּרֵדָה לֹא נַגִּיד שָׁלוֹם, נַגִּיד רַק לְהִתְרָאוֹת.

19 בְּהַצְלָחָה, בִּידִידוּת.

20 לְהִתְרָאוֹת. שִׁפְרָה רוֹזֶ'ה. □

Answers to Exercise 1

❶ He speaks good Hebrew, but he doesn't understand the latest *(contemporary)* slang. ❷ I do not like farewells at the airport. ❸ She got used to studying Hebrew half an hour every morning. ❹ They are not only friends, they are also business partners. ❺ In this family, the relationships between Dad, Mom and the children are really wonderful.

Targil sheni – Hashlem תַּרְגִּיל שֵׁנִי – הַשְׁלֵם

❶ Every summer they travel together abroad for a new fascinating adventure.

Kol [...] hem nos'im [...] lechutz la`aretz le[...] [...] chadashah.

כל --- הם נוסעים --- לחוץ לארץ ל______ _____ חדשה.

❷ To practice the new words they have learned at Ulpan, they do *(write)* exercises at home.

Kedey [...] `et [...] hachadashot shehem [...] ba`ulpan, hem kotvim [...] babayit.

כדי _____ את ______ החדשות שהם ____ באולפן, הם כותבים _______, בבית.

❸ For beginners, there are books and newspapers adapted in easy Hebrew.

[...] yesh [...] ve'itonim [...] be'ivrit [...].

______ יש _____ ועיתונים _______ בעברית ___ .

❹ Well? What do you say about our teacher *(fem.)*? Great!

[...]? Mah `atah [...] 'al hamorah [...]? [...]!

__? מה אתה ____ על המורה ____? _____!

❺ At the end of the year, each student received a video of Hebrew songs as a farewell present.

[...] [...] kol talmid qibel vide`o shel shirim [...] kematnat [...].

___ ____ כל תלמיד קיבל וידאו של שירים ______ כמתנת ____ .

Answers to Exercise 2

❶ – **qayitz** – **yachad** – **harpatqah merateqet** –

❶ - קיץ - יחד - הרפתקה מרתקת -

❷ – **letargel** – **hamilim** – **lamdu** – **targilim** –

❷ - לתרגל - המילים - למדו - תרגילים -

❸ **Lematchilim** – **sfarim** – **me'ubadim** – **qalah**

❸ למתחילים - ספרים - מעובדים - קלה

❹ **Nu** – **`omer** – **shelanu** – **Sababah**

❹ נו - אומר - שלנו - סבאבה

❺ **Besof hashanah** – **'ivriyim** – **predah**

❺ בסוף השנה - עבריים - פרדה

You've made it to the end! But ... is it really the end? **Tam velo nishlam!** !תַּם וְלֹא נִשְׁלַם Finished but not complete! *Having reached this far, you'll surely want to continue to improve your Hebrew. Here are some ideas you could try:*

• *If there is a Jewish community centre in your town, it is likely to offer modern Hebrew courses for different levels. A local university may also have suitable courses. If you can't find any classes that suit you, find a group of people interested in studying together – it's always easier when you're not on your own.*

• *If you prefer to study at home, you can use books including audio resources or online courses. Multimedia courses are the most effective, as they allow you to hear, see and speak Hebrew almost as if you were in Israel.*

• *A variety of* **`ulpanim** אוּלְפָּנִים *are available in Israel, providing intensive Hebrew studies for visitors as well as new immigrants. There are even Ulpanim for specific professions, such as for doctors, who need to learn specialized vocabulary.*

And last but not least – don't forget to continue the 'second wave' and go back to review a lesson each day until you've completed the whole book.

Second wave: lesson 36

Grammatical appendix

Contents

1 Some opening comments

The basic word order in Hebrew is the same as in English – subject, verb, object: **Hayeled `okhel tapuach.** הַיֶּלֶד אוֹכֵל תַּפּוּחַ. *The boy eats an apple.*

In certain cases, the object of the sentence is preceded by the Hebrew word **`et** אֶת, which has no equivalent in English. This little word must be placed before a direct object when it is definite: that is, when the object is preceded by **ha** הַ *the*, or is a proper noun (the name of a person or place, such as Moshe, Sarah, Jerusalem or China). The following examples illustrate when it is used:

Hi `okhelet** `et **ha'ugah. הִיא אוֹכֶלֶת אֶת הָעוּגָה.
She eats the cake.
But:
Hi `okhelet 'ugah. הִיא אוֹכֶלֶת עוּגָה.
She eats cake.
Hu `ohev** `et **Mikhal. הוּא אוֹהֵב אֶת מִיכַל.
He loves Mikhal.
But:
Hu `ohev banot. הוּא אוֹהֵב בָּנוֹת.
He loves girls.

2 Hebrew roots

The idea of forming words from other words is familiar to English speakers. Taking the word *act*, you can probably think of a whole string of related words: *actor, action, react, interaction, active, proactively* and so on. In English, however, it is not always predictable how such words will be formed.

In Hebrew, roots form the basis of the entire language, and different words are formed from roots in regular and predictable ways. A root is a sequence of Hebrew letters (usually three, but sometimes four). The root is not a word in its own right, but is used to create words by applying set patterns: adding certain vowel points to the root letters, and adding other letters before, after or in between the root letters.

A root usually carries an underlying meaning. In this course, we refer to the root meaning with the infinitive – *to write, to think* – although the root is not the same as the infinitive.

To illustrate the way roots work, let's take the example of the root כתב. Note that the first and third letters in this root can have two different sounds: **kaf** כ is pronounced **k** if it has a point inside it, and **kh** if it doesn't – and since the points are not usually included in modern Hebrew, over time you will need to know which is required in each context. Similarly, **bet** ב can be pronounced **b** or **v**. Having made that clear, the following list gives just some of dozens of Hebrew words that come from this root:

K**o**T**e**V	כּוֹתֵב	*he writes*
hitK**a**TV**ut**	הִתְכַּתְּבוּת	*correspondence*
K**a**T**a**V**ah**	כַּתָּבָה	*article (in a newspaper)*
KT**a**V	כְּתָב	*(a piece of) writing*
KT**u**B**ah**	כְּתוּבָּה	*marriage contract*
KT**o**V**et**	כְּתוֹבֶת	*address*
miK**H**T**a**V	מִכְתָּב	*letter (correspondence, not letter of the alphabet)*

Sometimes, the connections between words formed from the same root seem to have philosophical or moral significance. For example, from the root **[sh]-[l]-[m]**: שלם:

SH**a**L**o**M	שָׁלוֹם	*peace*
hiSHL**i**M	הִשְׁלִים	*he made peace, reconciled; completed, perfected*
miSH**ta**L**e**M	מִשְׁתַּלֵּם	*worthwhile*
muSHL**a**M	מוּשְׁלָם	*perfect*
SH**a**L**a**M	שַׁלָּם	*paymaster*
SH**a**L**e**M	שָׁלֵם	*complete*
SH**i**L**e**M	שִׁלֵּם	*he paid*
taSHL**u**M	תַּשְׁלוּם	*payment, instalment*

3 The definite article and nouns

3.1 The definite article

As in English, Hebrew has only one definite article: **ha** הַ *the*. This article is the same for masculine or feminine nouns in the singular or the plural. In Hebrew, a single letter cannot appear on its own as a separate word, so the definite article is attached to the word that follows it: **habayit** הַבַּיִת *the house*.

When used before a one-letter preposition, the definite article combines with it. For example: **hamerkaz** הַמֶּרְכָּז *the centre*; **bamerkaz** בַּמֶּרְכָּז *in the centre*. The preposition here is **b** בְּ *in*; all that remains of the definite article is the vowel **a**. Similarly, from the preposition **l** לְ *to*: **ha'ir** הָעִיר *the city*; **la'ir** לָעִיר *to the city*.

There is no indefinite article (*a, an*) in Hebrew. So, for example, **`otobus** אוֹטוֹבּוּס means both *bus* and *a bus*. If a noun is indefinite, it is not introduced by anything: הִיא אוֹכֶלֶת פְּרוּסַת עוּגָה. **Hi `okhelet prusat 'ugah.** *She is eating [a] slice of cake.*

3.2 Nouns

Every noun in Hebrew has a gender: either *masculine* **zakhar** זָכָר or *feminine* נְקֵבָה **neqevah**. Nouns may appear in the *singular* **yachid** יָחִיד or the *plural* **rabim** רַבִּים. There is also a 'dual' form, which is used in some cases to refer to nouns that naturally occur in pairs.

The masculine has no special ending. The following are all masculine nouns: **yeled** יֶלֶד *boy*; **malon** מָלוֹן *hotel*; **balshan** בַּלְשָׁן *linguist*. The plural form of masculine nouns almost always ends in **im** ִים : **yeladim** יְלָדִים *boys*; **balshanim** בַּלְשָׁנִים *linguists*.

Most feminine nouns have one of a small number of characteristic endings. The following are the commonest (the plural forms have the ending **ot** וֹת or **yot** יוֹת):

ah / ot	ָה / וֹת	**yaldah**	יַלְדָּה	*girl*
		yeladot	יְלָדוֹת	*girls*
at / ot	ַת / וֹת	**taba'at**	טַבַּעַת	*ring*
		taba'ot	טַבָּעוֹת	*rings*
et / ot	ֶת / וֹת	**ktovet**	כְּתוֹבֶת	*address*
		ktovot	כְּתוֹבוֹת	*addresses*
it / iyot	ִית / יוֹת	**balshanit**	בַּלְשָׁנִית	*linguist*
		balshaniyot	בַּלְשָׁנִיּוֹת	*linguists*
yah / yot	ָיה / יוֹת	**'aliyah**	עֲלִיָּה	*ascent (or wave of Jewish immigration to Israel)*
		'aliyot	עֲלִיּוֹת	*ascents*

Singular nouns ending in **ut** וּת are invariably feminine, and usually denote abstract concepts: **'atzma`ut** עַצְמָאוּת *independence*; **bri`ut** בְּרִיאוּת *health*. As in English, such nouns do not usually have a plural form.

A small number of feminine nouns do not have one of the characteristic endings: **`even** אֶבֶן *stone*; **'ir** עִיר *city*; **kaf** כַּף *spoon*.

Just to make your life as a learner a bit more interesting, some nouns have a singular or plural form that suggests they are of one gender, when in fact they are of the other:

laylah (masc.)	לַיְלָה	*night*	**leylot**	לֵילוֹת	*nights*
malon (masc.)	מָלוֹן	*hotel*	**melonot**	מְלוֹנוֹת	*hotels*
pri (masc.)	פְּרִי	*fruit*	**perot**	פֵּרוֹת	*fruits*
`even (fem.)	אֶבֶן	*stone*	**`avanim**	אֲבָנִים	*stones*
shanah (fem.)	שָׁנָה	*year*	**shanim**	שָׁנִים	*years*

Some other nouns only exist in the plural form (think of the English *scissors*):

chayim (masc.)	חַיִּים	*life*
mayim (masc.)	מַיִם	*water*
nisu`im (masc.)	נִשּׂוּאִים	*marriage*
panim (fem.)	פָּנִים	*face*
shamayim (masc.)	שָׁמַיִם	*sky*

If these nouns are qualified (accompanied) by an adjective, the adjective also appears in the plural: **chayim tovim** חַיִּים טוֹבִים *good life*; **mayim chamim** מַיִם חַמִּים *hot water*; **nis`uim me`usharim** נִשּׂוּאִים מְאוּשָּׁרִים *happy marriage*. The same is true with accompanying verbs: **mayim qarim nozlim** מַיִם קָרִים נוֹזְלִים *cold water runs*.

All names of countries, cities and languages are feminine, whatever their form and ending.

3.3 The dual form

As its name suggests, the dual form refers to two of something. The dual ending is always **yim** יִים – note the two **yods** יי – regardless of the gender of the noun. In Hebrew, only certain nouns have a dual form; most do not. For example, you cannot say '**melonayim**' to mean *two hotels* – the correct form is **shney melonot** (see the end of this section). As you can see from the following, many dual nouns refer to parts of the body that are usually referred to in pairs or to units of time.

When a dual form is accompanied by a verb, the verb takes the normal plural form:

Chodshayim 'ovrim maher. חוֹדשַׁיִים עוֹברִים מַהֵר.

Two months pass quickly.

The same is true of adjectives:

'eynayim gdolot עֵינַיִים גדוֹלוֹת

big eyes

Here are some frequently used dual nouns:

• **Parts of the body**

'ayin (fem.)	עַיִן	*eye*	**'eynayim**	עֵינַיִם	*two eyes*
regel (fem.)	רֶגֶל	*leg*	**raglayim**	רַגלַיִים	*two legs*
yad (fem.)	יָד	*hand*	**yadayim**	יָדַיִים	*two hands*

• **Objects**

mikhnasayim (masc.)	מִכנָסַיִים	*trousers*
mishkafayim (masc.)	מִשקָפַיִים	*eyeglasses*
`ofanayim (masc.)	אוֹפָנַיִים	*bicycle*

• **Units of time and number**

sha'ah (fem.)	שָׁעָה	*hour*	**she'atayim**	שעָתַיִים	*two hours*
yom (masc.)	יוֹם	*day*	**yomayim**	יוֹמַיִים	*two days*
shavu'a (masc.)	שָׁבוּעַ	*week*	**shvu'ayim**	שבוּעַיִים	*two weeks*
chodesh (masc.)	חוֹדֶשׁ	*month*	**chodshayim**	חוֹדשַׁיִים	*two months*
shanah (fem.)	שָׁנָה	*year*	**shnatayim**	שנָתַיִים	*two years*
pa'am (fem.)	פַּעַם	*time, once*	**pa'amayim**	פַּעֲמַיִים	*two times, twice*
me`ah (fem.)	מֵאָה	*hundred*	**matayim**	מָאתַיִים	*two hundred*
`elef	אֶלֶף	*thousand*	**'alpayim**	אַלפַּיִים	*two thousand*

To refer to two things that don't take the dual form:
• before a masculine noun use **shney** שְׁנֵי; before a feminine noun use **shtey** שְׁתֵי: **shney sfarim** שְׁנֵי סְפָרִים *two books*, **shtey daqot** שְׁתֵי דַקּוֹת *two minutes.*
• if it does not occur before a noun, use **shnayim** (masc.) שְׁנַיִים, **shtayim** (fem.) שְׁתַיִים:
Kamah yeladim yesh lekha? – Shnayim.
כַּמָה יְלָדִים יֵשׁ לְךָ? שְׁנַיִים.
How many children do you have? – Two.

3.4 The construct state

This construction is called **smikhut** סְמִיכוּת in Hebrew. The construct state is a way of combining two nouns to create a phrase for a particular concept, or to express a relationship of possession between the two nouns. It sounds more complicated than it is!

Let's take the word *school* as an example. The Hebrew word for *school* literally translates to 'house of book'. It would be possible to express this in Hebrew as **bayit** *house* **shel** *of* **sefer** *book* בַּיִת שֶׁל סֵפֶר. In fact, though, the construct state is used. The word **bayit** בַּיִת (in its absolute, i.e. independent, form) is shortened to its 'construct' form **beyt** בֵּית and is placed directly before the word for book, creating the phrase **beyt sefer** בֵּית סֵפֶר *school.*

If a construct expression is preceded by the definite article, this goes before the <u>second</u> word: **beyt hasefer** בֵּית הַסֵפֶר *the school.*

There are two kinds of construct expressions in Hebrew:

• Fixed constructs

These are set phrases that can be found in the dictionary. A fixed construct has a specific meaning that may go beyond the mere combination of the two nouns. We saw one example above: **beyt sefer** בֵּית סֵפֶר *school.* Although in theory the same Hebrew construct could logically have been used for *library* – another kind of 'house' that contains books – **beyt sefer** always refers to a school. (The Hebrew for *library* is **sifriyah** סִפְרִיָּה, which also comes from **sefer** *book.*) In other words, while it is useful to understand the relationship between the two nouns in a fixed construct and the meaning of the phrase as a whole, you need to learn it as a set phrase. Another example of a fixed construct is **`aruchat boqer** אֲרוּחַת בּוֹקֶר *breakfast* 'meal-of morning'. The absolute form of the word for *meal* is **`aruchah** אֲרוּחָה.

• **Free constructs**

These can't be found in the dictionary and are created as needed when speaking or writing. The connection between the two nouns is obvious. For example:
qir `avanim קִיר אֲבָנִים *stone wall*
baqbuq birah בַּקְבּוּק בִּירָה *beer bottle, bottle of beer*
tachanat deleq תַּחֲנַת דֶּלֶק *gas/petrol station.*

In each case, you could guess the meaning of the construct even if you had never seen it before (provided, of course, that you know what the two nouns in the construct mean when they appear on their own).

As you will have noticed, many nouns change form when they change from the absolute to the construct state. In feminine nouns ending in **ah** ה, the ending changes to **`at** ת_ in the construct (**`aruchat boqer**, **tachanat deleq**). Other nouns can have more minor changes, for example, in the internal voweling of the word. The rules that dictate these changes are regular but very complex. The best advice we can give is to pay attention to constructs as you encounter them.

Note that if an adjective is used with a construct phrase, it comes after it (i.e. after the second word), but its gender and number need to agree with the first word: **`aruchat boqer tovah** אֲרוּחַת בּוֹקֶר טוֹבָה *a good breakfast* ('meal-of morning good').

3.5 Forming nouns from roots

Many different patterns are used to form nouns from roots. A very common pattern is to place the letter מ before the root of the verb, as in the following examples:

Verb	Root	Noun with מ prefix
chashav חָשַׁב *he thought*	חשב	**machshev** מַחְשֵׁב *computer*
qerar קֵרַר *he cooled*	קרר	**meqarer** מְקָרֵר *refrigerator*
katav כָּתַב *he wrote*	כתב	**mikhtav** מִכְתָּב *letter (correspondence)*

4 Adjectives

In Hebrew, the adjective comes after the noun it describes, and its form varies according to the gender and number of the noun:

talmid tov	תַלְמִיד טוֹב	*a good pupil* (male)
talmidim tovim	תַלְמִידִים טוֹבִים	*good pupils* (male or both genders)
talmidah tovah	תַלְמִידָה טוֹבָה	*a good pupil* (female)
talmidot tovot	תַלְמִידוֹת טוֹבוֹת	*good pupils* (female)

As the above example shows, the masculine singular is the basic form of the adjective. The masculine plural adjective ends in **im** ים. The feminine form often ends in **ah** ָה, and sometimes in **t** ת. The feminine plural form ends in **ot** וֹת or **yot** יוֹת.

When the definite article is added to the noun, it must also be added to any accompanying adjectives:

bayit yafeh בַּיִת יָפֶה *a beautiful house*

habayit hayafeh הַבַּיִת הַיָפֶה *the beautiful house*

habayit hayafeh vehagadol הַבַּיִת הַיָפֶה וְהַגָדוֹל *the beautiful and big house* ('the-house the-beautiful and-the-big')

Remember that there is no present tense of *to be* in Hebrew, so **habayit yafeh** הַבַּיִת יָפֶה also means *The house [is] beautiful.*

As mentioned in section 3.3, adjectives that qualify a dual noun take the plural form:

yadayim gdolot יָדַיִים גדולוֹת *big hands*

mikhnasayim qtzarim מִכנָסַיִים קְצָרִים *short trousers*

If an adjective refers to both a masculine and a feminine noun, the masculine form is used:

Hayeled vehayaldah qtanim. הַיֶלֶד וְהַיַלדָה קְטַנִים.

The boy and the girl are small.

See section 3.4 for using adjectives with construct phrases.

4.1 Comparatives

• *As ... as* expressions are formed with the word **kmo** כּמוֹ *as*:

Hi yafah kmo `ima shelah. הִיא יָפָה כּמוֹ אִמָא שֶׁלָה.

She is as beautiful as her mother. ('She beautiful as mother of-her.')

Instead of **kmo** כְּמוֹ, the shorter form **k** כְּ can be used:
taba'at yeqarah kedirah טַבַּעַת יְקָרָה כְּדִירָה
a ring as expensive as an apartment

• *More ... than* expressions place the adverb **yoter** יוֹתֵר *more* before the adjective, and the preposition **mi** מִ *from* before the second part of the comparison (where English uses *than*).
Hasefer hazeh yoter gadol mishelkha.
This book is bigger than yours. הַסֵּפֶר הַזֶּה יוֹתֵר גָּדוֹל מִשֶּׁלְּךָ.

A slightly longer construction using **yoter me`asher** יוֹתֵר מֵאֲשֶׁר *more than* is also used:
Hatisah leLondon yoter qtzarah me`asher hatisah leRio.
הַטִּיסָה לְלוֹנדוֹן יוֹתֵר קְצָרָה מֵאֲשֶׁר הַטִּיסָה לְרִיוֹ.
The flight to London is shorter than the flight to Rio.
Hashanah hi 'ovedet yoter me`asher lifney shanah.
הַשָּׁנָה הִיא עוֹבֶדֶת יוֹתֵר מֵאֲשֶׁר לִפְנֵי שָׁנָה.
This year she is working more than last year.

As in this example, the preposition **mi** מִ sometimes takes the form **me** מֵ. Don't worry about it!

• *Less... than* expressions use the adverb **pachot** פָּחוֹת *less* in exactly the same way as **yoter**:
Hasapah shel savta pachot nochah mishelkha.
הַסַּפָּה שֶׁל סַבְתָּא פָּחוֹת נוֹחָה מִשֶּׁלְּךָ.
Grandmother's sofa is less comfortable than yours.

Here, too, the longer form with **me`asher** מֵאֲשֶׁר is also used:
Hu 'oved pachot me`asher lifney shanah.
הוּא עוֹבֵד פָּחוֹת מֵאֲשֶׁר לִפְנֵי שָׁנָה.
He works less than last year.

4.2 Superlatives

• *The biggest, the most ....:* This meaning is expressed by the adjective (preceded by the article **ha** הַ) followed by the adverb **beyoter** בְּיוֹתֵר *most*:
Zeh hakelev hagadol beyoter. זֶה הַכֶּלֶב הַגָּדוֹל בְּיוֹתֵר.
This is the biggest dog.

Hasefer hame'anyen beyoter sheqarati hashanah ...
הַסֵּפֶר הַמְעַנְיֵן בְּיוֹתֵר שֶׁקָּרָאתִי הַשָּׁנָה...
The most interesting book I've read this year ...('The-book the-interesting in-most that-I-read the-year ...')

• *The smallest, the least ...:* To convey this sense, **hapachot** הַפָּחוֹת *the least* (**ha** הַ *the* + **pachot** פָּחוֹת *less*) is followed by the relevant adjective:
Hu hapachot chakham bakitah. הוּא הַפָּחוֹת חָכָם בַּכִּתָּה.
He is the least intelligent in the class.
Hen hapachot chakhamot bakitah. הֵן הַפָּחוֹת חֲכָמוֹת בַּכִּתָּה.
They (fem.) *are the least intelligent in the class.*
Zot hamekhonit hapachot mehirah besugah.
זֹאת הַמְּכוֹנִית הַפָּחוֹת מְהִירָה בְּסוּגָהּ.
This is the least fast car of its type.

5 Adverbs

Some Hebrew adverbs do not have any obvious connection to other words, such as **'etmol** אֶתְמוֹל *yesterday*. Many, however, are formed by combining a preposition and an adjective or noun.
• **kamuvan** כַּמּוּבָן *naturally, obviously* is formed from **k** כּ *as*, and **muvan** מוּבָן *understood*
• **beseder** בְּסֵדֶר *all right, okay* is formed from **b** בּ *in* and **seder** סֵדֶר *order*
• **mechadash** מֵחָדָשׁ *again, over again* is formed from מ *from* and **chadash** חָדָשׁ *new.*

The suffix **-ah** ָה is used to indicate direction of movement. In English, we often say simply 'to turn left', but in Hebrew, when movement is involved, the idea of 'turning to or towards' conveyed by this suffix must be included. The suffix can be added to an adjective, noun or even a proper noun such as a place name.
• **smolah** שְׂמֹאלָה *to the left* is formed from **smol** שְׂמֹאל *left* and the suffix **ah** ָה
• **yaminah** יָמִינָה *to the right* (**yamin** יָמִין *right*)
• **habaytah** הַבַּיְתָה *homewards, home* (**bayit** בַּיִת *house, home*)
• **Yerushalaymah** יְרוּשָׁלַיְמָה *to Jerusalem, towards Jerusalem* (**Yerushalayim** יְרוּשָׁלַיִם *Jerusalem*).

The position of an adverb varies, but the common adverb **gam** גַּם *also, too* always comes before the word it relates to:
Hu 'oved vegam lomed. הוּא עוֹבֵד וְגַם לוֹמֵד.
He works and also studies.

6 Personal pronouns

6.1 Subject pronouns

The subject forms of the personal pronouns in Hebrew are:

`ani	אֲנִי	*I* (masc./fem.)
`atah	אַתָּה	*you* (masc. sing.)
`at	אַתְּ	*you* (fem. sing.)
hu	הוּא	*he*
hi	הִיא	*she*
`anachnu	אֲנַחְנוּ	*we* (masc./fem.)
`atem	אַתֶּם	*you* (masc. pl.)
`aten	אַתֶּן	*you* (fem. pl.)
hem	הֵם	*they* (masc.)
hen	הֵן	*they* (fem.)

Note that the first-person pronouns (*I* and *we*) have the same form whether the subject is male or female, whereas the second- and third-persons have distinct forms for each gender. If the subject refers to a group of mixed gender, the masculine form is used.

6.2 Object pronouns

There are two types of object pronouns, indirect and direct objects.

• **Indirect objects** are the equivalent of the underlined words in the following English phrases: *he gave the book <u>to me</u>, they sent the letter <u>to you</u>.* The indirect object pronouns in Hebrew are:

li	לִי	*to me* (masc./fem.)
lekha	לְךָ	*to you* (masc. sing.)
lakh	לָךְ	*to you* (fem. sing.)
lo	לוֹ	*to him*
lah	לָהּ	*to her*
lanu	לָנוּ	*to us* (masc./fem.)
lakhem	לָכֶם	*to you* (masc. pl.)
lakhen	לָכֶן	*to you* (fem. pl.)
lahem	לָהֶם	*to them* (masc.)
lahen	לָהֶן	*to them* (fem.)

Note that the endings are identical to those in the declension of the preposition **shel** שֶׁל *of* (see section 8 on 'Possessive adjectives'). Many prepositions decline in an identical or similar way.

• **Direct objects** are the equivalent of the underlined words in the following English phrases: *the children saw us, she heard them, the film bored me.*

In Hebrew, the particle **`et** אֶת is used before the direct object, so direct object pronouns are formed by adding personal suffixes to this particle:

`oti	אוֹתִי	*me*	**`otanu**	אוֹתָנוּ	*us*
`otkha	אוֹתְךָ	*you* (masc. sing.)	**`etkhem**	אֶתְכֶם	*you* (masc. pl.)
`otakh	אוֹתָךְ	*you* (fem. sing.)	**`etkhen**	אֶתְכֶן	*you* (fem. pl.)
`oto	אוֹתוֹ	*him*	**`otam**	אוֹתָם	*them* (masc.)
`otah	אוֹתָהּ	*her*	**`otan**	אוֹתָן	*them* (fem.)

`Ani `ohev `otakh. אֲנִי אוֹהֵב אוֹתָךְ.
I love you. (a man talking to a woman)
`Ani `ohevet `otkha. אֲנִי אוֹהֶבֶת אוֹתְךָ.
I love you. (a woman talking to a man)

7 'This', 'that', 'these', 'those'

• **Demonstrative adjectives**
These are used to indicate something specific and always precede the noun they refer to (e.g. *this room, that girl, those people*, etc.). The demonstrative adjectives in Hebrew are **zeh** זֶה (masc.), **zot** זֹאת (fem.) and **`eleh** אֵלֶּה (plural). Since a noun preceded by a demonstrative adjective is always definite, both usually take the article **ha** הַ: **hacheder hazeh** הַחֶדֶר הַזֶּה *this room* ('the-room the-this').

• **Demonstrative pronouns**
These are used to indicate something specific, but replace the noun they refer to. For example:
Zeh tamar gadol aval hahu' mehagan gadol yoter.
זֶה תָּמָר גָּדוֹל אֲבָל הָהוּא מֵהַגַּן גָּדוֹל יוֹתֵר.
This is a big date palm, but that one from the garden is bigger.

Note that in this example, **ha** is combined with the personal pronoun **hu** הוּא *he*, *it* (here referring to **tamar** *date palm*) in order to form the word for *that one*. Here are all the forms:

zeh	זֶה	*this, this one* (masc. sing.)	**hahu**	הָהוּא	*that, that one* (masc. sing)
zot	זֹאת	*this, this one* (fem. sing.)	**hahi**	הָהִיא	*that, that one* (fem. sing.)
`eleh	אֵלֶּה	*these, these ones* (plural)	**hahem**	הָהֵם	*those, those ones* (masc. pl.)
			hahen	הָהֵן	*those, those ones* (fem. pl.)

As in English, one form is used to refer to things that are closer in distance or time, and the other to things farther away.
`At rotzah `et hachultzah hazot? Lo, `ani rotzah `et hahi.
אַתְּ רוֹצָה אֶת הַחוּלְצָה הַזֹּאת? לֹא, אֲנִי רוֹצָה אֶת הָהִיא.
Do you want this shirt? No, I want that one.

8 Possessive adjectives ('my', 'your', 'his', 'her', etc.)

There are two ways in Hebrew to express ownership or possession.

• The first is by using the word **shel** שֶׁל *of*, combined with the suffix for the appropriate person. For example: **hamisrad sheli** הַמִּשְׂרָד שֶׁלִּי *my office* ('office of-me'). Here is the full declension for any possible possessor:

sheli	שֶׁלִּי	*my*
shelkha	שֶׁלְּךָ	*your* (masc. sing.)
shelakh	שֶׁלָּךְ	*your* (fem. sing.)
shelo	שֶׁלּוֹ	*his, its*
shelah	שֶׁלָּהּ	*her, its*
shelanu	שֶׁלָּנוּ	*our*
shelakhem	שֶׁלָּכֶם	*your* (masc. pl.)
shelakhen	שֶׁלָּכֶן	*your* (fem. pl.)
shelahem	שֶׁלָּהֶם	*their* (masc.)
shelahen	שֶׁלָּהֶן	*their* (fem.)

• The other way is by attaching the suffix for the appropriate person to the noun itself. For example: **misradi** מִשְׂרָדִי *my office*. There is no difference in meaning between these two ways of expressing possession. The forms with **shel** are much more common in speech, whereas the forms consisting of a noun with a possessive suffix are formal and literary. Here is the full declension with the noun **misrad** מִשְׂרָד *office*:

misradi	מִשְׂרָדִי	*my office*
misradkha	מִשְׂרָדְךָ	*your office* (masc. sing.)
misradekh	מִשְׂרָדֵךְ	*your office* (fem. sing.)
misrado	מִשְׂרָדוֹ	*his office*
misradah	מִשְׂרָדָהּ	*her office*
misradenu	מִשְׂרָדֵנוּ	*our office*
misradkhem	מִשְׂרַדְכֶם	*your office* (masc. pl.)
misradkhen	מִשְׂרַדְכֶן	*your office* (fem. pl.)
misradam	מִשְׂרָדָם	*their office* (masc.)
misradan	מִשְׂרָדָן	*their office* (fem.)

The above example is a case in which the noun stays the same, but some nouns change form when these suffixes are added. For example: **sefer** סֵפֶר *book* and its plural form **sfarim** סְפָרִים *books*.

sifri	סִפְרִי	*my book*
sifrekha	סִפְרְךָ	*your book* (masc. sing.)
sifrekh	סִפְרֵךְ	*your book* (fem. sing.)
sifro	סִפְרוֹ	*his book*
sifrah	סִפְרָהּ	*her book*
sifrenu	סִפְרֵנוּ	*our book*
sifrekhem	סִפְרְכֶם	*your book* (masc. pl.)
sifrekhen	סִפְרְכֶן	*your book* (fem. pl.)
sifram	סִפְרָם	*their book* (masc.)
sifran	סִפְרָן	*their book* (fem.)

sfaray	סְפָרַי	*my books*
sfarekha	סְפָרֶיךָ	*your books* (masc. sing.)
farayikh	סְפָרַיִךְ	*your books* (fem. sing.)
sfarav	סְפָרָיו	*his books*
fareha	סְפָרֶיהָ	*her books*
fareynu	סְפָרֵינוּ	*our books*
ifreykhem	סִפְרֵיכֶם	*your books* (masc. pl.)
ifreykhen	סִפְרֵיכֶן	*your books* (fem. pl.)
ifreyhem	סִפְרֵיהֶם	*their books* (masc.)
ifreyhen	סִפְרֵיהֶן	*their books* (fem.)

These forms are not easy to learn. Get used to reading them (you're less likely to hear them), but remember that you can always use the simpler construction with **shel** שֶׁל.

9 Prepositions

Here are the main prepositions:

shel	שֶׁל	*of*
be	בְּ	*in*
ba	בַּ	*in the*
'im	עִם	*with*
`etzel	אֵצֶל	*at, by (a person)*
'ad	עַד	*until*
`el	אֶל	*towards*
'al	עַל	*on*
me'al	מֵעַל	*above*
tachat	תַחַת	*under*
mitachat	מִתַחַת	*below*
bli	בְּלִי	*without*
kedey	כְּדֵי	*in order to*
biglal	בִּגְלַל	*because of*
bishvil	בִּשְׁבִיל	*for, in order that*
me`achorey	מֵאֲחוֹרֵי	*behind*
lifney	לִפְנֵי	*in front of*
'al yad	עַל - יַד	*by, next to*
min, me-, mi-	מִן מֵ, מִ	*from*
le-, la-, …	לְ, לַ…	*to*
`et	אֶת	used before a definite direct object
beyn	בֵּין	*between*
`aval	אֲבָל	*but*

As we saw with the preposition **shel** שֶׁל *of* in section 8, Hebrev prepositions decline by attaching the suffix for the appropriat person. For example, here is the declension of the prepositio **`etzel** אֵצֶל, which means *at* in the sense of *at the house of, at m place* (like the French word *chez*).

`etzli	אֶצְלִי	*at mine* ('at-me')
`etzlekha	אֶצְלְךָ	*at yours* ('at-you[masc.]')

`etzlekh	אֶצְלֵךְ	*at yours* ('at-you[fem.]')
`etzlo	אֶצְלוֹ	*at his* ('at-him')
`etzlah	אֶצְלָה	*at hers* ('at-her')
`etzlenu	אֶצְלֵנוּ	*at ours* ('at-us')
`etzlekhem	אֶצְלְכֶם	*at yours* ('at-you[masc. pl.]')
`etzlekhen	אֶצְלְכֶן	*at yours* ('at-you[fem. pl.]')
`etzlam	אֶצְלָם	*at theirs* ('at-them[masc.]')
`etzlan	אֶצְלָן	*at theirs* ('at-them[fem.]')

10 Negation

• Negative sentences are usually formed using **lo** לֹא, which means both *no* and *not*, and comes before the word it negates:

`Ani lo mevin.   אֲנִי לֹא מֵבִין.
I don't understand.

Zot lo hamizvadah sheli.   זֹאת לֹא הַמִּזְוָדָה שֶׁלִּי.
This isn't my suitcase.

• **`al** אַל is used with future tense forms in a negative imperative sense: **`Al tafria' li!** אַל תַּפְרִיעַ לִי! *Don't bother me!*

• **`eyn** אֵין *there is/are not* is the negative equivalent of **yesh** יֵשׁ *there is/are.*

• Three other words – **`af** אַף, **klum** כְּלוּם and **shum** שׁוּם – have a negative sense when they are combined with **lo** לֹא or **`eyn** אֵין:
• **`af** אַף is usually used before a noun: **`af pa'am** אַף פַּעַם *never* (not once), **`af `echad** אַף אֶחָד *no one.* (When **`af** אַף is not accompanied by a negative particle, it means *even, also.*)
• **klum** כְּלוּם means *nothing, nothing at all*: **Lo shama'ti klum.** לֹא שָׁמַעְתִּי כְּלוּם. *I didn't hear anything.*
• **shum** שׁוּם is used before a noun: **shum davar** שׁוּם דָּבָר *nothing.*

11 Questions

• In spoken Hebrew, a question is often formed simply by changing the tone of voice:

`Atah `ohev `oti.   אַתָּה אוֹהֵב אוֹתִי.   *You love me.*

But with a rising tone towards the end of the phrase it becomes:

`Atah `ohev `oti?   אַתָּה אוֹהֵב אוֹתִי?   *Do you love me?*

• Hebrew also uses question words that are quite similar to their English equivalents:
Mi? ?מִי *Who?*
Mah? ?מַה *What?*

A preposition can be attached to either of these question words. For example: **Bameh?** בַּמֶּה *With what?* **Lemi?** לְמִי *To whom?*

• *Which/what* needs to agree with the gender and number of what it refers to:

`Eyzeh?	?אֵיזֶה	(masc. sing.)
`Eyzo?	?אֵיזוֹ	(fem. sing.)
`Eylu?	?אֵילוּ	(masc. pl.)
`Eleh?	?אֵלֶה	(fem. pl.)

• Interrogative adverbs – *how, when, why*, etc.

`Eykh?	?אֵיךְ	*How?*
Matay?	?מָתַי	*When?*
Lamah?	?לָמָה	*Why?*
`Eyfoh?	?אֵיפֹה	*Where?*
Me`ayin?	?מֵאַיִן	*From where?*
Kamah?	?כַּמָּה	*How many?*

• One particular kind of question deserves special mention, since the Hebrew way of asking it is very different from English. To ask someone how old they are, you use an expression that literally means 'The son of how many are you?' or, to a woman, 'The daughter of how many are you?'

Bat kamah `at?	?בַּת כַּמָּה אַת	*How old are you?* (to a female)
Ben kamah `atah?	?בֶּן כַּמָּה אַתָּה	*How old are you?* (to a male)
Bnot kamah hen?	?בנוֹת כַּמָּה הֵן	*How old are they?* (several females)
Bney kamah hem?	?בְּנֵי כַּמָּה הֵם	*How old are they?* (several males, or both genders)

The answers to these questions also include the word *son/daughter*:
`Ani bat shiv'im ushmoneh. .אֲנִי בַּת שִׁבעִים וּשׁמוֹנֶה
I (fem.) *am 78 years old.* ('I am daughter of seventy eight.')
`Ani ben esrim. .אֲנִי בֶּן עֶשׂרִים
I (masc.) *am 20 years old.*

12 Verbs

In most Hebrew dictionaries, verbs are listed according to the third-person masculine singular of the past tense (e.g. *he wrote, he walked*). This is the simplest verbal form and, in many cases, is closest to the underlying root of the word. If dictionaries presented verbs in the infinitive, all the verbs in the language would be crowded under the letter **lamed** לְ – **ledaber** לְדַבֵּר *to speak*, **lilmod** לִלְמוֹד *to learn*, **likhtov** לִכְתּוֹב *to write* – just as if all English infinitives were listed under 'to'.

So, for example, the Hebrew dictionary entry **katav** כָּתַב (*he wrote*), from the root כתב, is equivalent to the dictionary entry *write* (as in *to write*) in an English dictionary. The entry **diber** דִּבֵּר (*he spoke*), from the root דבר, is equivalent to the entry *speak*.

Although different groups of verbs have slightly different conjugations in the past tense, there are underlying patterns. In particular, note the similarity between the suffixes used to form the different conjugations and the corresponding subject pronoun. For example, *we spoke* is **dibarnu** דִּבַּרְנוּ; the **nu** נוּ ending is also seen in the pronoun **`anachnu** אֲנַחְנוּ *we*. All the first- and second-person forms have this similarity, which helps explain why it is not usually necessary to use the pronoun with these conjugations. The third-person singular and plural do not have this similarity, so the pronouns are almost always used with these conjugations.

12.1 Past tense

There is just one past tense in Hebrew – it corresponds to all the different past tense forms in English. Many Hebrew verbs follow one of two patterns in the past tense (in describing the patterns, we've used the letter X to stand for any consonant):

• Pattern XaXaX: **halakh** הָלַךְ *he went* (*has gone, was going*, etc.)

(`ani) halakhti	הָלַכְתִּי	*I went*
(`atah) halakhta	הָלַכְתָּ	*you went* (masc. sing.)
(`at) halakht	הָלַכְתְּ	*you went* (fem. sing.)
(hu) halakh	הָלַךְ	*he/it went*
(hi) halkhah	הָלְכָה	*she/it went*
(`anachnu) halakhnu	הָלַכְנוּ	*we went*
(`atem) halakhtem	הֲלַכְתֶּם	*you went* (masc. pl.)

(`aten) halakhten הֲלַכְתֶּן *you went* (fem. pl.)
(hem) halkhu הָלְכוּ *they went* (masc.)
(hen) halkhu הָלְכוּ *they went* (fem.)

• Pattern XiXeX: **diber** דִּבֵּר *he spoke* (*has spoken, was speaking*, etc.)

(`ani) dibarti דִּבַּרְתִּי *I spoke*
(`atah) dibarta דִּבַּרְתָּ *you spoke* (masc. sing.)
(`at) dibart דִּבַּרְת *you spoke* (fem. sing.)
(hu) diber דִּבֵּר *he spoke*
(hi) dibrah דִּבְּרָה *she spoke*
(`anachnu) dibarnu דִּבַּרְנוּ *we spoke*
(`atem) dibartem דִּבַּרְתֶּם *you spoke* (masc. pl.)
(`aten) dibarten דִּבַּרְתֶּן *you spoke* (fem. pl.)
(hem) dibru דִּבְּרוּ *they spoke* (masc.)
(hen) dibru דִּבְּרוּ *they spoke* (fem.)

12.2 Present tense

The present tense has just four forms: masculine singular (used for *I, you, he, it* when masculine), feminine singular (*I, you, she, it* when feminine), masculine plural (*we, you, they* when masculine) and feminine plural (*we, you, they* when feminine). Since each verb form can be used for several persons and the conjugation doesn't specify which, they are always used with a specific pronoun: **`ani qore`** אֲנִי קוֹרֵא *I read*, **hu kotev** הוּא כּוֹתֵב *he writes.*

• Pattern XaXaX: in the present tense, the characteristic vowel pattern is **o - e** in the singular. The plural forms end in **-im** ים and **-ot** וֹת (endings that are also used for the plural form of nouns).

katav *to write*

	masculine	feminine
singular	**kotev** כּוֹתֵב	**kotevet** כּוֹתֶבֶת
plural	**kotvim** כּוֹתְבִים	**kotvot** כּוֹתבוֹת

`ahav אָהַב *to love*

	masculine	feminine
singular	**`ohev** אוֹהֵב	**`ohevet** אוֹהֶבֶת
plural	**`ohavim** אוֹהֲבִים	**`ohavot** אוֹהֲבוֹת

If the third root letter is **h** ה, the singular forms in the present tense end in **-eh** ֶה and **-ah** ָה, as with the roots שתה *to drink*, קנה *to buy* and ראה *to see*:

	masculine	feminine
singular	**shoteh** שׁוֹתֶה	**shotah** שׁוֹתָה
	qoneh קוֹנֶה	**qonah** קוֹנָה
	ro`eh רוֹאֶה	**ro`ah** רוֹאָה
plural	**shotim** שׁוֹתִים	**shotot** שׁוֹתוֹת
	qonim קוֹנִים	**qonot** קוֹנוֹת
	ro`im רוֹאִים	**ro`ot** רוֹאוֹת

• Pattern XiXeX: the characteristic vowel pattern in these verbs is **a - e** in the singular. The plural forms end in the suffixes **-im** ים and **-ot** וֹת. The distinguishing feature of these verbs in the present tense is that **me** מְ is prefixed to the root. Examples of this pattern include the roots נשק *to kiss* and צלם *to photograph*:

	masculine	feminine
singular	**menasheq** מְנַשֵּׁק	**menasheqet** מְנַשֶּׁקֶת
	metzalem מְצַלֵּם	**metzalemet** מְצַלֶּמֶת
plural	**menashqim** מְנַשְּׁקִים	**menashqot** מְנַשְּׁקוֹת
	metzalmim מְצַלְּמִים	**metzalmot** מְצַלְּמוֹת

In many cases, the present tense forms of the verb can also be used as nouns, as the following examples illustrate:

shomer שׁוֹמֵר *guard* (m.) **shomeret** שׁוֹמֶרֶת *guard* (f.)
shomrim שׁוֹמְרִים *guards* (m.) **shomrot** שׁוֹמְרוֹת *guards* (f.)
me'ashen מְעַשֵּׁן *smoker* (m.) **me'ashenet** מְעַשֶּׁנֶת *smoker* (f.)
me'ashnim מְעַשְּׁנִים *smokers* (m.) **me'ashnot** מְעַשְּׁנוֹת *smokers* (f.)

The masculine plural of the present tense is often used to refer to an impersonal or general subject. Take the following example:
`Omrim she`atah shoteh raq mayim.
אוֹמְרִים שֶׁאַתָּה שׁוֹתֶה רַק מַיִם.
They say that you only drink water.

Note that a similar construction can be used in English, which also uses the plural of the present tense, but the pronoun *they* must be included. *They say that it will be a cold winter.*

12.3 Future tense

While the main feature of the past tense are the personal suffixes for the different persons and genders (**-ti** תִי **-ta** תָ **-t** ת, etc.), the future tense is formed by adding prefixes to the stem in all the forms (some also have a suffix).

(I)	**`alef**	א
(you, masc. sing.*)*	**t-**	ת
(you, fem. sing.*)*	**t- (+ i)**	ת...י
(he)	**y-**	י
(she)	**t-**	ת
(we)	**n-**	נ
(you, masc. pl.*)*	**t- (+ u)**	ת...ו
(you, fem, pl.*)*	**t- (+ u)**	ת...ו
(they, masc.*)*	**y- (+ u)**	י...ו
(they, fem.*)*	**y- (+ u)**	י...ו

Since each conjugated form is unique, the subject pronoun doesn't have to be used with the verb, but it is usually included anyway in spoken Hebrew.

• Pattern XaXaX: **katav** כָּתַב *to write*

(`ani) `ekhtov	אֶכתוֹב	*I will write*
(`atah) tikhtov	תִכתוֹב	*you will write* (masc. sing.)
(`at) tikhtevi	תִכתְבִי	*you will write* (fem. sing.)
(hu) yikhtov	יִכתוֹב	*he will write*
(hi) tikhtov	תִכתוֹב	*she will write*
(`anachnu) nikhtov	נִכתוֹב	*we will write*
(`atem) tikhtevu	תִכתְבוּ	*you will write* (masc. pl.)
(`aten) tikhtevu	תִכתְבוּ	*you will write* (fem. pl.)
(hem) yikhtevu	יִכתְבוּ	*they will write* (masc.)
(hen) yikhtevu	יִכתְבוּ	*they will write* (fem.)

gamar גָּמַר *to finish*

(`ani) `egmor	אֶגמוֹר	*I will finish*
(`atah) tigmor	תִגמוֹר	*you will finish* (masc. sing.)
(`at) tigmeri	תִגמְרִי	*you will finish* (fem. sing.)
(hu) yigmor	יִגמוֹר	*he/it will finish*
(hi) tigmor	תִגמוֹר	*she/it will finish*
(`anachnu) nigmor	נִגמוֹר	*we will finish*
(`atem) tigmeru	תִגמְרוּ	*you will finish* (masc. pl.)
(`aten) tigmeru	תִגמְרוּ	*you will finish* (fem. pl.)
(hem) yigmeru	יִגמְרוּ	*they will finish* (masc.)
(hen) yigmeru	יִגמְרוּ	*they will finish* (fem.)

• Pattern XiXeX: **tiyel** טִיֵּל *to take a walk*

(`ani) atayel	אֲטַיֵּל	*I will take a walk*
(`atah) tetayel	תְטַיֵּל	*you will take a walk* (m. sing.)
(`at) tetayli	תְטַילִי	*you will take a walk* (f. sing.)
(hu) yetayel	יְטַיֵּל	*he will take a walk*
(hi) tetayel	תְטַיֵּל	*she will take a walk*
(`anachnu) netayel	נְטַיֵּל	*we will take a walk*
(`atem) tetaylu	תְטַילוּ	*you will take a walk* (masc. pl.)
(`aten) tetaylu	תְטַילוּ	*you will take a walk* (fem. pl.)
(hem) yetaylu	יְטַילוּ	*they will take walk* (masc.)
(hen) yetaylu	יְטַילוּ	*they will take a walk* (fem.)

biqer בִּקֵר *to visit*

(`ani) 'avaqer	אֲבַקֵר	*I will visit*
(`atah) tevaqer	תְבַקֵר	*you will visit* (masc. sing.)
(`at) tevaqri	תְבַקרִי	*you will visit* (fem. sing.)
(hu) yevaqer	יְבַקֵר	*he will visit*
(hi) tevaqer	תְבַקֵר	*she will visit*
(`anachnu) nevaqer	נְבַקֵר	*we will visit*
(`atem) tevaqru	תְבַקרוּ	*you will visit* (masc. pl.)
(`aten) tevaqru	תְבַקרוּ	*you will visit* (fem. pl.)
(hem) yevaqru	יְבַקרוּ	*they will visit* (masc.)
(hen) yevaqru	יְבַקרוּ	*they will visit* (fem.)

12.4 Imperative

The imperative is the verb form used in commands (e.g. *Walk! Eat! Drink!*). The imperative is similar in form to the future tense, as the following examples show:

• Pattern XaXaX: **katav** כָּתַב *to write*

Imperative:	Future:
ktov (masc. sing.) כתוֹב	**tikhtov** (masc. sing.) תִכתוֹב
kitvi (fem. sing.) כִּתבִי	**tikhtevi** (fem. sing.) תִכתְבִי
kitvu (masc./fem. pl.) כִּתבוּ	**tikhtevu** (masc./fem. pl.) תִכתְבוּ

• Pattern XiXeX: **diber** דִבֵּר *to speak*

Imperative:	Future:
daber (masc. sing.) דַבֵּר	**tedaber** (masc. sing.) תְדַבֵּר
dabri (fem. sing.) דַבּרִי	**tedabri** (fem. sing.) תְדַבּרִי
dabru (masc./fem. pl.) דַברוּ	**tedabru** (masc./fem. pl.) תְדַברוּ

For the negative imperative (or prohibitions, e.g. *Don't walk! Don't eat! Don't drink!*), the negative particle **`al** אַל is placed before the appropriate future tense form:

`Al tetayel poh! !אַל תְטַיֵל פֹּה *Don't take a walk here!* (to a man)

`Al ta'asi `et zeh! !אַל תַעֲשִׂי אֶת זֶה *Don't do that!* (to a woman)

13 The verb 'to be'

לִהְיוֹת **liheyot** *to be* is used only in the past and future. In the present, Hebrew uses verbless constructions, as the following examples show:

`At yafah. .אַת יָפָה *You are beautiful.* ('You beautiful.')

`Atah ra'ev? ?אַתָה רָעֵב *Are you hungry?* ('You hungry?')

Hayom cham. .הַיוֹם חַם *Today it is hot.* ('Today hot.')

Zeh yoter miday yaqar. .זֶה יוֹתֵר. מִדַי יָקָר *That is too expensive.* ('That more than-enough expensive.')

13.1 Past

(The subject pronoun is not usually used with these forms, except in the third-person.):

hayiti הָיִיתִי *I was*
hayita הָיִיתָ *you were* (masc. sing.)
hayit הָיִית *you were* (fem. sing.)
hayah הָיָה *he/it was*
haytah הָיְתָה *she/it was*
hayinu הָיִינוּ *we were*
hayitem הָיִיתֶם *you were* (masc. pl)
hayiten הָיִיתֶן *you were* (fem. pl.)
hayu הָיוּ *they were* (masc.)
hayu הָיוּ *they were* (fem.)

13.2 Future

`eheyeh אֶהְיֶה *I will be*
tiheyeh תִהְיֶה *you will be* (masc. sing.)
tiheyi תִהְיִי *you will be* (fem. sing.)
yiheyeh יִהְיֶה *he/it will be*
tiheyeh תִהְיֶה *she/it will be*
niheyeh נִהְיֶה *we will be*
tiheyu תִהְיוּ *you will be* (masc. pl.)
tiheyu תִהְיוּ *you will be* (fem. pl.)
yiheyu יִהְיוּ *they will be* (masc.)
yiheyu יִהְיוּ *they will be* (fem.)

13.3 Imperative

heyeh הֱיֵה *Be!* (masc. sing.)
heyi הֱיִי *Be!* (fem. sing)
heyu הֱיוּ *Be!* (masc./fem. pl.)

14 The verb 'to have' and the idea of possession

Hebrew does not have a verb *to have* in the sense of owning or possessing something. Hebrew gets around this by saying something like 'There is to me a problem', meaning 'I have a problem'. Let's look at how this works in the different tenses.

14.1 Present tense

• To say that someone has something, you simply use the particle **yesh** יֵשׁ *there is* or *there are*, followed by the relevant indirect object pronoun (these are formed from the preposition **l** לְ *for* and the suffix for the appropriate person):

Yesh li be'ayah. יֵשׁ לִי בְּעָיָה.
I have ('There-is for-me') *a problem.*
Yesh lekha mekhonit? יֵשׁ לְךָ מְכוֹנִית?
Do you have ('There-is for-you') *a car?*

If this construction is used with a noun rather than a pronoun, simply attach **l** לְ to the noun:

Yesh leba'ali misradim gdolim beTel Aviv.
יֵשׁ לְבַעְלִי מִשְׂרָדִים גדוֹלִים בְּתֵל אָבִיב.
My husband has ('There-is for-my-husband') *large offices in Tel Aviv.*

• To create the negative form (*I do not have ...*), just replace **yesh** יֵשׁ with **`eyn** אֵין *there is/are not*:

`Eyn lakh maqom? אֵין לָךְ מָקוֹם?
Don't you have ('There-is-not for-you') *space?*
`Eyn latalmidim sfarim. אֵין לַתַּלְמִידִים ספָרִים.
The pupils don't have ('There-is-not for-pupils') *books.*

14.2 Past and future tenses

• To express the idea of possession in the past and future tenses, the appropriate form of the verb לִהְיוֹת **liheyot** *to be* is used and the preposition **l** לְ is added as a prefix to the noun or pronoun that indicates the possessor:

LeDan hayu na'alayim shchorot. לְדָן הָיוּ נָעֲלַיִים שחוֹרוֹת.
Dan had ('For-Dan were') *black shoes.*
Yiheyeh lakhen gan yafeh baqayitz haba.
יִהְיֶה לָכֶן גַּן יָפֶה בַּקַּיִץ הַבָּא.
You'll have ('It-will-be for-you') *a beautiful garden next summer.*

• To create the negative form, **lo** לֹא is used:

LeQeren lo hayah `af yafeh. לְקֶרֶן לֹא הָיָה אַף יָפֶה.
Keren did not have ('For-Keren not was') *a beautiful nose.*
Lo yiheyeh lanu znan machar. לֹא יִהְיֶה לָנוּ זמַן מָחָר.
We will not have time tomorrow.

15 Linking words and phrases

In all languages, a vital role is played by the usually short words used to define the relationship between different words, phrases or ideas. Examples of these conjunctions and relative pronouns in English include *and*, *but*, *which* and *that*. In this section, we review the main words that perform this function in Hebrew.

15.1 Coordinating conjunctions

• *And* in Hebrew is **v** ו. Like all single-letter words in Hebrew, it must be attached to the following word:

`Adam veChavah אָדָם וְחַוָּה *Adam and Eve*
Hu qoneh vemokher. הוּא קוֹנֶה וְמוֹכֵר. *He buys and sells.*

The word **v** ו is pronounced in various ways: **ve** וְ, **va** וַ, **vi** וִ, or וּ, depending on the letter that follows it.

Cheyfah viYrushalayim חֵיפָה וִירוּשָׁלַיִם *Haifa and Jerusalem*
`Aharon uMosheh אַהֲרוֹן וּמֹשֶׁה *Aaron and Moses.*

If in doubt, you can always say **ve** and you will be understood, even if strict grammar requires one of the other forms.

• *Or* in Hebrew is **o** אוֹ:
`Atah ba o `atah nish`ar? אַתָּה בָּא אוֹ אַתָּה נִשְׁאָר?
Are you coming or are you staying?

• *But* is **`aval** אֲבָל:
Cham aval `ani lo shoteh. חַם אֲבָל אֲנִי לֹא שׁוֹתֶה.
It's hot, but I'm not drinking.

15.2 Subordinating conjunctions and relative pronouns

To link a relative clause to a main clause, English uses relative pronouns such as *that, which* and *who: the book that I read, the man who saw me*, etc. The main Hebrew word that corresponds to this is **she** שֶׁ, which also has a longer but identical equivalent: **`asher** אֲשֶׁר. The following examples show the wide range of contexts in which this word is used (note that **she-** שֶׁ is attached to the word that follows it):

Ha`ishah shehaytah bamalon. הָאִשָּׁה שֶׁהָיְתָה בַּמָּלוֹן.
The woman who was in the hotel.*

* Note that **she** can only be used to mean *who* when this is a relative pronoun – that is, where it could be replaced with *that*. When *who* is a question word, the word **mi** מִי must be used:
Mi ha`ishah bamalon? מִי הָאִשָּׁה בַּמָּלוֹן?
Who is the woman in the hotel?

Hatzalachat shelaqachti mehashulchan.

הַצַּלַּחַת שֶׁלָּקַחְתִּי מֵהַשּׁוּלְחָן.

The plate that* I took from the table.

* Note that in English we often leave out the relative pronoun: *The plate I took from the table*. In Hebrew, however, either **she** or **`asher** must be used.

Hatzalachat `asher laqachti.

הַצַּלַּחַת אֲשֶׁר לָקַחְתִּי.

The plate that I took from the table.

The meaning here is exactly the same as in the previous example with **she**, but this version is more formal and literary.

Zeh nakhon shehi nesu`ah?

זֶה נָכוֹן שֶׁהִיא נְשׂוּאָה?

Is it true that she is married?

`Amru shehabgadim sham zolim.

אָמְרוּ שֶׁהַבְּגָדִים שָׁם זוֹלִים.

They said that the clothes there are cheap.

Hebrew also has a large number of expressions that are combined with **she** שׁ to form linking words and phrases:

mipney she-	-מִפְּנֵי שֶׁ	*because*
'ad she-	-עַד שֶׁ	*until*
kshe-	-כְּשֶׁ	*when*
bizman she-	-בִּזְמַן שֶׁ	*while*
lifney she-	-לִפְנֵי שֶׁ	*before*
`acharey she-	-אַחֲרֵי שֶׁ	*after*
be`ofen she-	-בְּאוֹפֶן שֶׁ	*in a way that*
kedey she-	-כְּדֵי שֶׁ	*in order to*
kmo she-	-כְּמוֹ שֶׁ	*just as*
lamaqom she-	-לַמָּקוֹם שֶׁ	*to the place that*
mehamaqom she-	-מֵהַמָּקוֹם שֶׁ	*from the place that*
bemaqom she-	-בְּמָקוֹם שֶׁ	*in a place that*

16 Numbers

16.1 Cardinal numbers

Hebrew cardinal numbers (e.g. *one, two, three*, etc.) are a bit more complicated than English numbers because, for the most part, they need to agree with the gender of the noun they qualify. Before we explain the forms for this, here are some other points to note:

• **`Efes** אֶפֶס *zero* is always masculine.

• Most numbers come before the noun; the number *one* is unique in coming after the noun it qualifies: **sefer `echad** סֵפֶר אֶחָד *one book*, **she`elah `achat** שְׁאֵלָה אַחַת *one question.*

• The number *two*, not surprisingly, has a similar form to dual nouns: **shnayim** (m.) שְׁנַיִים or **shtayim** (f.) שְׁתַּיִים. But, when it comes before a noun, it is in the construct state: **shney sfarim** שְׁנֵי סְפָרִים *two books*, **shtey she`elot** שְׁתֵּי שְׁאֵלוֹת *two questions.*

Important: When using numbers for general counting purposes, the feminine forms are used (e.g. when children are playing a game, or when counting the number of people present). This is why the page numbers appear in the feminine form.

The numbers up to 19 must agree in gender with the noun they qualify.

	Masculine		Feminine	
	`echad	אֶחָד	**`achat**	אַחַת
	shnayim	שְׁנַיִים	**shtayim**	שְׁתַּיִים
	shloshah	שְׁלוֹשָׁה	**shalosh**	שָׁלוֹשׁ
	`arba'ah	אַרְבָּעָה	**`arba'**	אַרְבַּע
	chamishah	חֲמִישָּׁה	**chamesh**	חָמֵשׁ
	shishah	שִׁשָּׁה	**shesh**	שֵׁשׁ
	shiv'ah	שִׁבְעָה	**sheva'**	שֶׁבַע
	shmonah	שְׁמוֹנָה	**shmoneh**	שְׁמוֹנֶה
	tish'ah	תִּשְׁעָה	**tesha'**	תֵּשַׁע
0	**'asarah**	עֲשָׂרָה	**'eser**	עֶשֶׂר
1	**`achad 'asar**	אַחַד עָשָׂר	**`achat 'esreh**	אַחַת עֶשְׂרֵה
2	**shneym 'asar**	שְׁנֵים עָשָׂר	**shteym 'esreh**	שְׁתֵּים עֶשְׂרֵה
3	**shloshah 'asar**	שְׁלוֹשָׁה עָשָׂר	**shlosh 'esreh**	שְׁלוֹשׁ עֶשְׂרֵה
4	**`arba'ah 'asar**	אַרְבָּעָה עָשָׂר	**`arba' 'esreh**	אַרְבַּע עֶשְׂרֵה
5	**chamishah 'asar**	חֲמִישָּׁה עָשָׂר	**chamesh 'esreh**	חֲמֵשׁ עֶשְׂרֵה
6	**shishah 'asar**	שִׁשָּׁה עָשָׂר	**shesh 'esreh**	שֵׁשׁ עֶשְׂרֵה
7	**shiv'ah 'asar**	שִׁבְעָה עָשָׂר	**shva' 'esreh**	שְׁבַע עֶשְׂרֵה
8	**shmonah 'asar**	שְׁמוֹנָה עָשָׂר	**shmoneh 'esreh**	שְׁמוֹנֶה עֶשְׂרֵה
9	**tish'ah 'asar**	תִּשְׁעָה עָשָׂר	**tsha' 'esreh**	תְּשַׁע עֶשְׂרֵה

The words for the tens have only one form, used for both masculine and feminine nouns:

20	**'esrim**	עֶשְׂרִים	*60*	**shishim**	שִׁשִּׁים
30	**shloshim**	שְׁלוֹשִׁים	*70*	**shiv'im**	שִׁבְעִים
40	**`arba'im**	אַרְבָּעִים	*80*	**shmonim**	שְׁמוֹנִים
50	**chamishim**	חֲמִישִּׁים	*90*	**tish'im**	תִּשְׁעִים

However, when units are added to the tens, the units need to agree with the gender of the noun qualified:

21	**'esrim ve`echad** (masc.)	עֶשְׂרִים וְאֶחָד
	'esrim ve`achat (fem.)	עֶשְׂרִים וְאַחַת
22	**'esrim ushnayim**	עֶשְׂרִים וּשְׁנַיִם
	'esrim ushtayim	עֶשְׂרִים וּשְׁתַּיִם
35	**shloshim vachamishah**	שְׁלוֹשִׁים וַחֲמִישָּׁה
	shloshim vechamesh	שְׁלוֹשִׁים וְחָמֵשׁ
73	**shiv'im ushloshah**	שִׁבְעִים וּשְׁלוֹשָׁה
	shiv'im veshalosh	שִׁבְעִים וְשָׁלוֹשׁ
100	**me`ah**	מֵאָה
200	**matayim**	מָאתַיִם
300	**shlosh me`ot**	שְׁלוֹשׁ מֵאוֹת
400	**`arba' me`ot**	אַרְבַּע מֵאוֹת
500	**chamesh me`ot**	חֲמֵשׁ מֵאוֹת
600	**shesh me`ot**	שֵׁשׁ מֵאוֹת
700	**shva' me`ot**	שְׁבַע מֵאוֹת
800	**shmoneh me`ot**	שְׁמוֹנֶה מֵאוֹת
900	**tsha' me`ot**	תְּשַׁע מֵאוֹת
1000	**`elef**	אֶלֶף
2000	**`alpayim**	אַלְפַּיִם
3000	**shloshet `alafim**	שְׁלוֹשֶׁת אֲלָפִים
4000	**`arba'at `alafim**	אַרְבַּעַת אֲלָפִים
5000	**chameshet `alafim**	חֲמֵשֶׁת אֲלָפִים
6000	**sheshet `alafim**	שֵׁשֶׁת אֲלָפִים
7000	**shiv'at `alafim**	שִׁבְעַת אֲלָפִים
8000	**shmonat `alafim**	שְׁמוֹנַת אֲלָפִים

9000	**tish'at `alafim**	תִּשְׁעַת אֲלָפִים
10,000	**'aseret `alafim**	עֲשֶׂרֶת אֲלָפִים
11,000	**`achad 'asar `elef**	אֶלֶף עָשָׂר אַחַד
12,000	**shneym 'asar `elef**	שְׁנֵים עָשָׂר אֶלֶף
20,000	**'esrim `elef**	עֶשְׂרִים אֶלֶף
100,000	**me`ah `elef**	מֵאָה אֶלֶף

16.2 Ordinal numbers

Ordinal numbers (e.g. *first, second, third*, etc.) function as adjectives. Like other Hebrew adjectives, they come after the word they refer to and vary according to the number and gender of the word they qualify:

1st	**rishon / rishonah**	רִאשׁוֹן, רִאשׁוֹנָה
	rishonim / rishonot	רִאשׁוֹנִים, רִאשׁוֹנוֹת
2nd	**sheni / shniyah**	שֵׁנִי, שְׁנִיָּה
3rd	**shlishi / shlishit**	שְׁלִישִׁי, שְׁלִישִׁית
4th	**revi'i / revi'it**	רְבִיעִי, רְבִיעִית
5th	**chamishi / chamishit**	חֲמִישִׁי, חֲמִישִׁית
6th	**shishi / shishit**	שִׁשִּׁי, שִׁשִּׁית
7th	**shvi'i / shvi'it**	שְׁבִיעִי, שְׁבִיעִית
8th	**shmini / shminit**	שְׁמִינִי, שְׁמִינִית
9th	**tshi'i / tshi'it**	תְּשִׁיעִי, תְּשִׁיעִית
10th	**'asiri / 'asirit**	עֲשִׂירִי, עֲשִׂירִית

Since we've mentioned **rishon** רִאשׁוֹן *first*, we should probably also note the word for *last*:

`acharon / `acharonah (sing.) אַחֲרוֹן, אַחֲרוֹנָה

`acharonim / `acharonot (pl.) אַחֲרוֹנִים, אַחֲרוֹנוֹת

Zot hapa'am harishonah veha`acharonah.
זֹאת הַפַּעַם הָרִאשׁוֹנָה וְהָאַחֲרוֹנָה.
This is the first and last time.

Grammatical index

The reference numbers for each entry occur in pairs: the first number refers to the lesson, the second to the note or section of the lesson in which the explanation can be found. Reference numbers in bold indicate review lessons. GA refers to the Grammatical Appendix.

Glossaries

We've provided a three-way glossary to make it easier to look up words:
- Transliteration – Hebrew – English
- English – Transliteration – Hebrew
- Hebrew – Transliteration – English

Each noun is followed by its gender, and sometimes the plural form is given, particularly if it is irregular or more common than the singular form. Adjectives are given in their singular masculine and feminine form. As is usual in Hebrew dictionaries, verbs are presented in the third-person masculine singular past tense form. We've also included the infinitive, which always begins with **l-**, in square brackets. For example, הצר is defined as *to want*, though this verb form actually means *he wanted*. The form in square brackets [לרצות] is the infinitive *to want*.

The Hebrew words in the glossary appear without their vowel points. As mentioned in the lessons, some Hebrew words change spelling when they appear without the vowel points. A **yod** or a **vav** is added to hint at the vowel sound (for example, י to represent an *[i]* sound, ו to represent an *[o]* sound, two וו to represent a *[v]*, and so on). Don't be confused if you notice this type of discrepancy between the entries in the glossary and the vowel-marked words in the lessons.

Key to abbreviations:

(f.) feminine	*(m.)* masculine
(sing.) singular	*(pl.)* plural
(adj.) adjective	*(adv.)* adverb

Each word appears with the number of the lesson in which it first occurs.

Transliteration – Hebrew - English

This glossary lists the words according to the transliterations used in the course. We've listed all words beginning with ` (the Hebrew letter **`alef**) and **'** (the letter **'ayin**) separately at the beginning of the glossary. There are also separate sections for words beginning with **chet** (**CH**), with **shin** (**SH**) and with **tsadi** (**TZ**), as the transliteration in these cases is a letter combination. However, words beginning with **samekh** and **sin** appear together under **S**, and words beginning with **tav** and **tet** appear together under **T**, since our transcription method does not distinguish between these letters (as there is no phonetic difference).

` (`alef)

`aba	אבא	dad 19
`ach	אח	brother 19
`ach *(m.)*	אח	fireplace 83
`achar kakh	אחר כך	after that, then 69
`acharey	אחרי	after 26
`acharey hatzohorayim	אחרי הצהרים	afternoon 62
`acharon** *(m.)*, **`acharonah *(f.)*	אחרון, אחרונה	last 45
`achat *(f.)*	אחת	one (number) 23
`acher** *(m.)*, **`acheret *(f.)*	אחר, אחרת	another 47
`achot	אחות	sister 19
`adom** *(m.)*, **`adumah *(f.)*	אדום, אדומה	red 27
`adoni	אדוני	sir 52
`af *(m.)*	אף	nose 65
`af	אף	no (negative particle) 75
`af `echad	אף אחד	no one 74
`af pa'am	אף פעם	never 70
`afah [le`efot]	אפה [לאפות]	to bake 79
`afilu	אפילו	even 41
`afiyah *(f.)*	אפיה	baking 79
`afor** *(m.)*, **`aforah *(f.)*	אפור, אפורה	grey 64
`agrah *(f.)*	אגרה	tax 53
`agudal *(m.)*	אגודל	thumb, toe 73
`ahav [le`ehov]	אהב [לאהוב]	to love 31; to like 52
`ahavah *(f.)*	אהבה	love 27
`akh	אך	but 67
`akhal [le`ekhol]	אכל [לאכול]	to eat 20
`al	אל	do not 47
`alchuti** *(m.)*, **`alchutit *(f.)*	אלחוטי, אלחוטית	wireless (cordless) 13
`aluf** *(m.)*, **`alufah *(f.)*	אלוף, אלופה	champion 71
`amar [lomar]	אמר [לומר]	to say 30
`ambatyah *(f.)*	אמבטיה	bath 83
`anachnu *(m./f.)*	אנחנו	we 9
`ani *(m./f.)*	אני	I 5

`aretz *(f.)*	ארץ	land 25
`ari *(m.)*	ארי	lion 69
`arokh** *(m.)*, **`arukah *(f.)*	ארוך, ארוכה	long 43
`arubah *(f.)*	ארובה	chimney 67
`aruchah *(f.)*	ארוחה	meal 24
`aruchat 'erev *(f.)*	ארוחת ערב	dinner 24
`asar [le`esor]	אסר [לאסור]	to arrest, to prohibit (ban) 66
`asimon *(m.)*	אסימון	token 73
`asur** *(m.)*, **`asurah *(f.)*	אסור, אסורה	forbidden, prohibited 66
`at *(f. sing.)*	את	you 4
`atah *(m. sing.)*	אתה	you 4
`atar *(m.)*	אתר	site / website 60
`atem *(m. pl.)*	אתם	you 9
`aten *(f. pl.)*	אתן	you 10
`Atunah *(f.)*	אתונה	Athens 44
`av	אב	father 63
`aval	אבל	but 10
`avir *(m.)*	אויר	air 68
`aviv *(m.)*	אביב	spring (the season) 18
`avoqado *(m.)*	אבוקדו	avocado 51
`avtachah *(f.)*	אבטחה	security 60
`az	אז	so 15
`echad *(m.)*	אחד	one (number) 58
`efer *(m.)*	אפר	ash 64
`efshar	אפשר	possible 24
`ela	אלא	but 80
`elef	אלף	thousand 45
`eleh *(m./f.)*	אלה	these 17
`eleqtroni** *(m.)*, **`eleqtronit *(f.)*	אלקטרוני, אלקטרונית	electronic 22
`elohim *(m.)*	אלהים	God 59
`em	אם	mother 62
`emet *(f.)*	אמת	truth 52
`eqologi** *(m.)*, **`eqologit *(f.)*	אקולוגי, אקולוגית	ecological 71
`eretz *(f.)*	ארץ	country 53
`eruach *(m.)*	ארוח	hospitality 83
`esh *(f.)*	אש	fire 20
`et	את	particle before direct definite object 17
`etmol	אתמול	yesterday 31
`etz- (+ li/lekh etc.)	-אצל	among, at, by (+ pronoun) 36
`etzba'** *(f.)*, **`etzba'ot *(pl.)*	אצבע, אצבעות	finger 82
`Eyfoh?	איפה?	Where? 13
`Eykh?	איך?	How? 36
`eykhut *(f.)*	איכות	quality 82
`eylu *(pl.)*	אילו	which 38
`eyn	אין	there is/are no 6
`eyn-sof	אין-סוף	infinite 81

`Eyzeh?** *(m.)*, **`Eyzo? *(f.)*	איזה?, איזו?	What? 32; Which? 33
`ezrach** *(m.)*, **`ezrachit *(f.)*	אזרח, אזרחית	citizen 82
`ezrachut *(f.)*	אזרחות	citizenship 82
`i-`efshar	אי-אפשר	impossible 24
`ibed [le`abed]	אבד [לאבד]	to lose 73
`im	אם	if 41
`ima	אמא	mum 19
`imen [le`amen]	אמן [לאמן]	to practice, to train 79
`internet *(m.)*	אינטרנט	internet 9
`ish	איש	man 67
`ishah	אשה	wife, woman 12
`itztadyon *(m.)*	איצטדיון	stadium 71
`o	או	or 10
`ofan *(m.)*	אופן	wheel 31
`ofanayim *(m.)*	אופניים	bicycle 31
`ofnah *(f.)*	אופנה	fashion 61
`ofnati** *(m.)*, **`ofnatit *(f.)*	אופנתי, אופנתית	fashionable 61
`okhel *(m.)*	אוכל	food 48
`olimpi** *(m.)*, **`olimpit *(f.)*	אולימפי, אולימפית	Olympian 71
`ometz *(m.)*	אומץ	courage 54
`oniyah *(f.)*	אוניה	boat, ship 34
`or *(m.)*	אור	light 1
`oreach** *(m.)*, **`orachat *(f.)*	אורח, אורחת	guest 75
`oren *(m.)*	אורן	pine 80
`ot *(f.)*	אות	letter (of the alphabet) 57
`oto** *(m.)*, **`otah *(f.)*	אותו, אותה	same 30
`otobus *(m.)*	אוטובוס	bus 33
`ulam *(m.)*	אולם	hall 72
`ulay	אולי	maybe, perhaps 22
`ulpan *(m.)*	אולפן	Ulpan 8

' ('ayin)

'ad	עד	until 26
'adi *(m.)*	עדי	jewel 54
'adinut *(f.)*	עדינות	gentleness 79
'agvaniyah *(f.)*	עגבניות	tomato 76
'akhbar *(m.)*	עכבר	mouse 81
'akhshav	עכשיו	now 50
'akhshavi *(m.)*, **'akhshavit** *(f.)*	עכשווי, עכשווית	contemporary 71
'al	על	about, on 20
'al ha`esh	על האש	barbecue 20
'al yad	על יד	by, next to 68
'alah [la'alot]	עלה [לעלות]	to ascend, to climb, to go up 67
'aliyah *(f.)*	עליה	ascent 1
'am *(m.)*	עם	people (nation) 59
'amad [la'amod]	עמד [לעמוד]	to stand 78
'anah [la'anot]	ענה [לענות]	to reply 43; to answer 45
'anivah *(f.)*	עניבה	tie (necktie) 48
'aqev *(m.)*	עקב	heel 73
'aravi *(m.)*, **'aravit** *(f.)*	ערבי, ערבית	Arab *(adj.)* 82

'asah [la'asot]	עשה [לעשות]	to do 37
'ashir *(m.)*, **'ashirah** *(f.)*	עשיר, עשירה	rich 45
'atid *(m.)*	עתיד	future 57
'atiq *(m.)*, **'atiqah** *(f.)*	עתיק, עתיקה	antique, old 38
'atzar [la'atzor]	עצר [לעצור]	to stop 83
'atzmah *(f.)*	עצמה	herself 67
'atzmo *(m.)*	עצמו	himself 67
'atzor *(m.)*	עצור	stop 51
'atzuv *(m.)*, **'atzuvah** *(f.)*	עצוב, עצובה	sad 85
'avad [la'avod]	עבד [לעבוד]	to work 24
'avar [la'avor]	עבר [לעבור]	to cross 5; to move (house) 37
'avodah *(f.)*	עבודה	work 37
'ayef *(m.)*, **'ayefah** *(f.)*	עייף, עייפה	tired 12
'ayin *(f.)*, **'eynayim** *(pl.)*	עין, עיניים	eye 38
'azar [la'azor]	עזר [לעזור]	to help 22
'eden *(m.)*	עדן	delight 61
'erev *(m.)*	ערב	evening 10
'eseq *(m.)*, **'asaqim** *(pl.)*	עסק, עסקים	business 59
'etz *(m.)*	עץ	wood 83
'etzah *(f.)*	עצה	advice 78
'etzem *(m.)*	עצם	bone, self 70
'im	עם	with 18
'iqar *(m.)*, **'iqarit** *(f.)*	עיקר, עיקרית	the main (thing) 68
'ir *(f.)*	עיר	city 58
'irbev [le'arbev]	ערבב [לערבב]	to mix 55
'isqah *(f.)*	עסקה	deal (bargain) 83
'iton *(m.)*	עיתון	newspaper 52
'iver *(m.)*, **'iveret** *(f.)*	עיוור, עיוורת	blind 80
'ivrit *(f.)*	עברית	Hebrew 5
'od	עוד	more 27; yet 32
'od lo	עוד לא	not yet 32
'olam *(m.)*	עולם	world 47
'oleh chadash *(m.)*, **'olah chadashah** *(f.)*	עולה חדש, עולה חדשה	new immigrant 82
'oqetz *(m.)*	עוקץ	sting 80
'oteq *(m.)*	עותק	copy 81
'ugah *(f.)*	עוגה	cake 10

B

ba [lavo]	בא [לבוא]	to come 15
ba'al	בעל	husband 18
ba'al *(m.)*, **ba'alat** *(f.)*	בעל / בעלת	master / mistress (owner) 18
bachar [livchor]	בחר [לבחור]	to choose, to vote 82
balagan *(m.)*	בלגן	mess 17; disorder 27
balaganist *(m.)*, **balaganistit** *(f.)*	בלגניסט, בלגניסטית	messy guy/woman 17
balal [livlol]	בלל [לבלול]	to mix up (jumble) 59
balshan *(m.)*, **balshanit** *(f.)*	בלשן, בלשנית	linguist 62
banah [livnot]	בנה [לבנות]	to build 58
bar	בר	son 16

bar mitzvah *(m.)*, **bat mitzvah** *(f.)*	בר מצווה, בת מצווה	Bar Mitzvah / Bat Mitzvah 16
bari *(m.)*, **bri`ah** *(f.)*	בריא, בריאה	healthy 76
bat	בת	daughter 9
batlan *(m.)*, **batlanit** *(f.)*	בטלן, בטלנית	layabout 74
batuach *(m.)*, **betuchah** *(f.)*	בטוח, בטוחה	sure 43
batzal *(m.)*	בצל	onion 76
batzeq *(m.)*	בצק	pastry 79
bayit *(m.)*	בית	home, house 19
bchirah *(f.)*	בחירה	choice 82
bchirot *(f. pl.)*	בחירות	elections 82
bdichah *(f.)*	בדיחה	joke 44
be-	-ב	by 10; in 11, 77
be'ad	בעד	for (in favour of) 73
be'ayah *(f.)*	בעיה	problem 13
bediyuq	בדיוק	exactly 52
be'etzem	בעצם	actually 75
beged *(m.)*	בגד	clothing (item of) 64
be'iqar	בעיקר	mainly, in particular 65
bekhol maqom	בכל מקום	everywhere 68
ben	בן	son 9
ben `adam *(m.)*	בן אדם	person 23
be'od	בעוד	in (+ period of time) 27
beqarov	בקרוב	soon 16
beqitzur	בקיצור	in short 82
berekh [levarekh]	ברך [לברך]	to congratulate 57
beseder	בסדר	okay, in order 6; all right 17
besisi *(m.)*, **besisit** *(f.)*	בסיסי, בסיסית	basic 79
Bete`avon!	בתיאבון!	Bon appétit! 55
beten *(f.)*	בטן	stomach 78
bevaqashah	בבקשה	please 10
beyn	בין	among, between 44
beynle`umi** *(m.)*, **beynle`umit *(f.)*	בינלאומי, בינלאומית	international 44
beyntayim	בינתיים	in the meantime 79
beyoter	ביותר	most 32
beyt *(m.)*	בית	house 10
beyt cholim *(m.)*	בית חולים	hospital 51
beyt kneset *(m.)*	בית כנסת	synagogue 37
beyt sefer *(m.)*	בית ספר	school 37
beyt shimush *(m.)*	בית שימוש	toilet (restroom) 37
bgadim *(m. pl.)*	בגדים	clothes 64
bifnim	בפנים	inside 79
biglal	בגלל	because of (due to) 27
bilah [levalot]	בילה [לבלות]	to have a good time, to spend (time) 39
bilti	בלתי	not 66
biqer [levaqer]	בקר [לבקר]	to visit 51
biqesh [levaqesh]	ביקש [לבקש]	to request 52
biqtah *(f.)*	בקתה	cabin 83

birah *(f.)* בירה beer 4
bishvil בשביל for 25
bitachon *(m.)* ביטחון security 53; confidence 73
bitel [levatel] ביטל [לבטל] to cancel 52
bli בלי without 57
bocher *(m.)*, **bocheret** *(f.)* בוחר, בוחרת voter 82
boded *(m.)*, **bodedah** *(f.)* בודד, בודדה lonely 75
boqer *(m.)* בוקר morning 1
botz *(m.)* בוץ mud 11
brekhah *(f.)* ברכה pool 20
bri`ut *(f.)* בריאות health 76
brit *(f.)* ברית covenant 30
brit milah *(f.)* ברית מילה circumcision 30
briyot *(m. pl.)* בריות people 80

CH

chadar sheynah *(f.)* חדר שינה bedroom 83
chadash *(m.)*, **chadashah** *(f.)* חדש, חדשה new 6
chadashot *(f. pl.)* חדשות news 33
chadish *(m.)*, **chadishah** *(f.)* חדיש, חדישה latest (newest) 38
chafirah *(f.)* חפירה excavation 44
chag *(m.)* חג holiday (festival) 36
chagag [lachgog] חגג [לחגוג] to celebrate 38
chakham *(m.)*, **chakhamah** *(f.)* חכם, חכמה intelligent, wise 67
chalal *(m.)* חלל space (outer) 31
chalav *(m.)* חלב milk 79
chalon *(m.)*, **chalonot** *(pl.)* חלון, חלונות window 68
chaluqah *(f.)* חלוקה share (distribution) 69
cham חם father-in-law 36
cham *(m.)*, **chamah** *(f.)* חם, חמה hot 27
chamam *(m.)* חמם Turkish bath 45
chamim *(m.)*, **chamimah** *(f.)* חמים, חמימה warm 36
chamor *(m.)* חמור donkey 69
chamot חמות mother-in-law 36
chamud *(m.)*, **chamudah** *(f.)* חמוד, חמודה darling 45
chanayah *(f.)* חניה parking 60
chanukah *(f.)* חנוכה dedication 38
chanukat bayit *(f.)* חנוכת בית housewarming, inauguration 38
chanut *(f.)* חנות shop 25
charuz *(m.)* חרוז rhyme 64
chasah *(f.)* חסה lettuce 76
chaser *(m.)*, **chaserah** *(f.)* חסר, חסרה missing (lacking) 85
chashav [lachashov] חשב [לחשוב] to think 32
chashuv *(m.)*, **chashuvah** *(f.)* חשוב, חשובה important 68
chatan *(m.)* חתן groom 18

chatikh *(m.)*, **chatikhah** *(f.)*	חתיך, חתיכה	hot guy/woman 15
chatikhah *(f.)*	חתיכה	piece 15
chatunah *(f.)*	חתונה	marriage (ceremony), wedding 18
chaval	חבל	what a pity 6
chavayah *(f.)*	חוויה	experience 81
chaver *(m.)*, **chaverah** *(f.)*	חבר, חברה	friend 20; member (of an organization) 48
chavilah *(f.)*	חבילה	package 40
chayah *(f.)*	חיה	animal 69
chayal *(m.)*, **chayelet** *(f.)*	חייל, חיילת	soldier 71
chay-bar *(m.)*	חי-בר	animal reserve 83
chayim *(m. pl.)*	חיים	life 69
chazaq *(m.)*, **chazaqah** *(f.)*	חזק, חזקה	stiff, strong 79
chazar [lachazor]	חזר [לחזור]	to come back, to return 47; to repeat 78
cheder *(m.)*	חדר	room 17
chelbon *(m.)*	חלבון	egg white 79
cheleq *(m.)*	חלק	part 58
chelmon *(m.)*	חלמון	egg yolk 79
chem`ah *(f.)*	חמאה	butter 79
chen *(m.)*	חן	grace 38
chetzi	חצי	half 53
chevreman *(m.)*, **chevremanit** *(f.)*	חברמן, חברמנית	cool (laid back) 29
chidush *(m.)*	חידוש	innovation 57
chikah [lechakot]	חיכה [לחכות]	to wait 74
chileq [lechaleq]	חלק [לחלק]	to divide, to share 69
chiloni *(m.)*, **chilonit** *(f.)*	חילוני, חילונית	secular 82
chipes [lechapes]	חיפש [לחפש]	to look for, to search 50
chizuq *(m.)*	חיזוק	reinforcement 78
chodesh *(m.)*	חודש	month 29
chof *(m.)*	חוף	beach 15
chofen *(m.)*	חופן	handful 79
chofshi *(m.)*, **chofshit** *(f.)*	חופשי, חופשית	free (not held down) 78
chol *(m.)*	חול	sand 39
choleh *(m.)*, **cholah** *(f.)*	חולה, חולה	ill, sick 51
chom *(m.)*	חום	heat 43
chometz *(m.)*	חומץ	vinegar 76
choref *(m.)*	חורף	winter 41
choshekh *(m.)*	חושך	darkness 72
chovev *(m.)*, **chovevet** *(f.)*	חובב, חובבת	amateur 25
chufshah *(f.)*	חופשה	holiday (vacation) 83
chultzah *(f.)*	חולצה	shirt 64
chumus *(m.)*	חומוס	hummus 27; chickpea(s) 55
chut *(m.)*	חוט	wire 44
chutz	חוץ	outside of 25
chutz la`aretz	חוץ לארץ	abroad 25

D

dag *(m.)*	דג	fish 83
daq *(m.)*, **daqah** *(f.)*	דק, דקה	thin 76

daqah *(f.)*	דקה	minute 79
darash [lidrosh]	דרש [לדרוש]	to demand 73
darkon *(m.)*	דרכון	passport 26
darom	דרום	south 56
dati *(m.)*, **datit** *(f.)*	דתי, דתית	religious 46
davar *(m.)*	דבר	word 58; thing 73
davqa	דווקא	just, precisely, rather 68
day	די	it is enough 81
de'ah *(f.)*	דיעה	opinion 71
deleq *(m.)*	דלק	gas, petrol 50
delet *(f.)*	דלת	door 46
dereg *(m.)*	דרג	grade (echelon) 83
derekh *(f.)*	דרך	road 50
dfus *(m.)*	דפוס	print(ing) 57
diber [ledaber]	דבר [לדבר]	to speak 8; to talk 13
dibur *(m.)*	דיבור	speech (speaking) 8
diburit *(f.)*	דיבורית	hands-free set 13
dietah *(f.)*	דיאטה	diet 16
dirah *(f.)*	דירה	apartment 37
disq *(m.)*	דיסק	disk 81
do`ar *(m.)*	דואר	post (mail) 22; post office 29
dor *(m.)*	דור	generation 81
dover *(m.)*, **doveret** *(f.)*	דובר, דוברת	speaker (of a particular language) 82
dugmah *(f.)*	דוגמה	example 43
dugman *(m.)*, **dugmanit** *(f.)*	דוגמן, דוגמנית	fashion model 75
du-leshoni *(m.)*	דו-לשוני	bilingual 62
du-siach *(m.)*	דו-שיח	dialogue 73
dvash *(m.)*	דבש	honey 80
dvorah *(f.)*	דבורה	bee 80

F

falafel *(m.)*	פלאפל	falafel 27
festival *(m.)*	פסטיבל	festival 27
figurah *(f.)*	פיגורה	figure 75
filter *(m.)*	פילטר	filter 11
fiziqah *(f.)*	פיזיקה	physics 43
frayer *(m.)*, **frayerit** *(f.)*	פראיר, פראירית	sucker 73

G

gadol *(m.)*, **gdolah** *(f.)*	גדול, גדולה	big 19
gag *(m.)*	גג	roof 67
gal *(m.)*	גל	wave (in the sea) 61
Galil	גליל	Galilee 83
gal'in *(m.)*	גלעין	pit (stone of fruit) 76
gam	גם	also 13
gam … vegam …	גם … וגם …	as well as, both 27
gan *(m.)*	גן	garden 37
gan 'eden *(m.)*	גן עדן	paradise (Garden of Eden) 46
gan-yeladim *(m.)*	גן-ילדים	kindergarten 37
ganaz [lignoz]	גנז [לגנוז]	to hide (stash) 72

gar [lagur]	גר [לגור]	to live (reside), to stay (somewhere) 51
gar'inim *(m. pl.)*	גרעינים	seeds 20
garush *(m.)*, **grushah** *(f.)*	גרוש, גרושה	divorced 74
gav *(m.)*	גב	back (the part of the body) 78
gavi'a *(m.)*	גביע	cup (trophy) 73
ge`eh** *(m.)*, **ge`ah *(f.)*	גאה, גאה	proud 52
ge`ografyah *(f.)*	גיאוגרפיה	geography 26
gerev *(f.)*	גרב	sock 64
gever	גבר	man 50
gezer *(m.)*	גזר	carrot 76
gibor *(m.)*, **giborah** *(f.)*	גיבור, גיבורה	hero 71
gil *(m.)*	גיל	age 30; joy 61
glidah *(f.)*	גלידה	ice cream 67
golmi *(m.)*, **golmit** *(f.)*	גולמי, גולמית	raw (plain or untreated) 55
govah *(m.)*	גובה	height, level 73
guf *(m.)*	גוף	body 43
gveret	גברת	lady 52
gvinah *(f.)*	גבינה	cheese 10
gvirti	גבירתי	madam 51

H

ha-	ה-	the 9
Ha`im?	האם?	particle for forming yes/no questions 67
ha'arakhah *(f.)*	הערכה	consideration, esteem 73
haba *(m.)*, **haba`ah** *(f.)*	הבא, הבאה	next (coming) 40
habaytah	הביתה	towards home 40
hafta'ah *(f.)*	הפתעה	surprise 34
hafukh *(m.)*, **hafukhah** *(f.)*	הפוך, הפוכה	reversed 11
hakhanah *(f.)*	הכנה	preparation 54
hakhi	הכי	most 75
halakh [lalekhet]	הלך [ללכת]	to go 18; to walk 29
hamcha`ah *(f.)*	המחאה	cheque 32
handasah *(f.)*	הנדסה	engineering 40
haqladah *(f.)*	הקלדה	typing 81
har *(m.)*	הר	mountain 83
harbeh	הרבה	a lot 27; many / much 50
harpatqah *(f.)*	הרפתקה	adventure 85
hatchalah *(f.)*	התחלה	beginning 85
hatmadah *(f.)*	התמדה	perseverance 78
hatov *(m.)*, **hatovah** *(f.)* **beyoter**	הטוב, הטובה ביותר	best 32
hatza'ah *(f.)*	הצעה	suggestion 83
hatzlachah *(f.)*	הצלחה	success 57
hayah [liheyot]	היה [להיות]	to be 35
hazmanah *(f.)*	הזמנה	invitation 24; reservation (booking) 60
he'edif [leha'adif]	העדיף [להעדיף]	to prefer 50
he'ez [leha'ez]	העז [להעז]	to dare 71
hechlit [lehachlit]	החליט [להחליט]	to decide 82
hekhin [lehakhin]	הכין [להכין]	to prepare 54

hem *(m.)*	הם	they 13
hen *(f.)*	הן	they 13
herim [leharim]	הרים [להרים]	to raise 73
hesir [lehasir]	הסיר [להסיר]	to remove, to take off 48
hevi` [lehavi`]	הביא [להביא]	to bring 74
hevin [lehavin]	הבין [להבין]	to understand 16
heykhal *(m.)*	היכל	palace, shrine 72
heziq [lehaziq]	הזיק [להזיק]	to damage, to hurt 78
hi	היא	it *(f.)*, she 8
hidpis [lehadpis]	הדפיס [להדפיס]	to print 81
higi'a [lehagi'a]	הגיע [להגיע]	to arrive, to reach 38
higid [lehagid]	הגיד [להגיד]	to tell 52
higish [lehagish]	הגיש [להגיש]	to serve 76
hikir [lehakir]	היכיר [להכיר]	to meet (become acquainted) 34; to know (be acquainted with) 37
hineh	הנה	here 67
hiqlid [lehaqlid]	הקליד [להקליד]	to type 81
hiqlit [lehaqlit]	הקליט [להקליט]	to record, to save to 81
hiqtzif [lehaqtzif]	הקציף [להקציף]	to beat (eggs), to whip (cream) 79
hirgish [lehargish]	הרגיש [להרגיש]	to feel 47
hisbir [lehasbir]	הסביר [להסביר]	to explain 67
hish`ir [lehash`ir]	השאיר [להשאיר]	to leave 79
hishlim [lehashlim]	השלים [להשלים]	to supplement 81
hishmin [lehashmin]	השמין [להשמין]	to fatten (gain weight) 52
hishta'amem [lehishta'amem]	השתעמם [להשתעמם]	to be bored 82
hishtadel [lehishtadel]	השתדל [להשתדל]	to try 85
hishtage'a [lehishtage'a]	השתגע [להשתגע]	to go crazy 41
histakel [lehistakel]	הסתכל [להסתכל]	to look 80
histori *(m.)*, **historit** *(f.)*	הסטורי, הסטורית	historical 34
histovev [lehistovev]	הסתובב [להסתובב]	to wander 50
hit'amel [lehit'amel]	התעמל [להתעמל]	to work out 78
hit'amlut *(f.)*	התעמלות	workout 78
hit'anyen [lehit'anyen]	התעניין [להתעניין]	to be interested 71
hitchaten [lehitchaten]	התחתן [להתחתן]	to get married 34
hitchayvut *(f.)*	היתחיבות	commitment 85
hitkavetz [lehitkavetz]	התכווץ [להתכווץ]	to contract 43
hitkonen [lehitkonen]	התכונן [להתכונן]	to prepare oneself (be prepared) 54
hitlahev [lehitlahev]	התלהב [להתלהב]	to be excited 65
hitnasah [lehitnasot]	התנסה [להתנסות]	to experience, to try 83
hitpalel [lehitpalel]	התפלל [להתפלל]	to pray 46
hitpaneq [lehitpaneq]	התפנק [להתפנק]	to spoil oneself 83
hitqarer [lehitqarer]	התקרר [להתקרר]	to cool down 79
hitrachetz [lehitrachetz]	התרחץ [להתרחץ]	to wash (oneself) 67
hitrachev [lehitrachev]	התרחב [להתרחב]	to expand 43
hitragel [lehitragel]	התרגל [להתרגל]	to get used to 85
hitrakez [lehitrakez]	התרכז [להתרכז]	to concentrate 78
hitzbi'a [lehatzbi'a]	הצביע [להצביע]	to vote 82
hitzi'a [lehatzi'a]	הציע [להציע]	to suggest 78; to offer 79

hitzliach [lehatzliach]	הצליח [להצליח]	to succeed 57
hivtiach [lehavtiach]	הבטיח [להבטיח]	to promise 78
hizdamnut *(f.)*	הזדמנות	opportunity 73
hizkir [lehazkir]	הזכיר [להזכיר]	to recall 72
hizmin [lehazmin]	הזמין [להזמין]	to invite 32
hodi'a [lehodi'a]	הודיע [להודיע]	to announce 53
hofi'a [lehofi'a]	הופיע [להופיע]	to appear 81
horeh *(m.)*, **horim** *(pl.)*	הורה, הורים	parent 75
hosif [lehosif]	הוסיף [להוסיף]	to add 53
hu	הוא	he, it *(m.)* 8
huledet *(f.)*	הולדת	birth 32

K

ka`asher	כאשר	when 29
ka'as *(m.)*	כעס	anger 80
ka'as [likh'os]	כעס [לכעוס]	to be angry 69
kachol *(m.)*, **kchulah** *(f.)*	כחול, כחולה	blue 64
kadur *(m.)*	כדור	ball 19
kaduregel *(m.)*	כדורגל	football (soccer) 19
kadursal *(m.)*	כדורסל	basketball 19
kaduryad *(m.)*	כדוריד	handball 19
kaf *(f.)*	כף	spoon (tablespoon) 55
kafri *(m.)*, **kafrit** *(f.)*	כפרי, כפרית	rural 83
kakh	כך	if so 67
kakhah	ככה	like that, so 3
kakhah, kakhah	ככה, ככה	not bad 3
kalal [likhlol]	כלל [ליכלול]	to include 83
kamah	כמה	how many 23
kapit *(f.)*	כפית	teaspoon 55
kartis *(m.)*	כרטיס	ticket 26
katav [likhtov]	כתב [לכתוב]	to correspond with, to write 22
katom *(m.)*, **ktumah** *(f.)*	כתום, כתומה	orange (colour) 65
kaved *(m.)*, **kvedah** *(f.)*	כבד, כבדה	heavy 57
kavod *(m.)*	כבוד	honour 57
kazeh	כזה	such (like this) 68
keday	כדאי	worthwhile (to be worth it) 53
kedey	כדי	in order to 53
kef *(m.)*	כיף	fun 20
ken	כן	yes 22
kenes *(m.)*	כנס	conference 44
kesef *(m.)*	כסף	money 32
kfar *(m.)*	כפר	village 39
ki	כי	because 16
kibah [lekhabot]	כיבה [לכבות]	to turn off 45
kirayim *(m. pl.)*	כיריים	stove top 83
kis *(m.)*	כיס	pocket 80
kise` *(m.)*	כיסא	chair 17
klomar	כלומר	that's to say 78
klum *(m.)*	כלום	nothing 73
kmo	כמו	like 18
kneset *(f.)*	כנסת	Knesset (Israel's parliament) 48
knisah *(f.)*	כניסה	entrance 72

kol	כל	all 27; each, every 31
kolbo *(m.)*	כלבו	minimarket 83
kos *(f.)*	כוס	cup, glass 55
kosher *(m.)*	כושר	fitness 71
kotel *(m.)*	כותל	Western Wall 44
ktav *(m.)*	כתב	writing 57
ktovet *(f.)*	כתובת	address 22
kursah *(f.)*	כורסה	armchair 38
kvar	כבר	already 27

L

lachut *(f.)*	לחות	humidity 75
lakhen	לכן	therefore 65
lamad [lilmod]	למד [ללמוד]	to learn 5; to study 26
Lamah?	למה?	Why? 12
lamrot she-	למרות ש-	although 65
laqach [laqachat]	לקח [לקחת]	to take 41
lashon *(m.)*, **leshonot** *(pl.)*	לשון, לשונות	language 58
latinit *(f.)*	לטינית	Latin (language) 5
lavan *(m.)*, **levanah** *(f.)*	לבן, לבנה	white 64
lavash [lilbosh]	לבש [ללבוש]	to dress, to wear 18
laylah *(m.)*	לילה	night 27
le-	ל-	to 9; for 9, 16; towards 18
Le`an?	לאן?	To where? 18
le`at	לאט	slowly 78
le`om *(m.)*	לאום	nation 44
le`umi** *(m.)*, **le`umit *(f.)*	לאומי, לאומית	national 44
lechem *(m.)*	לחם	bread 55
lefachot	לפחות	at least 85
lefi	לפי	according to 53
lehavah *(f.)*	להבה	flame 65
Lehishtame'a!	להשתמע!	Speak to you soon! 74
Lehit!	להת!	Bye! 22
Lehitra`ot!	להתראות!	Goodbye!, See you soon! 6
le'itim qrovot	לעיתים קרובות	often 79
le'itim rechoqot	לעיתים רחוקות	rarely 79
lelo	ללא	without 73
lema'elah	למעלה	on top 73
lemashal	למשל	for example 78
lematah	למטה	at the bottom 73
lev *(m.)*	לב	heart 31
levad	לבד	alone 66
leytzan *(m.)*, **leytzanit** *(f.)*	ליצן, ליצנית	clown 65
lif'amim	לפעמים	sometimes 79
lifney	לפני	before 26; ago 29
ligah *(f.)*	ליגה	league 73
likhvod	לכבוד	in honour of 34
limed [lelamed]	לימד [ללמד]	to teach 40
limon *(m.)*	לימון	lemon 55
limud *(m.)*	לימוד	learning (study) 57
liqer *(m.)*	ליקר	liqueur 79
litef [lelatef]	ליטף [ללטף]	to caress 47

lo לא no 8
lo-yutzlach לא-יוצלח good-for-nothing 74

M

ma`agar *(m.)* מאגר reservoir (stockpile) 81
ma`agar meyda' *(m.)* מאגר מידע database 81
ma`amatz *(m.)* מאמץ effort 57
ma'agal *(m.)* מעגל circle 78
ma'alah *(f.)* מעלה degree 79
ma'alit *(f.)* מעלית elevator / lift 41
ma'arav *(m.)* מערב west 50
ma'arekhet *(f.)* מערכת campaign 82
machar מחר tomorrow 33
machshev *(m.)* מחשב computer 9
machshev nayad *(m.)* מחשב נייד laptop 9
machshev nisa *(m.)* מחשב נישא laptop 9
mador *(m.)* מדור column (newspaper) 52
madpeset *(f.)* מדפסת printer 81
madregah *(f.)* מדרגה step (on a staircase) 83
magaf *(m.)* מגף boot 64
Mah? מה? What?, Which? 3
mahapakh *(m.)* מהפך upheaval 73
mahapekhah *(f.)* מהפכה revolution 53
makhar [limkor] מכר [למכור] to sell 53
makhur *(m.)*, **mekhurah** *(f.)* מכור, מכורה addicted 75
mal`akh *(m.)* מלאך angel 46
male *(m.)*, **mele`ah** *(f.)* מלא, מלאה complete, full 60
malon *(m.)* מלון hotel 51
mamash ממש really 36
manah [limnot] מנה [למנות] to count 82
manuy *(m.)*, **menuyah** *(f.)* מנוי, מנויה subscriber 52
maqom *(m.)* מקום place 66
maqor *(m.)*, **meqorot** *(pl.)* מקור, מקורות source 85
masa' *(m.)* מסע trek 26
maspiq מספיק enough 39
matanah *(f.)* מתנה present (gift) 32
Matay? מתי? When? 24
matchil *(m.)*, **matchilah** *(f.)* מתחיל, מתחילה beginner 85
matkon *(m.)* מתכון recipe 79
matoq *(m.)*, **metuqah** *(f.)* מתוק, מתוקה sweet 79
matza [limtzo] מצא [למצוא] to find 38
matza [limtzo] chen מצא [למצוא] חן to like (find pleasing) 38
matzchiq *(m.)*, **matzchiqah** *(f.)* מצחיק, מצחיקה funny 65
matzeget *(f.)* מצגת computer presentation 81
matzlemah *(f.)* מצלמה camera 25
matzpun *(m.)* מצפון conscience 82
ma'ukh *(m.)*, **me'ukhah** *(f.)* מעוך, מעוכה crushed 55
mayim *(m. pl.)* מיים water 27
mazag [limzog] מזג [למזוג] to pour 68
mazal *(m.)* מזל luck 16

Mazal tov!	מזל טוב!	Congratulations! 16, 30
mazgan *(m.)*	מזגן	air-conditioner 68
me-	מ-	from 8
me`amen** *(m.)*, **me`amenet *(f.)*	מאמן, מאמנת	coach, trainer 71
Me`ayin?	מאין?	From where? 15
me`az	מאז	since (temporal) 59
me`od	מאוד	very 23
me`urgan** *(m.)*, **me`urgenet *(f.)*	מאורגן, מאורגנת	organized, ready 73
me`uvzar** *(m.)*, **me`uvzeret *(f.)*	מאובזר, מאובזרת	equipped 83
me'anyen *(m.)*, **me'anyenet** *(f.)*	מעניין, מעניינת	interesting 44
me'arah *(f.)*	מערה	cave 72
me'ayef *(m.)*, **me'ayefet** *(f.)*	מעייף, מעייפת	tiring 12
mechir *(m.)*	מחיר	price 53
mechubar *(m.)*, **mechuberet** *(f.)*	מחובר, מחוברת	connected (tied to) 75
mediach-kelim *(m.)*	מדיח-כלים	dishwasher 83
mefateh *(m.)*, **mefatah** *(f.)*	מפתה, מפתה	tempting 83
megilah *(f.)*	מגילה	scroll 72
megurim *(m. pl.)*	מגורים	living 83
me'il *(m.)*	מעיל	coat 41
mekhinah *(f.)*	מכינה	preparatory course 54
mekhonit *(f.)*	מכונית	car 13
mekhubad *(m.)*, **mekhubedet** *(f.)*	מכובד, מכובדת	respected 80
melach *(m.)*	מלח	salt 55
melafefon *(m.)*	מלפפון	cucumber 76
melakhah *(f.)*	מלאכה	handicraft 83
melukhlakh *(m.)*, **melukhlekhet** *(f.)*	מלוכלך, מלוכלכת	dirty 67
menahel *(m.)*, **menahelet** *(f.)*	מנהל, מנהלת	manager 53
meqarer *(m.)*	מקרר	refrigerator 83
mequlqal *(m.)*, **mequlqelet** *(f.)*	מקולקל, מקולקלת	broken, out of order 68
merateq *(m.)*, **merateqet** *(f.)*	מרתק, מרתקת	fascinating 85
merchaq *(m.)*	מרחק	distance 83
merkaz *(m.)*	מרכז	centre 51
merkaz ha'ir *(m.)*	מרכז העיר	city centre 58
meshekh *(m.)*	משך	duration, during 62; over (the course of) 73
mesibah *(f.)*	מסיבה	party 34
mesunan *(m.)*, **mesunenet** *(f.)*	מסונן, מסוננת	strained (sieved) 79
mesuyam *(m.)*, **mesuyemet** *(f.)*	מסוים, מסוימת	certain 83
met [lamut]	מת [למות]	to die 46
metoraf *(m.)*, **metorefet** *(f.)*	מטורף, מטורפת	crazy 75
metzuyan *(m.)*, **metzuyenet** *(f.)*	מצויין, מצויינת	excellent 25
metzuyanut *(f.)*	מצויינות	excellence 73
me'ubad *(m.)*, **me'ubedet** *(f.)*	מעובד, מעובדת	adapted 85
me'udkan *(m.)*, **me'udkenet** *(f.)*	מעודכן, מעודכנת	updated (up-to-date) 81
mevugar *(m.)*, **mevugeret** *(f.)*	מבוגר, מבוגרת	adult 65
mevuqash *(m.)*, **mevuqeshet** *(f.)*	מבוקש, מבוקשת	desired 81
meyda' *(m.)*	מידע	information 81
meyuchad *(m.)*, **meyuchedet** *(f.)*	מיוחד, מיוחדת	special 75
mezeg *(m.)*	מזג	temperament 68

mezeg `avir *(m.)* מזג אוויר weather 68
mezuman *(m.)* מזומן cash 32
Mi? מי? Who? 18
midbar *(m.)* מדבר desert 50
midrachov *(m.)* מדרחוב pedestrian street 51
midrakhah *(f.)* מדרכה pavement, sidewalk 51
midsha`ah *(f.)* מדשאה lawn 83
miflagah *(f.)* מפלגה political party 82
migdal *(m.)* מגדל tower 58
migrash *(m.)* מגרש field (sports) 73
mikhnasayim *(m.)* מכנסיים trousers 64
mikhseh *(m.)* מכסה lid 72
mikhshol *(m.)* מכשול obstacle 80
mikhtav *(m.)* מכתב letter (correspondence) 27
milah *(f.)* מילה circumcision 30
milah *(f.)*, **milim** *(pl.)* מילה, מילים word 71
milchamah *(f.)* מלחמה war 72
milon *(m.)* מילון dictionary 71
mipney she- מפני ש- because 27
miqledet *(f.)* מקלדת keyboard 81
miqrogal *(m.)* מיקרוגל microwave 83
miqtzo'a *(m.)* מקצוע profession 62
mirpeset *(f.)* מרפסת balcony 39
mis'adah *(f.)* מסעדה restaurant 68
mischaq *(m.)* משחק game 19
mishehu *(m.)* מישהו someone 33
mishpachah *(f.)* משפחה family 19
mishpat *(m.)* משפט law 40
mishqal *(m.)* משקל scale (for weighing), weight 53
misrad *(m.)* משרד office 53
mitah *(f.)* מטה bed 17
mitbach *(m.)* מטבח kitchen 39
mitologi *(m.)*, **mitologit** *(f.)* מיתולוגי, מיתולוגית mythological 71
mitologyah *(f.)* מיתולוגיה mythology 71
mitqan *(m.)* מתקן facility 83
mitz *(m.)* מיץ juice 11
mitzpeh *(m.)* מצפה vantage point 83
mitzpor *(m.)* מצפור lookout 83
Mitzrayim *(f.)* מצרים Egypt 50
mitzvah *(f.)* מצווה commandment 16
mivchar *(m.)* מבחר choice 82
mivneh *(m.)* מבנה building, structure 72
mizrach *(m.)* מזרח east 50
mizug *(m.)* מיזוג mixture 68
mizug `avir *(m.)* מיזוג אוויר air-conditioning 68
mizvadah *(f.)* מזוודה suitcase 23
mo'adon *(m.)* מועדון club 60
moda'ah *(f.)* מודעה advertisement, announcement 60
molad *(m.)* מולד birth 41
moreh *(m.)*, **morah** *(f.)* מורה, מורה teacher 43
mukhan *(m.)*, **mukhanah** *(f.)* מוכן, מוכנה ready 54

mul מול facing, in front of 68
mumcheh *(m.)*, **mumchit** *(f.)* מומחה, מומחית expert, specialist 81
muqdam מוקדם early 72
musag *(m.)* מושג concept 81
musiqah *(f.)* מוסיקה music 71
mutar *(m.)*, **muteret** *(f.)* מותר, מותרת permitted 66
mutzlach *(m.)*, **mutzlachat** *(f.)* מוצלח, מוצלחת successful 85
muzah *(f.)* מוזה muse 71
muze`on *(m.)* מוזיאון museum 71

N

na'al *(f.)* נעל shoe 64
nafal [lifol] נפל [לפול] to fall 29
nafotz [lafutz] נפוץ [לפוץ] to be dispersed, to be scattered 58
nahag [linhog] נהג [לנהוג] to drive 46
na'im *(m.)*, **ne'imah** *(f.)* נעים, נעימה pleasant 26
nakhon *(m.)*, **nekhonah** *(f.)* נכון, נכונה correct, right (proper) 40
naqi *(m.)*, **neqiyah** *(f.)* נקי, נקייה clean 67
nasa' [linso'a] נסע [לנסוע] to travel 33; to drive 50
natan [latet] נתן [לתת] to give 43
natun *(m.)*, **netunim** *(pl.)* נתון, נתונים data 81
nayad *(m.)*, **nayedet** *(f.)* נייד, ניידת mobile *(adj.)* 13
ne'elam [lehe'alem] נעלם [להעלם] to disappear 82
nefilah *(f.)* נפילה fall (the act of falling) 73
nehag *(m.)*, **naheget** *(f.)* נהג, נהגת driver 46
nehedar *(m.)*, **nehederet** *(f.)* נהדר, נהדרת wonderful 41
neheneh [lehanot] נהנה [להנות] to enjoy 76
nekhdah נכדה granddaughter 30
nekhed נכד grandson 30
nequdah *(f.)* נקודה dot 22; point 57
nes *(m.)* נס miracle 11
neshamah *(f.)* נשמה soul 46
neshimah *(f.)* נשימה breath 83
nesi'ah *(f.)* נסיעה travel (journey), trip 53
nifgash [lehipagesh] נפגש [להפגש] to meet 44
nifrad [lehipared] נפרד [להפרד] to break up 40
nihel [lenahel] ניהל [לנהל] to manage (direct) 73
nikar *(m.)*, **nikeret** *(f.)* נכר, נכרת distinguished 80
nikhnas [lehikanes] נכנס [להכנס] to enter, to go into 46
nikhshal [lehikashel] נכשל [להכשל] to fail 54
nim`as (+ li/lekha/lakh etc.) נמאס לי ... to be fed up 78
nimratz *(m.)*, **nimretzet** *(f.)* נמרץ, נמרצת dynamic 73
niqah [lenaqot] ניקה [לנקות] to clean 67
niqud *(m.)* ניקוד vowel point 57
nisa *(m.)*, **niset** *(f.)* נשא, נשאת portable 9
nishba' [lehishava'] נשבע [להשבע] to swear (make an oath) 66
nishmar [lehishamer] נשמר [להישמר] to maintain 85
nishqal [lehishaqel] נשקל [להשקל] to be weighed 53
nisu`im *(m. pl.)* נישואים marriage (institution) 34
niteq [lenateq] ניתק [לנתק] to cut off 74
nitzachon *(m.)* ניצחון victory 73

nitzeach [lenatzeach]	נצח [לנצח]	to win 73
nivchar [lehibacher]	נבחר [להבחר]	to be elected 82
noach *(m.)*, **nochah** *(f.)*	נוח, נוחה	comfortable 83
nof *(m.)*	נוף	landscape, view (scenery) 68
nofesh *(m.)*	נופש	holiday (vacation) 39
nolad [lehivaled]	נולד [להולד]	to be born 30
nosaf *(m.)*, **nosefet** *(f.)*	נוסף, נוספת	further 60; additional 81
nose *(m.)*	נושא	subject 82
nose'a *(m.)*, **nosa'at** *(f.)*	נוסע, נוסעת	passenger 46; traveller 53
noy *(m.)*	נוי	beauty 61
Nu?	נו?!	Well?! 22
nudniq *(m.)*, **nudniqit** *(f.)*	נודניק, נודניקית	pest (irritating guy/woman) 29

P

pa'am *(f.)*	פעם	once 58
pa'amayim *(f.)*	פעמיים	twice 58
pachot ... m-	פחות ... מ-	less … than 77
pan *(m.)*, **panim** *(pl.)*	פן, פנים	side, face 65
panah [lifnot]	פנה [לפנות]	to turn 51
parus *(m.)*, **prusah** *(f.)*	פרוס, פרוסה	sliced 76
parvah *(f.)*	פרווה	fur 41
pashat [lifshot]	פשט [לפשוט]	to stretch, to take off 83
pashat [lifshot] `et haregel	פשט [לפשוט] את הרגל	to go bankrupt 83
pashut *(m.)*, **pshutah** *(f.)*	פשוט, פשוטה	simple / simply 85
patach [liftoach]	פתח [לפתוח]	to open 71
patar [liftor]	פתר [לפתור]	to solve 62
peh *(m.)*	פה	mouth 73
pelefon *(m.)*	פלאפון	mobile/cell phone 45
pereg *(m.)*	פרג	poppy / poppyseed 10
petrozilyah *(f.)*	פטרוזיליה	parsley 55
pilpel *(m.)*	פלפל	pepper 55
pinah *(f.)*	פינה	corner 83
pisgah *(f.)*	פסגה	top (summit) 73
pitah *(f.)*	פיתה	pita bread 55
pitgam *(m.)*	פתגם	proverb 80
pitpet [lefatpet]	פטפט [לפטפט]	to chat 20
pitput *(m.)*	פטפוט	chit-chat 13
pnay *(m.)*	פנאי	free time, leisure 62
pney *(m. pl.)*	פני	the face of, the surface of 58
pnim *(m.)*	פנים	inside (interior) 78
poh	פה	here 17
polanit *(f.)*	פולנית	Polish (the language) 8
Polanyah *(f.)*	פולניה	Poland 8
prat *(m.)*	פרט	detail 60
predah *(f.)*	פרדה	parting (farewell) 85
pri *(m.)*, **perot** *(pl.)*	פרי, פירות	fruit 79
pshitat regel *(f.)*	פשיטת רגל	bankruptcy 83

Q

qabalah *(f.)*	קבלה	receipt 75
qadimah	קדימה	forwards 51

qadum *(m.)*, **qdumah** *(f.)*	קדום, קדומה	ancient 72
qafatz [liqfotz]	קפץ [לקפוץ]	to jump 85
qafeh *(m.)*	קפה	café, coffee 10
qafeteriah *(f.)*	קפטריה	cafeteria 11
qal *(m.)*, **qalah** *(f.)*	קל, קלה	easy, light (in weight) 76
qam [laqum]	קם [לקום]	to arise, to get up, to rise 82
qanah [liqnot]	קנה [לקנות]	to buy, to shop 12
qanqan *(m.)*	קנקן	pot (jug) 72
qanyon *(m.)*	קניון	shopping centre / mall 12
qar *(m.)*, **qarah** *(f.)*	קר, קרה	cold, cool (temperature) 41
qara` [liqro`]	קרא [לקרוא]	to read 57
qarah [liqrot]	קרה [לקרות]	to happen 29
qaramel *(m.)*	קרמל	caramel 51
qasheh *(m.)*, **qashah** *(f.)*	קשה, קשה	difficult 67
qashiach *(m.)*, **qeshichah** *(f.)*	קשיח, קשיחה	hard (rigid) 81
qashur *(m.)*, **qshurah** *(f.)*	קשור, קשורה	close (attached to) 75
qatan *(m.)*, **qtanah** *(f.)*	קטן, קטנה	little, small 19
qatzar *(m.)*, **qtzarah** *(f.)*	קצר, קצרה	short 43
qatzefet *(f.)*	קצפת	whipped cream 79
qatzutz *(m.)*, **qtzutzah** *(f.)*	קצוץ, קצוצה	chopped 55
qayitz *(m.)*	קיץ	summer 39
qe'arah *(f.)*	קערה	bowl 76
qedem *(m.)*	קדם	the East 58
qemach *(m.)*	קמח	flour 79
qeren *(m.)*	קרן	ray 61
qeresh *(m.)*	קרש	board 76
qesher *(m.)*, **qsharim** *(pl.)*	קשר, קשרים	contact 85
qetzef *(m.)*	קצף	foam 79
qibel [leqabel]	קבל [לקבל]	to receive 54
qibutz *(m.)*	קבוץ	kibbutz 34
qipel [leqapel]	קיפל [לקפל]	to fold/roll up 48
qir *(m.)*	קיר	wall 72
qirqas *(m.)*	קרקס	circus 65
qishur *(m.)*	קשור	link 81
qitzur *(m.)*	קצור	shortcut 73
qlaf *(m.)*	קלף	playing card 66
qlasi *(m.)*, **qlasit** *(f.)*	קלסי, קלסית	classical (typical) 82
qniyah *(f.)*	קניה	purchase 12
qniyot *(f. pl.)*	קניות	shopping (purchases) 12
qol *(m.)*, **qolot** *(pl.)*	קול, קולות	sound, voice 81
qolno'a *(m.)*	קולנוע	cinema, movie theatre 31
qomedyah *(f.)*	קומדיה	comedy 31
qor *(m.)*	קור	cold *(noun)* 43
qore`** *(m.)*, **qor`ah *(f.)*	קורא, קוראה	reader 57
qovetz *(m.)*	קובץ	computer file 81
qovetz qol *(m.)*, **qivtzey qol** *(pl.)*	קובץ קול, קבצי קול	sound file 81
qrem *(m.)*	קרם	cream 51
qtzat	קצת	a little 53
qubiyah *(f.)*	קוביה	cube 76
qupah *(f.)*	קופה	cash register/till 31
qvutzah *(f.)*	קבוצה	team 71

R

ra`ah [lir`ot]	ראה [לראות]	to see 23
rabah *(f.)*	רבה	great (in amount), very much 24
rachav *(m.)*, **rechavah** *(f.)*	רחב, רחבה	wide 80
radyo *(m.)*	רדיו	radio 75
ra'ev *(m.)*, **re'evah** *(f.)*	רעב, רעבה	hungry 67
rahit *(m.)*	רהיט	furniture 38
ramah *(f.)*	רמה	level 83
ramzor *(m.)*	רמזור	traffic light 51
raq	רק	only (merely) 8
ratuv *(m.)*, **retuvah** *(f.)*	רטוב, רטובה	wet 76
ratzah [lirtzot]	רצה [לרצות]	to want 9
rav *(m.)*	רב	rabbi 46
razah [lirzot]	רזה [לירזות]	to become thin (lose weight) 53
razeh *(m.)*, **razah** *(f.)*	רזה, רזה	thin 53
re`ayon** *(m.)*, **re`ayonot *(pl.)*	ראיון, ראיונות	interview 75
rechov *(m.)*, **rechovot** *(pl.)*	רחוב, רחובות	street 51
refu`ah *(f.)*	רפואה	medicine 40
rega' *(m.)*	רגע	moment 73
regel *(f.)*	רגל	foot 19; leg 83
retzu'ah *(f.)*	רצועה	strip 76
rishmi *(m.)*, **rishmit** *(f.)*	רשמי, רשמית	official 48
rofe *(m.)*, **rofah** *(f.)*	רופא, רופאה	doctor 51
rofe shinayim *(m.)*, **rof`at shinayim** *(f.)*	רופא שיניים, רופאת שיניים	dentist 80
ron *(m.)*	רון	joy 54
rosh *(m.)*	ראש	head 24
rotev *(m.)*	רוטב	salad dressing, sauce 76
rusit *(f.)*	רוסית	Russian (the language) 8
Rusyah *(f.)*	רוסיה	Russia 8

S

saba	סבא	grandfather 30
Sababah!	סבאבה!	Great! 85
sachah [lischot]	שחה [לשחות]	to swim 15
sachqan *(m.)*, **sachqanit** *(f.)*	שחקן, שחקנית	player 73
sadeh *(m.)*	שדה	field 23
safah *(f.)*	שפה	language, lip 58
safar [lispor]	ספר [לספור]	to count 47
sakhar [liskor]	שכר [לשכור]	to rent 39
sakin *(f.)*, **sakinim** *(pl.)*	סכין, סכינים	knife 76
sal *(m.)*	סל	basket 19
salat *(m.)*	סלט	salad 27
samakh [lismokh]	סמך [לסמוך]	to rely 73
sameach *(m.)*, **smechah** *(f.)*	שמח, שמחה	happy 80
samikh *(m.)*, **smikhah** *(f.)*	סמיך, סמיכה	thick 79
sapah *(f.)*	ספה	sofa 38
saqit *(f.)*	שקית	packet 79
saqran *(m.)*, **saqranit** *(f.)*	סקרן, סקרנית	curious 83
sar *(m.)*, **sarah** *(f.)*	שר, שרה	minister (government) 48
satan *(m.)*	שטן	devil 80

saviv	סביב	around 66
savta	סבתא	grandmother 30
scharchoret *(f.)*	סחרחורת	dizziness 75
sdeh te'ufah *(m.)*	שדה תעופה	airport 23
seder *(m.)*	סדר	order 17
seder yom *(m.)*	סדר יום	agenda, routine 75
sefer *(m.)*	ספר	book 37
seret *(m.)*	סרט	film, movie 65
sfaradi *(m.)*, **sfaradiyah** *(f.)*	ספרדי, ספרדיה	Sephardi 82
sibah *(f.)*	סיבה	reason 34
sicheq [lesacheq]	שחק [לשחק]	to play 19
sichrer [lesachrer]	סחרר [לסחרר]	to make dizzy, to faze 73
sider [lesader]	סדר [לסדר]	to order (arrange), to tidy 17
sidrah *(f.)*	סדרה	series 78
sidur *(m.)*	סידור	arrangement (organization) 53
simel [lesamel]	סמל [לסמל]	to symbolize 72
simlah *(f.)*	שמלה	dress 16
sipur *(m.)*	ספור	story 73
sleng *(m.)*	סלנג	slang 85
slichah *(f.)*	סליחה	excuse [me] 23
smali *(m.)*, **smalit** *(f.)*	שמאלי, שמאלית	left *(adj.)* 51
smol	שמאל	left *(adv.)* 56
smolah	שמאלה	to the left 51
sof *(m.)*	סוף	end 20
sof shavu'a *(m.)*	סוף שבוע	weekend 20
sof sof	סוף סוף	at last 20
sokhnut *(f.)*	סוכנות	agency 53
sportivi *(m.)*, **sportivit** *(f.)*	ספורטיבי, ספורטיבית	sporty 19
sukar *(m.)*	סוכר	sugar 11
sukrazit *(f.)*	סוכרזית	sweetener 11
svivah *(f.)*	סביבה	environment 82

SH

sha`al [lish`ol]	שאל [לשאול]	to ask 43
sha'ah *(f.)*	שעה	hour, time (in reference to the clock) 33
sha'ar *(m.)*	שער	gate 85
shabat *(f.)*	שבת	Saturday, Shabbat 8
shachar *(m.)*	שחר	dawn 64
shachmat *(m.)*	שחמט	chess 62
shachor *(m.)*, **shchorah** *(f.)*	שחור, שחורה	black 64
shakhen *(m.)*, **shkhenah** *(f.)*	שכן, שכנה	neighbour 37
shalach [lishloach]	שלח [לשלוח]	to send 54
shalav *(m.)*, **shlabim** *(pl.)*	שלב, שלבים	stage (phase) 79
shalem *(m.)*, **shlemah** *(f.)*	שלם, שלמה	entire 72
shalom *(m.)*	שלום	hello, peace 2
shalvah *(f.)*	שלווה	tranquillity 71; calm 83
sham	שם	there 15
shama' [lishmo'a]	שמע [לשמוע]	to hear, to listen 6
shamayim *(m. pl.)*	שמיים	sky 27; heavens 58
shanah *(f.)*	שנה	year 30
shaqet *(m.)*, **shqetah** *(f.)*	שקט, שקטה	calm 73
shar [lashir]	שר [לשיר]	to sing 65
sharvul *(m.)*	שרוול	sleeve 48

shatach [lishtoach]	שטח [לשטוח]	to flatten, to roll out, to spread 79
shatah [lishtot]	שתה [לשתות]	to drink 4
shavar [lishbor]	שבר [לשבור]	to break 31
shavat [lishbot]	שבת [לשבות]	to strike (stop work) 33
shaveh *(m.)*, **shavah** *(f.)*	שווה, שווה	equal 69
shavu'a *(m.)*	שבוע	week 20
she-	-ש	that, which, who 23
she`elah *(f.)*	שאלה	question 45
shebo *(m.)*, **shebah** *(f.)*	שבו, שבה	in which 77
shefa' *(f.)*	שפע	abundance, plenty 60
shekhunah *(f.)*	שכונה	neighbourhood 73
shel	של	of 8
shelanu *(m./f.)*	שלנו	our 30
shem *(m.)*	שם	name 51
shemen *(m.)*	שמן	oil 52
shen *(f.)*	שן	clove (of garlic), tooth 55
sheqel *(m.)*	שקל	shekel (Israeli unit of currency) 45
sherutim *(m. pl.)*	שירותים	toilet 83
shevu'on *(m.)*	שבועון	weekly newspaper/ magazine 52
shgi`ah *(f.)*	שגיאה	mistake 85
shichrer [leshachrer]	שחרר [לשחרר]	to free, to release 66
shidreg [leshadreg]	שדרג [לשדרג]	to upgrade 83
shir *(m.)*	שיר	poem, song 61
shirah *(f.)*	שירה	poetry, singing 60
shitah *(f.)*	שיטה	method 82
shi'ur *(m.)*	שיעור	lesson 43
shkhunati *(m.)*, **shkhunatit** *(f.)*	שכונתי, שכונתית	neighbourhood *(adj.)* 73
shlish *(m.)*	שליש	third (fraction) 55
shmurah *(f.)*	שמורה	reserve 83
shmurat teva' *(f.)*	שמורת טבע	nature reserve 83
shniyah *(f.)*	שניה	second (unit of time) 81
shoqolad *(m.)*	שוקולד	chocolate 10
shoresh *(m.)*	שורש	root 71
shoter *(m.)*, **shoteret** *(f.)*	שוטר, שוטרת	police officer 66
shpitz *(m.) (slang)*	שפיץ	point (tip), summit 73
shtut *(f.)*	שטות	nonsense 47
shu'al *(m.)*	שועל	fox 69
shulchan *(m.)*	שולחן	table 17
shum	שום	no (negative particle) 75
shum *(m.)*	שום	garlic 55
shutaf *(m.)*, **shutafah** *(f.)*	שותף, שותפה	partner 85
shuv	שוב	again 31
shvil *(m.)*	שביל	path 83
shvitah *(f.)*	שביתה	strike (labour dispute) 33

T

ta`arikh *(m.)*	תאריך	date (on the calendar) 83
ta'ah [lit'ot]	טעה [לטעות]	to be mistaken, to be wrong 50
ta'am *(m.)*	טעם	taste 76

ta'arovet *(f.)*	תערובת	mixture 79
taba'at *(f.)*	טבעת	ring (jewellery) 45
tachanah *(f.)*	תחנה	station 50
tachtit *(f.)*	תחתית	bottom 73
tafas [litpos]	תפס [לתפוס]	to catch 83
tafrit *(m.)*	תפריט	menu 68
ta'im *(m.)*, **te'imah** *(f.)*	טעים, טעימה	tasty 36
tal *(m.)*	טל	dew 61
talmid *(m.)*, **talmidah** *(f.)*	תלמיד, תלמידה	student 46
tamid	תמיד	always 36
tamrur *(m.)*	תמרור	road sign 51
Tanakh *(m.)*	תנ"ך	Bible 57
tanakhi *(m.)*, **tanakhit** *(f.)*	תנכי, תנכית	Biblical 57
tanur *(m.)*	תנור	oven 79
tapuach *(m.)*	תפוח	apple 11
tapuz *(m.)*	תפוז	orange (fruit) 11
taraf [litrof]	טרף [לטרוף]	to devour 69
targil *(m.)*	תרגיל	exercise 85
tari *(m.)*, **triyah** *(f.)*	טרי, טריה	fresh 76
tarmilay *(m.)*, **tarmila`it** *(f.)*	תרמילאי, תרמילאית	backpacker 26
tas [latus]	טס [לטוס]	to fly (by plane) 23
tashbetz *(m.)*	תשבץ	crossword 62
tashchetz *(m.)*	תשחץ	arrow word puzzle 62
tayar *(m.)*, **tayeret** *(f.)*	תייר, תיירת	tourist 39
tayarut *(f.)*	תיירות	tourism 53
tchinah *(f.)*	טחינה	tahini (sesame paste) 27
te`avon *(m.)*	תאבון	appetite 55
teh *(m.)*	תה	tea 4
tekhniyon *(m.)*	טכניון	Technion (institute of technology) 40
telefon *(m.)*	טלפון	telephone 13
televizyah *(f.)*	טלביזיה	television 68
te'udah *(f.)*	תעודה	certificate, document 72
te'ufah *(f.)*	תעופה	flight 23
teva' *(m.)*	טבע	nature 83
tevah *(f.)*	תיבה	box 71
tfilah *(f.)*	תפילה	prayer 16
tikhnen [letakhnen]	תכנן [לתכנן]	to plan 79
Tikhon *(m.)*	תיכון	Mediterranean 53
tinoq *(m.)*, **tinoqet** *(f.)*	תינוק, תינוקת	baby 61
tiqen [letaqen]	תיקן [לתקן]	to fix, to repair 68
tirgel [letargel]	תרגל [לתרגל]	to practice 85
tisah *(f.)*	טיסה	flight (airplane) 23
tiskel [letaskel]	תסכל [לתסכל]	to frustrate 75
tiyel [letayel]	טיל [לטיל]	to walk (for pleasure) 83
tmunah *(f.)*	תמונה	photograph 23
todah *(f.)*	תודה	thank you 4
toren *(m.)*	תורן	mast 80
tov *(m.)*, **tovah** *(f.)*	טוב, טובה	good 1
tqufah *(f.)*	תקופה	period (of time) 44
trufah *(f.)*	תרופה	medicine 71
tshuvah *(f.)*	תשובה	reply 54
turqi *(m.)*, **turqit** *(f.)*	טורקי, טורקית	Turkish *(adj.)* 11
tut *(m.)*	תות	strawberry 79

TZ

tzachaq [litzchoq]	צחק [לצחוק]	to laugh 51
tzad *(m.)*	צד	side 82
tzad [latzud]	צד [לצוד]	to hunt 69
tzag *(m.)*	צג	screen (e.g. computer) 81
tza'ir *(m.)*, **tze'irah** *(f.)*	צעיר, צעירה	young 30
tzalam *(m.)*, **tzalemet** *(f.)*	צלם, צלמת	photographer 25
tzameret *(f.)*	צמרת	top (upper part) 75
tzar *(m.)*, **tzarah** *(f.)*	צר, צרה	narrow 80
tzarfati *(m.)*, **tzarfatit** *(f.)*	צרפתי, צרפתית	French *(adj.)* 82
tzarikh *(m.)*, **tzrikhah** *(f.)*	צריך, צריכה	to need 25
tzava *(m.)*	צבא	army 26
tzavta *(m.)*	צוותא	togetherness 60
tzayid *(m.)*	צייד	hunt *(noun)* 69
tzedeq *(m.)*	צדק	justice 69
tzela' *(f.)*	צלע	rib 47
tzeva' *(m.)*	צבע	colour 64
tzevet *(m.)*	צוות	team 81
tzibur *(m.)*	ציבור	public 60
tziburi *(m.)*, **tziburit** *(f.)*	ציבורי, ציבורית	public *(adj.)* 66
tzilem [letzalem]	צלם [לצלם]	to photograph 25
tziltzel [letzaltzel]	צלצל [לצלצל]	to ring 45
tzilum *(m.)*	צילום	photography 25
tzimchoni *(m.)*, **tzimchonit** *(f.)*	צמחוני, צמחונית	vegetarian 76
tzimuq *(m.)*	צימוק	raisin 79
tziv'oni *(m.)*, **tziv'onit** *(f.)*	צבעוני, צבעונית	colourful 65
tziyer [letzayer]	צייר [לצייר]	to draw 78
tzlil *(m.)*	צליל	sound 61
tznonit *(f.)*	צנונית	radish 76
tzodeq *(m.)*, **tzodeqet** *(f.)*	צודק, צודקת	fair (right), just 69
tzohorayim *(m. pl.)*	צהרים	noon 62
tzolelet *(f.)*	צוללת	submarine 39
tzurah *(f.)*	צורה	shape 72

U

u-	-ו	and 36

V

vanil *(m.)*	וניל	vanilla 79
vatiq *(m.)*, **vatiqah** *(f.)*	וותיק, וותיקה	senior (older in age) 82
ve-	-ו	and 8
video *(m.)*	וידאו	video 19

Y

ya'ad *(m.)*	יעד	destination, objective 60
yachad	יחד	together 60
yachas *(m.)*	יחס	relationship 36
yachid *(m.)*, **yechidah** *(f.)*	יחיד, יחידה	only (sole) 47
yad *(f.)*	יד	hand 19
yada' [lada'at]	ידע [לדעת]	to know (a fact) 41
yadu'a *(m.)*	ידוע	well known 74
yafeh *(m.)*, **yafah** *(f.)*	יפה, יפה	beautiful, pretty 16
yahalom *(m.)*	יהלום	diamond 45

ya'il *(m.)*, **ye'ilah** *(f.)*	יעיל, יעילה	effective 73
ya'il [leho'il]	יעיל [להועיל]	to be useful 78
yakhol *(m.)*, **yekholah** *(f.)*	יכול, יכולה	to be able to, can 22
yam *(m.)*	ים	sea 15
yamin	ימין	right *(adv.)* 56
yaminah	ימינה	to the right 51
yaqar *(m.)*, **yeqarah** *(f.)*	יקר, יקרה	expensive 38; dear (cherished) 74
yarad [laredet]	ירד [לרדת]	to descend, to go down 72
yarchon *(m.)*	ירחון	monthly journal 52
Yarden *(m.)*	ירדן	Jordan 50
yaroq *(m.)*, **yeruqah** *(f.)*	ירוק, ירוקה	green 64
yashan *(m.)*, **yeshanah** *(f.)*	ישן, ישנה	old 82
yashan [lishon]	ישן [לישון]	to sleep 46
yashav [lashevet]	ישב [לשבת]	to sit 38
yashir *(m.)*, **yeshirah** *(f.)*	ישיר, ישירה	direct 53
yashvan *(m.)*	ישבן	buttocks 78
yatza [latzet]	יצא [לצאת]	to come out 67; to go out 74
yedidut *(f.)*	ידידות	friendship 85
ye'ilut *(f.)*	יעילות	efficiency 78
yeled *(m.)*, **yaldah** *(f.)*	ילד, ילדה	child 25
yemani *(m.)*, **yemanit** *(f.)*	ימני, ימנית	right *(adj.)* 56
yereq *(m.)*	ירק	vegetable 64
Yerushalayim	ירושלים	Jerusalem 23
yesh	יש	there is/are 10
yesh (+ **li/lekha/lakh** etc.)	יש ...	to have (to possess) 28
yeshivah *(f.)*	ישיבה	meeting, Yeshiva (religious school) 67; sitting 78
yetzi`ah *(f.)*	יציאה	departure 34
yevani *(m.)*, **yevanit** *(f.)*	יווני, יוונית	Greek *(adj.)* 44
yidish *(f.)*	אידיש	Yiddish (the language) 8
yisra`eli** *(m.)*, **yisra`elit *(f.)*	ישראלי, ישראלית	Israeli *(adj.)* 44
yitaron *(m.)*	יתרון	advantage 81
yitzer [leyatzer]	יצר [ליצר]	to create, to produce 71
yofi *(m.)*	יופי	beauty 61
Yofi!	יופי!	Great! 38
yom *(m.)*	יום	day 24
yom huledet *(m.)*	יום הולדת	birthday 32
yoter ... m-	יותר ... מ-	more ... than 77
yovel *(m.)*	יובל	jubilee 34

Z

zahav *(m.)*	זהב	gold 11
zakhar [lizkor]	זכר [לזכור]	to remember 67
zaquf *(m.)*, **zequfah** *(f.)*	זקוף, זקופה	straight 78
zayit *(m.)*	זית	olive 76
zaz [lazuz]	זז [לזוז]	to move 68
zeh *(m.)*	זה	this 17
zehut *(f.)*	זהות	identity 82
zekhukhit *(f.)*	זכוכית	glass (material) 39
zineq [lezaneq]	זינק [לזנק]	to soar 73
zman *(m.)*	זמן	time 75
zol *(m.)*, **zolah** *(f.)*	זול, זולה	cheap 38
zot *(f.)*	זאת	this 17
zug *(m.)*	זוג	couple 60; pair 60

English - Transliteration – Hebrew

Note that although the verbs are shown in the infinitive form in English, the Hebrew verbs are shown in the third-person masculine singular past tense, followed by the infinitive in square brackets. In Hebrew dictionaries it is standard to list the verbs in this way.

A

English	Transliteration	Hebrew
able to (to be ~) 22	**yakhol** *(m.)*, **yekholah** *(f.)*	יכול, יכולה
about 20	**'al**	על
abroad 25	**chutz la`aretz**	חוץ לארץ
abundance 60	**shefa'** *(f.)*	שפע
according to 53	**lefi**	לפי
actually 75	**be'etzem**	בעצם
adapted 85	**me'ubad** *(m.)*, **me'ubedet** *(f.)*	מעובד, מעובדת
add (to ~) 53	**hosif [lehosif]**	הוסיף [להוסיף]
addicted 75	**makhur** *(m.)*, **mekhurah** *(f.)*	מכור, מכורה
additional 81	**nosaf** *(m.)*, **nosefet** *(f.)*	נוסף, נוספת
address 22	**ktovet** *(f.)*	כתובת
adult 65	**mevugar** *(m.)*, **mevugeret** *(f.)*	מבוגר, מבוגרת
advantage 81	**yitaron** *(m.)*	יתרון
adventure 85	**harpatqah** *(f.)*	הרפתקה
advertisement 60	**moda'ah** *(f.)*	מודעה
advice 78	**'etzah** *(f.)*	עצה
after 26	**`acharey**	אחרי
after that 69	**`achar kakh**	אחר כך
afternoon 62	**`acharey hatzohorayim**	אחרי הצהרים
again 31	**shuv**	שוב
age 30	**gil** *(m.)*	גיל
agency 53	**sokhnut** *(f.)*	סוכנות
agenda 75	**seder yom** *(m.)*	סדר יום
ago 29	**lifney**	לפני
air 68	**`avir** *(m.)*	אויר
air-conditioner 68	**mazgan** *(m.)*	מזגן
air-conditioning 68	**mizug `avir** *(m.)*	מיזוג אוויר
airport 23	**sdeh te'ufah** *(m.)*	שדה תעופה
all 27	**kol**	כל
all right 17	**beseder**	בסדר
alone 66	**levad**	לבד
already 27	**kvar**	כבר
also 13	**gam**	גם
although 65	**lamrot she-**	למרות ש-
always 36	**tamid**	תמיד
amateur 25	**chovev** *(m.)*, **chovevet** *(f.)*	חובב, חובבת
among 44	**beyn**	בין
among (+ pronoun) 36	**`etz- (+ li/lekh** etc.)	אצל-
ancient 72	**qadum** *(m.)*, **qdumah** *(f.)*	קדום, קדומה
and 8, 36	**u-; ve-**	ו-; ו-
angel 46	**mal`akh** *(m.)*	מלאך
anger 80	**ka'as** *(m.)*	כעס

angry (to be ~) 69	**ka'as [likh'os]**	כעס [לכעוס]
animal 69	**chayah** *(f.)*	חיה
announce (to ~) 53	**hodi'a [lehodi'a]**	הודיע [להודיע]
announcement 60	**moda'ah** *(f.)*	מודעה
another 47	**`acher** *(m.)*, **`acheret** *(f.)*	אחר, אחרת
answer (to ~) 45	**'anah [la'anot]**	ענה [לענות]
antique 38	**'atiq** *(m.)*, **'atiqah** *(f.)*	עתיק, עתיקה
apartment 37	**dirah** *(f.)*	דירה
appear (to ~) 81	**hofi'a [lehofi'a]**	הופיע [להופיע]
appetite 55	**te`avon** *(m.)*	תאבון
apple 11	**tapuach** *(m.)*	תפוח
Arab *(adj.)* 82	**'aravi** *(m.)*, **'aravit** *(f.)*	ערבי, ערבית
arise (to ~) 82	**qam [laqum]**	קם [לקום]
armchair 38	**kursah** *(f.)*	כורסה
army 26	**tzava** *(m.)*	צבא
around 66	**saviv**	סביב
arrangement (organization) 53	**sidur** *(m.)*	סידור
arrest (to ~) 66	**`asar [le`esor]**	אסר [לאסור]
arrive (to ~) 38	**higi'a [lehagi'a]**	הגיע [להגיע]
arrow word puzzle 62	**tashchetz** *(m.)*	תשחץ
as well as 27	**gam … vegam …**	גם … וגם…
ascend (to ~) 67	**'alah [la'alot]**	עלה [לעלות]
ascent 1	**'aliyah** *(f.)*	עליה
ash 64	**`efer** *(m.)*	אפר
ask (to ~) 43	**sha`al [lish`ol]**	שאל [לשאול]
at (+ pronoun) 36	**`etz- (+ li/lekh** etc.)	אצל-
Athens 44	**`Atunah** *(f.)*	אתונה
avocado 51	**`avoqado** *(m.)*	אבוקדו

B

baby 61	**tinoq** *(m.)*, **tinoqet** *(f.)*	תינוק, תינוקת
back (the part of the body) 78	**gav** *(m.)*	גב
backpacker 26	**tarmilay** *(m.)*, **tarmila`it** *(f.)*	תרמילאי, תרמילאית
bake (to ~) 79	**`afah [le`efot]**	אפה [לאפות]
baking 79	**`afiyah** *(f.)*	אפיה
balcony 39	**mirpeset** *(f.)*	מרפסת
ball 19	**kadur** *(m.)*	כדור
bankrupt (to go ~) 83	**pashat [lifshot] `et haregel**	פשט [לפשוט] את הרגל
bankruptcy 83	**pshitat regel** *(f.)*	פשיטת רגל
Bar Mitzvah / Bat Mitzvah 16	**bar mitzvah** *(m.)*, **bat mitzvah** *(f.)*	בר מצווה, בת מצווה
barbecue 20	**'al ha`esh**	על האש
basic 79	**besisi** *(m.)*, **besisit** *(f.)*	בסיסי, בסיסית
basket 19	**sal** *(m.)*	סל
basketball 19	**kadursal** *(m.)*	כדורסל
bath 83	**`ambatyah** *(f.)*	אמבטיה
be (to ~) 35	**hayah [liheyot]**	היה [להיות]
beach 15	**chof** *(m.)*	חוף
beat (eggs) (to ~) 79	**hiqtzif [lehaqtzif]**	הקציף [להקציף]
beautiful 16	**yafeh** *(m.)*, **yafah** *(f.)*	יפה, יפה
beauty 61	**noy** *(m.)*, **yofi** *(m.)*	נוי, יופי

because 16, 27	**ki; mipney she**	כי-; מפני ש-
because of (due to) 27	**biglal**	בגלל
bed 17	**mitah** *(f.)*	מטה
bedroom 83	**chadar sheynah** *(f.)*	חדר שינה
bee 80	**dvorah** *(f.)*	דבורה
beer 4	**birah** *(f.)*	בירה
before 26	**lifney**	לפני
beginner 85	**matchil** *(m.)*, **matchilah** *(f.)*	מתחיל, מתחילה
beginning 85	**hatchalah** *(f.)*	התחלה
best 32	**hatov** *(m.)*, **hatovah** *(f.)* **beyoter**	הטוב, הטובה ביותר
between 44	**beyn**	בין
Bible 57	**Tanakh** *(m.)*	תנ"ך
Biblical 57	**tanakhi** *(m.)*, **tanakhit** *(f.)*	תנכי, תנכית
bicycle 31	**`ofanayim** *(m.)*	אופניים
big 16	**gadol** *(m.)*, **gdolah** *(f.)*	גדול, גדולה
bilingual 62	**du-leshoni** *(m.)*	דו-לשוני
birth 32, 41	**huledet** *(f.)*; **molad** *(m.)*	הולדת; מולד
birthday 32	**yom huledet** *(m.)*	יום הולדת
black 64	**shachor** *(m.)*, **shchorah** *(f.)*	שחור, שחורה
blind 80	**'iver** *(m.)*, **'iveret** *(f.)*	עיוור, עיוורת
blue 64	**kachol** *(m.)*, **kchulah** *(f.)*	כחול, כחולה
board 76	**qeresh** *(m.)*	קרש
boat 34	**`oniyah** *(f.)*	אוניה
body 43	**guf** *(m.)*	גוף
Bon appétit! 55	**Bete`avon!**	בתיאבון!
bone 70	**'etzem** *(m.)*	עצם
book 37	**sefer** *(m.)*	ספר
boot 64	**magaf** *(m.)*	מגף
bored (to be ~) 82	**hishta'amem [lehishta'amem]**	השתעמם [להשתעמם]
born (to be ~) 30	**nolad [lehivaled]**	נולד [להולד]
both 27	**gam … vegam …**	גם ... וגם ...
bottom 73	**tachtit** *(f.)*	תחתית
bottom (at the ~) 73	**lematah**	למטה
bowl 76	**qe'arah** *(f.)*	קערה
box 71	**tevah** *(f.)*	תיבה
bread 55	**lechem** *(m.)*	לחם
break (to ~) 31	**shavar [lishbor]**	שבר [לשבור]
break up (to ~) 40	**nifrad [lehipared]**	נפרד [להפרד]
breath 83	**neshimah** *(f.)*	נשימה
bring (to ~) 74	**hevi` [lehavi`]**	הביא [להביא]
broken 68	**mequlqal** *(m.)*, **mequlqelet** *(f.)*	מקולקל, מקולקלת
brother 19	**`ach**	אח
build (to ~) 58	**banah [livnot]**	בנה [לבנות]
building 72	**mivneh** *(m.)*	מבנה
bus 33	**`otobus** *(m.)*	אוטובוס
business 59	**'eseq** *(m.)*, **'asaqim** *(pl.)*	עסק, עסקים
but 10, 67, 80	**`aval; `akh; `ela**	אבל; אך; אלא
butter 79	**chem`ah** *(f.)*	חמאה
buttocks 78	**yashvan** *(m.)*	ישבן
buy (to ~) 12	**qanah [liqnot]**	קנה [לקנות]
by 10, 68	**be-; al yad**	ב-; על יד

by (+ pronoun) 36	**`etz- (+ li/lekh** etc.)	אצל-
Bye! 22	**Lehit!**	להת!

C

cabin 83	**biqtah** *(f.)*	בקתה
café 10	**qafeh** *(m.)*	קפה
cafeteria 11	**qafeteriah** *(f.)*	קפטריה
cake 10	**'ugah** *(f.)*	עוגה
calm 73	**shaqet** *(m.)*, **shqetah** *(f.)*	שקט, שקטה
calm *(noun)* 83	**shalvah** *(f.)*	שלווה
camera 25	**matzlemah** *(f.)*	מצלמה
campaign 82	**ma'arekhet** *(f.)*	מערכת
can (able to) 22	**yakhol** *(m.)*, **yekholah** *(f.)*	יכול, יכולה
cancel (to ~) 52	**bitel [levatel]**	ביטל [לבטל]
car 13	**mekhonit** *(f.)*	מכונית
caramel 51	**qaramel** *(m.)*	קרמל
card (playing ~) 66	**qlaf** *(m.)*	קלף
caress (to ~) 47	**litef [lelatef]**	ליטף [ללטף]
carrot 76	**gezer** *(m.)*	גזר
cash 32	**mezuman** *(m.)*	מזומן
cash register/till 31	**qupah** *(f.)*	קופה
catch (to ~) 83	**tafas [litpos]**	תפס [לתפוס]
cave 72	**me'arah** *(f.)*	מערה
celebrate (to ~) 38	**chagag [lachgog]**	חגג [לחגוג]
centre 51	**merkaz** *(m.)*	מרכז
certain 83	**mesuyam** *(m.)*, **mesuyemet** *(f.)*	מסוים, מסוימת
certificate 72	**te'udah** *(f.)*	תעודה
chair 17	**kise`** *(m.)*	כיסא
champion 71	**`aluf** *(m.)*, **`alufah** *(f.)*	אלוף, אלופה
chat (to ~) 20	**pitpet [lefatpet]**	פטפט [לפטפט]
cheap 38	**zol** *(m.)*, **zolah** *(f.)*	זול, זולה
cheese 10	**gvinah** *(f.)*	גבינה
cheque 32	**hamcha`ah** *(f.)*	המחאה
chess 62	**shachmat** *(m.)*	שחמט
chickpea(s) 55	**chumus** *(m.)*	חומוס
child 25	**yeled** *(m.)*, **yaldah** *(f.)*	ילד, ילדה
chimney 67	**`arubah** *(f.)*	ארובה
chit-chat13	**pitput** *(m.)*	פטפוט
chocolate 10	**shoqolad** *(m.)*	שוקולד
choice 82	**bchirah** *(f.)*, **mivchar** *(m.)*	בחירה, מבחר
choose (to ~) 82	**bachar [livchor]**	בחר [לבחור]
chopped 55	**qatzutz** *(m.)*, **qtzutzah** *(f.)*	קצוץ, קצוצה
cinema 31	**qolno'a** *(m.)*	קולנוע
circle 78	**ma'agal** *(m.)*	מעגל
circumcision 30	**brit milah** *(f.)*, **milah** *(f.)*	ברית מילה, מילה
circus 65	**qirqas** *(m.)*	קרקס
citizen 82	**`ezrach** *(m.)*, **`ezrachit** *(f.)*	אזרח, אזרחית
citizenship 82	**`ezrachut** *(f.)*	אזרחות
city 58	**'ir** *(f.)*	עיר
city centre 58	**merkaz ha'ir** *(m.)*	מרכז העיר
classical (typical) 82	**qlasi** *(m.)*, **qlasit** *(f.)*	קלסי, קלסית
clean 67	**naqi** *(m.)*, **neqiyah** *(f.)*	נקי, נקייה

clean (to ~) 67	**niqah [lenaqot]**	ניקה [לנקות]
climb (to ~) 67	**'alah [la'alot]**	עלה [לעלות]
close (attached to) 75	**qashur** *(m.)*, **qshurah** *(f.)*	קשור, קשורה
clothes 64	**bgadim** *(m. pl.)*	בגדים
clothing (item of) 64	**beged** *(m.)*	בגד
clove (of garlic) 55	**shen** *(f.)*	שן
clown 65	**leytzan** *(m.)*, **leytzanit** *(f.)*	ליצן, ליצנית
club 60	**mo'adon** *(m.)*	מועדון
coach 71	**me`amen** *(m.)*, **me`amenet** *(f.)*	מאמן, מאמנת
coat 41	**me'il** *(m.)*	מעיל
coffee 10	**qafeh** *(m.)*	קפה
cold 41	**qar** *(m.)*, **qarah** *(f.)*	קר, קרה
cold *(noun)* 43	**qor** *(m.)*	קור
colour 64	**tzeva'** *(m.)*	צבע
colourful 65	**tziv'oni** *(m.)*, **tziv'onit** *(f.)*	צבעוני, צבעונית
column (newspaper) 52	**mador** *(m.)*	מדור
come (to ~) 15	**ba [lavo]**	בא [לבוא]
come back (to ~) 47	**chazar [lachazor]**	חזר [לחזור]
come out (to ~) 67	**yatza [latzet]**	יצא [לצאת]
comedy 31	**qomedyah** *(f.)*	קומדיה
comfortable 83	**noach** *(m.)*, **nochah** *(f.)*	נוח, נוחה
commandment 16	**mitzvah** *(f.)*	מצווה
commitment 85	**hitchayvut** *(f.)*	היתחיבות
complete 60	**male** *(m.)*, **mele`ah** *(f.)*	מלא, מלאה
computer 9	**machshev** *(m.)*	מחשב
concentrate (to ~) 78	**hitrakez [lehitrakez]**	התרכז [להתרכז]
concept 81	**musag** *(m.)*	מושג
conference 44	**kenes** *(m.)*	כנס
confidence 73	**bitachon** *(m.)*	ביטחון
congratulate (to ~) 57	**berekh [levarekh]**	ברך [לברך]
Congratulations! 16, 30	**Mazal tov!**	מזל טוב!
connected (tied to) 75	**mechubar** *(m.)*, **mechuberet** *(f.)*	מחובר, מחוברת
conscience 82	**matzpun** *(m.)*	מצפון
consideration 73	**ha'arakhah** *(f.)*	הערכה
contact 85	**qesher** *(m.)*, **qsharim** *(pl.)*	קשר, קשרים
contemporary 71	**'akhshavi** *(m.)*, **'akhshavit** *(f.)*	עכשווי, עכשווית
contract (to ~) 43	**hitkavetz [lehitkavetz]**	התכווץ [להתכווץ]
cool (laid back) 29	**chevreman** *(m.)*, **chevremanit** *(f.)*	חברמן, חברמנית
cool (temperature) 41	**qar** *(m.)*, **qarah** *(f.)*	קר, קרה
cool down (to ~) 79	**hitqarer [lehitqarer]**	התקרר [להתקרר]
copy 81	**'oteq** *(m.)*	עותק
corner 83	**pinah** *(f.)*	פינה
correct 40	**nakhon** *(m.)*, **nekhonah** *(f.)*	נכון, נכונה
correspond with (to ~) 22	**katav [likhtov]**	כתב [לכתוב]
count (to ~) 47, 82	**safar [lispor]; manah [limnot]**	ספר [לספור]; מנה [למנות]
country 53	**`eretz** *(f.)*	ארץ
couple 60	**zug** *(m.)*	זוג
courage 54	**`ometz** *(m.)*	אומץ
covenant 30	**brit** *(f.)*	ברית
crazy 75	**metoraf** *(m.)*, **metorefet** *(f.)*	מטורף, מטורפת
crazy (to go ~) 41	**hishtage'a [lehishtage'a]**	השתגע [להשתגע]

cream 51	**qrem** *(m.)*	קרם
create (to ~) 71	**yitzer [leyatzer]**	יצר [ליצר]
cross (to ~) 5	**'avar [la'avor]**	עבר [לעבור]
crossword 62	**tashbetz** *(m.)*	תשבץ
crushed 55	**ma'ukh** *(m.)*, **me'ukhah** *(f.)*	מעוך, מעוכה
cube 76	**qubiyah** *(f.)*	קוביה
cucumber 76	**melafefon** *(m.)*	מלפפון
cup 55	**kos** *(f.)*	כוס
cup (trophy) 73	**gavi'a** *(m.)*	גביע
curious 83	**saqran** *(m.)*, **saqranit** *(f.)*	סקרן, סקרנית
cut off (to ~) 74	**niteq [lenateq]**	ניתק [לנתק]

D

dad 19	**`aba**	אבא
damage (to ~) 78	**heziq [lehaziq]**	הזיק [להזיק]
dare (to ~) 71	**he'ez [leha'ez]**	העז [להעז]
darkness 72	**choshekh** *(m.)*	חושך
darling 45	**chamud** *(m.)*, **chamudah** *(f.)*	חמוד, חמודה
data 81	**natun** *(m.)*, **netunim** *(pl.)*	נתון, נתונים
database 81	**ma`agar meyda'** *(m.)*	מאגר מידע
date (on the calendar) 83	**ta`arikh** *(m.)*	תאריך
daughter 9	**bat**	בת
dawn 64	**shachar** *(m.)*	שחר
day 24	**yom** *(m.)*	יום
deal (bargain) 83	**'isqah** *(f.)*	עסקה
dear (cherished) 74	**yaqar** *(m.)*, **yeqarah** *(f.)*	יקר, יקרה
decide (to ~) 82	**hechlit [lehachlit]**	החליט [להחליט]
dedication 38	**chanukah** *(f.)*	חנוכה
degree 79	**ma'alah** *(f.)*	מעלה
delight 61	**'eden** *(m.)*	עדן
demand (to ~) 73	**darash [lidrosh]**	דרש [לדרוש]
dentist 80	**rofe shinayim** *(m.)*, **rof`at shinayim** *(f.)*	רופא שיניים, רופאת שיניים
departure 34	**yetzi`ah** *(f.)*	יציאה
descend (to ~) 72	**yarad [laredet]**	ירד [לרדת]
desert 50	**midbar** *(m.)*	מדבר
desired 81	**mevuqash** *(m.)*, **mevuqeshet** *(f.)*	מבוקש, מבוקשת
destination 60	**ya'ad** *(m.)*	יעד
detail 60	**prat** *(m.)*	פרט
devil 80	**satan** *(m.)*	שטן
devour (to ~) 69	**taraf [litrof]**	טרף [לטרוף]
dew 61	**tal** *(m.)*	טל
dialogue 73	**du-siach** *(m.)*	דו-שיח
diamond 45	**yahalom** *(m.)*	יהלום
dictionary 71	**milon** *(m.)*	מילון
die (to ~) 46	**met [lamut]**	מת [למות]
diet 16	**dietah** *(f.)*	דיאטה
difficult 67	**qasheh** *(m.)*, **qashah** *(f.)*	קשה, קשה
dinner 24	**`aruchat 'erev** *(f.)*	ארוחת ערב
direct 53	**yashir** *(m.)*, **yeshirah** *(f.)*	ישיר, ישירה
dirty 67	**melukhlakh** *(m.)*, **melukhlekhet** *(f.)*	מלוכלך, מלוכלכת
disappear (to ~) 82	**ne'elam [lehe'alem]**	נעלם [להעלם]

dishwasher 83	**mediach-kelim** *(m.)*	מדיח-כלים
disk 81	**disq** *(m.)*	דיסק
disorder 27	**balagan** *(m.)*	בלגן
dispersed (to be ~) 58	**nafotz [lafutz]**	נפוץ [לפוץ]
distance 83	**merchaq** *(m.)*	מרחק
distinguished 80	**nikar** *(m.)*, **nikeret** *(f.)*	נכר, נכרת
divide (to ~) 69	**chileq [lechaleq]**	חלק [לחלק]
divorced 74	**garush** *(m.)*, **grushah** *(f.)*	גרוש, גרושה
dizziness 75	**scharchoret** *(f.)*	סחרחורת
dizzy (to make ~) 73	**sichrer [lesachrer]**	סחרר [לסחרר]
do (to ~) 37	**'asah [la'asot]**	עשה [לעשות]
do not 47	**`al**	אל
doctor 51	**rofe** *(m.)*, **rofah** *(f.)*	רופא, רופאה
document 72	**te'udah** *(f.)*	תעודה
donkey 69	**chamor** *(m.)*	חמור
door 46	**delet** *(f.)*	דלת
dot 22	**nequdah** *(f.)*	נקודה
draw (to ~) 78	**tziyer [letzayer]**	צייר [לצייר]
dress 16	**simlah** *(f.)*	שמלה
dress (to ~) 18	**lavash [lilbosh]**	לבש [ללבוש]
dressing (salad ~) 76	**rotev** *(m.)*	רוטב
drink (to ~) 4	**shatah [lishtot]**	שתה [לשתות]
drive (to ~) 46, 50	**nahag [linhog];**	נהג [לנהוג]
	nasa' [linso'a]	נסע [לנסוע]
driver 46	**nehag** *(m.)*, **naheget** *(f.)*	נהג, נהגת
duration 62	**meshekh** *(m.)*	משך
during 62	**meshekh** *(m.)*	משך
dynamic 73	**nimratz** *(m.)*, **nimretzet** *(f.)*	נמרץ, נמרצת

E

each 31	**kol**	כל
early 72	**muqdam**	מוקדם
east 50	**mizrach** *(m.)*	מזרח
East (the ~) 58	**qedem** *(m.)*	קדם
easy 76	**qal** *(m.)*, **qalah** *(f.)*	קל, קלה
eat (to ~) 20	**`akhal [le`ekhol]**	אכל [לאכול]
ecological 71	**`eqologi** *(m.)*, **`eqologit** *(f.)*	אקולוגי, אקולוגית
effective 73	**ya'il** *(m.)*, **ye'ilah** *(f.)*	יעיל, יעילה
efficiency 78	**ye'ilut** *(f.)*	יעילות
effort 57	**ma`amatz** *(m.)*	מאמץ
egg white 79	**chelbon** *(m.)*	חלבון
egg yolk 79	**chelmon** *(m.)*	חלמון
Egypt 50	**Mitzrayim** *(f.)*	מצרים
elected (to be ~) 82	**nivchar [lehibacher]**	נבחר [להבחר]
elections 82	**bchirot** *(f. pl.)*	בחירות
electronic 22	**`eleqtroni** *(m.)*, **`eleqtronit** *(f.)*	אלקטרוני, אלקטרונית
elevator / lift 41	**ma'alit** *(f.)*	מעלית
end 20	**sof** *(m.)*	סוף
engineering 40	**handasah** *(f.)*	הנדסה
enjoy (to ~) 76	**neheneh [lehanot]**	נהנה [להנות]
enough 39	**maspiq**	מספיק

enough (it is ~) 81	**day**	די
enter (to ~) 46	**nikhnas [lehikanes]**	נכנס [להכנס]
entire 72	**shalem** *(m.)*, **shlemah** *(f.)*	שלם, שלמה
entrance 72	**knisah** *(f.)*	כניסה
environment 82	**svivah** *(f.)*	סביבה
equal 69	**shaveh** *(m.)*, **shavah** *(f.)*	שווה, שווה
equipped 83	**me\`uvzar** *(m.)*, **me\`uvzeret** *(f.)*	מאובזר, מאובזרת
esteem 73	**ha'arakhah** *(f.)*	הערכה
even 41	**\`afilu**	אפילו
evening 10	**'erev** *(m.)*	ערב
every 31	**kol**	כל
everywhere 68	**bekhol maqom**	בכל מקום
exactly 52	**bediyuq**	בדיוק
example 43	**dugmah** *(f.)*	דוגמה
example (for ~) 78	**lemashal**	למשל
excavation 44	**chafirah** *(f.)*	חפירה
excellence 73	**metzuyanut** *(f.)*	מצויינות
excellent 25	**metzuyan** *(m.)*, **metzuyenet** *(f.)*	מצויין, מצויינת
excited (to be ~) 65	**hitlahev [lehitlahev]**	התלהב [להתלהב]
excuse [me] 23	**slichah** *(f.)*	סליחה
exercise 85	**targil** *(m.)*	תרגיל
expand (to ~) 43	**hitrachev [lehitrachev]**	התרחב [להתרחב]
expensive 38	**yaqar** *(m.)*, **yeqarah** *(f.)*	יקר, יקרה
experience 81	**chavayah** *(f.)*	חוויה
experience (to ~) 83	**hitnasah [lehitnasot]**	התנסה [להתנסות]
expert 81	**mumcheh** *(m.)*, **mumchit** *(f.)*	מומחה, מומחית
explain (to ~) 67	**hisbir [lehasbir]**	הסביר [להסביר]
eye 38	**'ayin** *(f.)*, **'eynayim** *(pl.)*	עין, עיניים

F

face 65	**pan** *(m.)*, **panim** *(pl.)*	פן, פנים
face of (the ~) 58	**pney** *(m. pl.)*	פני
facility 83	**mitqan** *(m.)*	מתקן
facing 68	**mul**	מול
fail (to ~) 54	**nikhshal [lehikashel]**	נכשל [להכשל]
fair (right) 69	**tzodeq** *(m.)*, **tzodeqet** *(f.)*	צודק, צודקת
falafel 27	**falafel** *(m.)*	פלאפל
fall (the act of falling) 73	**nefilah** *(f.)*	נפילה
fall (to ~) 29	**nafal [lifol]**	נפל [לפול]
family 19	**mishpachah** *(f.)*	משפחה
fascinating 85	**merateq** *(m.)*, **merateqet** *(f.)*	מרתק, מרתקת
fashion 61	**\`ofnah** *(f.)*	אופנה
fashionable 61	**\`ofnati** *(m.)*, **\`ofnatit** *(f.)*	אופנתי, אופנתית
father 63	**\`av**	אב
father-in-law 36	**cham**	חם
fatten (to ~) (gain weight) 52	**hishmin [lehashmin]**	השמין [להשמין]
faze (to ~) 73	**sichrer [lesachrer]**	סחרר [לסחרר]
fed up (to be ~) 78	**nim\`as (+ li/lekha/lakh** etc.)	נמאס לי ...
feel (to ~) 47	**hirgish [lehargish]**	הרגיש [להרגיש]
festival 27	**festival** *(m.)*	פסטיבל

field 23	**sadeh** *(m.)*	שדה
field (sports) 73	**migrash** *(m.)*	מגרש
figure 75	**figurah** *(f.)*	פיגורה
file (computer ~) 81	**qovetz** *(m.)*	קובץ
film 65	**seret** *(m.)*	סרט
filter 11	**filter** *(m.)*	פילטר
find (to ~) 38	**matza [limtzo]**	מצא [למצוא]
finger 82	**`etzba'** *(f.)*, **`etzba'ot** *(pl.)*	אצבע, אצבעות
fire 20	**`esh** *(f.)*	אש
fireplace 83	**`ach** *(m.)*	אח
fish 83	**dag** *(m.)*	דג
fitness 71	**kosher** *(m.)*	כושר
fix (to ~) 68	**tiqen [letaqen]**	תיקן [לתקן]
flame 65	**lehavah** *(f.)*	להבה
flatten (to ~) 79	**shatach [lishtoach]**	שטח [לשטוח]
flight 23	**te'ufah** *(f.)*	תעופה
flight (airplane) 23	**tisah** *(f.)*	טיסה
flour 79	**qemach** *(m.)*	קמח
fly (to ~) (by plane) 23	**tas [latus]**	טס [לטוס]
foam 79	**qetzef** *(m.)*	קצף
fold/roll up (to ~) 48	**qipel [leqapel]**	קיפל [לקפל]
food 48	**`okhel** *(m.)*	אוכל
foot 19	**regel** *(f.)*	רגל
football (soccer) 19	**kaduregel** *(m.)*	כדורגל
for 9, 16, 25	**le-; bishvil**	ל-; בשביל
for (in favour of) 73	**be'ad**	בעד
forbidden 66	**`asur** *(m.)*, **`asurah** *(f.)*	אסור, אסורה
forwards 51	**qadimah**	קדימה
fox 69	**shu'al** *(m.)*	שועל
free (not held down) 78	**chofshi** *(m.)*, **chofshit** *(f.)*	חופשי, חופשית
free (to ~) 66	**shichrer [leshachrer]**	שחרר [לשחרר]
free time 62	**pnay** *(m.)*	פנאי
French *(adj.)* 82	**tzarfati** *(m.)*, **tzarfatit** *(f.)*	צרפתי, צרפתית
fresh 76	**tari** *(m.)*, **triyah** *(f.)*	טרי, טריה
friend 20	**chaver** *(m.)*, **chaverah** *(f.)*	חבר, חברה
friendship 85	**yedidut** *(f.)*	ידידות
from 8	**me-**	מ-
front of (in ~) 68	**mul**	מול
fruit 79	**pri** *(m.)*, **perot** *(pl.)*	פרי, פירות
frustrate (to ~) 75	**tiskel [letaskel]**	תסכל [לתסכל]
full 60	**male** *(m.)*, **mele`ah** *(f.)*	מלא, מלאה
fun 20	**kef** *(m.)*	כיף
funny 65	**matzchiq** *(m.)*, **matzchiqah** *(f.)*	מצחיק, מצחיקה
fur 41	**parvah** *(f.)*	פרווה
furniture 38	**rahit** *(m.)*	רהיט
further 60	**nosaf** *(m.)*, **nosefet** *(f.)*	נוסף, נוספת
future 57	**'atid** *(m.)*	עתיד

G

Galilee 83	**Galil**	גליל
game 19	**mischaq** *(m.)*	משחק

garden 37 — **gan** *(m.)* — גן
garlic 55 — **shum** *(m.)* — שום
gas 50 — **deleq** *(m.)* — דלק
gate 85 — **sha'ar** *(m.)* — שער
generation 81 — **dor** *(m.)* — דור
gentleness 79 — **'adinut** *(f.)* — עדינות
geography 26 — **ge`ografyah** *(f.)* — גיאוגרפיה
get up (to ~) 82 — **qam [laqum]** — קם [לקום]
give (to ~) 43 — **natan [latet]** — נתן [לתת]
glass (drinking ~) 55 — **kos** *(f.)* — כוס
glass (material) 39 — **zekhukhit** *(f.)* — זכוכית
go (to ~) 18 — **halakh [lalekhet]** — הלך [ללכת]
go down (to ~) 72 — **yarad [laredet]** — ירד [לרדת]
go into (to ~) 46 — **nikhnas [lehikanes]** — נכנס [להכנס]
go out (to ~) 74 — **yatza [latzet]** — יצא [לצאת]
go up (to ~) 67 — **'alah [la'alot]** — עלה [לעלות]
God 59 — **`elohim** *(m.)* — אלהים
gold 11 — **zahav** *(m.)* — זהב
good 1 — **tov** *(m.)*, **tovah** *(f.)* — טוב, טובה
Goodbye! 6 — **Lehitra`ot!** — להתראות!
good-for-nothing 74 — **lo-yutzlach** — לא-יוצלח
grace 38 — **chen** *(m.)* — חן
grade (echelon) 83 — **dereg** *(m.)* — דרג
granddaughter 30 — **nekhdah** — נכדה
grandfather 30 — **saba** — סבא
grandmother 30 — **savta** — סבתא
grandson 30 — **nekhed** — נכד
great (in amount) 24 — **rabah** *(f.)* — רבה
Great! 38, 85 — **Yofi!; Sababah!** — יופי!; סבאבה!
Greek *(adj.)* 44 — **yevani** *(m.)*, **yevanit** *(f.)* — יווני, יוונית
green 64 — **yaroq** *(m.)*, **yeruqah** *(f.)* — ירוק, ירוקה
grey 64 — **`afor** *(m.)*, **`aforah** *(f.)* — אפור, אפורה
groom 18 — **chatan** *(m.)* — חתן
guest 75 — **`oreach** *(m.)*, **`orachat** *(f.)* — אורח, אורחת

H

half 53 — **chetzi** — חצי
hall 72 — **`ulam** *(m.)* — אולם
hand 19 — **yad** *(f.)* — יד
handball 19 — **kaduryad** *(m.)* — כדוריד
handful 79 — **chofen** *(m.)* — חופן
handicraft 83 — **melakhah** *(f.)* — מלאכה
hands-free set 13 — **diburit** *(f.)* — דיבורית
happen (to ~) 29 — **qarah [liqrot]** — קרה [לקרות]
happy 80 — **sameach** *(m.)*, **smechah** *(f.)* — שמח, שמחה
hard (rigid) 81 — **qashiach** *(m.)*, **qeshichah** *(f.)* — קשיח, קשיחה
have (to ~) (to possess) 28 — **yesh (+ li/lekha/lakh** etc.) — יש ...
have a good time (to ~) 39 — **bilah [levalot]** — בילה [לבלות]
he 8 — **hu** — הוא
head 24 — **rosh** *(m.)* — ראש
health 76 — **bri`ut** *(f.)* — בריאות
healthy 76 — **bari** *(m.)*, **bri`ah** *(f.)* — בריא, בריאה

hear (to ~) 6	**shama' [lishmo'a]**	שמע [לשמוע]
heart 31	**lev** *(m.)*	לב
heat 43	**chom** *(m.)*	חום
heavens 58	**shamayim** *(m. pl.)*	שמיים
heavy 57	**kaved** *(m.)*, **kvedah** *(f.)*	כבד, כבדה
Hebrew 5	**'ivrit** *(f.)*	עברית
heel 73	**'aqev** *(m.)*	עקב
height 73	**govah** *(m.)*	גובה
hello 2	**shalom** *(m.)*	שלום
help (to ~) 22	**'azar [la'azor]**	עזר [לעזור]
here 17, 67	**poh; hineh**	פה; הנה
hero 71	**gibor** *(m.)*, **giborah** *(f.)*	גיבור, גיבורה
herself 67	**'atzmah** *(f.)*	עצמה
hide (to ~) (stash) 72	**ganaz [lignoz]**	גנז [לגנוז]
himself 67	**'atzmo** *(m.)*	עצמו
historical 34	**histori** *(m.)*, **historit** *(f.)*	הסטורי, הסטורית
holiday (festival) 36	**chag** *(m.)*	חג
holiday (vacation) 39, 83	**nofesh** *(m.)*; **chufshah** *(f.)*	נופש; חופשה
home 19	**bayit** *(m.)*	בית
home (towards ~) 40	**habaytah**	הביתה
honey 80	**dvash** *(m.)*	דבש
honour 57	**kavod** *(m.)*	כבוד
honour of (in ~) 34	**likhvod**	לכבוד
hospital 51	**beyt cholim** *(m.)*	בית חולים
hospitality 83	**`eruach** *(m.)*	ארוח
hot 27	**cham** *(m.)*, **chamah** *(f.)*	חם, חמה
hot guy/woman 15	**chatikh** *(m.)*, **chatikhah** *(f.)*	חתיך, חתיכה
hotel 51	**malon** *(m.)*	מלון
hour 33	**sha'ah** *(f.)*	שעה
house 10, 19	**bayit** *(m.)*; **beyt** *(m.)*	בית; בית
housewarming 38	**chanukat bayit** *(f.)*	חנוכת בית
how many 23	**kamah**	כמה
How? 36	**`Eykh?**	איך?
humidity 75	**lachut** *(f.)*	לחות
hummus 27	**chumus** *(m.)*	חומוס
hungry 67	**ra'ev** *(m.)*, **re'evah** *(f.)*	רעב, רעבה
hunt (to ~) 69	**tzad [latzud]**	צד [לצוד]
hunt (noun) 69	**tzayid** *(m.)*	צייד
hurt (to ~) 78	**heziq [lehaziq]**	הזיק [להזיק]
husband 18	**ba'al**	בעל

I

I 5	**`ani** *(m./f.)*	אני
ice cream 67	**glidah** *(f.)*	גלידה
identity 82	**zehut** *(f.)*	זהות
if 41	**`im**	אם
ill 51	**choleh** *(m.)*, **cholah** *(f.)*	חולה, חולה
immigrant (new ~) 82	**oleh chadash** *(m.)*, **'olah chadashah** *(f.)*	עולה חדש, עולה חדשה
important 68	**chashuv** *(m.)*, **chashuvah** *(f.)*	חשוב, חשובה
impossible 24	**`i-`efshar**	אי-אפשר

in 11, 77 **be-** ב-
in (+ period of time) 27 **be'od** בעוד
inauguration 38 **chanukat bayit** *(f.)* חנוכת בית
include (to ~) 83 **kalal [likhlol]** כלל [ליכלול]
infinite 81 **`eyn-sof** אין-סוף
information 81 **meyda'** *(m.)* מידע
innovation 57 **chidush** *(m.)* חידוש
inside 79 **bifnim** בפנים
inside (interior) 78 **pnim** *(m.)* פנים
intelligent 67 **chakham** *(m.)*, **chakhamah** *(f.)* חכם, חכמה
interested (to be ~) 71 **hit'anyen [lehit'anyen]** התעניין [להתעניין]
interesting 44 **me'anyen** *(m.)*, **me'anyenet** *(f.)* מעניין, מעניינת
international 44 **beynle`umi** *(m.)*, **beynle`umit** *(f.)* בינלאומי, בינלאומית
internet 9 **`internet** *(m.)* אינטרנט
interview 75 **re`ayon** *(m.)*, **re`ayonot** *(pl.)* ראיון, ראיונות
invitation 24 **hazmanah** *(f.)* הזמנה
invite (to ~) 32 **hizmin [lehazmin]** הזמין [להזמין]
Israeli *(adj.)* 44 **yisra`eli** *(m.)*, **yisra`elit** *(f.)* ישראלי, ישראלית
it *(f.)* 8 **hi** היא
it *(m.)* 8 **hu** הוא

J

Jerusalem 23 **Yerushalayim** ירושלים
jewel 54 **'adi** *(m.)* עדי
joke 44 **bdichah** *(f.)* בדיחה
Jordan 50 **Yarden** *(m.)* ירדן
joy 54, 61 **ron** *(m.)*; **gil** *(m.)* רון; גיל
jubilee 34 **yovel** *(m.)* יובל
juice 11 **mitz** *(m.)* מיץ
jump (to ~) 85 **qafatz [liqfotz]** קפץ [לקפוץ]
just 68 **davqa** דווקא
just (equitable) 69 **tzodeq** *(m.)*, **tzodeqet** *(f.)* צודק, צודקת
justice 69 **tzedeq** *(m.)* צדק

K

keyboard 81 **miqledet** *(f.)* מקלדת
kibbutz 34 **qibutz** *(m.)* קבוץ
kindergarten 37 **gan-yeladim** *(m.)* גן-ילדים
kitchen 39 **mitbach** *(m.)* מטבח
Knesset (Israel's parliament) 48 **kneset** *(f.)* כנסת
knife 76 **sakin** *(f.)*, **sakinim** *(pl.)* סכין, סכינים
know (to ~) (a fact) 41 **yada' [lada'at]** ידע [לדעת]
know (to ~) (be acquainted with) 37 **hikir [lehakir]** היכיר [להכיר]
known (well ~) 74 **yadu'a** *(m.)* ידוע

L

lady 52 **gveret** גברת
land 25 **`aretz** *(f.)* ארץ
landscape 68 **nof** *(m.)* נוף

language 58	**lashon** *(m.)*, **leshonot** *(pl.)*, **safah** *(f.)*	לשון, לשונות, שפה
laptop 9	**machshev nayad** *(m.)*, **machshev nisa** *(m.)*	מחשב נייד, מחשב נישא
last 45	**`acharon** *(m.)*, **`acharonah** *(f.)*	אחרון, אחרונה
last (at ~) 20	**sof sof**	סוף סוף
latest (newest) 38	**chadish** *(m.)*, **chadishah** *(f.)*	חדיש, חדישה
Latin (language) 5	**latinit** *(f.)*	לטינית
laugh (to ~) 51	**tzachaq [litzchoq]**	צחק [לצחוק]
law 40	**mishpat** *(m.)*	משפט
lawn 83	**midsha`ah** *(f.)*	מדשאה
layabout 74	**batlan** *(m.)*, **batlanit** *(f.)*	בטלן, בטלנית
league 73	**ligah** *(f.)*	ליגה
learn (to ~) 5	**lamad [lilmod]**	למד [ללמוד]
learning (study) 57	**limud** *(m.)*	לימוד
least (at ~) 85	**lefachot**	לפחות
leave (to ~) 79	**hish`ir [lehash`ir]**	השאיר [להשאיר]
left (to the ~) 51	**smolah**	שמאלה
left *(adj.)* 51	**smali** *(m.)*, **smalit** *(f.)*	שמאלי, שמאלית
left *(adv.)* 56	**smol**	שמאל
leg 83	**regel** *(f.)*	רגל
leisure 62	**pnay** *(m.)*	פנאי
lemon 55	**limon** *(m.)*	לימון
less … than 77	**pachot ... m-**	פחות ... מ-
lesson 43	**shi'ur** *(m.)*	שיעור
letter (message) 27	**mikhtav** *(m.)*	מכתב
letter (of alphabet) 57	**`ot** *(f.)*	אות
lettuce 76	**chasah** *(f.)*	חסה
level 73, 83	**govah** *(m.)*; **ramah** *(f.)*	גובה; רמה
lid 72	**mikhseh** *(m.)*	מכסה
ife 69	**chayim** *(m. pl.)*	חיים
ight 1	**`or** *(m.)*	אור
ight (in weight) 76	**qal** *(m.)*, **qalah** *(f.)*	קל, קלה
ike 18	**kmo**	כמו
ike (to ~) 52	**`ahav [le`ehov]**	אהב [לאהוב]
ike (to ~) (find pleasing) 38	**matza [limtzo] chen**	מצא [למצוא] חן
ike that 3	**kakhah**	ככה
inguist 62	**balshan** *(m.)*, **balshanit** *(f.)*	בלשן, בלשנית
nk 81	**qishur** *(m.)*	קשור
ion 69	**`ari** *(m.)*	ארי
p 58	**safah** *(f.)*	שפה
iqueur 79	**liqer** *(m.)*	ליקר
isten (to ~) 6	**shama' [lishmo'a]**	שמע [לשמוע]
ittle 19	**qatan** *(m.)*, **qtanah** *(f.)*	קטן, קטנה
ittle (a ~) 53	**qtzat**	קצת
ve (to ~) (reside) 51	**gar [lagur]**	גר [לגור]
iving 83	**megurim** *(m. pl.)*	מגורים
onely 75	**boded** *(m.)*, **bodedah** *(f.)*	בודד, בודדה
ong 43	**`arokh** *(m.)*, **`arukah** *(f.)*	ארוך, ארוכה
ook (to ~) 80	**histakel [lehistakel]**	הסתכל [להסתכל]
ook for (to ~) 50	**chipes [lechapes]**	חיפש [לחפש]
ookout 83	**mitzpor** *(m.)*	מצפור

lose (to ~) 73	**`ibed [le`abed]**	אבד [לאבד]
lot (a ~) 27	**harbeh**	הרבה
love 27	**`ahavah** *(f.)*	אהבה
love (to ~) 31	**`ahav [le`ehov]**	אהב [לאהוב]
luck 16	**mazal** *(m.)*	מזל

M

madam 51	**gvirti**	גבירתי
main (thing) (the ~) 68	**'iqar** *(m.)*, **'iqarit** *(f.)*	עיקר, עיקרית
mainly 65	**be'iqar**	בעיקר
maintain (to ~) 85	**nishmar [lehishamer]**	נשמר [להישמר]
man 50, 67	**gever; `ish**	גבר; איש
manage (to ~) (direct) 73	**nihel [lenahel]**	ניהל [לנהל]
manager 53	**menahel** *(m.)*, **menahelet** *(f.)*	מנהל, מנהלת
many / much 50	**harbeh**	הרבה
marriage (ceremony) 18	**chatunah** *(f.)*	חתונה
marriage (institution) 34	**nisu`im** *(m. pl.)*	נישואים
married (to get ~) 34	**hitchaten [lehitchaten]**	התחתן [להתחתן]
mast 80	**toren** *(m.)*	תורן
master / mistress (owner) 18	**ba'al** *(m.)*, **ba'alat** *(f.)*	בעל / בעלת
maybe 22	**`ulay**	אולי
meal 24	**`aruchah** *(f.)*	ארוחה
meantime (in the ~) 79	**beyntayim**	בינתיים
medicine 40, 71	**refu`ah** *(f.)*; **trufah** *(f.)*	רפואה; תרופה
Mediterranean 40, 71	**Tikhon** *(m.)*	תיכון
meet (to ~) 44	**nifgash [lehipagesh]**	נפגש [להפגש]
meet (to ~) (become acquainted) 34	**hikir [lehakir]**	היכיר [להכיר]
meeting 67	**yeshivah** *(f.)*	ישיבה
member (of an organization) 48	**chaver** *(m.)*, **chaverah** *(f.)*	חבר, חברה
menu 68	**tafrit** *(m.)*	תפריט
mess 17	**balagan** *(m.)*	בלגן
messy guy/woman 17	**balaganist** *(m.)*, **balaganistit** *(f.)*	בלגניסט, בלגניסטית
method 82	**shitah** *(f.)*	שיטה
microwave 83	**miqrogal** *(m.)*	מיקרוגל
milk 79	**chalav** *(m.)*	חלב
minimarket 83	**kolbo** *(m.)*	כלבו
minister (government) 48	**sar** *(m.)*, **sarah** *(f.)*	שר, שרה
minute 79	**daqah** *(f.)*	דקה
miracle 11	**nes** *(m.)*	נס
missing (lacking) 85	**chaser** *(m.)*, **chaserah** *(f.)*	חסר, חסרה
mistake 85	**shgi`ah** *(f.)*	שגיאה
mistaken (to be ~) 50	**ta'ah [lit'ot]**	טעה [לטעות]
mix (to ~) 55	**'irbev [le'arbev]**	ערבב [לערבב]
mix up (to ~) (jumble) 59	**balal [livlol]**	בלל [לבלול]
mixture 68, 79	**mizug** *(m.)*; **ta'arovet** *(f.)*	מיזוג; תערובת
mobile *(adj.)* 13	**nayad** *(m.)*, **nayedet** *(f.)*	נייד, ניידת
mobile/cell phone 45	**pelefon** *(m.)*	פלאפון
model (fashion ~) 75	**dugman** *(m.)*, **dugmanit** *(f.)*	דוגמן, דוגמנית
moment 73	**rega'** *(m.)*	רגע

money 32	**kesef** *(m.)*	כסף
month 29	**chodesh** *(m.)*	חודש
monthly journal 52	**yarchon** *(m.)*	ירחון
more 27	**'od**	עוד
more … than 77	**yoter ... m-**	יותר ... מ-
morning 1	**boqer** *(m.)*	בוקר
most 32, 75	**beyoter; hakhi**	ביותר; הכי
mother 62	**`em**	אם
mother-in-law 36	**chamot**	חמות
mountain 83	**har** *(m.)*	הר
mouse 81	**'akhbar** *(m.)*	עכבר
mouth 73	**peh** *(m.)*	פה
move (to ~) 68	**zaz [lazuz]**	זז [לזוז]
move (house) (to ~) 37	**'avar [la'avor]**	עבר [לעבור]
movie 65	**seret** *(m.)*	סרט
movie theatre 31	**qolno'a** *(m.)*	קולנוע
mud 11	**botz** *(m.)*	בוץ
mum / mom 19	**`ima**	אמא
muse 71	**muzah** *(f.)*	מוזה
museum 71	**muze`on** *(m.)*	מוזיאון
music 71	**musiqah** *(f.)*	מוסיקה
mythological 71	**mitologi** *(m.)*, **mitologit** *(f.)*	מיתולוגי, מיתולוגית
mythology 71	**mitologyah** *(f.)*	מיתולוגיה

N

name 51	**shem** *(m.)*	שם
narrow 80	**tzar** *(m.)*, **tzarah** *(f.)*	צר, צרה
nation 44	**le`om** *(m.)*	לאום
national 44	**le`umi** *(m.)*, **le`umit** *(f.)*	לאומי, לאומית
nature 83	**teva'** *(m.)*	טבע
nature reserve 83	**shmurat teva'** *(f.)*	שמורת טבע
need (to ~) 25	**tzarikh** *(m.)*, **tzrikhah** *(f.)*	צריך, צריכה
neighbour 37	**shakhen** *(m.)*, **shkhenah** *(f.)*	שכן, שכנה
neighbourhood	**shekhunah** *(f.)*	שכונה
neighbourhood *(adj.)* 73	**shkhunati** *(m.)*, **shkhunatit** *(f.)*	שכונתי, שכונתית
never 70	**`af pa'am**	אף פעם
new 6	**chadash** *(m.)*, **chadashah** *(f.)*	חדש, חדשה
news 33	**chadashot** *(f. pl.)*	חדשות
newspaper 52	**'iton** *(m.)*	עיתון
next (coming) 40	**haba** *(m.)*, **haba`ah** *(f.)*	הבא, הבאה
next to 68	**'al yad**	על יד
night 27	**laylah** *(m.)*	לילה
no 8	**lo**	לא
no (negative particle) 75	**`af, shum**	אף, שום
no one 74	**`af `echad**	אף אחד
nonsense 47	**shtut** *(f.)*	שטות
noon 62	**tzohorayim** *(m. pl.)*	צהרים
nose 65	**`af** *(m.)*	אף
not 66	**bilti**	בלתי
not bad 3	**kakhah, kakhah**	ככה, ככה
nothing 73	**klum** *(m.)*	כלום
now 50	**'akhshav**	עכשיו

O

objective 60	**ya'ad** *(m.)*	יעד
obstacle 80	**mikhshol** *(m.)*	מכשול
of 8	**shel**	של
offer (to ~) 79	**hitzi'a [lehatzi'a]**	הציע [להציע]
office 53	**misrad** *(m.)*	משרד
official 48	**rishmi** *(m.)*, **rishmit** *(f.)*	רשמי, רשמית
often 79	**le'itim qrovot**	לעיתים קרובות
oil 52	**shemen** *(m.)*	שמן
okay 6	**beseder**	בסדר
old 38, 82	**'atiq** *(m.)*, **'atiqah** *(f.)*; **yashan** *(m.)*, **yeshanah** *(f.)*	עתיק, עתיקה; ישן, ישנה
olive 76	**zayit** *(m.)*	זית
Olympian 71	**\`olimpi** *(m.)*, **\`olimpit** *(f.)*	אולימפי, אולימפית
on 20	**'al**	על
once 58	**pa'am** *(f.)*	פעם
one (number) 23, 58	**\`achat** *(f.)*; **\`echad** *(m.)*	אחת; אחד
onion 76	**batzal** *(m.)*	בצל
only (merely) 8	**raq**	רק
only (sole) 47	**yachid** *(m.)*, **yechidah** *(f.)*	יחיד, יחידה
open (to ~) 71	**patach [liftoach]**	פתח [לפתוח]
opinion 71	**de'ah** *(f.)*	דיעה
opportunity 73	**hizdamnut** *(f.)*	הזדמנות
or 10	**\`o**	או
orange (colour) 65	**katom** *(m.)*, **ktumah** *(f.)*	כתום, כתומה
orange (fruit) 11	**tapuz** *(m.)*	תפוז
order 17	**seder** *(m.)*	סדר
order (in ~) 6	**beseder**	בסדר
order (to ~) (arrange) 17	**sider [lesader]**	סדר [לסדר]
order to (in ~) 53	**kedey**	כדי
organized 73	**me\`urgan** *(m.)*, **me\`urgenet** *(f.)*	מאורגן, מאורגנת
our 30	**shelanu** *(m./f.)*	שלנו
out of order 68	**mequlqal** *(m.)*, **mequlqelet** *(f.)*	מקולקל, מקולקלת
outside of 25	**chutz**	חוץ
oven 79	**tanur** *(m.)*	תנור
over (the course of) 73	**meshekh** *(m.)*	משך

P

package 40	**chavilah** *(f.)*	בילה
packet 79	**saqit** *(f.)*	שקית
pair 60	**zug** *(m.)*	ג
palace 72	**heykhal** *(m.)*	יכל
paradise (Garden of Eden) 46	**gan 'eden** *(m.)*	ן עדן
parent 75	**horeh** *(m.)*, **horim** *(pl.)*	ורה, הורים
parking 60	**chanayah** *(f.)*	ניה
parsley 55	**petrozilyah** *(f.)*	טרוזיליה
part 58	**cheleq** *(m.)*	לק
particular (in ~) 65	**be'iqar**	עיקר
parting (farewell) 85	**predah** *(f.)*	רדה
partner 85	**shutaf** *(m.)*, **shutafah** *(f.)*	ותף, שותפה

party 34	**mesibah** *(f.)*	מסיבה
party (political ~) 82	**miflagah** *(f.)*	מפלגה
passenger 46	**nose'a** *(m.)*, **nosa'at** *(f.)*	נוסע, נוסעת
passport 26	**darkon** *(m.)*	דרכון
pastry 79	**batzeq** *(m.)*	בצק
path 83	**shvil** *(m.)*	שביל
pavement 51	**midrakhah** *(f.)*	מדרכה
peace 2	**shalom** *(m.)*	שלום
pedestrian street 51	**midrachov** *(m.)*	מדרחוב
people 80	**briyot** *(m. pl.)*	בריות
people (nation) 59	**'am** *(m.)*	עם
pepper 55	**pilpel** *(m.)*	פלפל
perhaps 22	**`ulay**	אולי
period (of time) 44	**tqufah** *(f.)*	תקופה
permitted 66	**mutar** *(m.)*, **muteret** *(f.)*	מותר, מותרת
perseverance 78	**hatmadah** *(f.)*	התמדה
person 23	**ben `adam** *(m.)*	בן אדם
pest (irritating guy/woman) 29	**nudniq** *(m.)*, **nudniqit** *(f.)*	נודניק, נודניקית
petrol 50	**deleq** *(m.)*	דלק
photograph 23	**tmunah** *(f.)*	תמונה
photograph (to ~) 25	**tzilem [letzalem]**	צלם [לצלם]
photographer 25	**tzalam** *(m.)*, **tzalemet** *(f.)*	צלם, צלמת
photography 25	**tzilum** *(m.)*	צילום
physics 43	**fiziqah** *(f.)*	פיזיקה
piece 15	**chatikhah** *(f.)*	חתיכה
pine 80	**`oren** *(m.)*	אורן
pit (stone of fruit) 76	**gal'in** *(m.)*	גלעין
pita bread 55	**pitah** *(f.)*	פיתה
pity (what a ~) 6	**chaval**	חבל
place 66	**maqom** *(m.)*	מקום
plan (to ~) 79	**tikhnen [letakhnen]**	תכנן [לתכנן]
play (to ~) 19	**sicheq [lesacheq]**	שחק [לשחק]
player 73	**sachqan** *(m.)*, **sachqanit** *(f.)*	שחקן, שחקנית
pleasant 26	**na'im** *(m.)*, **ne'imah** *(f.)*	נעים, נעימה
please 10	**bevaqashah**	בבקשה
plenty 60	**shefa'** *(f.)*	שפע
pocket 80	**kis** *(m.)*	כיס
poem 61	**shir** *(m.)*	שיר
poetry 60	**shirah** *(f.)*	שירה
point 57	**nequdah** *(f.)*	נקודה
point (tip) 73	**shpitz** *(m.) (slang)*	שפיץ
Poland 8	**Polanyah** *(f.)*	פולניה
olice officer 66	**shoter** *(m.)*, **shoteret** *(f.)*	שוטר, שוטרת
Polish (the language) 8	**polanit** *(f.)*	פולנית
ool 20	**brekhah** *(f.)*	ברכה
oppy / poppyseed 10	**pereg** *(m.)*	פרג
ortable 9	**nisa** *(m.)*, **niset** *(f.)*	נשא, נשאת
ossible 24	**`efshar**	אפשר
ost (mail) 22	**do`ar** *(m.)*	דואר
ost office 29	**do`ar** *(m.)*	דואר
ot (jug) 72	**qanqan** *(m.)*	קנקן

pour (to ~) 68	**mazag [limzog]**	מזג [למזוג]
practice (to ~) 79, 85	**`imen [le`amen];** **tirgel [letargel]**	אמן [לאמן]; תרגל [לתרגל]
pray (to ~) 46	**hitpalel [lehitpalel]**	התפלל [להתפלל]
prayer 16	**tfilah** *(f.)*	תפילה
precisely 68	**davqa**	דווקא
prefer (to ~) 50	**he'edif [leha'adif]**	העדיף [להעדיף]
preparation 54	**hakhanah** *(f.)*	הכנה
preparatory course 54	**mekhinah** *(f.)*	מכינה
prepare (to ~) 54	**hekhin [lehakhin]**	הכין [להכין]
prepare oneself (to ~) (be prepared) 54	**hitkonen [lehitkonen]**	התכונן [להתכונן]
present (gift) 32	**matanah** *(f.)*	מתנה
presentation (computer ~) 81	**matzeget** *(f.)*	מצגת
pretty 16	**yafeh** *(m.)*, **yafah** *(f.)*	יפה, יפה
price 53	**mechir** *(m.)*	מחיר
print (to ~) 81	**hidpis [lehadpis]**	הדפיס [להדפיס]
print(ing) 57	**dfus** *(m.)*	דפוס
printer 81	**madpeset** *(f.)*	מדפסת
problem 13	**be'ayah** *(f.)*	בעיה
produce (to ~) 71	**yitzer [leyatzer]**	יצר [ליצר]
profession 62	**miqtzo'a** *(m.)*	מקצוע
prohibit (to ~) (ban) 66	**`asar [le`esor]**	אסר [לאסור]
prohibited 66	**`asur** *(m.)*, **`asurah** *(f.)*	אסור, אסורה
promise (to ~) 78	**hivtiach [lehavtiach]**	הבטיח [להבטיח]
proud 52	**ge`eh** *(m.)*, **ge`ah** *(f.)*	גאה, גאה
proverb 80	**pitgam** *(m.)*	פתגם
public 60	**tzibur** *(m.)*	ציבור
public *(adj.)* 66	**tziburi** *(m.)*, **tziburit** *(f.)*	ציבורי, ציבורית
purchase 12	**qniyah** *(f.)*	קניה

Q

quality 82	**`eykhut** *(f.)*	איכות
question 45	**she`elah** *(f.)*	שאלה

R

rabbi 46	**rav** *(m.)*	ב
radio 75	**radyo** *(m.)*	דיו
radish 76	**tznonit** *(f.)*	נונית
raise (to ~) 73	**herim [leharim]**	רים [להרים]
raisin 79	**tzimuq** *(m.)*	ימוק
rarely 79	**le'itim rechoqot**	עיתים רחוקות
rather 68	**davqa**	ווקא
raw (plain or untreated) 55	**golmi** *(m.)*, **golmit** *(f.)*	ולמי, גולמית
ray 61	**qeren** *(m.)*	רן
reach (to ~) 38	**higi'a [lehagi'a]**	גיע [להגיע]
read (to ~) 57	**qara` [liqro`]**	רא [לקרוא]
reader 57	**qore`** *(m.)*, **qor`ah** *(f.)*	ורא, קוראה
ready 54, 73	**mukhan** *(m.)*, **mukhanah** *(f.)*; **me`urgan** *(m.)*, **me`urgenet** *(f.)*	וכן, מוכנה; אורגן, אורגנת

really 36	**mamash**	ממש
reason 34	**sibah** *(f.)*	סיבה
recall (to ~) 72	**hizkir [lehazkir]**	הזכיר [להזכיר]
receipt 75	**qabalah** *(f.)*	קבלה
receive (to ~) 54	**qibel [leqabel]**	קבל [לקבל]
recipe 79	**matkon** *(m.)*	מתכון
record (to ~) 81	**hiqlit [lehaqlit]**	הקליט [להקליט]
red 27	**`adom** *(m.)*, **`adumah** *(f.)*	אדום, אדומה
refrigerator 83	**meqarer** *(m.)*	מקרר
reinforcement 78	**chizuq** *(m.)*	חיזוק
relationship 36	**yachas** *(m.)*	יחס
release (to ~) 66	**shichrer [leshachrer]**	שחרר [לשחרר]
religious 46	**dati** *(m.)*, **datit** *(f.)*	דתי, דתית
rely (to ~) 73	**samakh [lismokh]**	סמך [לסמוך]
remember (to ~) 67	**zakhar [lizkor]**	זכר [לזכור]
remove (to ~) 48	**hesir [lehasir]**	הסיר [להסיר]
rent (to ~) 39	**sakhar [liskor]**	שכר [לשכור]
repair (to ~) 68	**tiqen [letaqen]**	תיקן [לתקן]
repeat (to ~) 78	**chazar [lachazor]**	חזר [לחזור]
reply 54	**tshuvah** *(f.)*	תשובה
reply (to ~) 43	**'anah [la'anot]**	ענה [לענות]
request (to ~) 52	**biqesh [levaqesh]**	ביקש [לבקש]
reservation (booking) 60	**hazmanah** *(f.)*	הזמנה
reserve 83	**shmurah** *(f.)*	שמורה
reserve (animal ~) 83	**chay-bar** *(m.)*	חי-בר
reservoir (stockpile) 81	**ma`agar** *(m.)*	מאגר
respected 80	**mekhubad** *(m.)*, **mekhubedet** *(f.)*	מכובד, מכובדת
restaurant 68	**mis'adah** *(f.)*	מסעדה
return (to ~) 47	**chazar [lachazor]**	חזר [לחזור]
reversed 11	**hafukh** *(m.)*, **hafukhah** *(f.)*	הפוך, הפוכה
revolution 53	**mahapekhah** *(f.)*	מהפכה
rhyme 64	**charuz** *(m.)*	חרוז
rib 47	**tzela'** *(f.)*	צלע
rich 45	**'ashir** *(m.)*, **'ashirah** *(f.)*	עשיר, עשירה
right (proper) 40	**nakhon** *(m.)*, **nekhonah** *(f.)*	נכון, נכונה
right (to the ~) 51	**yaminah**	ימינה
right *(adj.)* 56	**yemani** *(m.)*, **yemanit** *(f.)*	ימני, ימנית
right *(adv.)* 56	**yamin**	ימין
ring (jewellery) 45	**taba'at** *(f.)*	טבעת
ring (to ~) 45	**tziltzel [letzaltzel]**	צלצל [לצלצל]
rise (to ~) 82	**qam [laqum]**	קם [לקום]
road 50	**derekh** *(f.)*	דרך
roll out (to ~) 79	**shatach [lishtoach]**	שטח [לשטוח]
roof 67	**gag** *(m.)*	גג
room 17	**cheder** *(m.)*	חדר
root 71	**shoresh** *(m.)*	שורש
routine 75	**seder yom** *(m.)*	סדר יום
rural 83	**kafri** *(m.)*, **kafrit** *(f.)*	כפרי, כפרית
Russia 8	**Rusyah** *(f.)*	רוסיה
Russian (the language) 8	**rusit** *(f.)*	רוסית

S

sad 85	**'atzuv** *(m.)*, **'atzuvah** *(f.)*	עצוב, עצובה
salad 27	**salat** *(m.)*	סלט

salt 55 | **melach** *(m.)* | מלח
same 30 | **`oto** *(m.)*, **`otah** *(f.)* | אותו, אותה
sand 39 | **chol** *(m.)* | חול
Saturday 8 | **shabat** *(f.)* | שבת
sauce 76 | **rotev** *(m.)* | רוטב
save to (to ~) 81 | **hiqlit [lehaqlit]** | הקליט [להקליט]
say (to ~) 30 | **`amar [lomar]** | אמר [לומר]
scale (for weighing) 53 | **mishqal** *(m.)* | משקל
scattered (to be ~) 58 | **nafotz [lafutz]** | נפוץ [לפוץ]
school 37 | **beyt sefer** *(m.)* | בית ספר
screen (e.g. computer) 81 | **tzag** *(m.)* | צג
scroll 72 | **megilah** *(f.)* | מגילה
sea 15 | **yam** *(m.)* | ים
search (to ~) 50 | **chipes [lechapes]** | חיפש [לחפש]
second (unit of time) 81 | **shniyah** *(f.)* | שניה
secular 82 | **chiloni** *(m.)*, **chilonit** *(f.)* | חילוני, חילונית
security 53, 60 | **bitachon** *(m.)*; **`avtachah** *(f.)* | ביטחון; אבטחה
see (to ~) 23 | **ra`ah [lir`ot]** | ראה [לראות]
See you soon! 6 | **Lehitra`ot!** | להתראות!
seeds 20 | **gar'inim** *(m. pl.)* | גרעינים
self 70 | **'etzem** *(m.)* | עצם
sell (to ~) 53 | **makhar [limkor]** | מכר [למכור]
send (to ~) 54 | **shalach [lishloach]** | שלח [לשלוח]
senior (older in age) 82 | **vatiq** *(m.)*, **vatiqah** *(f.)* | וותיק, וותיקה
Sephardi 82 | **sfaradi** *(m.)*, **sfaradiyah** *(f.)* | ספרדי, ספרדיה
series 78 | **sidrah** *(f.)* | סדרה
serve (to ~) 76 | **higish [lehagish]** | הגיש, להגיש
Shabbat 8 | **shabat** *(f.)* | שבת
shape 72 | **tzurah** *(f.)* | צורה
share (distribution) 69 | **chaluqah** *(f.)* | חלוקה
share (to ~) 69 | **chileq [lechaleq]** | חלק [לחלק]
she 8 | **hi** | היא
shekel (Israeli unit of currency) 45 | **sheqel** *(m.)* | שקל
ship 34 | **`oniyah** *(f.)* | אוניה
shirt 64 | **chultzah** *(f.)* | חולצה
shoe 64 | **na'al** *(f.)* | נעל
shop 25 | **chanut** *(f.)* | חנות
shop (to ~) 12 | **qanah [liqnot]** | קנה [לקנות]
shopping (purchases) 12 | **qniyot** *(f. pl.)* | קניות
shopping centre / mall 12 | **qanyon** *(m.)* | קניון
short 43 | **qatzar** *(m.)*, **qtzarah** *(f.)* | קצר, קצרה
short (in ~) 82 | **beqitzur** | בקיצור
shortcut 73 | **qitzur** *(m.)* | קיצור
shrine 72 | **heykhal** *(m.)* | היכל
sick 51 | **choleh** *(m.)*, **cholah** *(f.)* | חולה, חולה
side 65, 82 | **pan** *(m.)*, **panim** *(pl.)*; **tzad** *(m.)* | פן, פנים; צד
sidewalk 51 | **midrakhah** *(f.)* | מדרכה
sign (road ~) 51 | **tamrur** *(m.)* | תמרור
simple / simply 85 | **pashut** *(m.)*, **pshutah** *(f.)* | פשוט, פשוטה
since (temporal) 59 | **me`az** | מאז

sing (to ~) 65	**shar [lashir]**	שר [לשיר]
singing 60	**shirah** *(f.)*	שירה
sir 52	**`adoni**	אדוני
sister 19	**`achot**	אחות
sit (to ~) 38	**yashav [lashevet]**	ישב [לשבת]
site / website 60	**`atar** *(m.)*	אתר
sitting 78	**yeshivah** *(f.)*	ישיבה
sky 27	**shamayim** *(m. pl.)*	שמיים
slang 85	**sleng** *(m.)*	סלנג
sleep (to ~) 46	**yashan [lishon]**	ישן [לישון]
sleeve 48	**sharvul** *(m.)*	שרוול
sliced 76	**parus** *(m.)*, **prusah** *(f.)*	פרוס, פרוסה
slowly 78	**le`at**	לאט
small 19	**qatan** *(m.)*, **qtanah** *(f.)*	קטן, קטנה
so 3, 15	**kakhah; `az**	ככה; אז
so (if ~) 67	**kakh**	כך
soar (to ~) 73	**zineq [lezaneq]**	זינק [לזנק]
sock 64	**gerev** *(f.)*	גרב
sofa 38	**sapah** *(f.)*	ספה
soldier 71	**chayal** *(m.)*, **chayelet** *(f.)*	חייל, חיילת
solve (to ~) 62	**patar [liftor]**	פתר [לפתור]
someone 33	**mishehu** *(m.)*	מישהו
sometimes 79	**lif'amim**	לפעמים
son 9, 16	**ben; bar**	בן; בר
song 61	**shir** *(m.)*	שיר
soon 16	**beqarov**	בקרוב
soul 46	**neshamah** *(f.)*	נשמה
sound 61, 81	**tzlil** *(m.)*; **qol** *(m.)*, **qolot** *(pl.)*	צליל; קול, קולות
sound file 81	**qovetz qol** *(m.)*, **qivtzey qol** *(pl.)*	קובץ קול, קבצי קול
source 85	**maqor** *(m.)*, **meqorot** *(pl.)*	מקור, מקורות
south 56	**darom**	דרום
space (outer) 31	**chalal** *(m.)*	חלל
speak (to ~) 8	**diber [ledaber]**	דבר [לדבר]
Speak to you soon! 74	**Lehishtame'a!**	להשתמע!
speaker (of a particular language) 82	**dover** *(m.)*, **doveret** *(f.)*	דובר, דוברת
special 75	**meyuchad** *(m.)*, **meyuchedet** *(f.)*	מיוחד, מיוחדת
specialist 81	**mumcheh** *(m.)*, **mumchit** *(f.)*	מומחה, מומחית
speech (speaking) 8	**dibur** *(m.)*	דיבור
spend (time) (to ~) 39	**bilah [levalot]**	בילה [לבלות]
spoil oneself (to ~) 83	**hitpaneq [lehitpaneq]**	התפנק [להתפנק]
spoon (tablespoon) 55	**kaf** *(f.)*	כף
sporty 19	**sportivi** *(m.)*, **sportivit** *(f.)*	ספורטיבי, ספורטיבית
spread (to ~) 79	**shatach [lishtoach]**	שטח [לשטוח]
spring (the season) 18	**`aviv** *(m.)*	אביב
stadium 71	**`itztadyon** *(m.)*	איצטדיון
stage (phase) 79	**shalav** *(m.)*, **shlabim** *(pl.)*	שלב, שלבים
stand (to ~) 78	**'amad [la'amod]**	עמד [לעמוד]
station 50	**tachanah** *(f.)*	תחנה
stay (somewhere) (to ~) 51	**gar [lagur]**	גר [לגור]
step (on a staircase) 83	**madregah** *(f.)*	מדרגה

stiff 79	**chazaq** *(m.)*, **chazaqah** *(f.)*	חזק, חזקה
sting 80	**'oqetz** *(m.)*	עוקץ
stomach 78	**beten** *(f.)*	בטן
stop 51	**'atzor** *(m.)*	עצור
stop (to ~) 83	**'atzar [la'atzor]**	עצר [לעצור]
story 73	**sipur** *(m.)*	ספור
stove top 83	**kirayim** *(m. pl.)*	כיריים
straight 78	**zaquf** *(m.)*, **zequfah** *(f.)*	זקוף, זקופה
strained (sieved) 79	**mesunan** *(m.)*, **mesunenet** *(f.)*	מסונן, מסוננת
strawberry 79	**tut** *(m.)*	תות
street 51	**rechov** *(m.)*, **rechovot** *(pl.)*	רחוב, רחובות
stretch (to ~) 83	**pashat [lifshot]**	פשט [לפשוט]
strike (labour dispute) 33	**shvitah** *(f.)*	שביתה
strike (to ~) (stop work) 33	**shavat [lishbot]**	שבת [לשבות]
strip 76	**retzu'ah** *(f.)*	רצועה
strong 79	**chazaq** *(m.)*, **chazaqah** *(f.)*	חזק, חזקה
structure 72	**mivneh** *(m.)*	מבנה
student 46	**talmid** *(m.)*, **talmidah** *(f.)*	תלמיד, תלמידה
study (to ~) 26	**lamad [lilmod]**	למד [ללמוד]
subject 82	**nose** *(m.)*	נושא
submarine 39	**tzolelet** *(f.)*	צוללת
subscriber 52	**manuy** *(m.)*, **menuyah** *(f.)*	מנוי, מנויה
succeed (to ~) 57	**hitzliach [lehatzliach]**	הצליח [להצליח]
success 57	**hatzlachah** *(f.)*	הצלחה
successful 85	**mutzlach** *(m.)*, **mutzlachat** *(f.)*	מוצלח, מוצלחת
such (like this) 68	**kazeh**	כזה
sucker 73	**frayer** *(m.)*, **frayerit** *(f.)*	פראיר, פראירית
sugar 11	**sukar** *(m.)*	סוכר
suggest (to ~) 78	**hitzi'a [lehatzi'a]**	הציע [להציע]
suggestion 83	**hatza'ah** *(f.)*	הצעה
suitcase 23	**mizvadah** *(f.)*	מזוודה
summer 39	**qayitz** *(m.)*	קיץ
summit 73	**shpitz** *(m.) (slang)*	שפיץ
supplement (to ~) 81	**hishlim [lehashlim]**	השלים [להשלים]
sure 43	**batuach** *(m.)*, **betuchah** *(f.)*	בטוח, בטוחה
surface of (the ~) 58	**pney** *(m. pl.)*	פני
surprise 34	**hafta'ah** *(f.)*	הפתעה
swear (to ~) (make an oath) 66	**nishba' [lehishava']**	נשבע [להשבע]
sweet 79	**matoq** *(m.)*, **metuqah** *(f.)*	מתוק, מתוקה
sweetener 11	**sukrazit** *(f.)*	סוכרזית
swim (to ~) 15	**sachah [lischot]**	שחה [לשחות]
symbolize (to ~) 72	**simel [lesamel]**	סמל [לסמל]
synagogue 37	**beyt kneset** *(m.)*	בית כנסת

T

table 17	**shulchan** *(m.)*	שולחן
tahini (sesame paste) 27	**tchinah** *(f.)*	טחינה
take (to ~) 41	**laqach [laqachat]**	לקח [לקחת]
take off (to ~) 48, 83	**hesir [lehasir];** **pashat [lifshot]**	הסיר [להסיר]; פשט [לפשוט]
talk (to ~) 13	**diber [ledaber]**	דבר [לדבר]

taste 76	**ta'am** *(m.)*	טעם
tasty 36	**ta'im** *(m.)*, **te'imah** *(f.)*	טעים, טעימה
tax 53	**`agrah** *(f.)*	אגרה
tea 4	**teh** *(m.)*	תה
teach (to ~) 40	**limed [lelamed]**	לימד [ללמד]
teacher 43	**moreh** *(m.)*, **morah** *(f.)*	מורה, מורה
team 71, 81	**qvutzah** *(f.)*; **tzevet** *(m.)*	קבוצה; צוות
teaspoon 55	**kapit** *(f.)*	כפית
Technion (institute of technology) 40	**tekhniyon** *(m.)*	טכניון
telephone 13	**telefon** *(m.)*	טלפון
television 68	**televizyah** *(f.)*	טלביזיה
tell (to ~) 52	**higid [lehagid]**	הגיד [להגיד]
temperament 68	**mezeg** *(m.)*	מזג
tempting 83	**mefateh** *(m.)*, **mefatah** *(f.)*	מפתה, מפתה
thank you 4	**todah** *(f.)*	תודה
that 23	**she-**	ש-
that's to say 78	**klomar**	כלומר
the 9	**ha-**	ה-
then 69	**`achar kakh**	אחר כך
there 15	**sham**	שם
there is/are 10	**yesh**	יש
there is/are no 6	**`eyn**	אין
therefore 65	**lakhen**	לכן
these 17	**`eleh** *(m./f.)*	אלה
they 13	**hem** *(m.)*, **hen** *(f.)*	הם, הן
thick 79	**samikh** *(m.)*, **smikhah** *(f.)*	סמיך, סמיכה
thin 53, 76	**razeh** *(m.)*, **razah** *(f.)*; **daq** *(m.)*, **daqah** *(f.)*	רזה, רזה; דק, דקה
thin (to become ~) (lose weight) 53	**razah [lirzot]**	רזה [לירזות]
thing 73	**davar** *(m.)*	דבר
think (to ~) 32	**chashav [lachashov]**	חשב [לחשוב]
third (fraction) 55	**shlish** *(m.)*	שליש
this 17	**zeh** *(m.)*, **zot** *(f.)*	זה, זאת
thousand 45	**`elef**	אלף
thumb 73	**`agudal** *(m.)*	אגודל
ticket 26	**kartis** *(m.)*	כרטיס
tidy (to ~) 17	**sider [lesader]**	סדר [לסדר]
tie (necktie) 48	**'anivah** *(f.)*	עניבה
time 75	**zman** *(m.)*	זמן
time (in reference to the clock) 33	**sha'ah** *(f.)*	שעה
tired 12	**'ayef** *(m.)*, **'ayefah** *(f.)*	עייף, עייפה
tiring 12	**me'ayef** *(m.)*, **me'ayefet** *(f.)*	מעייף, מעייפת
to 9	**le-**	ל-
toe 73	**`agudal** *(m.)*	אגודל
together 60	**yachad**	יחד
togetherness 60	**tzavta** *(m.)*	צוותא
toilet 83	**sherutim** *(m. pl.)*	שירותים
toilet (restroom) 37	**beyt shimush** *(m.)*	בית שימוש

token 73	**`asimon** *(m.)*	אסימון
tomato 76	**'agvaniyah** *(f.)*	עגבניות
tomorrow 33	**machar**	מחר
tooth 55	**shen** *(f.)*	שן
top (on ~) 73	**lema'elah**	למעלה
top (summit) 73	**pisgah** *(f.)*	פסגה
top (upper part) 75	**tzameret** *(f.)*	צמרת
tourism 53	**tayarut** *(f.)*	תיירות
tourist 39	**tayar** *(m.)*, **tayeret** *(f.)*	תייר, תיירת
towards 18	**le-**	ל-
tower 58	**migdal** *(m.)*	מגדל
traffic light 51	**ramzor** *(m.)*	רמזור
train (to ~) 79	**`imen [le`amen]**	אמן [לאמן]
trainer 71	**me`amen** *(m.)*, **me`amenet** *(f.)*	מאמן, מאמנת
tranquillity 71	**shalvah** *(f.)*	שלווה
travel (journey) 53	**nesi'ah** *(f.)*	נסיעה
travel (to ~) 33	**nasa' [linso'a]**	נסע [לנסוע]
traveller 53	**nose'a** *(m.)*, **nosa'at** *(f.)*	נוסע, נוסעת
trek 26	**masa'** *(m.)*	מסע
trip 53	**nesi'ah** *(f.)*	נסיעה
trousers 64	**mikhnasayim** *(m.)*	מכנסיים
truth 52	**`emet** *(f.)*	אמת
try (to ~) 83, 85	**hitnasah [lehitnasot];** **hishtadel [lehishtadel]**	התנסה [להתנסות]; השתדל [להשתדל]
Turkish *(adj.)* 11	**turqi** *(m.)*, **turqit** *(f.)*	טורקי, טורקית
Turkish bath 45	**chamam** *(m.)*	חמם
turn (to ~) 51	**panah [lifnot]**	פנה [לפנות]
turn off (to ~) 45	**kibah [lekhabot]**	כיבה [לכבות]
twice 58	**pa'amayim** *(f.)*	פעמיים
type (to ~) 81	**hiqlid [lehaqlid]**	הקליד [להקליד]
typing 81	**haqladah** *(f.)*	הקלדה

U

Ulpan 8	**`ulpan** *(m.)*	אולפן
understand (to ~) 16	**hevin [lehavin]**	הבין [להבין]
until 26	**'ad**	עד
updated (up-to-date) 81	**me'udkan** *(m.)*, **me'udkenet** *(f.)*	מעודכן, מעודכנת
upgrade (to ~) 83	**shidreg [leshadreg]**	שדרג [לשדרג]
upheaval 73	**mahapakh** *(m.)*	מהפך
used to (to get ~) 85	**hitragel [lehitragel]**	התרגל [להתרגל]
useful (to be ~) 78	**ya'il [leho'il]**	יעיל [להועיל]

V

vanilla 79	**vanil** *(m.)*	וניל
vantage point 83	**mitzpeh** *(m.)*	מצפה
vegetable 64	**yereq** *(m.)*	ירק
vegetarian 76	**tzimchoni** *(m.)*, **tzimchonit** *(f.)*	צמחוני, צמחונית
very 23	**me`od**	מאוד
very much 24	**rabah** *(f.)*	רבה
victory 73	**nitzachon** *(m.)*	ניצחון
video 19	**video** *(m.)*	וידאו

view (scenery) 68	**nof** *(m.)*	נוף
village 39	**kfar** *(m.)*	כפר
vinegar 76	**chometz** *(m.)*	חומץ
visit (to ~) 51	**biqer [levaqer]**	בקר [לבקר]
voice 81	**qol** *(m.)*, **qolot** *(pl.)*	קול, קולות
vote (to ~) 82	**bachar [livchor],** **hitzbi'a [lehatzbi'a]**	בחר [לבחור], הצביע [להצביע]
voter 82	**bocher** *(m.)*, **bocheret** *(f.)*	בוחר, בוחרת
vowel point 57	**niqud** *(m.)*	ניקוד

W

wait (to ~) 74	**chikah [lechakot]**	חיכה [לחכות]
walk (to ~) 29	**halakh [lalekhet]**	הלך [ללכת]
walk (to ~) (for pleasure) 83	**tiyel [letayel]**	טיל [לטיל]
wall 72	**qir** *(m.)*	קיר
Wall (Western ~) 44	**kotel** *(m.)*	כותל
wander (to ~) 50	**histovev [lehistovev]**	הסתובב [להסתובב]
want (to ~) 9	**ratzah [lirtzot]**	רצה [לרצות]
war 72	**milchamah** *(f.)*	מלחמה
warm 36	**chamim** *(m.)*, **chamimah** *(f.)*	חמים, חמימה
wash (oneself) (to ~) 67	**hitrachetz [lehitrachetz]**	התרחץ [להתרחץ]
water 27	**mayim** *(m. pl.)*	מיים
wave (in the sea) 61	**gal** *(m.)*	גל
we 9	**\`anachnu** *(m./f.)*	אנחנו
wear (to ~) 18	**lavash [lilbosh]**	לבש [ללבוש]
weather 68	**mezeg \`avir** *(m.)*	מזג אוויר
wedding 18	**chatunah** *(f.)*	חתונה
week 20	**shavu'a** *(m.)*	שבוע
weekend 20	**sof shavu'a** *(m.)*	סוף שבוע
weekly (e.g. magazine) 52	**shevu'on** *(m.)*	שבועון
weighed (to be ~) 53	**nishqal [lehishaqel]**	נשקל [להשקל]
weight 53	**mishqal** *(m.)*	משקל
Well? 22	**Nu?**	נו?
west 50	**ma'arav** *(m.)*	מערב
wet 76	**ratuv** *(m.)*, **retuvah** *(f.)*	רטוב, רטובה
What? 3, 32	**Mah?; \`Eyzeh?** *(m.)*, **\`Eyzo?** *(f.)*	מה?; איזה?, איזו?
wheel 31	**\`ofan** *(m.)*	אופן
when 29	**ka\`asher**	כאשר
When? 24	**Matay?**	מתי?
Where? 13	**\`Eyfoh?**	איפה?
where? (From ~) 15	**Me\`ayin?**	מאין?
where? (To ~) 18	**Le\`an?**	לאן?
which 23, 38	**she-; \`eylu** *(pl.)*	ש-; אילו
which (in ~) 77	**shebo** *(m.)*, **shebah** *(f.)*	שבו, שבה
Which? 3, 33	**Mah?; \`Eyzeh?** *(m.)*, **\`Eyzo?** *(f.)*	מה?; איזה?, איזו?
whip (cream) (to ~) 79	**hiqtzif [lehaqtzif]**	הקציף [להקציף]
whipped cream 79	**qatzefet** *(f.)*	קצפת
white 64	**lavan** *(m.)*, **levanah** *(f.)*	לבן, לבנה
who 23	**she-**	ש-
Who? 18	**Mi?**	מי?

Why? 12	**Lamah?**	למה?
wide 80	**rachav** *(m.)*, **rechavah** *(f.)*	רחב, רחבה
wife 12	**`ishah**	אשה
win (to ~) 73	**nitzeach [lenatzeach]**	נצח [לנצח]
window 68	**chalon** *(m.)*, **chalonot** *(pl.)*	חלון, חלונות
winter 41	**choref** *(m.)*	חורף
wire 44	**chut** *(m.)*	חוט
wireless (cordless) 13	**`alchuti** *(m.)*, **`alchutit** *(f.)*	אלחוטי, אלחוטית
wise 68	**chakham** *(m.)*, **chakhamah** *(f.)*	חכם, חכמה
with 18	**'im**	עם
without 57, 73	**bli; lelo**	בלי; ללא
woman 12	**`ishah**	אשה
wonderful 41	**nehedar** *(m.)*, **nehederet** *(f.)*	נהדר, נהדרת
wood 83	**'etz** *(m.)*	עץ
word 58, 71	**davar** *(m.)*; **milah** *(f.)*, **milim** *(pl.)*	דבר; מילה, מילים
work 37	**'avodah** *(f.)*	עבודה
work (to ~) 24	**'avad [la'avod]**	עבד [לעבוד]
work out (to ~) 78	**hit'amel [lehit'amel]**	התעמל [להתעמל]
workout 78	**hit'amlut** *(f.)*	התעמלות
world 47	**'olam** *(m.)*	עולם
worthwhile (to be worth it) 53	**keday**	כדאי
write (to ~) 22	**katav [likhtov]**	כתב [לכתוב]
writing 57	**ktav** *(m.)*	כתב
wrong (to be ~) 50	**ta'ah [lit'ot]**	טעה [לטעות]

Y

year 30	**shanah** *(f.)*	שנה
yes 22	**ken**	כן
Yeshiva (religious school) 67	**yeshivah** *(f.)*	ישיבה
yesterday 31	**`etmol**	אתמול
yet 32	**'od**	עוד
yet (not ~) 32	**'od lo**	עוד לא
Yiddish (the language) 8	**yidish** *(f.)*	אידיש
you 4, 9, 10	**`at** *(f. sing.)*, **`atah** *(m. sing.)*; **`atem** *(m. pl.)*; **`aten** *(f. pl.)*	את, אתה; אתם; אתן
young 30	**tza'ir** *(m.)*, **tze'irah** *(f.)*	צעיר, צעירה

Hebrew – Transliteration – English

This glossary is organized in Hebrew alphabetical order. Note that it reads from right to left! As in everyday written Hebrew, the words appear without the vowel points, as well as without the dots that distinguish between **bet** and **vet** (which both appear as ב), **kaf** and **khaf** (כ), **pe** and **fe** (פ) and **shin** and **sin** (ש).

		א
father	**`av** 63	אב
dad	**`aba** 19	אבא
to lose	**`ibed [le`abed]** 73	אבד [לאבד]
avocado	**`avoqado** *(m.)* 51	אבוקדו
security	**`avtachah** *(f.)* 60	אבטחה
spring (the season)	**`aviv** *(m.)* 18	אביב
but	**`aval** 10	אבל
thumb, toe	**`agudal** *(m.)* 73	אגודל
tax	**`agrah** *(f.)* 53	אגרה
red	**`adom** *(m.)*, **`adumah** *(f.)* 27	אדום, אדומה
sir	**`adoni** 52	אדוני
to love; to like	**`ahav [le`ehov]** 31, 52	אהב [לאהוב]
love	**`ahavah** *(f.)* 27	אהבה
or	**`o** 10	או
bus	**`otobus** *(m.)* 33	אוטובוס
air	**`avir** *(m.)* 68	אויר
food	**`okhel** *(m.)* 48	אוכל
maybe, perhaps	**`ulay** 22	אולי
Olympian	**`olimpi** *(m.)*, **`olimpit** *(f.)* 71	אולימפי, אולימפית
hall	**`ulam** *(m.)* 72	אולם
Ulpan	**`ulpan** *(m.)* 8	אולפן
courage	**`ometz** *(m.)* 54	אומץ
boat, ship	**`oniyah** *(f.)* 34	אוניה
wheel	**`ofan** *(m.)* 31	אופן
bicycle	**`ofanayim** *(m.)* 31	אופניים
fashion	**`ofnah** *(f.)* 61	אופנה
fashionable	**`ofnati** *(m.)*, **`ofnatit** *(f.)* 61	אופנתי, אופנתית
light	**`or** *(m.)* 1	אור
guest	**`oreach** *(m.)*, **`orachat** *(f.)* 75	אורח, אורחת
pine	**`oren** *(m.)* 80	אורן
letter (of the alphabet)	**`ot** *(f.)* 57	אות
same	**`oto** *(m.)*, **`otah** *(f.)* 30	אותו, אותה
so	**`az** 15	אז
citizen	**`ezrach** *(m.)*, **`ezrachit** *(f.)* 82	אזרח, אזרחית
citizenship	**`ezrachut** *(f.)* 82	אזרחות
brother; fireplace	**`ach** 19, 83	אח
one (number)	**`echad** *(m.)* 58	אחד
sister	**`achot** 19	אחות
after that, then	**`achar kakh** 69	אחר כך
another	**`acher** *(m.)*, **`acheret** *(f.)* 47	אחר, אחרת
last	**`acharon** *(m.)*, **`acharonah** *(f.)* 45	אחרון, אחרונה

after	**`acharey** 26	אחרי
afternoon	**`acharey hatzohorayim** 62	אחרי הצהרים
one (number)	**`achat** *(f.)* 23	אחת
impossible	**`i-`efshar** 23	אי-אפשר
Yiddish (the language)	**yidish** *(f.)* 8	אידיש
What?; Which?	**`Eyzeh?** *(m.)*, **`Eyzo?** *(f.)* 32, 33	איזה?, איזו?
How?	**`Eykh?** 36	איך?
quality	**`eykhut** *(f.)* 82	איכות
which	**`eylu** *(pl.)* 38	אילו
there is/are no	**`eyn** 6	אין
infinite	**`eyn-sof** 81	אין-סוף
internet	**`internet** *(m.)* 9	אינטרנט
Where?	**`Eyfoh?** 13	איפה?
stadium	**`itztadyon** *(m.)* 71	איצטדיון
man	**`ish** 67	איש
but	**`akh** 67	אך
to eat	**`akhal [le`ekhol]** 20	אכל [לאכול]
do not	**`al** 47	אל
but	**`ela** 80	אלא
these	**`eleh** *(m./f.)* 17	אלה
God	**`elohim** *(m.)* 59	אלהים
champion	**`aluf** *(m.)*, **`alufah** *(f.)* 71	אלוף, אלופה
wireless (cordless)	**`alchuti** *(m.)*, **`alchutit** *(f.)* 13	אלחוטי, אלחוטית
thousand	**`elef** 45	אלף
electronic	**`eleqtroni** *(m.)*, **`eleqtronit** *(f.)* 22	אלקטרוני, אלקטרונית
if	**`im** 41	אם
mother	**`em** 62	אם
mum / mom	**`ima** 19	אמא
bath	**`ambatyah** *(f.)* 83	אמבטיה
to practice, to train	**`imen [le`amen]** 79	אמן [לאמן]
to say	**`amar [lomar]** 30	אמר [לומר]
truth	**`emet** *(f.)* 52	אמת
we	**`anachnu** *(m./f.)* 9	אנחנו
I	**`ani** *(m./f.)* 5	אני
forbidden, prohibited	**`asur** *(m.)*, **`asurah** *(f.)* 66	אסור, אסורה
token	**`asimon** *(m.)* 73	אסימון
to arrest, to prohibit (ban)	**`asar [le`esor]** 66	אסר [לאסור]
nose	**`af** *(m.)* 65	אף
no (negative particle)	**`af** 75	אף
no one	**`af `echad** 74	אף אחד
never	**`af pa'am** 70	אף פעם
to bake	**`afah [le`efot]** 79	אפה [לאפות]
grey	**`afor** *(m.)*, **`aforah** *(f.)* 64	אפור, אפורה
baking	**`afiyah** *(f.)* 79	אפיה
even	**`afilu** 41	אפילו
ash	**`efer** *(m.)* 64	אפר
possible	**`efshar** 24	אפשר
finger	**`etzba'** *(f.)*, **`etzba'ot** *(pl.)* 82	אצבע, אצבעות
at, by, among (+ pronoun)	**`etz- (+ li/lekh** etc.**)** 36	אצל-
ecological	**`eqologi** *(m.)*, **`eqologit** *(f.)* 71	אקולוגי, אקולוגית
chimney	**`arubah** *(f.)* 67	ארובה

hospitality	**`eruach** *(m.)* 83	ארוח
meal	**`aruchah** *(f.)* 24	ארוחה
dinner	**`aruchat 'erev** *(f.)* 24	ארוחת ערב
long	**`arokh** *(m.)*, **`arukah** *(f.)* 43	ארוך, ארוכה
lion	**`ari** *(m.)* 69	ארי
land; country	**`aretz** *(f.)* 25, 53	ארץ
fire	**`esh** *(f.)* 20	אש
wife, woman	**`ishah** 12	אשה
you	**`at** *(f. sing.)* 4	את
particle before direct definite object	**`et** 17	את
you	**`atah** *(m. sing.)* 4	אתה
Athens	**`Atunah** *(f.)* 44	אתונה
you	**`atem** *(m. pl.)* 9	אתם
you	**`aten** *(f. pl.)* 10	אתן
yesterday	**`etmol** 31	אתמול
site / website	**`atar** *(m.)* 60	אתר

ב

by; in	**be-** 10, 11, 77	ב-
to come	**ba [lavo]** 15	בא [לבוא]
please	**bevaqashah** 10	בבקשה
clothing (item of)	**beged** *(m.)* 64	בגד
clothes	**bgadim** *(m. pl.)* 64	בגדים
because of (due to)	**biglal** 27	בגלל
exactly	**bediyuq** 52	בדיוק
joke	**bdichah** *(f.)* 44	בדיחה
lonely	**boded** *(m.)*, **bodedah** *(f.)* 75	בודד, בודדה
voter	**bocher** *(m.)*, **bocheret** *(f.)* 82	בוחר, בוחרת
mud	**botz** *(m.)* 11	בוץ
morning	**boqer** *(m.)* 1	בוקר
choice	**bchirah** *(f.)* 82	בחירה
elections	**bchirot** *(f. pl.)* 82	בחירות
to choose, to vote	**bachar [livchor]** 82	בחר [לבחור]
sure	**batuach** *(m.)*, **betuchah** *(f.)* 43	בטוח, בטוחה
layabout	**batlan** *(m.)*, **batlanit** *(f.)* 74	בטלן, בטלנית
stomach	**beten** *(f.)* 78	בטן
most	**beyoter** 32	ביותר
security; confidence	**bitachon** *(m.)* 53, 73	ביטחון
to cancel	**bitel [levatel]** 52	ביטל [לבטל]
to have a good time, to spend (time)	**bilah [levalot]** 39	בילה [לבלות]
among, between	**beyn** 44	בין
international	**beynle`umi** *(m.)*, **beynle`umit** *(f.)* 44	בינלאומי, בינלאומית
in the meantime	**beyntayim** 79	בינתיים
to request	**biqesh [levaqesh]** 52	ביקש [לבקש]
beer	**birah** *(f.)* 4	בירה
house; home	**beyt** *(m.)* 10, 19	בית
hospital	**beyt cholim** *(m.)* 51	בית חולים
synagogue	**beyt kneset** *(m.)* 37	בית כנסת
school	**beyt sefer** *(m.)* 37	בית ספר

toilet (restroom)	**beyt shimush** *(m.)* 37	בית שימוש
everywhere	**bekhol maqom** 68	בכל מקום
mess; disorder	**balagan** *(m.)* 17, 27	בלגן
messy guy/woman	**balaganist** *(m.)*, **balaganistit** *(f.)* 17	בלגניסט, בלגניסטית
without	**bli** 57	בלי
to mix up (jumble)	**balal [livlol]** 59	בלל [לבלול]
linguist	**balshan** *(m.)*, **balshanit** *(f.)* 62	בלשן, בלשנית
not	**bilti** 66	בלתי
son	**ben** 9	בן
person	**ben `adam** *(m.)* 23	בן אדם
to build	**banah [livnot]** 58	בנה [לבנות]
in order; all right, okay	**beseder** 6, 17	בסדר
basic	**besisi** *(m.)*, **besisit** *(f.)* 79	בסיסי, בסיסית
for (in favour of)	**be'ad** 73	בעד
in (+ period of time)	**be'od** 27	בעוד
problem	**be'ayah** *(f.)* 13	בעיה
mainly, in particular	**be'iqar** 65	בעיקר
husband	**ba'al** 18	בעל
master / mistress (owner)	**ba'al** *(m.)*, **ba'alat** *(f.)* 18	בעל / בעלת
actually	**be'etzem** 75	בעצם
inside	**bifnim** 79	בפנים
onion	**batzal** *(m.)* 76	בצל
pastry	**batzeq** *(m.)* 79	בצק
in short	**beqitzur** 82	בקיצור
to visit	**biqer [levaqer]** 51	בקר [לבקר]
soon	**beqarov** 16	בקרוב
cabin	**biqtah** *(f.)* 83	בקתה
son	**bar** 16	בר
Bar Mitzvah / Bat Mitzvah	**bar mitzvah** *(m.)*, **bat mitzvah** *(f.)* 16	בר מצווה, בת מצווה
healthy	**bari** *(m.)*, **bri`ah** *(f.)* 76	בריא, בריאה
health	**bri`ut** *(f.)* 76	בריאות
people	**briyot** *(m. pl.)* 80	בריות
covenant	**brit** *(f.)* 30	ברית
circumcision	**brit milah** *(f.)* 30	ברית מילה
to congratulate	**berekh [levarekh]** 57	ברך [לברך]
pool	**brekhah** *(f.)* 20	ברכה
for	**bishvil** 25	בשביל
daughter	**bat** 9	בת
Bon appétit!	**Bete`avon!** 55	בתיאבון!

ג

proud	**ge`eh** *(m.)*, **ge`ah** *(f.)* 52	גאה, גאה
back (the part of the body)	**gav** *(m.)* 78	גב
cheese	**gvinah** *(f.)* 10	גבינה
cup (trophy)	**gavi'a** *(m.)* 73	גביע
madam	**gvirti** 51	גבירתי
man	**gever** 50	גבר
lady	**gveret** 52	גברת
roof	**gag** *(m.)* 67	גג
big	**gadol** *(m.)*, **gdolah** *(f.)* 19	גדול, גדולה

height, level	**govah** *(m.)* 73	גובה
raw (plain or untreated)	**golmi** *(m.)*, **golmit** *(f.)* 55	גולמי, גולמית
body	**guf** *(m.)* 43	גוף
carrot	**gezer** *(m.)* 76	גזר
geography	**ge`ografyah** *(f.)* 26	גיאוגרפיה
hero	**gibor** *(m.)*, **giborah** *(f.)* 71	גיבור, גיבורה
age; joy	**gil** *(m.)* 30, 61	גיל
wave (in the sea)	**gal** *(m.)* 61	גל
ice cream	**glidah** *(f.)* 67	גלידה
Galilee	**Galil** 83	גליל
pit (stone of fruit)	**gal'in** *(m.)* 76	גלעין
also	**gam** 13	גם
as well as, both	**gam ... vegam ...** 27	גם ... וגם ...
garden	**gan** *(m.)* 37	גן
kindergarten	**gan-yeladim** *(m.)* 37	גן-ילדים
paradise (Garden of Eden)	**gan 'eden** *(m.)* 46	גן עדן
to hide (stash)	**ganaz [lignoz]** 72	גנז [לגנוז]
to live (reside), to stay (somewhere)	**gar [lagur]** 51	גר [לגור]
sock	**gerev** *(f.)* 64	גרב
divorced	**garush** *(m.)*, **grushah** *(f.)* 74	גרוש, גרושה
seeds	**gar'inim** *(m. pl.)* 20	גרעינים

ד

bee	**dvorah** *(f.)* 80	דבורה
word; thing	**davar** *(m.)* 58, 73	דבר
to speak; to talk	**diber [ledaber]** 8, 13	דבר [לדבר]
honey	**dvash** *(m.)* 80	דבש
fish	**dag** *(m.)* 83	דג
bilingual	**du-leshoni** *(m.)* 62	דו-לשוני
dialogue	**du-siach** *(m.)* 73	דו-שיח
post (mail); post office	**do`ar** *(m.)* 22, 29	דואר
speaker (of a particular language)	**dover** *(m.)*, **doveret** *(f.)* 82	דובר, דוברת
example	**dugmah** *(f.)* 43	דוגמה
fashion model	**dugman** *(m.)*, **dugmanit** *(f.)* 75	דוגמן, דוגמנית
precisely, rather	**davqa** 68	דווקא
generation	**dor** *(m.)* 81	דור
it is enough	**day** 81	די
diet	**dietah** *(f.)* 16	דיאטה
speech (speaking)	**dibur** *(m.)* 8	דיבור
hands-free set	**diburit** *(f.)* 13	דיבורית
disk	**disq** *(m.)* 81	דיסק
opinion	**de'ah** *(f.)* 71	דיעה
apartment	**dirah** *(f.)* 37	דירה
gas, petrol	**deleq** *(m.)* 50	דלק
door	**delet** *(f.)* 46	דלת
print(ing)	**dfus** *(m.)* 57	דפוס
thin	**daq** *(m.)*, **daqah** *(f.)* 76	דק, דקה

minute	**daqah** *(f.)* 79	דקה
grade (echelon)	**dereg** *(m.)* 83	דרג
south	**darom** 56	דרום
road	**derekh** *(f.)* 50	דרך
passport	**darkon** *(m.)* 26	דרכון
to demand	**darash [lidrosh]** 73	דרש [לדרוש]
religious	**dati** *(m.)*, **datit** *(f.)* 46	דתי, דתית

ה

the	**ha-** 9	ה-
particle for forming yes/no questions	**Ha`im?** 67	האם?
next (coming)	**haba** *(m.)*, **haba`ah** *(f.)* 40	הבא, הבאה
to promise	**hivtiach [lehavtiach]** 78	הבטיח [להבטיח]
to bring	**hevi` [lehavi`]** 74	הביא [להביא]
to understand	**hevin [lehavin]** 16	הבין [להבין]
towards home	**habaytah** 40	הביתה
to arrive, to reach	**higi'a [lehagi'a]** 38	הגיע [להגיע]
to serve	**higish [lehagish]** 76	הגיש, להגיש
to print	**hidpis [lehadpis]** 81	הדפיס [להדפיס]
he, it *(m.)*	**hu** 8	הוא
to announce	**hodi'a [lehodi'a]** 53	הודיע [להודיע]
birth	**huledet** *(f.)* 32	הולדת
to add	**hosif [lehosif]** 53	הוסיף [להוסיף]
to appear	**hofi'a [lehofi'a]** 81	הופיע [להופיע]
parent	**horeh** *(m.)*, **horim** *(pl.)* 75	הורה, הורים
opportunity	**hizdamnut** *(f.)* 73	הזדמנות
to damage, to hurt	**heziq [lehaziq]** 78	הזיק [להזיק]
to recall	**hizkir [lehazkir]** 72	הזכיר [להזכיר]
to invite	**hizmin [lehazmin]** 32	הזמין [להזמין]
invitation; reservation (booking)	**hazmanah** *(f.)* 24, 60	הזמנה
to decide	**hechlit [lehachlit]** 82	החליט [להחליט]
best	**hatov** *(m.)*, **hatovah** *(f.)* **beyoter** 32	הטוב, הטובה ביותר
it *(f.)*, she	**hi** 8	היא
to tell	**higid [lehagid]** 52	הגיד [להגיד]
to be	**hayah [liheyot]** 35	היה [להיות]
to meet (become acquainted); to know (be acquainted with)	**hikir [lehakir]** 34, 37	היכיר [להכיר]
palace, shrine	**heykhal** *(m.)* 72	היכל
commitment	**hitchayvut** *(f.)* 85	היתחיבות
most	**hakhi** 75	הכי
to prepare	**hekhin [lehakhin]** 54	הכין [להכין]
preparation	**hakhanah** *(f.)* 54	הכנה
to go; to walk	**halakh [lalekhet]** 18, 29	הלך [ללכת]
they	**hem** *(m.)* 13	הם
they	**hen** *(f.)* 13	הן
cheque	**hamcha`ah** *(f.)* 32	המחאה
engineering	**handasah** *(f.)* 40	הנדסה
here	**hineh** 67	הנה

to explain	**hisbir [lehasbir]** 67	הסביר [להסביר]
historical	**histori** *(m.)*, **historit** *(f.)* 34	הסטורי, הסטורית
to remove, to take off	**hesir [lehasir]** 48	הסיר [להסיר]
to wander	**histovev [lehistovev]** 50	הסתובב [להסתובב]
to look	**histakel [lehistakel]** 80	הסתכל [להסתכל]
to prefer	**he'edif [leha'adif]** 50	העדיף [להעדיף]
to dare	**he'ez [leha'ez]** 71	העיז [להעיז]
consideration, esteem	**ha'arakhah** *(f.)* 73	הערכה
reversed	**hafukh** *(m.)*, **hafukhah** *(f.)* 11	הפוך, הפוכה
surprise	**hafta'ah** *(f.)* 34	הפתעה
to vote	**hitzbi'a [lehatzbi'a]** 82	הצביע [להצביע]
to suggest; to offer	**hitzi'a [lehatzi'a]** 78, 79	הציע [להציע]
success	**hatzlachah** *(f.)* 57	הצלחה
to succeed	**hitzliach [lehatzliach]** 57	הצליח [להצליח]
suggestion	**hatza'ah** *(f.)* 83	הצעה
typing	**haqladah** *(f.)* 81	הקלדה
to type	**hiqlid [lehaqlid]** 81	הקליד [להקליד]
to record, to save to	**hiqlit [lehaqlit]** 81	הקליט [להקליט]
to beat (eggs), to whip (cream)	**hiqtzif [lehaqtzif]** 79	הקציף [להקציף]
mountain	**har** *(m.)* 83	הר
a lot; many / much	**harbeh** 27, 50	הרבה
to feel	**hirgish [lehargish]** 47	הרגיש [להרגיש]
to raise	**herim [leharim]** 73	הרים [להרים]
adventure	**harpatqah** *(f.)* 85	הרפתקה
to leave	**hish`ir [lehash`ir]** 79	השאיר [להשאיר]
to supplement	**hishlim [lehashlim]** 81	השלים [להשלים]
to fatten (gain weight)	**hishmin [lehashmin]** 52	השמין [להשמין]
to go crazy	**hishtage'a [lehishtage'a]** 41	השתגע [להשתגע]
to try	**hishtadel [lehishtadel]** 85	השתדל [להשתדל]
to be bored	**hishta'amem [lehishta'amem]** 82	השתעמם [להשתעמם]
beginning	**hatchalah** *(f.)* 85	התחלה
to get married	**hitchaten [lehitchaten]** 34	התחתן [להתחתן]
to contract	**hitkavetz [lehitkavetz]** 43	התכווץ [להתכווץ]
to prepare oneself (be prepared)	**hitkonen [lehitkonen]** 54	התכונן [להתכונן]
to be excited	**hitlahev [lehitlahev]** 65	התלהב [להתלהב]
perseverance	**hatmadah** *(f.)* 78	התמדה
to experience, to try	**hitnasah [lehitnasot]** 83	התנסה [להתנסות]
to work out	**hit'amel [lehit'amel]** 78	התעמל [להתעמל]
workout	**hit'amlut** *(f.)* 78	התעמלות
to be interested	**hit'anyen [lehit'anyen]** 71	התעניין [להתעניין]
to pray	**hitpalel [lehitpalel]** 46	התפלל [להתפלל]
to spoil oneself	**hitpaneq [lehitpaneq]** 83	התפנק [להתפנק]
to cool down	**hitqarer [lehitqarer]** 79	התקרר [להתקרר]
to get used to	**hitragel [lehitragel]** 85	התרגל [להתרגל]
to expand	**hitrachev [lehitrachev]** 43	התרחב [להתרחב]
to wash (oneself)	**hitrachetz [lehitrachetz]** 67	התרחץ [להתרחץ]
to concentrate	**hitrakez [lehitrakez]** 78	התרכז [להתרכז]

ה

and	**ve-** 8, 36	ו-
senior (older in age)	**vatiq** *(m.)*, **vatiqah** *(f.)* 82	וותיק, וותיקה
video	**video** *(m.)* 19	וידאו
vanilla	**vanil** *(m.)* 79	וניל

ז

this	**zot** *(f.)* 17	זאת
this	**zeh** *(m.)* 17	זה
gold	**zahav** *(m.)* 11	זהב
identity	**zehut** *(f.)* 82	זהות
couple, pair	**zug** *(m.)* 60	זוג
cheap	**zol** *(m.)*, **zolah** *(f.)* 38	זול, זולה
to move	**zaz [lazuz]** 68	זז [לזוז]
to soar	**zineq [lezaneq]** 73	זינק [לזנק]
olive	**zayit** *(m.)* 76	זית
glass (material)	**zekhukhit** *(f.)* 39	זכוכית
to remember	**zakhar [lizkor]** 67	זכר [לזכור]
time	**zman** *(m.)* 75	זמן
straight	**zaquf** *(m.)*, **zequfah** *(f.)* 78	זקוף, זקופה

ח

package	**chavilah** *(f.)* 40	חבילה
what a pity	**chaval** 6	חבל
friend; member (of an organization)	**chaver** *(m.)*, **chaverah** *(f.)* 20, 48	חבר, חבֵרה
cool (laid back)	**chevreman** *(m.)*, **chevremanit** *(f.)* 29	חברמן, חברמנית
holiday (festival)	**chag** *(m.)* 36	חג
to celebrate	**chagag [lachgog]** 38	חגג [לחגוג]
latest (newest)	**chadish** *(m.)*, **chadishah** *(f.)* 38	חדיש, חדישה
room	**cheder** *(m.)* 17	חדר
bedroom	**chadar sheynah** *(f.)* 83	חדר שינה
new	**chadash** *(m.)*, **chadashah** *(f.)* 6	חדש, חדשה
news	**chadashot** *(f. pl.)* 33	חדשות
amateur	**chovev** *(m.)*, **chovevet** *(f.)* 25	חובב, חובבת
month	**chodesh** *(m.)* 29	חודש
experience	**chavayah** *(f.)* 81	חוויה
wire	**chut** *(m.)* 44	חוט
sand	**chol** *(m.)* 39	חול
ill, sick	**choleh** *(m.)*, **cholah** *(f.)* 51	חולה, חולה
shirt	**chultzah** *(f.)* 64	חולצה
heat	**chom** *(m.)* 43	חום
hummus; chickpea(s)	**chumus** *(m.)* 27, 55	חומוס
vinegar	**chometz** *(m.)* 76	חומץ
beach	**chof** *(m.)* 15	חוף
handful	**chofen** *(m.)* 79	חופן
holiday (vacation)	**chufshah** *(f.)* 83	חופשה
free (not held down)	**chofshi** *(m.)*, **chofshit** *(f.)* 78	חופשי, חופשית
outside of	**chutz** 25	חוץ
abroad	**chutz la`aretz** 25	חוץ לארץ
winter	**choref** *(m.)* 41	חורף

darkness	**choshekh** *(m.)* 72	חושך
stiff, strong	**chazaq** *(m.)*, **chazaqah** *(f.)* 79	חזק, חזקה
to return; to repeat	**chazar [lachazor]** 47, 78	חזר [לחזור]
animal reserve	**chay-bar** *(m.)* 83	חי-בר
innovation	**chidush** *(m.)* 57	חידוש
animal	**chayah** *(f.)* 69	חיה
reinforcement	**chizuq** *(m.)* 78	חיזוק
soldier	**chayal** *(m.)*, **chayelet** *(f.)* 71	חייל, חיילת
life	**chayim** *(m. pl.)* 69	חיים
to wait	**chikah [lechakot]** 74	חיכה [לחכות]
secular	**chiloni** *(m.)*, **chilonit** *(f.)* 82	חילוני, חילונית
to look for, to search	**chipes [lechapes]** 50	חיפש [לחפש]
intelligent, wise	**chakham** *(m.)*, **chakhamah** *(f.)* 67	חכם, חכמה
milk	**chalav** *(m.)* 79	חלב
egg white	**chelbon** *(m.)* 79	חלבון
window	**chalon** *(m.)*, **chalonot** *(pl.)* 68	חלון, חלונות
share (distribution)	**chaluqah** *(f.)* 69	חלוקה
space (outer)	**chalal** *(m.)* 31	חלל
egg yolk	**chelmon** *(m.)* 79	חלמון
part	**cheleq** *(m.)* 58	חלק
to divide, to share	**chileq [lechaleq]** 69	חלק [לחלק]
father-in-law	**cham** 36	חם
hot	**cham** *(m.)*, **chamah** *(f.)* 27	חם, חמה
butter	**chem`ah** *(f.)* 79	חמאה
darling	**chamud** *(m.)*, **chamudah** *(f.)* 45	חמוד, חמודה
donkey	**chamor** *(m.)* 69	חמור
mother-in-law	**chamot** 36	חמות
warm	**chamim** *(m.)*, **chamimah** *(f.)* 36	חמים, חמימה
Turkish bath	**chamam** *(m.)* 45	חמם
grace	**chen** *(m.)* 38	חן
dedication	**chanukah** *(f.)* 38	חנוכה
housewarming, inauguration	**chanukat bayit** *(f.)* 38	חנוכת בית
shop	**chanut** *(f.)* 25	חנות
parking	**chanayah** *(f.)* 60	חניה
lettuce	**chasah** *(f.)* 76	חסה
missing (lacking)	**chaser** *(m.)*, **chaserah** *(f.)* 85	חסר, חסרה
excavation	**chafirah** *(f.)* 44	חפירה
half	**chetzi** 53	חצי
rhyme	**charuz** *(m.)* 64	חרוז
to think	**chashav [lachashov]** 32	חשב [לחשוב]
important	**chashuv** *(m.)*, **chashuvah** *(f.)* 68	חשוב, חשובה
marriage (ceremony), wedding	**chatunah** *(f.)* 18	חתונה
hot guy/woman	**chatikh** *(m.)*, **chatikhah** *(f.)* 15	חתיך, חתיכה
piece	**chatikhah** *(f.)* 15	חתיכה
groom	**chatan** *(m.)* 18	חתן

ט

nature	**teva'** *(m.)* 83	טבע
ring (jewellery)	**taba'at** *(f.)* 45	טבעת
good	**tov** *(m.)*, **tovah** *(f.)* 1	טוב, טובה

Turkish *(adj.)*	**turqi** *(m.)*, **turqit** *(f.)* 11	טורקי, טורקית
tahini (sesame paste)	**tchinah** *(f.)* 27	טחינה
to walk (for pleasure)	**tiyel [letayel]** 83	טיל [לטיל]
flight (airplane)	**tisah** *(f.)* 23	טיסה
Technion (institute of technology)	**tekhniyon** *(m.)* 40	טכניון
dew	**tal** *(m.)* 61	טל
television	**televizyah** *(f.)* 68	טלביזיה
telephone	**telefon** *(m.)* 13	טלפון
to fly (by plane)	**tas [latus]** 23	טס [לטוס]
to be mistaken, to be wrong	**ta'ah [lit'ot]** 50	טעה [לטעות]
tasty	**ta'im** *(m.)*, **te'imah** *(f.)* 36	טעים, טעימה
taste	**ta'am** *(m.)* 76	טעם
fresh	**tari** *(m.)*, **triyah** *(f.)* 76	טרי, טריה
to devour	**taraf [litrof]** 69	טרף [לטרוף]

י

hand	**yad** *(f.)* 19	יד
well known	**yadu'a** *(m.)* 74	ידוע
friendship	**yedidut** *(f.)* 85	ידידות
to know (a fact)	**yada' [lada'at]** 41	ידע [לדעת]
diamond	**yahalom** *(m.)* 45	יהלום
jubilee	**yovel** *(m.)* 34	יובל
Greek *(adj.)*	**yevani** *(m.)*, **yevanit** *(f.)* 44	יווני, יוונית
day	**yom** *(m.)* 24	יום
birthday	**yom huledet** *(m.)* 32	יום הולדת
beauty	**yofi** *(m.)* 61	יופי
Great!	**Yofi!** 38	יופי!
more … than	**yoter ... m-** 77	יותר ... מ-
together	**yachad** 60	יחד
only (sole)	**yachid** *(m.)* , **yechidah** *(f.)* 47	יחיד, יחידה
relationship	**yachas** *(m.)* 36	יחס
to be able to, can	**yakhol** *(m.)*, **yekholah** *(f.)* 22	יכול, יכולה
child	**yeled** *(m.)*, **yaldah** *(f.)* 25	ילד, ילדה
sea	**yam** *(m.)* 15	ים
right *(adv.)*	**yamin** 56	ימין
to the right	**yaminah** 51	ימינה
right *(adj.)*	**yemani** *(m.)*, **yemanit** *(f.)* 56	ימני, ימנית
destination, objective	**ya'ad** *(m.)* 60	יעד
to be useful	**ya'il [leho'il]** 78	יעיל [להועיל]
effective	**ya'il** *(m.)*, **ye'ilah** *(f.)* 73	יעיל, יעילה
efficiency	**ye'ilut** *(f.)* 78	יעילות
beautiful, pretty	**yafeh** *(m.)*, **yafah** *(f.)* 16	יפה, יפה
to come out; to go out	**yatza [latzet]** 67, 74	יצא [לצאת]
departure	**yetzi`ah** *(f.)* 34	יציאה
to create, to produce	**yitzer [leyatzer]** 71	יצר [ליצר]
expensive; dear (cherished)	**yaqar** *(m.)*, **yeqarah** *(f.)* 38, 74	יקר, יקרה
to descend, to go down	**yarad [laredet]** 72	ירד [לרדת]
Jordan	**Yarden** *(m.)* 50	ירדן
green	**yaroq** *(m.)*, **yeruqah** *(f.)* 64	ירוק, ירוקה
Jerusalem	**Yerushalayim** 23	ירושלים

monthly journal	**yarchon** *(m.)* 52	ירחון
vegetable	**yereq** *(m.)* 64	ירק
there is/are	**yesh** 10	יש
to have (to possess)	**yesh (+ li/lekha/lakh** etc.**)** 28	יש...
to sit	**yashav [lashevet]** 38	ישב [לשבת]
buttocks	**yashvan** *(m.)* 78	ישבן
Yeshiva (religious school); sitting	**yeshivah** *(f.)* 67, 78	ישיבה
direct	**yashir** *(m.)*, **yeshirah** *(f.)* 53	ישיר, ישירה
to sleep	**yashan [lishon]** 46	ישן [לישון]
old	**yashan** *(m.)*, **yeshanah** *(f.)* 82	ישן, ישנה
Israeli *(adj.)*	**yisra`eli** *(m.)*, **yisra`elit** *(f.)* 44	ישראלי, ישראלית
advantage	**yitaron** *(m.)* 81	יתרון

כ

when	**ka`asher** 29	כאשר
heavy	**kaved** *(m.)*, **kvedah** *(f.)* 57	כבד, כבדה
honour	**kavod** *(m.)* 57	כבוד
already	**kvar** 27	כבר
worthwhile (to be worth it)	**keday** 53	כדאי
ball	**kadur** *(m.)* 19	כדור
football (soccer)	**kaduregel** *(m.)* 19	כדורגל
handball	**kaduryad** *(m.)* 19	כדוריד
basketball	**kadursal** *(m.)* 19	כדורסל
in order to	**kedey** 53	כדי
cup, glass	**kos** *(f.)* 55	כוס
armchair	**kursah** *(f.)* 38	כורסה
fitness	**kosher** *(m.)* 71	כושר
Western Wall	**kotel** *(m.)* 44	כותל
such (like this)	**kazeh** 68	כזה
blue	**kachol** *(m.)*, **kchulah** *(f.)* 64	כחול, כחולה
because	**ki** 16	כי
to turn off	**kibah [lekhabot]** 45	כיבה [לכבות]
pocket	**kis** *(m.)* 80	כיס
chair	**kise`** *(m.)* 17	כיסא
fun	**kef** *(m.)* 20	כיף
stove top	**kirayim** *(m. pl.)* 83	כיריים
if so	**kakh** 67	כך
like that, so	**kakhah** 3	ככה
not bad	**kakhah, kakhah** 3	ככה, ככה
all; each, every	**kol** 27, 31	כל
minimarket	**kolbo** *(m.)* 83	כלבו
nothing	**klum** *(m.)* 73	כלום
that's to say	**klomar** 78	כלומר
to include	**kalal [likhlol]** 83	כלל [ליכלול]
how many	**kamah** 23	כמה
like	**kmo** 18	כמו
yes	**ken** 22	כן
entrance	**knisah** *(f.)* 72	כניסה
conference	**kenes** *(m.)* 44	כנס
Knesset (Israel's parliament)	**kneset** *(f.)* 48	כנסת

money	**kesef** *(m.)* 32	כסף
anger	**ka'as** *(m.)* 80	כעס
to be angry	**ka'as [likh'os]** 69	כעס [לכעוס]
spoon (tablespoon)	**kaf** *(f.)* 55	כף
teaspoon	**kapit** *(f.)* 55	כפית
village	**kfar** *(m.)* 39	כפר
rural	**kafri** *(m.)*, **kafrit** *(f.)* 83	כפרי, כפרית
ticket	**kartis** *(m.)* 26	כרטיס
writing	**ktav** *(m.)* 57	כתב
to correspond with, to write	**katav [likhtov]** 22	כתב [לכתוב]
address	**ktovet** *(f.)* 22	כתובת
orange (colour)	**katom** *(m.)*, **ktumah** *(f.)* 65	כתום, כתומה

ל

to; for, towards	**le-** 9, 16, 18	ל-
no	**lo** 8	לא
good-for-nothing	**lo-yutzlach** 74	לא-יוצלח
nation	**le`om** *(m.)* 44	לאום
national	**le`umi** *(m.)*, **le`umit** *(f.)* 44	לאומי, לאומית
slowly	**le`at** 78	לאט
To where?	**Le`an?** 18	לאן?
heart	**lev** *(m.)* 31	לב
alone	**levad** 66	לבד
white	**lavan** *(m.)*, **levanah** *(f.)* 64	לבן, לבנה
to dress, to wear	**lavash [lilbosh]** 18	לבש [ללבוש]
flame	**lehavah** *(f.)* 65	להבה
Speak to you soon!	**Lehishtame'a!** 74	להשתמע!
Bye!	**Lehit!** 22	להת!
Goodbye!, See you soon!	**Lehitra`ot!** 6	להתראות!
humidity	**lachut** *(f.)* 75	לחות
bread	**lechem** *(m.)* 55	לחם
Latin (language)	**latinit** *(f.)* 5	לטינית
league	**ligah** *(f.)* 73	ליגה
to caress	**litef [lelatef]** 47	ליטף [ללטף]
night	**laylah** *(m.)* 27	לילה
to teach	**limed [lelamed]** 40	לימד [ללמד]
learning (study)	**limud** *(m.)* 57	לימוד
lemon	**limon** *(m.)* 55	לימון
clown	**leytzan** *(m.)*, **leytzanit** *(f.)* 65	ליצן, ליצנית
liqueur	**liqer** *(m.)* 79	ליקר
in honour of	**likhvod** 34	לכבוד
therefore	**lakhen** 65	לכן
without	**lelo** 73	ללא
to learn; to study	**lamad [lilmod]** 5, 26	למד [ללמוד]
Why?	**Lamah?** 12	למה?
at the bottom	**lematah** 73	למטה
on top	**lema'elah** 73	למעלה
although	**lamrot she-** 65	למרות ש-

for example	**lemashal** 78	למשל
often	**le'itim qrovot** 79	לעיתים קרובות
rarely	**le'itim rechoqot** 79	לעיתים רחוקות
at least	**lefachot** 85	לפחות
according to	**lefi** 53	לפי
before; ago	**lifney** 26, 29	לפני
sometimes	**lif'amim** 79	לפעמים
to take	**laqach [laqachat]** 41	לקח [לקחת]
language	**lashon** *(m.)*, **leshonot** *(pl.)* 58	לשון, לשונות

מ

from	**me-** 8	מ-
reservoir (stockpile)	**ma`agar** *(m.)* 81	מאגר
database	**ma`agar meyda'** *(m.)* 81	מאגר מידע
equipped	**me`uvzar** *(m.)*, **me`uvzeret** *(f.)* 83	מאובזר, מאובזרת
very	**me`od** 23	מאוד
organized, ready	**me`urgan** *(m.)*, **me`urgenet** *(f.)* 73	מאורגן, מאורגנת
since (temporal)	**me`az** 59	מאז
From where?	**Me`ayin?** 15	מאין?
coach, trainer	**me`amen** *(m.)*, **me`amenet** *(f.)* 71	מאמן, מאמנת
effort	**ma`amatz** *(m.)* 57	מאמץ
adult	**mevugar** *(m.)*, **mevugeret** *(f.)* 65	מבוגר, מבוגרת
desired	**mevuqash** *(m.)*, **mevuqeshet** *(f.)* 81	מבוקש, מבוקשת
choice	**mivchar** *(m.)* 82	מבחר
building, structure	**mivneh** *(m.)* 72	מבנה
tower	**migdal** *(m.)* 58	מגדל
living	**megurim** *(m. pl.)* 83	מגורים
scroll	**megilah** *(f.)* 72	מגילה
boot	**magaf** *(m.)* 64	מגף
field (sports)	**migrash** *(m.)* 73	מגרש
desert	**midbar** *(m.)* 50	מדבר
column (newspaper)	**mador** *(m.)* 52	מדור
dishwasher	**mediach-kelim** *(m.)* 83	מדיח-כלים
printer	**madpeset** *(f.)* 81	מדפסת
step (on a staircase)	**madregah** *(f.)* 83	מדרגה
pedestrian street	**midrachov** *(m.)* 51	מדרחוב
pavement, sidewalk	**midrakhah** *(f.)* 51	מדרכה
lawn	**midsha`ah** *(f.)* 83	מדשאה
What?, Which?	**Mah?** 3	מה?
upheaval	**mahapakh** *(m.)* 73	מהפך
revolution	**mahapekhah** *(f.)* 53	מהפכה
advertisement, announcement	**moda'ah** *(f.)* 60	מודעה
muse	**muzah** *(f.)* 71	מוזה
museum	**muze`on** *(m.)* 71	מוזיאון
ready	**mukhan** *(m.)*, **mukhanah** *(f.)* 54	מוכן, מוכנה
facing, in front of	**mul** 68	מול
birth	**molad** *(m.)* 41	מולד
expert, specialist	**mumcheh** *(m.)*, **mumchit** *(f.)* 81	מומחה, מומחית
music	**musiqah** *(f.)* 71	מוסיקה
club	**mo'adon** *(m.)* 60	מועדון

successful	**mutzlach** *(m.)*, **mutzlachat** *(f.)* 85	מוצלח, מוצלחת
early	**muqdam** 72	מוקדם
teacher	**moreh** *(m.)*, **morah** *(f.)* 43	מורה, מורה
concept	**musag** *(m.)* 81	מושג
permitted	**mutar** *(m.)*, **muteret** *(f.)* 66	מותר, מותרת
temperament	**mezeg** *(m.)* 68	מזג
to pour	**mazag [limzog]** 68	מזג [למזוג]
weather	**mezeg `avir** *(m.)* 68	מזג אוויר
air-conditioner	**mazgan** *(m.)* 68	מזגן
suitcase	**mizvadah** *(f.)* 23	מזוודה
cash	**mezuman** *(m.)* 32	מזומן
luck	**mazal** *(m.)* 16	מזל
Congratulations!	**Mazal tov!** 16, 30	מזל טוב!
east	**mizrach** *(m.)* 50	מזרח
connected (tied to)	**mechubar** *(m.)*, **mechuberet** *(f.)* 75	מחובר, מחוברת
price	**mechir** *(m.)* 53	מחיר
tomorrow	**machar** 33	מחר
computer	**machshev** *(m.)* 9	מחשב
laptop	**machshev nayad** *(m.)* 9	מחשב נייד
laptop	**machshev nisa** *(m.)* 9	מחשב נישא
kitchen	**mitbach** *(m.)* 39	מטבח
bed	**mitah** *(f.)* 17	מטה
crazy	**metoraf** *(m.)*, **metorefet** *(f.)* 75	מטורף, מטורפת
Who?	**Mi?** 18	מי?
information	**meyda'** *(m.)* 81	מידע
special	**meyuchad** *(m.)*, **meyuchedet** *(f.)* 75	מיוחד, מיוחדת
mixture	**mizug** *(m.)* 68	מיזוג
air-conditioning	**mizug `avir** *(m.)* 68	מיזוג אוויר
water	**mayim** *(m. pl.)* 27	מים
circumcision	**milah** *(f.)* 30	מילה
word	**milah** *(f.)*, **milim** *(pl.)* 71	מילה, מילים
dictionary	**milon** *(m.)* 71	מילון
juice	**mitz** *(m.)* 11	מיץ
microwave	**miqrogal** *(m.)* 83	מיקרוגל
someone	**mishehu** *(m.)* 33	מישהו
mythological	**mitologi** *(m.)*, **mitologit** *(f.)* 71	מיתולוגי, מיתולוגית
mythology	**mitologyah** *(f.)* 71	מיתולוגיה
respected	**mekhubad** *(m.)*, **mekhubedet** *(f.)* 80	מכובד, מכובדת
car	**mekhonit** *(f.)* 13	מכונית
addicted	**makhur** *(m.)*, **mekhurah** *(f.)* 75	מכור, מכורה
preparatory course	**mekhinah** *(f.)* 54	מכינה
trousers	**mikhnasayim** *(m.)* 64	מכנסיים
lid	**mikhseh** *(m.)* 72	מכסה
to sell	**makhar [limkor]** 53	מכר [למכור]
obstacle	**mikhshol** *(m.)* 80	מכשול
letter (message)	**mikhtav** *(m.)* 27	מכתב
complete, full	**male** *(m.)*, **mele`ah** *(f.)* 60	מלא, מלאה
angel	**mal`akh** *(m.)* 46	מלאך
handicraft	**melakhah** *(f.)* 83	מלאכה
dirty	**melukhlakh** *(m.)*, **melukhlekhet** *(f.)* 67	מלוכלך, מלוכלכת
hotel	**malon** *(m.)* 51	מלון

salt	**melach** *(m.)* 55	מלח
war	**milchamah** *(f.)* 72	מלחמה
cucumber	**melafefon** *(m.)* 76	מלפפון
really	**mamash** 36	ממש
to count	**manah [limnot]** 82	מנה [למנות]
manager	**menahel** *(m.)*, **menahelet** *(f.)* 53	מנהל, מנהלת
subscriber	**manuy** *(m.)*, **menuyah** *(f.)* 52	מנוי, מנויה
certain	**mesuyam** *(m.)*, **mesuyemet** *(f.)* 83	מסוים, מסוימת
strained (sieved)	**mesunan** *(m.)*, **mesunenet** *(f.)* 79	מסונן, מסוננת
party	**mesibah** *(f.)* 34	מסיבה
trek	**masa'** *(m.)* 26	מסע
restaurant	**mis'adah** *(f.)* 68	מסעדה
enough	**maspiq** 39	מספיק
circle	**ma'agal** *(m.)* 78	מעגל
adapted	**me'ubad** *(m.)*, **me'ubedet** *(f.)* 85	מעובד, מעובדת
updated (up-to-date)	**me'udkan** *(m.)*, **me'udkenet** *(f.)* 81	מעודכן, מעודכנת
crushed	**ma'ukh** *(m.)*, **me'ukhah** *(f.)* 55	מעוך, מעוכה
tiring	**me'ayef** *(m.)*, **me'ayefet** *(f.)* 12	מעייף, מעייפת
coat	**me'il** *(m.)* 41	מעיל
degree	**ma'alah** *(f.)* 79	מעלה
elevator / lift	**ma'alit** *(f.)* 41	מעלית
interesting	**me'anyen** *(m.)*, **me'anyenet** *(f.)* 44	מעניין, מעניינת
west	**ma'arav** *(m.)* 50	מערב
cave	**me'arah** *(f.)* 72	מערה
campaign	**ma'arekhet** *(f.)* 82	מערכת
political party	**miflagah** *(f.)* 82	מפלגה
because	**mipney she-** 27	מפני ש-
tempting	**mefateh** *(m.)*, **mefatah** *(f.)* 83	מפתה, מפתה
to find	**matza [limtzo]** 38	מצא [למצוא]
to like (find pleasing)	**matza [limtzo] chen** 38	מצא [למצוא] חן
computer presentation	**matzeget** *(f.)* 81	מצגת
commandment	**mitzvah** *(f.)*16	מצווה
excellent	**metzuyan** *(m.)*, **metzuyenet** *(f.)* 25	מצויין, מצויינת
excellence	**metzuyanut** *(f.)* 73	מצויינות
funny	**matzchiq** *(m.)*, **matzchiqah** *(f.)* 65	מצחיק, מצחיקה
camera	**matzlemah** *(f.)* 25	מצלמה
vantage point	**mitzpeh** *(m.)* 83	מצפה
conscience	**matzpun** *(m.)* 82	מצפון
lookout	**mitzpor** *(m.)* 83	מצפור
Egypt	**Mitzrayim** *(f.)* 50	מצרים
broken, out of order	**mequlqal** *(m.)*, **mequlqelet** *(f.)* 68	מקולקל, מקולקלת
place	**maqom** *(m.)* 66	מקום
source	**maqor** *(m.)*, **meqorot** *(pl.)* 85	מקור, מקורות
keyboard	**miqledet** *(f.)* 81	מקלדת
profession	**miqtzo'a** *(m.)* 62	מקצוע
refrigerator	**meqarer** *(m.)* 83	מקרר
distance	**merchaq** *(m.)* 83	מרחק
centre	**merkaz** *(m.)* 51	מרכז
city centre	**merkaz ha'ir** *(m.)* 58	מרכז העיר
balcony	**mirpeset** *(f.)* 39	מרפסת
fascinating	**merateq** *(m.)*, **merateqet** *(f.)* 85	מרתק, מרתקת

game	**mischaq** *(m.)* 19	משחק
during; over (the course of)	**meshekh** *(m.)* 62, 73	משך
family	**mishpachah** *(f.)* 19	משפחה
law	**mishpat** *(m.)* 40	משפט
scale (for weighing), weight	**mishqal** *(m.)* 53	משקל
office	**misrad** *(m.)* 53	משרד
to die	**met [lamut]** 46	מת [למות]
sweet	**matoq** *(m.)*, **metuqah** *(f.)* 79	מתוק, מתוקה
beginner	**matchil** *(m.)*, **matchilah** *(f.)* 85	מתחיל, מתחילה
When?	**Matay?** 24	מתי?
recipe	**matkon** *(m.)* 79	מתכון
present (gift)	**matanah** *(f.)* 32	מתנה
facility	**mitqan** *(m.)* 83	מתקן

נ

to be elected	**nivchar [lehibacher]** 82	נבחר [להבחר]
to drive	**nahag [linhog]** 46	נהג [לנהוג]
driver	**nehag** *(m.)*, **naheget** *(f.)* 46	נהג, נהגת
wonderful	**nehedar** *(m.)*, **nehederet** *(f.)* 41	נהדר, נהדרת
to enjoy	**neheneh [lehanot]** 76	נהנה [להנות]
Well?!	**Nu?** 22	נו?
pest (irritating guy/ woman)	**nudniq** *(m.)*, **nudniqit** *(f.)* 29	נודניק, נודניקית
comfortable	**noach** *(m.)*, **nochah** *(f.)* 83	נוח, נוחה
beauty	**noy** *(m.)* 61	נוי
to be born	**nolad [lehivaled]** 30	נולד [להולד]
passenger; traveller	**nose'a** *(m.)*, **nosa'at** *(f.)* 46, 53	נוסע, נוסעת
further; additional	**nosaf** *(m.)*, **nosefet** *(f.)* 60, 81	נוסף, נוספת
landscape, view	**nof** *(m.)* 68	נוף
holiday (vacation)	**nofesh** *(m.)* 39	נופש
subject	**nose** *(m.)* 82	נושא
to manage (direct)	**nihel [lenahel]** 73	ניהל [לנהל]
mobile *(adj.)*	**nayad** *(m.)*, **nayedet** *(f.)* 13	נייד, ניידת
victory	**nitzachon** *(m.)* 73	ניצחון
to clean	**niqah [lenaqot]** 67	ניקה [לנקות]
vowel point	**niqud** *(m.)* 57	ניקוד
marriage (institution)	**nisu`im** *(m. pl.)* 34	נישואים
to cut off	**niteq [lenateq]** 74	ניתק [לנתק]
grandson	**nekhed** 30	נכד
granddaughter	**nekhdah** 30	נכדה
correct, right	**nakhon** *(m.)*, **nekhonah** *(f.)* 40	נכון, נכונה
to enter, to go into	**nikhnas [lehikanes]** 46	נכנס [להכנס]
distinguished	**nikar** *(m.)*, **nikeret** *(f.)* 80	נכר, נכרת
to fail	**nikhshal [lehikashel]** 54	נכשל [להכשל]
to be fed up	**nim`as** (+ **li/lekha/lakh** etc.) 78	נמאס לי ...
dynamic	**nimratz** *(m.)*, **nimretzet** *(f.)* 73	נמרץ, נמרצת
miracle	**nes** *(m.)* 11	נס
travel (journey), trip	**nesi'ah** *(f.)* 53	נסיעה
to travel; to drive	**nasa' [linso'a]** 33, 50	נסע [לנסוע]
pleasant	**na'im** *(m.)*, **ne'imah** *(f.)* 26	נעים, נעימה
shoe	**na'al** *(f.)* 64	נעל

to disappear	**ne'elam [lehe'alem]** 82	נעלם [להעלם]
to meet	**nifgash [lehipagesh]** 44	נפגש [להפגש]
to be dispersed, to be scattered	**nafotz [lafutz]** 58	נפוץ [לפוץ]
fall (the act of falling)	**nefilah** *(f.)* 73	נפילה
to fall	**nafal [lifol]** 29	נפל [לפול]
to break up	**nifrad [lehipared]** 40	נפרד [להפרד]
to win	**nitzeach [lenatzeach]** 73	נצח [לנצח]
dot; point	**nequdah** *(f.)* 22, 57	נקודה
clean	**naqi** *(m.)*, **neqiyah** *(f.)* 67	נקי, נקייה
portable	**nisa** *(m.)*, **niset** *(f.)* 9	נשא, נשאת
to swear (make an oath)	**nishba' [lehishava']** 66	נשבע [להשבע]
breath	**neshimah** *(f.)* 83	נשימה
soul	**neshamah** *(f.)* 46	נשמה
to maintain	**nishmar [lehishamer]** 85	נשמר [להישמר]
to be weighed	**nishqal [lehishaqel]** 53	נשקל [להשקל]
data	**natun** *(m.)*, **netunim** *(pl.)* 81	נתון, נתונים
to give	**natan [latet]** 43	נתן [לתת]

ס

grandfather	**saba** 30	סבא
Great!	**Sababah!** 85	סבאבה!
around	**saviv** 66	סביב
environment	**svivah** *(f.)* 82	סביבה
grandmother	**savta** 30	סבתא
order	**seder** *(m.)* 17	סדר
to order (arrange), to tidy	**sider [lesader]** 17	סדר [לסדר]
agenda, routine	**seder yom** *(m.)* 75	סדר יום
series	**sidrah** *(f.)* 78	סדרה
agency	**sokhnut** *(f.)* 53	סוכנות
sugar	**sukar** *(m.)* 11	סוכר
sweetener	**sukrazit** *(f.)* 11	סוכרזית
end	**sof** *(m.)* 20	סוף
at last	**sof sof** 20	סוף סוף
weekend	**sof shavu'a** *(m.)* 20	סוף שבוע
dizziness	**scharchoret** *(f.)* 75	סחרחורת
to make dizzy, to faze	**sichrer [lesachrer]** 73	סחרר [לסחרר]
reason	**sibah** *(f.)* 34	סיבה
arrangement (organization)	**sidur** *(m.)* 53	סידור
knife	**sakin** *(f.)*, **sakinim** *(pl.)* 76	סכין, סכינים
basket	**sal** *(m.)* 19	סל
salad	**salat** *(m.)* 27	סלט
excuse [me]	**slichah** *(f.)* 23	סליחה
slang	**sleng** *(m.)* 85	סלנג
thick	**samikh** *(m.)*, **smikhah** *(f.)* 79	סמיך, סמיכה
to rely	**samakh [lismokh]** 73	סמך [לסמוך]
to symbolize	**simel [lesamel]** 72	סמל [לסמל]
sofa	**sapah** *(f.)* 38	ספה
story	**sipur** *(m.)* 73	ספור
sporty	**sportivi** *(m.)*, **sportivit** *(f.)* 19	ספורטיבי, ספורטיבית

book	**sefer** *(m.)* 37	ספר
to count	**safar [lispor]** 47	ספר [לספור]
Sephardi	**sfaradi** *(m.)*, **sfaradiyah** *(f.)* 82	ספרדי, ספרדיה
curious	**saqran** *(m.)*, **saqranit** *(f.)* 83	סקרן, סקרנית
film, movie	**seret** *(m.)* 65	סרט

ע

to work	**'avad [la'avod]** 24	עבד [לעבוד]
work	**'avodah** *(f.)* 37	עבודה
to cross; to move (house)	**'avar [la'avor]** 37	עבר [לעבור]
Hebrew	**'ivrit** *(f.)* 5	עברית
tomato	**'agvaniyah** *(f.)* 76	עגבניות
until	**'ad** 26	עד
jewel	**'adi** *(m.)* 54	עדי
gentleness	**'adinut** *(f.)* 79	עדינות
delight	**'eden** *(m.)* 61	עדן
cake	**'ugah** *(f.)* 10	עוגה
more; yet	**'od** 27, 32	עוד
not yet	**'od lo** 32	עוד לא
new immigrant	**'oleh chadash** *(m.)*, **'olah chadashah** *(f.)* 82	עולה חדש, עולה חדשה
world	**'olam** *(m.)* 47	עולם
sting	**'oqetz** *(m.)* 80	עוקץ
copy	**'oteq** *(m.)* 81	עותק
to help	**'azar [la'azor]** 22	עזר [לעזר]
blind	**'iver** *(m.)*, **'iveret** *(f.)* 80	עיוור, עיוורת
tired	**'ayef** *(m.)*, **'ayefah** *(f.)* 12	עייף, עייפה
eye	**'ayin** *(f.)*, **'eynayim** *(pl.)* 38	עין, עיניים
the main (thing)	**'iqar** *(m.)*, **'iqarit** *(f.)* 68	עיקר, עיקרית
city	**'ir** *(f.)* 58	עיר
newspaper	**'iton** *(m.)* 52	עיתון
mouse	**'akhbar** *(m.)* 81	עכבר
now	**'akhshav** 50	עכשיו
contemporary	**'akhshavi** *(m.)*, **'akhshavit** *(f.)* 71	עכשווי, עכשווית
about, on	**'al** 20	על
barbecue	**'al ha`esh** 20	על האש
by, next to	**'al yad** 68	על יד
to climb, to go up	**'alah [la'alot]** 67	עלה [לעלות]
ascent	**'aliyah** *(f.)* 1	עליה
with	**'im** 18	עם
people (nation)	**'am** 59	עם
to stand	**'amad [la'amod]** 78	עמד [לעמוד]
to reply; to answer	**'anah [la'anot]** 43, 45	ענה [לענות]
tie (necktie)	**'anivah** *(f.)* 48	עניבה
business	**'eseq** *(m.)*, **'asaqim** *(pl.)* 59	עסק, עסקים
deal (bargain)	**'isqah** *(f.)* 83	עסקה
wood	**'etz** *(m.)* 83	עץ
advice	**'etzah** *(f.)* 78	עצה
sad	**'atzuv** *(m.)*, **'atzuvah** *(f.)* 85	עצוב, עצובה
stop	**'atzor** *(m.)* 51	עצור
bone, self	**'etzem** *(m.)* 70	עצם

herself	**'atzmah** *(f.)* 67	עצמה
himself	**'atzmo** *(m.)* 67	עצמו
to stop	**'atzar [la'atzor]** 83	עצר [לעצור]
heel	**'aqev** *(m.)* 73	עקב
evening	**'erev** *(m.)* 10	ערב
to mix	**'irbev [le'arbev]** 55	ערבב [לערבב]
Arab *(adj.)*	**'aravi** *(m.)*, **'aravit** *(f.)* 82	ערבי, ערבית
to do	**'asah [la'asot]** 37	עשה [לעשות]
rich	**'ashir** *(m.)*, **'ashirah** *(f.)* 45	עשיר, עשירה
future	**'atid** *(m.)* 57	עתיד
antique, old	**'atiq** *(m.)*, **'atiqah** *(f.)* 38	עתיק, עתיקה

פ

here	**poh** 17	פה
mouth	**peh** *(m.)* 73	פה
Poland	**Polanyah** *(f.)* 8	פולניה
Polish (the language)	**polanit** *(f.)* 8	פולנית
less … than	**pachot ... m-** 77	פחות ... מ-
chit-chat	**pitput** *(m.)* 13	פטפוט
to chat	**pitpet [lefatpet]** 20	פטפט [לפטפט]
parsley	**petrozilyah** *(f.)* 55	פטרוזיליה
figure	**figurah** *(f.)* 75	פיגורה
physics	**fiziqah** *(f.)* 43	פיזיקה
filter	**filter** *(m.)* 11	פילטר
corner	**pinah** *(f.)* 83	פינה
pita bread	**pitah** *(f.)* 55	פיתה
mobile/cell phone	**pelefon** *(m.)* 45	פלאפון
falafel	**falafel** *(m.)* 27	פלאפל
pepper	**pilpel** *(m.)* 55	פלפל
side, face	**pan** *(m.)*, **panim** *(pl.)* 65	פן, פנים
free time, leisure	**pnay** *(m.)* 62	פנאי
to turn	**panah [lifnot]** 51	פנה [לפנות]
the face of, the surface of	**pney** *(m. pl.)* 58	פני
inside (interior)	**pnim** *(m.)* 78	פנים
top (summit)	**pisgah** *(f.)* 73	פסגה
festival	**festival** *(m.)* 27	פסטיבל
once	**pa'am** *(f.)* 58	פעם
twice	**pa'amayim** *(f.)* 58	פעמיים
sucker	**frayer** *(m.)*, **frayerit** *(f.)*	פראיר, פראירית
poppy / poppyseed	**pereg** *(m.)* 10	פרג
parting (farewell)	**predah** *(f.)* 85	פרדה
fur	**parvah** *(f.)* 41	פרווה
sliced	**parus** *(m.)*, **prusah** *(f.)* 76	פרוס, פרוסה
detail	**prat** *(m.)* 60	פרט
fruit	**pri** *(m.)*, **perot** *(pl.)* 79	פרי, פירות
simple / simply	**pashut** *(m.)*, **pshutah** *(f.)* 85	פשוט, פשוטה
to stretch, to take off	**pashat [lifshot]** 83	פשט [לפשוט]
to go bankrupt	**pashat [lifshot] `et haregel** 83	פשט [לפשוט] את הרגל
bankruptcy	**pshitat regel** *(f.)* 83	פשיטת רגל
proverb	**pitgam** *(m.)* 80	פתגם

to open	**patach [liftoach]** 71	פתח [לפתוח]
to solve	**patar [liftor]** 62	פתר [לפתור]

צ

army	**tzava** *(m.)* 26	צבא
colour	**tzeva'** *(m.)* 64	צבע
colourful	**tziv'oni** *(m.)*, **tziv'onit** *(f.)* 65	צבעוני, צבעונית
screen (e.g. computer)	**tzag** *(m.)* 81	צג
side	**tzad** *(m.)* 82	צד
to hunt	**tzad [latzud]** 69	צד [לצוד]
justice	**tzedeq** *(m.)* 69	צדק
noon	**tzohorayim** *(m. pl.)* 62	צהרים
fair (right), just	**tzodeq** *(m.)*, **tzodeqet** *(f.)* 69	צודק, צודקת
team	**tzevet** *(m.)* 81	צוות
togetherness	**tzavta** *(m.)* 60	צוותא
submarine	**tzolelet** *(f.)* 39	צוללת
shape	**tzurah** *(f.)* 72	צורה
to laugh	**tzachaq [litzchoq]** 51	צחק [לצחוק]
public	**tzibur** *(m.)* 60	ציבור
public *(adj.)*	**tziburi** *(m.)*, **tziburit** *(f.)* 66	ציבורי, ציבורית
hunt *(noun)*	**tzayid** *(m.)* 69	צייד
to draw	**tziyer [letzayer]** 78	צייר [לצייר]
photography	**tzilum** *(m.)* 25	צילום
raisin	**tzimuq** *(m.)* 79	צימוק
sound	**tzlil** *(m.)* 61	צליל
to photograph	**tzilem [letzalem]** 25	צלם [לצלם]
photographer	**tzalam** *(m.)*, **tzalemet** *(f.)* 25	צלם, צלמת
rib	**tzela'** *(f.)* 47	צלע
to ring	**tziltzel [letzaltzel]** 45	צלצל [לצלצל]
vegetarian	**tzimchoni** *(m.)*, **tzimchonit** *(f.)* 76	צמחוני, צמחונית
top (upper part)	**tzameret** *(f.)* 75	צמרת
radish	**tznonit** *(f.)* 76	צנונית
young	**tza'ir** *(m.)*, **tze'irah** *(f.)* 30	צעיר, צעירה
narrow	**tzar** *(m.)*, **tzarah** *(f.)* 80	צר, צרה
to need	**tzarikh** *(m.)*, **tzrikhah** *(f.)* 25	צריך, צריכה
French *(adj.)*	**tzarfati** *(m.)*, **tzarfatit** *(f.)* 82	צרפתי, צרפתית

ק

kibbutz	**qibutz** *(m.)* 34	קבוץ
team	**qvutzah** *(f.)* 71	קבוצה
to receive	**qibel [leqabel]** 54	קבל [לקבל]
receipt	**qabalah** *(f.)* 75	קבלה
ancient	**qadum** *(m.)*, **qdumah** *(f.)* 72	קדום, קדומה
forwards	**qadimah** 51	קדימה
the East	**qedem** *(m.)* 58	קדם
cube	**qubiyah** *(f.)* 76	קוביה
computer file	**qovetz** *(m.)* 81	קובץ
sound file	**qovetz qol** *(m.)*, **qivtzey qol** *(pl.)* 81	קובץ קול, קבצי קול
sound, voice	**qol** *(m.)*, **qolot** *(pl.)* 81	קול, קולות
cinema, movie theatre	**qolno'a** *(m.)* 31	קולנוע
comedy	**qomedyah** *(f.)* 31	קומדיה

cash register/till	**qupah** *(f.)* 31	קופה
cold *(noun)*	**qor** *(m.)* 43	קור
reader	**qore`** *(m.)*, **qor`ah** *(f.)* 57	קורא, קוראה
little, small	**qatan** *(m.)*, **qtanah** *(f.)* 19	קטן, קטנה
to fold/roll up	**qipel [leqapel]** 48	קיפל [לקפל]
summer	**qayitz** *(m.)* 39	קיץ
wall	**qir** *(m.)* 72	קיר
easy, light (in weight)	**qal** *(m.)*, **qalah** *(f.)* 76	קל, קלה
classical (typical)	**qlasi** *(m.)*, **qlasit** *(f.)* 82	קלסי, קלסית
playing card	**qlaf** *(m.)* 66	קלף
to get up, to rise	**qam [laqum]** 82	קם [לקום]
flour	**qemach** *(m.)* 79	קמח
to buy, to shop	**qanah [liqnot]** 12	קנה [לקנות]
purchase	**qniyah** *(f.)* 12	קניה
shopping centre / mall	**qanyon** *(m.)* 12	קניון
shopping (purchases)	**qniyot** *(f. pl.)* 12	קניות
pot (jug)	**qanqan** *(m.)* 72	קנקן
bowl	**qe'arah** *(f.)* 76	קערה
café, coffee	**qafeh** *(m.)* 10	קפה
cafeteria	**qafeteriah** *(f.)* 11	קפטריה
to jump	**qafatz [liqfotz]** 85	קפץ [לקפוץ]
chopped	**qatzutz** *(m.)*, **qtzutzah** *(f.)* 55	קצוץ, קצוצה
shortcut	**qitzur** *(m.)* 73	קצור
foam	**qetzef** *(m.)* 79	קצף
whipped cream	**qatzefet** *(f.)* 79	קצפת
short	**qatzar** *(m.)*, **qtzarah** *(f.)* 43	קצר, קצרה
a little	**qtzat** 53	קצת
cold, cool (temperature)	**qar** *(m.)*, **qarah** *(f.)* 41	קר, קרה
to read	**qara` [liqro`]** 57	קרא [לקרוא]
to happen	**qarah [liqrot]** 29	קרה [לקרות]
cream	**qrem** *(m.)* 51	קרם
caramel	**qaramel** *(m.)* 51	קרמל
ray	**qeren** *(m.)* 61	קרן
circus	**qirqas** *(m.)* 65	קרקס
board	**qeresh** *(m.)* 76	קרש
difficult	**qasheh** *(m.)*, **qashah** *(f.)* 67	קשה, קשה
link	**qishur** *(m.)* 81	קשור
close (attached to)	**qashur** *(m.)*, **qshurah** *(f.)* 75	קשור, קשורה
hard (rigid)	**qashiach** *(m.)*, **qeshichah** *(f.)* 81	קשיח, קשיחה
contact	**qesher** *(m.)*, **qsharim** *(pl.)* 85	קשר, קשרים

ר

to see	**ra`ah [lir`ot]** 23	ראה [לראות]
interview	**re`ayon** *(m.)*, **re`ayonot** *(pl.)* 75	ראיון, ראיונות
head	**rosh** *(m.)* 24	ראש
rabbi	**rav** *(m.)* 46	רב
great (in amount), very much	**rabah** *(f.)* 24	רבה
foot; leg	**regel** *(f.)* 19, 83	רגל
moment	**rega'** *(m.)* 73	רגע
radio	**radyo** *(m.)* 75	רדיו
furniture	**rahit** *(m.)* 38	רהיט

salad dressing, sauce	**rotev** *(m.)* 76	רוטב
joy	**ron** *(m.)* 54	רון
Russia	**Rusyah** *(f.)* 8	רוסיה
Russian (the language)	**rusit** *(f.)* 8	רוסית
doctor	**rofe** *(m.)*, **rofah** *(f.)* 51	רופא, רופאה
dentist	**rofe shinayim** *(m.)*, **rof`at shinayim** *(f.)* 80	רופא שיניים, רופאת שיניים
to become thin (lose weight)	**razah [lirzot]** 53	רזה [לירזות]
thin	**razeh** *(m.)*, **razah** *(f.)* 53	רזה, רזה
wide	**rachav** *(m.)*, **rechavah** *(f.)* 80	רחב, רחבה
street	**rechov** *(m.)*, **rechovot** *(pl.)* 51	רחוב, רחובות
wet	**ratuv** *(m.)*, **retuvah** *(f.)* 76	רטוב, רטובה
level	**ramah** *(f.)* 83	רמה
traffic light	**ramzor** *(m.)* 51	רמזור
hungry	**ra'ev** *(m.)*, **re'evah** *(f.)* 67	רעב, רעבה
medicine	**refu`ah** *(f.)* 40	רפואה
to want	**ratzah [lirtzot]** 9	רצה [לרצות]
strip	**retzu'ah** *(f.)* 76	רצועה
only (merely)	**raq** 8	רק
official	**rishmi** *(m.)*, **rishmit** *(f.)* 48	רשמי, רשמית

ש

which, who	**she-** 23	-ש
to ask	**sha`al [lish`ol]** 43	שאל [לשאול]
question	**she`elah** *(f.)* 45	שאלה
in which	**shebo** *(m.)*, **shebah** *(f.)* 77	שבו, שבה
week	**shavu'a** *(m.)* 20	שבוע
weekly (e.g. magazine)	**shevu'on** *(m.)* 52	שבועון
path	**shvil** *(m.)* 83	שביל
strike (labour dispute)	**shvitah** *(f.)* 33	שביתה
to break	**shavar [lishbor]** 31	שבר [לשבור]
Saturday, Shabbat	**shabat** *(f.)* 8	שבת
to strike (stop work)	**shavat [lishbot]** 33	שבת [לשבות]
mistake	**shgi`ah** *(f.)* 85	שגיאה
field	**sadeh** *(m.)* 23	שדה
airport	**sdeh te'ufah** *(m.)* 23	שדה תעופה
to upgrade	**shidreg [leshadreg]** 83	שדרג [לשדרג]
again	**shuv** 31	שוב
equal	**shaveh** *(m.)*, **shavah** *(f.)* 69	שווה, שווה
police officer	**shoter** *(m.)*, **shoteret** *(f.)* 66	שוטר, שוטרת
table	**shulchan** *(m.)* 17	שולחן
garlic	**shum** *(m.)* 55	שום
no (negative particle)	**shum** 75	שום
fox	**shu'al** *(m.)* 69	שועל
chocolate	**shoqolad** *(m.)* 10	שוקולד
root	**shoresh** *(m.)* 71	שורש
partner	**shutaf** *(m.)*, **shutafah** *(f.)* 85	שותף, שותפה
to swim	**sachah [lischot]** 15	שחה [לשחות]
black	**shachor** *(m.)*, **shchorah** *(f.)* 64	שחור, שחורה
chess	**shachmat** *(m.)* 62	שחמט
to play	**sicheq [lesacheq]** 19	שחק [לשחק]
player	**sachqan** *(m.)*, **sachqanit** *(f.)* 73	שחקן, שחקנית

dawn	**shachar** *(m.)* 64	שחר
to free, to release	**shichrer [leshachrer]** 66	שחרר [לשחרר]
nonsense	**shtut** *(f.)* 47	שטות
to roll out, to spread	**shatach [lishtoach]** 79	שטח [לשטוח]
devil	**satan** *(m.)* 80	שטן
method	**shitah** *(f.)* 82	שיטה
lesson	**shi'ur** *(m.)* 43	שיעור
poem, song	**shir** *(m.)* 61	שיר
poetry, singing	**shirah** *(f.)* 60	שירה
toilet	**sherutim** *(m. pl.)* 83	שירותים
neighbourhood	**shekhunah** *(f.)* 73	שכונה
neighbourhood *(adj.)*	**shkhunati** *(m.)*, **shkhunatit** *(f.)* 73	שכונתי, שכונתית
neighbour	**shakhen** *(m.)*, **shkhenah** *(f.)* 37	שכן, שכנה
to rent	**sakhar [liskor]** 39	שכר [לשכור]
of	**shel** 8	של
stage (phase)	**shalav** *(m.)*, **shlabim** *(pl.)* 79	שלב, שלבים
tranquillity; calm	**shalvah** *(f.)* 71, 81	שלווה
hello, peace	**shalom** *(m.)* 2	שלום
to send	**shalach [lishloach]** 54	שלח [לשלוח]
third (fraction)	**shlish** *(m.)* 55	שליש
entire	**shalem** *(m.)*, **shlemah** *(f.)* 72	שלם, שלמה
our	**shelanu** *(m./f.)* 30	שלנו
there	**sham** 15	שם
name	**shem** *(m.)* 51	שם
left *(adv.)*	**smol** 56	שמאל
to the left	**smolah** 51	שמאלה
left *(adj.)*	**smali** *(m.)*, **smalit** *(f.)* 51	שמאלי, שמאלית
reserve	**shmurah** *(f.)* 83	שמורה
nature reserve	**shmurat teva'** *(f.)* 83	שמורת טבע
happy	**sameach** *(m.)*, **smechah** *(f.)* 80	שמח, שמחה
sky; heavens	**shamayim** *(m. pl.)* 27, 58	שמיים
dress	**simlah** *(f.)* 16	שמלה
oil	**shemen** *(m.)* 52	שמן
to hear, to listen	**shama' [lishmo'a]** 6	שמע [לשמוע]
clove (of garlic), tooth	**shen** *(f.)* 55	שן
year	**shanah** *(f.)* 30	שנה
second (unit of time)	**shniyah** *(f.)* 81	שניה
hour, time (in ref. to the clock)	**sha'ah** *(f.)* 33	שעה
gate	**sha'ar** *(m.)* 85	שער
language, lip	**safah** *(f.)* 58	שפה
point (tip), summit	**shpitz** *(m.) (slang)* 73	שפיץ
abundance, plenty	**shefa'** *(f.)* 60	שפע
calm	**shaqet** *(m.)*, **shqetah** *(f.)* 73	שקט, שקטה
packet	**saqit** *(f.)* 79	שקית
shekel (Israeli unit of currency)	**sheqel** *(m.)* 45	שקל
to sing	**shar [lashir]** 65	שר [לשיר]
minister (government)	**sar** *(m.)*, **sarah** *(f.)* 48	שר, שרה
sleeve	**sharvul** *(m.)* 48	שרוול
to drink	**shatah [lishtot]** 4	שתה [לשתות]

ת

appetite	**te`avon** *(m.)* 55	תאבון
date (on the calendar)	**ta`arikh** *(m.)* 83	תאריך
tea	**teh** *(m.)* 4	תה
thank you	**todah** *(f.)* 4	תודה
mast	**toren** *(m.)* 80	תורן
strawberry	**tut** *(m.)* 79	תות
station	**tachanah** *(f.)* 50	תחנה
bottom	**tachtit** *(f.)* 73	תחתית
box	**tevah** *(f.)* 71	תיבה
tourist	**tayar** *(m.)*, **tayeret** *(f.)* 39	תייר, תיירת
tourism	**tayarut** *(f.)* 53	תיירות
Mediterranean	**Tikhon** *(m.)* 53	תיכון
baby	**tinoq** *(m.)*, **tinoqet** *(f.)* 61	תינוק, תינוקת
to fix, to repair	**tiqen [letaqen]** 68	תיקן [לתקן]
to plan	**tikhnen [letakhnen]** 79	תכנן [לתכנן]
student	**talmid** *(m.)*, **talmidah** *(f.)* 46	תלמיד, תלמידה
photograph	**tmunah** *(f.)* 23	תמונה
always	**tamid** 36	תמיד
road sign	**tamrur** *(m.)* 51	תמרור
Bible	**Tanakh** *(m.)* 57	תנ"ך
Biblical	**tanakhi** *(m.)*, **tanakhit** *(f.)* 57	תנכי, תנכית
oven	**tanur** *(m.)* 79	תנור
to frustrate	**tiskel [letaskel]** 75	תסכל [לתסכל]
certificate, document	**te'udah** *(f.)* 72	תעודה
flight	**te'ufah** *(f.)* 23	תעופה
mixture	**ta'arovet** *(f.)* 79	תערובת
orange (fruit)	**tapuz** *(m.)* 11	תפוז
apple	**tapuach** *(m.)* 11	תפוח
prayer	**tfilah** *(f.)* 16	תפילה
to catch	**tafas [litpos]** 83	תפס [לתפוס]
menu	**tafrit** *(m.)* 68	תפריט
period (of time)	**tqufah** *(f.)* 44	תקופה
exercise	**targil** *(m.)* 85	תרגיל
to practice	**tirgel [letargel]** 85	תרגל [לתרגל]
medicine	**trufah** *(f.)* 71	תרופה
backpacker	**tarmilay** *(m.)*, **tarmila`it** *(f.)* 26	תרמילאי, תרמילאית
crossword	**tashbetz** *(m.)* 62	תשבץ
arrow word puzzle	**tashchetz** *(m.)* 62	תשחץ
reply	**tshuvah** *(f.)* 54	תשובה

Also available from Assimil:

Yiddish (With Ease Series)

Edition number 3383 : Hebrew
Printed in Slovenia - February 2015